VOX
Super-Mini
SPANISH
and
ENGLISH
Dictionary

Third Edition

New York   Chicago   San Francisco   Lisbon   London   Madrid   Mexico City
Milan   New Delhi   San Juan   Seoul   Singapore   Sydney   Toronto

The McGraw·Hill Companies

1 2 3 4 5 6 7 8 9 10 11 12   QLM/QLM   1 9 8 7 6 5 4 3 2

ISBN 978-0-07-178866-3
MHID 0-07-178866-2

e-ISBN 978-0-07-178865-6
e-MHID 0-07-178865-4

Library of Congress Cataloging-in-Publication Data
Vox super-mini Spanish and English dictionary. — 3rd ed.
    p. cm. — (Vox dictionaries)
  ISBN 978-0-07-178866-3 (acid-free paper) —
  ISBN 0-07-178866-2 (acid-free paper)
  1. Spanish language—Dictionaries—English. 2. English language
—Dictionaries—Spanish. I. McGraw-Hill Companies. II. Title: Spanish
and English dictionary.
  PC4680.V698 2012
  463'.21—dc23

                                                        2012006297

Dirección editorial: Jordi Induráin Pons
Coordinación editorial: Mª José Simón Aragón

Diccionario:
Coordinación de la obra: Andrew Hastings
Redacción: Isabel Ferrer Marrades, Victoria Ordóñez Diví, Jose Mª Ruiz
Vaca, Stephen Waller
VOX (y su logotipo) es marca registrada de Larousse Editorial
www.vox.es

Contents

Abbreviations Used in This Dictionary

abbreviation, acronym	*abbr, abr*	abreviatura, sigla
adjective	*adj*	adjetivo
adverb	*adv*	adverbio
somebody	algn	alguien
architecture	ARCH, ARQ	arquitectura
slang	*arg*	argot
auxiliary	*aux*	auxiliar
commercial	COMM, COM	comercio
computing	COMPUT	informática
conditional	*cond*	conticional
conjunction	*conj*	conjunción
determiner	*det*	determinante
euphemism	*euf, euph*	eufemismo
familiar	*fam*	familiar
figurative	*fig*	uso figurado
finance	FIN	finanzas
formal	*fml*	formal
future	*fut*	futuro
British English	GB	inglés británico
geography	GEOG	geografía
history	HIST	historia
indicative	*ind*	indicativo
computing	INFORM	informática
interjection	*interj*	interjección
invariable	*inv*	invariable
ironic	*iron, irón*	irónico
law	JUR	derecho
mathematics	MATH, MAT	matemáticas
medicine	MED	medicina
music	MUS, MÚS	música

Abreviaturas usadas
en el diccionario

noun	*n*	nombre
femenine noun	*nf*	nombre femenino
masculine noun	*nm*	nombre masculino
masc, and fem. noun	*nm,f*	nombre masc. y fem.
masc. or fem. noun	*nm & f*	género ambiguo
plural noun	*npl*	nombre plural
number	*num*	número
pejorative	*pej, pey*	peyorativo
perfect	*perf*	perfecto
person	*pers*	persona
phrase	*phr*	locución
pluperfect	*pluperf*	pluscuamperfecto
politics	POL	política
past participle	*pp*	participio pasado
preposition	*prep*	preposición
present	*pres*	presente
pronoun	*pron*	pronombre
past	*pt*	pasado
somebody	sb	alguien
singular	*sing*	singular
slang	*sl*	argot
sport	SP	deportes
something	*sth*	algo
American English	US	inglés de América
intransitive verb	*vi*	verbo intransitivo
reflexive verb	*vpr*	verbo pronominal
transitive verb	*vt*	verbo transitivo
vulgar	*vulg*	vulgar
see	→	véase
registered trademark	®	marca registrada

Fonética

Todas las entradas inglesas en este diccionario llevan transcripción fonética basada en el sistema de la Asociación Fonética Internacional (AFI). He aquí una relación de los símbolos empleados. El símbolo ' delante de una sílaba indica que es ésta la acentuada.

Las consonantes

[p]	pan [pæn], happy ['hæpɪ], slip [slɪp].
[b]	big [bɪg], habit ['hæbɪt], stab [stæb].
[t]	top [tɒp], sitting ['sɪtɪŋ], bit [bɪt].
[d]	drip [drɪp], middle ['mɪdəl], rid [rɪd].
[k]	card [kɑːd], maker ['meɪkəʳ], sock [sɒk].
[g]	god [gɒd], mugger ['mʌgəʳ], dog [dɒg].
[tʃ]	chap [tʃæp], hatchet ['hætʃɪt], beach [biːtʃ].
[dʒ]	jack [dʒæk], digest [daɪ'dʒest], wage [weɪdʒ].
[f]	wish [wɪʃ], coffee ['kɒfɪ], wife [waɪf].
[v]	very ['verɪ], never ['nevəʳ], give [gɪv].
[θ]	thing [θɪŋ], cathode ['kæθəʊd], filth [fɪlθ].
[ð]	they [ðeɪ], father ['fɑːðəʳ], loathe [ləʊð].
[s]	spit [spɪt], stencil ['stensəl], niece [niːs].
[z]	zoo ['zuː], weasel ['wiːzəl], buzz [bʌz].
[ʃ]	show [ʃəʊ], fascist [fæ'ʃɪst], gush [gʌʃ].
[ʒ]	gigolo ['ʒɪgələʊ], pleasure ['pleʒəʳ], massage ['mæsɑːʒ].
[h]	help [help], ahead [ə'hed].
[m]	moon [muːn], common ['kɒmən], came [keɪm].
[n]	nail [neɪl], counter ['kaʊntəʳ], shone [ʃɒn].
[ŋ]	linger ['lɪŋgəʳ], sank [sæŋk], thing [θɪŋ].
[l]	light [laɪt], illness ['ɪlnəs], bull [bʊl].
[r]	rug [rʌg], merry ['merɪ].
[j]	young [jʌŋ], university [juːnɪ'vɛːsɪtɪ], Europe ['jʊərəp].
[w]	want [wɒnt], rewind [riː'waɪnd].
[x]	loch [lɒx].
[ʳ]	se llama *"linking r"* y se encuentra únicamente a final de palabra. Se pronuncia sólo cuando la palabra siguiente empieza por una vocal: **mother and father came** ['mʌðər ən 'fɑːðə keɪm].

Las vocales y los diptongos

[iː]   sheep [ʃiːp], sea [siː], scene [siːn], field [fiːld].

[ɪ]   ship [ʃɪp], pity ['pɪtɪ], roses ['rəʊzɪz], babies ['beɪbɪz], college ['kɒlɪdʒ].

[e]   shed [ʃed], instead [ɪn'sted], any ['enɪ], bury ['berɪ], friend [frend].

[æ]   fat [fæt], thank [θæŋk], plait [plæt].

[ɑː]   rather ['rɑːðəʳ], car [kɑːʳ], heart [hɑːt], clerk [klɑːk], palm [pɑːm], aunt [ɑːnt].

[ɒ]   lock [lɒk], wash [wɒʃ], trough [trɒf], because [bɪ'kɒz].

[ɔː]   horse [hɔːs], straw [strɔː], fought [fɔːt], cause [kɔːz], fall [fɔːl], boar [bɔːʳ], door [dɔːʳ].

[ʊ]   look [lʊk], pull [pʊl], woman ['wʊmən], should [ʃʊd].

[uː]   loop [luːp], do [duː], soup [suːp], elude [i'luːd], true [truː], shoe [ʃuː], few [fjuː].

[ʌ]   cub [kʌb], ton [tʌn], young [jʌŋ], flood [flʌd], does [dʌz].

[ɛː]   third [θɛːd], herd [hɛːd], heard [hɛːd], curl [kɛːl], word [wɛːd], journey ['dʒɛːnɪ].

[ə]   actor ['æktəʳ], honour ['ɒnəʳ], about [ə'baʊt].

[ə]   opcional. En algunos casos se pronuncia y en otros se omite: trifle ['traɪfəl].

[eɪ]   cable ['keɪbəl], way [weɪ], plain [pleɪn], freight [freɪt], prey [preɪ], great [greɪt].

[əʊ]   go [gəʊ], toad [təʊd], toe [təʊ], though [ðəʊ], snow [snəʊ].

[aɪ]   lime [laɪm], thigh [θaɪ], height [haɪt], lie [laɪ], try [traɪ], either ['aɪðəʳ].

[aʊ]   house [haʊs], cow [kaʊ].

[ɔɪ]   toy [tɔɪ], soil [sɔɪl].

[ɪə]   near [nɪəʳ], here [hɪəʳ], sheer [ʃɪəʳ], idea [aɪ'dɪə], museum [mjuː'zɪəm], weird [wɪəd], pierce [pɪəs].

[eə]   hare [heəʳ], hair [heəʳ], wear [weəʳ].

[ʊə]   pure [pjʊəʳ], during ['djʊərɪŋ], tourist ['tʊərɪst].

English - Spanish

A

a [eɪ, ə] *det* un, una.

A [eɪ] *abbr* **1** sobresaliente *(calificación)*. **2** la *(nota musical)*.

abandon [ə'bændən] *vt* abandonar.

abattoir ['æbətwɑːʳ] *n* matadero.

abbey ['æbɪ] *n* abadía.

abbreviation [əbriːvɪ'eɪʃən] *n* abreviatura.

abdomen ['æbdəmən] *n* abdomen.

abduct [æb'dʌkt] *vt* raptar, secuestrar.

ability [ə'bɪlɪtɪ] *n* **1** capacidad. **2** talento, aptitud.

able ['eɪbəl] *adj* hábil, capaz. • **to be able to 1** poder. **2** saber: *he was able to drive when he was sixteen*, sabía conducir a los dieciséis años.

abnormal [æb'nɔːməl] *adj* **1** anormal. **2** inusual.

aboard [ə'bɔːd] *adv* a bordo.

abort [ə'bɔːt] *vi* abortar.

abortion [ə'bɔːʃən] *n* aborto *(provocado)*.

about [ə'baʊt] *prep* **1** de, sobre, acerca de. **2** por, en: *he's somewhere about the house*, está por algún rincón de la casa. ▶ *adv* **1** alrededor de. **2** por aquí, por ahí: *there was nobody about*, no había nadie. • **to be about to...** estar a punto de...

above [ə'bʌv] *prep* **1** por encima de. **2** más de, más que: *above 5,000 people*, más de 5.000 personas. ▶ *adv* arriba. • **above all** sobre todo.

abridged [ə'brɪdʒd] *adj* abreviado,-a.

abroad [ə'brɔːd] *adv* **1** al extranjero. **2** en el extranjero.

absent ['æbsənt] *adj* ausente.

absent-minded [æbsənt'maɪndɪd] *adj* distraído,-a.

absolute ['æbsəluːt] *n* absoluto,-a.

absorb [əb'zɔːb] *vt* absorber.

abstain [əb'steɪn] *vi* abstenerse.

abstract ['æbstrækt] *adj* abstracto,-a. ▶ *n* resumen, sinopsis.

abundant [ə'bʌndənt] *adj* abundante.

abuse [ə'bjuːs] *n* **1** insultos. **2** malos tratos. **3** abuso.

abyss [ə'bɪs] *n* abismo.

academic [ækə'demɪk] *adj* académico,-a. ▶ *n* profesor, -ra de universidad. ▪ **academic year** curso escolar.

academy [ə'kædəmɪ] *n* academia.

accelerate [æk'seləreɪt] *vt-vi* acelerar.

accelerator [æk'seləreɪtəʳ] *n* acelerador.

accent ['æksənt] *n* acento.

accept [ək'sept] *vt* aceptar.

access ['ækses] *n* acceso. ▶ *vt* COMPUT acceder a.

accessory [æk'sesərɪ] *n* **1** accesorio. **2** cómplice.

accident ['æksɪdənt] *n* accidente.

accident-prone ['æksɪdəntprəʊn] *adj* propenso,-a a los accidentes.

acclaim [ə'kleɪm] *vt* aclamar.

accommodation [əkɒmə'deɪʃən] *n* alojamiento.

accompany [ə'kʌmpənɪ] *vt* acompañar.

accomplish [ə'kʌmplɪʃ] *vt* lograr, conseguir.

according to [ə'kɔːdɪŋtʊ] *prep* según.

accordion [ə'kɔːdɪən] *n* acordeón.

account [ə'kaʊnt] *n* **1** cuenta. **2** relato, versión. **3** importancia. • **on account** a cuenta; **on account of** por, a causa de.

to account for *vi* explicar.

accounting [ə'kaʊntɪŋ] *n* contabilidad.

accumulate [ə'kjuːmjʊleɪt] *vt-vi* acumular(se).

accurate ['ækjʊrət] *adj* exacto,-a, preciso,-a.

accusation [ækjuː'zeɪʃən] *n* acusación.

accuse [ə'kjuːz] *vt* acusar.

accustom [ə'kʌstəm] *vt* acostumbrar.

accustomed [ə'kʌstəmd] *adj* acostumbrado,-a. • **to get accustomed to** acostumbrarse a.

ace [eɪs] *n* as.

ache [eɪk] *n* dolor. ▶ *vi* doler.

achieve [ə'tʃiːv] *vt* lograr.

acid ['æsɪd] *n* ácido. ▶ *adj* ácido,-a. ▪ **acid rain** lluvia ácida.

acknowledge [ək'nɒlɪdʒ] *vt* **1** reconocer. **2** agradecer.

acknowledgement [ək'nɒlɪdʒmənt] *n* **1** reconocimiento. **2** acuse de recibo.

acne ['æknɪ] *n* acné.

acorn ['eɪkɔːn] *n* bellota.

acoustic [ə'kuːstɪk] *adj* acústico,-a.

acquaint [ə'kweɪnt] *vt* informar, poner al corriente.

acquaintance [ə'kweɪntəns] *n* conocido,-a.

acquire [ə'kwaɪəʳ] *vt* **1** adquirir *(posesiones)*. **2** obtener, conseguir *(información)*.

acquit [ə'kwɪt] *vt* absolver.

acre ['eɪkəʳ] *n* acre.

acrobat ['ækrəbæt] *n* acróbata.

acronym ['ækrənɪm] *n* sigla.

across [ə'krɒs] *prep* **1** a través de: *to swim across a river*, cruzar un río a nado. **2** al otro lado de: *they live across the* *road*, viven enfrente. ► *adv* de un lado a otro.

act [ækt] *n* **1** acto. **2** número: *tonight's first act is a clown*, el primer número de la noche es un payaso. **3** (*Act of Parliament*) ley. ► *vi* actuar. ■ **act of God** fuerza mayor.

acting ['æktɪŋ] *n* actuación. ► *adj* en funciones.

action ['ækʃən] *n* acción. ● **out of action** fuera de servicio; **to bring an action against SB** entablar una demanda contra ALGN.

active ['æktɪv] *adj* activo,-a.

activity [æk'tɪvɪtɪ] *n* actividad.

actor ['æktə'] *n* actor.

actress ['æktrəs] *n* actriz.

actual ['æktʃʊəl] *adj* **1** real. **2** exacto,-a: *those were her actual words*, esas fueron sus palabras exactas.

actually ['æktjʊəlɪ] *adv* **1** en realidad, de hecho. **2** de verdad: *have you actually seen a ghost?*, ¿de verdad que has visto un fantasma?

acute [ə'kju:t] *adj* agudo,-a.

ad [æd] *n fam* anuncio.

adamant ['ædəmənt] *adj* firme, inflexible.

adapt [ə'dæpt] *vt-vi* adaptar(se).

adaptor [ə'dæptə'] *n* ladrón (*enchufe*).

add [æd] *vt* añadir. ► *vt-vi* sumar.

to add to *vt* aumentar.

to add up *vt-vi* sumar. ► *vi fig* cuadrar: *his version doesn't add up*, su versión no cuadra.

adder ['ædə'] *n* víbora.

addict ['ædɪkt] *n* adicto,-a.

addition [ə'dɪʃən] *n* adición. ● **in addition to** además de.

additive ['ædɪtɪv] *n* aditivo.

address [ə'dres] *n* **1** dirección. **2** discurso. **3** conferencia. ► *vt* dirigirse a. ■ **address book** agenda.

adept [ə'dept] *adj* experto,-a.

adequate ['ædɪkwət] *adj* adecuado,-a, satisfactorio,-a.

adjective ['ædʒɪktɪv] *n* adjetivo.

adjourn [ə'dʒɜːn] *vt* aplazar.

adjust [ə'dʒʌst] *vt* ajustar (*temperatura*). ► *vi* adaptarse.

adjustable [ə'dʒʌstəbəl] *adj* regulable. ■ **adjustable spanner** llave inglesa.

adjustment [ə'dʒʌstmənt] *n* ajuste.

administration [ədmɪnɪs'treɪʃən] *n* administración.

administrator [əd'mɪnɪstreɪtə'] *n* administrador,-ra.

admiral ['ædmərəl] *n* almirante.

admiration [ædmɪ'reɪʃən] *n* admiración.

admire [əd'maɪə'] *vt* admirar.

admission [əd'mɪʃən] *n* **1** ingreso (*en hospital, institución*). **2** entrada: *"Admission free"*, "Entrada gratuita".

admit [ədˈmɪt] vt **1** admitir. **2** ingresar (en hospital).

adolescent [ædəˈlesənt] adj-n adolescente.

adopt [əˈdɒpt] vt adoptar.

adore [əˈdɔːʳ] vt adorar.

adorn [əˈdɔːn] vt adornar.

adrift [əˈdrɪft] adj a la deriva.

adult [ˈædʌlt] adj-n adulto,-a.

adulterate [əˈdʌltəreɪt] vt adulterar.

advance [ədˈvɑːns] n **1** avance. **2** anticipo, adelanto (de dinero). ► vt **1** avanzar (tropas). **2** ascender (empleado). **3** adelantar (reunión). **4** anticipar (dinero). ► vi avanzar. • **in advance** por adelantado.

advantage [ədˈvɑːntɪdʒ] n ventaja.

adventure [ədˈventʃəʳ] n aventura. ▪ **adventure playground** parque infantil.

adverb [ˈædvɜːb] n adverbio.

adversary [ˈædvəsərɪ] n adversario,-a.

adversity [ədˈvɜːsɪtɪ] n adversidad.

advert [ˈædvɜːt] n fam anuncio.

advertise [ˈædvətaɪz] vt anunciar. ► vi hacer publicidad.

advertisement [ədˈvɜːtɪsmənt] n anuncio.

advice [ədˈvaɪs] n consejos.

advise [ədˈvaɪz] vt aconsejar. • **to advise against** STH desaconsejar algo.

adviser [ədˈvaɪzəʳ] n asesor,-a.

advocate [ˈædvəkət] n partidario,-a.

aerial [ˈeərɪəl] n antena.

aerodynamic [eərəʊdaɪˈnæmɪk] adj aerodinámico,-a.

aeroplane [ˈeərəpleɪn] n avión.

aerosol [ˈeərəsɒl] n aerosol.

aesthetic [iːsˈθetɪk] adj estético,-a.

affair [əˈfeəʳ] n **1** asunto. **2** caso: the Watergate affair, el caso Watergate. **3** lío, aventura (amorosa).

affect [əˈfekt] vt afectar.

affection [əˈfekʃən] n afecto.

affectionate [əˈfekʃənət] adj afectuoso,-a.

affiliated [əˈfɪlɪeɪtɪd] adj afiliado,-a.

affirmative [əˈfɜːmətɪv] adj afirmativo,-a.

affluent [ˈæfluənt] adj rico,-a, próspero,-a.

afford [əˈfɔːd] vt permitirse: I can't afford to pay £750 for a coat, no puedo permitirme pagar 750 libras por un abrigo.

afraid [əˈfreɪd] adj temeroso,-a. • **to be afraid** tener miedo.

afresh [əˈfreʃ] adv de nuevo.

after [ˈɑːftəʳ] prep **1** después de. **2** detrás de: the police are after us, la policía nos está persiguiendo. ► adv después. ► conj después de que. • **after all** al fin y al cabo.

after-effect [ˈɑːftərɪfekt] n efecto secundario.

afternoon [ɑːftəˈnuːn] *n* tarde: *good afternoon*, buenas tardes.

after-sales [ˈɑːftəˈseɪlz] *adj* posventa.

aftershave [ˈɑːftəʃeɪv] *n* loción para después del afeitado.

afterwards [ˈɑːftəwədz] *adv* después, luego.

again [əˈgen, əˈgeɪn] *prep* de nuevo, otra vez.

against [əˈgenst, əˈgeɪnst] *prep* contra.

age [eɪdʒ] *n* edad. ► *vi-vt* envejecer. • **of age** mayor de edad; **under age** menor de edad.

aged [eɪdʒd] *adj* **1** de… años: *a boy aged ten*, un niño de diez años. **2** viejo,-a, anciano,-a.

agency [ˈeɪdʒənsi] *n* agencia.

agenda [əˈdʒendə] *n* orden del día.

agent [ˈeɪdʒənt] *n* agente.

ages [ˈeɪdʒɪz] *npl* años, siglos: *it's ages since she left*, hace años que se marchó.

aggressive [əˈgresɪv] *adj* agresivo,-a.

agility [əˈdʒɪlɪti] *n* agilidad.

agitate [ˈædʒɪteɪt] *vt* agitar.

ago [əˈgəʊ] *adv* hace: *a long time ago*, hace mucho tiempo.

agonize [ˈægənaɪz] *vi* atormentarse, angustiarse.

agony [ˈægəni] *n* **1** dolor. **2** angustia.

agree [əˈgriː] *vi-vt* **1** estar de acuerdo. **2** ponerse de acuerdo, acordar. **3** acceder, consentir: *will he agree to our request?*, ¿accederá a nuestra petición? **4** concordar, encajar: *the two men's stories don't agree*, las historias de los dos hombres no encajan. **5** sentar bien *(comida)*.

agreeable [əˈgriːəbəl] *adj* agradable.

agreement [əˈgriːmənt] *n* acuerdo.

agriculture [ˈægrɪkʌltʃəˈ] *n* agricultura.

ahead [əˈhed] *adv* delante.

aid [eɪd] *n* ayuda, auxilio. ► *vt* ayudar, auxiliar.

AIDS [eɪdz] *abbr* SIDA.

ailment [ˈeɪlmənt] *n* dolencia, achaque.

aim [eɪm] *n* **1** puntería. **2** meta, objetivo. • **to take aim** apuntar.

to aim at *vt* apuntar a.

to aim to *vt* tener la intención de, proponerse.

air [eəˈ] *n* aire. ► *vt* **1** airear. **2** ventilar. ■ **air hostess** azafata.

airbag [ˈeəbæg] *n* airbag.

air-conditioned [eəkənˈdɪʃənd] *adj* con aire acondicionado, climatizado,-a.

aircraft [ˈeəkrɑːft] *n* avión. ■ **aircraft carrier** portaaviones.

airline [ˈeəlaɪn] *n* compañía aérea.

airplane ['eəplein] n US avión.
airport ['eəpɔːt] n aeropuerto.
airsick ['eəsɪk] adj mareado,-a *(en el avión).*
airstrip ['eəstrɪp] n pista de aterrizaje.
airtight ['eətaɪt] adj hermético,-a.
airy ['eəri] adj bien ventilado,-a.
aisle [aɪl] n 1 pasillo. 2 nave lateral.
alarm [əˈlɑːm] n alarma. ► vt alarmar. ▪ **alarm clock** despertador.
album ['ælbəm] n álbum.
alcohol ['ælkəhɒl] n alcohol.
alcoholic [ælkəˈhɒlɪk] adj alcohólico,-a.
ale [eɪl] n cerveza.
alert [əˈlɜːt] adj alerta. ► n alarma, aviso: *bomb alert,* aviso de bomba. ► vt alertar.
algae ['ældʒiː] npl algas.
alibi ['ælɪbaɪ] n coartada.
alien ['eɪlɪən] adj 1 extranjero, -a. 2 extraterrestre.
alight [əˈlaɪt] adj encendido,-a.
to alight on vt 1 posarse en. 2 darse cuenta de.
align [əˈlaɪn] vt-vi alinear(se).
alike [əˈlaɪk] adj igual. ► adv igual, de la misma forma. ● **to look alike** parecerse.
alimony ['ælɪmənɪ] n pensión alimenticia.
alive [əˈlaɪv] adj vivo,-a.
all [ɔːl] adj todo,-a, todos,-as. ► pron 1 todo, la totalidad.

2 lo único. 3 todos, todo el mundo. ► adv 1 completamente, muy: *you're all dirty!,* ¡estás todo sucio! 2 empatados, iguales: *the score was three all,* empataron a tres. ●
after all después de todo; **all right 1** bueno,-a. 2 bien: *are you all right?,* ¿estás bien?; **at all** en absoluto; **not at all 1** en absoluto. 2 no hay de qué, de nada: *Thank you very much. –Not at all,* Muchas gracias. –De nada.
allege [əˈledʒ] vt alegar.
alleged [əˈledʒd] adj presunto,-a, supuesto,-a.
allergy ['ælədʒɪ] n alergia.
alley ['ælɪ] n callejuela, callejón.
alligator ['ælɪgeɪtə] n caimán.
allocate ['æləkeɪt] vt asignar.
allow [əˈlaʊ] vt 1 permitir, dejar. 2 admitir: *dogs are not allowed in,* no se admiten perros. 3 conceder, dar, asignar.
to allow for vt tener en cuenta.
allowance [əˈlaʊəns] n 1 prestación, subsidio, dietas. 2 US paga semanal.
alloy ['ælɔɪ] n aleación.
ally ['ælaɪ] n aliado,-a. ► vt-vi aliar(se).
almond ['ɑːmənd] n almendra.
almost ['ɔːlməʊst] adv casi.
alone [əˈləʊn] adj solo,-a.
along [əˈlɒŋ] prep a lo largo de, por. ► adv hacia delante:

she was walking along, iba caminando. • **all along** desde el principio; • **along with** junto con; **come along!** ¡ven!, ¡venid!

alongside [əlɒŋ'saɪd] *prep* al lado de. ► *adv* al costado.

aloof [ə'luːf] *adj* distante.

aloud [ə'laʊd] *adv* en voz alta.

alphabet ['ælfəbet] *n* alfabeto.

already [ɔːl'redɪ] *adv* ya.

also ['ɔːlsəʊ] *adv* también.

altar ['ɔːltə'] *n* altar.

alter ['ɔːltə'] *vt* **1** cambiar, modificar. **2** arreglar *(ropa)*.

alternate [*(adj)* ɔːl'tɜːnət, *(vb)* 'ɔːltɜːneɪt] *adj* alterno,-a. ► *vt-vi* alternar(se).

alternative [ɔːl'tɜːnətɪv] *adj* alternativo,-a. ► *n* alternativa.

although [ɔːl'ðəʊ] *conj* aunque.

altogether [ɔːltə'geðə'] *adv* **1** del todo, completamente. **2** en conjunto, en total. • **in the altogether** en cueros.

always ['ɔːlweɪz] *adv* siempre.

amateur ['æmətə'] *adj-n* aficionado,-a.

amaze [ə'meɪz] *vt* asombrar.

amazing [ə'meɪzɪŋ] *adj* asombroso.

ambassador [æm'bæsədə'] *n* embajador,-ra.

amber ['æmbə'] *n* ámbar.

ambience ['æmbɪəns] *n* ambiente.

ambiguous [æm'bɪgjʊəs] *adj* ambiguo,-a.

ambition [æm'bɪʃən] *n* ambición.

ambitious [æm'bɪʃəs] *adj* ambicioso,-a.

ambulance ['æmbjʊləns] *n* ambulancia.

ambush ['æmbʊʃ] *n* emboscada. ► *vt* tender una emboscada a.

ameba [ə'miːbə] *n* US ameba.

amend [ə'mend] *vt* enmendar.

amenities [ə'miːnɪtɪz] *npl* servicios, instalaciones.

amiable ['eɪmɪəbəl] *adj* amable.

amid [ə'mɪd] *prep* en medio de, entre.

ammonia [ə'məʊnɪə] *n* amoníaco.

ammunition [æmjʊ'nɪʃən] *n* municiones.

amoeba [æ'miːbə] *n* ameba.

among [ə'mʌŋ] *prep* entre.

amongst [ə'mʌŋst] *prep* entre.

amount [ə'maʊnt] *n* cantidad.

to amount to *vt* ascender a.

ampere ['æmpeə'] *n* amperio.

amphibian [æm'fɪbɪən] *n* anfibio.

ample ['æmpəl] *adj* **1** abundante. **2** amplio,-a *(habitación)*.

amplifier ['æmplɪfaɪə'] *n* amplificador.

amplify ['æmplɪfaɪ] *vt* amplificar.

amputate ['æmpjʊteɪt] *vt* amputar.

amuse [ə'mjuːz] *vt* entretener, divertir.

amusement [ə'mjuːzmənt] *n* diversión, entretenimiento. ▪ **amusement park** parque de atracciones.

amusing [ə'mjuːzɪŋ] *adj* divertido,-a.

an [ən, æn] *det* un,-a.

anaemia [ə'niːmɪə] *n* GB anemia.

anaesthesia [ænəs'θiːzɪə] *n* GB anestesia.

anal ['eɪnəl] *adj* anal.

analgesic [ænəl'dʒiːzɪk] *adj* analgésico,-a. ► *n* analgésico.

analyse ['ænəlaɪz] *vt* analizar.

analysis [ə'næləsɪs] *n* análisis.

anarchy ['ænəkɪ] *n* anarquía.

anatomy [ə'nætəmɪ] *n* anatomía.

ancestor ['ænsəstəʳ] *n* antepasado.

anchor ['æŋkəʳ] *n* ancla. ► *vt-vi* anclar.

anchovy ['æntʃəvɪ] *n* anchoa.

ancient ['eɪnʃənt] *adj* antiguo, -a, histórico,-a.

and [ænd, ənd] *conj* y, e.

anecdote ['ænɪkdəʊt] *n* anécdota.

anemia [ə'niːmɪə] *n* US anemia.

anesthesia [ænəs'θiːzɪə] *n* US anestesia.

angel ['eɪndʒəl] *n* ángel.

anger ['æŋgəʳ] *n* cólera, ira.

angle ['æŋgəl] *n* ángulo.

angler ['æŋgləʳ] *n* pescador,-ra (de caña). ▪ **angler fish** rape.

angling ['æŋglɪŋ] *n* pesca (con caña).

angry ['æŋgrɪ] *adj* enfadado,-a.

anguish ['æŋgwɪʃ] *n* angustia.

animal ['ænɪməl] *n* animal.

animate ['ænɪmeɪt] *vt* animar.

ankle ['æŋkəl] *n* tobillo.

annex [(*vb*) ə'neks(*n*) 'æneks] *vt* anexar. ► *n* US anexo.

annexe ['æneks] *n* GB anexo.

annihilate [ə'naɪəleɪt] *vt* aniquilar.

anniversary [ænɪ'vɜːsərɪ] *n* aniversario.

announce [ə'naʊns] *vt* anunciar.

announcement [ə'naʊnsmənt] *n* anuncio.

announcer [ə'naʊnsəʳ] *n* presentador,-ra, locutor,-ra.

annoy [ə'nɔɪ] *vt* molestar.

anonymous [ə'nɒnɪməs] *adj* anónimo,-a.

anorexia [ænə'reksɪə] *n* anorexia.

another [ə'nʌðəʳ] *adj-pron* otro,-a.

answer ['ɑːnsəʳ] *n* respuesta. ► *vt-vi* responder, contestar.

to answer back *vt-vi* replicar (con insolencia).

to answer for *vt* responder por, responder de.

answering machine ['ɑːnsərɪŋməʃiːn] *n* contestador automático.

ant [ænt] *n* hormiga. ■ **ant hill** hormiguero.

antelope ['æntɪləʊp] *n* antílope.

antenna [æn'tenə] *n* antena.

anthem ['ænθəm] *n* himno.

antibiotic [æntɪbaɪ'ɒtɪk] *n* antibiótico. ► *adj* antibiótico,-a.

antibody ['æntɪbɒdɪ] *n* anticuerpo.

anticipate [æn'tɪsɪpeɪt] *vt* 1 esperar: *we anticipate problems*, esperamos problemas. 2 prever: *as anticipated*, de acuerdo con lo previsto.

anticlockwise [æntɪ'klɒkwaɪz] *adj* en el sentido contrario al de las agujas del reloj.

antifreeze ['æntɪfriːz] *n* anticongelante.

antique [æn'tiːk] *adj* antiguo, -a. ► *n* antigüedad. ■ **antique shop** anticuario, tienda de antigüedades.

antiseptic [æntɪ'septɪk] *adj* antiséptico,-a. ► *n* antiséptico.

antivirus [æntɪ'vaɪrəs] *adj* antivirus.

antlers ['æntləʳ] *npl* cornamenta.

anus ['eɪnəs] *n* ano.

anvil ['ænvɪl] *n* yunque.

anxious ['æŋkʃəs] *adj* ansioso,-a.

any ['enɪ] *adj* algún,-una, ningún,-una *(con el verbo negativo)*, cualquier,-ra, todo,-a: *any fool knows that*, cualquier tonto sabe eso. ► *pron* alguno,-a, ninguno,-a *(con el verbo negativo)*, cualquiera: *I asked for some records, but they hadn't got any left*, pedí unos discos pero ya no quedaba ninguno. ► *adv*: *I don't work there any more*, ya no trabajo allí.

anybody ['enɪbɒdɪ] *pron* alguien, alguno,-a, nadie *(con el verbo negativo)*, cualquiera: *don't tell anybody*, no se lo digas a nadie.

anyhow ['enɪhaʊ] *adv* 1 en todo caso. 2 bueno, pues. 3 de cualquier forma.

anyone ['enɪwʌn] *pron* → anybody.

anything ['enɪθɪŋ] *pron* algo, alguna cosa, nada *(con el verbo negativo)*, cualquier cosa, todo cuanto: *do you want anything else?*, ¿quieres algo más?

anyway ['enɪweɪ] *adv* → anyhow.

anywhere ['enɪweəʳ] *adv* 1 (en) algún sitio, a algún sitio. 2 (en) ningún sitio, a ningún sitio *(con el verbo negativo)*. 3 donde sea, en cualquier sitio, a donde sea, a cualquier sitio: *I'd go anywhere with you*, iría a cualquier sitio contigo.

aorta [eɪ'ɔːtə] *n* aorta.

apart [ə'pɑːt] *adv* separado,-a.
• **apart from** aparte de, excepto, menos.

apartment [ə'pɑːtmənt] *n* piso, apartamento.

apathy ['æpəθɪ] *n* apatía.

ape [eɪp] *n* simio. ▶ *vt* imitar.

aperitif [əperɪ'tiːf] *n* aperitivo.

apiece [ə'piːs] *adv* cada uno,-a.

apologize [ə'pɒlədʒaɪz] *vi* disculparse, pedir perdón.

apology [ə'pɒlədʒɪ] *n* disculpa.

appal [ə'pɔːl] *vt* GB horrorizar.

appall [ə'pɔːl] *vt* US horrorizar.

apparatus [æpə'reɪtəs] *n* equipo, aparatos.

apparent [ə'pærənt] *adj* **1** evidente. **2** aparente.

appeal [ə'piːl] *n* **1** llamamiento. **2** petición, súplica. **3** atractivo. **4** apelación *(contra sentencia judicial)*. ▶ *vi* **1** pedir, solicitar, suplicar. **2** atraer: *it doesn't appeal to me*, no me atrae. **3** apelar *(contra sentencia judicial)*.

appealing [ə'piːlɪŋ] *adj* atractivo.

appear [ə'pɪəʳ] *vi* **1** aparecer. **2** parecer: *this appears to be a mistake*, parece que esto es un error.

appearance [ə'pɪərəns] *n* **1** aparición. **2** apariencia, aspecto.

appendicitis [əpendɪ'saɪtɪs] *n* apendicitis.

appendix [ə'pendɪks] *n* apéndice.

appetizer ['æpɪtaɪzəʳ] *n* aperitivo.

appetizing ['æpɪtaɪzɪŋ] *adj* apetitoso,-a.

applaud [ə'plɔːd] *vt-vi* aplaudir.

applause [ə'plɔːz] *n* aplausos.

apple ['æpəl] *n* manzana. ▪ **apple pie** tarta de manzana.

appliance [ə'plaɪəns] *n* aparato.

applicant ['æplɪkənt] *n* candidato,-a, solicitante.

application [æplɪ'keɪʃən] *n* **1** solicitud. **2** aplicación. ▪ **application form** impreso de solicitud.

apply [ə'plaɪ] *vt* aplicar. ▶ *vi* **1** aplicarse. **2** dirigirse, presentarse, solicitar: *to apply for a job*, solicitar un trabajo.

appointment [ə'pɔɪntmənt] *n* **1** cita, hora: *I've got an appointment with the doctor*, tengo hora con el médico. **2** nombramiento.

appraise [ə'preɪz] *vt* valorar.

appreciate [ə'priːʃɪeɪt] *vt* **1** agradecer. **2** entender. **3** valorar, apreciar.

apprehension [æprɪ'henʃən] *n* **1** detención, captura. **2** aprensión, recelo.

apprehensive [æprɪ'hensɪv] *adj* aprensivo.

apprentice [ə'prentɪs] *n* aprendiz,-za.

approach [ə'prəʊtʃ] *n* **1** aproximación, acercamiento. **2** entrada, acceso *(a un lugar)*. **3** enfoque *(de un problema)*. ▶ *vt* **1** acercarse a, aproximarse a.

2 enfocar, abordar *(un problema)*. ■ **approach road** vía de acceso.

appropriate [ə'prəʊprɪət] *adj* apropiado,-a.

approval [ə'pruːvəl] *n* aprobación. • **on approval** a prueba.

approve [ə'pruːv] *vt* aprobar. **to approve of** aprobar.

approximate [ə'prɒksɪmət] *adj* aproximado,-a.

apricot ['eɪprɪkɒt] *n* albaricoque.

April ['eɪprɪl] *n* abril. ■ **April Fool's day** el día de los Inocentes *(celebrado el 1 de abril)*.

apron ['eɪprən] *n* delantal.

apt [æpt] *adj* apropiado,-a.

aquarium [ə'kweərɪəm] *n* acuario.

Arab ['ærəb] *adj* árabe. ► *n* árabe.

arbitrate ['ɑːbɪtreɪt] *vt-vi* arbitrar.

arc [ɑːk] *n* arco.

arcade [ɑː'keɪd] *n* **1** galería comercial. **2** salón recreativo. ■ **arcade game** videojuego.

arch [ɑːtʃ] *n* arco.

archaeology [ɑːkɪ'ɒlədʒɪ] *n* arqueología.

archery ['ɑːtʃərɪ] *n* tiro con arco.

archipelago [ɑːkɪ'pelɪgəʊ] *n* archipiélago.

architect ['ɑːkɪtekt] *n* arquitecto,-a.

architecture ['ɑːkɪtektʃə'] *n* arquitectura.

archive ['ɑːkaɪv] *n* archivo.

are [ɑː', ə'] *pres* → be.

area ['eərɪə] *n* área.

arena [ə'riːnə] *n* **1** estadio. **2** ruedo *(de plaza de toros)*.

argue ['ɑːgjuː] *vi* **1** discutir. **2** argüir, argumentar.

argument ['ɑːgjʊmənt] *n* **1** discusión, disputa. **2** argumento.

arise [ə'raɪz] *vi* **1** surgir, provenir de. **2** presentarse.

aristocrat ['ærɪstəkræt] *n* aristócrata.

arithmetic [ə'rɪθmətɪk] *n* aritmética.

ark [ɑːk] *n* arca.

arm [ɑːm] *n* **1** brazo. **2** manga. **3** arma.

armchair [ɑːm'tʃeə'] *n* sillón.

armour ['ɑːmə'] (US **armor**) *n* **1** armadura. **2** blindaje.

armpit ['ɑːmpɪt] *n* sobaco, axila.

army ['ɑːmɪ] *n* ejército.

aroma [ə'rəʊmə] *n* aroma.

arose [ə'rəʊz] *pt* → arise.

around [ə'raʊnd] *adv* alrededor. ► *prep* alrededor de.

arouse [ə'raʊz] *vt* despertar.

arrange [ə'reɪndʒ] *vt* **1** arreglar, colocar, ordenar. **2** planear, organizar, concertar.

arrangement [ə'reɪndʒmənt] *n* **1** arreglo *(floral, musical)*. **2** acuerdo, arreglo. ► *npl* **arrangements** planes, preparativos.

arrears [ə'rɪəz] *npl* atrasos.

arrest [ə'rest] n arresto. ► vt arrestar, detener: **to be under arrest**, estar detenido.

arrival [ə'raɪvəl] n llegada.

arrive [ə'raɪv] vi llegar.

arrow ['ærəʊ] n flecha.

arse [ɑːs] n GB vulg culo.

arson ['ɑːsən] n incendio provocado.

art [ɑːt] n arte. ► npl **arts** letras. ■ **arts and crafts** artes y oficios.

artery ['ɑːterɪ] n arteria.

artichoke ['ɑːtɪtʃəʊk] n alcachofa.

article ['ɑːtɪkəl] n artículo. ■ **leading article** editorial.

artificial [ɑːtɪ'fɪʃəl] adj artificial.

artisan ['ɑːtɪzæn] n artesano,-a.

artist ['ɑːtɪst] n artista.

as [æz, əz] prep como. ► conj **1** mientras, cuando: **she sang as she painted**, cantaba mientras pintaba. **2** como, ya que, puesto que: **as the hotel was full, we had to look for another**, como el hotel estaba completo, tuvimos que buscar otro. **3** como: **as you know**, como sabes. • **as... as 1** tan... como: **as big as an elephant**, tan grande como un elefante. **2** tanto como: **he works as little as possible**, trabaja lo mínimo posible; **as for** en cuanto a; **as if** como si; **as of** desde; **as though** como si; **as yet** hasta ahora.

asbestos [æs'bestəs] n amianto.

ascend [ə'send] vt-vi ascender, subir.

ascent [ə'sent] n subida.

ascribe [əs'kraɪb] vt atribuir.

ash[1] [æʃ] n ceniza.

ash[2] [æʃ] n fresno.

ashamed [ə'ʃeɪmd] adj avergonzado,-a.

ashore [ə'ʃɔːʳ] adv en tierra, a tierra. • **to go ashore** desembarcar.

ashtray ['æʃtreɪ] n cenicero.

aside [ə'saɪd] adv al lado, a un lado. ► n aparte (en teatro).

ask [ɑːsk] vt **1** preguntar. **2** pedir. **3** invitar, convidar: **they asked me to dinner**, me invitaron a cenar.

to ask after vt preguntar por.

to ask for vt pedir.

to ask out vt invitar a salir.

asleep [ə'sliːp] adj-adv dormido,-a: **to fall asleep**, dormirse.

asparagus [æs'pærəgəs] n espárragos.

aspect ['æspekt] n **1** aspecto. **2** orientación (de edificio).

asphalt ['æsfælt] n asfalto.

aspire [əs'paɪəʳ] vi aspirar.

aspirin® ['æspɪrɪn] n aspirina®.

ass [æs] n burro,-a, asno,-a.

assailant [ə'seɪlənt] n agresor,-ra.

assault [ə'sɔːlt] n **1** asalto (militar). **2** agresión (a persona).

assemble [ə'sembəl] vt montar, armar. ► vi reunirse.

assembly [ə'semblɪ] *n* **1** reunión, asamblea. **2** montaje, ensamblaje. ▪ **assembly hall** salón de actos.

assert [ə'sɜːt] *vt* **1** afirmar. **2** imponer *(autoridad)*.

assess [ə'ses] *vt* valorar.

asset ['æset] *n* ventaja, baza. ▶ *npl* **assets** bienes.

assign [ə'saɪn] *vt* asignar.

assignment [ə'saɪnmənt] *n* **1** misión. **2** tarea, trabajo.

assist [ə'sɪst] *vt* ayudar.

assistant [ə'sɪstənt] *n* ayudante. ▪ **assistant manager** subdirector,-ra.

associate [(*n*) ə'səʊsɪət, (*vb*) ə'səʊsɪeɪt] *n* socio,-a. ▶ *vt-vi* asociar(se). • **to associate with SB** relacionarse con ALGN.

association [əsəʊsɪ'eɪʃən] *n* asociación.

assortment [ə'sɔːtmənt] *n* surtido.

assume [ə'sjuːm] *vt* **1** suponer. **2** tomar, asumir *(responsabilidad)*. **3** adoptar *(actitud)*.

assurance [ə'ʃʊərəns] *n* **1** garantía. **2** seguro.

assure [ə'ʃʊəʳ] *vt* asegurar.

asthma ['æsmə] *n* asma.

astonish [əs'tɒnɪʃ] *vt* asombrar.

astray [ə'streɪ] *adj-adv* extraviado,-a. • **to go astray 1** extraviarse. **2** descarriarse.

astrology [əs'trɒlədʒɪ] *n* astrología.

astronaut ['æstrənɔːt] *n* astronauta.

astronomy [əs'trɒnəmɪ] *n* astronomía.

astute [əs'tjuːt] *adj* astuto,-a, sagaz.

asylum [ə'saɪləm] *n* **1** asilo, refugio. **2** manicomio.

at [æt, ət] *prep* en, a: *at home*, en casa; *at night*, por la noche; *at the beginning/end*, al principio/final; *at 50 miles an hour*, a 50 millas la hora.

ate [et, eɪt] *pt* → eat.

atheist ['eɪθɪɪst] *n* ateo,-a.

athlete ['æθliːt] *n* atleta.

athletics [æθ'letɪks] *n* atletismo.

atlas ['ætləs] *n* atlas.

atmosphere ['ætməsfɪəʳ] *n* atmósfera.

atom ['ætəm] *n* átomo. ▪ **atom bomb** bomba atómica.

atrocity [ə'trɒsɪtɪ] *n* atrocidad.

attach [ə'tætʃ] *vt* **1** sujetar. **2** atar. **3** pegar. **4** adjuntar.

attachment [ə'tætʃmənt] *n* **1** accesorio. **2** archivo adjunto, anexo. **3** cariño, apego.

attack [ə'tæk] *n* ataque. ▶ *vt* atacar.

attain [ə'teɪn] *vt* lograr.

attempt [ə'tempt] *n* intento. ▶ *vt* intentar.

attend [ə'tend] *vt* asistir a.

to attend to *vt* ocuparse de

attendance [ə'tendəns] *n* **1** asistencia. **2** asistentes.

attention [əˈtenʃən] *n* atención.

attic [ˈætɪk] *n* desván.

attitude [ˈætɪtjuːd] *n* actitud.

attorney [əˈtɜːnɪ] *n* US aboga-do,-a. ■ **Attorney General** GB Fiscal General.

attract [əˈtrækt] *vt* atraer.

aubergine [ˈəʊbəʒiːn] *n* GB be-renjena.

auction [ˈɔːkʃən] *n* subasta. ► *vt* subastar.

audience [ˈɔːdɪəns] *n* **1** públi-co, espectadores. **2** audien-cia *(de televisión)*.

audit [ˈɔːdɪt] *n* auditoría. ► *vt* auditar.

August [ˈɔːgəst] *n* agosto.

aunt [ɑːnt] *n* tía.

authentic [ɔːˈθentɪk] *adj* au-téntico,-a.

author [ˈɔːθəʳ] *n* autor,-ra.

authority [ɔːˈθɒrɪtɪ] *n* autori-dad. ● **on good authority** de buena tinta.

authorize [ˈɔːθəraɪz] *vt* auto-rizar.

automatic [ɔːtəˈmætɪk] *adj* au-tomático,-a.

automaton [ɔːˈtɒmətən] *n* au-tómata.

automobile [ˈɔːtəməbiːl] *n* au-tomóvil.

autopsy [ˈɔːtɒpsɪ] *n* autopsia.

autoteller [ˈɔːtəʊtələʳ] *n* cajero automático.

autumn [ˈɔːtəm] *n* otoño.

auxiliary [ɔːgˈzɪljərɪ] *adj* auxi-liar.

available [əˈveɪləbəl] *adj* dis-ponible.

avalanche [ˈævəlɑːnʃ] *n* alud, avalancha.

avenge [əˈvendʒ] *vt* vengar.

avenue [ˈævənjuː] *n* avenida.

average [ˈævərɪdʒ] *n* promedio, media. ► *adj* medio,-a. ● **on av-erage** por término medio.

aviation [eɪvɪˈeɪʃən] *n* aviación.

avocado [ævəˈkɑːdəʊ] *n* agua-cate.

avoid [əˈvɔɪd] *vt* evitar.

awake [əˈweɪk] *adj* despierto, -a. ► *vt-vi* despertar(se).

awaken [əˈweɪkən] *vt-vi* → awake.

award [əˈwɔːd] *n* **1** premio. **2** beca. ► *vt* otorgar, conceder.

aware [əˈweəʳ] *adj* consciente. ● **to be aware of** ser cons-ciente de.

away [əˈweɪ] *adv* lejos, fuera: *he lives 4 km away*, vive a 4 km de aquí.

awful [ˈɔːful] *adj* horrible.

awkward [ˈɔːkwəd] *adj* **1** torpe *(gesto)*. **2** difícil, complicado, -a. **3** embarazo-so,-a, delica-do,-a *(situación)*.

awning [ˈɔːnɪŋ] *n* toldo.

awoke [əˈwəʊk] *pt* → awake.

awoken [əˈwəʊkən] *pp* → awake.

ax [æks] *n* US hacha.

axe [æks] *n* GB hacha.

axis [ˈæksɪs] *n* eje.

axle [ˈæksəl] *n* eje.

B

baa [bɑː] *vi* balar.
B & B [ˈbiːənˈbiː] *abbr (bed and breakfast)* hostal familiar.
babble [ˈbæbəl] *vt-vi* balbucear.
baby [ˈbeɪbɪ] *n* bebé, niño,-a.
baby-sitter [ˈbeɪbɪsɪtəˈ] *n* canguro.
bachelor [ˈbætʃələˈ] *n* soltero.
back [bæk] *adj* trasero,-a, posterior. ► *n* **1** espalda. **2** lomo *(de animal)*. **3** respaldo *(de silla)*. **4** fondo, parte de atrás. **5** defensa *(en deportes)*. ► *adv* **1** atrás, hacia atrás, hace. **2** de vuelta. ► *vt* **1** apoyar, respaldar. **2** financiar. **3** dar marcha atrás a *(coche)*. ► *vi* retroceder. •**back to front** al revés. ▪**back pay** atrasos; **back street** callejuela.
backbone [ˈbækbəun] *n* columna vertebral.
background [ˈbækɡraʊnd] *n* **1** fondo *(de imagen)*. **2** *fig* origen, formación.
backhand [ˈbækhænd] *n* revés.
backpack [ˈbækpæk] *n* mochila.
backstroke [ˈbækstrəuk] *n* espalda *(en natación)*.
backup [ˈbækʌp] *n* apoyo. ▪ **backup copy** copia de seguridad.
backward [ˈbækwəd] **1** *adj* hacia atrás. **2** atrasado,-a, retrasado. ► *adv* → backwards.

backwards [ˈbækwədz] *adv* **1** hacia atrás. **2** al revés. • **backwards and forwards** de acá para allá.
bacon [ˈbeɪkən] *n* beicon.
bad [bæd] *adj* **1** malo,-a, mal. **2** grave: *a bad accident*, un accidente grave. **3** fuerte *(dolor de cabeza)*. • **to go bad** echarse a perder, pudrirse; **to go from bad to worse** ir de mal en peor.
bade [beɪd] *pt* → bid.
badge [bædʒ] *n* **1** insignia. **2** chapa.
badger [ˈbædʒəˈ] *n* tejón.
bad-tempered [bædˈtempəd] *adj*. • **to be bad-tempered** tener mal carácter, estar de mal humor.
bag [bæg] *n* **1** bolsa, saco. **2** bolso.
baggage [ˈbæɡɪdʒ] *n* equipaje.
baggy [ˈbæɡɪ] *adj* holgado,-a.
bagpipes [ˈbæɡpaɪps] *npl* gaita.
bail [beɪl] *n* fianza.
bait [beɪt] *n* cebo.
bake [beɪk] *vt* cocer al horno. ▪ **baked beans** alubias cocidas con salsa de tomate.
baker [ˈbeɪkəˈ] *n* panadero,-a.
baker's [ˈbeɪkəz] *n* panadería.
bakery [ˈbeɪkərɪ] *n* panadería.
balance [ˈbæləns] *n* **1** equilibrio. **2** balanza. **3** saldo, balance. ► *vi* mantenerse en equilibrio.
balcony [ˈbælkənɪ] *n* balcón.

bald [bɔːld] *adj* calvo,-a.

ball [bɔːl] *n* **1** pelota, balón, bola. **2** ovillo. **3** baile, fiesta.

ballet ['bæleɪ] *n* ballet. ▪ **ballet dancer** bailarín, bailarina.

balloon [bə'luːn] *n* globo.

ballot ['bælət] *n* **1** votación. **2** papeleta. ▪ **ballot box** urna.

ballpoint pen ['bɔːlpɔɪnt pen] *n* bolígrafo.

ballroom ['bɔːlruːm] *n* sala de baile.

balm [baːm] *n* bálsamo.

ban [bæn] *n* prohibición. ▸ *vt* prohibir.

banana [bə'naːnə] *n* plátano.

band [bænd] *n* **1** banda. **2** cinta, tira. **3** raya, franja.

bandage ['bændɪdʒ] *n* venda, vendaje. ▸ *vt* vendar.

bandit ['bændɪt] *n* bandido,-a.

bandstand ['bændstænd] *n* quiosco de música.

bang [bæŋ] *n* **1** golpe. **2** porrazo, estampido, estallido, portazo. ▸ *vt-vi* golpear.

banger ['bæŋəʳ] *n* **1** petardo. **2** GB *fam* salchicha.

bangle ['bæŋɡəl] *n* pulsera.

banish ['bænɪʃ] *vt* desterrar.

banister ['bænɪstəʳ] *n* barandilla.

bank¹ [bæŋk] *n* banco. ▪ **bank account** cuenta bancaria; **bank holiday** GB día festivo.

bank² [bæŋk] *n* **1** banco *(para sentarse)*. **2** ribera, orilla *(de río)*.

banker ['bæŋkəʳ] *n* banquero,-a.

banknote ['bæŋknəʊt] *n* billete de banco.

bankrupt ['bæŋkrʌpt] *adj* en quiebra, en bancarrota.

banner ['bænəʳ] *n* **1** estandarte. **2** pancarta.

banquet ['bæŋkwɪt] *n* banquete.

baptize [bæp'taɪz] *vt* bautizar.

bar [baːʳ] *n* **1** barra. **2** pastilla *(de jabón)*. **3** tableta *(de chocolate)*. **4** bar.

barb [baːb] *n* **1** púa. **2** lengüeta.

barbecue ['baːbəkjuː] *n* barbacoa.

barber's ['baːbəs] *n* barbería.

barbiturate [baː'bɪtʃərət] *n* barbitúrico.

bare [beəʳ] *adj* **1** desnudo,-a, descubierto,-a. **2** mero,-a: *a bare 10%*, solo el 10%.

barely ['beəlɪ] *adv* apenas.

bargain ['baːɡən] *n* **1** trato. **2** ganga. ▸ *vi* **1** negociar. **2** regatear.

bark¹ [baːk] *n* ladrido. ▸ *vi* ladrar.

bark² [baːk] *n* corteza *(de árbol)*.

barley ['baːlɪ] *n* cebada.

barmaid ['baːmeɪd] *n* camarera.

barman ['baːmən] *n* camarero, barman.

barn [baːn] *n* granero.

barnacle ['baːnəkəl] *n* bálano.

baroque [bə'rɒk] *adj* barroco,-a.

barracks ['bærəks] *n* cuartel.
barrel ['bærəl] *n* **1** barril, tonel, cuba. **2** cañón *(de fusil)*.
barren ['bærən] *adj* estéril.
barricade [bærɪ'keɪd] *n* barricada
barrier ['bærɪəʳ] *n* barrera.
barrister ['bærɪstəʳ] *n* abogado,-a *(en tribunales superiores)*.
barter ['bɑːtəʳ] *n* trueque.
base [beɪs] *n* base. ► *vt* basar.
baseball ['beɪsbɔːl] *n* béisbol.
basement ['beɪsmənt] *n* sótano.
basic ['beɪsɪk] *adj* básico,-a.
basin ['beɪsən] *n* **1** cuenco. **2** lavabo. **3** cuenca.
basis ['beɪsɪs] *n* base: **on a weekly basis**, semanalmente.
basket ['bɑːskɪt] *n* cesta, cesto.
basketball ['bɑːskɪtbɔːl] *n* baloncesto.
bass[1] [bæs] *n* lubina.
bass[2] [beɪs] *n* bajo *(cantante, instrumento)*.
bassoon [bə'suːn] *n* fagot.
bat[1] [bæt] *n* murciélago.
bat[2] [bæt] *n* bate.
batch [bætʃ] *n* lote.
bath [bɑːθ] *n* **1** baño. **2** bañera. ► *vt* bañar. ► *vi* bañarse. ► *npl* **baths** piscina *(pública)*.
bathe [beɪð] *vi* bañarse. ► *vt* lavar *(herida)*.
bathing ['beɪðɪŋ] *n* baño. ■ **bathing costume** traje de baño, bañador; **bathing suit** traje de baño.

bathrobe ['bɑːθrəub] *n* albornoz.
bathroom ['bɑːθruːm] *n* cuarto de baño.
bathtub ['bɑːθtʌb] *n* bañera.
baton ['bætən] *n* **1** porra *(de policía)*. **2** batuta *(música)*. **3** testigo *(carrera de relevos)*.
batter[1] ['bætəʳ] *n* rebozado.
batter[2] ['bætəʳ] *vt* apalear.
battery ['bætərɪ] *n* **1** batería. **2** pila.
battle ['bætəl] *n* batalla.
battlements ['bætəlmənts] *npl* almenas.
battleship ['bætəlʃɪp] *n* acorazado.
bauble ['bɔːbəl] *n* baratija.
baulk [bɔːk] *vt* → balk.
bay[1] [beɪ] *n* bahía, golfo.
bay[2] [beɪ] *n* laurel.
bay[3] [beɪ] *n* hueco. ■ **loading bay** cargadero; **parking bay** plaza de parking.
be [biː] *vi* **1** ser: **she's clever**, es inteligente. **2** estar: **how are you?**, ¿cómo estás? **3** tener: **I'm cold**, tengo frío. **4** hacer: **it's sunny**, hace sol. ► *aux* **1** be + *pres participle* estar: **it is raining**, está lloviendo. **2** be + *past participle* ser: **he was sacked**, fue despedido, lo despidieron. **3** be + *infinitive*: **the King is to visit Egypt**, el Rey visitará Egipto. ●**there is/are** hay.
beach [biːtʃ] *n* playa. ► *vt* varar, embarrancar.

bead [bi:d] *n* **1** cuenta *(de collar)*. **2** gota *(de sudor)*.

beak [bi:k] *n* pico.

beam [bi:m] *n* **1** viga. **2** rayo *(de luz)*. ► *vi* sonreír.

bean [bi:n] *n* **1** alubia, judía, haba. **2** grano *(de café)*.

bear[1] [beə'] *n* oso.

bear[2] [beə'] *vt* soportar.

beard [bɪəd] *n* barba.

bearer ['beərə'] *n* **1** portador, -ra. **2** titular.

bearing ['beərɪŋ] *n* cojinete.

beast [bi:st] *n* bestia, animal.

beat [bi:t] *vt* **1** golpear. **2** batir *(huevos, alas, récord)*. **3** vencer, derrotar. ► *vi* latir *(corazón)*. ► *n* **1** latido. **2** ritmo. ► *adj fam* agotado,-a.

beautician [bju:'tɪʃən] *n* esteticista.

beautiful ['bju:tɪfʊl] *adj* **1** bonito,-a. **2** maravilloso,-a.

beauty ['bju:tɪ] *n* belleza. ■ **beauty contest** concurso de belleza; **beauty spot 1** lunar. **2** lugar pintoresco.

beaver ['bi:və'] *n* castor.

became [bɪ'keɪm] *pt* → become.

because [bɪ'kɒz] *conj* porque. ► *prep* **because of** a causa de.

become [bɪ'kʌm] *vi* **1** convertirse en. **2** volverse. • **to become of** ser de.

bed [bed] *n* **1** cama. **2** macizo *(de flores)*. **3** lecho, cauce *(de río)*, fondo *(del mar)*.

bed and breakfast [bedən-'brekfəst] *n* hostal familiar.

bedroom ['bedru:m] *n* dormitorio.

bedside ['bedsaɪd] *n* cabecera. ■ **bedside table** mesita de noche.

bedspread ['bedspred] *n* colcha.

bee [bi:] *n* abeja.

beech [bi:tʃ] *n* haya.

beef [bi:f] *n* carne de vaca.

beefburger ['bi:fbɜ:gə'] *n* hamburguesa.

beefsteak ['bi:fsteɪk] *n* bistec.

beehive ['bi:haɪv] *n* colmena.

been [bi:n, bɪn] *pp* → be.

beer [bɪə'] *n* cerveza.

beetle ['bi:təl] *n* escarabajo.

beetroot ['bi:tru:t] *n* remolacha.

before [bɪ'fɔ:'] *prep* **1** antes de. **2** delante de, ante. ► *conj* antes de + *inf*, antes de que + *subj*: *before you go*, antes de irte, antes de que te vayas. ► *adv* **1** antes. **2** anterior.

beforehand [bɪ'fɔ:hænd] *adv* de antemano.

beg [beg] *vi* mendigar. ► *vt* pedir, suplicar, rogar.

began [bɪ'gæn] *pt* → begin.

beggar ['begə'] *n* mendigo,-a.

begin [bɪ'gɪn] *vt-vi* empezar, comenzar. • **to begin with** para empezar.

beginner [bɪ'gɪnə'] *n* principiante.

beginning [bɪˈgɪnɪŋ] *n* principio.

begun [bɪˈgʌn] *pp* → begin.

behave [bɪˈheɪv] *vi* comportarse, portarse. • **to behave oneself** portarse bien.

behaviour [bɪˈheɪvjəʳ] (US **behavior**) *n* conducta, comportamiento.

behead [bɪˈhed] *vt* decapitar.

behind [bɪˈhaɪnd] *prep* detrás de. ▶ *adv* **1** detrás. **2** atrasado, -a: *he's behind with his work*, va atrasado con el trabajo.

beige [beɪʒ] *adj-n* beige.

belch [beltʃ] *n* eructo.

belief [bɪˈliːf] *n* creencia.

believe [bɪˈliːv] *vt-vi* creer.

bell [bel] *n* **1** campana. **2** timbre: *to ring the bell*, tocar el timbre.

bellboy [ˈbelbɔɪ] *n* botones.

bellow [ˈbeləʊ] *n* bramido.

belly [ˈbelɪ] *n* vientre, barriga. ■ **belly button** *fam* ombligo.

belong [bɪˈlɒŋ] *vi* **1** pertenecer. **2** ser socio,-a.

belongings [bɪˈlɒŋɪŋz] *npl* pertenencias.

below [bɪˈləʊ] *prep* debajo de, por debajo de. ▶ *adv* abajo. • **below zero** bajo cero.

belt [belt] *n* **1** cinturón. **2** correa.

bench [bentʃ] *n* **1** banco (*asiento*). **2** banquillo.

bend [bend] *n* curva. ▶ *vt* doblar. ▶ *vi* **1** doblarse. **2** torcer.

to bend over *vi* inclinarse.

beneath [bɪˈniːθ] *prep* bajo, debajo de, por debajo de. ▶ *adv* abajo, debajo.

benefit [ˈbenɪfɪt] *n* **1** beneficio. **2** subsidio. ▶ *vt-vi* beneficiar(se).

benign [bɪˈnaɪn] *adj* benigno,-a.

bent [bent] *pt-pp* → bend.

bequest [bɪˈkwest] *n* legado.

beret [ˈbereɪ] *n* boina.

berry [ˈberɪ] *n* baya.

berth [bɜːθ] *n* **1** amarradero. **2** litera.

beside [bɪˈsaɪd] *prep* al lado de, junto a.

besides [bɪˈsaɪdz] *prep* **1** además de. **2** aparte de. ▶ *adv* además.

besiege [bɪˈsiːdʒ] *vt* sitiar.

best [best] *adj* mejor. ▶ *adv* mejor. ▶ *n* lo mejor. • **all the best!** ¡que te vaya bien!; **at best** en el mejor de los casos; **to do one's best** esmerarse. ■ **best man** ayudante del novio (*en boda*).

bet [bet] *n* apuesta. ▶ *vt-vi* apostar.

betray [bɪˈtreɪ] *vt* traicionar.

better [ˈbetəʳ] *adj* mejor. ▶ *adv* mejor. ▶ *vt* mejorar. • **had better** más vale que + *subj*: *we'd better be going*, más vale que nos vayamos, deberíamos irnos; **to get better** mejorar, ponerse mejor. ■ **better half** media naranja.

betting [ˈbetɪŋ] *n* apuestas.

between [bɪ'twiːn] *prep* entre. ▶ *adv* en medio, entre medio.

beverage ['bevərɪdʒ] *n* bebida.

beware [bɪ'weə'] *vi* tener cuidado.

bewilder [bɪ'wɪldə'] *vt* desconcertar, confundir.

bewitch [bɪ'wɪtʃ] *vt* hechizar.

beyond [bɪ'jɒnd] *prep* más allá de, al otro lado de. ▶ *adv* más allá.

bias ['baɪəs] *n* parcialidad, prejuicio.

bib [bɪb] *n* babero.

biceps ['baɪseps] *n* bíceps.

bicycle ['baɪsɪkəl] *n* bicicleta.

bid [bɪd] *n* **1** puja. **2** intento. **3** oferta. ▶ *vt-vi* pujar.

bidet ['biːdeɪ] *n* bidé.

big [bɪg] *adj* grande, gran.
■ **big brother** hermano mayor; **big game** caza mayor; **big sister** hermana mayor.

bike [baɪk] *n* **1** *fam* bici. **2** *fam* moto.

bikini [bɪ'kiːnɪ] *n* biquini.

bile [baɪl] *n* bilis, hiel.

bill [bɪl] *n* **1** factura, cuenta. **2** proyecto de ley. **3** US billete de banco. **4** cartel, póster.
● **to top the bill** encabezar el reparto. ■ **bill of exchange** letra de cambio.

billboard ['bɪlbɔːd] *n* US valla publicitaria.

billiards ['bɪlɪədz] *n* billar.

billion ['bɪlɪən] *n* mil millones.

bin [bɪn] *n* cubo de la basura, papelera.

bind [baɪnd] *vt* **1** atar. **2** ligar *(salsa)*. **3** obligar. **4** encuadernar.

binder ['baɪndə'] *n* carpeta.

binoculars [bɪ'nɒkjʊləz] *npl* gemelos.

biography [baɪ'ɒgrəfɪ] *n* biografía.

biology [baɪ'ɒlədʒɪ] *n* biología.

birch [bɜːtʃ] *n* abedul.

bird [bɜːd] *n* ave, pájaro. ■ **bird of prey** ave de rapiña.

birdseed ['bɜːdsiːd] *n* alpiste.

bird's-eye view [bɜːdzaɪ'vjuː] *n* vista aérea.

Biro® ['baɪrəʊ] *n* GB boli.

birth [bɜːθ] *n* nacimiento. ● **to give birth to** dar a luz a. ■ **birth certificate** partida de nacimiento.

birthday ['bɜːθdeɪ] *n* cumpleaños.

birthmark ['bɜːθmɑːk] *n* antojo.

birthplace ['bɜːθpleɪs] *n* lugar de nacimiento.

biscuit ['bɪskɪt] *n* GB galleta.

bishop ['bɪʃəp] *n* **1** obispo. **2** alfil *(en ajedrez)*.

bison ['baɪsən] *n* bisonte.

bit[1] [bɪt] *n* trozo, pedacito. ● **a bit** un poco, algo.

bit[2] [bɪt] *n* bit.

bit[3] [bɪt] *n* broca.

bit[4] [bɪt] *pt* → bite.

bitch [bɪtʃ] *n* **1** hembra, perra. **2** *pej* bruja, arpía.

bite [baɪt] *n* **1** mordisco. **2** picadura. **3** mordedura. **4** bocado. ► *vt-vi* **1** morder(se). **2** picar.

bitten ['bɪtən] *pp* → bite.

bitter ['bɪtə'] *adj* amargo,-a *(sabor)*. ► *n* cerveza amarga. ► *npl* **bitters** bíter.

black [blæk] *adj-n* negro,-a. ■ **black coffee** café solo; **black eye** ojo morado.

blackberry ['blækbəri] *n* mora, zarzamora.

blackboard ['blækbɔːd] *n* pizarra.

blackhead ['blækhed] *n* espinilla.

blackmail ['blækmeɪl] *n* chantaje.

blacksmith ['blæksmɪθ] *n* herrero.

bladder ['blædə'] *n* vejiga.

blade [bleɪd] *n* **1** hoja, filo, cuchilla. **2** pala *(de remo)*. **3** brizna *(de hierba)*.

blame [bleɪm] *n* culpa. ► *vt* culpar, echar la culpa a. • **to put the blame on** echar la culpa a.

bland [blænd] *adj* soso,-a.

blank [blæŋk] *adj* en blanco. ■ **blank cartridge** cartucho de fogueo.

blanket ['blæŋkɪt] *n* manta.

blast [blɑːst] *n* **1** ráfaga *(de aire)*. **2** chorro *(de agua)*. **3** explosión, voladura. • **at full blast** a todo volumen. ■ **blast furnace** alto horno.

blaze [bleɪz] *n* **1** incendio. **2** fogata, hoguera. ► *vi* **1** arder. **2** brillar con fuerza.

bleach [bliːtʃ] *n* lejía.

bleat [bliːt] *n* balido.

bled [bled] *pt-pp* → bleed.

bleed [bliːd] *vi* sangrar.

bleep [bliːp] *n* pitido.

bleeper ['bliːpə'] *n* busca.

blend [blend] *n* mezcla ► *vt-vi* mezclarse.

blender ['blendə'] *n* batidora.

bless [bles] *vt* bendecir.

blew [bluː] *pt* → blow.

blind [blaɪnd] *adj* ciego,-a. ► *n* persiana. ► *vt* cegar.

blink [blɪŋk] *vi* parpadear.

blister ['blɪstə'] *n* ampolla.

block [blɒk] *n* bloque. ► *vt* **1** obstruir, cegar. **2** bloquear. ■ **block letters** mayúsculas.

blog [blɒg] *n* blog.

blond [blɒnd] *adj-n* rubio,-a.

blood [blʌd] *n* sangre. ■ **blood group** grupo sanguíneo; **blood pressure** tensión arterial.

bloodhound ['blʌdhaʊnd] *n* sabueso.

bloom [bluːm] *n* flor. ► *vi* florecer.

blossom ['blɒsəm] *n* flor. ► *vi* florecer.

blot [blɒt] *n* borrón.

blotch [blɒtʃ] *n* **1** mancha. **2** borrón.

blouse [blaʊz] *n* blusa.

blow[1] [bləʊ] *n* golpe.

blow² [bləʊ] *vi* **1** soplar *(viento).* **2** sonar *(silbato).* **3** fundirse *(fusible).* ▶ *vt* tocar *(cláxon, trompeta, etc).* • **to blow one's nose** sonarse la nariz.

to blow up *vt* **1** hacer explotar. **2** hinchar, inflar. **3** ampliar *(foto).* ▶ *vt* hacer explosión, explotar.

blowout [ˈbləʊaʊt] *n* reventón.

blue [bluː] *adj* **1** azul. **2** triste, deprimido,-a. **3** verde *(película).* ▶ *n* azul. • **out of the blue** de forma inesperada, como llovido del cielo. ▪ **the blues 1** melancolía. **2** el blues *(música).*

blueberry [ˈbluːbərɪ] *n* arándano.

bluff [blʌf] *n* farol.

blunder [ˈblʌndəˈ] *n* metedura de pata.

blunt [blʌnt] *adj* **1** desafilado,-a. **2** franco,-a.

blurred [blɜːd] *adj* borroso,-a.

blush [blʌʃ] *n vi* ruborizarse.

boar [bɔːˈ] *n.* ▪ **wild boar** jabalí.

board [bɔːd] *n* **1** tabla, tablero. **2** tablón de anuncios. **3** junta, consejo. ▶ *vt* subirse a, embarcar en. • **on board** a bordo. ▪ **full board** pensión completa; **half board** media pensión.

boarding [ˈbɔːdɪŋ] *n.* ▪ **boarding card** tarjeta de embarque; **boarding house** casa de huéspedes.

boast [bəʊst] *vi* jactarse.

boat [bəʊt] *n* barco, barca.

bobbin [ˈbɒbɪn] *n* bobina.

body [ˈbɒdɪ] *n* **1** cuerpo. **2** organismo, entidad.

body-building [ˈbɒdɪbɪldɪŋ] *n* culturismo.

bodyguard [ˈbɒdɪɡɑːd] *n* guardaespaldas.

bodywork [ˈbɒdɪwɜːk] *n* carrocería.

bog [bɒɡ] *n* pantano.

boil¹ [bɔɪl] *n* furúnculo.

boil² [bɔɪl] *vt-vi* hervir.

boiler [ˈbɔɪləˈ] *n* caldera.

boiling [ˈbɔɪlɪŋ] *adj* hirviente.

bold [bəʊld] *adj* valiente. ▪ **bold type** negrita.

bolt [bəʊlt] *n* **1** cerrojo, pestillo. **2** perno, tornillo.

bomb [bɒm] *n.* bomba. ▶ *vt* bombardear. ▪ **bomb scare** amenaza de bomba.

bombshell [ˈbɒmʃel] *n* **1** obús. **2** bombazo, bomba.

bond [bɒnd] *n* **1** lazo, vínculo. **2** bono, obligación.

bone [bəʊn] *n* **1** hueso. **2** espina *(de pescado).*

bonfire [ˈbɒnfaɪəˈ] *n* hoguera.

bonnet [ˈbɒnɪt] *n* **1** gorro, gorra. **2** capó.

bonus [ˈbəʊnəs] *n* prima.

bony [ˈbəʊnɪ] *adj* **1** huesudo, -a. **2** lleno,-a de espinas.

boo [buː] *vt-vi* abuchear.

booby trap [ˈbuːbɪtræp] *n* trampa explosiva.

book [bʊk] *n* libro. ▶ *vt* **1** reservar. **2** multar, amonestar.

bow

bookcase ['bʊkkeɪs] n librería, estantería.

booking ['bʊkɪŋ] n reserva. ■ **booking office** taquilla.

booklet ['bʊklət] n folleto.

bookshelf ['bʊkʃelf] n estante. ► npl **bookshelves** librería, estantería.

bookshop ['bʊkʃɒp] n librería.

bookstore ['bʊkstɔːʳ] n librería.

boom[1] [buːm] n estruendo.

boom[2] [buːm] n fig boom, auge.

boost [buːst] n empuje. ► vt 1 aumentar (ventas). 2 estimular, impulsar (producción).

boot [buːt] n 1 bota. 2 GB maletero. ► vt-vi arrancar (ordenador). • **to boot** además.

booth [buːð] n 1 cabina. 2 barraca, caseta (de feria).

bootlegger ['buːtlegəʳ] n contrabandista.

border ['bɔːdəʳ] n 1 frontera. 2 borde, margen.

bore[1] [bɔːʳ] pt → bear.

bore[2] [bɔːʳ] n calibre. ► vt horadar, taladrar.

bore[3] [bɔːʳ] n 1 pelmazo,-a. 2 lata.

bored [bɔːd] adj aburrido,-a.

boring ['bɔːrɪŋ] adj aburrido,-a.

born [bɔːn] pp → bear. • **to be born** nacer.

borne [bɔːn] pp → bear.

borough ['bʌrə] n 1 distrito. 2 municipio.

borrow ['bɒrəʊ] vt tomar prestado,-a, pedir prestado,-a.

boss [bɒs] n jefe,-a.

botany ['bɒtənɪ] n botánica.

botch [bɒtʃ] n chapuza.

both [bəʊθ] adj-pron ambos, -as, los/las dos. ► conj tanto.

bother ['bɒðəʳ] n molestia. ► vt 1 molestar. 2 preocupar. ► vi molestarse. preocuparse. • **not to be bothered** dar igual, no tener ganas.

bottle ['bɒtəl] n 1 botella. 2 biberón. ► vt embotellar. ■ **bottle bank** contenedor de vidrio; **bottle opener** abrebotellas.

bottom ['bɒtəm] n 1 fondo (del mar, calle). 2 culo (de botella, trasero). 3 bajo (de vestido). ► adj de abajo.

bought [bɔːt] pt-pp → buy.

bounce [baʊns] n bote. ► vi 1 rebotar. 2 ser rechazado por el banco (cheque).

bound[1] [baʊnd] pt-pp → bind.

bound[2] [baʊnd] adj seguro: *it's bound to happen*, tiene que pasar. • **bound for** con destino a, con rumbo a.

bound[3] [baʊnd] vi saltar.

boundary ['baʊndərɪ] n límite, frontera.

bounds [baʊndz] npl límites.

bouquet [buːˈkeɪ] n 1 ramillete. 2 aroma.

boutique [buːˈtiːk] n boutique.

bow[1] [baʊ] n reverencia.

bow[2] [bəʊ] n arco. ■ **bow tie** pajarita.

bow[3] [baʊ] n proa.

bowel ['bauəl] *n* intestino.
bowl[1] [bəul] *n* **1** escudilla, cuenco. **2** palangana, barreño.
bowl[2] [bəul] *n* bocha.
bowler ['bəulə'] *n* lanzador,-ra *(críquet).* ■ **bowler hat** bombín.
bowling ['bəulɪŋ] *n* bolos. ■ **bowling alley** bolera.
box[1] [bɒks] *n* **1** caja, cajón, cajetilla, estuche. **2** palco *(en teatro).* ■ **box office** taquilla.
box[2] [bɒks] *vi* boxear.
boxing ['bɒksɪŋ] *n* boxeo.
boy [bɔɪ] *n* niño, chico, muchacho, joven.
boyfriend ['bɔɪfrend] *n* novio.
brace [breɪs] *n* aparato *(de dientes).* ▶ *npl* GB **braces** tirantes.
bracelet ['breɪslət] *n* pulsera.
bracket ['brækɪt] *n* **1** paréntesis. **2** soporte.
brag [bræg] *vi* fanfarronear.
braid [breɪd] *n* US trenza.
brain [breɪn] *n* cerebro.
brake [breɪk] *n* freno. ▶ *vt-vi* frenar.
bramble ['bræmbəl] *n* zarza.
branch [brɑːntʃ] *n* **1** rama. **2** sucursal. ▶ *vi* bifurcarse.
brand [brænd] *n* marca.
brand-new [bræn'njuː] *adj* completamente nuevo.
brandy ['brændɪ] *n* brandy.
brass [brɑːs] *n* **1** latón. **2** instrumentos de metal.
brassiere ['bræzɪə'] *n* sujetador, sostén.
brave [breɪv] *adj* valiente

brawl [brɔːl] *n* reyerta, pelea.
breach [briːtʃ] *n* **1** brecha. **2** incumplimiento *(de contrato).*
bread [bred] *n* pan.
breadth [bredθ] *n* anchura.
break [breɪk] *n* **1** ruptura. **2** interrupción, pausa, descanso. ▶ *vt* **1** romper. **2** batir *(récord).* **3** no cumplir *(promesa).* **4** comunicar *(noticias).* ▶ *vi* **1** romperse. **2** estallar *(tormenta).*
to break down *vt* **1** echar abajo, derribar. **2** desglosar. ▶ *vi* averiarse.
to break in *vt* domar. ▶ *vi* entrar a robar.
to break out *vi* **1** escaparse *(prisioneros).* **2** estallar *(guerra).*
to break up *vi* **1** disolverse *(multitud).* **2** separarse. **3** empezar las vacaciones.
breakdown ['breɪkdaun] *n* **1** avería. **2** crisis nerviosa
breakfast ['brekfəst] *n* desayuno. • **to have breakfast** desayunar.
breakwater ['breɪkwɔːtə'] *n* rompeolas.
breast [brest] *n* **1** pecho. **2** pechuga *(de pollo).*
breaststroke ['breststrəuk] *n* braza.
breath [breθ] *n* aliento. • **out of breath** sin aliento; **to hold your breath** contener la respiración.
Breathalyser® ['breθəlaɪzə'] *n* alcoholímetro.

breathe [briːð] *vt-vi* respirar.
breathing ['briːðɪŋ] *n* respiración.
bred [bred] *pt-pp* → breed.
breed [briːd] *n* raza. ► *vt* criar
breeze [briːz] *n* brisa.
brew [bruː] *n* brebaje. ► *vt* 1 hacer *(cerveza)*. 2 preparar *(té)*. ► *vi* reposar *(té)*.
brewery ['bruəri] *n* cervecería.
bribe [braib] *n* soborno.
brick [brik] *n* ladrillo.
bricklayer ['brikleiə'] *n* albañil.
bride [braid] *n* novia *(el día de la boda)*.
bridegroom ['braidgruːm] *n* novio *(el día de la boda)*.
bridesmaid ['braidzmeid] *n* dama de honor.
bridge [bridʒ] *n* puente.
bridle ['braidəl] *n* brida.
brief [briːf] *adj* breve. ► *n* informe.
briefcase ['briːfkeis] *n* maletín, cartera.
briefs [briːfs] *npl* 1 calzoncillos. 2 bragas.
brigade [bri'geid] *n* brigada.
bright [brait] *adj* 1 brillante. 2 despejado *(día)*. 3 vivo,-a *(color)*.
brilliant ['briljənt] *adj* 1 brillante. 2 *fam* estupendo,-a.
brim [brim] *n* borde.
bring [briŋ] *vt* 1 traer. 2 llevar.
to bring about *vt* causar.
to bring back *vt* devolver.
to bring down *vt* derribar.

to bring in *vt* 1 introducir. 2 producir.
to bring on *vt* provocar.
to bring out *vt* sacar.
to bring round *vt* hacer volver en sí.
to bring up *vt* 1 criar, educar. 2 plantear. 3 devolver, vomitar.
bristle ['brisəl] *n* cerda.
brittle ['britəl] *adj* quebradizo,-a, frágil.
broad [brɔːd] *adj* ancho,-a, amplio,-a, extenso,-a. ■ **broad bean** haba.
broadcast ['brɔːdkɑːst] emitir, transmitir.
broadcasting ['brɔːdkɑːstɪŋ] *n* 1 radiodifusión. 2 transmisión.
broccoli ['brɒkəli] *n* brécol.
brochure ['brəʊʃə'] *n* folleto.
broil [brɔil] *vt* US asar a la parrilla.
broke [brəʊk] *pt* → break. ► *adj fam* sin blanca.
broken ['brəʊkən] *pp* → break. ► *adj* 1 roto,-a. 2 chapurreado,-a *(lenguaje)*.
bronchitis [brɒŋ'kaitəs] *n* bronquitis.
bronze [brɒnz] *n* bronce.
brooch [brəʊtʃ] *n* broche.
brook [brʊk] *n* arroyo.
broom [bruːm] *n* escoba.
broth [brɒθ] *n* caldo.
brother ['brʌðə'] *n* hermano.
brother-in-law ['brʌðərinlɔː] *n* cuñado.
brought [brɔːt] *pt-pp* → bring.

brow [braʊ] *n* **1** ceja. **2** frente. **3** cresta, cima.

brown [braʊn] *adj* **1** marrón. **2** castaño,-a *(pelo)*. **3** moreno,-a *(piel)*. **4** integral *(arroz, pan)*.

browse [braʊz] *vi* mirar, hojear. • **to browse the Web** navegar por la Web.

browser ['braʊzə'] *n* navegador *(programa)*.

bruise [bruːz] *n* morado.

brunette [bruːˈnet] *n* morena.

brush [brʌʃ] *n* **1** cepillo. **2** pincel. **3** brocha. **4** maleza. ► *vt* cepillar.

Brussels sprouts ['brʌsəlz] *n pl* coles de Bruselas.

brutal ['bruːtəl] *adj* brutal.

bubble ['bʌbəl] *n* burbuja. ▪ **bubble bath** gel de baño; **bubble gum** chicle.

buck [bʌk] *n* US *fam* dólar.

bucket ['bʌkɪt] *n* cubo.

buckle ['bʌkəl] *n* hebilla. ► *vt* abrochar *(con hebilla)*. ► *vi* combarse, doblarse.

bud [bʌd] *n* yema, capullo.

buddy ['bʌdɪ] *n* US *fam* colega.

budgerigar ['bʌdʒərɪgaː'] *n* periquito.

budget ['bʌdʒɪt] *n* presupuesto. ► *vt-vi* presupuestar.

buffalo ['bʌfələʊ] *n* búfalo.

buffer ['bʌfə'] *n* **1** tope *(para trenes)*. **2** memoria intermedia.

buffet ['bʌfeɪ] *n* **1** bar, cantina. **2** bufet libre. ▪ **buffet car** vagón restaurante.

bug [bʌg] *n* **1** bicho. **2** error *(en programa)*.

build [bɪld] *vt* construir.

to build up *vt-vi* acumular(se).

building ['bɪldɪŋ] *n* edificio. ▪ **building site** obra; **building society** sociedad de ahorro para la vivienda.

built [bɪlt] *pt-pp* → build.

built-in [bɪltˈɪn] *adj* **1** empotrado,-a. **2** incorporado,-a.

bulb [bʌlb] *n* **1** bulbo. **2** bombilla.

bulk [bʌlk] *n* mayor parte. • **in bulk** a granel, al por mayor.

bull [bʊl] *n* toro.

bullet ['bʊlɪt] *n* bala.

bulletin ['bʊlɪtɪn] *n* boletín.

bullfight ['bʊlfaɪt] *n* corrida de toros.

bullfighter ['bʊlfaɪtə'] *n* torero,-a.

bullring ['bʊlrɪŋ] *n* plaza de toros.

bumblebee ['bʌmbəlbiː] *n* abejorro.

bump [bʌmp] *n* **1** chichón. **2** bache *(en carretera)*. **3** choque, golpe. ► *vt-vi* chocar.

to bump into *vt* tropezar con.

bumper ['bʌmpə'] *n* GB parachoques.

bun [bʌn] *n* **1** panecillo, bollo. **2** moño.

bunch [bʌntʃ] *n* **1** manojo. **2** ramo. **3** racimo. **4** grupo.

bundle ['bʌndəl] *n* **1** fardo. **2** haz. **3** fajo.

byte

bung [bʌŋ] *n* tapón.

bunion [ˈbʌnjən] *n* juanete.

bunk [bʌŋk] *n* litera *(en un barco o tren)*. ■ **bunk bed** litera *(en una habitación)*.

buoy [bɔɪ] *n* boya.

burden [ˈbɜːdən] *n* carga. ► *vt* cargar.

bureaucracy [bjʊəˈrɒkrəsɪ] *n* burocracia.

burger [ˈbɜːgəʳ] *n* hamburguesa.

burglar [ˈbɜːgləʳ] *n* ladrón,-ona.

burglary [ˈbɜːglərɪ] *n* robo.

burial [ˈberɪəl] *n* entierro.

burn [bɜːn] *n* quemadura. ► *vt* quemar. ► *vi* arder, quemarse.

burner [ˈbɜːnəʳ] *n* quemador.

burnt [bɜːnt] *pt-pp* → burn.

burrow [ˈbʌrəʊ] *n* madriguera.

burst [bɜːst] *n* **1** explosión. **2** reventón. ► *vt-vi* reventar(se).

bury [ˈberɪ] *vt* enterrar.

bus [bʌs] *n* autobús. ■ **bus stop** parada de autobús.

bush [bʊʃ] *n* arbusto.

business [ˈbɪznəs] *n* **1** los negocios. **2** negocio, empresa. **3** asunto.

businessman [ˈbɪznəsmən] *n* hombre de negocios, empresario.

businesswoman [ˈbɪznəswʊmən] *n* mujer de negocios, empresaria.

bust¹ [bʌst] *n* busto.

bust² [bʌst] *vt-vi fam* romper, romperse.

busy [ˈbɪzɪ] *adj* **1** ocupado,-a. **2** concurrido,-a *(calle)*. **3** que comunica *(teléfono)*.

but [bʌt] *conj* **1** pero. **2** sino: *not two, but three*, no dos, sino tres. ► *prep* excepto, salvo, menos. ● **but for** si no hubiese sido por, si no fuese por.

butane [ˈbjuːteɪn] *n* butano.

butcher [ˈbʊtʃəʳ] *n* carnicero,-a.

butler [ˈbʌtləʳ] *n* mayordomo.

butt [bʌt] *n* **1** colilla. **2** culata.

butter [ˈbʌtəʳ] *n* mantequilla.

butterfly [ˈbʌtəflaɪ] *n* mariposa.

buttock [ˈbʌtək] *n* nalga.

button [ˈbʌtən] *n* botón. ► *vt-vi* abrochar(se).

buttonhole [ˈbʌtənhəʊl] *n* ojal.

buy [baɪ] *vt* comprar.

buyer [ˈbaɪəʳ] *n* comprador,-ra.

buzz [bʌz] *n*

buzzer [ˈbʌzəʳ] *n* timbre.

by [baɪ] *prep* **1** por. **2** en: *by car/train*, en coche/tren. **3** para: *I need it by ten*, lo necesito para las diez. **4** de: *by day/night*, de día/noche. **5** junto a, al lado de: *sit by me*, siéntate a mi lado. ► *adv* de largo. ● **by and by** con el tiempo.

bye [baɪ] *interj fam* ¡adiós!, ¡hasta luego!

bypass [ˈbaɪpɑːs] *n* **1** variante *(carretera)*. **2** by-pass.

by-product [ˈbaɪprɒdʌkt] *n* subproducto, derivado.

byte [baɪt] *n* byte.

C

cab [kæb] *n* **1** taxi. **2** cabina.
cabbage ['kæbɪdʒ] *n* col.
cabin ['kæbɪn] *n* **1** cabaña. **2** camarote. **3** cabina.
cabinet ['kæbɪnət] *n* **1** gabinete. **2** armario, vitrina.
cable ['keɪbəl] *n* cable. ■ **cable car** teleférico; **cable television** televisión por cable.
cache [kæʃ] *n* **1** alijo. **2** caché.
cactus ['kæktəs] *n* cactus.
café ['kæfeɪ] *n* cafetería.
cafeteria [kæfə'tɪərɪə] *n* cafetería.
cage [keɪdʒ] *n* jaula.
cagoule [kə'guːl] *n* chubasquero.
cake [keɪk] *n* pastel, tarta.
calculate ['kælkjəleɪt] *vt* calcular.
calculating ['kælkjəleɪtɪŋ] *adj* calculador,-ra. ■ **calculating machine** calculadora.
calendar ['kælɪndə'] *n* calendario.
calf[1] [kɑːf] *n* ternero,-a.
calf[2] [kɑːf] *n* pantorrilla.
call [kɔːl] *n* **1** grito. **2** llamada. **3** demanda: *there's not much call for it*, no tiene mucha demanda. **4** visita. ► *vt-vi* **1** llamar. *vi* **2** llamar. **3** pasar: *call at the butcher's*, pásate por la carnicería. **4** efectuar parada: *this train calls at Selby and York*, este tren efectúa parada da en Selby y York. ● **on call** de guardia. ■ **call box** GB cabina telefónica.
to call for *vt* pasar a buscar.
to call off *vt* suspender.
to call on *vt* visitar.
to call out *vt-vi* gritar.
caller ['kɔːlə'] *n* **1** visita, visitante. **2** persona que llama.
calm [kɑːm] *adj* **1** en calma *(mar)*. **2** tranquilo,-a *(persona)*. ► *vt* calmar.
calorie ['kælərɪ] *n* caloría.
camcorder ['kæmkɔːdə'] *n* videocámara.
came [keɪm] *pt* → come.
camel ['kæməl] *n* camello.
camera ['kæmərə] *n* cámara.
camomile ['kæməmaɪl] *n* manzanilla.
camouflage ['kæməflɑːʒ] *n* camuflaje. ► *vt* camuflar.
camp [kæmp] *n* campamento. ► *vi* acampar. ■ **camp bed** cama plegable; **camp site** camping, campamento.
campaign [kæm'peɪn] *n* campaña.
camper ['kæmpə'] *n* **1** campista. **2** US caravana.
can[1] [kæn] *aux* **1** poder. **2** saber.
can[2] [kæn] *n* lata.
canal [kə'næl] *n* canal.
canary [kə'neərɪ] *n* canario.
cancel ['kænsəl] *vt* **1** cancelar *(pedido)*. **2** anular *(contrato)*.

cancer ['kænsə'] *n* cáncer.

candidate ['kændɪdət] *n* candidato,-a.

candle ['kændəl] *n* vela.

candy ['kændɪ] *n* US caramelo.

cane [keɪn] *n* **1** caña. **2** bastón, vara.

canine ['keɪnaɪn] *adj* canino,-a.

canister ['kænɪstə'] *n* bote, lata.

cannon ['kænən] *n* cañón.

cannot ['kænɒt] *aux* → can.

canoe [kə'nuː] *n* canoa.

canopy ['kænəpɪ] *n* dosel.

can't [kɑːnt] *aux* contracción de **can** + **not**.

canteen [kæn'tiːn] *n* cantina.

canvas ['kænvəs] *n* **1** lona. **2** lienzo.

canyon ['kænjən] *n* cañón.

cap [kæp] *n* **1** gorro, gorra. **2** capuchón, chapa, tapa.

capable ['keɪpəbəl] *adj* capaz.

capacity [kə'pæsɪtɪ] *n* capacidad.

cape¹ [keɪp] *n* capa corta.

cape² [keɪp] *n* cabo.

caper ['keɪpə'] *n* alcaparra.

capital ['kæpɪtəl] *n* **1** capital. **2** mayúscula.

capitalism ['kæpɪtəlɪzəm] *n* capitalismo.

capricious [kə'prɪʃəs] *adj* caprichoso,-a.

capsize [kæp'saɪz] *vi* volcar.

capsule ['kæpsjuːl] *n* cápsula.

captain ['kæptɪn] *n* capitán.

caption ['kæpʃən] *n* leyenda, pie de foto.

captive ['kæptɪv] *adj-n* cautivo,-a.

captivity [kæp'tɪvɪtɪ] *n* cautiverio, cautividad.

capture ['kæptʃə'] *n* captura. ► *vt* capturar.

car [kɑː'] *n* **1** coche, automóvil. **2** vagón, coche *(de ferrocarril)*. ■ **car park** aparcamiento; **car wash** túnel de lavado.

caramel ['kærəmel] *n* caramelo.

carat ['kærət] *n* quilate.

caravan [kærə'væn] *n* caravana.

carbon ['kɑːbən] *n* carbono.

carburettor [kɑːbə'retə'] *n* carburador.

carcass ['kɑːkəs] *n* res muerta.

card [kɑːd] *n* **1** carta, naipe. **2** tarjeta, felicitación. **3** ficha. **4** carnet, carné *(de socio)*. **5** cartulina.

cardboard ['kɑːdbɔːd] *n* cartón.

cardiac ['kɑːdɪæk] *adj* cardíaco,-a. ■ **cardiac arrest** paro cardíaco.

cardigan ['kɑːdɪgən] *n* rebeca.

cardphone ['kɑːdfəʊn] *n* teléfono de tarjeta.

care [keə'] *n* **1** cuidado. **2** asistencia: *health care*, asistencia sanitaria. ► *vi* preocuparse: *I don't care*, me tiene sin cuidado. ● **take care!** ¡cuidado!; **to take care of 1** cuidar, cuidar de. **2** ocuparse de.

to care for *vt* cuidar.

career [kə'rɪə'] *n* carrera.

careful ['keəfʊl] *adj* cuidadoso,-a. ● **to be careful** tener cuidado.

caress [kə'res] *n* caricia. ► *vt* acariciar.

caretaker ['keəteɪkə'] *n* conserje.

cargo ['kɑːgəʊ] *n* carga.

caries ['keərɪz] *n* caries.

carnation [kɑː'neɪʃən] *n* clavel.

carol ['kærəl] *n* villancico.

carp [kɑːp] *n* carpa *(pez)*.

carpenter ['kɑːpɪntə'] *n* carpintero.

carpet ['kɑːpɪt] *n* moqueta, alfombra.

carriage ['kærɪdʒ] *n* **1** carruaje. **2** vagón, coche *(de ferrocarril)*. ■ **carriage paid** portes pagados.

carrier ['kærɪə'] *n* **1** transportista. **2** portador,-ra *(de enfermedad)*. ■ **carrier bag** bolsa *(de plástico o papel)*.

carrot ['kærət] *n* zanahoria.

carry ['kærɪ] *vt* llevar.

to carry on *vt* seguir.

to carry out *vt* llevar a cabo.

carsick ['kɑːsɪk] *adj* mareado, -a *(en un coche)*.

cart [kɑːt] *n* **1** carro. **2** carretilla.

cartilage ['kɑːtɪlɪdʒ] *n* cartílago.

carton ['kɑːtən] *n* **1** envase de cartón. **2** cartón.

cartoon [kɑː'tuːn] *n* **1** caricatura. **2** dibujos animados. **3** historieta, tira cómica.

cartridge ['kɑːtrɪdʒ] *n* **1** cartucho. **2** recambio *(para estilográfica)*.

carve [kɑːv] *vt* **1** tallar. **2** trinchar *(carne)*.

case¹ [keɪs] *n* caso. ●**in any case** en cualquier caso; **in case** por si; **in case of** en caso de; **just in case** por si acaso.

case² [keɪs] *n* **1** maleta. **2** caja. **3** estuche, funda.

cash [kæʃ] *n* dinero en efectivo. ► *vt* cobrar *(talón)*. ● **cash down** al contado; **cash on delivery** contra reembolso. ■ **cash desk** caja; **cash dispenser** cajero automático; **cash register** caja registradora.

cash-and-carry [kæʃən'kærɪ] *n* autoservicio al por mayor.

cashier [kæ'ʃɪə'] *n* cajero,-a.

cashmere [kæʃ'mɪə'] *n* cachemira.

casino [kə'siːnəʊ] *n* casino.

cask [kɑːsk] *n* tonel, barril.

casserole ['kæsərəʊl] *n* **1** cazuela. **2** guiso.

cassette [kə'set] *n* casete. ■ **cassette player/ recorder** casete.

cast [kɑːst] *n* **1** reparto *(de película, etc)*. **2** molde.► *vt* **1** lanzar. **2** dar el papel de. **3** moldear. ● **to be cast away** naufragar. ■ **cast iron** hierro colado.

castle ['kɑːsəl] *n* **1** castillo. **2** torre *(ajedrez)*.

casual ['kæʒjʊəl] *adj* **1** fortuito,-a, casual *(encuentro)*. **2** informal *(ropa)*.

casualty ['kæʒjʊəltɪ] *n* **1** víctima. **2** baja *(soldado)*. ▪ **casualty department** urgencias.

cat [kæt] *n* gato,-a.

catalogue ['kætəlɒg] (US **catalog**) *n* GB catálogo.

cataract ['kætərækt] *n* catarata.

catarrh [kəˈtɑːʰ] *n* catarro.

catastrophe [kəˈtæstrəfɪ] *n* catástrofe.

catch [kætʃ] *vt* coger. ▶ *n* **1** parada *(de pelota)*. **2** pesca. **3** cierre, pestillo.

category ['kætəgərɪ] *n* categoría.

cater ['keɪtəʰ] *vt* **1** proveer comida. **2** atender.

caterpillar ['kætəpɪləʰ] *n* oruga.

cathedral [kəˈθiːdrəl] *n* catedral.

Catholic ['kæθəlɪk] *adj-n* católico,-a.

cattle ['kætəl] *n* ganado vacuno.

caught [kɔːt] *pt-pp* → catch.

cauliflower ['kɒlɪflaʊəʰ] *n* coliflor.

cause [kɔːz] *n* causa. ▶ *vt* causar.

caution ['kɔːʃən] *n* **1** precaución. **2** aviso, advertencia.

cautious ['kɔːʃəs] *adj* prudente.

cavalry ['kævəlrɪ] *n* caballería.

cave [keɪv] *n* cueva. ▪ **cave painting** pintura rupestre.

cavern ['kævən] *n* caverna.

caviar ['kævɪɑːʰ] *n* caviar.

cavity ['kævɪtɪ] *n* cavidad.

CD ['siː'diː] *abbr (compact disc)* disco compacto, CD. ▪ **CD player** reproductor de discos compactos.

cease [siːs] *vt-vi* cesar.

cease-fire [siːsˈfaɪəʰ] *n* alto el fuego.

cedar ['siːdəʰ] *n* cedro.

ceiling ['siːlɪŋ] *n* techo.

celebrate ['selɪbreɪt] *vt-vi* celebrar.

celebration [selɪˈbreɪʃən] *n* celebración.

celery ['selərɪ] *n* apio.

cell [sel] *n* **1** celda. **2** célula.

cellar ['seləʰ] *n* **1** sótano. **2** bodega *(para vino)*.

cello ['tʃeləʊ] *n* violoncelo.

cellophane® ['seləfeɪn] *n* celofán®.

cellphone ['selfəʊn] *n* teléfono móvil.

cement [sɪˈment] *n* cemento. ▪ **cement mixer** hormigonera.

cemetery ['semətrɪ] *n* cementerio.

censorship ['sensəʃɪp] *n* censura.

census ['sensəs] *n* censo.

cent [sent] *n* centavo, céntimo. • **per cent** por ciento.

centigrade ['sentɪgreɪd] *adj* centígrado.

centimetre ['sentımi:tə'] (US **centimeter**) n centímetro.

central ['sentrəl] adj central. ▪ **central heating** calefacción central.

centre ['sentə'] (US **center**) n centro. ► vt-vi centrar. ▪ **centre forward** delantero centro.

century ['sentʃərı] n siglo.

ceramics [sə'ræmıks] npl cerámica.

cereal ['sıərıəl] n cereal.

cerebral ['serıbrəl] adj cerebral.

ceremony ['serımənı] n ceremonia.

certain ['sɜːtən] adj **1** seguro,-a. **2** cierto,-a, alguno,-a. ● **for certain** con toda seguridad; **to make certain of** asegurarse de.

certificate [sə'tıfıkət] n certificado.

cesspit ['sespıt] n pozo negro.

chafe [tʃeıf] vt rozar, escoriar.

chain [tʃeın] n cadena.

chair [tʃeə'] n **1** silla. **2** sillón. ▪ **chair lift** telesilla.

chairman ['tʃeəmən] n presidente.

chairwoman ['tʃeəwumən] n presidenta.

chalet ['ʃæleı] n chalet, chalé.

chalk [tʃɔːk] n tiza.

challenge ['tʃælındʒ] n reto, desafío. ► vt retar, desafiar.

challenger ['tʃælındʒə'] n rival.

chamber ['tʃeımbə'] n cámara.

chambermaid ['tʃeımbəmeıd] n camarera.

chameleon [kə'mi:lıən] n camaleón.

champion ['tʃæmpıən] n campeón,-ona.

championship ['tʃæmpıənʃıp] n campeonato.

chance [tʃɑːns] n **1** azar. **2** oportunidad. ● **by chance** por casualidad; **to take a chance** arriesgarse.

chancellor ['tʃɑːnsələ'] n canciller. ▪ **Chancellor of the Exchequer** GB ministro,-a de Economía y Hacienda.

change [tʃeındʒ] n cambio. ► vt-vi cambiar. ► vi cambiarse de ropa. ● **for a change** para variar; **to change into** convertirse en, transformarse en.

changing ['tʃeındʒıŋ] adj. ▪ **changing room** vestuario.

channel ['tʃænəl] n canal (cauce de agua). ► vt canalizar.

chaos ['keıɒs] n caos.

chap [tʃæp] n fam tío, tipo.

chapel ['tʃæpəl] n capilla.

chapter ['tʃæptə'] n capítulo.

character ['kærəktə'] n **1** carácter. **2** personaje.

characteristic [kærəktə'rıstık] adj característico,-a. ► n característica.

charcoal ['tʃɑːkəʊl] n **1** carbón vegetal. **2** carboncillo.

charge [tʃɑːdʒ] *n* **1** precio, coste. **2** cargo, acusación *(formal)*. **3** carga. ► *vt* **1** cobrar. **2** acusar *(de delito)*. **3** cargar. ● **to be in charge of** estar a cargo de; **to bring a charge against SB** formular una acusación contra ALGN; **to take charge of** hacerse cargo de.

charger [ˈtʃɑːdʒəʳ] *n* cargador *(de batería)*.

charity [ˈtʃærɪtɪ] *n* caridad.

charm [tʃɑːm] *n* **1** encanto. **2** amuleto *(de la suerte)*. ► *vt* encantar.

chart [tʃɑːt] *n* **1** tabla, gráfico, diagrama. **2** carta de navegación. ■ **the charts** los cuarenta principales.

charter [ˈtʃɑːtəʳ] *n* **1** carta, estatutos. **2** flete. ► *vt* fletar. ■ **charter flight** vuelo chárter.

chase [tʃeɪs] *n* persecución. ► *vt* perseguir.

chassis [ˈʃæsɪ] *n* chasis.

chat [tʃæt] *n* charla. ► *vi* **1** charlar. **2** chatear. ■ **chat show** programa de entrevistas.

chatter [ˈtʃætəʳ] *n* **1** cháchara, parloteo. **2** castañeteo *(de dientes)*. ► *vi* **1** charlar, parlotear. **2** castañetear *(dientes)*.

chauffeur [ˈʃəʊfəʳ] *n* chófer.

cheap [tʃiːp] *adj* barato,-a.

cheat [tʃiːt] *n* tramposo,-a. ► *vi* **1** hacer trampa. **2** copiar *(en un examen)*. ► *vt-vi* engañar, timar.

check [tʃek] *n* **1** comprobación, verificación. **2** US → cheque. **3** US nota, cuenta. **4** jaque. ► *vt* **1** comprobar, verificar. **2** dar jaque a.

to check in *vi* **1** facturar *(en aeropuerto)*. **2** dejar los datos *(en hotel)*.

checkbook [ˈtʃekbʊk] *n* US talonario de cheques.

checked [tʃekt] *adj* a cuadros.

checkers [ˈtʃekəz] *npl* US damas.

checkmate [ˈtʃekmeɪt] *n* jaque mate. ► *vt* dar mate a.

checkout [ˈtʃekaʊt] *n* caja.

checkup [ˈtʃekʌp] *n* chequeo.

cheek [tʃiːk] *n* **1** mejilla. **2** *fig* descaro.

cheekbone [ˈtʃiːkbəʊn] *n* pómulo.

cheer [tʃɪəʳ] *n* viva. ► *vt-vi* vitorear.

to cheer up *vt-vi* animar(se).

cheerful [ˈtʃɪəfʊl] *adj* alegre.

cheers [tʃɪəz] *interj* **1** ¡salud! **2** ¡gracias! **3** ¡adiós!, ¡hasta luego!

cheese [tʃiːz] *n* queso.

cheesecake [ˈtʃiːzkeɪk] *n* tarta de queso.

cheetah [ˈtʃiːtə] *n* guepardo.

chemist [ˈkemɪst] *n* **1** químico,-a. **2** GB farmacéutico,-a.

chemistry [ˈkemɪstrɪ] *n* química.

chemist's [ˈkemɪsts] *n* farmacia.

cheque [tʃek] *n* cheque, talón.

chequebook [ˈtʃekbʊk] *n* talonario de cheques.

cherish ['tʃerɪʃ] *vt* **1** apreciar, valorar. **2** abrigar *(esperanza)*.

cherry ['tʃerɪ] *n* cereza.

chess [tʃes] *n* ajedrez.

chessboard ['tʃesbɔːd] *n* tablero de ajedrez.

chest [tʃest] *n* **1** pecho. **2** cofre, arca. ■ **chest of drawers** cómoda, cajonera.

chestnut ['tʃesnʌt] *n* **1** castaña *(fruto)*. **2** castaño *(color)*.

chew [tʃuː] *vt* masticar.

chewing gum ['tʃuːɪŋɡʌm] *n* chicle.

chicken ['tʃɪkɪn] *n* **1** pollo *(carne)*. **2** gallina *(ave)*.

chickenpox ['tʃɪkɪnpɒks] *n* varicela.

chickpea ['tʃɪkpiː] *n* garbanzo.

chicory ['tʃɪkərɪ] *n* achicoria.

chief [tʃiːf] *n* jefe.

chilblain ['tʃɪlbleɪn] *n* sabañón.

child [tʃaɪld] *n* **1** niño,-a. **2** hijo, hija. ■ **only child** hijo,-a único,-a.

childbirth ['tʃaɪldbɜːθ] *n* parto.

childhood ['tʃaɪldhʊd] *n* infancia.

children ['tʃɪldrən] *npl* → child.

chill [tʃɪl] *adj* frío,-a. ► *n* resfriado. ► *vt-vi* enfriar(se).

chimney ['tʃɪmnɪ] *n* chimenea.

chimpanzee [tʃɪmpæn'ziː] *n* chimpancé.

chin [tʃɪn] *n* barbilla, mentón.

china ['tʃaɪnə] *n* porcelana.

chip [tʃɪp] *n* **1** patata frita. **2** chip. **3** astilla, lasca *(de madera)*. **4** ficha *(en casino)*. ► *vt-vi* **1** astillarse *(madera)*. **2** resquebrajarse *(piedra)*. **3** desconcharse *(pintura)*.

chiropodist [kɪ'rɒpədɪst] *n* podólogo,-a.

chitchat ['tʃɪttʃæt] *n* cháchara.

chocolate ['tʃɒkələt] *n* **1** chocolate. **2** bombón.

choice [tʃɔɪs] *n* elección.

choir ['kwaɪə'] *n* coro.

choke [tʃəʊk] *n* estárter. ► *vi* ahogarse.

cholera ['kɒlərə] *n* cólera.

choose [tʃuːz] *vt* escoger.

chop [tʃɒp] *n* chuleta *(carne)*. ► *vt* cortar.

chopsticks ['tʃɒpstɪks] *npl* palillos chinos.

chord [kɔːd] *n* acorde.

chorus ['kɔːrəs] *n* **1** coro. **2** estribillo.

chose [tʃəʊz] *pt* → choose.

chosen ['tʃəʊzən] *pp* → choose.

christen ['krɪsən] *vt* bautizar.

christening ['krɪsənɪŋ] *n* bautizo.

Christian ['krɪstɪən] *adj-n* cristiano,-a. ■ **Christian name** nombre de pila.

Christmas ['krɪsməs] *n* Navidad. ■ **Christmas card** tarjeta de Navidad, christmas; **Christmas Eve** Nochebuena.

chronic ['krɒnɪk] *adj* crónico,-a.

chronicle ['krɒnɪkəl] *n* crónica.

chronology [krə'nɒlədʒɪ] *n* cronología.

chuck [tʃʌk] vt **1** tirar *(objeto)*. **2** dejar *(novio, trabajo)*.

chunk [tʃʌŋk] n *fam* cacho.

church [tʃɜːtʃ] n iglesia.

chute [ʃuːt] n tobogán.

cider ['saɪdəʳ] n sidra.

cigar [sɪˈgaːʳ] n puro.

cigarette [sɪgəˈret] n cigarrillo.
▪ **cigarette case** pitillera; **cigarette holder** boquilla; **cigarette lighter** encendedor.

cinder ['sɪndəʳ] n ceniza.

cinema ['sɪnəmə] n cine.

cinnamon ['sɪnəmən] n canela.

cipher ['saɪfəʳ] n código.

circle ['sɜːkəl] n **1** círculo. **2** anfiteatro *(en teatro)*.

circuit ['sɜːkɪt] n circuito.

circumference [səˈkʌmfərəns] n circunferencia.

circumstance ['sɜːkəmstəns] n circunstancia.

circus ['sɜːkəs] n **1** circo. **2** GB glorieta, rotonda.

cistern ['sɪstən] n cisterna.

citizen ['sɪtɪzən] n ciudadano,-a.

citric ['sɪtrɪk] adj cítrico,-a.

city ['sɪtɪ] n ciudad.

civil ['sɪvəl] adj **1** civil. **2** cortés, educado,-a. ▪ **civil servant** funcionario,-a; **civil service** administración pública.

civilization [sɪvɪlaɪˈzeɪʃən] n civilización.

claim [kleɪm] n **1** reivindicación. **2** derecho. **3** afirmación. ► vt **1** afirmar. **2** reclamar.

clam [klæm] n almeja.

clap [klæp] n **1** aplauso. **2** ruido seco. **3** palmada. ► vt-vi aplaudir.

clarinet [klærɪˈnet] n clarinete.

clash [klæʃ] n **1** choque. **2** estruendo. ► vi **1** chocar. **2** coincidir *(fechas)*. **3** desentonar *(colores)*.

class [klaːs] n clase.

classic ['klæsɪk] adj clásico,-a.

classification [klæsɪfɪˈkeɪʃən] n clasificación.

classify ['klæsɪfaɪ] vt clasificar.

classmate ['klaːsmeɪt] n compañero,-a de clase.

classroom ['klaːsruːm] n clase.

clause [klɔːz] n **1** cláusula. **2** oración.

clavicle ['klævɪkəl] n clavícula.

claw [klɔː] n **1** garra *(de ave)*. **2** uña *(de gato)*. **3** pinza *(de cangrejo)*.

clay [kleɪ] n arcilla, barro.

clean [kliːn] adj limpio,-a. ► vt limpiar.

cleaner's ['kliːnəz] n tintorería.

cleanse [klenz] vt limpiar.

clear [klɪəʳ] adj **1** claro,-a. **2** transparente *(vidrio)*. **3** despejado,-a *(cielo, vista)*. ► vt **1** despejar. **2** levantar, recoger *(mesa)*. **3** absolver *(acusado)*. **4** salvar *(obstáculo)*. ▪ **in the clear 1** fuera de peligro. **2** fuera de toda sospecha.

to clear up vt **1** aclarar. **2** ordenar, recoger. ► vi mejorar, despejarse *(tiempo)*.

clearance ['klɪərəns] *n.* ■ **clearance sale** liquidación.

clearing ['klɪərɪŋ] *n* claro.

cleavage ['kliːvɪdʒ] *n* escote.

clef [klef] *n* clave *(música)*.

clerk [klɑːk, US klɜːrk] *n* **1** oficinista. **2** US dependiente,-a.

clever ['klevəʳ] *adj* listo,-a.

click [klɪk] *n* chasquido.

client ['klaɪənt] *n* cliente.

cliff [klɪf] *n* acantilado.

climate ['klaɪmət] *n* clima.

climb [klaɪm] *n* subida, escalada. ► *vt* **1** subir *(escalera)*. **2** trepar a *(árbol)*. **3** escalar.

clinic ['klɪnɪk] *n* clínica.

clip[1] [klɪp] *n* clip, fragmento *(de película)*. ► *vt* recortar *(barba)*.

clip[2] [klɪp] *n* **1** clip. **2** pasador.

clippers ['klɪpəz] *npl* cortaúñas.

cloak [kləʊk] *n* capa.

cloakroom ['kləʊkruːm] *n* **1** guardarropa. **2** GB servicios.

clock [klɒk] *n* reloj.

clod [klɒd] *n* terrón.

clog [klɒg] *n* zueco.

cloister ['klɔɪstəʳ] *n* claustro.

close[1] [kləʊs] *adj* **1** cercano,-a. **2** íntimo,-a *(amigo)*. **3** detenido,-a *(examen)*. ► *adv* cerca.

close[2] [kləʊz] *vt-vi* cerrar(se). ■ **close season** temporada de veda.

closet ['klɒzɪt] *n* US armario.

close-up ['kləʊsʌp] *n* primer plano.

closing ['kləʊzɪŋ] *n* cierre.

clot [klɒt] *n* coágulo.

cloth [klɒθ] *n* **1** tela. **2** trapo.

clothes [kləʊðz] *npl* ropa.

cloud [klaʊd] *n* nube.

cloudy ['klaʊdɪ] *adj* nublado,-a.

clove[1] [kləʊv] *n* clavo *(especie)*.

clove[2] [kləʊv] *n* diente *(de ajo)*.

clover ['kləʊvəʳ] *n* trébol.

clown [klaʊn] *n* payaso.

club [klʌb] *n* **1** club, sociedad. **2** palo *(de golf)*. **3** trébol *(cartas)*.

clue [kluː] *n* pista, indicio.

clumsy ['klʌmzɪ] *adj* torpe.

cluster ['klʌstəʳ] *n* grupo.

clutch [klʌtʃ] *n* embrague. ► *vt* agarrar.

coach [kəʊtʃ] *n* **1** autocar. **2** coche *(de tren, de caballos)*. **3** entrenador,-ra. ► *vt* entrenar. ■ **coach station** estación de autobuses.

coal [kəʊl] *n* carbón.

coalition [kəʊə'lɪʃən] *n* coalición.

coarse [kɔːs] *adj* basto,-a.

coast [kəʊst] *n* costa, litoral.

coastguard ['kəʊstgɑːd] *n* guardacostas.

coastline ['kəʊstlaɪn] *n* litoral.

coat [kəʊt] *n* **1** abrigo *(prenda)*. **2** capa *(de pintura)*. **3** pelaje *(de animal)*. ► *vt* cubrir.

cob [kɒb] *n* mazorca.

cobble ['kɒbəl] *n* adoquín.

cobweb ['kɒbweb] *n* telaraña.

cock [kɒk] *n* gallo.

cockle ['kɒkəl] *n* berberecho.

cockpit ['kɒkpɪt] *n* cabina del piloto.

cockroach ['kɒkrəʊtʃ] *n* cucaracha.

cocktail ['kɒkteɪl] *n* cóctel.

cocoa ['kəʊkəʊ] *n* cacao.

coconut ['kəʊkənʌt] *n* coco.

cocoon [kə'kuːn] *n* capullo.

cod [kɒd] *n* bacalao.

code [kəʊd] *n* **1** código. **2** prefijo *(de teléfono)*. ► *vt* codificar.

coffee ['kɒfɪ] *n* café. ■ **coffee shop** cafetería.

coffeepot ['kɒfɪpɒt] *n* cafetera.

coffin ['kɒfɪn] *n* ataúd.

coherent [kəʊ'hɪərənt] *adj* coherente.

cohesion [kəʊ'hiːʒən] *n* cohesión.

coin [kɔɪn] *n* moneda.

coincidence [kəʊ'ɪnsɪdəns] *n* coincidencia.

coke [kəʊk] *n* refesco de cola.

colander ['kʌləndəʳ] *n* colador.

cold [kəʊld] *adj* frío,-a. ► *n* **1** frío. **2** resfriado, catarro. • **to catch a cold** resfriarse. ■ **cold sore** herpes.

collaboration [kəlæbə'reɪʃən] *n* colaboración.

collapse [kə'læps] *n* **1** derrumbamiento. **2** fracaso *(de plan)*. **3** colapso *(de persona)*. ► *vi* derrumbarse.

collapsible [kə'læpsəbəl] *adj* plegable.

collar ['kɒləʳ] *n* **1** cuello *(de camisa)*. **2** collar *(de perro)*.

collarbone ['kɒləbəʊn] *n* clavícula.

colleague ['kɒliːg] *n* colega.

collect [kə'lekt] *vt* **1** reunir *(objetos)*. **2** coleccionar *(sellos)*. **3** recaudar *(impuestos)*. **4** ir a buscar *(persona)*. ► *vi* acumularse. • **to call collect** US llamar a cobro revertido.

collection [kə'lekʃən] *n* **1** colección *(de sellos)*. **2** colecta *(de dinero)*. **3** recogida *(de correo)*. **4** recaudación *(de impuestos)*.

college ['kɒlɪdʒ] *n* centro de educación superior.

collide [kə'laɪd] *vi* chocar.

collision [kə'lɪʒən] *n* colisión.

colloquial [kə'ləʊkwɪəl] *adj* coloquial.

cologne [kə'ləʊn] *n* colonia.

colon¹ ['kəʊlən] *n* colon.

colon² ['kəʊlən] *n* dos puntos.

colonel ['kɜːnəl] *n* coronel.

colonial [kə'ləʊnɪəl] *adj* colonial.

colony ['kɒlənɪ] *n* colonia.

colour ['kʌləʳ] (US **color**) *n* color. ► *vt* colorear, pintar.

colour-blind ['kʌləblaɪnd] (US **color-blind**) *adj* daltónico,-a.

colouring ['kʌlərɪŋ] (US **coloring**) *n* **1** colorante. **2** colorido.

colt [kəʊlt] *n* potro.

column ['kɒləm] *n* columna.

coma ['kəʊmə] *n* coma.

comb [kəʊm] *n* peine. ► *vt* peinar.

combat ['kɒmbæt] *n* combate.

combination [kɒmbɪˈneɪʃən] *n* combinación.

combine [kəmˈbaɪn] *vt-vi* combinar(se).

come [kʌm] *vi* **1** venir. **2** llegar.

to come apart *vi* romperse.

to come back *vi* volver.

to come from *vt* ser de.

to come in *vi* **1** entrar: *come in!*, ¡adelante! **2** llegar *(tren)*.

to come off *vi* **1** tener lugar. **2** desprenderse, caerse *(pieza)*. **3** quitarse *(mancha)*.

to come on *vi* progresar.

to come out *vi* salir.

to come round *vi* **1** volver en sí. **2** hacer una visita.

to come up *vi* **1** surgir *(tema)*. **2** acercarse. **3** salir *(sol)*.

comeback [ˈkʌmbæk] *n fam* reaparición.

comedy [ˈkɒmədɪ] *n* comedia.

comet [ˈkɒmɪt] *n* cometa.

comfort [ˈkʌmfət] *n* **1** comodidad. **2** consuelo.

comfortable [ˈkʌmfətəbəl] *adj* cómodo,-a. • **to make oneself comfortable** ponerse cómodo,-a.

comic [ˈkɒmɪk] *adj-n* cómico, -a. ▶ *n* tebeo, cómic.

comma [ˈkɒmə] *n* coma.

command [kəˈmɑːnd] *n* **1** orden. **2** mando. **3** comando, instrucción. **4** dominio. ▶ *vt-vi* mandar.

commander [kəˈmɑːndəʳ] *n* comandante.

commemorate [kəˈmeməreɪt] *vt* conmemorar.

comment [ˈkɒment] *n* comentario. ▶ *vi* comentar.

commerce [ˈkɒmɜːs] *n* comercio.

commercial [kəˈmɜːʃəl] *adj* comercial. ▶ *n* anuncio.

commission [kəˈmɪʃən] *n* comisión.

commissioner [kəˈmɪʃənəʳ] *n* comisario.

commit [kəˈmɪt] *vt* cometer. • **to commit oneself** comprometerse.

commitment [kəˈmɪtmənt] *n* compromiso.

committee [kəˈmɪtɪ] *n* comité, comisión.

commodity [kəˈmɒdɪtɪ] *n* producto, artículo.

common [ˈkɒmən] *adj* común.

communicate [kəˈmjuːnɪkeɪt] *vt-vi* comunicar(se).

communiqué [kəˈmjuːnɪkeɪ] *n* comunicado.

communism [ˈkɒmjənɪzəm] *n* comunismo.

community [kəˈmjuːnɪtɪ] *n* comunidad.

commute [kəˈmjuːt] *vi* desplazarse diariamente de casa al lugar de trabajo. ▶ *vt* conmutar.

compact [kəmˈpækt] *adj* compacto,-a. ▪ **compact disc** disco compacto.

company [ˈkʌmpənɪ] *n* compañía.

compare [kəm'peə'] *vt-vi* comparar(se).

compartment [kəm'pɑ:tmənt] *n* compartim(i)ento.

compass ['kʌmpəs] *n* **1** brújula. **2** compás.

compatible [kəm'pætɪbəl] *adj* compatible.

compel [kəm'pel] *vt* obligar.

compensate ['kɒmpənseɪt] *vt* compensar.

compere ['kɒmpeə'] *n* GB presentador,-ra.

compete [kəm'pi:t] *vi* competir.

competence ['kɒmpɪtəns] *n* competencia.

competent ['kɒmpɪtənt] *adj* competente.

competition [kɒmpə'tɪʃən] *n* **1** competición. **2** competencia.

complain [kəm'pleɪn] *vt* quejarse.

complaint [kəm'pleɪnt] *n* **1** queja. **2** dolencia.

complement ['kɒmplɪmənt] *n* complemento.

complete [kəm'pli:t] *adj* completo,-a. ► *vt* completar.

complex ['kɒmpleks] *adj* complejo,-a. ► *n* complejo.

complexion [kəm'plekʃən] *n* cutis, tez.

complicate ['kɒmplɪkeɪt] *vt* complicar.

compliment [(*n*) 'kɒmplɪmənt, (*vb*) 'kɒmplɪment] *n* cumplido. ► *vt* felicitar.

component [kəm'pəʊnənt] *adj-n* componente.

composed [kəm'pəʊzd] *adj* sereno,-a.

composer [kəm'pəʊzə'] *n* compositor,-ra.

composition [kɒmpə'zɪʃən] *n* composición.

compost ['kɒmpɒst] *n* abono.

compound ['kɒmpaʊnd] *adj* compuesto,-a. ► *n* compuesto.

comprehensive [kɒmprɪ'hensɪv] *adj* **1** completo,-a. **2** amplio,-a. ■ **comprehensive insurance** seguro a todo riesgo.

compress ['kɒmpres] *n* compresa. ► *vt* comprimir.

comprise [kəm'praɪz] *vt* constar de.

compromise ['kɒmprəmaɪz] *n* acuerdo. ► *vi* llegar a un acuerdo.

compulsory [kəm'pʌlsərɪ] *adj* obligatorio,-a.

computer [kəm'pju:tə'] *n* ordenador. ■ **computer science** informática.

computing [kəm'pju:tɪŋ] *n* informática.

con [kɒn] *n fam* timo.

conceal [kən'si:l] *vt* ocultar.

conceit [kən'si:t] *n* vanidad.

conceive [kən'si:v] *vt-vi* concebir.

concentrate ['kɒnsəntreɪt] *vt-vi* concentrar(se).

concentration [kɒnsən'treɪʃən] *n* concentración.

concept ['kɒnsept] *n* concepto.

concern [kən'sɜːn] *n* **1** preocupación. **2** negocio, empresa. ► *vt* **1** afectar, concernir. **2** preocupar. **3** tener que ver con. • **as far as I'm concerned** por lo que a mí se refiere; **to whom it may concern** a quien corresponda.

concerning [kən'sɜːnɪŋ] *prep* referente a, sobre, acerca de.

concert ['kɒnsət] *n* concierto. ■ **concert house** sala de conciertos.

concise [kən'saɪs] *adj* conciso,-a.

conclude [kən'kluːd] *vt-vi* concluir.

conclusion [kən'kluːʒən] *n* conclusión.

concrete ['kɒnkriːt] *adj* concreto,-a. ► *n* hormigón. ■ **concrete mixer** hormigonera.

condemn [kən'dem] *vt* condenar.

condition [kən'dɪʃən] *n* **1** condición. **2** circunstancia. **3** afección (*médica*). ► *vt* **1** condicionar. **2** acondicionar. • **in bad/good condition** en mal/buen estado; **to be out of condition** no estar en forma.

conditioner [kən'dɪʃənəʳ] *n* suavizante.

condolences [kən'dəʊlənsɪz] *npl* pésame.

conduct [(*n*) 'kɒndəkt, (*vb*) kən'dʌkt] *n* **1** conducta. **2** dirección. ► *vt* **1** dirigir, llevar a cabo. **2** comportarse. ► *vt-vi* dirigir (*orquesta*).

conductor [kən'dʌktəʳ] *n* **1** director,-ra (*de orquesta*). **2** cobrador (*de autobús*). **3** conductor (*de calor, electricidad*).

cone [kəʊn] *n* cono.

confectionery [kən'fekʃənərɪ] *n* dulces.

conference ['kɒnfərəns] *n* congreso. ■ **conference call** teleconferencia.

confess [kən'fes] *vt-vi* confesar(se).

confidence ['kɒnfɪdəns] *n* **1** confianza. **2** confidencia (*secreto*).

confirm [kən'fɜːm] *vt* confirmar.

conflict ['kɒnflɪkt] *n* conflicto.

conform [kən'fɔːm] *vi* **1** conformarse. **2** ajustarse.

confusion [kən'fjuːʒən] *n* confusión.

congenial [kən'dʒiːnɪəl] *adj* agradable.

congratulate [kən'grætjəleɪt] *vt* felicitar.

congratulations [kəngrætjə'leɪʃəns] *npl* felicidades.

congress ['kɒŋgres] *n* congreso.

conjunction [kən'dʒʌŋkʃən] *n* conjunción.

conjurer ['kʌndʒərəʳ] *n* mago,-a, prestidigitador,-ra.

conjuror ['kʌndʒərəʳ] *n* mago,-a, prestidigitador,-ra.

connect [kə'nekt] vt conectar.
► vi enlazar *(vuelos)*.

connection [kə'nekʃən] n conexión.

connoisseur [kɒnə'sɜːʳ] n entendido,-a.

conquer ['kɒŋkəʳ] vt conquistar.

conquest ['kɒŋkwest] n conquista.

conscience ['kɒnʃəns] n conciencia.

conscious ['kɒnʃəs] adj consciente.

consent [kən'sent] n consentimiento. ► vi consentir.

consequence ['kɒnsɪkwəns] n consecuencia.

conservation [kɒnsə'veɪʃən] n conservación.

conservative [kən'sɜːvətɪv] adj-n conservador,-ra.

conservatory [kən'sɜːvətrɪ] n 1 invernadero. 2 conservatorio.

consider [kən'sɪdəʳ] vt considerar.

considerable [kən'sɪdərəbəl] adj considerable.

consist [kən'sɪst] vi consistir.

consistent [kən'sɪstənt] adj 1 consecuente. 2 constante.

consolation [kɒnsə'leɪʃən] n consuelo.

console ['kɒnsəʊl] n consola.

consonant ['kɒnsənənt] n consonante.

conspicuous [kəns'pɪkjuəs] adj llamativo,-a, visible.

conspiracy [kən'spɪrəsɪ] n conspiración.

constable ['kʌnstəbəl] n policía.

constant ['kɒnstənt] adj constante.

constipation [kɒnstɪ'peɪʃən] n estreñimiento.

constituency [kən'stɪtjʊənsɪ] n circunscripción.

constitution [kɒnstɪ'tjuːʃən] n constitución.

constraint [kən'streɪnt] n 1 coacción. 2 limitación.

construction [kən'strʌkʃən] n construcción.

consul ['kɒnsəl] n cónsul.

consulate ['kɒnsjələt] n consulado.

consult [kən'sʌlt] vt-vi consultar.

consume [kən'sjuːm] vt consumir.

consumer [kən'sjuːməʳ] n consumidor,-ra. ■ **consumer goods** bienes de consumo.

contact ['kɒntækt] n contacto. ■ **contact lens** lentilla.

contagious [kən'teɪdʒəs] adj contagioso,-a.

contain [kən'teɪn] vt contener.

container [kən'teɪnəʳ] n 1 recipiente. 2 contáiner.

contamination [kəntæmɪ'neɪʃən] n contaminación.

contemporary [kən'tempərərɪ] adj-n contemporáneo,-a.

contempt [kən'tempt] n desprecio, menosprecio. ■ **con-**

-tempt of court desacato a la autoridad.

contend [kən'tend] *vi* 1 luchar. 2 enfrentarse a.

content¹ [kən'tent] *adj* contento,-a.

content² ['kɒntent] *n* contenido.

contents ['kɒntents] *npl* contenido.

contest ['kɒntest] *n* 1 concurso. 2 contienda.

contestant [kən'testənt] *n* 1 concursante. 2 candidato,-a.

context ['kɒntekst] *n* contexto.

continent ['kɒntɪnənt] *n* continente.

continental [kɒntɪ'nentəl] *adj* 1 continental. 2 GB europeo,-a.

continuation [kəntɪnju'eɪʃən] *n* continuación.

continue [kən'tɪnjuː] *vt-vi* continuar.

contraceptive [kɒntrə'septɪv] *adj* anticonceptivo,-a. ► *n* anticonceptivo.

contract [(n) 'kɒntrækt, (vb) kən'trækt] *n* 1 contrato. ► *vi* contraerse. ► *vt* contraer *(enfermedad, matrimonio)*.

contradiction [kɒntrə'dɪkʃən] *n* contradicción.

contrary ['kɒntrərɪ] *adj* contrario,a. ■ **contrary to** en contra de, al contrario de; **on the contrary** al contrario.

contrast ['kɒntræst] *n* contraste.

contribute [kən'trɪbjuːt] *vt-vi* contribuir. ► *vi* colaborar *(en periódico)*.

contributor [kən'trɪbjətəʳ] *n* 1 contribuyente. 2 colaborador,-ra *(en periódico)*.

control [kən'trəʊl] *n* 1 control. 2 mando. ► *vt* 1 controlar. 2 dominar. ■ **control tower** torre de control.

controller [kən'trəʊləʳ] *n* 1 controlador,-ra. 2 director, -ra de programación.

convenience [kən'viːnɪəns] *n* conveniencia. ■ **convenience food** plato precocinado.

convenient [kən'viːnɪənt] *adj* conveniente.

convent ['kɒnvənt] *n* convento.

convention [kən'venʃən] *n* convención.

conversation [kɒnvə'seɪʃən] *n* conversación.

convert [(n) 'kɒnvɜːt, (vb) kən'vɜːt] *n* converso,-a. ► *vt-vi* converti(se).

convertible [kən'vɜːtəbəl] *adj* convertible. ► *adj-n* descapotable *(coche)*.

convey [kən'veɪ] *vt* 1 transportar. 2 comunicar *(idea)*.

conveyor belt [kən'veɪəbelt] *n* cinta transportadora.

convict [(n) 'kɒnvɪkt, (vb) kən'vɪkt] *n* preso,-a. ► *vt* declarar culpable.

conviction [kən'vɪkʃən] *n* 1 convicción. 2 condena.

convince [kən'vɪns] *vt* convencer.

convoy ['kɒnvɔɪ] *n* convoy.

cook [kʊk] *n* cocinero,-ra. ► *vt* cocinar.

cooker ['kʊkəʳ] *n* cocina *(aparato)*.

cookery ['kʊkərɪ] *n* cocina *(arte)*.

cookie ['kʊkɪ] *n* US galleta.

cool [kuːl] *adj* 1 fresco,-a *(bebida)*. 2 tranquilo,-a *(persona)*. 3 *sl* en la onda. ► *vt* refrescar. ► *vi* enfriarse.

coop [kuːp] *n* gallinero.

cooperation [kəʊɒpə'reɪʃən] *n* cooperación.

cooperative [kəʊ'ɒpərətɪv] *adj* dispuesto,-a a colaborar. ► *n* cooperativa.

coordinate [kəʊ'ɔːdɪneɪt] *vt* coordinar.

cop [kɒp] *n fam* poli.

cope [kəʊp] *vi* arreglárselas. **to cope with** *vt* poder con, hacer frente a.

copper ['kɒpəʳ] *n* cobre.

copy ['kɒpɪ] *n* copia. ► *vt-vi* copiar.

coral ['kɒrəl] *n* coral.

cord [kɔːd] *n* cuerda, cordón.

corduroy ['kɔːdərɔɪ] *n* pana.

core [kɔːʳ] *n* 1 núcleo, centro. 2 corazón *(de manzana)*.

cork [kɔːk] *n* corcho. ■ **cork oak** alcornoque.

corkscrew ['kɔːkskruː] *n* sacacorchos.

corn[1] [kɔːn] *n* 1 maíz. 2 cereales. ■ **corn on the cob** mazorca, maíz tierno.

corn[2] [kɔːn] *n* callo *(dureza)*.

cornea ['kɔːnɪə] *n* córnea.

corner ['kɔːnəʳ] *n* esquina, rincón. ■ **corner kick** córner.

cornet ['kɔːnɪt] *n* 1 corneta. 2 GB cucurucho.

cornflakes ['kɔːnfleɪks] *npl* copos de maíz.

cornstarch ['kɔːnstɑːtʃ] *n* harina de maíz, maicena.

corporal ['kɔːpərəl] *n* cabo *(militar)*. ► *adj* corporal.

corporation [kɔːpə'reɪʃən] *n* corporación.

corpse [kɔːps] *n* cadáver.

corpuscle ['kɔːpəsəl] *n* glóbulo.

correct [kə'rekt] *adj* 1 correcto,-a. 2 exacto,-a. 3 formal. ► *vt* corregir.

correction [kə'rekʃən] *n* corrección.

correspond [kɒrɪs'pɒnd] *vi* 1 coincidir, corresponderse. 2 escribirse, cartearse.

correspondence [kɒrɪs'pɒndəns] *n* correspondencia.

corridor ['kɒrɪdɔːʳ] *n* pasillo.

corrosion [kə'rəʊʒən] *n* corrosión.

corruption [kə'rʌpʃən] *n* corrupción.

corset ['kɔːsɪt] *n* corsé.

cosmetic [kɒz'metɪk] *n* cosmético. ■ **cosmetic surgery** cirugía estética.

cost [kɒst] n coste, costo, precio. ► vi costar, valer. • **at all costs** a toda costa; **at the cost of** a costa de; **whatever the cost** cueste lo que cueste.

costume ['kɒstjuːm] n traje, disfraz. ▪ **costume jewellery** (US **jewelry**) bisutería.

cosy ['kəʊzɪ] adj acogedor,-ra.

cot [kɒt] n cuna.

cottage ['kɒtɪdʒ] n casa de campo. ▪ **cottage cheese** requesón.

cotton ['kɒtən] n algodón. ▪ **cotton wool** algodón hidrófilo.

couch [kaʊtʃ] n canapé, sofá.

couchette [kuːʃet] n litera.

cough [kɒf] n tos. ► vi toser. ▪ **cough mixture** jarabe para la tos.

could [kʊd, kəd] pt → can.

council ['kaʊnsəl] n 1 ayuntamiento. 2 consejo.

count[1] [kaʊnt] n conde.

count[2] [kaʊnt] n cuenta, recuento. ► vt-vi contar.

to count on vt contar con.

countdown ['kaʊntdaʊn] n cuenta atrás.

counter ['kaʊntə'] n 1 mostrador (de tienda). 2 ficha (de juego).

counterfeit ['kaʊntəfɪt] adj falso,-a, falsificado,-a. ► n falsificación. ► vt falsificar.

counterpane ['kaʊntəpeɪn] n colcha, cubrecama.

counterpart ['kaʊntəpɑːt] n homólogo,-a.

countess ['kaʊntəs] n condesa.

country ['kʌntrɪ] n 1 país. 2 campo. 3 tierra, región.

countryside ['kʌntrɪsaɪd] n 1 campo. 2 paisaje.

county ['kaʊntɪ] n condado.

coup [kuː] n golpe de estado.

couple ['kʌpəl] n 1 par (de cosas). 2 pareja (de personas). ► vt enganchar, conectar.

coupon ['kuːpɒn] n cupón.

courage ['kʌrɪdʒ] n valor.

courgette [kʊəʒet] n calabacín.

courier ['kʊərɪə'] n 1 mensajero,-a. 2 guía turístico,-a.

course [kɔːs] n 1 rumbo (de barco, avión). 2 curso (de río). 3 curso. 4 plato. 5 campo (de golf). • **in due course** a su debido tiempo; **of course** desde luego, por supuesto. ▪ **first course** primer plato; **main course** plato principal.

court [kɔːt] n 1 tribunal, juzgado. 2 pista (de tenis). 3 patio. 4 corte (de rey).

courteous ['kɜːtɪəs] adj cortés.

courtyard ['kɔːtjɑːd] n patio.

cousin ['kʌzən] n primo,-a.

cove [kəʊv] n cala, ensenada.

cover ['kʌvə'] n 1 cubierta, funda. 2 tapa (de cazuela). 3 cubierta (de libro), portada (de revista). 4 cobertura (de seguro). ► vt 1 cubrir. 2 tapar (con

tapa). **3** asegurar *(con seguro).* ●
under cover of al amparo de,
al abrigo de. ■ **cover charge**
precio del cubierto.

to cover up *vt* tapar.

covet ['kʌvət] *vt* codiciar.

cow [kaʊ] *n* vaca.

coward ['kaʊəd] *n* cobarde.

cowboy ['kaʊbɔɪ] *n* vaquero.

cowshed ['kaʊʃed] *n* establo.

crab [kræb] *n* cangrejo.

crack [kræk] *vt* **1** rajar, agrietar
(suelo). **2** forzar *(caja fuerte).* **3**
cascar *(huevo, nuez).* **4** soltar
(chiste). ► *vi* **1** rajarse, agri-
etarse. **2** quebrarse *(voz).* **3**
hundirse *(persona).* **4** crujir. ►
n **1** raja *(en taza).* **2** grieta *(en
pared).* **3** chasquido *(de látigo).*

cracker ['krækə'] *n* galleta salada.

cradle ['kreɪdəl] *n* cuna.

craft [krɑːft] *n* **1** arte, oficio. **2**
artesanía. **3** embarcación. ■ **a
pleasure craft** un barco de
recreo.

craftsman ['krɑːftsmən] *n* artesano.

crag [kræg] *n* risco, peñasco.

cramp [kræmp] *n* calambre. ►
cramps *npl* retortijones.

crane [kreɪn] *n* **1** grulla común. **2** grúa.

crash [kræʃ] *vi* estrellarse *(avión,
coche).* ► *n* **1** estallido, estrépito
(ruido). **2** accidente. ■ **crash
course** curso intensivo.

crate [kreɪt] *n* caja.

crawfish ['krɔːfɪʃ] *n* langosta.

crawl [krɔːl] *vi* arrastrarse
(adulto), gatear *(bebé).* ► *n* crol.

crayfish ['kreɪfɪʃ] *n* cangrejo de
río.

craze [kreɪz] *n* manía, moda.

crazy ['kreɪzɪ] *adj fam* loco,-a.

cream [kriːm] *n* crema, nata.

crease [kriːs] *n* arruga.

create [kriː'eɪt] *vt* crear.

creature ['kriːtʃə'] *n* criatura.

crèche [kreʃ] *n* guardería.

credible ['kredɪbəl] *adj* creíble.

credit ['kredɪt] *n* **1** mérito,
reconocimiento. **2** crédito,
haber. ► *vt* **1** creer, dar crédito
a. **2** abonar, ingresar. ► *npl*
credits créditos *(de película).* ●
on credit a crédito. ■ **credit
card** tarjeta de crédito.

creed [kriːd] *n* credo.

creek [kriːk] *n* **1** GB cala. **2** US
riachuelo.

creep [kriːp] *vi* arrastrarse *(insecto),* deslizarse *(animal).*

creeper ['kriːpə'] *n* enredadera.

crème caramel [kremkærə-
'mel] *n* flan.

crept [krept] *pt-pp* → creep.

crescent ['kresənt] *n* medialu-
na. ► creciente *(luna).*

crest [krest] *n* cresta.

crevice ['krevɪs] *n* raja, grieta.

crew [kruː] *n* **1** tripulación. **2**
equipo. ■ **crew cut** pelado al
cero.

crib [krɪb] *n* cuna. ► *vt fam* copiar, plagiar.

crick [krɪk] n tortícolis.
cricket¹ [ˈkrɪkɪt] n grillo *(insecto)*.
cricket² [ˈkrɪkɪt] n críquet.
crime [kraɪm] n **1** crimen. **2** delito.
criminal [ˈkrɪmɪnəl] adj-n criminal. ▪ **criminal record** antecedentes penales.
crinkle [ˈkrɪŋkəl] vt-vi arrugar(se).
cripple [ˈkrɪpəl] n lisiado,-a, inválido,-a. ► vt paralizar.
crisis [ˈkraɪsɪs] n crisis.
crisp [krɪsp] adj **1** crujiente *(pan)*. **2** fresco,-a *(lechuga)*. **3** frío,-a y seco,-a *(tiempo)*. ► n GB patata frita *(de bolsa)*.
criterion [kraɪˈtɪərɪən] n criterio.
critic [ˈkrɪtɪk] n crítico,-a.
critical [ˈkrɪtɪkəl] adj crítico,-a.
criticize [ˈkrɪtɪsaɪz] vt-vi criticar.
crockery [ˈkrɒkərɪ] n loza.
crocodile [ˈkrɒkədaɪl] n cocodrilo.
crocus [ˈkrəʊkəs] n azafrán *(planta, flor)*.
crook [krʊk] n **1** gancho. **2** cayado. **3** fam delincuente.
crooked [ˈkrʊkɪd] adj **1** torcido,-a. **2** tortuoso,-a *(camino)*.
crop [krɒp] n **1** cultivo, cosecha. **2** pelado corto.
cross [krɒs] n **1** cruz. **2** cruce; vt cruzar, atravesar. ► vi cruzar(se).
to cross off vt borrar, tachar.
to cross out vt borrar, tachar.

to cross over vi cruzar.
crossbar [ˈkrɒsbɑːʳ] n travesaño.
crossbow [ˈkrɒsbəʊ] n ballesta.
cross-country [krɒsˈkʌntrɪ] adj-adv campo través. ▪ **cross-country race** cros.
cross-eyed [ˈkrɒsaɪd] adj bizco,-a.
crossing [ˈkrɒsɪŋ] n **1** cruce *(de carretera)*. **2** travesía *(en barco)*.
crossroads [ˈkrɒsrəʊdz] n encrucijada, cruce.
crossword [ˈkrɒswɜːd] n crucigrama.
crotch [krɒtʃ] n entrepierna.
crotchet [ˈkrɒtʃɪt] n negra *(nota)*.
crouch [kraʊtʃ] vi agacharse, agazaparse.
crow [krəʊ] n cuervo.
crowbar [ˈkrəʊbɑːʳ] n palanca.
crowd [kraʊd] n **1** multitud, gentío. **2** público. **3** gente.
crowded [ˈkraʊdɪd] adj abarrotado,-a.
crown [kraʊn] n **1** corona *(de monarca)*. **2** copa *(de árbol, sombrero)*. ► vt coronar.
crucifix [ˈkruːsɪfɪks] n crucifijo.
crude [kruːd] n **1** grosero,-a *(chiste)*. **2** crudo,-a *(petróleo)*.
cruel [ˈkruːəl] adj cruel.
cruet [ˈkruːɪt] n vinagreras.
cruise [kruːz] vi hacer un crucero *(viaje)*. ► n crucero *(viaje)*.
cruiser [ˈkruːzəʳ] n crucero *(barco)*.

crumb [krʌm] *n* miga.

crumble ['krʌmbəl] *vt* desmigar. ► *vi* desmoronarse, deshacerse.

crumple ['krʌmpəl] *vt-vi* arrugar(se).

crunch [krʌntʃ] ► *vi* crujir. ► *n* crujido.

crusade [kruːˈseɪd] *n* cruzada.

crush [krʌʃ] *n* aglomeración, gentío. ► *vt* **1** aplastar. **2** triturar.

crust [krʌst] *n* corteza.

crutch [krʌtʃ] *n* muleta.

cry [kraɪ] *vt-vi* gritar. ► *vi* llorar. ► *n* **1** grito. **2** llanto.

to cry out *vi* gritar.

crypt [krɪpt] *n* cripta.

crystal ['krɪstəl] *n* cristal.

cub [kʌb] *n* cachorro,-a.

cube [kjuːb] *n* **1** cubo. **2** terrón *(de azúcar)*. ■ **cube root** raíz cúbica.

cubic ['kjuːbɪk] *adj* cúbico,-a.

cuckoo ['kukuː] *n* cuco común.

cucumber ['kjuːkʌmbəʳ] *n* pepino.

cuddle ['kʌdəl] *vt-vi* abrazar(se). ► *n* abrazo.

cue[1] [kjuː] *n* **1** señal. **2** pie *(en teatro)*.

cue[2] [kjuː] *n* taco *(de billar)*.

cuff [kʌf] *n* puño. ■ **cuff links** gemelos *(de camisa)*.

cul-de-sac ['kʌldəsæk] *n* calle sin salida.

culminate ['kʌlmɪneɪt] *vt* culminar.

culprit ['kʌlprɪt] *n* culpable.

cultivate ['kʌltɪveɪt] *vt* cultivar.

cultivated ['kʌltɪveɪtɪd] *adj* **1** culto,-a *(persona)*. **2** cultivado,-a *(tierra)*.

culture ['kʌltʃəʳ] *n* cultura.

cumbersome ['kʌmbəsəm] *adj* **1** voluminoso. **2** incómodo,-a.

cumin ['kʌmɪn] *n* comino.

cunning ['kʌnɪŋ] *adj* astuto,-a.

cup [kʌp] *n* **1** taza. **2** copa.

cupboard ['kʌbəd] *n* armario.

curb [kɜːb] *n* freno, restricción. ► *vt* refrenar, contener.

curd [kɜːd] *n* cuajada. ■ **curd cheese** requesón.

cure [kjʊəʳ] *vt* curar. ► *n* cura.

curfew ['kɜːfjuː] *n* toque de queda.

curious ['kjʊərɪəs] *adj* **1** curioso,-a. **2** extraño.

curl [kɜːl] *vt-vi* rizar(se). ► *n* **1** rizo, bucle. **2** espiral.

currant ['kʌrənt] *n* pasa.

currency ['kʌrənsɪ] *n* moneda.

current ['kʌrənt] *adj* **1** actual *(precio)*. **2** en curso, corriente *(mes)*. **3** común *(idea)*. ► *n* corriente. ■ **current account** cuenta corriente; **current affairs** temas de actualidad.

curriculum [kəˈrɪkjələm] *n* plan de estudios. ■ **curriculum vitae** currículum.

curse [kɜːs] *n* **1** maldición, maleficio. **2** palabrota. ► *vt-vi* maldecir.

cursor ['kɜːsəʳ] n cursor.
curtail [kɜːˈteɪl] vt reducir.
curtain ['kɜːtən] n 1 cortina. 2 telón. • **to draw the curtains** correr las cortinas.
curve [kɜːv] n curva.
cushion ['kʊʃən] n cojín, almohadón. ► vt fig amortiguar.
custard ['kʌstəd] n natillas.
custom ['kʌstəm] n costumbre.
customer ['kʌstəməʳ] n cliente. ■ **customer services** servicio de atención al cliente.
customs ['kʌstəmz] n aduana. ■ **customs duties** derechos de aduana, aranceles.
cut [kʌt] vt 1 cortar. 2 tallar (piedra, vidrio). 3 dividir. 4 recortar. ► n 1 corte, incisión. 2 parte (ganancias). 3 rebaja, recorte. ■ **cold cuts** fiambres.
to cut down vt 1 talar, cortar. 2 fig reducir: **to cut down on smoking**, fumar menos.
to cut in vi interrumpir.
to cut off vt 1 cortar (electricidad). 2 aislar.
to cut out vt 1 recortar, cortar. 2 eliminar, suprimir.
cute [kjuːt] adj mono,-a, guapo,-a.
cutlery ['kʌtləri] n cubiertos, cubertería.
cutlet ['kʌtlət] n chuleta.
cuttlefish ['kʌtəlfɪʃ] n sepia.
cycle ['saɪkəl] n ciclo. ► vi ir en bicicleta.
cycling ['saɪklɪŋ] n ciclismo.

cyclist ['saɪklɪst] n ciclista.
cyclone ['saɪkləʊn] n ciclón.
cylinder ['sɪlɪndəʳ] n 1 cilindro. 2 bombona.
cynical ['sɪnɪkəl] adj cínico,-a.
cypress ['saɪprəs] n ciprés.
cyst [sɪst] n quiste.
czar [zɑːʳ] n zar.

D

dad [dæd] n fam papá.
daddy ['dædɪ] n fam papá.
daffodil ['dæfədɪl] n narciso.
daft [dɑːft] adj fam tonto,-a.
daily ['deɪlɪ] adj diario,-a, cotidiano,-a. ► adv diariamente. ► n diario.
dairy ['deərɪ] n 1 vaquería. 2 lechería.
daisy ['deɪzɪ] n margarita.
dam [dæm] n 1 dique. 2 embalse, presa.
damage ['dæmɪdʒ] vt dañar. ► n daño.
damn [dæm] interj fam ¡maldito,-a sea! ► adj fam maldito,-a.
damp [dæmp] adj húmedo,-a. ► n humedad.
dance [dɑːns] n baile, danza. ► vt-vi bailar.
dancer ['dɑːnsəʳ] n bailarín,-ina.
dandelion ['dændɪlaɪən] n diente de león.

dandruff ['dændrʌf] *n* caspa.
danger ['deɪndʒəʳ] *n* peligro.
dare [deəʳ] *vi* atreverse. • **I dare say...** creo que; **don't you dare!** ¡ni se te ocurra!
dark [dɑːk] *adj* **1** oscuro,-a. **2** moreno,-a *(pelo, piel)*. ► *n* **1** oscuridad. • **to grow dark** anochecer. • **to grow dark** anochecer.
darkness ['dɑːknəs] *n* oscuridad.
darling ['dɑːlɪŋ] *n* querido,-a, cariño.
darn [dɑːn] *n* zurcido. ► *vt* zurcir.
dart [dɑːt] *n* dardo.
dartboard ['dɑːtbɔːd] *n* diana.
dash [dæʃ] *n* **1** poco, pizca *(de sal)*. **2** chorro *(de líquido)*.
dashboard ['dæʃbɔːd] *n* salpicadero.
data ['deɪtə] *npl* datos, información. ▪ **data base** base de datos; **data processing** procesamiento de datos.
date[1] [deɪt] *n* **1** fecha. **2** cita, compromiso. • **out of date** anticuado,-a.
date[2] [deɪt] *n* dátil.
dated ['deɪtɪd] *adj* anticuado,-a.
daughter ['dɔːtəʳ] *n* hija.
daughter-in-law ['dɔːtərɪnlɔː] *n* nuera.
daunt [dɔːnt] *vt* intimidar.
dawn [dɔːn] *n* amanecer.
day [deɪ] *n* **1** día. **2** jornada. **3** época, tiempo. • **by day** de día. ▪ **day off** día libre.

daybreak ['deɪbreɪk] *n* alba.
daylight ['deɪlaɪt] *n* luz de día.
daytime *n* día.
dazzle ['dæzəl] *vt* deslumbrar.
dead [ded] *adj* **1** muerto,-a. **2** sordo,-a *(ruido)*. **3** total, absoluto,-a: **dead silence**, silencio total. ▪ **dead end** callejón sin salida.
deadline ['dedlaɪn] *n* fecha límite, hora límite.
deadlock ['dedlɒk] *n* punto muerto.
deaf [def] *adj* sordo,-a.
deaf-and-dumb [defən'dʌm] *adj* sordomudo,-a.
deal [diːl] *n* **1** trato, pacto. **2** cantidad: **a great deal of noise**, mucho ruido. ► *vt* **1** dar, asestar *(golpe)*. **2** repartir *(cartas)*. ► *vi* comerciar.
to deal with *vt* **1** tratar con. **2** abordar, ocuparse de *(problema)*. **3** tratar de *(tema)*.
dealer ['diːləʳ] *n* **1** comerciante. **2** traficante *(de drogas)*.
dealt [delt] *pt-pp* → deal.
dear [dɪəʳ] *adj* **1** querido,-a. **2** caro,-a *(precio)*. • **Dear Sir** Muy señor mío, Estimado señor.
death [deθ] *n* muerte. ▪ **death penalty** pena de muerte.
debate [dɪ'beɪt] *n* debate. ► *vt-vi* debatir.
debit ['debɪt] *n* débito. ► *vt* cargar en cuenta.
debris ['deɪbriː] *n* escombros.
debt [det] *n* deuda.

debug [diːˈbʌg] *vt* depurar.

debut [ˈdeɪbjuː] *n* estreno.

decade [ˈdekeɪd] *n* década.

decadence [ˈdekədəns] *n* decadencia.

decaffeinated [dɪˈkæfɪneɪtɪd] *adj* descafeinado,-a.

decay [dɪˈkeɪ] *n* **1** descomposición *(de cuerpo)*. **2** caries *(de diente)*. **3** *fig* decadencia *(de sociedad)*. ▶ *vi* **1** descomponerse *(cuerpo)*. **2** deteriorarse *(edificio)*. **3** cariarse *(diente)*.

deceased [dɪˈsiːst] *adj-n* fallecido,-a.

deceive [dɪˈsiːv] *vt* engañar.

December [dɪˈsembəʳ] *n* diciembre.

decent [ˈdiːsənt] *adj* decente.

deception [dɪˈsepʃən] *n* engaño, mentira.

decide [dɪˈsaɪd] *vt-vi* decidir(se).

decimal [ˈdesɪməl] *adj-n* decimal.

decision [dɪˈsɪʒən] *n* decisión.

decisive [dɪˈsaɪsɪv] *adj* **1** decisivo,-a. **2** decidido,-a *(persona)*.

deck [dek] *n* **1** cubierta *(de barco)*. **2** piso *(de autobús)*. **3** US baraja.

deckchair [ˈdektʃeəʳ] *n* tumbona.

declare [dɪˈkleəʳ] *vt* declarar.

decorate [ˈdekəreɪt] *vt* decorar, adornar. ▶ *vt-vi* pintar, empapelar.

decoration [dekəˈreɪʃən] *n* **1** decoración. **2** condecoración.

decrease [dɪˈkriːs] *n* disminución. ▶ *vt-vi* disminuir.

decree [dɪˈkriː] *n* decreto.

dedicate [ˈdedɪkeɪt] *vt* dedicar.

deduce [dɪˈdjuːs] *vt* deducir.

deduct [dɪˈdʌkt] *vt* restar.

deed [diːd] *n* **1** acto. **2** hazaña. **3** escritura *(de propiedad)*.

deep [diːp] *adj* hondo,-a, profundo,-a.

deer [dɪəʳ] *n* ciervo.

default [dɪˈfɔːlt] *n* negligencia. ▪ **default settings** valores por defecto.

defeat [dɪˈfiːt] *n* derrota. ▶ *vt* derrotar.

defect [*(n)* ˈdiːfekt, *(vb)* dɪˈfekt] *n* defecto. ▶ *vi* desertar.

defence [dɪˈfens] *n* defensa.

defend [dɪˈfend] *vt* defender.

defer [dɪˈfɜːʳ] *vt* aplazar.

deficient [dɪˈfɪʃənt] *adj* deficiente.

deficit [ˈdefɪsɪt] *n* déficit.

define [dɪˈfaɪn] *vt* definir.

definition [defɪˈnɪʃən] *n* definición.

definitive [dɪˈfɪnɪtɪv] *adj* definitivo,-a.

deflate [dɪˈfleɪt] *vt-vi* desinflar(se), deshinchar(se).

deflect [dɪˈflekt] *vt-vi* desviar(se).

defrost [diːˈfrɒst] *vt-vi* descongelar(se).

defy [dɪˈfaɪ] *vt* desafiar.

degree [dɪˈgriː] *n* **1** grado. **2** título, licenciatura. ● **to some**

depot

degree hasta cierto punto. ■
honorary degree doctorado "honoris causa".

delay [dɪ'leɪ] n retraso. ► vt aplazar.

delegation [delɪ'geɪʃən] n delegación.

delete [dɪ'liːt] vt borrar.

deliberate [dɪ'lɪbəreɪt] vt-vi deliberar.

delicacy ['delɪkəsɪ] n 1 delicadeza. 2 manjar (exquisito).

delicate ['delɪkət] adj delicado,-a.

delicatessen [delɪkə'tesən] n charcutería selecta.

delicious [dɪ'lɪʃəs] adj delicioso,-a.

delight [dɪ'laɪt] n placer, delicia.

delighted [dɪ'laɪtɪd] adj encantado,-a.

deliver [dɪ'lɪvəˈ] vt 1 entregar, (mercancía). 2 dar (golpe, patada). 3 pronunciar (discurso). 4 traer al mundo.

delivery [dɪ'lɪvərɪ] n 1 entrega. 2 parto. ■ **delivery man** repartidor.

delude [dɪ'luːd] vt engañar.

demand [dɪ'maːnd] n 1 reclamación, petición. 2 demanda. ► vt exigir, reclamar.

democracy [dɪ'mɒkrəsɪ] n democracia.

democrat ['deməkræt] n demócrata.

demolish [dɪ'mɒlɪʃ] vt derribar, demoler.

demon ['diːmən] n demonio.

demonstrate ['demənstreɪt] vt 1 demostrar. 2 mostrar. ► vi manifestarse.

demonstration [demən'streɪʃən] n 1 demostración. 2 manifestación.

denial [dɪ'naɪəl] n negativa.

denim ['denɪm] n tela vaquera.

denounce [dɪ'naʊns] vt denunciar.

dense [dens] adj denso,-a.

dent [dent] n abolladura. ► vt abollar.

dentist ['dentɪst] n dentista.

deny [dɪ'naɪ] vt negar.

deodorant [diː'əʊdərənt] n desodorante.

department [dɪ'paːtmənt] n 1 departamento, sección. 2 ministerio. ■ **department store** grandes almacenes.

departure [dɪ'paːtʃəˈ] n 1 partida, marcha (de persona). 2 salida (de tren, avión).

depend [dɪ'pend] vi depender.

to depend on vt confiar en.

deplore [dɪ'plɔːˈ] vt deplorar.

deploy [dɪ'plɔɪ] vt fig desplegar.

deport [dɪ'pɔːt] vt deportar.

deposit [dɪ'pɒzɪt] n 1 depósito. 2 yacimiento (minerales). 3 poso (en vino). ► vt 1 depositar. 2 ingresar. ■ **deposit account** cuenta de ahorros.

depot ['depəʊ] n 1 almacén. 2 depósito.

depress [dɪ'pres] *vt* deprimir.

depression [dɪ'preʃən] *n* depresión.

deprive [dɪ'praɪv] *vt* privar.

depth [depθ] *n* profundidad.

deputy ['depjətɪ] *n* **1** sustituto,-a, suplente. **2** diputado,-a.

derive [dɪ'raɪv] *vt-vi* derivar(se).

derogatory [dɪ'rɒgətərɪ] *adj* despectivo,-a.

descend [dɪ'send] *vt-vi* bajar.

descendant [dɪ'sendənt] *n* descendiente.

descent [dɪ'sent] *n* **1** descenso, bajada. **2** pendiente.

describe [dɪ'skraɪb] *vt* describir.

description [dɪ'skrɪpʃən] *n* descripción.

desert[1] ['dezət] *n* desierto.

desert[2] [dɪ'zɜːt] *vt* abandonar, dejar. ▶ *vi* desertar.

deserve [dɪ'zɜːv] *vt* merecerse.

design [dɪ'zaɪn] *n* diseño. ▶ *vt-vi* diseñar.

desire [dɪ'zaɪə'] *n* deseo. ▶ *vt* desear.

desk [desk] *n* **1** pupitre. **2** escritorio, mesa *(de trabajo)*.

desktop ['desktɒp] *n* escritorio. ▪ **desktop computer** ordenador de sobremesa; **desktop publishing** autoedición.

despair [dɪs'peə'] *n* desesperación. ▶ *vi* desesperarse.

despatch [dɪs'pætʃ] *vt-n* → dispatch.

desperate ['despərət] *adj* desesperado,-a.

desperation [despə'reɪʃən] *n* desesperación.

despicable [dɪ'spɪkəbəl] *adj* despreciable.

despise [dɪ'spaɪz] *vt* despreciar.

despite [dɪ'spaɪt] *prep* a pesar de.

dessert [dɪ'zɜːt] *n* postre.

destination [destɪ'neɪʃən] *n* destino.

destiny ['destɪnɪ] *n* destino.

destroy [dɪ'strɔɪ] *vt* destruir.

destruction [dɪ'strʌkʃən] *n* destrucción.

detach [dɪ'tætʃ] *vt* separar.

detail ['diːteɪl] *n* detalle.

detect [dɪ'tekt] *vt* detectar.

detective [dɪ'tektɪv] *n* detective.

detention [dɪ'tenʃən] *n* detención.

detergent [dɪ'tɜːdʒənt] *n* detergente.

determine [dɪ'tɜːmɪn] *vt* determinar.

deterrent [dɪ'terənt] *adj* disuasivo,-a. ▶ *n* fuerza disuasoria.

detest [dɪ'test] *vt* detestar.

detour ['diːtʊə'] *n* desvío.

devaluation [diːvæljuː'eɪʃən] *n* devaluación.

develop [dɪ'veləp] *vt* **1** desarrollar. **2** revelar *(carrete)*. ▶ *vi* desarrollarse.

development [dɪ'veləpmənt] *n* **1** desarrollo. **2** revelado *(de carrete)*.

deviate ['diːvɪeɪt] *vi* desviarse.

device [dɪ'vaɪs] *n* mecanismo, dispositivo.

devil ['devəl] *n* diablo.

devise [dɪ'vaɪz] *vt* idear.

devoted [dɪ'vəʊtɪd] *adj* fiel.

devotion [dɪ'vəʊʃən] *n* dedicación.

dew [djuː] *n* rocío.

dexterity [dek'sterɪtɪ] *n* destreza, habilidad.

diabetes [daɪə'biːtiːz] *n* diabetes.

diagnosis [daɪəg'nəʊsɪs] *n* diagnóstico.

diagonal [daɪ'ægənəl] *n* diagonal.

diagram ['daɪəgræm] *n* diagrama, esquema, gráfico.

dial ['daɪəl] *n* **1** esfera *(de reloj)*. **2** dial *(de radio)*. **3** teclado *(de teléfono)*. ► *vt* marcar. ■ **dialling code** prefijo telefónico; **dialling tone** señal de marcar.

dialect ['daɪəlekt] *n* dialecto.

dialogue ['daɪəlɒg] (US **dialog**) *n* diálogo.

diameter [daɪ'æmɪtə'] *n* diámetro.

diamond ['daɪəmənd] *n* diamante.

diaper ['daɪəpə'] *n* US pañal.

diarrhoea [daɪə'rɪə] *n* diarrea.

diary ['daɪərɪ] *n* **1** diario. **2** agenda.

dice [daɪs] *n* dado.

dictate [dɪk'teɪt] *vt* dictar. ► *vi* mandar.

dictation [dɪk'teɪʃən] *n* dictado.

dictator [dɪk'teɪtə'] *n* dictador, -ra.

dictionary ['dɪkʃənərɪ] *n* diccionario.

did [dɪd] *pt* → do.

die [daɪ] *vi* morir.

to die away *vi* desvanecerse.

diesel ['diːzəl] *n* gasoil, diesel.

diet ['daɪət] *n* dieta, régimen. ● **to go on a diet** ponerse a régimen.

differ ['dɪfə'] *vi* diferir.

difference ['dɪfərəns] *n* diferencia.

different ['dɪfərənt] *adj* diferente, distinto,-a.

difficult ['dɪfɪkəlt] *adj* difícil.

dig [dɪg] *vt* **1** cavar *(hoyo)*, excavar *(túnel)*. **2** clavar, hincar *(con uñas)*.

to dig out/up *vt* desenterrar.

digest ['daɪdʒest] *n* resumen.

digestion [dɪ'dʒestʃən] *n* digestión.

digestive [daɪ'dʒestɪv] *adj* digestivo,-a. ■ **digestive tract** aparato digestivo.

dignity ['dɪgnɪtɪ] *n* dignidad.

dike [daɪk] *n* US → dyke.

diligence ['dɪlɪdʒəns] *n* diligencia.

dilute [daɪ'luːt] *vt* diluir.

dim [dɪm] *adj* **1** débil, difuso, -a, tenue. **2** oscuro,-a. **3** borroso,-a. **4** *fam* tonto,-a. ► *vt* **1** bajar, atenuar. **2** *fig* difuminar.

dime [daɪm] *n* US moneda de diez centavos.

dimension [dɪ'menʃən] *n* dimensión.

dimple ['dɪmpəl] *n* hoyuelo.

din [dɪn] *n* alboroto.

dine [daɪn] *vi* cenar.

diner ['daɪnəʳ] *n* **1** comensal. **2** US restaurante barato.

dinghy ['dɪŋgɪ] *n* bote.

dingy ['dɪndʒɪ] *adj* **1** sucio,-a, sórdido,-a. **2** deslucido,-a, deslustrado,-a *(ropa)*.

dining car ['daɪnɪŋkɑːʳ] *n* coche restaurante.

dining room ['daɪnɪŋruːm] *n* comedor.

dinner ['dɪnəʳ] *n* comida, cena. • **to have dinner** cenar. ■ **dinner jacket** esmoquin; **dinner table** mesa de comedor.

dinosaur ['daɪnəsɔːʳ] *n* dinosaurio.

dip [dɪp] *n vt* sumergir, bañar.

diploma [dɪ'pləʊmə] *n* diploma.

diplomacy [dɪ'pləʊməsɪ] *n* diplomacia.

direct [dɪ'rekt, daɪ'rekt] *adj* directo,-a. ► *vt* dirigir.

direction [dɪ'rekʃən, daɪ'rekʃən] *n* dirección. ► *npl* **directions** instrucciones de uso, modo de empleo.

director [dɪ'rektəʳ, daɪ'rektəʳ] *n* director,-ra.

directory [dɪ'rektərɪ, daɪ'rektərɪ] *n* **1** guía telefónica. **2** callejero.

dirt [dɜːt] *n* suciedad.

dirty ['dɜːtɪ] *adj* **1** sucio,-a. **2** verde *(chiste)*. ► *vt-vi* ensuciar(se). ■ **dirty trick** cochinada; **dirty word** palabrota.

disabled [dɪs'eɪbəld] *adj* minusválido,-a, incapacitado,-a.

disadvantage [dɪsəd'vɑːntɪdʒ] *n* desventaja.

disagree [dɪsə'griː] *vi* **1** discrepar. **2** sentar mal *(comida)*.

disappear [dɪsə'pɪəʳ] *vi* desaparecer.

disappoint [dɪsə'pɔɪnt] *vt* decepcionar, defraudar.

disaster [dɪ'zɑːstəʳ] *n* desastre.

disc [dɪsk] *n* disco. ■ **disc brake** freno de disco; **disc jockey** disc-jockey.

discard [dɪs'kɑːd] *vt* desechar.

discern [dɪ'sɜːn] *vt* discernir.

discharge [(*n*) 'dɪstʃɑːdʒ, (*vb*) dɪs'tʃɑːdʒ] *n* **1** descarga. **2** liberación *(de preso)*. **3** alta *(de paciente)*. ► *vt* **1** liberar *(preso)*. **2** dar de alta *(paciente)*. **3** licenciar *(soldado)*.

discipline ['dɪsɪplɪn] *n* disciplina.

disco ['dɪskəʊ] *n fam* discoteca.

discolour [dɪs'kʌləʳ] (US **discolor**) *vt-vi* desteñir(se).

disconnect [dɪskə'nekt] *vt* desconectar.

discotheque ['dɪskətek] *n* discoteca.

discount [(*n*) 'dɪskaʊnt, (*vb*) dɪs'kaʊnt] *n* descuento. ► *vt* descontar.

discourage [dɪs'kʌrɪdʒ] vt **1** desanimar. **2** disuadir.

discover [dɪ'skʌvə'] vt descubrir.

discovery [dɪ'skʌvərɪ] n descubrimiento.

discriminate [dɪ'skrɪmɪneɪt] vi discriminar.

discus ['dɪskəs] n disco.

discuss [dɪ'skʌs] vt-vi discutir.

discussion [dɪ'skʌʃən] n discusión.

disease [dɪ'ziːz] n enfermedad.

disembark [dɪsɪm'baːk] vt-vi desembarcar.

disgrace [dɪs'greɪs] n **1** desgracia. **2** escándalo, vergüenza.

disguise [dɪs'gaɪz] n disfraz. ► vt disfrazar.

disgusting [dɪs'gʌstɪŋ] adj asqueroso,-a, repugnante.

dish [dɪʃ] n plato, fuente (para servir). ● **to do the dishes** lavar los platos.

dishcloth ['dɪʃklɒθ] n trapo de cocina.

dishevelled [dɪ'ʃevəld] adj **1** despeinado,-a (pelo). **2** desarreglado,-a (aspecto).

dishwasher ['dɪʃwɒʃə'] n lavavajillas.

disinfectant [dɪsɪn'fektənt] n desinfectante.

disk [dɪsk] n disco. ■ **disk drive** unidad de disco.

dislike [dɪs'laɪk] n aversión, antipatía. ► vt no gustar.

dislodge [dɪs'lɒdʒ] vt desalojar.

dismal ['dɪzməl] adj triste.

dismantle [dɪs'mæntəl] vt-vi desmontar(se), desarmar(se).

dismiss [dɪs'mɪs] vt **1** despedir (empleado). **2** descartar, desechar.

disobey [dɪsə'beɪ] vt-vi desobedecer.

disorder [dɪs'ɔːdə'] n desorden.

dispatch [dɪs'pætʃ] n **1** despacho, parte. **2** reportaje (de corresponsalía). **3** envío. ► vt enviar.

dispenser [dɪ'spensə'] n máquina expendedora.

display [dɪ'spleɪ] n **1** exposición (de artículos). **2** exhibición (de fuerzas). **3** visualización (en pantalla). ► vt mostrar, exponer.

disposable [dɪ'spəʊzəbəl] adj desechable.

dispute [(n) 'dɪspjuːt, (vb) dɪ'spjuːt] n discusión, disputa. ► vt cuestionar.

disqualify [dɪs'kwɒlɪfaɪ] vt descalificar.

disrupt [dɪs'rʌpt] vt trastornar.

dissatisfied [dɪs'sætɪsfaɪd] adj descontento,-a.

dissident ['dɪsɪdənt] adj-n disidente.

dissolve [dɪ'zɒlv] vt-vi disolver(se).

dissuade [dɪ'sweɪd] vt disuadir.

distance ['dɪstəns] n distancia. ▶ vt distanciar. • **from a distance** desde lejos; **in the distance** a lo lejos.

distinction [dɪ'stɪŋkʃən] n distinción.

distinguish [dɪ'stɪŋgwɪʃ] vt-vi distinguir(se).

distort [dɪ'stɔːt] vt deformar.

distract [dɪ'strækt] vt distraer.

distraction [dɪ'strækʃən] n distracción.

distress [dɪ'stres] n angustia. ▶ vt afligir. ■ **distress call/signal** señal de socorro.

distribute [dɪ'strɪbjuːt] vt distribuir.

distribution [dɪstrɪ'bjuːʃən] n distribución.

district ['dɪstrɪkt] n distrito. ■ **district council** municipio.

disturb [dɪ'stɜːb] vt molestar.

ditch [dɪtʃ] n 1 zanja, cuneta. 2 acequia (para agua).

dive [daɪv] n 1 zambullida. 2 buceo. 3 picado (pájaro, avión). 4 fam antro. ▶ vi 1 tirarse de cabeza (al agua). 2 bucear (bajo el agua). 3 bajar en picado (pájaro, avión).

diver ['daɪvə'] n 1 buceador,-ra. 2 saltador,-ra (de trampolín).

diversion [daɪ'vɜːʃən] n 1 desvío, desviación. 2 distracción.

diversity [daɪ'vɜːsɪtɪ] n diversidad.

divert [daɪ'vɜːt] vt 1 desviar. 2 distraer.

divide [dɪ'vaɪd] vt-vi dividir(se).

diving ['daɪvɪŋ] n 1 submarinismo. 2 saltos de trampolín. ■ **diving board** trampolín.

division [dɪ'vɪʒən] n división.

divorce [dɪ'vɔːs] n divorcio. ▶ vt-vi divorciarse (de).

dizzy ['dɪzɪ] adj mareado,-a.

do [duː] aux: *do you smoke?*, ¿fumas?; *I don't want to dance*, no quiero bailar; *you don't smoke, do you?*, no fumas, ¿verdad? ▶ vt 1 hacer, realizar: *what are you doing?*, ¿qué haces? 2 ser suficiente: *ten packets will do us*, con diez paquetes tenemos suficiente. • **how do you do?** 1 ¿cómo está usted? (saludo). 2 mucho gusto, encantado,-a (respuesta).

to do up vt 1 fam abrocharse, atar. 2 envolver. 3 arreglar, renovar.

dock¹ [dɒk] n 1 muelle (en puerto). 2 banquillo (de los acusados).

dockyard ['dɒkjɑːd] n astillero.

doctor ['dɒktə'] n médico,-a.

document ['dɒkjəmənt] n documento.

documentary [dɒkjə'mentərɪ] adj-n documental.

does [dʌz] 3rd pers sing pres → do.

dog [dɒg] n perro,-a.

do-it-yourself [duːɪtjɔː'self] n bricolaje.

dole [dəʊl] *n* GB *fam* subsidio de desempleo. • **to be on the dole** estar en el paro.

doll [dɒl] *n* muñeca.

dollar ['dɒlə'] *n* dólar.

dolphin ['dɒlfɪn] *n* delfín.

domain [də'meɪn] *n* dominio.

domestic [də'mestɪk] *adj* **1** doméstico,-a *(animal)*. **2** nacional *(vuelo)*.

dominate ['dɒmɪneɪt] *vt-vi* dominar.

domino ['dɒmɪnəʊ] *n* ficha de dominó. ► *npl* **dominoes** dominó.

donate [dəʊ'neɪt] *vt* donar, hacer un donativo de.

done [dʌn] *pp* → do.

donkey ['dɒŋkɪ] *n* burro,-a.

donor ['dəʊnə'] *n* donante.

don't [dəʊnt] *aux* contracción de *do + not*.

door [dɔː'] *n* puerta. • **to answer the door** abrir la puerta.

doorbell ['dɔːbel] *n* timbre.

doorman ['dɔːmən] *n* portero.

door-to-door [dɔːtə'dɔː] *adj* a domicilio.

doorway ['dɔːweɪ] *n* entrada, portal.

dosage ['dəʊsɪdʒ] *n* posología.

dose [dəʊs] *n* dosis.

dot [dɒt] *n* punto.

double ['dʌbəl] *adj-adv* doble. ► *n* doble. ► *vt-vi* doblar(se). ► *npl* **doubles** dobles. ■ **double bass** contrabajo; **double bed** cama de matrimonio; **double**

chin papada; **double room** habitación doble.

double-decker [dʌbəl'dekə'] *n* GB autobús de dos pisos.

doubt [daʊt] *n* duda. ► *vt* dudar. • **no doubt** sin duda.

dough [dəʊ] *n* **1** masa *(de pan)*. **2** *fam* pasta *(dinero)*.

doughnut ['dəʊnʌt] *n* rosquilla, donut.

dove[1] [dʌv] *n* paloma.

dove[2] [dəʊv] *pt* US → dive.

down[1] [daʊn] *prep* abajo, hacia abajo. ► *adv* **1** abajo, hacia abajo, al suelo. **2** estropeado,-a: *the computer is down*, el ordenador está estropeado. ► *adj fam* deprimido. ■ **down payment** entrada.

down[2] [daʊn] *n* **1** plumón. **2** vello, pelusa, pelusilla.

downhill [daʊn'hɪl] *adv* cuesta abajo. ► *adj* en pendiente.

download ['daʊn'ləʊd] *vt* bajar, descargar.

downpour ['daʊnpɔː'] *n* chaparrón.

downstairs [daʊn'steəz] *adv* abajo: *to go downstairs*, bajar la escalera. ► *adj* de la planta baja, de abajo.

downstream [daʊn'striːm] *adv* río abajo.

downtown [daʊn'taʊn] US *adv* al/en el centro de la ciudad. ► *adj* del centro de la ciudad.

downward ['daʊnwəd] *adj* **1** descendente. **2** a la baja.

downwards ['daʊnwədz] *adv* hacia abajo.

doze [dəʊz] *n* cabezada.

dozen ['dʌzən] *n* docena.

draft [drɑːft] *n* **1** borrador. **2** letra de cambio, giro. **3** US → draught.

draftsman ['drɑːftsmən] *n* US → draughtsman.

drag [dræg] *n fam* calada. ► *vt* **1** arrastrar. **2** rastrear, dragar. • **in drag** vestido de mujer.

dragon ['drægən] *n* dragón.

drain [dreɪn] *n* desagüe, alcantarilla. ► *vt* **1** drenar *(pantano)*. **2** desecar *(lago)*. **3** apurar *(vaso)*. **4** vaciar *(depósito)*. **5** escurrir *(verduras)*. ► *vi* escurrirse.

drainpipe ['dreɪnpaɪp] *n* (tubería de) desagüe.

drama ['drɑːmə] *n* **1** drama. **2** teatro, arte dramático.

drank [dræŋk] *pt* → drink.

drastic ['dræstɪk] *adj* drástico,-a.

draught [drɑːft] *n* **1** corriente de aire. **2** trago. ► *npl* **draughts** GB damas. • **on draught** a presión, de barril.

draughtsman ['drɑːftsmən] *n* delineante.

draw [drɔː] *n* **1** sorteo. **2** empate. ► *vt* **1** dibujar *(línea, círculo)*. **2** tirar de. **3** correr *(cortinas)*. **4** cobrar *(sueldo)*. **5** extender *(talón)*. **6** sacar *(conclusión)*.

to draw apart separarse.

to draw back *vi* retroceder.

to draw in *vi* apartarse.

to draw on *vt* recurrir a.

drawback ['drɔːbæk] *n* inconveniente.

drawer ['drɔːə'] *n* cajón.

drawing ['drɔːɪŋ] *n* dibujo. ■ **drawing pin** GB chincheta; **drawing room** sala de estar.

drawn [drɔːn] *pp* → draw.

dreadful ['dredfʊl] *adj* espantoso,-a.

dream [driːm] *n* sueño. ► *vt-vi* soñar.

dreamt [dremt] *pt-pp* → dream.

dress [dres] *n* **1** vestido. **2** ropa. ► *vt* **1** vestir. **2** vendar *(herida)*. **3** aliñar *(ensalada)*. ► *vi* vestirse. ■ **dress rehearsal** ensayo general *(con trajes)*.

to dress up *vi* disfrazarse.

dresser ['dresə'] *n* **1** GB aparador. **2** US tocador.

dressing ['dresɪŋ] *n* **1** vendaje. **2** aliño *(de ensalada)*. ■ **dressing gown** bata; **dressing table** tocador.

drew [druː] *pt* → draw.

dribble ['drɪbəl] *n* **1** gotas. **2** baba. ► *vi* **1** gotear *(líquido)*. **2** babear *(bebé)*. ► *vt* driblar, regatear *(en fútbol)*.

drier ['draɪə'] *n* → dryer.

drift [drɪft] *n* **1** flujo. **2** ventisquero *(de nieve)*. **3** *fig* significado. ► *vi* ir a la deriva.

drill [drɪl] *n* **1** taladro. **2** broca. **3** ejercicio. **4** fresa *(de dentista)*. ► *vt* taladrar.

drink [drɪŋk] *n* bebida, copa. ►
vt-vi beber.

drinking ['drɪŋkɪŋ] *n*. ▪ **drinking
water** agua potable.

drip [drɪp] *n* **1** goteo. **2** gota a
gota *(de suero)*. ► *vi* gotear.

drive [draɪv] *n* **1** paseo en
coche. **2** camino de entrada.
3 drive *(golf, tenis)*. **4** transmisión *(en motor)*. **5** tracción
(en coche). **6** unidad de disco.
► *vt* **1** conducir. **2** llevar,
acompañar: *I'll drive you
home*, te llevaré a casa. **3** volver: *you drive me mad*, me
vuelves loco.

driven ['drɪvən] *pp* → drive.

driver ['draɪvəʳ] *n* conductor,
-ra. ▪ **driver's license** US permiso de conducir.

driving ['draɪvɪŋ] *adj*. ▪ **driving
licence** GB permiso de con-
ducir; **driving school** autoescuela.

drizzle ['drɪzəl] *n* llovizna.
► *vi* lloviznar.

dromedary ['drɒmədərɪ] *n*
dromedario.

drop [drɒp] *n* **1** gota. **2** pastilla. **3** pendiente, desnivel. **4**
caída. ► *vt* **1** dejar caer: *he
dropped the glass*, se le cayó el vaso. **2** *fam* romper
con. **3** abandonar *(hábito)*. **4**
no seleccionar, excluir *(de
equipo)*. ► *vi* **1** caerse *(persona)*. **2** bajar *(precios, voz)*. **3**
amainar *(viento)*.

to drop off *vi* **1** *fam* quedarse
dormido,-a. **2** disminuir.

to drop out *vi* **1** dejar los estudios. **2** retirarse *(de un partido)*.

dropper ['drɒpəʳ] *n* cuentagotas.

drought [draʊt] *n* sequía.

drove [drəʊv] *pt* → drive.

drown [draʊn] *vt-vi* ahogar(se).

drug [drʌg] *n* **1** medicamento. **2** droga. ► *vt* drogar. ● **to
be on/take drugs** drogarse.
▪ **drug addict** drogadicto,-a;
drug pusher traficante de
drogas.

drugstore ['drʌgstɔːʳ] *n* US establecimiento donde se com-
pran medicamentos, periódicos, comida etc.

drum [drʌm] *n* **1** tambor. **2**
bidón *(contenedor)*. ► *vi* tocar el
tambor. ► *npl* **drums** batería.

drumstick ['drʌmstɪk] *n* **1** ba-
queta. **2** muslo *(de pollo)*.

drunk [drʌŋk] *pp* → drink. ►
adj-n borracho,-a.

dry [draɪ] *adj* seco,-a. ► *vt-vi*
secar(se).

dry-clean [draɪ'kliːn] *vt* limpiar
en seco.

dry-cleaners [draɪ'kliːnəz] *n*
tintorería.

dryer ['draɪəʳ] *n* secadora.

dual ['djuːəl] *adj* dual. ▪ **dual
carriageway** autovía.

dub [dʌb] *vt* doblar *(película)*.

duchess ['dʌtʃəs] *n* duquesa.

duck [dʌk] *n* pato,-a.

duct [dʌkt] *n* conducto.

due [djuː] *adj* **1** debido,-a *(dinero)*. **2** pagadero,-a. **3** esperado,-a: *the train is due at five*, el tren debe llegar a las cinco. ► *npl* **dues** cuota. ● **to be due to** deberse a. ■ **due date** vencimiento.

duel ['djuːəl] *n* duelo.

duet [djuːˈet] *n* dúo.

dug [dʌg] *pt-pp* → dig.

duke [djuːk] *n* duque.

dull [dʌl] *adj* **1** apagado,-a *(color)*. **2** gris *(día)*. **3** sordo,-a *(sonido)*. **4** torpe *(persona)*. **5** pesado,-a *(película)*.

dumb [dʌm] *adj* mudo,-a.

dummy ['dʌmɪ] *n* **1** imitación. **2** maniquí. **3** GB chupete.

dump [dʌmp] *n* vertedero, basurero. ► *vt* tirar: *"No dumping"*, "Prohibido tirar basuras".

dune [djuːn] *n* duna.

dungarees [dʌngəˈriːz] *n* pantalones de peto, mono.

dungeon ['dʌndʒən] *n* mazmorra.

duo ['djuːəʊ] *n* dúo.

duplicate [*(adj-n)* 'djuːplɪkət, *(vb)* 'djuːplɪkeɪt] *adj* duplicado, -a. ► *n* duplicado. ► *vt* duplicar.

duration [djʊəˈreɪʃən] *n* duración.

during ['djʊərɪŋ] *prep* durante.

dusk [dʌsk] *n* anochecer.

dust [dʌst] *n* polvo. ► *vt* quitar el polvo a.

dustbin ['dʌstbɪn] *n* GB cubo de la basura.

duster ['dʌstər] *n* **1** paño, trapo. **2** borrador *(de pizarra)*.

dustman ['dʌstmən] *n* GB basurero.

dustpan ['dʌstpæn] *n* recogedor.

duty ['djuːtɪ] *n* **1** deber, obligación. **2** impuesto. **3** guardia. ● **to be on/off duty** estar/no estar de servicio/ guardia.

duty-free ['djuːtɪfriː] *adj* libre de impuestos.

duvet ['duːveɪ] *n* edredón.

dwarf [dwɔːf] *n* enano,-a.

dwelling ['dwelɪŋ] *n* morada.

dye [daɪ] *n* tinte. ► *vt-vi* teñir(se).

dynamic [daɪˈnæmɪk] *adj* dinámico,-a.

dynasty ['dɪnəstɪ] *n* dinastía.

dyslexia [dɪsˈleksɪə] *n* dislexia.

E

each [iːtʃ] *adj* cada. ► *pron* cada uno,-a. ● **each other** el/la uno,-a al/a la otro,-a: *we love each other*, nos queremos.

eager ['iːgər] *adj* ansioso,-a, impaciente. ● **to be eager for SB to do STH** estar deseando que ALGN haga algo.

eagle ['iːgəl] *n* águila.

ear¹ [ɪəʳ] n **1** oreja. **2** oído.

ear² [ɪəʳ] n espiga *(de trigo)*.

earache ['ɪəreɪk] n dolor de oídos.

eardrum ['ɪədrʌm] n tímpano.

early ['ɜːlɪ] adj temprano,-a. ► adv temprano.

earn [ɜːn] vt **1** ganar *(dinero)*. **2** merecer(se).

earnings ['ɜːnɪŋz] npl ingresos.

earphones ['ɪəfəʊnz] npl auriculares.

earplug ['ɪəplʌg] n tapón.

earring ['ɪərɪŋ] n pendiente.

earth [ɜːθ] n tierra. ■ **the Earth** la Tierra.

earthquake ['ɜːθkweɪk] n terremoto.

earthworm ['ɜːθwɜːm] n lombriz.

ease [iːz] n **1** facilidad. **2** tranquilidad. **3** comodidad. ► vt aliviar, calmar. ► vi disminuir. ● **at ease** relajado,-a.

to ease off vi disminuir.

easel ['iːzəl] n caballete.

easily ['iːzɪlɪ] adv **1** fácilmente. **2** con mucho.

east [iːst] n este, oriente. ► adj oriental, del este. ► adv hacia el este.

Easter ['iːstəʳ] n **1** Pascua. **2** Semana Santa.

eastern ['iːstən] adj oriental, del este.

easy ['iːzɪ] adj fácil. ● **take it easy!** ¡tranquilo,-a! ■ **easy chair** sillón.

easy-going [iːzɪ'gəʊɪŋ] adj tranquilo,-a.

eat [iːt] vt-vi comer.

to eat out vi comer fuera.

eaten ['iːtən] pp → eat.

ebb [eb] n reflujo.

ebony ['ebənɪ] n ébano.

echo ['ekəʊ] n eco.

ecology [ɪ'kɒlədʒɪ] n ecología.

economical [iːkə'nɒmɪkəl] adj barato,-a, económico,-a.

economize [ɪ'kɒnəmaɪz] vi ahorrar.

economy [ɪ'kɒnəmɪ] n economía.

ecosystem ['iːkəʊsɪstəm] n ecosistema.

eczema ['eksɪmə] n eccema.

edge [edʒ] n **1** borde. **2** canto *(de moneda)*. **3** filo *(de navaja)*. ● **on edge** nervioso,-a; **to have the edge on/over SB** llevar ventaja a ALGN.

edible ['edɪbəl] adj comestible.

edition [ɪ'dɪʃən] n edición.

editor ['edɪtəʳ] n **1** editor,-ra. **2** director,-ra *(de periódico)*.

editorial [edɪ'tɔːrɪəl] adj-n editorial.

educate ['edjʊkeɪt] vt educar.

education [edjʊ'keɪʃən] n educación.

eel [iːl] n anguila.

effect [ɪ'fekt] n efecto. ► vt efectuar. ● **to come into effect** entrar en vigor.

effective [ɪ'fektɪv] adj **1** eficaz *(medicamento)*. **2** efectivo,-a.

effervescent [efə'vesənt] *adj* efervescente.

efficiency [ɪ'fɪʃənsɪ] *n* **1** eficiencia *(de persona)*. **2** eficacia *(de producto)*. **3** rendimiento *(de máquina)*.

effort ['efət] *n* esfuerzo.

egg [eg] *n* huevo. ▪ **boiled egg** huevo pasado por agua; **egg cup** huevera; **fried egg** huevo frito; **hard-boiled egg** huevo duro.

eggplant ['egplɑːnt] *n* US berenjena.

egoist ['iːgəʊɪst] *n* egoísta.

eiderdown ['aɪdədaʊn] *n* edredón.

eight [eɪt] *num* ocho.

eighteen [eɪ'tiːn] *num* dieciocho.

eighteenth [eɪ'tiːnθ] *adj* decimoctavo,-a.

eighth [eɪtθ] *adj* octavo,-a.

eightieth ['eɪtɪɪθ] *adj* octogésimo,-a.

eighty ['eɪtɪ] *num* ochenta.

either ['aɪðə', 'iːðə'] *adj* **1** cualquiera. **2** ni el uno/la una ni el otro/la otra, ninguno,-a: *I don't like either of them*, no me gusta ninguno de los dos. **3** cada, los/las dos, ambos, -as: *with a gun in either hand*, con una pistola en cada mano. ▶ *conj* o. ▶ *adv* tampoco. ▶ *pron* cualquiera de los dos.

eject [ɪ'dʒekt] *vt* expulsar.

elaborate [ɪ'læbərət] *adj* **1** detallado,-a. **2** complicado,-a.

elastic [ɪ'læstɪk] *adj* elástico,-a.

elbow ['elbəʊ] *n* codo.

elder ['eldə'] *adj-n* mayor.

elderly ['eldəlɪ] *adj* mayor, anciano,-a.

eldest ['eldɪst] *adj* mayor.

elect [ɪ'lekt] *vt* elegir.

election [ɪ'lekʃən] *n* elección.

electric [ɪ'lektrɪk] *adj* eléctrico, -a. ▪ **electric shock** descarga eléctrica.

electrical [ɪ'lektrɪkəl] *adj* eléctrico,-a. ▪ **electrical appliance** electrodoméstico.

electricity [ɪlek'trɪsɪtɪ] *n* electricidad.

electron [ɪ'lektrɒn] *n* electrón.

electronic [ɪlek'trɒnɪk] *adj* electrónico,-a. ▪ **electronic mail** correo electrónico.

elegant ['elɪgənt] *adj* elegante.

element ['elɪmənt] *n* elemento.

elephant ['elɪfənt] *n* elefante.

elevator ['elɪveɪtə'] *n* US ascensor.

eleven [ɪ'levən] *num* once.

eleventh [ɪ'levənθ] *adj* undécimo,-a.

eliminate [ɪ'lɪmɪneɪt] *vt* eliminar.

elk [elk] *n* alce.

elm [elm] *n* olmo.

else [els] *adv* otro, más. ▪ **or else** si no: *hurry up or else you'll be late*, date prisa o llegarás tarde.

elsewhere [els'weə^r] *adv* en otro sitio.

e-mail ['i:meɪl] *n* correo electrónico. ► *vt* enviar un correo electrónico a.

embankment [ɪm'bæŋkmənt] *n* 1 terraplén. 2 dique *(de río)*.

embark [ɪm'bɑːk] *vt-vi* embarcar(se).

embarrass [ɪm'bærəs] *vt* avergonzar. ● **to be embarrassed** sentir vergüenza.

embarrassing [ɪm'bærəsɪŋ] *adj* embarazoso,-a.

embassy ['embəsi] *n* embajada.

embrace [ɪm'breɪs] *n* abrazo. ► *vt* abrazar.

embroidery [ɪm'brɔɪdəri] *n* bordado.

embryo ['embriəʊ] *n* embrión.

emerald ['emərəld] *n* esmeralda.

emerge [ɪ'mɜːdʒ] *vi* emerger.

emergency [ɪ'mɜːdʒənsi] *n* 1 emergencia. 2 urgencia *(médica)*. ■ **emergency exit** salida de emergencia.

emery ['eməri] *n* esmeril. ■ **emery board** lima de uñas.

emigration [emɪ'greɪʃən] *n* emigración.

emission [ɪ'mɪʃən] *n* emisión.

emit [ɪ'mɪt] *vt* emitir.

emotion [ɪ'məʊʃən] *n* emoción.

emperor ['empərə^r] *n* emperador.

emphasis ['emfəsɪs] *n* énfasis.

empire ['empaɪə^r] *n* imperio.

employ [ɪm'plɔɪ] *vt* emplear.

employee [emplɔɪ'iː, emplɔɪ'iː] *n* empleado,-a, trabajador,-ra.

employer [em'plɔɪə^r] *n* patrón,-ona.

employment [ɪm'plɔɪmənt] *n* empleo.

empress ['emprəs] *n* emperatriz.

empty ['empti] *adj* 1 vacío,-a. 2 libre. ► *vt-vi* vaciar(se).

enable [ɪ'neɪbəl] *vt* permitir.

enamel [ɪ'næməl] *n* esmalte.

encircle [ɪn'sɜːkəl] *vt* rodear.

enclose [ɪn'kləʊz] *vt* 1 cercar, rodear. 2 adjuntar.

encounter [ɪn'kaʊntə^r] *n* encuentro. ► *vt* encontrarse con.

encourage [ɪn'kʌrɪdʒ] *vt* 1 animar. 2 fomentar.

encouraging [ɪn'kʌrɪdʒɪŋ] *adj* alentador,-ra.

encyclopedia [ensaɪklə'piːdɪə] *n* enciclopedia.

end [end] *n* 1 fin, final. 2 extremo, punta. 3 objeto, objetivo. ► *vt-vi* acabar(se), terminar(se).

endanger [ɪn'deɪndʒə^r] *vt* poner en peligro.

ending ['endɪŋ] *n* final.

endive ['endaɪv] *n* endibia.

endless ['endləs] *adj* interminable.

endorse [ɪn'dɔːs] *vt* 1 endosar *(talón)*. 2 aprobar.

endurance [ın'djʊərəns] *n* resistencia.

enemy ['enəmı] *n* enemigo,-a.

energy ['enədʒı] *n* energía.

enforce [ın'fɔːs] *vt* hacer cumplir.

engaged [ın'geıdʒd] *adj* **1** prometido,-a. **2** ocupado,-a *(servicio)*. **3** comunicando *(teléfono)*.

engagement [ın'geıdʒmənt] *n* **1** petición de mano, noviazgo. **2** compromiso, cita.

engine ['endʒın] *n* **1** motor. **2** máquina, locomotora.

engineer [endʒı'nıər] *n* **1** ingeniero,-a. **2** US maquinista.

engrave [ın'greıv] *vt* grabar.

enhance [ın'hɑːns] *vt* realzar.

enjoy [ın'dʒɔı] *vt* gozar de, disfrutar de. • **to enjoy oneself** divertirse, pasarlo bien.

enlargement [ın'lɑːdʒmənt] *n* ampliación.

enough ['ınʌf] *adj* bastante, suficiente. ▸ *adv* bastante. ▸ *pron* suficiente. • **that's enough!** iya basta!

enquire [ıŋ'kwaıər] *vi* **1** preguntar. **2** investigar.

enquiry [ıŋ'kwaıərı] *n* **1** pregunta. **2** investigación.

enrol [ın'rəʊl] *vt-vi* matricular(se).

entail [ın'teıl] *vt* implicar.

entangle [ın'tæŋgəl] *vt* enredar.

enter ['entər] *vt* entrar en. ▸ *vi* entrar.

enterprise ['entəpraız] *n* empresa.

entertain [entə'teın] *vt* entretener, divertir.

entertainment [entə'teınmənt] *n* entretenimiento.

enthusiasm [ın'θjuːzıæzəm] *n* entusiasmo.

entice [ın'taıs] *vt* seducir.

entire [ın'taıər] *adj* entero,-a.

entrails ['entreılz] *npl* entrañas.

entrance ['entrəns] *n* entrada.

entrepreneur [ɒntrəprə'nɜːr] *n* empresario,-a.

entrust [ın'trʌst] *vt* confiar.

entry ['entrı] *n* entrada. • **"No entry"** "Prohibida la entrada".

envelope ['envələʊp] *n* sobre.

envious ['envıəs] *adj* envidioso,-a.

environment [ın'vaırənmənt] *n* medio ambiente.

envy ['envı] *vt* envidiar.

epidemic [epı'demık] *n* epidemia.

epilepsy ['epılepsı] *n* epilepsia.

episode ['epısəʊd] *n* episodio.

equal ['iːkwəl] *adj* igual. ▸ *vt* **1** ser igual a, equivaler a. **2** igualar.

equation [ı'kweıʒən] *n* ecuación.

equator [ı'kweıtər] *n* ecuador.

equip [ı'kwıp] *vt* equipar.

equipment [ı'kwıpmənt] *n* equipo.

equivalent [ı'kwıvələnt] *adj-n* equivalente.

era ['ɪərə] *n* era.

erase [ɪ'reɪz] *vt* borrar.

eraser [ɪ'reɪzə'] *n* **1** US goma de borrar. **2** borrador *(de pizarra)*.

erosion [ɪ'rəʊʒən] *n* erosión.

erotic [ɪ'rɒtɪk] *adj* erótico,-a.

errand ['erənd] *n* encargo, recado.

erratic [ɪ'rætɪk] *adj* inconstante.

error ['erə'] *n* error.

eruption [ɪ'rʌpʃən] *n* erupción.

escalator ['eskəleɪtə'] *n* escalera mecánica.

escape [ɪ'skeɪp] *n* fuga. ► *vi* escaparse. ► *vt* evitar.

escort [ɪ'skɔːt] *vt* **1** acompañar. **2** escoltar.

especial [ɪ'speʃəl] *adj* especial.

essay ['eseɪ] *n* **1** redacción, trabajo. **2** ensayo.

essence ['esəns] *n* esencia.

essential [ɪ'senʃəl] *adj* esencial.

establish [ɪ'stæblɪʃ] *vt* establecer.

estate [ɪ'steɪt] *n* **1** finca. **2** urbanización. ■ **estate agent** GB agente inmobiliario,-a; **estate car** GB coche familiar.

estimate [*(n)* 'estɪmət, *(vb)* 'estɪmeɪt] *n* **1** cálculo. **2** presupuesto. ► *vt* calcular.

estuary ['estjʊəri] *n* estuario.

eternity [ɪ'tɜːnəti] *n* eternidad.

ethic ['eθɪk] *n* ética.

eucalyptus [juːkə'lɪptəs] *n* eucalipto.

euphemism ['juːfəmɪzəm] *n* eufemismo.

euro ['jʊərəʊ] *n* euro.

evade [ɪ'veɪd] *vt* evadir.

evaluate [ɪ'væljʊeɪt] *vt* evaluar.

evaporate [ɪ'væpəreɪt] *vt-vi* evaporar(se).

eve [iːv] *n* víspera, vigilia.

even ['iːvən] *adj* **1** llano,-a, liso,-a *(superficie)*. **2** uniforme *(color)*. **3** igualado,-a *(puntuación)*. **4** par *(número)*. ► *adv* **1** hasta, incluso. **2** siquiera: *not even John was there*, ni siquiera John estaba allí. **3** aún, todavía. ● **even if** aunque; **even so** incluso; **even though** aunque.

evening ['iːvənɪŋ] *n* tarde, noche. ● **good evening!** ¡buenas tardes!, ¡buenas noches!

event [ɪ'vent] *n* **1** suceso, acontecimiento. **2** prueba *(deportiva)*. ● **in any event** pase lo que pase; **in the event of** en caso de.

eventually [ɪ'ventʃʊəli] *adv* finalmente.

ever ['evə'] *adv* **1** nunca, jamás. **2** alguna vez. ● **for ever** para siempre; **hardly ever** casi nunca.

evergreen ['evəgriːn] *adj* de hoja perenne. ■ **evergreen oak** encina.

everlasting [evə'lɑːstɪŋ] *adj* eterno,-a.

every ['evri] *adj* cada, todos,-as

everybody ['evrɪbɒdi] *pron* todos,-as, todo el mundo.

everyday ['evrɪdeɪ] *adj* diario,-a, de todos los días.

everyone ['evrɪwʌn] *pron* → everybody.

everything ['evrɪθɪŋ] *pron* todo.

everywhere ['evrɪweə'] *adv* **1** en/por todas partes. **2** a todas partes.

evidence ['evɪdəns] *n* pruebas. • **to give evidence** prestar declaración.

evident ['evɪdənt] *adj* evidente.

evil ['iːvəl] *adj* malo,-a. ▸ *n* mal.

evoke [ɪˈvəʊk] *vt* evocar.

evolution [iːvəˈluːʃən] *n* evolución.

exact [ɪgˈzækt] *adj* exacto,-a.

exaggerate [ɪgˈzædʒəreɪt] *vt-vi* exagerar.

exam [ɪgˈzæm] *n fam* examen.

examination [ɪgzæmɪˈneɪʃən] *n* **1** examen. **2** reconocimiento, chequeo. **3** interrogatorio.

examine [ɪgˈzæmɪn] *vt* examinar.

example [ɪgˈzɑːmpəl] *n* ejemplo. • **for example** por ejemplo.

excellent ['eksələnt] *adj* excelente.

except [ɪkˈsept] *prep* excepto.

excess [ɪkˈses] *n* exceso.

exchange [ɪksˈtʃeɪndʒ] *n* **1** cambio. **2** intercambio. ▸ *vt* cambiar, intercambiar. ▪ **exchange rate** tipo de cambio.

excite [ɪkˈsaɪt] *vt* **1** entusiasmar. **2** excitar *(sexualmente)*.

exclamation [ekskləˈmeɪʃən] *n* exclamación. ▪ **exclamation mark** signo de admiración.

exclude [ɪkˈskluːd] *vt* excluir.

exclusive [ɪkˈskluːsɪv] *adj* **1** exclusivo,-a. **2** selecto,-a.

excursion [ɪkˈskɜːʒən] *n* excursión.

excuse [*(n)* ɪkˈskjuːs, *(vb)* ɪkˈskjuːz] *n* disculpa, excusa. ▸ *vt* perdonar, disculpar. • **excuse me!** ¡perdone!, ¡por favor!

execute ['eksɪkjuːt] *vt* ejecutar.

executive [ɪgˈzekjətɪv] *adj-n* ejecutivo,-a.

exempt [ɪgˈzempt] *adj* exento,-a, libre. ▸ *vt* eximir.

exercise ['eksəsaɪz] *n* ejercicio. ▪ **exercise book** cuaderno.

exhaust [ɪgˈzɔːst] *vt* agotar. ▪ **exhaust pipe** tubo de escape.

exhausted [ɪgˈzɔːstɪd] *adj* agotado,-a.

exhibit [ɪgˈzɪbɪt] *n* objeto en exposición. ▸ *vt* **1** exponer. **2** mostrar, dar muestras de, manifestar.

exhibition [eksɪˈbɪʃən] *n* exposición.

exile ['eksaɪl] *n* exilio. ▸ *vt* exiliar.

exist [ɪgˈzɪst] *vi* existir.

exit ['egsɪt] *n* salida.

exotic [egˈzɒtɪk] *adj* exótico,-a.

expand [ɪk'spænd] *vt-vi* ampliar(se).

expansion [ɪk'spænʃən] *n* expansión.

expect [ɪk'spekt] *vt* esperar. • **to be expecting** *fam* estar embarazada.

expedition [ekspɪ'dɪʃən] *n* expedición.

expel [ɪk'spel] *vt* expulsar.

expenditure [ɪk'spendɪtʃəʳ] *n* gasto.

expense [ɪk'spens] *n* gasto.

expensive [ɪk'spensɪv] *adj* caro,-a.

experience [ɪk'spɪərɪəns] *n* experiencia. ► *vt* experimentar.

experiment [ɪk'sperɪmənt] *n* experimento.

expert ['ekspɜːt] *adj-n* experto,-a.

expire [ɪk'spaɪəʳ] *vi* **1** vencer *(contrato)*. **2** caducar *(pasaporte)*.

expiry [ɪk'spaɪərɪ] *n* vencimiento. ▪ **expiry date** fecha de caducidad.

explain [ɪk'spleɪn] *vt-vi* explicar.

explanation [eksplə'neɪʃən] *n* explicación.

explode [ɪk'spləʊd] *vi* estallar.

explore [ɪk'splɔːʳ] *vt* explorar.

explosion [ɪk'spləʊʒən] *n* explosión.

explosive [ɪk'spləʊsɪv] *adj* explosivo,-a. ► *n* explosivo.

export [*(n)* 'ekspɔːt, *(vb)* ɪk'spɔːt] *n* exportación.► *vt* exportar.

expose [ɪk'spəʊz] *vt* exponer.

express [ɪk'spres] *adj* **1** expreso,-a *(tren)*. **2** urgente *(correo)*. ► *vt* expresar.

expression [ɪk'spreʃən] *n* expresión.

extend [ɪk'stend] *vt* extender.

extension [ɪk'stenʃən] *n* extensión.

extent [ɪk'stent] *n* extensión, alcance. • **to a certain extent** hasta cierto punto.

external [ek'stɜːnəl] *adj* externo,-a.

extinct [ɪk'stɪŋkt] *adj* **1** extinto,-a. **2** extinguido,-a.

extra ['ekstrə] *adj-n* extra. ▪ **extra charge** suplemento; **extra time** prórroga.

extract [ɪk'strækt] *vt* extraer.

extraordinary [ɪk'strɔːdənrɪ] *adj* extraordinario,-a.

extravagant [ɪk'strævəgənt] *adj* **1** derrochador,-ra. **2** exagerado,-a, excesivo,-a.

extreme [ɪk'striːm] *adj* **1** extremo,-a. **2** excepcional *(caso)*. ► *n* extremo.

extremity [ɪk'stremɪtɪ] *n* extremidad.

eye [aɪ] *n* ojo.

eyebrow ['aɪbraʊ] *n* ceja.

eyelash ['aɪlæʃ] *n* pestaña.

eyelid ['aɪlɪd] *n* párpado.

eyeshadow ['aɪʃædəʊ] *n* sombra de ojos.

eyewitness ['aɪwɪtnəs] *n* testigo presencial.

F

fable ['feɪbəl] n fábula.
fabric ['fæbrɪk] n tela, tejido.
fabulous ['fæbjələs] adj fabuloso,-a.
facade [fə'sɑːd] n fachada.
façade [fə'sɑːd] n fachada.
face [feɪs] n 1 cara. 2 superficie. ► vt 1 dar a: *the house faces west*, la casa da al oeste. 2 afrontar, enfrentarse con/a. ● **face down** boca abajo; **face up** boca arriba; **to lose face** desprestigiarse. ■ **face cream** crema facial; **face value** valor nominal.
to face up to vt afrontar.
facelift ['feɪslɪft] n lifting.
facility [fə'sɪlɪti] n facilidad. ► npl **facilities** instalaciones, servicios.
fact [fækt] n hecho. ● **in fact** de hecho.
factor ['fæktə'] n factor.
factory ['fæktəri] n fábrica.
faculty ['fækəlti] n facultad.
fade [feɪd] vt desteñir.
to fade away vi desvanecerse.
fag [fæg] n 1 fam lata, rollo. 2 GB fam pitillo.
fail [feɪl] n suspenso. ► vt-vi 1 fallar. 2 suspender. ► vi 1 fracasar. 2 quebrar, hacer bancarrota.
failing ['feɪlɪŋ] n defecto, fallo. ► prep a falta de.

failure ['feɪljə'] n 1 fracaso. 2 quiebra. 3 fallo, avería. 4 hecho de no hacer algo.
faint [feɪnt] adj 1 débil. 2 pálido,-a. 3 vago,-a.
fair¹ [feə'] adj 1 justo,-a. 2 considerable: *he has a fair chance of getting the job*, tiene bastantes posibilidades de conseguir el trabajo. 3 rubio,-a, blanco,-a: *fair hair*, pelo rubio. ● **fair enough** de acuerdo, está bien. ■ **fair copy** copia en limpio; **fair play** juego limpio.
fair² [feə'] n feria, mercado.
fairground ['feəgraund] n recinto ferial, parque de atracciones.
fairly ['feəli] adv 1 justamente. 2 bastante.
fairy ['feəri] n hada. ■ **fairy tale** cuento de hadas.
faith [feɪθ] n fe.
faithful ['feɪθful] adj fiel.
faithfully ['feɪθfuli] adv. ● **yours faithfully** le saluda atentamente.
fake [feɪk] n falsificación. ► adj falso,-a, falsificado,-a. ► vt 1 falsificar. 2 fingir.
falcon ['fɔːlkən] n halcón.
fall [fɔːl] n 1 caída. 2 nevada. 3 US otoño. ► vi 1 caer, caerse. 2 bajar. ► npl **falls** cascada. ● **to fall short** no alcanzar; **to fall flat** salir mal.
to fall back vi retroceder.

to **fall down** *vt-vi* caer, caerse.

to **fall out** *vi* reñir, enfadarse.

fallen ['fɔːlən] *pp* → fall.

false [fɔːls] *adj* falso,-a. ■ **false alarm** falsa alarma; **false bottom** doble fondo; **false start** salida nula; **false teeth** dentadura postiza.

falsify ['fɔːlsɪfaɪ] *vt* falsificar.

fame [feɪm] *n* fama.

family ['fæmɪlɪ] *n* familia. ■ **family film** película apta para todos los públicos; **family name** apellido.

famine ['fæmɪn] *n* hambre.

famous ['feɪməs] *adj* famoso,-a.

fan [fæn] *n* **1** abanico. **2** ventilador *(eléctrico)*. **3** fan. ► *vt* abanicar, ventilar.

fanatic [fə'nætɪk] *adj-n* fanático,-a.

fancy ['fænsɪ] *n* **1** fantasía. **2** capricho. ► *adj* elegante. ► *vt* **1** imaginarse, figurarse. **2** apetecer: *I fancy an ice cream*, me apetece un helado. **3** gustar: *my friend fancies you*, le gustas a mi amigo. ■ **fancy dress** disfraz.

fang [fæŋ] *n* colmillo.

fantastic [fæn'tæstɪk] *adj* fantástico,-a.

fantasy ['fæntəsɪ] *n* fantasía.

far [fɑːʳ] *adj* **1** lejano,-a. **2** opuesto,-a, extremo,-a: *at the far end of the stadium*, en el otro extremo del estadio.

► *adv* **1** lejos. **2** mucho: *far better*, mucho mejor. • **as far as** hasta; **far away** lejos; **in so far as ...** en la medida en que ...; **so far 1** hasta ahora. **2** hasta cierto punto.

faraway ['fɑːrəweɪ] *adj* lejano,-a.

farce [fɑːs] *n* farsa.

fare [feəʳ] *n* tarifa, precio del billete/viaje.

farewell [feə'wel] *interj* ¡adiós! ► *n* despedida.

farm [fɑːm] *n* granja. ■ **farm labourer** jornalero,-a agrícola.

farmer ['fɑːməʳ] *n* agricultor, -ra, granjero,-a.

farming ['fɑːmɪŋ] *n* agricultura, ganadería. ■ **farming industry** industria agropecuaria.

farmyard ['fɑːmjɑːd] *n* corral.

fascinate ['fæsɪneɪt] *vt* fascinar.

fashion ['fæʃən] *n* **1** moda. **2** modo. • **in fashion** de moda; **out of fashion** pasado,-a de moda.

fashionable ['fæʃənəbəl] *adj* de moda.

fast¹ [fɑːst] *adj* **1** rápido,-a. **2** adelantado,-a: *my watch is fast*, mi reloj está adelantado. ► *adv* rápidamente, deprisa. ■ **fast food** comida rápida.

fast² [fɑːst] *vi* ayunar.

fasten ['fɑːsən] *vt* **1** sujetar. **2** atar. **3** abrochar.

fastener ['fɑːsənəʳ] *n* cierre.

fat [fæt] *adj* gordo,-a. ► *n* grasa.
fatal ['feɪtəl] *adj* **1** fatídico. **2** mortal.
fate [feɪt] *n* destino.
father ['fɑ:ðəʳ] *n* padre. ► *vt* engendrar. ■ **Father Christmas** Papá Noel.
father-in-law ['fɑ:ðərɪnlɔ:] *n* suegro.
fatten ['fætən] *vt* **1** cebar. **2** engordar.
faucet ['fɔ:sɪt] *n* US grifo.
fault [fɔ:lt] *n* **1** defecto. **2** culpa. **3** error, falta. **4** falla *(geológica)*. **5** falta *(en deporte)*.
fauna ['fɔ:nə] *n* fauna.
favour ['feɪvəʳ] (US **favor**) *n* favor. ► *vt* **1** favorecer. **2** estar a favor de.
favourite ['feɪvərɪt] (US **favorite**) *adj-n* preferido,-a.
fax [fæks] *n* fax. ► *vt* enviar por fax.
fear [fɪəʳ] *n* miedo, temor. ► *vt-vi* temer, tener miedo.
feast [fi:st] *n* **1** festín, banquete. **2** fiesta de guardar.
feat [fi:t] *n* proeza, hazaña.
feather ['feðəʳ] *n* pluma.
feature ['fi:tʃəʳ] *n* **1** rasgo, facción. **2** rasgo, característica. **3** artículo de fondo. ► *vt* **1** poner de relieve. **2** tener como protagonista. ■ **feature film** largometraje.
February ['februərɪ] *n* febrero.
fed [fed] *pt-pp* → feed.
federal ['fedərəl] *adj* federal.

federation [fedə'reɪʃən] *n* federación.
fed up [fed'ʌp] *adj fam* harto,-a.
fee [fi:] *n* honorarios, cuota, tarifa.
feeble ['fi:bəl] *adj* débil.
feed [fi:d] *n* pienso. ► *vt* alimentar, dar de comer a. ► *vi* alimentarse.
feel [fi:l] *n* tacto, sensación. ► *vt* **1** tocar, palpar. **2** sentir, notar. **3** creer: *I feel I ought to tell her*, creo que debería decírselo. ► *vi* **1** sentir(se), encontrarse: *do you feel ill?*, ¿te encuentras mal? **2** parecer: *it feels like leather*, parece piel. ● **to feel like** apetecer: *I feel like an ice cream*, me apetece un helado.
feeling ['fi:lɪŋ] *n* **1** sentimiento. **2** sensación.
feet [fi:t] *npl* → foot.
feign [feɪn] *vt* fingir.
feline ['fi:laɪn] *adj-n* felino,-a.
fell [fel] *pt* → fall.
fellow ['feləʊ] *n fam* tipo, tío.
felt[1] [felt] *pt-pp* → feel.
felt[2] [felt] *n* fieltro.
felt-tip pen ['felttɪp'pen] *n* rotulador.
female ['fi:meɪl] *n* **1** hembra. **2** mujer, chica: *a white female*, una mujer blanca. ► *adj* **1** femenino,-a. **2** mujer: *a female singer*, una cantante. **3** hembra: *a female elephant*, un elefante hembra.

feminine ['femɪnɪn] *adj* femenino,-a. ► *n* femenino.

fence [fens] *n* valla, cerca. ► *vi* practicar la esgrima. ► *vt* cercar.

fencing ['fensɪŋ] *n* esgrima.

fender ['fendəʳ] *n* 1 pantalla. 2 US parachoques.

fennel ['fenəl] *n* hinojo.

ferment [(*n*) 'fɜːmənt, (*vb*) fəˈment] *n* fermento. ► *vt-vi* fermentar.

fern [fɜːn] *n* helecho.

ferret ['ferɪt] *n* hurón.

ferry ['ferɪ] *n* transbordador, ferry. ► *vt-vi* transportar.

fertile ['fɜːtaɪl] *adj* fértil.

fervent ['fɜːvənt] *adj* ferviente.

festival ['festɪvəl] *n* 1 festival. 2 fiesta.

fetch [fetʃ] *vt* ir a buscar.

fetish ['fetɪʃ] *n* fetiche.

feudal ['fjuːdəl] *adj* feudal.

fever ['fiːvəʳ] *n* fiebre.

few [fjuː] *adj-pron* 1 pocos,-as. 2 **a few** unos,-as cuantos,-as, algunos,-as. • **as few as** solamente; **no fewer than** no menos de.

fiancé [fɪˈænseɪ] *n* prometido.

fiancée [fɪˈænseɪ] *n* prometida.

fib [fɪb] *n fam* bola.

fibre ['faɪbəʳ] (US **fiber**) *n* fibra.

fibreglass ['faɪbəɡlɑːs] (US **fiberglass**) *n* fibra de vidrio.

fiction ['fɪkʃən] *n* 1 novela, narrativa. 2 ficción.

fictitious [fɪkˈtɪʃəs] *adj* ficticio,-a.

fiddle ['fɪdəl] *n* 1 *fam* violín. 2 *fam* estafa, trampa. ► *vi fam* juguetear. ► *vt fam* falsificar.

fidelity [fɪˈdelɪtɪ] *n* fidelidad.

field [fiːld] *n* 1 campo. 2 yacimiento.

fierce [fɪəs] *adj* feroz.

fifteen [fɪfˈtiːn] *num* quince.

fifteenth [fɪfˈtiːnθ] *adj* decimoquinto,-a.

fifth [fɪfθ] *adj* quinto,-a.

fifty ['fɪftɪ] *num* cincuenta.

fig [fɪɡ] *n* higo.

fight [faɪt] *n* lucha, pelea. ► *vt-vi* pelearse, luchar.

to fight back *vi* resistir.

to fight off *vt* rechazar.

figure ['fɪɡəʳ] *n* 1 figura. 2 cifra, número. ► *vi* figurar. ► *vt* US suponer: *I figure she'll come,* supongo que vendrá. ■ **figure skating** patinaje artístico.

to figure out *vt fam* comprender, explicarse.

file [faɪl] *n* 1 lima. 2 carpeta. 3 archivo, expediente. 4 archivo, fichero. 5 fila. ► *vt* 1 limar. 2 archivar, fichar. ► *vi* desfilar. • **in single file** en fila india.

filing cabinet ['faɪlɪŋkæbɪnət] *n* archivador.

fill [fɪl] *vt* 1 llenar. 2 rellenar. 3 empastar.

to fill in *vt* rellenar.

fillet ['fɪlɪt] *n* filete.

filling ['fɪlɪŋ] *n* empaste. ■ **filling station** gasolinera.

film [fɪlm] *n* película. ► *vt*
rodar, filmar. ■ **film star** estrella de cine.

filter ['fɪltə'] *n* filtro. ► *vt-vi* fil-
trar(se).

filth [fɪlθ] *n* suciedad.

fin [fɪn] *n* aleta.

final ['faɪnəl] *adj* **1** final, último,-a. **2** definitivo,-a. ► *n* final. ► *npl* **finals** exámenes
finales.

finance ['faɪnæns] *vt* financiar. ► *n* finanzas.

find [faɪnd] *n* hallazgo. ► *vt* **1**
encontrar. **2** declarar: *he was
found guilty*, lo declararon
culpable.

to find out *vt-vi* averiguar.
► *vi* enterarse.

fine[1] [faɪn] *adj* **1** bien: *how are
you? –fine, thanks*, ¿cómo es-
tás? –bien, gracias. **2** excelente, magnífico: *that's a fine
building*, es un edificio magnífico. **3** bueno: *it's a fine
day*, hace buen día. ► *adv fam*
muy bien.

fine[2] [faɪn] *n* multa. ► *vt* multar, poner una multa a.

finger ['fɪŋgə'] *n* dedo.

fingerprint ['fɪŋgəprɪnt] *n* huella digital, huella dactilar.

fingertip ['fɪŋgətɪp] *n* punta
del dedo, yema del dedo.

finish ['fɪnɪʃ] *n* **1** fin, final. **2**
acabado. ► *vi-vt* acabar, ter-
minar. ● **a close finish** un final muy reñido.

finishing ['fɪnɪʃɪŋ] *adj* final. ■
finishing line línea de meta.

fir [fɜː'] *n* abeto.

fire [faɪə'] *n* **1** fuego. **2** incendio. **3** estufa. ► *vt* **1** disparar,
lanzar. **2** *fam* despedir, echar.
► *vi* disparar. ► *interj* ¡fuego!
● **to be on fire** estar ardiendo, estar en llamas. ■ **fire engine** coche de bomberos;
fire escape escalera de incendios; **fire extinguisher**
extintor; **fire station** parque
de bomberos; **fire hydrant**
boca de incendios.

fireman ['faɪəmən] *n* bombero.

fireplace ['faɪəpleɪs] *n* chimenea, hogar.

fireproof ['faɪəpruːf] *adj* a
prueba de fuego.

firewood ['faɪəwʊd] *n* leña.

fireworks ['faɪəwɜːks] *npl* fuegos artificiales.

firing ['faɪərɪŋ] *n* tiroteo. ■ **firing squad** pelotón de fusil-
amiento; **firing range** campo
de tiro.

firm[1] [fɜːm] *n* empresa, firma.

firm[2] [fɜːm] *adj* firme.

first [fɜːst] *adj* primero,-a. ►
adv **1** primero. **2** por primera
vez. ► *n* **1** primero,-a. **2** sobresaliente. ● **at first** al principio; **first of all** en primer lugar. ■ **first aid** primeros
auxilios; **first aid kit** botiquín
de primeros auxilios; **first floor**
1 GB primer piso. **2** US planta

baja; **first name** nombre de pila; **first degree** licenciatura.

first-class [ˈfɜːstklɑːs] *adj* de primera clase.

first-rate [ˈfɜːstreɪt] *adj* excelente.

fiscal [ˈfɪskəl] *adj* fiscal.

fish [fɪʃ] *n* **1** pez. **2** pescado. ▶ *vi* pescar. ■ **fish and chips** pescado con patatas; **fish finger** varita de pescado; **fish shop** pescadería.

fisherman [ˈfɪʃəmən] *n* pescador.

fishing [ˈfɪʃɪŋ] *n* pesca. ■ **fishing rod** caña de pescar.

fishmonger [ˈfɪʃmʌŋgəʳ] *n* GB pescadero,-a.

fishmonger's [ˈfɪʃmʌŋgəz] *n* GB pescadería.

fist [fɪst] *n* puño.

fistful [ˈfɪstfʊl] *n* puñado.

fit¹ [fɪt] *n* ataque, acceso.

fit² [fɪt] *vt* **1** ir bien a: *these shoes don't fit me, they're too big*, estos zapatos no me van bien, me quedan grandes. **2** poner, colocar: *the spy fitted a microphone under the table*, el espía puso un micrófono debajo de la mesa. ▶ *vi* caber, entrar: *this box won't fit in the car*, esta caja no va a entrar en el coche. ▶ *adj* **1** apto,-a, adecuado,-a. **2** en forma.

to fit in *vi* encajar.

fitness [ˈfɪtnəs] *n* buena forma *(física)*.

fitting [ˈfɪtɪŋ] *adj fml* apropiado,-a. ▶ *n* prueba *(de traje, etc)*. ▶ *npl* **fittings** accesorios. ■ **fitting room** probador.

five [faɪv] *num* cinco.

fix [fɪks] *vt* **1** fijar. **2** arreglar. **3** US preparar: *let me fix you a drink*, te prepararé una copa.

fizzy [ˈfɪzɪ] *adj* gaseoso,-a, con gas, espumoso,-a.

flag [flæg] *n* bandera.

flagpole [ˈflægpəʊl] *n* asta, mástil.

flagstone [ˈflægstəʊn] *n* losa.

flair [fleəʳ] *n* talento, don.

flake [fleɪk] *n* **1** copo. **2** escama. ▶ *vi* descamarse.

flame [fleɪm] *n* llama.

flamingo [fləˈmɪŋgəʊ] *n* flamenco *(ave)*.

flan [flæn] *n* tarta rellena.

flank [flæŋk] *n* flanco.

flannel [ˈflænəl] *n* franela.

flap [flæp] *n* **1** solapa. **2** faldón. ▶ *vt* batir. ▶ *vi* **1** agitarse. **2** ondear.

flare [fleəʳ] *n* **1** llamarada. **2** bengala. ▶ *vi* **1** llamear. **2** estallar.

flared [fleəd] *adj* acampanado,-a.

flash [flæʃ] *n* **1** destello. **2** flash *(de cámara, noticia)*. ▶ *vi* **1** brillar, destellar. **2** pasar como un rayo. ■ **flash of lightning** relámpago.

flashlight ['flæʃlaɪt] *n* linterna.
flask [flæsk] *n* termo.
flat¹ [flæt] *n* GB piso.
flat² [flæt] *adj* **1** llano,-a, plano,-a. **2** desinflado,-a, deshinchado,-a: *a flat tyre*, un neumático deshinchado. **3** descargado,-a: *a flat battery*, una batería descargada. **4** que ha perdido el gas: *this beer's flat!*, ¡esta cerveza no tiene gas! **5** rotundo,-a. ► *n* llanura. ► *adv*: *in ten seconds flat*, en diez segundos justos. ▪ **flat rate** precio fijo; **flat roof** azotea.
flatten ['flætən] *vt* allanar.
flatter ['flætə'] *vt* adular, halagar.
flautist ['flɔːtɪst] *n* flautista.
flavour ['fleɪvə'] (US **flavor**) *n* sabor. ► *vt* condimentar.
flavouring ['fleɪvərɪŋ] (US **flavoring**) *n* condimento.
flea [fliː] *n* pulga.
fleck [flek] *n* mota, punto.
flee [fliː] *vt* huir de. ► *vi* huir.
fleet [fliːt] *n* **1** armada. **2** flota.
flesh [fleʃ] *n* carne.
flew [fluː] *pt* → fly.
flex [fleks] *n* GB cable *(eléctrico)*. ► *vt* doblar, flexionar.
flexible ['fleksəbəl] *adj* flexible.
flick [flɪk] *n* movimiento rápido, coletazo, latigazo. ► *vt* **1** dar. **2** sacudir.
flicker ['flɪkə'] *n* **1** parpadeo. **2** *fig* indicio. ► *vi* parpadear.

flight [flaɪt] *n* **1** vuelo. **2** bandada. **3** tramo: *flight of stairs*, tramo de escalera. **4** huida, fuga.
fling [flɪŋ] *n* **1** lanzamiento. **2** juerga. **3** lío *(amoroso)*. ► *vt* arrojar, tirar, lanzar.
flint [flɪnt] *n* **1** pedernal. **2** piedra.
flip [flɪp] *n* voltereta.
flipper ['flɪpə'] *n* aleta.
flirt [flɜːt] *n* coqueto,-a. ► *vi* flirtear, coquetear.
float [fləʊt] *n* **1** flotador. **2** corcho. **3** carroza. ► *vi* flotar.
flock [flɒk] *n* **1** rebaño, bandada. **2** *fam* tropel.
flood [flʌd] *n* inundación. ► *vt* inundar. ► *vi* desbordarse.
floodlight ['flʌdlaɪt] *n* foco.
floor [flɔː'] *n* **1** suelo. **2** piso, planta: *my flat is on the fourth floor*, mi casa está en el cuarto piso. ● **to give/ have the floor** dar/tener la palabra.
floppy ['flɒpɪ] *adj* blando,-a, flexible. ▪ **floppy disk** disquete, disco flexible.
flora ['flɔːrə] *n* flora.
florist ['flɒrɪst] *n* florista. ▪ **florist's** floristería.
flounce [flaʊns] *n* volante *(de vestido)*.
flour [flaʊə'] *n* harina.
flourish ['flʌrɪʃ] *n* ademán, gesto. ► *vt* ondear, agitar. ► *vi* florecer.

flourishing ['flʌrɪʃɪŋ] *adj* floreciente, próspero,-a.

flow [fləʊ] *n* 1 flujo. 2 corriente: *the flow of traffic*, la circulación del tráfico. ► *vi* 1 fluir, manar. 2 circular: *traffic is flowing*, el tráfico circula con fluidez. 3 correr, fluir.
• **to flow into** desembocar en. ■ **flow chart** diagrama de flujo, organigrama.

flower [flaʊəʳ] *n* flor. ► *vi* florecer. ■ **flower bed** parterre.

flowerpot ['flaʊəpɒt] *n* maceta, tiesto.

flown [fləʊn] *pp* → fly.

flu [fluː] *n* gripe.

fluency ['fluːənsɪ] *n* fluidez.

fluent ['fluːənt] *adj* fluido,-a, suelto,-a: *she's fluent in French*, habla el francés con fluidez.

fluff [flʌf] *n* pelusa, lanilla.

fluffy ['flʌfɪ] *adj* mullido,-a.

fluid ['fluːɪd] *adj* fluido,-a. ► *n* fluido, líquido.

fluke [fluːk] *n fam* chiripa.

flung [flʌŋ] *pt-pp* → fling.

fluorescent [fluəˈresənt] *adj* fluorescente.

flurry ['flʌrɪ] *n* ráfaga: *a flurry of rain*, un chaparrón.

flush [flʌʃ] *n* rubor. ► *vt* 1 limpiar con agua. 2 *fig* hacer salir. ► *vi* ruborizarse. • **to flush the lavatory** tirar de la cadena *(del wáter)*.

flute [fluːt] *n* flauta.

flutter ['flʌtəʳ] *n* 1 agitación. 2 aleteo. 3 parpadeo. ► *vi* 1 ondear. 2 revolotear.

fly[1] [flaɪ] *vi* 1 volar. 2 ondear. 3 irse volando: *he flew down the stairs*, bajó la escalera volando. ► *vt* 1 pilotar *(avión)*. 2 izar. ► *npl* **flies** bragueta.

fly[2] [flaɪ] *n* mosca.

flying ['flaɪɪŋ] *n* 1 aviación. 2 vuelo. ► *adj* 1 volante. 2 rápido,-a. ■ **flying saucer** platillo volante.

flyover ['flaɪəʊvəʳ] *n* GB paso elevado.

foal [fəʊl] *n* potro,-a.

foam [fəʊm] *n* espuma. ■ **foam rubber** gomaespuma.

focus ['fəʊkəs] *n* foco. ► *vt* enfocar. ► *vi* centrarse. • **in focus** enfocado,-a; **out of focus** desenfocado,-a.

foetus ['fiːtəs] *n* feto.

fog [fɒg] *n* niebla. ► *vt-vi* empañar.

foggy ['fɒgɪ] *adj* de niebla.

foglamp ['fɒglæmp] *n* faro antiniebla.

foil [fɔɪl] *n* papel de aluminio.

fold[1] [fəʊld] *n* redil, aprisco.

fold[2] [fəʊld] *n* pliegue. ► *vt* doblar, plegar. ► *vi* doblarse, plegarse.

folder ['fəʊldəʳ] *n* carpeta.

folding ['fəʊldɪŋ] *adj* plegable: *a folding bed*, una cama plegable.

foliage ['fəʊlɪɪdʒ] *n fml* follaje.

folk [fəʊk] *adj* popular. ▶ *npl* **1** gente: *country folk*, gente del campo. **2 folks** *fam* familia. ■ **folk music** música popular; **folk song** canción popular.

folklore [ˈfəʊklɔːʳ] *n* folclor.

follow [ˈfɒləʊ] *vt-vi* seguir. ▶ *vt* perseguir. ▶ *vi* deducirse: *it follows that he's innocent*, se deduce que es inocente.

follower [ˈfɒləʊəʳ] *n* seguidor,-ra, discípulo,-a.

following [ˈfɒləʊɪŋ] *adj* siguiente. ▶ *n* seguidores. ▶ *prep* tras.

fond [fɒnd] *adj* **1** cariñoso,-a. **2** ser aficionado,-a: *he's fond of photography*, le gusta mucho la fotografía. ● **to be fond of SB** tenerle cariño a ALGN.

fondle [ˈfɒndəl] *vt* acariciar.

font [fɒnt] *n* pila bautismal.

food [fuːd] *n* comida, alimento. ■ **food poisoning** intoxicación alimenticia.

foodstuffs [ˈfuːdstʌfs] *npl* alimentos, comestibles, productos alimenticios.

fool [fuːl] *n* tonto,-a. ▶ *vt* engañar: *you can't fool me!*, ¡a mí no me engañas! ▶ *vi* bromear: *it wasn't true, I was just fooling*, no era verdad, solo bromeaba. ● **to make a fool of** poner en ridículo a; **to play the fool** hacer el tonto.

foolish [ˈfuːlɪʃ] *adj* estúpido,-a.

foot [fʊt] *n* **1** pie. **2** pata. ● **on foot** a pie.

football [ˈfʊtbɔːl] *n* fútbol. ■ **football pools** quinielas.

footballer [ˈfʊtbɔːləʳ] *n* futbolista.

footnote [ˈfʊtnəʊt] *n* nota a pie de página.

footpath [ˈfʊtpɑːθ] *n* sendero, camino.

footprint [ˈfʊtprɪnt] *n* huella, pisada.

footstep [ˈfʊtstep] *n* paso, pisada.

footwear [ˈfʊtweəʳ] *n* calzado.

for [fɔːʳ] *prep* **1** para: *it's for you*, es para ti. **2** por: *do it for me*, hazlo por mí. **3** por, durante: *for two weeks*, durante dos semanas. **4** para, hacia: *her feelings for him*, sus sentimientos hacia él. **5** desde hace: *I have lived in Spain for twenty years*, vivo en España desde hace veinte años. **6** como: *what do they use for fuel?*, ¿qué utilizan como combustible? **7** de: *"T" for Tony*, "T" de Toni. **8** for + object + inf: *it's time for you to go*, es hora de que te marches. ▶ *conj* ya que. ● **what for?** ¿para qué?

forbade [fɔːˈbeɪd] *pt* → forbid.

forbid [fəˈbɪd] *vt* prohibir.

forbidden [fəˈbɪdn] *pp* → forbid.

former

force [fɔːs] n fuerza. ► vt forzar. • **by force** a/por la fuerza; **to come into force** entrar en vigor.

forceps ['fɔːseps] npl fórceps.

ford [fɔːd] n vado. ► vt vadear.

forearm ['fɔːrɑːm] n antebrazo.

forecast ['fɔːkɑːst] n pronóstico, previsión. ► vt pronosticar.

forefinger ['fɔːfɪŋgəʳ] n dedo índice.

foreground ['fɔːgraʊnd] n primer plano.

forehead ['fɒrɪd, 'fɔːhed] n frente.

foreign ['fɒrɪn] adj 1 extranjero,-a. 2 exterior: *foreign policy*, política exterior. 3 ajeno, -a. ▪ **foreign exchange** GB; **Foreign Office** GB Ministerio de Asuntos Exteriores; **foreign currency** divisa.

foreigner ['fɒrɪnəʳ] n extranjero,-a.

foreman ['fɔːmən] n capataz.

foremost ['fɔːməʊst] adj principal.

forerunner ['fɔːrʌnəʳ] n precursor,-ra.

foresee [fɔːˈsiː] vt prever.

foresight ['fɔːsaɪt] n previsión.

forest ['fɒrɪst] n bosque, selva.

foretell [fɔːˈtel] vt presagiar, pronosticar.

foretold [fɔːˈtəʊld] pt-pp → foretell.

forever [fəˈrevəʳ] adv 1 siempre. 2 para siempre.

foreword ['fɔːwɜːd] n prólogo.

forfeit ['fɔːfɪt] n 1 pena, multa. 2 prenda.

forgave [fəˈgeɪv] pt → forgive.

forge [fɔːdʒ] n fragua. ► vt 1 falsificar. 2 forjar, fraguar.

forgery ['fɔːdʒərɪ] n falsificación.

forget [fəˈget] vt olvidar, olvidarse de. • **forget it!** ¡olvídalo!, ¡déjalo!; **to forget oneself** perder el control.

forgive [fəˈgɪv] vt perdonar.

forgot [fəˈgɒt] pt → forget.

forgotten [fəˈgɒtən] pp → forget.

fork [fɔːk] n 1 tenedor. 2 horca, horquilla. 3 bifurcación.

form [fɔːm] n 1 forma. 2 impreso, formulario. 3 GB curso: *I'm in the third form*, hago tercero. ► vt-vi formar(se). • **off form** en baja forma; **on form** en forma. ▪ **form of address** tratamiento.

formal ['fɔːməl] adj 1 formal. 2 de etiqueta.

format ['fɔːmæt] n formato. ► vt formatear.

former ['fɔːməʳ] adj 1 primer, -a: *the former case*, el primer caso. 2 antiguo,-a, ex-: *the former champion*, el excampeón. ► pron **the former** aquél, aquélla.

formula ['fɔ:mjələ] *n* fórmula.

forsake [fə'seɪk] *vt* **1** *fml* abandonar. **2** renunciar a.

fort [fɔ:t] *n* fuerte, fortaleza.

forth [fɔ:θ] *adv* en adelante. • **and so forth** y así sucesivamente.

forthcoming [fɔ:θ'kʌmɪŋ] *adj* próximo,-a.

fortieth ['fɔ:tɪəθ] *adj* cuadragésimo,-a.

fortify ['fɔ:tɪfaɪ] *vt* **1** fortificar. **2** *fig* fortalecer.

fortnight ['fɔ:tnaɪt] *n* GB quincena, dos semanas.

fortress ['fɔ:trəs] *n* fortaleza.

fortunate ['fɔ:tʃənət] *adj* afortunado,-a.

fortune ['fɔ:tʃən] *n* **1** fortuna. **2** suerte.

fortune-teller ['fɔ:tʃəntelə'] *n* adivino,-a.

forty ['fɔ:tɪ] *num* cuarenta.

forward ['fɔ:wəd] *adv* **1** hacia adelante. **2** en adelante. ► *adj* **1** hacia adelante. **2** delantero, -a, frontal: *a forward position*, una posición delantera. **3** adelantado,-a: *forward planning*, planificación anticipada. ► *n* delantero,-a. ► *vt* remitir: *please forward*, remítase al destinatario. • **to put the clock forward** adelantar el reloj.

forwards ['fɔ:wədz] *adv* → forward.

fossil ['fɒsəl] *n* fósil.

foster ['fɒstə'] *adj* adoptivo,-a. ▪ **foster child** hijo,-a adoptivo,-a.

fought [fɔ:t] *pt-pp* → fight.

foul [faʊl] *adj* asqueroso,-a. ► *n* falta *(en deporte)*.

found¹ [faʊnd] *vt* fundar.

found² [faʊnd] *pt-pp* → find.

foundation [faʊn'deɪʃən] *n* **1** fundación. **2** fundamento, base. ► *npl* **foundations** cimientos.

foundry ['faʊndrɪ] *n* fundición.

fountain ['faʊntən] *n* fuente. ▪ **fountain pen** pluma estilográfica.

four [fɔ:'] *num* cuatro. • **on all fours** a gatas.

fourteen [fɔ:'ti:n] *num* catorce.

fourteenth [fɔ:'ti:nθ] *adj* decimocuarto,-a.

fourth [fɔ:θ] *adj* cuarto,-a.

fowl [faʊl] *n* ave de corral.

fox [fɒks] *n* zorro,-a.

foxy ['fɒksɪ] *adj fam* astuto,-a.

foyer ['fɔɪeɪ, 'fɔɪə'] *n* vestíbulo.

fraction ['frækʃən] *n* fracción.

fracture ['fræktʃə'] *n* fractura. ► *vt-vi* fracturar(se).

fragile ['frædʒaɪl] *adj* frágil.

fragment ['frægmənt] *n* fragmento.

frame [freɪm] *n* **1** armazón, armadura. **2** cuadro *(de bici)*. **3** montura *(de gafas)*. **4** marco *(de ventana)*. **5** fotograma. ► *vt* **1** enmarcar. ▪ **frame of mind** estado de ánimo.

framework ['freɪmwɜːk] *n* armazón, estructura.

franchise ['fræntʃaɪz] *n* franquicia.

frank [fræŋk] *adj* franco,-a.

frantic ['fræntɪk] *adj* frenético,-a.

fraud [frɔːd] *n* fraude.

fray [freɪ] *vi* deshilacharse, desgastarse.

freak [friːk] *n* **1** monstruo. **2** *sl* fanático,-a: *a film freak*, un fanático del cine. ► *adj* insólito,-a.

freckle ['frekəl] *n* peca.

free [friː] *adj* **1** libre. **2** gratuito,-a. ► *adv* **1** gratis. **2** suelto,-a. ► *vt* **1** poner en libertad. **2** soltar.

freedom ['friːdəm] *n* libertad.

freelance ['friːlɑːns] *adj* autónomo,-a, freelance.

freestyle ['friːstaɪl] *n* estilo libre.

freeway ['friːweɪ] *n* US autopista.

freeze [friːz] *n* **1** helada. **2** congelación *(de precios)*. ► *vt-vi* congelar(se).

freezer ['friːzə'] *n* congelador.

freight [freɪt] *n* **1** transporte. **2** carga, flete. ■ **freight train** tren de mercancías.

frenzy ['frenzɪ] *n* frenesí.

frequency ['friːkwənsɪ] *n* frecuencia.

frequent ['friːkwənt] *adj* frecuente.

fresco ['freskəʊ] *n* fresco.

fresh [freʃ] *adj* fresco,-a. ■ **fresh water** agua dulce.

freshen ['freʃən] *vt-vi* refrescar(se).

fret [fret] *vi* preocuparse.

friar [fraɪə'] *n* fraile.

friction ['frɪkʃən] *n* fricción.

Friday ['fraɪdɪ] *n* viernes.

fridge [frɪdʒ] *n* nevera, frigorífico.

fried [fraɪd] *adj* frito,-a.

friend [frend] *n* amigo,-a.

friendly ['frendlɪ] *adj* **1** simpático,-a. **2** acogedor,-ra. ■ **friendly game/match** partido amistoso.

friendship ['frendʃɪp] *n* amistad.

frieze [friːz] *n* friso.

frigate ['frɪgət] *n* fragata.

fright [fraɪt] *n* **1** susto. **2** miedo.

frighten ['fraɪtən] *vt* asustar.

frightened ['fraɪtənd] *adj* asustado,-a. • **to be frightened** tener miedo.

fringe [frɪndʒ] *n* **1** fleco. **2** flequillo.

frisk [frɪsk] *vt* registrar, cachear.

fritter ['frɪtə'] *n* buñuelo.

frivolous ['frɪvələs] *adj* frívolo,-a.

fro [frəʊ] *phr.* **to and fro** de un lado para otro.

frog [frɒg] *n* rana.

frogman ['frɒgmən] *n* hombre rana.

from [frɒm] *prep* **1** de: *the train from New York to Washington*, el tren de Nueva York a Washington. **2** de, desde: *from January to June*, desde enero hasta junio. **3** según, por: *from experience*, por experiencia. • **from now on** a partir de ahora.

front [frʌnt] *n* **1** parte delantera. **2** frente. **3** principio. **4** fachada. ► *adj* **1** delantero,-a, de delante. **2** primero. ► *vi* dar: *the window fronts onto the sea*, la ventana da al mar. • **in front of** delante de. ▪ **front door** puerta principal, puerta de entrada.

frontier [ˈfrʌntɪəʳ] *n* frontera.

frost [frɒst] *n* **1** escarcha. **2** helada. ► *vi* **to frost over** helarse, escarcharse.

froth [frɒθ] *n* espuma.

frown [fraʊn] *n* ceño. ► *vi* fruncir el ceño.

froze [frəʊz] *pt* → freeze.

frozen [ˈfrəʊzən] *pp* → freeze.

fruit [fruːt] *n* **1** fruta. **2** fruto. ▪ **fruit dish** frutero; **fruit machine** máquina tragaperras; **fruit salad** macedonia.

frustrate [frʌˈstreɪt] *vt* frustrar.

fry [fraɪ] *vt-vi* freír, freírse.

frying pan [ˈfraɪɪŋpæn] *n* sartén.

fudge [fʌdʒ] *n* dulce hecho con azúcar, leche y mantequilla.

fuel [fjʊəl] *n* combustible, carburante.

fugitive [ˈfjuːdʒɪtɪv] *adj-n* fugitivo,-a.

fulfil [fʊlˈfɪl] *vt* **1** cumplir. **2** realizar, efectuar. **3** satisfacer.

full [fʊl] *adj* **1** lleno,-a. **2** completo,-a. ► *adv* justo, de lleno. ▪ **full moon** luna llena; **full stop** GB punto.

full-time [fʊlˈtaɪm] *adj* de jornada completa. ► *adv* a jornada completa.

fume [fjuːm] *vi* echar humo. ► *npl* **fumes** humos.

fumigate [ˈfjuːmɪgeɪt] *vt* fumigar.

fun [fʌn] *n* diversión. ► *adj* divertido,-a. • **in/for fun** en broma; **to have fun** divertirse, pasarlo bien; **to make fun of** reírse de.

function [ˈfʌŋkʃən] *n* **1** función. **2** acto, ceremonia. ► *vi* funcionar.

fund [fʌnd] *n* fondo. ► *vt* patrocinar.

fundamental [fʌndəˈmentəl] *adj* fundamental.

funeral [ˈfjuːnərəl] *n* entierro, funerales. ▪ **funeral procession** cortejo fúnebre; **funeral parlor** US funeraria.

funfair [ˈfʌnfeəʳ] *n* GB feria, parque de atracciones.

fungus [ˈfʌŋgəs] *n* hongo.

funnel [ˈfʌnəl] *n* **1** embudo. **2** chimenea *(de barco)*.

funny ['fʌnɪ] *adj* **1** gracioso,-a, divertido,-a. **2** raro,-a, extraño,-a, curioso,-a.

fur [fɜːʳ] *n* **1** pelo, pelaje. **2** piel. ■ **fur coat** abrigo de pieles.

furious ['fjʊərɪəs] *adj* furioso,-a.

furnace ['fɜːnəs] *n* horno.

furnish ['fɜːnɪʃ] *vt* amueblar.

furnishings ['fɜːnɪʃɪŋz] *npl* **1** muebles, mobiliario. **2** accesorios.

furniture ['fɜːnɪtʃəʳ] *n* mobiliario, muebles. ● **a piece of furniture** un mueble. ■ **furniture van** camión de mudanzas.

further ['fɜːðəʳ] *comp* → far. ► *adj* **1** nuevo,-a: *until further notice*, hasta nuevo aviso. **2** adicional: *we need further information*, necesitamos más información. ► *adv* más.

furthermore [fɜːðəˈmɔːʳ] *adv fml* además.

furthest ['fɜːðɪst] *superl* → far.

fury ['fjʊərɪ] *n* **1** furia. **2** frenesí.

fuse [fjuːz] *n* **1** fusible, plomo. **2** mecha, espoleta. ► *vt-vi* **1** fusionar(se). **2** fundir(se).

fusion ['fjuːʒən] *n* fusión.

fuss [fʌs] *n* alboroto, jaleo. ● **to make a fuss** quejarse.

fussy ['fʌsɪ] *adj* quisquilloso,-a.

future ['fjuːtʃəʳ] *adj* futuro,-a. ► *n* futuro.

fuzz [fʌz] *n* pelusa.

fuzzy ['fʌzɪ] *adj* **1** rizado,-a, crespo,-a. **2** borroso,-a.

G

gabardine ['gæbədiːn] *n* gabardina.

gadget ['gædʒɪt] *n* aparato, chisme.

gaffe [gæf] *n* metedura de pata.

gag [gæg] *n* **1** mordaza. **2** chiste, broma.

gage [geɪdʒ] *n* US → gauge.

gain [geɪn] *n* ganancia, beneficio. ► *vt* **1** lograr. **2** engordar. **3** aumentar. ► *vi* adelantarse *(reloj)*.

gait [geɪt] *n* porte, andares.

gal [gæl] *abbr* (*gallon*) galón.

galaxy ['gæləksɪ] *n* galaxia.

gale [geɪl] *n* vendaval.

gallery ['gælərɪ] *n* **1** galería. **2** galería, gallinero *(en teatro)*.

galley ['gælɪ] *n* galera.

gallon ['gælən] *n* galón.

gallop ['gæləp] *n* galope. ► *vi* galopar.

gallows ['gæləʊz] *n* horca.

gamble ['gæmbəl] *vi* jugar. ► *vt* apostar, jugarse.

gambling ['gæmblɪŋ] *n* juego. ■ **gambling den** casa de juego.

game [geɪm] *n* **1** juego. **2** partido *(de tenis, fútbol, etc)*. **3** partida *(de cartas, ajedrez)*. **4** caza. ■ **game reserve** coto de caza.

gammon ['gæmən] *n* jamón.

gander ['gændəʳ] *n* ganso.

gang [gæŋ] *n* **1** banda *(de delincuentes)*. **2** pandilla *(de amigos)*. **3** cuadrilla, brigada *(de obreros)*.

gangrene ['gæŋgriːn] *n* gangrena.

gangster ['gæŋstə'] *n* gángster.

gangway ['gæŋweɪ] *n* **1** pasillo. **2** pasarela *(en barco)*.

gaol [dʒeɪl] *n* GB cárcel.

gap [gæp] *n* **1** abertura, hueco. **2** espacio. **3** blanco. **4** intervalo.

garage ['gærɑːʒ, 'gærɪdʒ] *n* **1** garaje. **2** taller mecánico. **3** gasolinera.

garbage ['gɑːbɪdʒ] *n* basura.

garden ['gɑːdən] *n* jardín.

gardener ['gɑːdənə'] *n* jardinero,-a.

gardening ['gɑːdənɪŋ] *n* jardinería.

gargle ['gɑːgəl] *vi* hacer gárgaras.

garlic ['gɑːlɪk] *n* ajo.

garment ['gɑːmənt] *n* prenda de vestir.

garnish ['gɑːnɪʃ] *n* guarnición. ► *vt* guarnecer.

garrison ['gærɪsən] *n* guarnición *(militar)*.

garrulous ['gærələs] *adj* locuaz.

garter ['gɑːtə'] *n* liga.

gas [gæs] *n* **1** gas. **2** US gasolina. ▪ **gas chamber** cámara de gas; **gas mask** máscara antigás; **gas station** gasolinera.

gash [gæʃ] *n* raja, corte. ► *vt* rajar, cortar.

gasoline ['gæsəliːn] *n* US gasolina.

gastronomy [gæs'trɒnəmɪ] *n* gastronomía.

gate [geɪt] *n* **1** puerta, verja. **2** puerta de embarque.

gateau ['gætəʊ] *n* pastel.

gatecrash ['geɪtkræʃ] *vt-vi fam* colarse.

gateway ['geɪtweɪ] *n* puerta.

gather ['gæðə'] *vt* **1** juntar, reunir *(personas)*. **2** recoger, coger *(flores, fruta)*. **3** recaudar *(impuestos)*. ► *vi* **1** reunirse *(personas)*. **2** acumularse *(nubes)*.

gauge [geɪdʒ] *n* GB **1** indicador. **2** medida estándar. **3** calibre. ► *vt* **1** medir, calibrar. **2** *fig* juzgar.

gaunt [gɔːnt] *adj* demacrado,-a.

gauze [gɔːz] *n* gasa.

gave [geɪv] *pt* → give.

gay [geɪ] *adj* **1** alegre. **2** vistoso,-a *(aspecto)*. **3** gay, homosexual. ► *n* gay, homosexual.

gaze [geɪz] *vi* mirar fijamente.

gazelle [gə'zel] *n* gacela.

gazette [gə'zet] *n* gaceta.

gear [gɪə'] *n* **1** engranaje. **2** marcha, velocidad: *reverse gear*, marcha atrás. **3** *fam* efectos personales, ropa, cosas, equipo. ▪ **gear lever** palanca de cambio.

gearbox ['gɪəbɒks] *n* caja de cambios.

geese [giːs] *npl* → goose.

gem [dʒem] *n* gema.

gen [dʒen] *n fam* información.

gender ['dʒendə'] *n* género.

gene [dʒiːn] *n* gen.

general ['dʒenərəl] *adj-n* general. • **in general** por lo general. ■ **general practitioner** médico,-a de cabecera; **the general public** el público.

generate ['dʒenəreɪt] *vt* generar.

generation [dʒenə'reɪʃən] *n* generación.

generous ['dʒenərəs] *adj* generoso,-a.

genetic [dʒə'netɪk] *adj* genético,-a.

genial ['dʒiːnɪəl] *adj* simpático,-a, afable.

genital ['dʒenɪtəl] *adj* genital.

genius ['dʒiːnɪəs] *n* genio.

genre ['ʒɒnrə] *n* género.

gent [dʒent] *n* **1** *fam* caballero. **2 gents** servicio de caballeros.

gentle ['dʒentəl] *adj* **1** amable *(persona)*. **2** suave *(brisa)*. **3** manso,-a *(animal)*.

gentleman ['dʒentəlmən] *n* caballero.

genuine ['dʒenjʊɪn] *adj* **1** genuino,-a. **2** sincero,-a *(sentimiento)*.

geography [dʒɪ'ɒgrəfɪ] *n* geografía.

geology [dʒɪ'ɒlədʒɪ] *n* geología.

geometry [dʒɪ'ɒmətrɪ] *n* geometría.

geranium [dʒə'reɪnɪəm] *n* geranio.

germ [dʒɜːm] *n* germen.

gerund ['dʒerənd] *n* gerundio.

gesture ['dʒestʃə'] *n* ademán, gesto. ► *vi* hacer gestos, hacer un ademán.

get [get] *vt* **1** obtener, conseguir. **2** recibir. **3** traer. **4** coger. **5** persuadir, convencer. **6** preparar, hacer. **7** *fam* entender. **8** comprar. **9** buscar, recoger. ► *vi* **1** ponerse, volverse: *to get better*, mejorar; *to get tired*, cansarse. **2** ir: *how do you get there?*, cómo se va hasta allí? **3** llegar: *we got to Seattle at six o'clock*, llegamos a Seattle a las seis. **4** llegar a: *I never got to see that film*, nunca llegué a ver esa película.

to get along *vi* arreglárselas.

to get along with *vt* llevarse (bien) con.

to get away *vi* escaparse.

to get back *vi* volver, regresar. ► *vt* recuperar.

to get down *vi* bajarse.

to get in *vi* **1** llegar. **2** entrar.

to get into *vt* **1** entrar en. **2** subir a *(coche)*.

to get off *vt* **1** quitar. **2** bajarse de *(coche)*. ► *vi* **1** bajarse *(de coche)*. **2** salir *(de viaje)*.

to get on vt **1** subir(se) a *(vehículo)*. **2** montar *(bicicleta)*. ► vi **1** llevarse bien. **2** seguir.

to get out vt **1** sacar *(objeto)*. **2** quitar *(mancha)*. ► vi salir: *get out of here!*, ¡sal de aquí!

to get over vt **1** recuperarse de. **2** salvar *(obstáculo)*.

to get through vi conseguir hablar *(por teléfono)*.

to get up vt-vi levantar(se).

getaway ['getəweɪ] n fuga.

gherkin ['gɜːkɪn] n pepinillo.

ghost [gəʊst] n fantasma.

giant ['dʒaɪənt] n gigante,-a.

gift [gɪft] n regalo, obsequio.

gild [gɪld] vt dorar.

gills [gɪlz] npl agallas.

gin [dʒɪn] n ginebra.

ginger ['dʒɪndʒəʳ] n jengibre.

gipsy ['dʒɪpsɪ] n gitano,-a.

giraffe [dʒɪˈrɑːf] n jirafa.

girdle ['gɜːdəl] n faja.

girl [gɜːl] n chica, muchacha, joven, niña.

girlfriend ['gɜːlfrend] n **1** novia. **2** US amiga, compañera.

giro ['dʒaɪrəʊ] n giro.

give [gɪv] vt dar. ► vi dar de sí, ceder. ● **to give way 1** ceder. **2** ceder el paso. ■ **give and take** toma y daca.

to give back vt devolver.

to give in vi ceder, rendirse. ► vt entregar *(deberes)*.

to give up vt dejar: *to give up smoking*, dejar de fumar. ► vi rendirse, entregarse.

glacier ['glæsɪəʳ, 'gleɪʃəʳ] n glaciar.

glad [glæd] adj feliz, contento, -a. ● **to be glad** alegrarse; **to be glad to do** STH tener mucho gusto en hacer algo.

glamour ['glæməʳ] (US **glamor**) n **1** atractivo. **2** encanto.

glance [glɑːns] n vistazo, mirada. ► vi echar un vistazo. ● **at first glance** a primera vista; **to take a glance** echar un vistazo.

gland [glænd] n glándula.

glass [glɑːs] n **1** vidrio, cristal. **2** vaso, copa. ► npl **glasses** gafas.

glaze [gleɪz] n vidriado *(cerámica)*. ► vt vidriar, esmaltar *(cerámica)*. ■ **double glazing** doble acristalamiento.

gleam [gliːm] n destello. ► vi relucir, brillar.

glen [glen] n cañada.

glide [glaɪd] vi **1** planear. **2** deslizarse.

glider ['glaɪdəʳ] n planeador.

glimpse [glɪmps] n visión fugaz. ► vt vislumbrar.

global ['gləʊbəl] adj global.

globe [gləʊb] n **1** globo. **2** globo terrestre.

gloomy ['gluːmɪ] adj **1** lóbrego,-a, oscuro *(lugar)*. **2** tristón,-ona, melancólico,-a *(voz)*. **3** pesimista, poco prometedor,-ra *(pronóstico)*.

glory ['glɔːrɪ] n gloria.

gone

glossary ['glɒsərɪ] *n* glosario.

glossy ['glɒsɪ] *adj* brillante.

glove [glʌv] *n* guante.

glow [gləʊ] *n* **1** luz suave: *the red glow of the fire*, la suave luz roja del fuego. **2** rubor.

glucose ['glu:kəʊz] *n* glucosa.

glue [glu:] *n* cola, pegamento. ► *vt* encolar, pegar.

glutton ['glʌtən] *n* glotón,-ona.

glycerine ['glɪsəʳɪn] *n* glicerina.

gnat [næt] *n* mosquito.

gnaw [nɔ:] *vt* roer.

go [gəʊ] *vi* **1** ir. **2** marcharse, irse, salir. **3** desaparecer. **4** ir, funcionar. **5** volverse, ponerse, quedarse: *he's gone deaf*, se ha vuelto sordo. **6** terminarse, acabarse. **7** pasar. ► *vt* hacer: *it goes tick-tock*, hace tic-tac. ► *n* **1** energía, empuje. **2** turno: *it's my go now*, ahora me toca a mí. **3** intento. ● **to be going to do** STH ir a hacer algo; **to have a go at** SB criticar a ALGN; **to make a go of** STH tener éxito en algo.

to go away *vi* marcharse.

to go back *vi* volver.

to go by *vi* pasar.

to go down *vi* **1** bajar. **2** deshincharse *(neumático)*.

to go in *vi* entrar.

to go off *vi* **1** irse, marcharse. **2** estallar *(bomba)*. **3** sonar *(alarma)*. **4** apagarse *(luz)*. **5** estropearse *(comida)*.

to go on *vi* **1** seguir. **2** pasar, suceder.

to go out *vi* **1** salir. **2** apagarse *(luz)*.

to go up *vi* **1** subir. **2** estallar.

goal [gəʊl] *n* **1** meta, portería. **2** gol, tanto. **3** fin, objeto.

goalkeeper ['gəʊlki:pəʳ] *n* portero, guardameta.

goat [gəʊt] *n* cabra.

goblet ['gɒblət] *n* copa.

god [gɒd] *n* dios.

godchild ['gɒdtʃaɪld] *n* ahijado,-a.

goddaughter ['gɒddɔ:təʳ] *n* ahijada.

goddess ['gɒdəs] *n* diosa.

godfather ['gɒdfɑ:ðəʳ] *n* padrino.

godmother ['gɒdmʌðəʳ] *n* madrina.

godparents ['gɒdpeərənts] *npl* padrinos.

godson ['gɒdsʌn] *n* ahijado.

goggles ['gɒgəls] *npl* gafas *(de esquí, buceo)*.

gold [gəʊld] *n* oro. ► *adj* **1** de oro. **2** dorado.

golden ['gəʊldən] *adj* **1** de oro. **2** dorado,-a.

goldfish ['gəʊldfɪʃ] *n* pez de colores.

goldsmith ['gəʊldsmɪθ] *n* orfebre.

golf [gɒlf] *n* golf. ■ **golf club 1** palo de golf. **2** club de golf; **golf course** campo de golf.

gone [gɒn] *pp* → go.

good [gʊd] *adj* bueno,-a. ► *interj* ¡bien! ► *n* bien. ► *npl* **goods** 1 bienes. 2 género, artículos. ● **as good as** prácticamente, como; **a good deal** bastante; **for good** para siempre; **to be good at** STH tener facilidad para algo, ser bueno en algo; **to do good** hacer bien.

goodbye [gʊd'baɪ] *n* adiós. ► *interj* ¡adiós! ● **to say goodbye to** despedirse de.

good-for-nothing ['gʊdfə-nʌθɪŋ] *adj-n* inútil.

good-looking [gʊd'lʊkɪŋ] *adj* guapo,-a.

goodwill [gʊd'wɪl] *n* buena voluntad.

goose [guːs] *n* ganso, oca. ■ **goose pimples** carne de gallina.

gooseberry ['gʊzbrɪ, 'guːsbərɪ] *n* grosella espinosa.

gooseflesh ['guːsfleʃ] *n* carne de gallina.

gorge [gɔːdʒ] *n* desfiladero.

gorgeous ['gɔːdʒəs] *adj* espléndido,-a.

gorilla [gə'rɪlə] *n* gorila.

go-slow [gəʊ'sləʊ] *n* huelga de celo.

gospel ['gɒspəl] *n* evangelio.

gossip ['gɒsɪp] *n* 1 cotilleo. 2 cotilla. ► *vi* cotillear. ■ **gossip column** crónica de sociedad.

got [gɒt] *pt-pp* → get.

gout [gaʊt] *n* gota *(enfermedad)*.

govern ['gʌvən] *vt* gobernar.

government ['gʌvənmənt] *n* gobierno.

gown [gaʊn] *n* 1 vestido largo. 2 toga *(de juez)*. 3 bata *(de médico)*.

grab [græb] *vt* asir, coger.

grace [greɪs] *n* gracia.

graceful ['greɪsfʊl] *adj* elegante.

grade [greɪd] *n* 1 grado. 2 clase, categoría. 3 US pendiente, cuesta. 4 US nota, calificación. 5 US curso.

gradual ['grædjʊəl] *adj* gradual.

graduate [(*n*) 'grædjʊət, (*vb*) 'grædjʊeɪt] *n* graduado,-a, licenciado,-a. ► *vt* graduar. ► *vi* graduarse.

graffiti [grə'fiːtɪ] *npl* pintadas, grafiti.

graft [grɑːft] *n* injerto. ► *vt* injertar.

grain [greɪn] *n* 1 grano. 2 cereales. 3 veta *(en madera)*.

gram [græm] *n* gramo.

grammar ['græmə'] *n* gramática. ■ **grammar school** GB instituto de enseñanza secundaria.

gramme [græm] *n* gramo.

granary ['grænərɪ] *n* granero.

grand [grænd] *adj* 1 grandioso,-a, espléndido,-a. 2 *fam* fenomenal, estupendo,-a. ■ **grand piano** piano de cola; **grand total** total.

grandchild ['græntʃaɪld] *n* nieto,-a.

granddaughter ['grændɔːtə'] *n* nieta.

grandfather ['grændfɑːðə'] *n* abuelo.

grandmother ['grænmʌðə'] *n* abuela.

grandparents ['grændpeərənts] *npl* abuelos.

grandson ['grændsʌn] *n* nieto.

grandstand ['grændstænd] *n* tribuna.

granite ['grænɪt] *n* granito.

grant [grɑːnt] *n* **1** beca. **2** subvención. ► *vt* **1** conceder. **2** reconocer, admitir. • **to take sth for granted** dar algo por sentado.

grape [greɪp] *n* uva.

grapefruit ['greɪpfruːt] *n* pomelo.

grapevine ['greɪpvaɪn] *n* vid.

graph [grɑːf] *n* diagrama. ■ **graph paper** papel cuadriculado.

graphic ['græfɪk] *adj* gráfico,-a.

graphite ['græfaɪt] *n* grafito.

grasp [grɑːsp] ► *vt* **1** asir, agarrar. **2** comprender. • **to have a good grasp of** dominar.

grass [grɑːs] *n* hierba.

grasshopper ['grɑːshɒpə'] *n* saltamontes.

grate[1] [greɪt] *vt* rallar.

grate[2] [greɪt] *n* rejilla, parrilla.

grateful ['greɪtfʊl] *adj* agradecido,-a.

grater ['greɪtə'] *n* rallador.

gratify ['grætɪfaɪ] *vt* complacer, satisfacer.

gratis ['grætɪs, 'grɑːtɪs] *adv* gratis.

gratitude ['grætɪtjuːd] *n* gratitud.

gratuity [grəˈtjuːɪtɪ] *n* propina.

grave[1] [greɪv] *n* tumba.

grave[2] [greɪv] *adj* grave.

gravel ['grævəl] *n* grava.

graveyard ['greɪvjɑːd] *n* cementerio.

gravity ['grævɪtɪ] *n* gravedad.

gravy ['greɪvɪ] *n* salsa *(de carne)*.

gray [greɪ] *adj* US → grey.

graze [greɪz] *n* roce, rasguño. ► *vt* rozar. ► *vi* pacer, pastar.

grease [griːs] *n* grasa. ► *vt* engrasar.

great [greɪt] *adj* **1** grande, gran. **2** *fam* estupendo,-a, fantástico,-a.

greed [griːd] *n* **1** codicia, avaricia. **2** gula, glotonería.

green [griːn] *adj* **1** verde. **2** novato,-a. ► *n* **1** verde. **2** green *(en golf)*. ► *npl* **greens** verduras. • **to be green with envy** morirse de envidia. ■ **green bean** judía verde.

greengrocer's ['griːngrəʊsəz] *n* verdulería.

greenhouse ['griːnhaʊs] *n* invernadero. ■ **greenhouse effect** efecto invernadero.

greet [griːt] *vt* **1** saludar, recibir *(persona)*. **2** acoger, recibir *(propuesta)*.

greeting ['griːtɪŋ] *n* saludo.
■ **greetings card** tarjeta de felicitación; **greetings from...** recuerdos de...

gremlin ['gremlɪn] *n* duende.

grenade [grə'neɪd] *n* granada.

grew [gruː] *pt* → grow.

grey [greɪ] *adj* 1 gris. 2 cano,-a *(pelo)*. ► *n* gris.

greyhound ['greɪhaʊnd] *n* galgo.

grid [grɪd] *n* reja, parrilla.

grief [griːf] *n* dolor, pena.

grill [grɪl] *n* 1 parrilla. 2 parrillada: *mixed grill*, parrillada de carne. ► *vt* asar a la parrilla.

grille [grɪl] *n* rejilla.

grim [grɪm] *adj* 1 terrible. 2 lúgubre *(lugar)*. 3 severo,-a, muy serio,-a *(persona)*.

grimace ['grɪməs] *n* mueca. ► *vi* hacer una mueca.

grind [graɪnd] *vt* 1 moler. 2 afilar *(cuchillo)*.

grinder ['graɪndə'] *n* molinillo.

grip [grɪp] *vt* asir, agarra. ► *n* 1 asimiento, apretón. 2 adherencia *(sujección de neumático)*.

grizzly bear [grɪzlɪ'beə'] *n* oso pardo.

groan [grəʊn] *n* gemido, quejido *(de dolor)*. ► *vi* 1 gemir, quejarse *(de dolor)*. 2 crujir *(puerta)*.

grocer ['grəʊsə'] *n* tendero,-a.

grocer's ['grəʊsəz] *n* tienda de comestibles.

groceries ['grəʊsərɪz] *npl* comestibles.

groin [grɔɪn] *n* ingle.

groom [gruːm] *n* novio.

groove [gruːv] *n* 1 ranura. 2 surco.

gross [grəʊs] *adj* bruto,-a *(peso, cantidad)*.

ground¹ [graʊnd] *n* 1 tierra, suelo. 2 terreno. 3 campo *(de fútbol, batalla)*. ► *npl* **grounds** 1 razón, motivo. 2 posos. ■ **ground floor** planta baja.

ground² [graʊnd] *pt-pp* → grind.

group [gruːp] *n* grupo. ► *vt* agrupar.

grove [grəʊv] *n* arboleda.

grow [grəʊ] *vi* crecer. ► *vt* 1 cultivar *(planta)*. 2 dejarse crecer *(pelo, bigote)*.

to grow up *vi* criarse, crecer.

grown [grəʊn] *pp* → grow.

grown-up ['grəʊnʌp] *adj-n* adulto,-a.

growth [grəʊθ] *n* crecimiento.

grub [grʌb] *n* larva.

grudge [grʌdʒ] *n* resentimiento, rencor.

grumble ['grʌmbəl] *n* queja.

grunt [grʌnt] *n* gruñido. ► *vi* gruñir.

guarantee [gærən'tiː] *n* garantía. ► *vt* garantizar.

guard [gɑːd] *n* 1 guardia. 2 jefe de tren. ► *vt* 1 guardar, proteger. 2 vigilar. • **on guard**

de guardia; **to stand guard** montar guardia. ▪ **guard dog** perro guardián.

guerrilla [gə'rɪlə] *n* guerrillero,-a.

guess [ges] *vt-vi* **1** adivinar. **2** *fam* suponer. ► *n* conjetura: **have a guess!**, ia ver si lo adivinas!

guest [gest] *n* **1** invitado,-a. **2** cliente,-a, huésped,-a.

guesthouse ['gesthaʊs] *n* casa de huéspedes, pensión.

guide [gaɪd] *n* guía. ► *vt* guiar.

guidebook ['gaɪdbʊk] *n* guía.

guideline ['gaɪdlaɪn] *n* pauta, directriz.

guilty ['gɪltɪ] *adj* culpable.

guinea ['gɪnɪ] *n*. ▪ **guinea pig** conejillo de Indias.

guitar [gɪ'taːʳ] *n* guitarra.

guitarist [gɪ'taːrɪst] *n* guitarrista.

gulf [gʌlf] *n* golfo.

gull [gʌl] *n* gaviota.

gullible ['gʌlɪbəl] *adj* crédulo,-a.

gulp [gʌlp] *n* trago.

gum[1] [gʌm] *n* encía.

gum[2] [gʌm] *n* goma.

gun [gʌn] *n* arma de fuego.

gunman ['gʌnmən] *n* pistolero.

gunpoint ['gʌnpɔɪnt]. ● **at gunpoint** a punta de pistola.

gunpowder ['gʌnpaʊdəʳ] *n* pólvora.

gunshot ['gʌnʃɒt] *n* disparo.

gust [gʌst] *n* ráfaga, racha.

gut [gʌt] *n* intestino, tripa. ► *npl* **guts 1** entrañas, vísceras. **2** *fam* agallas.

gutter ['gʌtəʳ] *n* **1** cuneta, alcantarilla *(en calle)*. **2** canalón, desagüe *(en tejado)*. ▪ **gutter press** prensa amarilla.

guy [gaɪ] *n fam* tipo, tío.

guzzle ['gʌzəl] *vt* zamparse.

gym [dʒɪm] *n* **1** *fam* gimnasio. **2** gimnasia. ▪ **gym shoes** zapatillas de deporte.

gymnastics [dʒɪm'næstɪks] *n* gimnasia.

gynaecology [gaɪnɪ'kɒlədʒɪ] (US **gynecology**) *n* ginecología.

gypsy ['dʒɪpsɪ] *adj-n* gitano,-a.

H

habit ['hæbɪt] *n* hábito.

habitat ['hæbɪtæt] *n* hábitat.

habitual [hə'bɪtjʊəl] *adj* habitual.

hack [hæk] *vt* COMPUT piratear.

had [hæd] *pt-pp* → have.

haemorrhage ['hemərɪdʒ] (US **hemorrhage**) *n* hemorragia.

haemorrhoids ['hemərɔɪdz] *npl* (US **hemorroids**) hemorroides.

hag [hæg] *n* bruja, arpía.

haggle ['hægəl] *vi* regatear.

hail¹ [heɪl] *vt* llamar.

hail² [heɪl] *n* granizo. ▸ *vi* granizar.

hair [heəʳ] *n* cabello, pelo.

haircut ['heəkʌt] *n* corte de pelo.

hairdresser ['heədresəʳ] *n* peluquero,-a. ■ **hairdresser's** peluquería.

hairdryer ['heədraɪəʳ] *n* secador de pelo.

hairpiece ['heəpiːs] *n* peluquín.

hairpin ['heəpɪn] *n* horquilla.

hairspray ['heəspreɪ] *n* laca.

hairstyle ['heəstaɪl] *n* peinado.

hake [heɪk] *n* merluza.

half [hɑːf] *n* **1** mitad: *the second half*, la segunda mitad. **2** medio: *a kilo and a half*, un kilo y medio. ▸ *adj* medio,-a. ▸ *adv* medio, a medias. ▸ *pron* mitad. **half past** y media: *it's half past two*, son las dos y media.

half-time [hɑːftaɪm] *n* descanso *(en partido)*.

halfway ['hɑːfweɪ] *adv* a mitad de camino.

hall [hɔːl] *n* **1** vestíbulo, entrada. **2** sala *(de conciertos)*. ■ **hall of residence** colegio mayor.

hallo [hə'ləʊ] *interj* → hello.

hallucination [həluːsɪ'neɪʃən] *n* alucinación.

halo ['heɪləʊ] *n* halo, aureola.

halt [hɔːlt] *n* alto, parada. ▸ *vt-vi* parar(se), cesar.

ham [hæm] *n* jamón.

hamburger ['hæmbɜːgəʳ] *n* hamburguesa.

hammer ['hæməʳ] *n* martillo.

hammock ['hæmək] *n* hamaca.

hand [hænd] *n* **1** mano. **2** trabajador,-ra, operario,-a. **3** tripulante *(de barco)*. **4** manecilla *(de reloj)*. **5** letra, caligrafía. ▸ *vt* dar, entregar. ● **at first hand** de primera mano; **at hand** a mano; **by hand** a mano; **hands up!** ¡manos arriba!; **on the one hand** por una parte; **on the other hand** por otra parte; **to hold hands** estar cogidos,-as de la mano; **to lend a hand** echar una mano.

to hand in *vt* entregar.

to hand out *vt* repartir.

to hand over *vt* entregar.

handbag ['hændbæg] *n* bolso.

handball ['hændbɔːl] *n* balonmano.

handbook ['hændbʊk] *n* manual.

handbrake ['hændbreɪk] *n* freno de mano.

handcuff ['hændkʌf] *vt* esposar. ▸ *npl* **handcuffs** esposas.

handful ['hændfʊl] *n* puñado.

handicap ['hændɪkæp] *n* **1** discapacidad, minusvalía. **2** desventaja, obstáculo. **3** hándicap. ▸ *vt* obstaculizar.

handicapped ['hændɪkæpt] *adj* minusválido,-a.

handicraft ['hændɪkrɑːft] *n* artesanía.

handkerchief ['hæŋkətʃiːf] *n* pañuelo.

handle ['hændəl] *n* **1** pomo *(de puerta)*. **2** tirador *(de cajón)*. **3** asa *(de taza)*. **4** mango *(de cuchillo)*. ► *vt* **1** manejar. **2** tratar *(gente, problema)*.

handlebar ['hændəlbɑːʳ] *n* manillar.

handmade [hænd'meɪd] *adj* hecho,-a a mano.

handout ['hændaʊt] *n* **1** folleto. **2** nota de prensa. **3** limosna.

handshake ['hændʃeɪk] *n* apretón de manos.

handsome ['hænsəm] *adj* guapo,-a.

handwritten ['hænd'rɪtən] *adj* escrito,-a a mano.

handy ['hændɪ] *adj* **1** práctico,-a, útil. **2** a mano.

hang [hæŋ] *vt-vi* colgar.

to hang about/around *vi* **1** esperar. **2** perder el tiempo.

to hang out *vt* tender.

to hang up *vt-vi* colgar *(teléfono)*.

hangar ['hæŋəʳ] *n* hangar.

hanger ['hæŋəʳ] *n* percha.

hang-glider ['hæŋglaɪdəʳ] *n* ala delta.

hangover ['hæŋəʊvəʳ] *n* resaca.

happen ['hæpən] *vi* ocurrir.

happiness ['hæpɪnəs] *n* felicidad.

happy ['hæpɪ] *adj* **1** feliz, alegre. **2** contento,-a: *happy birthday!*, ¡feliz cumpleaños!

harass ['hærəs] *vt* acosar.

harbour ['hɑːbəʳ] *(US* **harbor)** *n* puerto.

hard [hɑːd] *adj* **1** duro,-a *(material)*. **2** difícil *(pregunta, tema)*. ► *adv* fuerte, duro. ■ **hard court** pista rápida; **hard disk** disco duro; **hard shoulder** GB arcén.

hardly ['hɑːdlɪ] *adv* **1** apenas. **2** casi.

hardware ['hɑːdweəʳ] *n* **1** artículos de ferretería. **2** hardware, soporte físico. ■ **hardware store** ferretería.

hare [heəʳ] *n* liebre.

haricot bean [hærɪkəʊ'biːn] *n* alubia.

harm [hɑːm] *n* mal, daño, perjuicio. ► *vt* dañar, perjudicar, hacer daño.

harmony ['hɑːmənɪ] *n* armonía.

harp [hɑːp] *n* arpa.

harpoon [hɑː'puːn] *n* arpón.

harvest ['hɑːvɪst] *n* cosecha. ► *vt* cosechar.

has [hæz] *3rd pers sing pres →* have.

hash [hæʃ] *n* picadillo.

haste [heɪst] *n* prisa.

hat [hæt] *n* sombrero.

hatch [hætʃ] *n* escotilla.

hate [heɪt] *n* odio. ► *vt* odiar.
haughty ['hɔːtɪ] *adj* arrogante.
haul [hɔːl] *n* **1** botín. **2** redada *(de peces)*. ► *vt* tirar de, arrastrar.
haulage ['hɔːlɪdʒ] *n* transporte.
haunted ['hɔːntɪd] *adj* encantado,-a.
have [hæv] *vt* **1** tener. **2** comer, beber, fumar: *to have lunch*, comer. **3** tomar: *to have a bath*, bañarse. **4** hacer, mandar: *he had the house painted*, hizo pintar la casa. ► *aux* haber. • **have got** GB tener; **to have just** acabar de.
to have on *vt* llevar puesto, -a *(prenda)*.
haversack ['hævəsæk] *n* mochila.
hawk [hɔːk] *n* halcón.
hay [heɪ] *n* heno.
hay-fever ['heɪfiːvəʳ] *n* fiebre del heno, alergia.
hazard ['hæzəd] *n* riesgo, peligro. ► *vt* aventurar.
haze [heɪz] *n* neblina.
hazelnut ['heɪzəlnʌt] *n* avellana.
he [hiː] *pron* él. ► *adj* macho: *a he bear*, un oso macho.
head [hed] *n* **1** cabeza. **2** cabecera *(de cama, mesa)*. ► *vt* **1** encabezar *(procesión)*. **2** cabecear. **3** dirigir *(organización)*. • **heads or tails?** ¿cara o cruz?

to head for *vt* dirigirse hacia.
headache ['hedeɪk] *n* dolor de cabeza.
header ['hedəʳ] *n* cabezazo.
headlamp ['hedlæmp] *n* faro.
headland ['hedlənd] *n* cabo.
headlight ['hedlaɪt] *n* faro.
headline ['hedlaɪn] *n* titular.
headphones ['hedfəʊnz] *npl* auriculares.
headquarters ['hedkwɔːtəz] *npl* **1** sede, oficina principal. **2** cuartel general.
heal [hiːl] *vt-vi* curar(se).
health [helθ] *n* salud.
healthy ['helθɪ] *adj* **1** sano,-a. **2** saludable.
heap [hiːp] *n* montón.
hear [hɪəʳ] *vt-vi* oír.
heart [hɑːt] *n* corazón. ► *npl* **hearts** corazones. • **by heart** de memoria; **to lose heart** desanimarse. ■ **heart attack** ataque al corazón.
heartbeat ['hɑːtbiːt] *n* latido del corazón.
heartless ['hɑːtləs] *adj* cruel
heat [hiːt] *n* **1** calor. **2** calefacción. **3** eliminatoria *(en deporte)*. ► *vt-vi* calentar(se). • **on heat** en celo.
heater ['hiːtəʳ] *n* estufa, calefactor.
heather ['heðəʳ] *n* brezo.
heating ['hiːtɪŋ] *n* calefacción.
heaven ['hevən] *n* cielo.
heavy ['hevɪ] *adj* **1** pesado,-a. **2** fuerte *(lluvia, golpe)*. • **to be**

a heavy smoker fumar mucho.

heavyweight ['hevɪweɪt] *n* peso pesado.

hectare ['hektɑːʳ] *n* hectárea.

hedge [hedʒ] *n* seto.

hedgehog ['hedʒhɒg] *n* erizo.

heel [hiːl] *n* **1** talón. **2** tacón.

height [haɪt] *n* **1** altura. **2** altitud.

heir [eəʳ] *n* heredero.

heiress ['eəres] *n* heredera.

held [held] *pt-pp* → hold.

helicopter ['helɪkɒptəʳ] *n* helicóptero.

hell [hel] *n* infierno.

hello [he'ləʊ] *interj* **1** ¡hola! **2** ¡diga!, ¡dígame! *(por teléfono).*

helm [helm] *n* timón.

helmet ['helmɪt] *n* casco.

help [help] *n* ayuda. ► *interj* ¡socorro! ► *vt* ayudar. • **help yourself** sírvete tú mismo, -a; **I can't help it** no lo puedo evitar.

helping ['helpɪŋ] *n* ración.

hem [hem] *n* dobladillo.

hemp [hemp] *n* cáñamo.

hen [hen] *n* gallina.

hence [hens] *adv* **1** por eso. **2** de aquí a, dentro de.

hepatitis [hepə'taɪtəs] *n* hepatitis.

her [hɜːʳ] *pron* **1** la *(complemento - directo)*; le, se *(- indirecto).* **2** ella *(después de preposición).* ► *adj* su, sus, de ella.

herb [hɜːb] *n* hierba.

herd [hɜːd] *n* **1** manada *(de ganado).* **2** rebaño *(de cabras).*

here [hɪəʳ] *adv* aquí. • **here you are** aquí tienes.

heritage ['herɪtɪdʒ] *n* herencia.

hero ['hɪərəʊ] *n* héroe.

heroin ['herəʊɪn] *n* heroína *(droga).*

heroine ['herəʊɪn] *n* heroína.

herring ['herɪŋ] *n* arenque.

hers [hɜːz] *pron* (el) suyo, (la) suya, (los) suyos, (las) suyas.

herself [hɜː'self] *pron* se, ella misma. • **by herself** sola.

hesitate ['hezɪteɪt] *vi* dudar.

hi [haɪ] *interj* ¡hola!

hiccough ['hɪkʌp] *n* hipo. ► *vi* tener hipo.

hiccup ['hɪkʌp] *n* hipo. ► *vi* tener hipo.

hid [hɪd] *pt-pp* → hide.

hidden ['hɪdən] *pp* → hide.

hide[1] [haɪd] *vt-vi* esconder(se).

hide[2] [haɪd] *n* piel, cuero.

hierarchy ['haɪərɑːkɪ] *n* jerarquía.

high [haɪ] *adj* **1** alto,-a. **2** agudo,-a *(voz).* **3** fuerte *(viento).* • **high court** tribunal supremo; **high jump** salto de altura; **high school** instituto de enseñanza secundaria; **high street** GB calle mayor; **high tide** pleamar.

high-heeled ['haɪ'hiːld] *adj* de tacón alto.

highlight ['haɪlaɪt] *vt* hacer resaltar, poner de relieve.

highly ['haɪlɪ] *adv* muy.
Highness ['haɪnəs] *n* Alteza.
highway ['haɪweɪ] *n* US autovía. ■ **Highway Code** GB código de la circulación.
hijack ['haɪdʒæk] *n* secuestro. ► *vt* secuestrar.
hike [haɪk] *n* excursión. ► *vi* ir de excursión.
hill [hɪl] *n* colina.
hilt [hɪlt] *n* empuñadura.
him [hɪm] *pron* **1** lo *(complemento - directo)*; le, se *(- indirecto)*. **2** él *(después de preposición)*.
himself [hɪm'self] *pron* se, sí mismo. ● **by himself** solo.
hinder ['hɪndə'] *vt-vi* entorpecer, estorbar.
hinge [hɪndʒ] *n* bisagra.
hint [hɪnt] *n* **1** insinuación, indirecta. **2** consejo. **3** pista, indicio. ► *vt* insinuar. ► *vi* lanzar indirectas.
hip [hɪp] *n* cadera.
hippie ['hɪpɪ] *adj-n fam* hippie.
hippo(potamus) [hɪpə'pɒtəməs] *n* hipopótamo.
hippy ['hɪpɪ] *adj-n fam* hippie.
hire ['haɪə'] *n* alquiler. ► *vt* **1** alquilar. **2** contratar. ● **on hire purchase** compra a plazos.
his [hɪz] *adj* **1** su, sus. **2** de él. ► *pron* (el) suyo, (la) suya, (los) suyos, (las) suyas.
history ['hɪstərɪ] *n* historia.
hit [hɪt] *n* **1** golpe. **2** éxito. **3** visita *(a página web)*. ► *vt* golpear, pegar.

hitchhike ['hɪtʃhaɪk] *vi* hacer autoestop.
hive [haɪv] *n* colmena.
hoarding ['hɔːdɪŋ] *n* valla.
hoarse [hɔːs] *adj* ronco,-a.
hobby ['hɒbɪ] *n* afición, hobby.
hockey ['hɒkɪ] *n* hockey.
hog [hɒg] *n* cerdo.
hoist [hɔɪst] *n* **1** grúa. **2** montacargas. ► *vt* **1** levantar. **2** izar *(bandera)*.
hold [həʊld] *n* bodega *(de barco, avión)*. ► *vt* **1** aguantar, sostener, agarrar *(con la mano)*. **2** dar cabida a, tener capacidad para. **3** celebrar *(reunión)*. **4** mantener *(conversación)*.
to hold on *vi* esperar, no colgar *(por teléfono)*.
to hold up *vt* **1** atracar, asaltar. **2** levantar *(mano)*.
holder ['həʊldə'] *n* poseedor, -ra, titular *(de pasaporte)*.
hold-up ['həʊldʌp] *n* atraco.
hole [həʊl] *n* agujero, hoyo.
holiday ['hɒlɪdeɪ] *n* **1** fiesta. **2** vacaciones.
hollow ['hɒləʊ] *adj* hueco,-a. ► *n* hueco.
holly ['hɒlɪ] *n* acebo.
holy ['həʊlɪ] *adj* santo,-a, sagrado,-a.
home [həʊm] *n* hogar, casa. ■ **home help** asistenta; **Home Office** Ministerio del Interior; **home page** página inicial.
homeland ['həʊmlænd] *n* patria.

homeless ['həʊmləs] *adj* sin techo, sin hogar.

home-made ['həʊm'meɪd] *adj* casero,-a.

homework ['həʊmwɜːk] *n* deberes.

honest ['ɒnɪst] *adj* honrado,-a.

honey ['hʌnɪ] *n* miel.

honeymoon ['hʌnɪmuːn] *n* luna de miel.

honour ['ɒnəʳ] (US **honor**) *n* honor.

hood [hʊd] *n* **1** capucha. **2** capota *(de coche)*. **3** US capó *(de coche)*.

hoof [huːf] *n* **1** pezuña. **2** casco *(de caballo)*.

hook [hʊk] *n* **1** gancho. **2** anzuelo *(para pescar)*. ► *vt* enganchar. • **off the hook 1** descolgado,-a *(teléfono)*. **2** a salvo *(persona)*.

hoop [huːp] *n* aro.

hoot [huːt] *n* bocinazo. ► *vi* tocar la bocina.

hooter ['huːtəʳ] *n* bocina.

hoover ['huːvə'] *n* aspiradora.► *vt-vi* pasar la aspiradora (por).

hope [həʊp] *n* esperanza. ► *vt-vi* esperar.

hopeless ['həʊpləs] *adj* imposible, desesperado,-a, inútil.

horizon [hə'raɪzən] *n* horizonte.

horn [hɔːn] *n* **1** asta, cuerno. **2** bocina, cláxon.

horoscope ['hɒrəskəʊp] *n* horóscopo.

horror ['hɒrəʳ] *n* horror. ■ **horror film** película de terror.

hors d'oeuvre [ɔː'dɜːvrʲ] *n* entremés.

horse [hɔːs] *n* caballo.

horsepower ['hɔːspaʊəʳ] *n* caballo *(de vapor)*.

horseshoe ['hɔːsʃuː] *n* herradura.

hose [həʊz] *n* manguera.

hospital ['hɒspɪtəl] *n* hospital.

host [həʊst] *n* **1** anfitrión, -ona. **2** presentador, -ra.

hostage ['hɒstɪdʒ] *n* rehén.

hostel ['hɒstəl] *n* **1** hostal, albergue. **2** residencia *(en universidad)*.

hostess ['həʊstəs] *n* **1** anfitriona. **2** azafata *(de avión, programa)*. **3** camarera.

hostile ['hɒstaɪl] *adj* hostil.

hot [hɒt] *adj* **1** caliente. **2** caluroso,-a *(día, tiempo)*. **3** picante *(comida)*. • **to be hot 1** tener calor. **2** estar caliente. ■ **hot dog** perrito caliente.

hotchpotch ['hɒtʃpɒtʃ] *n fam* batiburrillo.

hotel [həʊ'tel] *n* hotel.

hound [haʊnd] *n* perro de caza.

hour [aʊəʳ] *n* **1** hora. **2** horario. • **on the hour** a la hora en punto.

house [haʊs] *n* casa.

housewife ['haʊswaɪf] *n* ama de casa.

housework ['haʊswɜːk] *n* tareas de la casa.

housing ['haʊzɪŋ] n vivienda.
■ **housing development/estate** urbanización.
how [haʊ] adv 1 cómo. 2 qué: *how beautiful you look!*, ¡qué guapa estás! ● **how about...?** ¿qué tal si...?; **how are you?** ¿cómo estás?; **how much** cuánto,-a; **how many** cuántos,-as.
however [haʊ'evəʳ] conj sin embargo, no obstante.
howl [haʊl] n aullido. ► vi aullar.
hub [hʌb] n cubo (de rueda).
hug [hʌg] n abrazo. ► vt abrazar.
huge [hju:dʒ] adj enorme.
hull [hʌl] n casco (de barco).
hullo [hʌ'ləʊ] interj → hello.
human ['hju:mən] adj humano,-a. ► n humano. ■ **human being** ser humano.
humanity [hju:'mænɪti] n humanidad.
humble ['hʌmbəl] adj humilde. ► vt humillar.
humid ['hju:mɪd] adj húmedo,-a.
humiliate [hju:'mɪlɪeɪt] vt humillar.
humility [hju:'mɪlɪti] n humildad.
hummingbird ['hʌmɪŋbɜːd] n colibrí.
humour ['hju:məʳ] (US **humor**) n humor.
hump [hʌmp] n giba, joroba.

hundred ['hʌndrəd] num cien, ciento.
hundredth ['hʌndrədθ] adj-n centésimo,-a.
hung [hʌŋ] pt-pp → hang.
hunger ['hʌŋgəʳ] n hambre.
hungry ['hʌŋgri] adj hambriento,-a. ● **to be hungry** tener hambre.
hunt [hʌnt] n caza. ► vt-vi cazar. ● **to hunt for** buscar.
hunter ['hʌntəʳ] n cazador.
hunting ['hʌntɪŋ] n caza.
hurdle ['hɜːdəl] n valla.
hurl [hɜːl] vt lanzar, arrojar.
hurricane ['hʌrɪkən, 'hʌrɪkeɪn] n huracán.
hurry ['hʌri] n prisa. ► vt meter prisa a. ► vi darse prisa. ● **to be in a hurry** tener prisa.
to hurry up vi darse prisa.
hurt [hɜːt] n daño, dolor. ► vt herir, hacer daño. ► vi doler. ● **to get hurt** hacerse daño.
husband ['hʌzbənd] n marido, esposo.
hush [hʌʃ] n quietud.
husk [hʌsk] n cáscara.
hut [hʌt] n 1 cabaña. 2 cobertizo.
hutch [hʌtʃ] n conejera.
hyaena [haɪ'i:nə] n hiena.
hydrant ['haɪdrənt] n boca de riego.
hydraulic [haɪ'drɔːlɪk] adj hidráulico,-a.
hydrofoil ['haɪdrəfɔɪl] n hidroala.

hydrogen [ˈhaɪdrədʒən] n hidrógeno.
hydroplane [ˈhaɪdrəpleɪn] n hidroavión.
hyena [haɪˈiːnə] n hiena.
hygiene [ˈhaɪdʒiːn] n higiene.
hymn [hɪm] n himno.
hypermarket [ˈhaɪpəmɑːkɪt] n hipermercado.
hyphen [ˈhaɪfən] n guion.
hypnotize [ˈhɪpnətaɪz] vt hipnotizar.
hypocrite [ˈhɪpəkrɪt] n hipócrita.
hypothesis [haɪˈpɒθəsɪs] n hipótesis.
hysteria [hɪˈstɪərɪə] n histeria.

I

I [aɪ] pron yo.
ice [aɪs] n 1 hielo. 2 helado. ■ ice cube cubito; ice lolly GB polo; ice rink pista de hielo.
iceberg [ˈaɪsbɜːg] n iceberg.
ice-cream [ˈaɪskriːm] n helado.
ice-skate [ˈaɪsskeɪt] vi patinar sobre hielo. ► n patín de hielo.
ice-skating [ˈaɪskeɪtɪŋ] n patinaje sobre hielo.
icicle [ˈaɪsɪkəl] n carámbano.
idea [aɪˈdɪə] n idea.
identify [aɪˈdentɪfaɪ] vt identificar.

identity [aɪˈdentɪtɪ] n identidad. ■ identity card carnet de identidad.
ideology [aɪdɪˈɒlədʒɪ] n ideología.
idiom [ˈɪdɪəm] n locución.
idiot [ˈɪdɪət] n idiota.
idle [ˈaɪdəl] adj perezoso,-a.
idol [ˈaɪdəl] n ídolo.
if [ɪf] conj 1 si: if you want, si quieres. 2 aunque: a clever if rather talkative child, un niño inteligente aunque demasiado hablador. • if only ojalá, si.
igloo [ˈɪgluː] n iglú.
ignition [ɪgˈnɪʃən] n 1 ignición. 2 encendido (de motor). ■ ignition key llave de contacto.
ignorant [ˈɪgnərənt] adj ignorante.
ignore [ɪgˈnɔːʳ] vt ignorar.
ill [ɪl] adj enfermo,-a.
illegal [ɪˈliːgəl] adj ilegal.
illiterate [ɪˈlɪtərət] adj-n 1 analfabeto,-a. 2 inculto,-a.
illness [ˈɪlnəs] n enfermedad.
illuminate [ɪˈluːmɪneɪt] vt iluminar.
illusion [ɪˈluːʒən] n ilusión.
illustration [ɪləsˈtreɪʃən] n 1 ilustración. 2 ejemplo.
image [ˈɪmɪdʒ] n imagen.
imagination [ɪmædʒɪˈneɪʃən] n imaginación.
imagine [ɪˈmædʒɪn] vt imaginar.
imitate [ˈɪmɪteɪt] vt imitar.

imitation [ɪmɪ'teɪʃən] *n* imitación.

immediate [ɪ'miːdɪət] *adj* inmediato,-a.

immense [ɪ'mens] *adj* inmenso,-a.

immerse [ɪ'mɜːs] *vt* sumergir.

immigrant ['ɪmɪɡrənt] *adj* inmigrante. ► *n* inmigrante.

immobile [ɪ'məʊbaɪl] *adj* inmóvil.

immunity [ɪ'mjuːnɪti] *n* inmunidad.

impact ['ɪmpækt] *n* impacto.

impassive [ɪm'pæsɪv] *adj* impasible, imperturbable.

imperative [ɪm'perətɪv] *adj* esencial, imprescindible. ► *n* imperativo.

imperfect [ɪm'pɜːfekt] *adj* defectuoso,-a. ► *n* imperfecto *(tiempo verbal)*.

imperial [ɪm'pɪərɪəl] *adj* imperial.

impersonal [ɪm'pɜːsənəl] *adj* impersonal.

impertinent [ɪm'pɜːtɪnənt] *adj* impertinente.

implant [ɪm'plɑːnt] *vt* implantar.

implausible [ɪm'plɔːzəbəl] *adj* inverosímil.

implement [(*n*) 'ɪmpləmənt, (*vb*) 'ɪmplɪment] *n* instrumento, utensilio. ► *vt* llevar a cabo, poner en práctica.

implicate ['ɪmplɪkeɪt] *vt* implicar.

implicit [ɪm'plɪsɪt] *adj* 1 implícito,-a. 2 absoluto,-a, incondicional.

implore [ɪm'plɔː] *vt* implorar.

impolite [ɪmpə'laɪt] *adj* maleducado,-a.

import [(*n*) 'ɪmpɔːt; (*vb*) ɪm'pɔːt] *n* 1 artículo de importación. 2 importación. ► *vt* importar.

importance [ɪm'pɔːtəns] *n* importancia.

important [ɪm'pɔːtənt] *adj* importante.

impossible [ɪm'pɒsɪbəl] *adj* imposible.

impress [ɪm'pres] *vt* 1 impresionar. 2 subrayar, recalcar.

impression [ɪm'preʃən] *n* 1 impresión. 2 imitación.

impressive [ɪm'presɪv] *adj* impresionante.

imprisonment [ɪm'prɪzənmənt] *n* 1 encarcelamiento. 2 cárcel.

improve [ɪm'pruːv] *vt* mejorar. ► *vi* mejorar, mejorarse.

improvement [ɪm'pruːvmənt] *n* 1 mejora, mejoría. 2 reforma.

improvise ['ɪmprəvaɪz] *vt-vi* improvisar.

impulse ['ɪmpʌls] *n* impulso.

impulsive [ɪm'pʌlsɪv] *adj* impulsivo,-a.

in [ɪn] *prep* 1 en: *in May*, en mayo; *in the box*, en la caja. 2 en, vestido,-a de: *the man in black*, el hombre vestido de negro. **3** por: *in the afternoon*, por la tarde. **4** al: *in doing that*, al hacer eso. **5** de: *the biggest in the world*, el más grande del mundo. ► *adv* **1** dentro. **2** en casa: *is Judith in?*, ¿está Judith? **3** de moda: *short skirts are in*, las faldas cortas están de moda. • **in so far as** en la medida en que; **in all** en total.

inaccurate [ɪnˈækjərət] *adj* inexacto,-a.

inadequate [ɪnˈædɪkwət] *adj* **1** insuficiente. **2** inepto,-a, incapaz *(persona)*.

inaugural [ɪˈnɔːgjʊrəl] *adj* inaugural.

inaugurate [ɪˈnɔːgjʊreɪt] *vt* **1** inaugurar *(edificio)*. **2** investir *(presidente)*.

incapacity [ɪnkəˈpæsɪti] *n* incapacidad.

incense [ˈɪnsens] *n* incienso.

incentive [ɪnˈsentɪv] *n* incentivo.

incessant [ɪnˈsesənt] *adj* incesante.

inch [ɪntʃ] *n* pulgada.

incidence [ˈɪnsɪdəns] *n* **1** índice *(frecuencia)*. **2** incidencia *(efecto)*.

incident [ˈɪnsɪdənt] *n* incidente.

incidental [ɪnsɪˈdentəl] *adj* accesorio,-a, secundario,-a.

incinerate [ɪnˈsɪnəreɪt] *vt* incinerar.

incision [ɪnˈsɪʒən] *n* incisión.

incisive [ɪnˈsaɪsɪv] *adj* incisivo,-a.

incisor [ɪnˈsaɪzəʳ] *n* incisivo *(diente)*.

incite [ɪnˈsaɪt] *vt* incitar.

inclination [ɪnklɪˈneɪʃən] *n* inclinación.

incline [ɪnˈklaɪn] *vt-vi* inclinar(se).

include [ɪnˈkluːd] *vt* incluir.

including [ɪnˈkluːdɪŋ] *prep* incluso, inclusive, incluido.

incoherent [ɪnkəʊˈhɪərənt] *adj* incoherente.

income [ˈɪnkʌm] *n* ingresos, renta. ▪ **income tax** impuesto sobre la renta; **income tax return** declaración de la renta.

incoming [ˈɪnkʌmɪŋ] *adj* entrante.

incompetent [ɪnˈkɒmpətənt] *adj* incompetente, inepto,-a.

inconclusive [ɪnkənˈkluːsɪv] *adj* no concluyente.

incongruous [ɪnˈkɒŋgrʊəs] *adj* incongruente.

inconsiderate [ɪnkənˈsɪdərət] *adj* desconsiderado,-a.

inconsistent [ɪnkənˈsɪstənt] *adj* incoherente.

inconspicuous [ɪnkənˈspɪkjʊəs] *adj* que pasa inadvertido,-a.

inconvenient [ɪnkənˈviːnɪənt] *adj* **1** mal situado,-a *(lugar)*. **2** inoportuno,-a *(momento)*.

incorporate [ɪnˈkɔːpəreɪt] *vt* incorporar.

increase [*(n)* 'ɪnkriːs, *(vb)* ɪn-'kriːs] *n* aumento. ► *vt-vi* aumentar, subir.

incredible [ɪn'kredɪbəl] *adj* increíble.

incur [ɪn'kɜːʳ] *vt* **1** incurrir en *(críticas)*. **2** contraer *(deuda)*.

indeed [ɪn'diːd] *adv* **1** en efecto, efectivamente. **2** realmente, de veras: *thank you very much indeed*, muchísimas gracias.

indefinite [ɪn'defɪnət] *adj* indefinido,-a.

indemnity [ɪn'demnɪtɪ] *n* indemnización.

independence [ɪndɪ'pendəns] *n* independencia.

independent [ɪndɪ'pendənt] *adj* independiente.

in-depth [ɪn'depθ] *adj* exhaustivo,-a, a fondo.

index ['ɪndeks] *n* índice. ► *vt* poner un índice a, catalogar. ▪ **index finger** dedo índice.

indicate ['ɪndɪkeɪt] *vt* indicar.

indicative [ɪn'dɪkətɪv] *adj* indicativo,-a. ► *n* indicativo.

indicator ['ɪndɪkeɪtəʳ] *n* **1** indicador. **2** intermitente *(de coche)*.

indigenous [ɪn'dɪdʒənəs] *adj* indígena.

indignant [ɪn'dɪgnənt] *adj* **1** indignado,-a *(persona)*. **2** de indignación *(mirada)*.

indistinct [ɪndɪ'stɪŋkt] *adj* **1** vago,-a *(recuerdo)*. **2** borroso,-a, poco definido,-a *(forma)*.

individual [ɪndɪ'vɪdjʊəl] *adj* **1** individual. **2** particular, personal *(estilo)*. ► *n* individuo.

indoor ['ɪndɔːʳ] *adj* **1** interior, de estar por casa *(ropa)*. **2** cubierto,-a *(pista de tenis)*. ▪ **indoor football** fútbol sala; **indoor pool** piscina cubierta.

indoors [ɪn'dɔːz] *adv* dentro.

indulgent [ɪn'dʌldʒənt] *adj* indulgente.

industrial [ɪn'dʌstrɪəl] *adj* industrial. ▪ **industrial estate** polígono industrial.

industrious [ɪn'dʌstrɪəs] *adj* trabajador,-ra, aplicado,-a.

industry ['ɪndʌstrɪ] *n* industria.

inedible [ɪn'edɪbəl] *adj* no comestible.

inequality [ɪnɪ'kwɒlətɪ] *n* desigualdad.

inexpensive [ɪnɪk'spensɪv] *adj* barato,-a, económico,-a.

infantry ['ɪnfəntrɪ] *n* infantería.

infect [ɪn'fekt] *vt* **1** infectar. **2** contagiar.

infection [ɪn'fekʃən] *n* **1** infección. **2** contagio.

infectious [ɪn'fekʃəs] *adj* infeccioso,-a, contagioso,-a.

inferior [ɪn'fɪərɪəʳ] *adj* inferior. ► *n* inferior.

infertile [ɪn'fɜːtaɪl] *adj* estéril.

infest [ɪn'fest] *vt* infestar.

infiltrate ['ɪnfɪltreɪt] *vt* infiltrarse en.

infinite ['ɪnfɪnət] *adj* infinito,-a.

infinitive [ɪnˈfɪnɪtɪv] *n* infinitivo.

infirm [ɪnˈfɜːm] *adj* débil, enfermizo,-a.

infirmary [ɪnˈfɜːmərɪ] *n* **1** hospital. **2** enfermería.

inflammable [ɪnˈflæməbəl] *adj* inflamable.

inflammation [ɪnfləˈmeɪʃən] *n* inflamación.

inflation [ɪnˈfleɪʃən] *n* inflación.

influence [ˈɪnfluəns] *n* influencia. ▶ *vt* influir en.

influenza [ɪnfluˈenzə] *n* gripe.

inform [ɪnˈfɔːm] *vt* informar.

information [ɪnfəˈmeɪʃən] *n* información.

infuriate [ɪnˈfjuərɪeɪt] *vt* enfurecer.

ingenious [ɪnˈdʒiːnɪəs] *adj* ingenioso,-a.

ingrained [ɪnˈgreɪnd] *adj* **1** incrustado,-a *(suciedad)*. **2** arraigado,-a *(costumbre)*.

ingredient [ɪnˈgriːdɪənt] *n* ingrediente.

inhabitant [ɪnˈhæbɪtənt] *n* habitante.

inherit [ɪnˈherɪt] *vt* heredar.

inheritance [ɪnˈherɪtəns] *n* herencia.

initial [ɪˈnɪʃəl] *adj-n* inicial.

initiate [ɪˈnɪʃɪeɪt] *vt* iniciar.

injection [ɪnˈdʒekʃən] *n* inyección.

injure [ˈɪndʒəʳ] *vt* herir.

injury [ˈɪndʒərɪ] *n* herida, lesión. ▪ **injury time** tiempo de descuento *(en partido)*.

ink [ɪŋk] *n* tinta.

inkjet printer [ˈɪŋkdʒetˈprɪntəʳ] *n* impresora de chorro de tinta.

inland [(*adj*) ˈɪnlənd, (*adv*) ɪnˈlænd] *adj* de tierra adentro. ▶ *adv* tierra adentro.

inlet [ˈɪnlet] *n* **1** cala, ensenada. **2** entrada.

inn [ɪn] *n* **1** posada, fonda, mesón. **2** taberna.

inner [ˈɪnəʳ] *adj* interior.

innocent [ˈɪnəsənt] *adj-n* inocente.

innovation [ɪnəˈveɪʃən] *n* innovación.

inpatient [ˈɪnpeɪʃənt] *n* paciente hospitalizado,-a.

input [ˈɪnput] *n* **1** entrada, inversión *(de dinero)*. **2** input, entrada *(de datos)*.

inquire [ɪnˈkwaɪəʳ] *vt* preguntar. ● **"Inquire within"** "Razón aquí".

inquiry [ɪnˈkwaɪərɪ] *n* **1** pregunta. **2** investigación. ● **"Inquiries"** "Información".

inquisitive [ɪnˈkwɪzɪtɪv] *adj* curioso,-a.

insane [ɪnˈseɪn] *adj* demente, loco,-a.

insect [ˈɪnsekt] *n* insecto.

insert [ɪnˈsɜːt] *vt* insertar.

inside [ɪnˈsaɪd] *adj* interior, interno,-a. ▶ *adv* **1** dentro *(posición)*. **2** adentro *(movimiento)*. ▶ *prep* dentro de. ● **inside out** de dentro afuera, al revés, del revés.

insight ['msaɪt] *n* **1** perspicacia, penetración. **2** idea.

insinuate [m'sɪnjʊeɪt] *vt* insinuar.

insist [m'sɪst] *vi* insistir.

insomnia [m'sɒmnɪə] *n* insomnio.

inspection [m'spekʃən] *n* **1** inspección. **2** registro *(a equipaje)*. **3** revista *(a tropas)*.

inspector [m'spektə'] *n* **1** inspector,-ra. **2** revisor,-ra *(en tren)*.

inspiration [mspɪ'reɪʃən] *n* inspiración.

install [m'stɔːl] (US **instal**) *vt* instalar.

instalment [m'stɔːlmənt] (US **installment**) *n* **1** plazo *(de pago)*. **2** fascículo *(de libro)*. **3** episodio *(de serie)*.

instance ['mstəns] *n* ejemplo. ● **for instance** por ejemplo.

instant ['mstənt] *n* instante. ► *adj* **1** inmediato,-a. **2** instantáneo,-a *(café)*.

instead [m'sted] *adv* en cambio. ● **instead of** en vez de.

instinct ['mstɪŋkt] *n* instinto.

institute ['mstɪtjuːt] *n* instituto.

institution [mstɪ'tjuːʃən] *n* institución.

instruction [m'strʌkʃən] *n* instrucción.

instrument ['mstrəmənt] *n* instrumento.

insulate ['msjəleɪt] *vt* aislar.

insult [*(n)* 'msʌlt, *(vb)* m'sʌlt] *n* insulto. ► *vt* insultar.

insurance [m'ʃʊərəns] *n* seguro. ■ **insurance policy** póliza de seguro.

insure [m'ʃʊə'] *vt* asegurar.

intake ['mteɪk] *n* consumo.

integral ['mtɪgrəl] *adj-n* integral.

integrity [m'tegrɪtɪ] *n* integridad.

intellectual [mtə'lektjʊəl] *adj-n* intelectual.

intelligence [m'telɪdʒəns] *n* inteligencia.

intelligent [m'telɪʒənt] *adj* inteligente.

intend [m'tend] *vt* tener la intención de, proponerse.

intense [m'tens] *adj* **1** intenso,-a. **2** muy serio,-a *(persona)*.

intensive [m'tensɪv] *adj* intensivo,-a. ■ **intensive care** cuidados intensivos.

intention [m'tenʃən] *n* intención.

interactive [mtər'æktɪv] *adj* interactivo,-a.

interchange ['mtətʃeɪndʒ] *n* **1** intercambio. **2** enlace.

intercom ['mtəkɒm] *n* interfono.

interest ['mtrəst] *n* interés. ► *vt* interesar. ■ **interest rate** tipo de interés.

interface ['mtəfeɪs] *n* interfaz.

interference [mtə'fɪərəns] *n* interferencia.

interior [m'tɪərɪə'] *adj-n* interior.

interjection [ɪntəˈdʒekʃən] *n* **1** interjección. **2** comentario.

interlude [ˈɪntəluːd] *n* **1** intermedio, descanso. **2** interludio *(en música)*.

intermediate [ɪntəˈmiːdɪət] *adj* intermedio,-a.

intermission [ɪntəˈmɪʃən] *n* intermedio, descanso.

internal [ɪnˈtɜːnəl] *adj* interior, interno,-a. ▪ **internal flight** vuelo nacional.

international [ɪntəˈnæʃənəl] *adj* internacional.

Internet [ˈɪntənet] *n* Internet.

interplay [ˈɪntəpleɪ] *n* interacción.

interpret [ɪnˈtɜːprət] *vt* interpretar. ▶ *vi* hacer de intérprete.

interrogation [ɪnterəˈɡeɪʃən] *n* interrogatorio.

interrogative [ɪntəˈrɒɡətɪv] *adj* interrogativo,-a.

interrupt [ɪntəˈrʌpt] *vt-vi* interrumpir.

interval [ˈɪntəvəl] *n* **1** intervalo. **2** descanso, intermedio *(en teatro, etc)*.

intervention [ɪntəˈvenʃən] *n* intervención.

interview [ˈɪntəvjuː] *n* entrevista. ▶ *vt* entrevistar.

interviewer [ˈɪntəvjuːəʳ] *n* entrevistador,-ra.

intestine [ɪnˈtestɪn] *n* intestino.

intimacy [ˈɪntɪməsɪ] *n* intimidad.

intimate [ˈɪntɪmət] *adj* íntimo,-a.

into [ˈɪntʊ] *prep* **1** en, dentro de. **2** dividido entre.

intonation [ɪntəˈneɪʃən] *n* entonación.

intoxicated [ɪnˈtɒksɪkeɪtɪd] *adj* ebrio,-a.

intranet [ˈɪntrənet] *n* intranet.

intransitive [ɪnˈtrænsɪtɪv] *adj* intransitivo,-a.

intrigue [ɪnˈtriːɡ] *n* intriga.

introduce [ɪntrəˈdjuːs] *vt* **1** introducir. **2** presentar.

introduction [ɪntrəˈdʌkʃən] *n* **1** introducción. **2** presentación.

intruder [ɪnˈtruːdəʳ] *n* intruso,-a.

intuition [ɪntjuːˈɪʃən] *n* intuición.

invade [ɪnˈveɪd] *vt* invadir.

invaluable [ɪnˈvæljʊəbəl] *adj* inestimable.

invasion [ɪnˈveɪʒən] *n* invasión.

invent [ɪnˈvent] *vt* inventar.

invention [ɪnˈvenʃən] *n* **1** invento *(cosa)*. **2** invención *(acción)*.

inventor [ɪnˈventəʳ] *n* inventor,-ra.

inventory [ˈɪnvəntrɪ] *n* inventario.

inversion [ɪnˈvɜːʒən] *n* inversión.

invert [ɪnˈvɜːt] *vt* invertir.

inverted [ɪnˈvɜːtɪd] *adj* invertido,-a. ▪ **inverted commas** comillas.

invest [ɪnˈvest] *vt-vi* invertir.

investigation [ɪnvestɪˈgeɪʃən] *n* investigación.

investment [ɪnˈvestmənt] *n* inversión.

invitation [ɪnvɪˈteɪʃən] *n* invitación.

invite [ɪnˈvaɪt] *vt* invitar.

inviting [ɪnˈvaɪtɪŋ] *adj* tentador,-ra, atractivo,-a.

invoice [ˈɪnvɔɪs] *n* factura. ▶ *vt* facturar.

involve [ɪnˈvɒlv] *vt* 1 involucrar. 2 afectar a. 3 suponer.

inward [ˈɪnwəd] *adj* interior. ▶ *adv* hacia adentro.

inwards [ˈɪnwədz] *adv* hacia adentro.

iris [ˈaɪrɪs] *n* 1 iris *(del ojo)*. 2 lirio.

iron [ˈaɪən] *n* 1 hierro. 2 plancha. ▶ *vt* planchar.

ironic [aɪˈrɒnɪk] *adj* irónico,-a.

ironmonger's [ˈaɪənmʌŋgəz] *n* ferretería.

irony [ˈaɪrənɪ] *n* ironía.

irrational [ɪˈræʃənəl] *adj* irracional.

irregular [ɪˈregjələʳ] *adj* irregular.

irrelevant [ɪˈreləvənt] *adj* irrelevante.

irresistible [ɪrɪˈzɪstəbəl] *adj* irresistible.

irresponsible [ɪrɪˈspɒnsəbəl] *adj* irresponsable.

irrigate [ˈɪrɪgeɪt] *vt* regar.

irritate [ˈɪrɪteɪt] *vt* irritar.

irritating [ˈɪrɪteɪtɪŋ] *adj* irritante, molesto,-a.

irritation [ɪrɪˈteɪʃən] *n* irritación.

is [ɪz] *3rd pers sing pres* → be.

Islamic [ɪzˈlæmɪk] *adj* islámico,-ca.

island [ˈaɪlənd] *n* isla.

isle [aɪl] *n* isla.

isolate [ˈaɪsəleɪt] *vt* aislar.

isolation [aɪsəˈleɪʃən] *n* aislamiento.

issue [ˈɪʃuː] *n* 1 asunto, tema. 2 edición *(de libro)*. 3 número *(de revista)*. 4 emisión *(de sellos, acciones)*. 5 expedición *(de pasaporte)*. ▶ *vt* 1 publicar *(libro)*. 2 emitir *(sellos, acciones)*. 3 expedir *(pasaporte)*.

isthmus [ˈɪsməs] *n* istmo.

it [ɪt] *pron* 1 él, ella, ello *(sujeto)*. 2 lo, la *(complemento - directo)*; le *(- indirecto)*. 3 él, ella, ello *(después de preposición)*.

italics [ɪˈtælɪks] *npl* cursiva.

itch [ɪtʃ] *n* picazón, picor. ▶ *vi* picar: *my leg itches*, me pica la pierna.

item [ˈaɪtəm] *n* 1 artículo, cosa. 2 asunto *(en agenda)*. 3 partida *(en factura)*. 4 noticia.

itinerary [aɪˈtɪnərərɪ] *n* itinerario.

its [ɪts] *adj* su, sus.

itself [ɪtˈself] *pron* 1 se *(reflexivo)*. 2 sí, sí mismo,-a *(después de preposición)*. ● **by itself** solo.

ivory [ˈaɪvərɪ] *n* marfil.

ivy [ˈaɪvɪ] *n* hiedra.

J

jab [dʒæb] *n* pinchazo, inyección. ► *vt* pinchar, clavar.

jabber ['dʒæbə'] *vi-vt* farfullar.

jack [dʒæk] *n* **1** gato *(para coche).* **2** jota, sota.

jackal ['dʒækɔːl] *n* chacal.

jacket ['dʒækɪt] *n* **1** chaqueta, americana. **2** cazadora. **3** sobrecubierta *(de libro).*

jack-knife ['dʒæknaɪf] *n* navaja.

jackpot ['dʒækpɒt] *n* premio gordo.

jade [dʒeɪd] *n* jade.

jaguar ['dʒægjʊə'] *n* jaguar.

jail [dʒeɪl] *n* cárcel, prisión. ► *vt* encarcelar.

jam¹ [dʒæm] *n* mermelada.

jam² [dʒæm] *n* **1** aprieto, apuro. **2** atasco. ► *vt* **1** atestar, apiñar. **2** embutir, meter. ► *vi* atascarse, bloquearse.

janitor ['dʒænɪtə'] *n* portero.

January ['dʒænjʊəri] *n* enero.

jar [dʒɑː'] *n* tarro, pote.

jargon ['dʒɑːgən] *n* jerga.

jasmin ['dʒæzmɪn] *n* jazmín.

jaundice ['dʒɔːndɪs] *n* ictericia.

jaunt [dʒɔːnt] *n* excursión.

javelin ['dʒævəlɪn] *n* jabalina.

jaw [dʒɔː] *n* mandíbula.

jazz [dʒæz] *n* jazz.

jealous ['dʒeləs] *adj* celoso,-a.
● **to be jealous of** SB tener celos de ALGN.

jealousy ['dʒeləsi] *n* celos.

jeans [dʒiːnz] *npl* vaqueros.

jeep® [dʒiːp] *n* jeep®.

jeer [dʒɪə'] *vi* **1** burlarse. **2** abuchear. ► *n* **1** burla. **2** abucheo.

jelly ['dʒelɪ] *n* **1** jalea. **2** gelatina.

jellyfish ['dʒelɪfɪʃ] *n* medusa.

jerk [dʒɜːk] *n* **1** tirón, sacudida. **2** *fam* imbécil. ► *vt* sacudir, tirar de.

jersey ['dʒɜːzɪ] *n* jersey, suéter.

jet [dʒet] *n* **1** reactor, jet. **2** chorro.

jet-lag ['dʒetlæg] *n* jet-lag.

jetty ['dʒetɪ] *n* malecón.

Jew [dʒuː] *n* judío.

jewel ['dʒuːəl] *n* **1** joya, alhaja. **2** piedra preciosa.

jeweller ['dʒuːələ'] (US **jeweler**) *n* joyero,-a. ■ **jeweller's** joyería.

jewellery ['dʒuːəlrɪ] (US **jewelery**) *n* joyas.

Jewish ['dʒuːɪʃ] *adj* judío,-a.

jigsaw ['dʒɪgsɔː] *n* rompecabezas.

jingle ['dʒɪŋgəl] *n* **1** tintineo. **2** melodía *(de anuncio).* ► *vi* tintinear.

jinx [dʒɪŋks] *n* gafe.

job [dʒɒb] *n* trabajo.

jobless ['dʒɒbləs] *adj* parado,-a, sin trabajo.

jockey ['dʒɒkɪ] *n* jockey.

jog [dʒɒg] *n* trote. ► *vt* empujar, sacudir. ► *vi* hacer footing, correr. • **to go for a jog** hacer footing.

jogging ['dʒɒgɪŋ] *n* footing.

join [dʒɔɪn] *vt* **1** juntar, unir. **2** reunirse con. **3** acompañar. **4** alistarse *(en ejército)*; ingresar *(en policía)*. **5** hacerse socio,-a *(de un club)*. **6** afiliarse a *(partido)*. ▶ *vi* confluir *(ríos)*.

joiner ['dʒɔɪnə'] *n* carpintero.

joint [dʒɔɪnt] *n* **1** junta, juntura, unión. **2** articulación *(de rodilla, cadera)*. ▶ *adj* conjunto,-a. ▪ **joint venture** empresa conjunta.

joke [dʒəʊk] *n* **1** chiste. **2** broma. ▶ *vi* bromear.

joker ['dʒəʊkə'] *n* **1** bromista. **2** comodín.

jolly ['dʒɒlɪ] *adj* alegre.

jolt [dʒəʊlt] *n* **1** sacudida. **2** sorpresa, susto. ▶ *vt* sacudir. ▶ *vi* dar una sacudida.

jotter ['dʒɒtə'] *n* GB bloc.

journal ['dʒɜːnəl] *n* **1** revista, publicación *(especializada)*. **2** diario.

journalism ['dʒɜːnəlɪzəm] *n* periodismo.

journalist ['dʒɜːnəlɪst] *n* periodista.

journey ['dʒɜːnɪ] *n* **1** viaje. **2** trayecto.

joy [dʒɔɪ] *n* gozo, alegría.

joyful ['dʒɔɪfʊl] *adj* alegre.

joystick ['dʒɔɪstɪk] *n* joystick.

judge [dʒʌdʒ] *n* juez, jueza. ▶ *vt-vi* juzgar.

judgement ['dʒʌdʒmənt] *n* juicio. fallo.

jug [dʒʌg] *n* jarro.

juggler ['dʒʌglə'] *n* malabarista.

juice [dʒuːs] *n* jugo; zumo.

jukebox ['dʒuːkbɒks] *n* máquina de discos.

July [dʒuːˈlaɪ] *n* julio.

jump [dʒʌmp] *n* salto. ▶ *vt-vi* saltar. ▶ *vi* dar un salto.

jumper ['dʒʌmpə'] *n* **1** GB jersey. **2** US pichi.

jump-suit ['dʒʌmpsuːt] *n* mono.

junction ['dʒʌŋkʃən] *n* **1** salida, acceso *(en autopista)*. **2** cruce.

June [dʒuːn] *n* junio.

jungle ['dʒʌŋgəl] *n* jungla.

juniper ['dʒuːnɪpə'] *n* enebro.

junk¹ [dʒʌŋk] *n* trastos. ▪ **junk food** comida basura; **junk mail** propaganda.

junk² [dʒʌŋk] *n* junco *(barco)*.

jury ['dʒʊərɪ] *n* jurado.

just¹ [dʒʌst] *adj* justo,-a.

just² [dʒʌst] *adv* **1** exactamente, justo. **2** solamente. **3** justo ahora. **4** justo. • **just now** ahora mismo.

justice ['dʒʌstɪs] *n* justicia.

justify ['dʒʌstɪfaɪ] *vt* justificar.

jute [dʒuːt] *n* yute.

juvenile ['dʒuːvɪnaɪl] *adj* **1** juvenil. **2** infantil. ▶ *n* menor.

juxtapose ['dʒʌkstəpəʊz] *vt* yuxtaponer.

kind

K

kangaroo [kæŋɡəˈruː] *n* canguro.

karate [kəˈrɑːtɪ] *n* kárate.

kayak [ˈkaɪæk] *n* kayac.

keel [kiːl] *n* quilla.

keen [kiːn] *adj* 1 entusiasta, muy aficionado,-a. 2 agudo,-a *(mente)*. 3 penetrante *(mirada)*. 4 cortante *(viento)*. 5 fuerte *(competencia)*. • **keen on** aficionado,-a a.

keep [kiːp] *vt* 1 guardar. 2 retener, entretener. 3 tener *(tienda, negocio)*. 4 llevar *(cuentas, diario)*. 5 cumplir *(promesa)*. 6 acudir a, no faltar a *(cita)*. 7 mantener. 8 criar *(gallinas, cerdos)*. ► *vi* 1 seguir, continuar. 2 conservarse bien • **to keep STH to oneself** guardar algo para sí.

to keep on *vi* seguir, continuar.

keg [keɡ] *n* barril.

kennel [ˈkenəl] *n* perrera, caseta para perros.

kept [kept] *pt-pp* → keep.

kerb [kɜːb] *n* bordillo.

kernel [ˈkɜːnəl] *n* 1 semilla *(de nuez, fruta)*. 2 *fig* núcleo.

ketchup [ˈketʃəp] *n* ketchup, catsup.

kettle [ˈketəl] *n* hervidor.

key [kiː] *n* 1 llave *(de cerradura)*. 2 clave *(de misterio)*. 3 tecla *(de teclado)*. 4 soluciones, respuestas *(de ejercicios)*. ► *adj* clave. ► *vt* teclear. ■ **key ring** llavero.

keyboard [ˈkiːbɔːd] *n* teclado.

keyhole [ˈkiːhəʊl] *n* ojo de la cerradura.

kick [kɪk] *n* 1 puntapié, patada. 2 coz. 3 emoción, sensación. ► *vt* 1 dar un puntapié a, dar una patada a. 2 dar coces a.

to kick out *vt* echar.

kick-off [ˈkɪkɒf] *n* saque inicial *(en fútbol, rugby)*.

kid[1] [kɪd] *n* 1 cabrito *(animal)*. 2 cabritilla *(piel)*. 3 *fam* niño,-a, chico,-a.

kid[2] [kɪd] *vt* tomar el pelo a. ► *vi* estar de broma: *you must be kidding!*, ¡debes de estar de broma!

kidnap [ˈkɪdnæp] *vt* secuestrar.

kidney [ˈkɪdnɪ] *n* riñón.

kill [kɪl] *vt* matar.

killer [ˈkɪlər] *n* asesino,-a.

kilo [ˈkiːləʊ] *n* kilo.

kilogram [ˈkɪləɡræm] *n* kilogramo.

kilometre [kɪˈlɒmɪtər] (US **kilometer**) *n* kilómetro.

kilt [kɪlt] *n* falda escocesa.

kin [kɪn] *n* parientes, familia.

kind [kaɪnd] *adj* simpático,-a, amable. ► *n* tipo, género, clase. • **a kind of** una especie de; **to be so kind as to** tener la bondad de.

kindergarten ['kındəgæːtən] n jardín de infancia.

king [kıŋ] n rey.

kingdom ['kıŋdəm] n reino.

kiosk ['kiːɒsk] n 1 quiosco. 2 GB cabina telefónica.

kiss [kıs] n beso. ► vt-vi besar(se).

kit [kıt] n 1 equipo. 2 petate. 3 maqueta, kit.

kitchen ['kıtʃın] n cocina.

kite [kaıt] n cometa.

kitty ['kıtı] n fam bote (de dinero).

kiwi ['kiːwiː] n kiwi.

knapsack ['næpsæk] n mochila.

knead [niːd] vt amasar.

knee [niː] n rodilla.

kneecap ['niːkæp] n rótula.

kneel [niːl] vi arrodillarse.

knelt [nelt] pt-pp → kneel.

knew [njuː] pt → know.

knickers ['nıkəz] npl bragas.

knick-knack ['nıknæk] n chuchería.

knife [naıf] n cuchillo.

knight [naıt] n 1 caballero. 2 caballo (ajedrez).

knit [nıt] vt tejer. ► vi hacer punto, tricotar.

knitting ['nıtıŋ] n punto.

knob [nɒb] n 1 pomo (de puerta). 2 tirador (de cajón). 3 botón (de radio).

knock [nɒk] n golpe. ► vt golpear. ► vi llamar.

to knock down vt 1 derribar (edificio). 2 atropellar.

to knock out vt 1 dejar sin conocimiento. 2 dejar fuera de combate (en boxeo).

to knock over vt volcar (vaso), atropellar (persona).

knockout ['nɒkaut] n K.O., fuera de combate.

knot [nɒt] n nudo. ► vt anudar.

know [nəu] vt-vi 1 conocer. 2 saber. • **as far as I know** que yo sepa.

know-how ['nəuhau] n conocimientos prácticos.

knowledge ['nɒlıdʒ] n conocimiento(s).

known [nəun] pp → know.

knuckle ['nʌkəl] n nudillo.

KO ['keı'əu] abbr (**knockout**) fuera de combate, KO.

koala [kəu'ɑːlə] n koala.

L

label ['leıbəl] n etiqueta. ► vt etiquetar.

laboratory [lə'bɒrətərı] n laboratorio.

labour ['leıbəˀ] (US **labor**) n 1 trabajo. 2 mano de obra.

labourer ['leıbərəˀ] (US **laborer**) n peón, obrero,-a.

lace [leıs] n 1 cordón (de zapato). 2 encaje.

lack [læk] n falta, carencia. ► vt faltar, carecer de.

lacquer ['lækə'] *n* laca.

lad [læd] *n* muchacho, chaval.

ladder ['lædə'] *n* **1** escalera de mano. **2** carrera *(en medias)*.

ladle ['leɪdəl] *n* cucharón.

lady ['leɪdɪ] *n* señora, dama.

ladybird ['leɪdɪbɜːd] *n* (US **ladybug**) *n* mariquita *(insecto)*.

lager ['lɑːgə'] *n* cerveza rubia.

lagoon [lə'guːn] *n* laguna.

laid [leɪd] *pt-pp* → lay.

lain [leɪn] *pp* → lie.

lair [leə'] *n* guarida.

lake [leɪk] *n* lago.

lamb [læm] *n* cordero.

lame [leɪm] *adj* cojo,-a.

lamp [læmp] *n* lámpara.

lamp-post ['læmppəʊst] *n* farola.

lampshade ['læmpʃeɪd] *n* pantalla *(de lámpara)*.

lance [lɑːns] *n* lanza.

land [lænd] *n* tierra. ► *vi* aterrizar. ► *vt-vi* desembarcar.

landing ['lændɪŋ] *n* **1** aterrizaje *(de avión)*. **2** descansillo, rellano *(en escalera)*. **3** desembarco *(de personas)*.

landlady ['lændleɪdɪ] *n* **1** propietaria, casera *(de vivienda)*. **2** dueña *(de pensión)*.

landlord ['lændlɔːd] *n* **1** propietario, casero *(de vivienda)*. **2** dueño *(de pensión)*.

landscape ['lændskeɪp] *n* paisaje.

landslide ['lændslaɪd] *n* desprendimiento de tierras.

lane [leɪn] *n* **1** camino. **2** carril *(de autopista)*. **3** calle *(en atletismo, natación)*.

language ['læŋgwɪdʒ] *n* **1** lenguaje. **2** lengua, idioma.

lantern ['læntən] *n* linterna.

lap[1] [læp] *n* regazo, rodillas.

lap[2] [læp] *n* **1** vuelta *(de carrera)*. **2** etapa *(de viaje)*.

lapel [lə'pel] *n* solapa.

lapse [læps] *n* **1** lapso *(de tiempo)*. **2** lapsus.

laptop ['læptɒp] *n* ordenador portátil.

lard [lɑːd] *n* manteca de cerdo.

large [lɑːdʒ] *adj* grande, gran. ● **at large** suelto,-a.

lark [lɑːk] *n* alondra.

larynx ['lærɪŋks] *n* laringe.

lash [læʃ] *n* **1** latigazo, azote. **2** pestaña.

last [lɑːst] *adj* **1** último,-a. **2** pasado,-a: *last night,* anoche. ► *adv* **1** por última vez. **2** en último lugar. ► *n* el/la último,-a. ► *vt-vi* durar. ● **at last** al fin, por fin; **last but one** penúltimo,-a.

latch [lætʃ] *n* pestillo.

late [leɪt] *adj* **1**: *in the late afternoon,* a media tarde. **2** difunto,-a. ► *adv* tarde. ● **to be late** llegar tarde; **to get late** hacerse tarde.

later ['leɪtə'] *adj* posterior *(fecha, edición)*. ► *adv* **1** más tarde. **2** después, luego.

latest ['leɪtɪst] *adj* último,-a.

lather ['lɑːðəʳ] n espuma.

laugh [lɑːf] n risa. ► vi reír, reírse. ● **to laugh at** reírse de

launch [lɔːntʃ] n lanzamiento. ► vt lanzar.

launder ['lɔːndəʳ] vt 1 lavar y planchar (ropa). 2 blanquear (dinero).

launderette [lɔːndəˈret] n lavandería automática.

laundry ['lɔːndrɪ] n 1 lavandería. 2 colada.

laurel ['lɒrəl] n laurel.

lavatory ['lævətərɪ] n servicios, aseo (público).

lavender ['lævɪndəʳ] n lavanda.

lavish ['lævɪʃ] adj generoso,-a.

law [lɔː] n 1 ley. 2 derecho (carrera).

lawn [lɔːn] n césped.

lawyer ['lɔːjəʳ] n abogado,-a.

lay¹ [leɪ] vt 1 poner, colocar. 2 poner (huevos).

lay² [leɪ] pt → lie.

lay-by ['leɪbaɪ] n área de descanso.

layer ['leɪəʳ] n capa, estrato.

layout ['leɪaʊt] n diseño.

lazy ['leɪzɪ] adj perezoso,-a.

lead¹ [led] n 1 plomo (metal). 2 mina (de lápiz).

lead² [liːd] n 1 delantera, cabeza. 2 correa (de perro). 3 papel principal. ► vt 1 llevar, conducir (sendero, guía). 2 liderar. ► vi 1 ir primero,-a. 2 tener el mando. 3 conducir (camino).

leader ['liːdəʳ] n líder.

leadership ['liːdəʃɪp] n liderazgo.

lead-free ['ledfriː] adj sin plomo.

leaf [liːf] n hoja.

leaflet ['liːflət] n folleto.

league [liːg] n liga.

leak [liːk] n 1 escape, fuga. 2 gotera.

lean [liːn] vi 1 apoyarse. 2 inclinarse (curva, pendiente).

to lean out vt-vi asomar(se).

leant [lent] pt-pp → lean.

leap [liːp] n salto, brinco. ► vi saltar, brincar. ■ **leap year** año bisiesto.

leapt [lept] pt-pp → leap.

learn [lɜːn] vt-vi aprender.

learner ['lɜːnəʳ] n estudiante.

learnt [lɜːnt] pt-pp → learn.

lease [liːs] n vt arrendar.

leash [liːʃ] n correa.

least [liːst] adj más mínimo, -a, menor. ► adv menos. ● **at least** por lo menos.

leather ['leðəʳ] n piel, cuero.

leave [liːv] vt 1 dejar (gen). 2 salir de (lugar). ► vi salir, marcharse, irse. ● **to be left** quedar.

lecture ['lektʃəʳ] n 1 conferencia. 2 clase (en universidad).

lecturer ['lektʃərəʳ] n 1 conferenciante. 2 profesor,-ra (universitario).

led [led] pt-pp → lead.

leech [liːtʃ] n sanguijuela.

leek [liːk] *n* puerro.

left[1] [left] *adj* izquierdo,-a. ▶ *n* izquierda. ▶ *adv* a la izquierda, hacia la izquierda.

left[2] [left] *pt-pp* → leave.

left-handed [left'hændɪd] *adj* zurdo,-a.

left-luggage office [left-'lʌgɪdʒ ɒfɪs] *n* consigna.

leftover *adj* sobrante.

leg [leg] *n* 1 pierna. 2 pata. 3 muslo *(de pollo)*.

legal ['liːgəl] *adj* legal.

legend ['ledʒənd] *n* leyenda.

leggings ['legɪŋz] *npl* mallas.

legitimate [lɪ'dʒɪtɪmət] *adj* legítimo,-a.

leisure ['leʒəʳ] *n* ocio

lemon ['lemən] *n* limón

lemonade [lemə'neɪd] *n* limonada.

lend [lend] *vt* dejar, prestar.

length [leŋθ] *n* 1 largo, longitud. 2 duración.

lens [lenz] *n* 1 lente *(de gafas)*. 2 objetivo *(de cámara)*.

lent [lent] *pt-pp* → lend.

Lent [lent] *n* Cuaresma.

lentil ['lentɪl] *n* lenteja.

leopard ['lepəd] *n* leopardo.

leotard ['liːətɑːd] *n* malla.

less [les] *adj-adv-prep* menos.

lesson ['lesən] *n* lección, clase.

let [let] *vt* 1 dejar. 2 arrendar, alquilar: *"To let"*, "Se alquila". ▶ *aux*: *let's go!*, ¡vamos!

to let in *vt* dejar entrar.

to let out *vt* 1 dejar salir, soltar. 2 alquilar.

letter ['letəʳ] *n* 1 letra. 2 carta. ▪ **letter box** buzón.

lettuce ['letɪs] *n* lechuga.

level ['levəl] *adj* 1 llano,-a. 2 nivelado,-a. 3 empatado,-a. ▶ *vt* nivelar. ▪ **level crossing** GB paso a nivel.

lever ['liːvəʳ] *n* palanca.

levy ['levɪ] *n* recaudación. ▶ *vt* recaudar.

liability [laɪə'bɪlɪtɪ] *n* responsabilidad. ▶ *npl* **liabilities** COMM pasivo.

liar ['laɪəʳ] *n* mentiroso,-a.

liberal ['lɪbərəl] *adj* liberal.

liberate ['lɪbəreɪt] *vt* liberar.

liberty ['lɪbətɪ] *n* libertad.

library ['laɪbrərɪ] *n* biblioteca.

lice [laɪs] *npl* → louse.

licence ['laɪsəns] *n* GB licencia, permiso.

license ['laɪsəns] *vt* autorizar. ▶ *n* US licencia, permiso.

lick [lɪk] *n* lamedura, lametón. ▶ *vt* lamer.

licorice ['lɪkərɪs] *n* US regaliz.

lid [lɪd] *n* tapa, tapadera.

lie[1] [laɪ] *n* mentira: *to tell lies*, decir mentiras. ▶ *vi* mentir.

lie[2] [laɪ] *vi* 1 acostarse, tumbarse. 2 estar situado,-a, encontrarse.

to lie back *vi* recostarse.

to lie down *vi* acostarse.

lieutenant [lef'tenənt] *n* teniente.

life [laɪf] *n* vida. • **for life** para toda la vida. ■ **life belt** salvavidas; **life imprisonment** cadena perpetua; **life jacket** chaleco salvavidas; **life sentence** cadena perpetua.

life-boat ['laɪfbəʊt] *n* bote salvavidas.

lifeguard ['laɪfgɑːd] *n* socorrista.

lifestyle ['laɪfstaɪl] *n* estilo de vida.

lifetime ['laɪftaɪm] *n* vida.

lift [lɪft] *n* GB ascensor. ► *vt-vi* levantar. • **to give SB a lift** llevar a ALGN en coche.

light[1] [laɪt] *n* **1** luz. **2** fuego *(para cigarrillo).* ► *vt-vi* encender(se). ► *vt* iluminar, alumbrar. ► *adj* claro,-a. ■ **light bulb** bombilla.

light[2] [laɪt] *adj* ligero,-a.

lighter ['laɪtə'] *n* encendedor.

lighthouse ['laɪthaʊs] *n* faro.

lighting ['laɪtɪŋ] *n* **1** iluminación. **2** alumbrado.

lightning ['laɪtənɪŋ] *n* rayo, relámpago.

like[1] [laɪk] *adj* semejante, parecido,-a. ► *prep* como. • **like this** así.

like[2] [laɪk] *vt* gustar: *I like wine,* me gusta el vino. • **as you like** como quieras.

likeable ['laɪkəbəl] *adj* simpático,-a, agradable.

likelihood ['laɪklɪhʊd] *n* probabilidad.

likely ['laɪklɪ] *adj* probable.

lily ['lɪlɪ] *n* lirio, azucena.

limb [lɪm] *n* miembro.

lime[1] [laɪm] *n* cal.

lime[2] [laɪm] *n* lima *(fruto).*

lime[3] [laɪm] *n* tilo *(árbol).*

limit ['lɪmɪt] *n* límite. ► *vt* limitar.

limited ['lɪmɪtɪd] *adj* limitado, -a. ■ **limited company** sociedad anónima.

limp[1] [lɪmp] *n* cojera. ► *vi* cojear.

limp[2] [lɪmp] *adj* flojo,-a.

limpet ['lɪmpɪt] *n* lapa.

line[1] [laɪn] *n* **1** línea. **2** raya *(en papel).* **3** cuerda, cordel. **4** sedal *(de pesca).* **5** US cola. **6** tendedero. ► *vt* alinear.

line[2] [laɪn] *vt* forrar.

lined [laɪnd] *adj* forrado,-a.

linen ['lɪnɪn] *n* **1** lino. **2** ropa blanca.

liner ['laɪnə'] *n* transatlántico.

linesman ['laɪnzmən] *n* juez de línea.

lingerie ['lɑːnʒəriː] *n* lencería.

lining ['laɪnɪŋ] *n* forro.

link [lɪŋk] *vt* unir, conectar. ► *n* **1** eslabón *(de cadena).* **2** enlace, conexión. ► *npl* **links** campo de golf.

linkage ['lɪŋkɪdʒ] *n* conexión.

lion ['laɪən] *n* león.

lioness ['laɪənəs] *n* leona.

lip [lɪp] *n* labio.

lipstick ['lɪpstɪk] *n* pintalabios, lápiz de labios.

log off

liqueur [lɪˈkjʊəʳ] n licor.
liquid [ˈlɪkwɪd] adj líquido,-a. ► n líquido.
liquor [ˈlɪkəʳ] n alcohol, bebida alcohólica.
liquorice [ˈlɪkərɪs] n GB regaliz.
list [lɪst] n lista. ► vt hacer una lista de.
listen [ˈlɪsən] vi escuchar.
listener [ˈlɪsənəʳ] n oyente.
lit [lɪt] pt-pp → light.
literal [ˈlɪtərəl] adj literal.
literature [ˈlɪtərɪtʃəʳ] n literatura.
litre [ˈliːtəʳ] (US **liter**) n litro.
litter [ˈlɪtəʳ] n **1** basura, papeles. **2** camada.
little [ˈlɪtəl] adj **1** pequeño,-a. **2** poco,-a. ► pron poco. ► adv poco.
live¹ [lɪv] vt-vi vivir.
live² [laɪv] adj **1** vivo,-a. **2** en directo (programa, transmisión).
to live on vt vivir de, alimentarse de. ► vi sobrevivir.
lively [ˈlaɪvlɪ] adj animado,-a.
liven up [laɪvənˈʌp] vt-vi animar(se).
liver [ˈlɪvəʳ] n hígado.
livestock [ˈlaɪvstɒk] n ganado.
living [ˈlɪvɪŋ] adj vivo,-a. ► n medio de vida: **what do you do for a living?**, ¿cómo te ganas la vida? ▪ **living room** sala de estar.
lizard [ˈlɪzəd] n lagarto (grande), lagartija (pequeño).

llama [ˈlɑːmə] n llama.
load [ləʊd] n carga. ► vt-vi cargar. ● **loads of...** montones de...
loaf [ləʊf] n pan, barra.
loan [ləʊn] n préstamo. ► vt prestar.
loathe [ləʊð] vt detestar.
lobby [ˈlɒbɪ] n **1** vestíbulo. **2** POL grupo de presión.
lobe [ləʊb] n lóbulo.
lobster [ˈlɒbstəʳ] n bogavante. ▪ **spiny lobster** langosta.
local [ˈləʊkəl] adj local.
loch [lɒk] n lago.
lock¹ [lɒk] n **1** cerradura (de puerta). **2** esclusa (en canal). ► vt cerrar con llave.
lock² [lɒk] n mecha, mechón.
locker [ˈlɒkəʳ] n taquilla, armario.
locksmith [ˈlɒksmɪθ] n cerrajero.
locomotive [ləʊkəˈməʊtɪv] n locomotora.
locust [ˈləʊkəst] n langosta.
lodge [lɒdʒ] vi alojarse, hospedarse. ► vt presentar (queja).
lodging [ˈlɒdʒɪŋ] n alojamiento.
loft [lɒft] n desván.
log [lɒg] n **1** tronco (para fuego). **2** COMPUT registro. ► vt registrar, anotar.
to log in/log on vi COMPUT entrar (en sistema).
to log off/log out vi COMPUT salir (del sistema).

logical ['lɒdʒɪkəl] *adj* lógico,-a.

loin [lɔɪn] *n* 1 lomo *(de cerdo)*. 2 solomillo *(de ternera)*.

lollipop ['lɒlɪpɒp] *n* 1 piruleta, pirulí. 2 polo.

loneliness ['ləʊnlɪnəs] *n* soledad.

lonely ['ləʊnlɪ] *adj* solitario,-a.

long[1] [lɒŋ] *adj* largo,-a. ► *adv* 1 mucho, mucho tiempo. 2 **no longer, not any longer**: *she doesn't work here any longer*, ya no trabaja aquí. ● **as long as** mientras, con tal de que; **so long** hasta la vista. ■ **long jump** salto de longitud.

long[2] [lɒŋ] *vi* **to long for** anhelar.

long-distance [lɒŋ'dɪstəns] *adj* 1 de larga distancia *(llamada)*. 2 de fondo *(corredor)*.

longing ['lɒŋɪŋ] *n* 1 ansia, anhelo. 2 nostalgia.

longitude ['lɒndʒɪtjuːd] *n* longitud.

long-playing [lɒŋ'pleɪɪŋ] *adj* de larga duración.

long-range [lɒŋ'reɪndʒ] *adj* 1 de largo alcance *(distancia)*. 2 a largo plazo *(tiempo)*.

long-sighted [lɒŋ'saɪtɪd] *adj* hipermétrope.

loo [luː] *n fam* váter, servicio.

look [lʊk] *vi* 1 mirar. 2 parecer: *it looks easy*, parece fácil. ► *n* 1 mirada, vistazo. 2 aspecto, apariencia.

to look after *vt* 1 ocuparse de. 2 cuidar.

to look at *vt* mirar.

to look for *vt* buscar.

to look forward to *vt* esperar *(con ansia)*.

to look like *vt* 1 parecer: *what does Sarah look like?*, ¿cómo es Sarah? 2 parecerse a: *he looks like his father*, se parece a su padre.

lookalike ['lʊkəlaɪk] *n* doble.

lookout ['lʊkaʊt] *n* 1 vigía. 2 atalaya.

loop [luːp] *n* 1 lazo. 2 curva. 3 COMPUT bucle.

loose [luːs] *adj* 1 suelto,-a. 2 flojo,-a. ► *vt* soltar.

loosen ['luːsən] *vt-vi* soltar(se), aflojar(se).

loot [luːt] *n* botín.

lop [lɒp] *vt* podar.

lord [lɔːd] *n* 1 señor. 2 lord. ● **the Lord's Prayer** el padrenuestro.

lorry ['lɒrɪ] *n* camión.

lose [luːz] *vt-vi* 1 perder. 2 atrasarse *(reloj)*.

loser ['luːzə'] *n* perdedor,-a.

loss [lɒs] *n* pérdida.

lost [lɒst] *pt-pp* → lose. ► *adj* perdido,-a. ● **to get lost** perderse. ■ **lost property** objetos perdidos.

lot [lɒt] *n* 1 US solar, terreno. 2 lote *(en subasta)*. 3 cantidad: *a lot*, mucho, muchísimo.

lotion ['ləʊʃən] *n* loción.

macaroni

lottery ['lɒtərɪ] *n* lotería.
loud [laud] *adj* **1** fuerte *(sonido)*. **2** alto,-a *(voz)*. ► *adv* fuerte, alto.
loudspeaker [laud'spi:kə'] *n* altavoz.
lounge [laundʒ] *n* salón, sala de estar.
louse [laus] *n* piojo.
love [lʌv] *n* **1** amor. **2** cero *(en tenis)*. ► *vt* **1** amar, querer. **2** gustar: *I love fish*, me encanta el pescado. ● **to be in love with** estar enamorado,-a de.
lovely ['lʌvlɪ] *adj* encantador, -ra.
low [ləʊ] *adj* bajo,-a. ► *adv* bajo. ■ **low tide** bajamar.
lower ['ləʊə'] *adj* inferior. ► *vt* bajar.
low-necked [ləʊ'nekt] *adj* escotado,-a.
loyal ['lɔɪəl] *adj* leal, fiel.
lozenge ['lɒzɪndʒ] *n* **1** rombo. **2** pastilla para la tos.
lubricant ['lu:brɪkənt] *n* lubricante.
luck [lʌk] *n* suerte.
lucky ['lʌkɪ] *adj* afortunado, -a, con suerte. ● **to be lucky** tener suerte. ■ **lucky charm** amuleto.
luggage ['lʌgɪdʒ] *n* equipaje. ■ **luggage rack** portaequipajes.
lull [lʌl] *n* momento de calma. ► *vt* adormecer, arrullar.
lullaby ['lʌləbaɪ] *n* canción de cuna, nana.
lumberjack ['lʌmbədʒæk] *n* leñador.
lump [lʌmp] *n* **1** pedazo, trozo. **2** terrón *(de azúcar)*. **3** bulto *(en cuerpo)*. **4** grumo *(en salsa)*.
lunar ['lu:nə'] *adj* lunar.
lunch [lʌntʃ] *n* comida. ► *vi* comer.
luncheon ['lʌntʃən] *n fml* almuerzo.
lung [lʌŋ] *n* pulmón.
lurch [lɜ:tʃ] *n* bandazo. ► *vi* **1** dar bandazos. **2** tambalearse.
lure [ljʊə'] *n* **1** señuelo. **2** *fig* atractivo. ► *vt* atraer.
lurid ['ljuərɪd] *adj* **1** chillón, -ona *(color)*. **2** horripilante, espeluznante *(detalles)*.
lush [lʌʃ] *adj* exuberante.
lust [lʌst] *n* lujuria.
luxury ['lʌkʃərɪ] *n* lujo.
lynch [lɪntʃ] *vt* linchar.
lynx [lɪŋks] *n* lince.
lyric ['lɪrɪk] *adj* lírico,-a. ► *npl* **lyrics** letra *(de canción)*.

M

mac [mæk] *n* impermeable.
macabre [mə'kɑ:brə] *adj* macabro,-a.
macaroni [mækə'rəʊnɪ] *n* macarrones.

machine [məˈʃiːn] *n* máquina, aparato. ∎ **machine gun** ametralladora.

mackerel [ˈmækrəl] *n* caballa.

mackintosh [ˈmækɪntɒʃ] *n* impermeable.

mad [mæd] *adj* 1 loco,-a. 2 furioso,-a, muy enfadado,-a *(persona)*.

madam [ˈmædəm] *n fml* señora.

madden [ˈmædən] *vt* enfurecer.

made [meɪd] *pt-pp* → make.

madness [ˈmædnəs] *n* locura.

magazine [mægəˈziːn] *n* revista.

maggot [ˈmægət] *n* larva.

magic [ˈmædʒɪk] *n* magia. ► *adj* mágico,-a.

magician [məˈdʒɪʃən] *n* mago,-a.

magnet [ˈmægnət] *n* imán.

magnetic [mægˈnetɪk] *adj* magnético,-a. ∎ **magnetic tape** cinta magnética.

magnify [ˈmægnɪfaɪ] *vt* aumentar, ampliar.

magnifying glass [ˈmægnɪfaɪɪŋglɑːs] *n* lupa.

magnitude [ˈmægnɪtjuːd] *n* magnitud.

mahogany [məˈhɒgənɪ] *n* caoba.

maid [meɪd] *n* 1 criada, sirvienta. 2 camarera *(en hotel)*. ∎ **maid of honour** dama de honor.

maiden [ˈmeɪdən] ► *adj* 1 soltera. 2 inaugural. ∎ **maiden name** apellido de soltera.

mail [meɪl] *n* correo. ► *vt* US echar al buzón. ∎ **mail order** venta por correo.

mailbox [ˈmeɪlbɒks] *n* US buzón.

mailman [ˈmeɪlmæn] *n* US cartero.

main [meɪn] *adj* principal. ► *n* 1 tubería principa. 2 red eléctrica. ∎ **main beam** viga maestra; **main office** oficina central; **main street** calle mayor.

maintain [meɪnˈteɪn] *vt* mantener.

maintenance [ˈmeɪntənəns] *n* 1 mantenimiento. 2 pensión alimenticia.

maisonette [meɪzəˈnet] *n* dúplex.

maize [meɪz] *n* maíz.

majesty [ˈmædʒəstɪ] *n* majestad.

major [ˈmeɪdʒəʳ] *adj* principal. ► *n* comandante.

majority [məˈdʒɒrɪtɪ] *n* mayoría.

make [meɪk] *vt* 1 hacer. 2 ganar: *how much do you make a year?*, ¿cuánto ganas al año? ► *n* marca.

to make up *vt* 1 inventar. 2 hacer, preparar *(cama, paquete)*. 3 maquillar. ► *vi* maquillarse.

maker ['meɪkə'] *n* fabricante.
make-up ['meɪkʌp] *n* 1 maquillaje. 2 composición. ▪ **make-up remover** desmaquillador.
malaria [mə'leərɪə] *n* malaria.
male [meɪl] *adj-n* macho. ▶ *adj* 1 varón. 2 masculino,-a. ▪ **male chauvinism** machismo.
malfunction [mæl'fʌnkʃən] *n* funcionamiento defectuoso.
malice ['mælɪs] *n* malicia.
malignant [mə'lɪgnənt] *adj* maligno,-a.
malt [mɔːlt] *n* malta.
mammal ['mæməl] *n* mamífero.
mammoth ['mæməθ] *n* mamut.
man [mæn] *n* hombre. ▶ *vt* 1 tripular *(nave)*. 2 servir.
manage ['mænɪdʒ] *vt* 1 dirigir *(negocio)*. 2 administrar *(propiedad)*. ▶ *vi* 1 poder. 2 arreglárselas. 3 conseguir.
management ['mænɪdʒmənt] *n* dirección, administración, gestión.
manager ['mænɪdʒə'] *n* 1 director,-ra, gerente *(de empresa)*. 2 administrador,-ra *(de propiedad)*. 3 entrenador *(de deportista)*.
manageress [mænɪdʒə'res] *n* directora, gerente.
mane [meɪn] *n* 1 crin *(de caballo)*. 2 melena *(de león)*.

mango ['mæŋgəʊ] *n* mango.
manhood ['mænhʊd] *n* 1 madurez. 2 hombría.
mania ['meɪnɪə] *n* manía.
manicure ['mænɪkjʊə'] *n* manicura.
manipulate [mə'nɪpjʊleɪt] *vt* manipular.
mankind [mæn'kaɪnd] *n* el género humano.
manly ['mænlɪ] *adj* viril.
man-made [mæn'meɪd] *adj* 1 artificial. 2 sintético,-a.
manner ['mænə'] *n* manera, modo. ▶ *npl* **manners** modales. • **in this manner** de esta manera, así; **to be bad manners** ser de mala educación.
mannerism ['mænərɪzəm] *n* peculiaridad.
manoeuvre [mə'nuːvə'] (US **maneuver**) *n* maniobra. ▶ *vt-vi* maniobrar.
manor ['mænə'] *n* señorío. ▪ **manor house** casa solariega.
manpower ['mænpaʊə'] *n* mano de obra.
mansion ['mænʃən] *n* mansión.
manual ['mænjʊəl] *adj-n* manual.
manufacture [mænjʊ'fæktʃə'] *n* fabricación, manufactura. ▶ *vt* 1 fabricar, manufacturar.
manufacturer [mænjʊ'fæktʃərə'] *n* fabricante.
manure [mə'njʊə'] *n* abono, estiércol.

many ['menɪ] *adj-pron* muchos,-as. ● **as many … as** tantos,-as … como; **how many?** ¿cuántos,-as?; **not many** pocos,-as; **too many** demasiados,-as.

map [mæp] *n* **1** mapa *(de país, región)*. **2** plano *(de ciudad)*.

maple ['meɪpəl] *n* arce.

marathon ['mærəθən] *n* maratón.

marble ['mɑːbəl] *n* **1** mármol. **2** canica.

march [mɑːtʃ] *n* marcha. ► *vi* marchar, caminar.

to march past *vi* desfilar.

March [mɑːtʃ] *n* marzo.

mare [meəʳ] *n* yegua.

margarine [mɑːdʒəˈriːn] *n* margarina.

margin ['mɑːdʒɪn] *n* margen.

marginal ['mɑːdʒɪnəl] *adj* marginal.

marine [məˈriːn] *adj* marino, -a, marítimo,-a. ► *n* soldado de infantería de marina.

marionette [mærɪəˈnet] *n* marioneta.

marital ['mærɪtəl] *adj* matrimonial. ■ **marital status** estado civil.

maritime ['mærɪtaɪm] *adj* marítimo,-a.

mark [mɑːk] *n* **1** marca, señal. **2** mancha. **3** nota. ► *vt* **1** marcar. **2** corregir, puntuar. ● **on your marks!** ¡preparados!

marker ['mɑːkəʳ] *n* rotulador.

market ['mɑːkɪt] *n* mercado.

marketing ['mɑːkɪtɪŋ] *n* márketing, mercadotecnia.

marmalade ['mɑːməleɪd] *n* mermelada *(de cítricos)*.

marquee [mɑːˈkiː] *n* carpa.

marriage ['mærɪdʒ] *n* **1** matrimonio. **2** boda.

married ['mærɪd] *adj* casado,-a. ● **to get married** casarse.

marrow ['mærəʊ] *n* **1** tuétano, médula. **2** GB calabacín.

marry ['mærɪ] *vt-vi* casar(se).

marsh [mɑːʃ] *n* **1** pantano, ciénaga. **2** marisma.

marshal ['mɑːʃəl] *n* **1** mariscal. **2** US jefe,-a de policía.

martial ['mɑːʃəl] *adj* marcial.

martyr ['mɑːtəʳ] *n* mártir.

marvellous ['mɑːvələs] *adj* maravilloso,-a.

mascara [mæˈskɑːrə] *n* rímel.

mascot ['mæskɒt] *n* mascota.

masculine ['mɑːskjʊlɪn] *adj* masculino,-a. ► *n* masculino.

mash [mæʃ] *vt* triturar. ► *n fam* puré de patatas.

mask [mɑːsk] *n* **1** máscara. **2** mascarilla. ■ **masked ball** baile de disfraces.

mason ['meɪsən] *n* albañil.

mass¹ [mæs] *n* masa. ● **to mass produce** fabricar en serie. ■ **mass media** medios de comunicación de masas; **mass production** fabricación en serie.

mass² [mæs] *n* misa.

massacre ['mæsəkəʳ] *n* masacre.

massage ['mæsɑːʒ] *n* masaje. ▶ *vt* dar masajes a.

massive ['mæsɪv] *adj* **1** macizo,-a, sólido,-a. **2** enorme.

mast [mɑːst] *n* mástil.

master ['mɑːstəʳ] *n* **1** señor, amo, dueño. **2** maestro. ▶ *vt* dominar. ▪ **master key** llave maestra.

masterpiece ['mɑːstəpiːs] *n* obra maestra.

mat [mæt] *n* **1** alfombrilla, felpudo. **2** salvamanteles.

match¹ [mætʃ] *n* cerilla.

match² [mætʃ] *n* partido. ▶ *vt-vi* hacer juego (con).

matchbox ['mætʃbɒks] *n* caja de cerillas.

mate¹ [meɪt] *n* mate *(en ajedrez)*.

mate² [meɪt] *n* **1** compañero, -a, colega. **2** pareja *(persona)*. **3** macho, hembra *(animal)*. ▶ *vt-vi* aparear(se).

material [mə'tɪərɪəl] *adj-n* material.

maternity [mə'tɜːnɪtɪ] *n* maternidad. ▪ **maternity leave** baja por maternidad.

mathematics [mæθə'mætɪks] *n* matemáticas.

matt [mæt] *adj* mate.

matter ['mætəʳ] *n* **1** materia. **2** asunto, cuestión. ▶ *vi* importar. • **as a matter of fact** en realidad; **it's a matter of...** es cuestión de...; **no matter...**: *I never win, no matter what I do*, nunca gano, haga lo que haga; **the matter**: *what's the matter?*, ¿qué pasa?

mattress ['mætrəs] *n* colchón.

mature [mə'tʃʊəʳ] *adj* maduro,-a. ▶ *vt-vi* madurar.

maximum ['mæksɪməm] *adj* máximo,-a. ▶ *n* máximo.

may [meɪ] *aux* poder: *he may come*, es posible que venga, puede que venga; *may I go?*, ¿puedo irme?

May [meɪ] *n* mayo.

maybe ['meɪbiː] *adv* quizá, quizás, tal vez.

mayonnaise [meɪə'neɪz] *n* mayonesa, mahonesa.

mayor [meəʳ] *n* alcalde.

maze [meɪz] *n* laberinto.

me [miː] *pron* **1** me, mí. **2** yo: *it's me!*, ¡soy yo! • **with me** conmigo.

meadow ['medəʊ] *n* prado.

meagre ['miːgəʳ] (US **meager**) *adj* escaso,-a.

meal [miːl] *n* comida.

mean¹ [miːn] *adj* tacaño,-a.

mean² [miːn] *vt* **1** querer decir, significar. **2** querer, tener intención de: *I didn't mean to do it*, lo hice sin querer.

mean³ [miːn] *n* media.

meaning ['miːnɪŋ] *n* sentido, significado.

means [miːnz] *npl* medios, recursos económicos. • **by all means!** ¡naturalmente!; **by no means** de ninguna manera. ▪ **means of transport** medio de transporte.

meant [ment] *pt-pp* → mean.

meantime ['miːntaɪm] *phr.* **in the meantime** mientras tanto.

meanwhile ['miːnwaɪl] *adv* mientras tanto, entretanto.

measles ['miːzəlz] *n* sarampión. ▪ **German measles** rubeola.

measure ['meʒəʳ] *n* **1** medida. **2** MUS compás. ▪ *vt* medir.

measurement ['meʒəmənt] *n* **1** medición. **2** medida.

meat [miːt] *n* carne.

meatball ['miːtbɔːl] *n* albóndiga.

mechanic [mɪ'kænɪk] *n* mecánico,-a.

mechanism ['mekənɪzəm] *n* mecanismo.

medal ['medəl] *n* medalla.

meddle ['medəl] *vi* entrometerse.

media ['miːdɪə] *npl* medios de comunicación.

medical ['medɪkəl] *adj* médico,-a. ▪ *n fam* chequeo. ▪ **medical record** historial médico.

medicine ['medɪsɪn] *n* **1** medicina. **2** medicamento.

mediocre [miːdɪ'əʊkəʳ] *adj* mediocre.

medium ['miːdɪəm] *n* medio. ▪ *adj* mediano,-a.

meet [miːt] *vt* **1** encontrar, encontrarse con *(por casualidad)*. **2** reunirse con, verse con. **3** conocer. ▪ *vi* **1** encontrarse. **2** reunirse, verse. • **pleased to meet you!** ¡encantado,-a de conocerle!

meeting ['miːtɪŋ] *n* **1** reunión. **2** POL mítin. **3** encuentro. ▪ **meeting point** lugar de encuentro.

megaphone ['megəfəʊn] *n* megáfono.

mellow ['meləʊ] *adj* **1** maduro,-a *(fruta)*. **2** suave *(color, voz)*.

melody ['melədɪ] *n* melodía.

melon ['melən] *n* melón.

melt [melt] *vt-vi* **1** derretir(se) *(hielo, nieve)*. **2** fundir(se) *(metal)*.

member ['membəʳ] *n* **1** miembro. **2** socio,-a *(de club)*.

memorandum [memə'rændəm] *n* memorándum.

memory ['memərɪ] *n* **1** memoria. **2** recuerdo. ▪ **memory card** tarjeta de memoria.

men [men] *npl* → man.

menace ['menəs] *n* amenaza.

mend [mend] *n* remiendo. ▪ *vt* **1** reparar, arreglar. **2** remendar *(ropa)*.

menstruation [menstrʊ'eɪʃən] *n* menstruación.

menswear ['menzweəʳ] *n* ropa de caballero.

mental ['mentəl] *adj* mental.
mention ['menʃən] *n* mención. ► *vt* mencionar.
menu ['menjuː] *n* **1** carta *(en restaurante)*. **2** COMPUT menú.
merchandise ['mɜːtʃəndaɪz] *n* mercancías, géneros.
merchant ['mɜːtʃənt] *n* comerciante.
mercy ['mɜːsɪ] *n* misericordia, compasión. • **at the mercy of** a la merced de.
mere [mɪəʳ] *adj* mero,-a.
merge [mɜːdʒ] *vt* unir, empalmar *(carreteras)*. ► *vt-vi* fusionar(se) *(empresas)*.
merger ['mɜːdʒəʳ] *n* fusión.
meringue [mə'ræŋ] *n* merengue.
merit ['merɪt] *n* mérito. ► *vt* merecer.
mermaid ['mɜːmeɪd] *n* sirena.
merry ['merɪ] *adj* alegre. • **Merry Christmas!** ¡Feliz Navidad!
merry-go-round ['merɪɡəʊraʊnd] *n* tiovivo, caballitos.
mesh [meʃ] *n* malla.
mess [mes] *n* desorden, lío.
to mess about/around *vi* gandulear.
to mess up *vt* **1** *fam* desordenar *(habitación)*. **2** estropear *(planes)*.
message ['mesɪdʒ] *n* mensaje.
messenger ['mesɪndʒəʳ] *n* mensajero,-a.
met [met] *pt-pp* → meet.

metabolism [me'tæbəlɪzəm] *n* metabolismo.
metal ['metəl] *n* metal. ► *adj* metálico,-a, de metal.
meteorite ['miːtɪəraɪt] *n* meteorito.
meter[1] ['miːtəʳ] *n* US → metre.
meter[2] ['miːtəʳ] *n* contador.
method ['meθəd] *n* método.
metre ['miːtəʳ] (US **meter**) *n* metro.
mew [mjuː] *n* maullido.
mezzanine ['mezəniːn] *n* entresuelo.
miaow [mɪ'aʊ] *vi* maullar.
mice [maɪs] *npl* → mouse.
microbe ['maɪkrəʊb] *n* microbio.
microchip ['maɪkrəʊtʃɪp] *n* microchip.
microphone ['maɪkrəfəʊn] *n* micrófono.
microprocessor [maɪkrəʊ'prəʊsesəʳ] *n* microprocesador.
microscope ['maɪkrəskəʊp] *n* microscopio.
microwave ['maɪkrəʊweɪv] *n* microondas *(horno)*.
midday [mɪd'deɪ] *n* mediodía.
middle ['mɪdəl] *adj* del medio, central. ► *n* **1** medio, centro *(de habitación)*. **2** mitad. ■ **middle age** mediana edad; **middle class** clase media.
middleman ['mɪdəlmən] *n* intermediario.
midnight ['mɪdnaɪt] *n* medianoche.

midway ['mɪdweɪ] *adv* a medio camino.

midwife ['mɪdwaɪf] *n* comadrona.

might [maɪt] *aux* → may.

migraine ['maɪgreɪn] *n* jaqueca, migraña.

migrate [maɪ'greɪt] *vi* emigrar.

mild [maɪld] *adj* **1** apacible *(persona)*. **2** suave *(clima)*.

mile [maɪl] *n* milla.

milestone ['maɪlstəʊn] *n* hito.

military ['mɪlɪtərɪ] *adj* militar.

milk [mɪlk] *n* leche. ▪ **milk chocolate** chocolate con leche; **milk shake** batido.

mill [mɪl] *n* **1** molino. **2** molinillo *(de café)*. **3** fábrica. ▶ *vt* moler.

millimetre ['mɪlimiːtəʳ] (US **millimeter**) *n* milímetro.

million ['mɪljən] *n* millón.

mime [maɪm] *n* **1** mímica. **2** mimo *(persona)*.

mimic ['mɪmɪk] *vt* imitar.

mince [mɪns] *n* GB carne picada. ▶ *vt* picar.

mind [maɪnd] *n* mente. ▶ *vt* **1** hacer caso de. **2** cuidar. **3** tener cuidado con. ▶ *vt-vi* importar. ● **never mind** no importa, da igual; **to change one's mind** cambiar de opinión; **to have STH in mind** estar pensando en algo; **to make up one's mind** decidirse.

mine¹ [maɪn] *n* mina.

mine² [maɪn] *pron* (el) mío, (la) mía, (los) míos, (las) mías.

miner ['maɪnəʳ] *n* minero,-a.

mineral ['mɪnərəl] *adj* mineral. ▶ *n* mineral.

minimum ['mɪnɪməm] *adj* mínimo,-a. ▶ *n* mínimo.

minister ['mɪnɪstəʳ] *n* **1** ministro,-a. **2** pastor,-ra *(cura)*.

ministry ['mɪnɪstrɪ] *n* **1** ministerio. **2** sacerdocio.

mink [mɪŋk] *n* visón.

minor ['maɪnəʳ] *adj* de poca importancia. ▶ *n* menor de edad.

minority [maɪ'nɒrɪtɪ] *n* minoría. ▶ *adj* minoritario,-a.

mint¹ [mɪnt] *vt* acuñar.

mint² [mɪnt] *n* menta.

minus ['maɪnəs] *prep* menos: *minus five degrees*, cinco grados bajo cero.

minute¹ ['mɪnɪt] *adj* diminuto,-a.

minute² ['mɪnɪt] *n* minuto. ▪ **minute hand** minutero.

miracle ['mɪrəkəl] *n* milagro.

mirage ['mɪraːʒ] *n* espejismo.

mirror ['mɪrəʳ] *n* espejo; retrovisor *(de coche)*.

miscarriage [mɪs'kærɪdʒ] *n* aborto *(espontáneo)*.

miscellaneous [mɪsɪ'leɪnɪəs] *adj* diverso,-a, variado,-a.

mischievous ['mɪstʃɪvəs] *adj* travieso,-a.

misdemeanour [mɪsdɪ'miːnəʳ] (US **misdemeanor**) *n* **1** fechoría. **2** delito menor.

miserable ['mɪzərəbəl] *adj* **1** triste. **2** desagradable *(tiempo)*. **3** miserable.

misery ['mɪzəri] *n* **1** tristeza, desdicha. **2** miseria.

misfire [mɪs'faɪəʳ] *vi* fallar.

misfortune [mɪs'fɔːtʃən] *n* infortunio, desgracia.

mishap ['mɪshæp] *n* percance.

misjudge [mɪs'dʒʌdʒ] *vt* juzgar mal.

mislaid [mɪs'leɪd] *pt-pp* → mislay.

mislay [mɪs'leɪ] *vt* extraviar.

mislead [mɪs'liːd] *vt* engañar.

misled [mɪs'led] *pt-pp* → mislead.

misprint ['mɪsprɪnt] *n* errata.

miss[1] [mɪs] *n* señorita.

miss[2] [mɪs] *n* fallo. ▶ *vt-vi* fallar. ▶ *vt* **1** perder: *he missed the train*, perdió el tren. **2** no oír, no entender, no ver. **3** echar de menos, añorar. **4** echar en falta. ▶ *vi* faltar.

missile ['mɪsaɪl] *n* misil. ▪ **missile launcher** lanzamisiles.

missing ['mɪsɪŋ] *adj* **1** perdido,-a *(objeto)*. **2** desaparecido, -a *(persona)*.

mission ['mɪʃən] *n* misión.

missionary ['mɪʃənəri] *n* misionero,-a.

mistake [mɪs'teɪk] *n* error. ▶ *vt* **1** entender mal. **2** confundir. ● **by mistake** por error, por equivocación; **to make a mistake** equivocarse.

mister ['mɪstəʳ] *n* señor.

mistletoe ['mɪzəltəʊ] *n* muérdago.

mistook [mɪs'tʊk] *pt* → mistake.

mistreat [mɪs'triːt] *vt* maltratar.

mistress ['mɪstrəs] *n* **1** ama, señora. **2** profesora. **3** amante.

mistrust [mɪs'trʌst] *n* desconfianza, recelo. ▶ *vt* desconfiar de.

misunderstand [mɪsʌndə'stænd] *vt-vi* entender mal.

misunderstanding [mɪsʌndə'stændɪŋ] *n* malentendido.

misunderstood [mɪsʌndə'stʊd] *pt-pp* → misunderstand.

misuse [*(n)* mɪs'juːs, *(vb)* mɪs'juːz] *n* **1** mal uso. **2** abuso *(de poder)*. ▶ *vt* **1** emplear mal. **2** abusar de *(de poder)*.

mitten ['mɪtən] *n* manopla.

mix [mɪks] *n* mezcla. ▶ *vt-vi* mezclar(se).

mixed [mɪkst] *adj* **1** variado, -a. **2** mixto,-a *(de ambos sexos)*.

mixer ['mɪksəʳ] *n* batidora.

mixture ['mɪkstʃəʳ] *n* mezcla.

moan [məʊn] *n* gemido, quejido. ▶ *vi* gemir.

moat [məʊt] *n* foso.

mobile ['məʊbaɪl] *adj-n* móvil. ▪ **mobile home** caravana, remolque; **mobile phone** móvil, teléfono móvil.

moccasin ['mɒkəsɪn] *n* mocasín.

mock [mɒk] *adj* **1** falso, de imitación. **2** de prueba, simulado,-a. ► *vt-vi* burlarse (de).

mockery [ˈmɒkəri] *n* burla.

model [ˈmɒdəl] *n* modelo. ■ **model home** US casa piloto.

modem [ˈməʊdəm] *n* módem.

moderate [ˈmɒdərət] *adj* moderado,-a. ► *vt-vi* moderar(se).

modern [ˈmɒdən] *adj* **1** moderno,-a.

modest [ˈmɒdɪst] *adj* modesto,-a.

modify [ˈmɒdɪfaɪ] *vt* modificar.

module [ˈmɒdjuːl] *n* módulo.

moist [mɔɪst] *adj* húmedo,-a.

moisture [ˈmɔɪstʃəˈ] *n* humedad.

mold [məʊld] *n* US → mould.

mole[1] [məʊl] *n* lunar.

mole[2] [məʊl] *n* topo *(animal)*.

molecule [ˈmɒləkjuːl] *n* molécula.

molest [məˈlest] *vt* **1** hostigar, acosar. **2** agredir sexualmente.

moment [ˈməʊmənt] *n* momento. • **just a moment** un momento.

monarchy [ˈmɒnəki] *n* monarquía.

monastery [ˈmɒnəstəri] *n* monasterio.

Monday [ˈmʌndɪ] *n* lunes.

money [ˈmʌni] *n* dinero. ■ **money order** giro postal.

moneybox [ˈmʌnɪbɒks] *n* hucha.

monitor [ˈmɒnɪtəˈ] *n* monitor.

monk [mʌŋk] *n* monje.

monkey [ˈmʌŋki] *n* mono. ■ **monkey wrench** llave inglesa.

monopoly [məˈnɒpəli] *n* monopolio.

monotonous [məˈnɒtənəs] *adj* monótono,-a.

monster [ˈmɒnstəˈ] *n* monstruo.

month [mʌnθ] *n* mes.

monthly [ˈmʌnθlɪ] *adj* mensual. ► *adv* mensualmente. ■ **monthly instalment** mensualidad.

monument [ˈmɒnjʊmənt] *n* monumento.

moo [muː] *n* mugido.

mood [muːd] *n* humor. • **to be in the mood for** tener ganas de.

moon [muːn] *n* luna. ■ **moon landing** alunizaje.

moonlight [ˈmuːnlaɪt] *n* luz de luna, claro de luna.

moor [mʊəˈ] *n* páramo.

Moor [mʊəˈ] *n* moro,-a.

mop [mɒp] *n* fregona.

moped [ˈməʊped] *n* ciclomotor.

moral [ˈmɒrəl] *adj* moral. ► *n* moraleja.

more [mɔːˈ] *adj-adv* más. • **not any more** ya no …; **more or less** más o menos.

moreover [mɔː'rəʊvəʳ] *adv fml* además.

morgue [mɔːg] *n* depósito de cadáveres.

morning ['mɔːnɪŋ] *n* mañana. • **good morning!** ¡buenos días!; **tomorrow morning** mañana por la mañana.

morphine ['mɔːfiːn] *n* morfina.

morsel ['mɔːsəl] *n* bocado.

mortal ['mɔːtəl] *adj-n* mortal.

mortar ['mɔːtəʳ] *n* mortero.

mortgage ['mɔːgɪdʒ] *n* hipoteca. ► *vt* hipotecar. ■ **mortgage loan** préstamo hipotecario.

mosaic [məˈzeɪɪk] *adj* mosaico.

mosque [mɒsk] *n* mezquita.

mosquito [məsˈkiːtəʊ] *n* mosquito.

moss [mɒs] *n* musgo.

most [məʊst] *adj* **1** más. **2** la mayoría. ► *adv* más. ► *pron* **1** la mayor parte. **2** la mayoría.

mostly ['məʊstlɪ] *adv* principalmente.

motel [məʊˈtel] *n* motel.

moth [mɒθ] *n* **1** mariposa nocturna. **2** polilla.

mother ['mʌðəʳ] *n* madre. ■ **mother tongue** lengua materna.

motherhood ['mʌðəhʊd] *n* maternidad.

mother-in-law ['mʌðərɪnlɔː] *n* suegra.

motif [məʊˈtiːf] *n* motivo.

motion ['məʊʃən] *n* movimiento. • **in slow motion** a cámara lenta. ■ **motion picture** película.

motive ['məʊtɪv] *n* motivo.

motor ['məʊtəʳ] *n* motor. ■ **motor racing** carreras de coches.

motorbike ['məʊtəbaɪk] *n fam* moto.

motorboat ['məʊtəbəʊt] *n* lancha motora.

motorcycle ['məʊtəsaɪkəl] *n* motocicleta.

motorist ['məʊtərɪst] *n* automovilista.

motorway ['məʊtəweɪ] *n* GB autopista.

motto ['mɒtəʊ] *n* lema.

mould[1] [məʊld] *n* GB moho.

mould[2] [məʊld] *n* GB molde. ► *vt* GB moldear, modelar .

mount [maʊnt] *n* montura. ► *vt* **1** montar a *(caballo)*. **2** montar en *(bicicleta)*. **3** enmarcar *(foto)*.

mountain ['maʊntən] *n* montaña. ■ **mountain bike** bicicleta de montaña; **mountain range** cordillera, sierra.

mourn [mɔːn] *vt* **1** llorar la muerte de. **2** echar de menos.

mourning ['mɔːnɪŋ] *n* luto.

mouse [maʊs] *n* ratón.

moustache [məsˈtɑːʃ] *n* bigote.

mouth [maʊθ] *n* **1** boca. **2** desembocadura *(de río)*.

mouthful ['mauθful] *n* bocado.
move [mu:v] *n* movimiento.
► *vt-vi* mover(se).
movement ['mu:vmənt] *n* movimiento.
movie ['mu:vi] *n* US película.
mow [məu] *vt* segar, cortar.
mower ['məuə'] *n* cortacésped.
much [mʌtʃ] *adj* mucho,-a.
► *adv-pron* mucho. • **how much?** ¿cuánto?
mud [mʌd] *n* barro, lodo.
muddle ['mʌdəl] *n* lío.
mudguard ['mʌdgɑːd] *n* guardabarros.
mug [mʌg] *n* **1** taza. **2** jarra.
mule [mju:l] *n* mulo,-a.
multiple ['mʌltɪpəl] *adj* múltiple.
multiply ['mʌltɪplaɪ] *vt-vi* multiplicar(se).
mum [mʌm] *n* GB *fam* mamá.
mumps [mʌmps] *n* paperas.
murder ['mɜːdə'] *n* asesinato. ► *vt* asesinar.
murderer ['mɜːdərə'] *n* asesino,-a.
murmur ['mɜːmə'] *n* murmullo. ► *vt-vi* murmurar.
muscle ['mʌsəl] *n* músculo.
muse [mju:z] *n* musa.
museum [mju:'zɪəm] *n* museo.
mushroom ['mʌʃrum] *n* seta, hongo, champiñón.
music ['mju:zɪk] *n* música. ■ **music hall** teatro de variedades; **music score** partitura; **music stand** atril.

musical ['mju:zɪkəl] *adj-n* musical.
musician [mju:'zɪʃən] *n* músico,-a.
mussel ['mʌsəl] *n* mejillón.
must¹ [mʌst] *aux* **1** deber, tener que. **2** deber de. ► *n fam* cosa imprescindible.
must² [mʌst] *n* mosto.
mustard ['mʌstəd] *n* mostaza.
mute [mju:t] *adj-n* mudo,-a.
mutiny ['mju:tɪnɪ] *n* motín.
mutton ['mʌtən] *n* carne de oveja.
mutual ['mju:tʃuəl] *adj* mutuo,-a.
muzzle ['mʌzəl] *n* **1** hocico. **2** bozal.
my [maɪ] *adj* mi, mis.
myopia [maɪ'əupɪə] *n* miopía.
myself [maɪ'self] *pron* **1** me. **2** mí. • **by myself** yo mismo, -a, yo solo,-a.
mystery ['mɪstərɪ] *n* misterio.
myth [mɪθ] *n* mito.
mythology [mɪ'θɒlədʒɪ] *n* mitología.

N

nail [neɪl] *n* **1** uña. **2** clavo. ► *vt* clavar. ■ **nail file** lima de uñas; **nail varnish** esmalte de uñas; **nail varnish remover** quitaesmaltes.

naive [naɪ'iːv] *adj* ingenuo,-a.
naked ['neɪkɪd] *adj* desnudo,-a.
name [neɪm] *n* nombre.
nanny ['nænɪ] *n* niñera.
nap [næp] *n* siesta.
nape [neɪp] *n* nuca, cogote.
napkin ['næpkɪn] *n* servilleta.
nappy ['næpɪ] *n* GB pañal.
narcotic [nɑːˈkɒtɪk] *adj* narcótico,-a. ► *n* narcótico.
narrate [nəˈreɪt] *vt* narrar.
narrow ['nærəʊ] *adj* estrecho,-a. ► *vt-vi* estrechar(se).
narrow-minded [nærəʊˈmaɪndɪd] *adj* estrecho,-a de miras.
nasal ['neɪzəl] *adj* nasal.
nasty ['nɑːstɪ] *adj* **1** desagradable, asqueroso,-a. **2** malo,-a.
nation ['neɪʃən] *n* nación.
national ['næʃnəl] *adj* nacional.
nationality [næʃəˈnælɪtɪ] *n* nacionalidad.
nationalize [næʃnəˈlaɪz] *vt* nacionalizar.
nationwide ['neɪʃənwaɪd] *adj-adv* a escala nacional.
native ['neɪtɪv] *adj* **1** natal. **2** originario,-a. **3** materno. ► *n* nativo,-a.
natural ['nætʃərəl] *adj* natural.
nature ['neɪtʃəʳ] *n* naturaleza.
naught [nɔːt] *n* nada.
naughty ['nɔːtɪ] *adj* **1** travieso,-a. **2** atrevido,-a.
nausea ['nɔːzɪə] *n* náuseas.
nautical ['nɔːtɪkəl] *adj* náutico,-a.

naval ['neɪvəl] *adj* naval.
nave [neɪv] *n* nave central.
navel ['neɪvəl] *n* ombligo.
navigate ['nævɪgeɪt] *vt* navegar por.
navigation [nævɪˈgeɪʃən] *n* navegación.
navy ['neɪvɪ] *n* armada. ▪ **navy blue** azul marino.
near [nɪəʳ] *adj* **1** cercano,-a. **2** próximo,-a. ► *adv* **1** cerca. **2** a punto de. ► *prep* cerca de.
nearby ['nɪəbaɪ] *adj* cercano,-a. ► *adv* cerca.
nearly ['nɪəlɪ] *adv* casi.
neat [niːt] *adj* **1** ordenado,-a. **2** pulcro,-a. **3** claro,-a. **4** solo,-a.
necessary ['nesɪsərɪ] *adj* necesario,-a.
necessity [nɪˈsesɪtɪ] *n* necesidad.
neck [nek] *n* cuello.
necklace ['nekləs] *n* collar.
neckline ['neklaɪn] *n* escote.
nectar ['nektəʳ] *n* néctar.
née [neɪ] *adj* de soltera.
need [niːd] *n* necesidad. ► *vt* **1** necesitar. **2** tener que. ► *aux* tener que: *you needn't do it if you don't want to*, no tienes que hacerlo si no quieres. •**in need** necesitado; **to be in need of** necesitar.
needle ['niːdəl] *n* aguja.
needless ['niːdləs] *adj* innecesario,-a. • **needless to say** huelga decir.

negation [nɪ'geɪʃən] n negación.

negative ['negətɪv] adj negativo,-a. ► n 1 negativa. 2 negativo (de foto).

neglect [nɪ'glekt] n descuido. ► vt descuidar.

neglectful [nɪ'glektfʊl] adj negligente, descuidado,-a.

negligée ['neglɪʒeɪ] n salto de cama.

negligent ['neglɪdʒənt] adj negligente.

negotiate [nɪ'gəʊʃɪeɪt] vt-vi negociar.

negotiation [nɪgəʊʃɪ'eɪʃən] n negociación.

negro ['niːgrəʊ] adj-n negro,-a.

neighbour ['neɪbə'] (US **neighbor**) n vecino,-a.

neighbourhood ['neɪbəhʊd] (US **neighborhood**) n vecindad.

neither ['naɪðə', 'niːðə'] adj-pron ninguno de los dos, ninguna de las dos. ► adv-conj 1 ni. 2 tampoco: I can't swim. –Neither can I, No sé nadar. –Yo tampoco. • neither... nor... ni... ni...

neon ['niːən] n neón.

nephew ['nevjuː] n sobrino.

nerve [nɜːv] n 1 nervio. 2 valor. 3 descaro: you've got a nerve!, ¡qué cara tienes!

nervous ['nɜːvəs] adj nervioso,-a. ▪ nervous breakdown depresión nerviosa.

nest [nest] n nido. ► vi anidar.

nestle ['nesəl] vi acomodarse.

net¹ [net] n 1 red. 2 the Net la Red. ► vt coger con red. ▪ Net user internauta.

net² [net] adj neto,-a.

netball ['netbɔːl] n especie de baloncesto femenino.

netting ['netɪŋ] n malla.

nettle ['netəl] n ortiga. ► vt irritar.

network ['netwɜːk] n red.

neurotic [njʊ'rɒtɪk] adj-n neurótico,-a.

neuter ['njuːtə'] adj neutro,-a. ► n neutro.

neutral ['njuːtrəl] adj 1 neutro,-a. 2 POL neutral. ► n punto muerto.

never ['nevə'] adv nunca, jamás.

never-ending [nevə'rendɪŋ] adj interminable.

nevertheless [nevəðə'les] adv sin embargo.

new [njuː] adj nuevo,-a. • as good as new como nuevo; new to STH nuevo en algo. ▪ New Year Año Nuevo; New Year's Eve Nochevieja.

newborn ['njuːbɔːn] adj recién nacido,-a.

newcomer ['njuːkʌmə'] n recién llegado,-a.

newly ['njuːlɪ] adv recién, recientemente.

newlywed ['njuːlɪwed] n recién casado,-a.

news [njuːz] *n* noticias. • **to break the news to SB** dar la noticia a ALGN. ■ **a piece of news** una noticia; **news bulletin** boletín informativo.

newsagent ['njuːzeɪdʒənt] *n* vendedor,-ra de periódicos. ■ **newsagent's** quiosco de periódicos.

newsflash ['njuːzflæʃ] *n* noticia de última hora.

newsgroup ['njuːzgruːp] *n* grupo de noticias.

newsletter ['njuːzletər] *n* hoja informativa.

newspaper ['njuːspeɪpər] *n* diario, periódico.

newt [njuːt] *n* tritón.

next [nekst] *adj* **1** próximo,-a. **2** de al lado: *he lives next door*, vive en la casa de al lado. ► *adv* luego, después. • **next to** al lado de. ■ **next of kin** pariente(s) más cercano(s).

nibble ['nɪbəl] *n* **1** mordisco. **2** bocadito. ► *vt-vi* mordisquear.

nice [naɪs] *adj* **1** amable, simpático,-a. **2** agradable. **3** bonito,-a, guapo,-a.

niche [niːʃ] *n* nicho.

nick [nɪk] *n* mella, muesca.

nickel ['nɪkəl] *n* **1** níquel. **2** US moneda de cinco centavos.

nickname ['nɪkneɪm] *n* apodo. ► *vt* apodar.

niece [niːs] *n* sobrina.

night [naɪt] *n* noche. • **good night** buenas noches *(despedida)*; **last night** anoche.

nightclub ['naɪtklʌb] *n* discoteca.

nightdress ['naɪtdres] *n* camisón.

nightgown ['naɪtgaʊn] *n* camisón.

nightingale ['naɪtɪŋgeɪl] *n* ruiseñor.

nightmare ['naɪtmeər] *n* pesadilla.

nil [nɪl] *n* nada, cero.

nimble ['nɪmbəl] *adj* ágil.

nine [naɪn] *num* nueve.

nineteen [naɪn'tiːn] *num* diecinueve.

nineteenth [naɪn'tiːnθ] *adj* decimonoveno,-a.

ninety ['naɪntɪ] *num* noventa.

ninth [naɪnθ] *adj* noveno,-a.

nip [nɪp] *n* **1** pellizco. **2** mordisco. ► *vt-vi* **1** pellizcar. **2** mordisquear.

nipple ['nɪpəl] *n* **1** pezón. **2** tetilla.

nit [nɪt] *n* liendre.

nite [naɪt] *n* US → night.

no [nəʊ] *adv* no. ► *adj* ninguno,-a, ningún: *I have no time*, no tengo tiempo; *he's no friend of mine*, no es amigo mío.

noble ['nəʊbəl] *adj* noble. ► *n* noble.

nobody ['nəʊbədɪ] *pron* nadie.

nod [nɒd] *n* **1** saludo *(con la cabeza)*. **2** señal de asentimiento. ► *vi* **1** saludar *(con la cabeza)*. **2** asentir *(con la cabeza)*.

noise [nɔɪz] *n* ruido, sonido.

noisy ['nɔɪzɪ] *adj* ruidoso,-a.

nomad ['nəʊmæd] *adj-n* nómada.

nominal ['nɒmɪnəl] *adj* **1** nominal. **2** simbólico,-a *(precio)*.

nominate ['nɒmɪneɪt] *vt* **1** nombrar. **2** proponer.

nonchalant ['nɒnʃələnt] *adj* **1** despreocupado. **2** impasible.

nonconformist [nɒnkən'fɔːmɪst] *adj-n* inconformista.

none [nʌn] *pron* **1** ninguno,-a. **2** nadie. **3** nada.

nonexistent [nɒnɪg'zɪstənt] *adj* inexistente.

nonplussed [nɒn'plʌst] *adj* perplejo,-a.

nonsense ['nɒnsəns] *n* tonterías.

nonsmoker [nɒn'sməʊkə'] *n* no fumador,-ra.

nonstick [nɒn'stɪk] *adj* antiadherente.

nonstop [nɒn'stɒp] *adj* directo,-a: *a nonstop flight*, un vuelo directo. ► *adv* sin parar.

noodle ['nuːdəl] *n* fideo.

noon [nuːn] *n* mediodía.

noone ['nəʊwʌn] *pron* nadie.

nor [nɔː'] *conj* **1** ni. **2** tampoco: *nor do I*, yo tampoco.

norm [nɔːm] *n* norma.

normal ['nɔːməl] *adj* normal.

north [nɔːθ] *n* norte. ► *adj* del norte. ► *adv* al norte.

northern ['nɔːðən] *adj* del norte, septentrional.

nose [nəʊz] *n* **1** nariz. **2** hocico, morro. **3** olfato.

nosey ['nəʊzɪ] *adj fam* curioso,-a.

nostalgia [nɒ'stældʒɪə] *n* nostalgia.

nostril ['nɒstrɪl] *n* fosa nasal.

not [nɒt] *adv* no.

notation [nəʊ'teɪʃən] *n* notación.

notch [nɒtʃ] *n* muesca. ► *vt* hacer muescas en.

note [nəʊt] *vt* **1** notar, observar. **2** apuntar, anotar. ► *n* **1** nota. **2** GB billete *(de banco)*. • **to note down** apuntar, tomar nota.

notebook ['nəʊtbʊk] *n* **1** libreta, cuaderno. **2** ordenador portátil.

nothing ['nʌθɪŋ] *pron* nada. • **for nothing 1** gratis, gratuitamente. **2** en vano, en balde; **if nothing else** al menos; **nothing but** tan solo.

notice ['nəʊtɪs] *n* **1** letrero. **2** anuncio. **3** aviso. ► *vt* notar, fijarse en, darse cuenta de. • **to take no notice of** no hacer caso de; **until further notice** hasta nuevo aviso.

noticeboard ['nəʊtɪsbɔːd] *n* tablón de anuncios.

notify ['nəʊtɪfaɪ] *vt* notificar.
notion ['nəʊʃən] *n* noción.
notwithstanding [nɒtwɪθ-'stændɪŋ] *adv* no obstante. ► *prep* a pesar de.
nougat ['nuːgɑː] *n* turrón blando.
nought [nɔːt] *n* cero.
noun [naʊn] *n* nombre.
nourish ['nʌrɪʃ] *vt* nutrir.
novel ['nɒvəl] *n* novela.
novelty ['nɒvəltɪ] *n* novedad.
November [nəʊvembəʳ] *n* noviembre.
now [naʊ] *adv* 1 ahora. 2 hoy en día. • **from now on** de ahora en adelante; **now and then** de vez en cuando.
nowadays ['naʊədeɪz] *adv* hoy día, hoy en día.
nowhere ['nəʊweəʳ] *adv* en/a ninguna parte.
noxious ['nɒkʃəs] *adj* nocivo,-a.
nozzle ['nɒzəl] *n* boquilla.
nuance [njuːˈɒns] *n* matiz.
nuclear ['njuːklɪəʳ] *adj* nuclear.
nucleus ['njuːklɪəs] *n* núcleo.
nude [njuːd] *adj* desnudo,-a. ► *n* desnudo.
nugget ['nʌgɪt] *n* pepita.
nuisance ['njuːsəns] *n* 1 molestia, fastidio, lata. 2 pesado,-a.
null [nʌl] *adj* nulo,-a.
numb [nʌm] *adj* entumecido,-a. ► *vt* entumecer.
number ['nʌmbəʳ] *n* número.
numberplate ['nʌmbəpleɪt] *n*

GB placa de la matrícula.
nun [nʌn] *n* monja.
nunnery ['nʌnərɪ] *n* convento *(de monjas)*.
nurse [nɜːs] *n* 1 enfermero,-a. 2 niñera.
nursery ['nɜːsrɪ] *n* 1 vivero. 2 guardería.
nut [nʌt] *n* 1 fruto seco. 2 tuerca. 3 *fam* chalado,-a.
nutcracker ['nʌtkrækəʳ] *n* cascanueces.
nutmeg ['nʌtmeg] *n* nuez moscada.
nutritious [njuːˈtrɪʃəs] *adj* nutritivo,-a.
nutshell ['nʌtʃel] *n* cáscara.
nylon ['naɪlɒn] *n* nilón, nailon.

O

O [əʊ] *n* cero.
oak [əʊk] *n* roble.
oar [ɔːʳ] *n* remo.
oarsman ['ɔːzmən] *n* remero.
oasis [əʊˈeɪsɪs] *n* oasis.
oath [əʊθ] *n* juramento.
oats [əʊts] *npl* avena.
obedient [əˈbiːdɪənt] *adj* obediente.
obese [əʊˈbiːs] *adj* obeso,-a.
obey [əˈbeɪ] *vt* obedecer.
object ['ɒbdʒɪkt] *n* objeto.
objective [əbˈdʒektɪv] *adj* objetivo,-a. ► *n* objetivo.

obligation [ɒblɪˈgeɪʃən] *n* obligación.

oblige [əˈblaɪdʒ] *vt* **1** obligar. **2** hacer un favor a.

oblivion [əˈblɪvɪən] *n* olvido.

obscene [ɒbˈsiːn] *adj* obsceno,-a.

obscure [əbsˈkjʊəʳ] *adj* oscuro,-a.

observatory [əbˈzɜːvətrɪ] *n* observatorio.

observe [əbˈzɜːv] *vt* observar.

obsess [əbˈses] *vt* obsesionar.

obstacle [ˈɒbstəkəl] *n* obstáculo.

obstinate [ˈɒbstɪnət] *adj* obstinado,-a.

obstruct [əbˈstrʌkt] *vt* obstruir.

obtain [əbˈteɪn] *vt* obtener.

obvious [ˈɒbvɪəs] *adj* obvio,-a.

occasion [əˈkeɪʒən] *n* ocasión.

occult [ˈɒkʌlt] *adj* oculto,-a.

occupant [ˈɒkjʊpənt] *n* ocupante *(de silla, vehículo)*.

occupation [ɒkjʊˈpeɪʃən] *n* **1** ocupación. **2** pasatiempo.

occupy [ˈɒkjʊpaɪ] *vt* ocupar.

occur [əˈkɜːʳ] *vi* ocurrir.

ocean [ˈəʊʃən] *n* océano.

o'clock [əˈklɒk] *adv: it's one o'clock*, es la una.

October [ɒkˈtəʊbəʳ] *n* octubre.

octopus [ˈɒktəpəs] *n* pulpo.

odd [ɒd] *adj* **1** extraño,-a, raro,-a. **2** impar. **3**: *thirty odd*, treinta y pico, treinta y tantos.

odds [ɒdz] *npl* probabilidades.

odour [ˈəʊdəʳ] (US **odor**) *n* olor.

oesophagus [iːˈsɒfəgəs] (US **esophagus**) *n* esófago.

of [ɒv, unstressed əv] *prep* de.

off [ɒf] *prep* **1** de. **2** cerca. **3**: *there's a button off your coat*, a tu abrigo le falta un botón. ▶ *adv* **1**: *he ran off*, se fue corriendo. **2**: *two days off*, dos días libres. ▶ *adj* **1** ausente, de baja. **2** apagado,-a *(aparato)*. **3** malo,-a, pasado,-a, agrio,-a.

offence [əˈfens] *n* **1** ofensa. **2** infracción, delito.

offend [əˈfend] *vt* ofender.

offensive [əˈfensɪv] *adj* ofensivo,-a. ▶ *n* ofensiva.

offer [ˈɒfəʳ] *n* oferta. ▶ *vt* ofrecer. • **on offer** de oferta.

office [ˈɒfɪs] *n* **1** despacho, oficina. **2** cargo. • **in office** en el poder; **to take office** tomar posesión del cargo. ■ **office hours** horario de oficina; **office worker** oficinista.

officer [ˈɒfɪsəʳ] *n* **1** oficial *(militar)*. **2** agente, policía.

official [əˈfɪʃəl] *adj* oficial. ▶ *n* funcionario,-a.

off-key [ɒfˈkiː] *adj* desafinado,-a.

off-licence [ˈɒflaɪsəns] *n* GB tienda de bebidas alcohólicas.

off-line [ˈɒflaɪn] *adj* COMPUT desconectado,-a.

offshoot ['ɒfʃuːt] *n* vástago, retoño *(de planta, árbol)*.

offside [ɒfsaɪd] *adj-adv* fuera de juego.

offspring ['ɔːfsprɪŋ] *n* descendiente.

often ['ɒfən] *adv* a menudo. • **how often…?** ¿cada cuánto…?

oil [ɔɪl] *n* 1 aceite. 2 petróleo. 3 óleo, pintura al óleo. ▪ **oil rig** plataforma petrolífera; **oil slick** marea negra; **oil tanker** petrolero; **oil well** pozo petrolífero.

oilcloth ['ɔɪlklɒθ] *n* hule.

oilfield ['ɔɪlfiːld] *n* yacimiento petrolífero.

ointment ['ɔɪntmənt] *n* ungüento.

okay [əʊ'keɪ] *interj* ¡vale!, ¡de acuerdo! ▶ *adj-adv* bien. ▶ *n* visto bueno.

old [əʊld] *adj* viejo,-a. • **how old are you?** ¿cuántos años tienes?; **to be… years old** tener… años. ▪ **old age** vejez.

old-fashioned [əʊld'fæʃənd] *adj* anticuado,-a.

olive ['ɒlɪv] *n* aceituna, oliva. ▪ **olive oil** aceite de oliva.

omelette ['ɒmlət] (US **omelet**) *n* tortilla.

omit [əʊ'mɪt] *vt* omitir.

on [ɒn] *prep* 1 en. 2 sobre. 3: *on Sunday*, el domingo; *he got on the bus*, se subió al autobús; *he's on the phone*, está al teléfono. ▶ *adv* 1 conectado, -a, encendido,-a *(luz, aparato)*. 2 abierto,-a *(grifo)*. 3 puesto,-a. • **and so on** y así sucesivamente; **on and off** de vez en cuando; **on and on** sin parar.

once [wʌns] *adv* 1 una vez. 2 antes, anteriormente. ▶ *conj* una vez que. • **at once** 1 enseguida. 2 a la vez. 3 de una vez; **once and for all** de una vez para siempre; **once upon a time** érase una vez.

one [wʌn] *adj* un, una. ▶ *num* uno. ▶ *pron* uno,-a. • **one another** el uno al otro.

oneself [wʌn'self] *pron* uno,-a mismo,-a, sí mismo,-a. • **by oneself** solo.

one-way ['wʌnweɪ] *adj* 1 de sentido único *(calle)*. 2 de ida *(billete)*.

onion ['ʌnɪən] *n* cebolla.

on-line ['ɒn'laɪn] *adj* COMPUT en línea.

onlooker ['ɒnlʊkəʳ] *n* espectador,-ra.

only ['əʊnlɪ] *adj* único,-a. ▶ *adv* solo, solamente, únicamente. ▶ *conj* pero. • **if only** ojalá; **only just** apenas.

onto ['ɒntʊ] *prep* sobre.

onwards ['ɒnwədz] *adv* adelante, hacia adelante.

opaque [əʊ'peɪk] *adj* opaco,-a.

open ['əʊpən] *adj* abierto,-a. ▶ *vt-vi* abrir(se). ▪ **open season** temporada de caza.

open-air ['əʊpəneəʳ] *adj* al aire libre.
opener ['əʊpənəʳ] *n* abridor.
opening ['əʊpənɪŋ] *n* abertura. ▪ **opening hours** horario de apertura; **opening night** noche de estreno.
open-minded [əʊpən'maɪndɪd] *adj* tolerante, abierto.
opera ['ɒpərə] *n* ópera. ▪ **opera house** ópera.
operate ['ɒpəreɪt] *vt* hacer funcionar. ▶ *vi* operar. ▪ **operating theatre** quirófano.
operation [ɒpə'reɪʃən] *n* operación.
operator ['ɒpəreɪtəʳ] *n* **1** operador,-a, telefonista. **2** operario,-a.
opinion [ə'pɪnɪən] *n* opinión.
opponent [ə'pəʊnənt] *n* adversario,-a.
opportunity [ɒpə'tjuːnɪtɪ] *n* oportunidad.
oppose [ə'pəʊz] *vt* oponerse a.
opposite ['ɒpəzɪt] *adj* **1** de enfrente. **2** opuesto,-a, contrario,-a. ▶ *prep* enfrente de, frente a. ▶ *adv* enfrente.
opposition [ɒpə'zɪʃən] *n* oposición.
oppress [ə'pres] *vt* oprimir.
opt [ɒpt] *vi* optar.
optical ['ɒptɪkəl] *adj* óptico,-a.
optician [ɒp'tɪʃən] *n* óptico, -a. ▪ **optician's** óptica.
optimist ['ɒptɪmɪst] *n* optimista.

optimistic [ɒptɪ'mɪstɪk] *adj* optimista.
option ['ɒpʃən] *n* opción.
or [ɔːʳ] *conj* **1** o. **2** ni. ▪ **or else** de lo contrario, si no.
oral ['ɔːrəl] *adj* oral. ▶ *n* examen oral.
orange ['ɒrɪndʒ] *n* naranja. ▪ **orange blossom** azahar.
orbit ['ɔːbɪt] *n* órbita.
orchard ['ɔːtʃəd] *n* huerto.
orchestra ['ɔːkɪstrə] *n* orquesta.
orchid ['ɔːkɪd] *n* orquídea.
order ['ɔːdəʳ] *n* **1** orden. **2** pedido. ▶ *vt* **1** ordenar. **2** pedir. ▪ **in order to** para, a fin de; **"Out of order"** "No funciona".
ordinal ['ɔːdɪnəl] *adj* ordinal. ▶ *n* ordinal.
ordinary ['ɔːdɪnərɪ] *adj* normal, corriente.
oregano [ɒrɪ'gaːnəʊ] *n* orégano.
organ ['ɔːgən] *n* órgano.
organism ['ɔːgənɪzəm] *n* organismo.
organization [ɔːgənaɪ'zeɪʃən] *n* organización. ▪ **organization chart** organigrama.
organize ['ɔːgənaɪz] *vt-vi* organizar(se).
orientation [ɔːrɪen'teɪʃən] *n* orientación.
origin ['ɒrɪdʒɪn] *n* origen.
original [ə'rɪdʒɪnəl] *adj-n* original.

orphan ['ɔːfən] n huérfano,-a.

ostrich ['ɒstrɪtʃ] n avestruz.

other ['ʌðə'] adj-pron otro,-a.
• **other than** aparte de, salvo; **the others** los demás.

otherwise ['ʌðəwaɪz] adv 1 de otra manera. 2 por lo demás. ► conj si no, de lo contrario.

otter ['ɒtə'] n nutria.

ought [ɔːt] aux deber.

ounce [aʊns] n onza.

our ['aʊə'] adj nuestro,-a, nuestros,-as.

ours ['aʊəz] pron (el) nuestro, (la) nuestra, (los) nuestros, (las) nuestras.

ourselves [aʊə'selvz] pron 1 nos. 2 nosotros,-as mismos, -as. • **by ourselves** solos.

out [aʊt] adv 1 fuera, afuera. 2 equivocado,-a. 3: **white socks are out**, los calcetines blancos ya no se llevan. 4 apagado,-a (luz). 5 fuera, eliminado,-a (jugador). 6 despedido,-a. ► prep **out of** 1 fuera de. 2 de: **made out of wood**, hecho,-a de madera. 3 sin: **we're out of tea**, se nos ha acabado el té. 4 de cada: **eight women out of ten**, ocho de cada diez mujeres.

outboard ['aʊtbɔːd] adj fueraborda.

outbreak ['aʊtbreɪk] n 1 estallido (de guerra). 2 comienzo (de hostilidades). 3 brote (de epidemia).

outburst ['aʊtbɜːst] n explosión.

outcast ['aʊtkɑːst] n marginado,-a.

outcome ['aʊtkʌm] n resultado.

outdated [aʊt'deɪtɪd] adj anticuado,-a.

outdoor [aʊt'dɔː'] adj al aire libre. ► adv **outdoors** fuera.

outer ['aʊtə'] adj exterior.

outfit ['aʊtfɪt] n 1 conjunto, traje. 2 equipo, grupo.

outgoing [aʊt'gəʊɪŋ] adj 1 saliente, cesante. 2 sociable.

outing ['aʊtɪŋ] n salida, excursión.

outlaw ['aʊtlɔː] n forajido,-a, proscrito,-a. ► vt prohibir.

outlay ['aʊtleɪ] n desembolso.

outlet ['aʊtlet] n 1 salida. 2 desagüe.

outline ['aʊtlaɪn] n 1 contorno. 2 resumen, esbozo. ► vt 1 perfilar. 2 resumir.

outlook ['aʊtlʊk] n 1 vista. 2 punto de vista.

outlying ['aʊtlaɪɪŋ] adj alejado,-a, remoto,-a.

outnumber [aʊt'nʌmbə'] vt exceder en número.

outpatient ['aʊtpeɪʃənt] n paciente externo,-a.

output ['aʊtpʊt] n 1 producción, rendimiento. 2 COMPUT salida.

outrage ['aʊtreɪdʒ] n indignación. ► vt ultrajar, atropellar.

outright ['aʊtraɪt] *adj* absoluto,-a.

outside [*(n-prep-adv)* aʊt'saɪd, *(adj)* 'aʊtsaɪd] *n* exterior. ▸ *prep* fuera de. ▸ *adv* fuera, afuera. ▸ *adj* exterior.

outsider [aʊt'saɪdə'] *n* forastero,-a.

outskirts ['aʊtskɜːts] *npl* afueras.

outstanding [aʊt'stændɪŋ] *adj* **1** destacado,-a. **2** pendiente.

outward ['aʊtwəd] *adj* **1** externo,-a. **2** de ida *(viaje)*. ▸ *adv* (**outward** o **outwards**) hacia fuera, hacia afuera.

oval ['əʊvəl] *adj* oval, ovalado,-a. ▸ *n* óvalo.

ovary ['əʊvərɪ] *n* ovario.

oven ['ʌvən] *n* horno.

over ['əʊvə'] *adv*: *come over here*, ven aquí; *over there*, allí; *he fell over*, se cayó. ▸ *adj* acabado,-a. ▸ *prep* **1** encima de, por encima de. **2** más de. **3** al otro lado de. **5** durante. **6** por. • **over and over again** una y otra vez; **over here** aquí; **over there** allí.

overall [*(adj)* 'əʊvərɔːl, *(adv)* əʊvər'ɔːl] *adj* global, total. ▸ *adv* **1** en total. **2** en conjunto. ▸ *npl* **overalls** mono.

overboard ['əʊvəbɔːd] *adv* por la borda.

overcame [əʊvə'keɪm] *pt* → overcome.

overcast ['əʊvəkɑːst] *adj* cubierto,-a, nublado,-a.

overcoat ['əʊvəkəʊt] *n* abrigo.

overcome [əʊvə'kʌm] *vt* **1** vencer, superar. **2** abrumar.

overdose ['əʊvədəʊs] *n* sobredosis.

overexposed [əʊvərɪk'spəʊʒd] *adj* sobreexpuesto,-a.

overflow [əʊvə'fləʊ] *vi* desbordarse.

overhaul [*(n)* 'əʊvəhɔːl, *(vb)* əʊvə'hɔːl] *n* revisión general. ▸ *vt* repasar, revisar.

overheat [əʊvə'hiːt] *vi* recalentarse.

overjoyed [əʊvə'dʒɔɪd] *adj* encantadísimo,-a.

overland ['əʊvəlænd] *adj-adv* por tierra.

overlap [əʊvə'læp] *vi* superponerse.

overleaf [əʊvə'liːf] *adv* al dorso, a la vuelta.

overlook [əʊvə'lʊk] *vt* **1** pasar por alto, no notar. **2** hacer la vista gorda a, disculpar, dejar pasar. **3** dar a, tener vistas a.

overnight [əʊvə'naɪt] *adj* de una noche. ▸ *adv* por la noche. • **to stay overnight** pasar la noche.

overran [əʊvə'ræn] *pt* → overrun.

overrate [əʊvə'reɪt] *vt* sobrevalorar.

overrule [əʊvə'ruːl] *vt* **1** desautorizar. **2** denegar.

overrun [əʊvə'rʌn] *vt* invadir. ► *vi* durar más de lo previsto.

overseas [əʊvə'si:z] *adj* de ultramar, del extranjero. ► *adv* en ultramar, en el extranjero.

oversee [əʊvə'si:] *vt* supervisar.

overshadow [əʊvə'ʃædəʊ] *vt fig* eclipsar, ensombrecer.

oversight ['əʊvəsaɪt] *n* descuido.

oversleep [əʊvə'sli:p] *vi* dormirse, quedarse dormido.

overstep [əʊvə'step] *vt* sobrepasar, pasar de.

overt ['əʊvɜːt, əʊ'vɜːt] *adj* declarado,-a, abierto,-a.

overtake [əʊvə'teɪk] *vt* adelantar.

overthrow [əʊvə'θrəʊ] *vt* derribar, derrocar.

overtime ['əʊvətaɪm] *n* horas extraordinarias, horas extra.

overture ['əʊvətjʊəʳ] *n* obertura.

overturn [əʊvə'tɜːn] *vt-vi* volcar.

overweight [əʊvə'weɪt] *adj* demasiado gordo,-a. • **to be overweight** tener exceso de peso.

overwhelm [əʊvə'welm] *vt* **1** arrollar, aplastar. **2** *fig* abrumar.

overwhelming [əʊvə'welmɪŋ] *adj* aplastante, arrollador,-ra.

overwork [əʊvə'wɜːk] *vi* trabajar demasiado. ► *vt* hacer trabajar demasiado.

overwrought [əʊvə'rɔːt] *adj* muy nervioso,-a.

ovulation [ɒvjʊ'leɪʃən] *n* ovulación.

ovum ['əʊvəm] *n* óvulo.

owe [əʊ] *vt* deber.

owing ['əʊɪŋ] *adj* que se debe. • **owing to** debido a, a causa de.

owl [aʊl] *n* búho, mochuelo, lechuza.

own [əʊn] *adj* propio,-a: *he has his own car*, tiene su propio coche. ► *pron*: *my/your/ his own*, lo mío/ tuyo/ suyo; *a room of my own*, una habitación para mí solo. ► *vt* poseer, ser dueño,-a de, tener. • **on one's own** solo, sin ayuda: *can you do it on your own?*, ¿puedes hacerlo solo?

to own up *vi* confesar.

owner ['əʊnəʳ] *n* dueño,-a, propietario,-a, poseedor,-ra.

ownership ['əʊnəʃɪp] *n* propiedad, posesión.

ox [ɒks] *n* buey.

oxide ['ɒksaɪd] *n* óxido.

oxidize ['ɒksɪdaɪz] *vt-vi* oxidar(se).

oxygen ['ɒksɪdʒən] *n* oxígeno. ▪ **oxygen mask** máscara de oxígeno.

oyster ['ɔɪstəʳ] *n* ostra.

oz [aʊns, 'aʊnsɪz] *abbr (ounce)* onza.

ozone ['əʊzəʊn] *n* ozono. ▪ **ozone layer** capa de ozono.

P

pace [peɪs] *n* **1** paso. **2** marcha, ritmo.

pacemaker ['peɪsmeɪkəʳ] *n* **1** liebre *(en carrera)*. **2** marcapasos.

pacific [pə'sɪfɪk] *adj* pacífico,-a.

pacify ['pæsɪfaɪ] *vt* pacificar, apaciguar.

pack [pæk] *n* **1** paquete. **2** baraja. **3** banda *(de ladrones)*. ► *vt* **1** empaquetar. **2** hacer *(maleta)*. **3** apretar.

package ['pækɪdʒ] *n* paquete. ▪ **package tour** viaje organizado.

packaging ['pækɪdʒɪŋ] *n* embalaje.

packet ['pækɪt] *n* paquete.

pact [pækt] *n* pacto.

pad [pæd] *n* **1** almohadilla. **2** taco, bloc *(de papel)*.

paddle ['pædəl] *n* pala *(para remar)*. ► *vt-vi* remar con pala.

padlock ['pædlɒk] *n* candado. ► *vt* cerrar con candado.

pagan ['peɪgən] *adj-n* pagano,-a.

page [peɪdʒ] *n* página.

paid [peɪd] *pt-pp* → pay.

pain [peɪn] *n* dolor. • **on pain of** so pena de.

painful ['peɪnfʊl] *adj* doloroso,-a.

painkiller ['peɪnkɪləʳ] *n* calmante, analgésico.

painless ['peɪnləs] *adj* indoloro,-a.

paint [peɪnt] *n* pintura. ► *vt-vi* pintar.

paintbrush ['peɪntbrʌʃ] *n* **1** brocha. **2** pincel.

painter ['peɪntəʳ] *n* pintor,-ra.

painting ['peɪntɪŋ] *n* **1** pintura. **2** cuadro.

pair [peəʳ] *n* **1** par. **2** pareja.

pajamas [pə'dʒæməz] *npl* US pijama.

pal [pæl] *n fam* camarada.

palace ['pæləs] *n* palacio.

palate ['pælət] *n* paladar.

pale [peɪl] *adj* pálido,-a.

palm[1] [pɑːm] *n* palma *(de la mano)*.

palm[2] [pɑːm] *n* palmera.

paltry ['pɔːltrɪ] *adj* mísero,-a, mezquino,-a.

pamper ['pæmpəʳ] *vt* mimar.

pamphlet ['pæmflət] *n* **1** folleto *(publicitario)*. **2** panfleto *(político)*.

pan [pæn] *n* cazo, olla.

pancake ['pænkeɪk] *n* crepe.

pancreas ['pæŋkrɪəs] *n* páncreas.

panda ['pændə] *n* oso panda, panda.

panel ['pænəl] *n* panel.

panic ['pænɪk] *n* pánico.

panther ['pænθəʳ] *n* pantera.

panties ['pæntɪz] *npl* bragas.

pantry ['pæntrɪ] *n* despensa.

pants [pænts] *npl* **1** calzoncillos. **2** bragas. **3** US pantalón.

paper ['peɪpə'] *n* papel. ► *vt* empapelar. • **on paper 1** por escrito. **2** sobre el papel.

paperclip ['peɪpəklɪp] *n* clip.

paperweight ['peɪpəweɪt] *n* pisapapeles.

paperwork ['peɪpəwɜːk] *n* papeleo.

par [pɑː'] *n* par *(en golf)*.

parachute ['pærəʃuːt] *n* paracaídas.

parade [pə'reɪd] *n* desfile. ► *vi* desfilar.

paradise ['pærədaɪs] *n* paraíso.

paragraph ['pærəgrɑːf] *n* párrafo.

parakeet ['pærəkiːt] *n* periquito.

parallel ['pærəlel] *adj* paralelo,-a. ► *n* **1** paralelo. **2** paralela.

paralysis [pə'rælɪsɪs] *n* parálisis.

parasite ['pærəsaɪt] *n* parásito,-a.

parasol [pærə'sɒl] *n* sombrilla.

parcel ['pɑːsəl] *n* paquete.

parchment ['pɑːtʃmənt] *n* pergamino.

pardon ['pɑːdən] *n* perdón. ► *vt* perdonar. • **I beg your pardon** le ruego me disculpe, perdón; **pardon?** ¿perdón?, ¿cómo dice?

pare [peə'] *vt* **1** pelar *(fruta)*. **2** cortar *(uñas)*.

parent ['peərənt] *n* padre, madre. ► *npl* **parents** padres.

parenthesis [pə'renθəsɪs] *n* paréntesis.

parish ['pærɪʃ] *n* parroquia.

park [pɑːk] *n* parque. ► *vt-vi* aparcar.

parking ['pɑːkɪŋ] *n* aparcamiento. • **"No parking"** "Prohibido aparcar". ■ **parking lot** US aparcamiento; **parking meter** parquímetro; **parking place** sitio para aparcar.

parliament ['pɑːləmənt] *n* parlamento.

parlour ['pɑːlə'] (US **parlor**) *n* salón.

parole [pə'rəʊl] *n* libertad condicional. • **on parole** en libertad condicional.

parquet ['pɑːkeɪ] *n* parqué.

parrot ['pærət] *n* loro.

parsley ['pɑːslɪ] *n* perejil.

parson ['pɑːsən] *n* párroco.

part [pɑːt] *n* **1** parte. **2** pieza *(de máquina)*. **3** papel *(en obra, etc)*. ► *vt-vi* separar(se).

partial ['pɑːʃəl] *adj* parcial.

participate [pɑː'tɪsɪpeɪt] *vi* participar.

participle ['pɑːtɪsɪpəl] *n* participio.

particle ['pɑːtɪkəl] *n* partícula.

particular [pə'tɪkjʊlə'] *adj* particular. ► *npl* **particulars** detalles, datos.

parting ['pɑːtɪŋ] *n* **1** despedida. **2** raya *(en pelo)*.

partition [pɑː'tɪʃən] *n* **1** partición. **2** tabique.

partner ['pɑːtnəʳ] *n* **1** compañero,-a. **2** socio,-a *(en negocio)*. **3** compañero,-ra. **4** pareja.

part-time [pɑːt'taɪm] *adj* de media jornada. ► *adv* a tiempo parcial.

party ['pɑːtɪ] *n* **1** fiesta. **2** partido *(político)*. **3** parte *(en contrato, etc)*.

pass [pɑːs] *n* **1** pase. **2** aprobado. ► *vt-vi* **1** pasar. **2** aprobar.

to pass by *vi* pasar cerca.

to pass out *vi* desmayarse.

passage ['pæsɪdʒ] *n* **1** pasaje. **2** paso *(de vehículo, tiempo)*.

passenger ['pæsɪndʒəʳ] *n* pasajero,-a.

passer-by [pɑːsə'baɪ] *n* transeúnte.

passion ['pæʃən] *n* pasión.

passive ['pæsɪv] *adj* pasivo, -a. ► *n* voz pasiva.

passport ['pɑːspɔːt] *n* pasaporte.

password ['pɑːswɜːd] *n* contraseña.

past [pɑːst] *adj* **1** pasado,-a. **2** último,-a. ► *adv* por delante. ► *n* pasado. ► *prep* **1** más allá de. **2** por delante de. **3** y: *five past six*, las seis y cinco. ■ **past participle** participio pasado; **past tense** pasado.

pasta ['pæstə] *n* pasta.

paste [peɪst] *n* **1** pasta. **2** engrudo; cola. ► *vt* pegar.

pastel ['pæstəl] *n* pastel.

pastime ['pɑːstaɪm] *n* pasatiempo.

pastry ['peɪstrɪ] *n* **1** masa. **2** pastel, pasta.

pasture ['pɑːstʃəʳ] *n* pasto.

pasty ['pæstɪ] *n* empanada.

patch [pætʃ] *n* parche.

pâté ['pæteɪ] *n* paté.

patent ['peɪtənt] *adj-n* patente. ► *vt* patentar. ■ **patent leather** charol.

paternity [pə'tɜːnɪtɪ] *n* paternidad.

path [pɑːθ] *n* camino, sendero.

pathway ['pɑːθweɪ] *n* camino, sendero.

patience ['peɪʃəns] *n* paciencia.

patient ['peɪʃənt] *adj* paciente. ► *n* paciente.

patio ['pætɪəʊ] *n* patio.

patrimony ['pætrɪmənɪ] *n* patrimonio.

patriot ['peɪtrɪət] *n* patriota.

patrol [pə'trəʊl] *n* patrulla. ► *vi-vt* patrullar. ■ **patrol car** coche patrulla.

patron ['peɪtrən] *adj*. ■ **patron saint** patrón,-ona.

pattern ['pætən] *n* **1** modelo. **2** patrón *(en costura)*. **3** dibujo, diseño *(en tela)*.

pause [pɔːz] *n* pausa.

pavement ['peɪvmənt] *n* acera.

pavillion [pə'vɪlɪən] *n* pabellón.

paw [pɔː] *n* **1** pata *(de animal)*. **2** garra, zarpa *(de tigre)*.

pawn¹ [pɔːn] *n* peón.

pawn² [pɔːn] vt empeñar.
pay [peɪ] n paga, sueldo. ► vt-vi pagar. ■ **pay phone** teléfono público.
to pay back vt devolver.
payment ['peɪmənt] n pago.
payroll ['peɪrəʊl] n nómina.
payslip ['peɪslɪp] n nómina.
pea [piː] n guisante.
peace [piːs] n paz.
peach [piːtʃ] n melocotón.
peacock ['piːkɒk] n pavo real.
peak [piːk] n 1 cima, pico (de montaña). 2 visera (de gorra). ► adj máximo,-a. ■ **peak hour** hora punta; **peak period** período de tarifa máxima; **peak season** temporada alta.
peanut ['piːnʌt] n cacahuete.
pear [peəʳ] n pera.
pearl [pɜːl] n perla.
peasant ['pezənt] n campesino,-a.
pebble ['pebəl] n guijarro.
peck [pek] vt picotear.
pedagogy ['pedəgɒdʒɪ] n pedagogía.
pedal ['pedəl] n pedal. ► vi pedalear.
peddler ['pedləʳ] n vendedor, -ra ambulante.
pedestrian [pɪ'destrɪən] n peatón. ■ **pedestrian crossing** paso de peatones; **pedestrian precinct** zona peatonal.
pediatrician [piːdɪə'trɪʃən] n pediatra.
peel [piːl] n piel. ► vt pelar.

peep [piːp] n ojeada, vistazo.
peep-hole ['piːphəʊl] n mirilla.
peg [peg] n 1 pinza (de colgar ropa). 2 percha, colgador.
pelican ['pelɪkən] n pelícano.
pellet ['pelɪt] n perdigón.
pelvis ['pelvɪs] n pelvis.
pen¹ [pen] n 1 bolígrafo. 2 pluma.
pen² [pen] n corral.
penalty ['penəltɪ] n 1 pena. 2 penalti. ■ **penalty area** área de castigo.
pence [pens] npl → penny.
pencil ['pensəl] n lápiz. ■ **pencil case** plumier; **pencil sharpener** sacapuntas.
penetrate ['penɪtreɪt] vt penetrar.
penguin ['peŋgwɪn] n pingüino.
peninsula [pə'nɪnsjʊlə] n península.
penis ['piːnɪs] n pene.
penknife ['pennaɪf] n 1 cortaplumas. 2 navaja.
penny ['penɪ] n 1 GB penique. 2 US centavo.
pension ['penʃən] n pensión.
pensioner ['penʃənəʳ] n jubilado,-a, pensionista.
penthouse ['penthaʊs] n ático.
people ['piːpəl] npl gente, personas.
pepper ['pepəʳ] n 1 pimienta. 2 pimiento.
peppermint ['pepəmɪnt] n 1 menta. 2 hierbabuena.

per [pɜːʳ] *prep* por.

percentage [pəˈsentɪdʒ] *n* porcentaje.

perception [pəˈsepʃən] *n* percepción.

perch [pɜːtʃ] *n* perca.

percolator [ˈpɜːkəleɪtəʳ] *n* cafetera de filtro.

perfect [ˈpɜːfɪkt] *adj* perfecto,-a.

perfection [pəˈfekʃən] *n* perfección.

perform [pəˈfɔːm] *vt* 1 hacer, realizar. 2 interpretar *(música)*. 3 representar *(obra de teatro)*. ► *vi* actuar *(actor)*.

performance [pəˈfɔːməns] *n* 1 ejecución. 2 interpretación, actuación *(de cantante, actor)*. 3 representación *(de obra)*. 4 rendimiento *(de coche)*.

performer [pəˈfɔːməʳ] *n* intérprete.

perfume [ˈpɜːfjuːm] *n* perfume.

perhaps [pəˈhæps] *adv* quizá, quizás, tal vez.

period [ˈpɪərɪəd] *n* 1 período. 2 clase. 3 US punto final.

peripheral [pəˈrɪfərəl] *n* COMPUT unidad periférica.

perishable [ˈperɪʃəbəl] *adj* perecedero,-a.

permanent [ˈpɜːmənənt] *adj* permanente.

permission [pəˈmɪʃən] *n* permiso.

permit [ˈpɜːmɪt] *vt* permitir.

perpendicular [pɜːpənˈdɪkjuləʳ] *adj-n* perpendicular.

persecution [pɜːsɪˈkjuːʃən] *n* persecución.

persist [pəˈsɪst] *vi* persistir.

person [ˈpɜːsən] *n* persona.

personal [ˈpɜːsənəl] *adj* personal. ■ **personal computer** ordenador personal; **personal organizer** agenda personal.

personnel [pɜːsəˈnel] *n* personal.

perspective [pəˈspektɪv] *n* perspectiva.

perspiration [pɜːspɪˈreɪʃən] *n* transpiración, sudor.

persuade [pəˈsweɪd] *vt* persuadir, convencer.

perversion [pəˈvɜːʃən] *n* 1 perversión. 2 tergiversación.

pervert [pəˈvɜːt] *vt* 1 pervertir. 2 tergiversar *(verdad, etc)*.

pessimism [ˈpesɪmɪzəm] *n* pesimismo.

pessimist [ˈpesɪmɪst] *n* pesimista.

pest [pest] *n* 1 insecto nocivo, plaga. 2 *fam* pelma.

pester [ˈpestəʳ] *vt* molestar.

pet [pet] *n* animal doméstico.

petal [ˈpetəl] *n* pétalo.

petition [pəˈtɪʃən] *n* petición

petrol [ˈpetrəl] *n* gasolina. ■ **petrol pump** surtidor de gasolina; **petrol station** gasolinera; **petrol tank** depósito de gasolina.

picture

petticoat ['petɪkəʊt] *n* **1** enaguas. **2** combinación.

petty ['petɪ] *adj* **1** insignificante. **2** mezquino,-a. ▪ **petty cash** dinero para gastos menores.

phantom ['fæntəm] *n* fantasma.

pharmacy ['fɑːməsɪ] *n* farmacia.

phase [feɪz] *n* fase.

pheasant ['fezənt] *n* faisán.

phenomenon [fɪ'nɒmɪnən] *n* fenómeno.

philosopher [fɪ'lɒsəfə'] *n* filósofo,-a.

philosophy [fɪ'lɒsəfɪ] *n* filosofía.

phobia ['fəʊbɪə] *n* fobia.

phone [fəʊn] *n-vt-vi fam* → telephone. ▪ **phone book** listín telefónico; **phone box** cabina telefónica.

phonecard ['fəʊnkɑːd] *n* tarjeta telefónica.

phonetics [fə'netɪks] *n* fonética.

photo ['fəʊtəʊ] *n fam* foto.

photocopier ['fəʊtəʊkɒpɪə'] *n* fotocopiadora.

photocopy ['fəʊtəʊkɒpɪ] *n* fotocopia. ▶ *vt* fotocopiar.

photograph ['fəʊtəgrɑːf] *n* fotografía. ▶ *vt-vi* fotografiar.

photographer [fə'tɒgrəfə'] *n* fotógrafo,-a.

photography [fə'tɒgrəfɪ] *n* fotografía.

phrasal verb [freɪzəl'vɜːb] *n* verbo con partícula.

phrase [freɪz] *n* frase.

physical ['fɪzɪkəl] *adj* físico,-a. ▪ **physical education** educación física.

physician [fɪ'zɪʃən] *n* médico,-a.

physicist ['fɪzɪsɪst] *n* físico,-a.

physics ['fɪzɪks] *n* física.

physiology [fɪzɪ'ɒlədʒɪ] *n* fisiología.

physiotherapy [fɪzɪəʊ'θerəpɪ] *n* fisioterapia.

pianist ['pɪənɪst] *n* pianista.

piano [pɪ'ænəʊ] *n* piano.

pick [pɪk] *vt* **1** escoger, elegir. **2** coger *(flores, fruta)*. **3** forzar *(cerradura)*.

to pick on *vt* meterse con.

to pick out *vt* **1** escoger. **2** distinguir.

to pick up *vt* **1** coger, recoger. **2** ir a buscar. **3** captar *(emisora de radio)*. **4** aprender *(lengua)*.

picket ['pɪkɪt] *n* piquete.

pickle ['pɪkəl] *n* **1** encurtido, escabeche. **2** aprieto. ▶ *vt* encurtir, escabechar.

pickpocket ['pɪkpɒkɪt] *n* carterista.

pick-up ['pɪkʌp] *n* **1** brazo del tocadiscos. **2** furgoneta.

picnic ['pɪknɪk] *n* merienda, picnic. ▶ *vi* ir de picnic.

picture ['pɪktʃə'] *n* **1** pintura, cuadro. **2** dibujo. **3** fotografía. **4** película. **5** imagen. ▶ vt **1** pintar, retratar. **2** imaginar, imaginarse. • **to take a picture** hacer una foto.

picturesque [pɪktʃəˈresk] *adj* pintoresco,-a.

pie [paɪ] *n* **1** pastel, tarta *(dulce)*. **2** pastel, empanada *(salado)*.

piece [piːs] *n* **1** trozo, pedazo. **2** pieza. **3** moneda. • **to take to pieces** desmontar; **in one piece 1** sano y salvo *(persona)*. **2** intacto,-a *(objeto)*.

pier [pɪəʳ] *n* muelle.

pierce [pɪəs] *vt* perforar.

pig [pɪg] *n* cerdo,-a.

pigeon [ˈpɪdʒɪn] *n* paloma.

pigeonhole [ˈpɪdʒɪnhəʊl] *n* casilla.

piglet [ˈpɪglət] *n* cochinillo.

pigment [ˈpɪgmənt] *n* pigmento.

pigsty [ˈpɪgstaɪ] *n* pocilga.

pigtail [ˈpɪgteɪl] *n* trenza.

pile [paɪl] *n* montón, pila.

pile-up [ˈpaɪlʌp] *n* choque en cadena.

piles [paɪlz] *npl* hemorroides.

pilgrim [ˈpɪlgrɪm] *n* peregrino,-a.

pill [pɪl] *n* píldora, pastilla.

pillar [ˈpɪləʳ] *n* pilar, columna.

pillow [ˈpɪləʊ] *n* almohada.

pilot [ˈpaɪlət] *adj-n* piloto. ▶ vt pilotar.

pimple [ˈpɪmpəl] *n* grano.

pin [pɪn] *n* **1** alfiler. **2** clavija.

pinafore [ˈpɪnəfɔːʳ] *n* delantal.

pincers [ˈpɪnsəz] *npl* **1** tenazas. **2** pinzas *(de cangrejo)*.

pinch [pɪntʃ] *n* **1** pellizco. **2** pizca. ▶ vt **1** pellizcar. **2** apretar *(zapatos)*.

pine [paɪn] *n* pino. ▪ **pine cone** piña; **pine nut** piñón.

pineapple [ˈpaɪnæpəl] *n* piña.

ping-pong [ˈpɪŋpɒŋ] *n* tenis de mesa, pimpón.

pink [pɪŋk] *adj-n* rosa. ▶ *n* clavel.

pint [paɪnt] *n* pinta.

pioneer [paɪəˈnɪəʳ] *n* pionero,-a.

pipe [paɪp] *n* **1** tubería, cañería *(de agua, gas)*. **2** pipa *(para fumar)*. ▶ *npl* **pipes** gaita.

pipeline [ˈpaɪplaɪn] *n* **1** tubería. **2** gasoducto. **3** oleoducto.

pirate [ˈpaɪərət] *n* pirata.

pistol [ˈpɪstəl] *n* pistola.

piston [ˈpɪstən] *n* pistón.

pit¹ [pɪt] *n* **1** hoyo, foso. **2** mina.

pit² [pɪt] *n* US hueso *(de fruta)*.

pitch [pɪtʃ] *n* **1** MUS tono. **2** campo, terreno *(de juego)*. ▶ vt **1** tirar, lanzar. **2** plantar, armar *(tienda de campaña)*.

pitcher¹ [ˈpɪtʃəʳ] *n* **1** GB cántaro. **2** US jarro.

pitcher² [ˈpɪtʃəʳ] *n* US lanzador,-ra *(de béisbol)*.

pitchfork [ˈpɪtʃfɔːk] *n* horca.

pity [ˈpɪtɪ] *n* pena, lástima.

pivot [ˈpɪvət] *n* pivote, eje.

pizza [ˈpiːtsə] *n* pizza.

placard ['plækɑːd] *n* pancarta.
placate [plə'keit] *vt* aplacar.
place [pleis] *n* **1** lugar, sitio. **2** asiento, sitio. **3** plaza *(en escuela, etc)*. ► *vt* colocar, poner, situar. ● **in place of** en vez de.
placenta [plə'sentə] *n* placenta.
plague [pleig] *n* plaga.
plain [plein] *adj* **1** claro,-a. **2** sencillo,-a. **3** liso,-a *(tejido)*. **4** sin leche *(chocolate)*. ► *n* llanura. ● **to make STH plain** dejar algo bien claro. ■ **plain yoghurt** yogur natural.
plaintiff ['pleintif] *n* demandante.
plait [plæt] *n* trenza.
plan [plæn] *n* **1** plan. **2** plano. ► *vt* planear, planificar.
plane[1] [plein] *n* **1** plano. **2** avión.
plane[2] [plein] *n* cepillo.
plane[3] [plein] *n* plátano *(árbol)*.
planet ['plænət] *n* planeta.
plank [plæŋk] *n* tablón, tabla.
plant [plɑːnt] *n* planta. ► *vt* plantar. ■ **plant pot** maceta, tiesto.
plaque [plæk] *n* placa.
plasma ['plæzmə] *n* plasma.
plaster ['plɑːstə'] *n* **1** yeso. **2** MED escayola. **3** esparadrapo, tirita®. ► *vt* enyesar. ■ **plaster cast** escayola.
plastic ['plæstik] *adj* plástico,-a. ► *n* plástico.
plasticine® ['plæstisiːn] *n* plastilina®.

plate [pleit] *n* **1** plato. **2** placa.
plateau ['plætəʊ] *n* meseta.
platform ['plætfɔːm] *n* **1** plataforma. **2** andén.
platoon [plə'tuːn] *n* pelotón.
play [plei] *n* **1** juego. **2** obra de teatro. ► *vt-vi* **1** jugar. **2** tocar: *he plays the piano*, toca el piano. ► *vt* **1** interpretar. **2** jugar a: *she plays tennis*, juega al tenis. **3** jugar contra *(equipo, adversario)*. **4** poner *(disco)*. ■ **play on words** juego de palabras.
player ['pleiə'] *n* **1** jugador,-ra. **2** actor, actriz. **3** músico,-a: *a piano player*, un pianista.
playground ['pleigraund] *n* patio de recreo.
playing field ['pleiŋfiːld] *n* campo de juego.
playmate ['pleimeit] *n* compañero,-a de juego.
play-off ['pleiɒf] *n* partido de desempate.
playtime ['pleitaim] *n* recreo.
plea [pliː] *n* petición, súplica.
plead [pliːd] *vi* suplicar. ► *vt* alegar. ● **to plead guilty** declararse culpable; **to plead not guilty** declararse inocente.
pleasant ['plezənt] *adj* **1** agradable *(tiempo)*. **2** simpático,-a, amable *(persona)*.
please [pliːz] *vt-vi* agradar, gustar. ► *interj* por favor. ● **as you please** como quieras.

pleased [pli:zd] *adj* contento, -a, satisfecho,-a. • **pleased to meet you!** ¡encantado,-a!, ¡mucho gusto!; **to be pleased to do STH** alegrarse de hacer algo.

pleasure ['pleʒəʳ] *n* placer. • **it's my pleasure** de nada, no hay de qué.

pleat [pli:t] *n* pliegue.

pledge [pledʒ] *n* **1** promesa. **2** prenda, señal.

plenty ['plentɪ] *n* abundancia. ► *pron* **1** muchos,-as. **2** de sobra.

pliers ['plaɪəz] *npl* alicates.

plot[1] [plɒt] *n* **1** complot. **2** trama, argumento.

plot[2] [plɒt] *n* parcela, terreno.

plough [plaʊ] *n* GB arado. ► *vt-vi* GB arar.

plow [plaʊ] *n-vt-vi* US → plough.

pluck [plʌk] *vt* **1** arrancar *(flor)*. **2** desplumar *(ave)*. • **to pluck one's eyebrows** depilarse las cejas.

plug [plʌg] *n* **1** tapón. **2** enchufe, clavija *(macho)*; toma *(hembra)*. **3** bujía. **to plug in** *vt-vi* enchufar(se).

plughole ['plʌghəʊl] *n* desagüe.

plum [plʌm] *n* ciruela.

plumber ['plʌməʳ] *n* fontanero,-a.

plural ['plʊərəl] *adj-n* plural.

plus [plʌs] *prep* más. ► *conj* además de que. ► *n* ventaja.

plywood ['plaɪwʊd] *n* contrachapado.

pneumonia [nju:'məʊnɪə] *n* neumonía, pulmonía.

poach [pəʊtʃ] *vt* **1** hervir. **2** escalfar *(huevos)*.

pocket ['pɒkɪt] *n* bolsillo. ■ **pocket money 1** dinero para gastos personales. **2** paga.

pod [pɒd] *n* vaina.

poem ['pəʊəm] *n* poema.

poet ['pəʊət] *n* poeta.

poetry ['pəʊətrɪ] *n* poesía.

point [pɔɪnt] *n* **1** punta. **2** punto. **3** coma: *5 point 66*, cinco coma sesenta y seis. **4** sentido. ► *vi* indicar, señalar. ► *vt* apuntar. • **on the point of** a punto de; **there's no point in...** no vale la pena...

point-blank [pɔɪnt'blæŋk] *adj* a quemarropa.

poison ['pɔɪzən] *n* veneno. ► *vt* envenenar.

poker ['pəʊkəʳ] *n* póquer.

polar ['pəʊləʳ] *adj* polar. ■ **polar bear** oso polar.

pole[1] [pəʊl] *n* **1** palo, poste. **2** pértiga. ■ **pole vault** salto con pértiga.

pole[2] [pəʊl] *n* polo.

polemic [pə'lemɪk] *adj* polémico,-a. ► *n* polémica.

police [pə'li:s] *npl* policía. ■ **police station** GB comisaría de policía.

policeman [pə'li:smən] *n* policía, guardia.

policewoman [pəˈliːswʊmən] *n* mujer policía.

policy [ˈpɒlɪsɪ] *n* 1 política. 2 póliza *(de seguros)*.

polish [ˈpɒlɪʃ] *n* 1 cera *(para muebles)*. 2 betún *(para zapatos)*. 3 esmalte *(para uñas)*. ► *vt* 1 sacar brillo a. 2 pulir.

polite [pəˈlaɪt] *adj* cortés, educado,-a.

politician [pɒlɪˈtɪʃən] *n* político,-a.

politics [ˈpɒlɪtɪks] *n* política.

poll [pəʊl] *n* 1 votación. 2 encuesta, sondeo.

pollen [ˈpɒlən] *n* polen.

pollution [pəˈluːʃən] *n* contaminación.

polo [ˈpəʊləʊ] *n* polo. ▪ **polo neck** cuello alto.

pomegranate [ˈpɒmɪgrænət] *n* granada *(fruta)*.

pomp [pɒmp] *n* pompa.

pond [pɒnd] *n* estanque.

pony [ˈpəʊnɪ] *n* poni.

ponytail [ˈpəʊnɪteɪl] *n* cola de caballo.

pool¹ [puːl] *n* 1 charco. 2 estanque. 3 piscina.

pool² [puːl] *n* 1 fondo común. 2 billar americano. ► *npl* **the pools** las quinielas.

poor [pʊəˈ] *adj* pobre.

popcorn [ˈpɒpkɔːn] *n* palomitas *(de maíz)*.

pope [pəʊp] *n* papa.

poplar [ˈpɒpləˈ] *n* álamo.

poppy [ˈpɒpɪ] *n* amapola.

popular [ˈpɒpjʊləˈ] *adj* popular.

populate [ˈpɒpjʊleɪt] *vt* poblar.

population [pɒpjʊˈleɪʃən] *n* población.

porcelain [ˈpɔːsəlɪn] *n* porcelana.

porch [pɔːtʃ] *n* pórtico.

porcupine [ˈpɔːkjʊpaɪn] *n* puerco espín.

pore [pɔːˈ] *n* poro.

pork [pɔːk] *n* carne de cerdo. ▪ **pork chop** chuleta de cerdo.

porridge [ˈpɒrɪdʒ] *n* gachas de avena.

port¹ [pɔːt] *n* puerto *(de mar)*.

port² [pɔːt] *n* babor.

port³ [pɔːt] *n* oporto *(vino)*.

portable [ˈpɔːtəbəl] *adj* portátil.

portal [ˈpɔːtəl] *n* COMPUT portal.

porter [ˈpɔːtəˈ] *n* 1 portero,-a. 2 mozo.

portfolio [pɔːtˈfəʊlɪəʊ] *n* 1 carpeta. 2 POL cartera.

portion [ˈpɔːʃən] *n* porción, ración.

portrait [ˈpɔːtreɪt] *n* retrato.

pose [pəʊz] *n* pose. ► *vt* plantear *(problema)*. 2 representar *(amenaza)*. ► *vi* posar *(como modelo)*.

position [pəˈzɪʃən] *n* 1 sitio, posición. 2 postura, actitud. 3 puesto, empleo. ► *vt* colocar.

positive [ˈpɒzɪtɪv] *adj* 1 positivo,-a. 2 seguro,-a.

possess [pə'zes] *vt* poseer, tener.

possibility [pɒsɪ'bɪlɪtɪ] *n* posibilidad.

possible ['pɒsɪbəl] *adj* posible.

post[1] [pəʊst] *n* poste.

post[2] [pəʊst] *n* puesto. ► *vt* destinar.

post[3] [pəʊst] *n* correo. ► *vt* **1** echar al correo *(carta)*. **2** poner *(anuncio)*. ■ **post office** oficina de correos; **post office box** apartado de correos.

postage ['pəʊstɪdʒ] *n* franqueo, porte.

postal ['pəʊstəl] *adj* postal.

postbox ['pəʊstbɒks] *n* buzón.

postcard ['pəʊstkɑːd] *n* tarjeta postal, postal.

postcode ['pəʊstkəʊd] *n* código postal.

poster ['pəʊstər] *n* póster.

posterior [pɒ'stɪərɪər] *adj* posterior.

postman ['pəʊstmən] *n* cartero.

postmark ['pəʊstmɑːk] *n* matasellos.

postpone [pəs'pəʊn] *vt* posponer.

postscript ['pəʊstskrɪpt] *n* posdata.

posture ['pɒstʃər] *n* postura.

postwoman ['pəʊstwʊmən] *n* cartera.

pot [pɒt] *n* **1** pote, tarro. **2** bote *(de pintura)*. **3** tetera. **4** cafetera. **5** olla. **6** maceta.

potato [pə'teɪtəʊ] *n* patata.

potent ['pəʊtənt] *adj* potente.

pothole ['pɒthəʊl] *n* **1** cueva. **2** bache *(de carretera)*.

pottery ['pɒtərɪ] *n* **1** alfarería. **2** cerámica.

potty ['pɒtɪ] *n* orinal *(de niño)*.

poultry ['pəʊltrɪ] *n* aves de corral.

pound[1] [paʊnd] *n* libra.

pound[2] [paʊnd] *n* **1** perrera. **2** depósito municipal *(de coches)*.

pour [pɔːʳ] *vt* verter, echar. ► *vi* llover a cántaros.

poverty ['pɒvətɪ] *n* pobreza.

powder ['paʊdəʳ] *n* polvo.

power ['paʊəʳ] *n* **1** fuerza. **2** poder, capacidad. **3** corriente *(eléctrica)*. **4** energía. **5** potencia. ■ **power cut** apagón; **power station** central eléctrica.

powerful ['paʊəfʊl] *adj* poderoso,-a.

practical ['præktɪkəl] *adj* práctico,-a.

practice ['præktɪs] *n* **1** práctica. **2** consulta *(de médico)*. **3** bufete *(de abogados)*. ► *vt-vi* US → practise.

practise ['præktɪs] *vt-vi* GB **1** practicar. **2** ejercer *(profesión)*. ► *vi* entrenar *(deportes)*.

practitioner [præk'tɪʃənəʳ] *n* médico,-a.

prairie ['preərɪ] *n* pradera.

praise [preɪz] *n* alabanza, elogio. ► *vt* alabar.

pram [præm] *n* GB cochecito de niño.

prank [præŋk] *n* travesura, broma.

prawn [prɔːn] *n* gamba.

pray [preɪ] *vi* orar, rezar.

prayer [preəʳ] *n* oración, plegaria. ▪ **prayer book** misal.

preach [priːtʃ] *vt-vi* predicar.

precaution [prɪˈkɔːʃən] *n* precaución.

precede [prɪˈsiːd] *vt-vi* preceder.

precious [ˈpreʃəs] *adj* precioso,-a. ▪ **precious stone** piedra preciosa.

precipice [ˈprecɪpɪs] *n* precipicio.

precise [prɪˈsaɪs] *adj* preciso,-a.

precision [prɪˈsɪʒən] *n* precisión.

precocious [prɪˈkəʊʃəs] *adj* precoz.

precooked [priːˈkʊkt] *vt* precocinado,-a.

predator [ˈpredətəʳ] *n* depredador.

predicament [prɪˈdɪkəmənt] *n* apuro, aprieto.

predict [prɪˈdɪkt] *vt* predecir.

predictable [prɪˈdɪktəbəl] *adj* previsible.

prediction [prɪˈdɪkʃən] *n* predicción.

predominate [prɪˈdɒmɪneɪt] *vi* predominar.

pre-empt [priːˈempt] *vt* adelantarse a.

prefabricated [priːˈfæbrɪkeɪtɪd] *adj* prefabricado,-a.

preface [ˈprefəs] *n* prefacio.

prefer [prɪˈfɜːʳ] *vt* preferir.

preference [ˈprefərəns] *n* preferencia.

prefix [ˈpriːfɪks] *n* prefijo.

pregnancy [ˈpregnənsɪ] *n* embarazo. ▪ **pregnancy test** prueba del embarazo.

pregnant [ˈpregnənt] *adj-n* embarazada.

prehistoric [priːhɪˈstɒrɪk] *n* prehistórico,-a.

prejudice [ˈpredʒədɪs] *n* prejuicio.

prejudicial [predʒəˈdɪʃəl] *adj* perjudicial.

prelude [ˈpreljuːd] *n* preludio.

premature [ˈpremətjʊəʳ] *adj* prematuro,-a.

premier [ˈpremɪəʳ] *adj* primero,-a. ▶ *n* primer,-ra ministro,-a.

première [ˈpremɪeəʳ] *n* estreno.

premise [ˈpremɪs] *n* premisa. ▶ *npl* **premises** local.

premium [ˈpriːmɪəm] *n* prima.

preoccupy [priːˈɒkjʊpaɪ] *vt* preocupar.

prepaid [priːˈpeɪd] *adj* pagado,-a por adelantado.

preparation [prepəˈreɪʃən] *n* **1** preparación. **2** preparado. ▶ *npl* **preparations** preparativos.

prepare [prɪˈpeəʳ] *vt-vi* preparar(se).

preposition [prepə'zıʃən] *n* preposición.

prerogative [prɪ'rɒɡətɪv] *n* prerrogativa.

preschool ['priːskuːl] *adj* preescolar.

prescribe [prɪs'kraɪb] *vt* **1** prescribir. **2** recetar.

prescription [prɪs'krɪpʃən] *n* receta médica. • **on prescription** con receta médica.

presence ['prezəns] *n* presencia.

present[1] ['prezənt] *adj* **1** presente. **2** actual. ▶ *n* presente. • **at present** actualmente; **for the present** por ahora.

present[2] [(*n*) 'prezənt, (*vb*) prɪ'zənt] *n* regalo. ▶ *vt* presentar.

presenter [prɪ'zentəʳ] *n* **1** locutor,-ra. **2** presentador,-ra.

presently ['prezəntlɪ] *adv* **1** GB pronto, dentro de poco. **2** US ahora.

preservation [prezə'veɪʃən] *n* conservación, preservación.

preservative [prɪ'zɜːvətɪv] *n* conservante.

preserve [prɪ'zɜːv] *n* **1** conserva *(de fruta, verdura)*. **2** confitura. **3** coto, vedado.

preside [prɪ'zaɪd] *vi* presidir.

president ['prezɪdənt] *n* presidente,-a.

press [pres] *n* **1** prensa. **2** imprenta. ▶ *vt* **1** pulsar, apretar *(botón)*. **2** prensar *(uvas, olivas)*. **3** planchar *(ropa)*. **4** pre-

sionar *(persona)*. ▶ *vi* apretar. ▪ **press briefing** rueda de prensa; **press release** comunicado de prensa.

pressing ['presɪŋ] *adj* urgente.

press-up ['presʌp] *n* flexión.

pressure ['preʃəʳ] *n* presión.

prestige [pres'tiːʒ] *n* prestigio.

presume [prɪ'zjuːm] *vt* suponer.

pretend [prɪ'tend] *vt-vi* **1** aparentar, fingir. **2** pretender. ▶ *adj* de mentira.

pretentious [prɪ'tenʃəs] *adj* pretencioso,-a.

pretext ['priːtekst] *n* pretexto.

pretty ['prɪtɪ] *adj* bonito,-a, mono,-a. ▶ *adv* bastante. • **pretty much** más o menos.

prevail [prɪ'veɪl] *vi* **1** predominar, imperar. **2** prevalecer.

prevent [prɪ'vent] *vt* impedir, evitar.

preview ['priːvjuː] *n* preestreno.

previous ['priːvɪəs] *adj* previo,-a.

prey [preɪ] *n* presa.

price [praɪs] *n* precio.

prick [prɪk] *n* pinchazo. ▶ *vt* pinchar.

prickle ['prɪkəl] *n* pincho, espina.

pride [praɪd] *n* orgullo.

priest [priːst] *n* sacerdote.

primary ['praɪmərɪ] *adj* **1** principal. **2** primario,-a.

prime [praim] *adj* **1** primero,-a. **2** selecto,-a, de primera. ■ **Prime Minister** primer,-a ministro,-a; **prime time** franja de mayor audiencia.

primitive ['primitiv] *adj* primitivo,-a.

prince [prins] *n* príncipe.

princess ['prinses] *n* princesa.

principal ['prinsipəl] *adj* principal. ► *n* director,-ra *(de colegio)*; rector,-ra *(de universidad)*.

principle ['prinsipəl] *n* principio.

print [print] *n* **1** huella. **2** copia *(fotografía)*. **3** estampado *(de tela)*. ► *vt* **1** imprimir. **2** sacar una copia de *(fotografía)*. **3** estampar *(tela)*. ● **in print** en catálogo; **out of print** descatalogado,-a.

printer ['printə'] *n* impresora.

print-out ['printaut] *n* copia impresa.

prior ['praiə'] *adj* anterior, previo,-a.

priority [prai'briti] *n* prioridad.

prison ['prizən] *n* prisión.

prisoner ['prizənə'] *n* **1** preso,-a. **2** prisionero,-a.

privacy ['praivəsi] *n* intimidad.

private ['praivət] *adj* privado,-a. ► *n* soldado raso. ■ **private eye** detective privado.

privilege ['privilidʒ] *n* privilegio.

prize [praiz] *n* premio.

probability [prɒbə'biliti] *n* probabilidad.

probation [prə'beiʃən] *n* libertad condicional.

probe [prəub] *n* sonda.

problem ['prɒbləm] *n* problema.

procedure [prə'si:dʒə'] *n* procedimiento.

proceed [prə'si:d] *vi* **1** continuar, proseguir. **2** proceder.

process ['prəuses] *n* proceso. ► *vt* **1** procesar. **2** revelar.

proclaim [prə'kleim] *vt* proclamar.

prodigious [prə'didʒəs] *adj* prodigioso,-a.

produce [*(vb)* prə'dju:s, *(n)* 'prɒdju:s] *vt* producir. ► *n* productos *(agrícolas)*.

product ['prɒdʌkt] *n* producto.

production [prə'dʌkʃən] *n* producción. ■ **production line** cadena de producción.

profession [prə'feʃən] *n* profesión.

professional [prə'feʃənəl] *adj-n* profesional.

professor [prə'fəsə'] *n* GB catedrático,-a de universidad.

proficiency [prə'fiʃənsi] *n* competencia.

profile ['prəufail] *n* perfil.

profit ['prɒfit] *n* ganancia, beneficio.

program ['prəugræm] *n* US programa. ► *vt* US programar.

programme ['prəʊgræm] *n* GB
programa. ▶ *vt* GB programar.
progress [(*n*) 'prəʊgres, (*vb*)
prə'gres] *n* progreso. ▶ *vi* progresar. • **in progress** en curso.
prohibit [prə'hɪbɪt] *vt* prohibir.
prohibition [prəʊɪ'bɪʃən] *n*
prohibición.
project [(*n*) 'prɒdʒekt, (*vb*) prə'dʒekt] *n* proyecto. ▶ *vt* proyectar.
projectile [prə'dʒektaɪl] *n*
proyectil.
projector [prə'dʒektə'] *n* proyector.
prologue ['prəʊlɒg] (US **prolog**) *n* prólogo.
promenade [prɒmə'nɑ:d] *n*
paseo marítimo.
prominent ['prɒmɪnənt] *adj*
prominente.
promise ['prɒmɪs] *n* promesa. ▶ *vt-vi* prometer.
promote [prə'məʊt] *vt* **1** promover. **2** promocionar.
promotion [prə'məʊʃən] *n*
promoción.
prompt [prɒmpt] *adj* **1** inmediato, -a, rápido,-a (*servicio, acción*). **2** puntual (*persona*). ▶ *adv* en punto. ▶ *vt* **1**
inducir, impulsar, incitar. **2**
apuntar (*en teatro*).
prompter ['prɒmptə'] *n* apuntador,-ra.
prone [prəʊn] *adj* boca abajo.
• **prone to** propenso,-a a.

prong [prɒŋ] *n* diente, punta.
pronoun ['prəʊnaʊn] *n* pronombre.
pronounce [prə'naʊns] *vt* pronunciar.
pronunciation [prənʌnsɪ'eɪʃən] *n* pronunciación.
proof [pru:f] *n* **1** prueba. **2**
graduación (*alcohólica*).
prop [prɒp] *n* puntal (*objeto*)
propaganda [prɒpə'gændə] *n*
propaganda.
propeller [prə'pelə'] *n* hélice.
proper ['prɒpə'] *adj* **1** adecuado,-a (*procedimiento*). **2** correcto,-a (*respuesta, conducta*). ■
proper noun nombre propio.
property ['prɒpətɪ] *n* propiedad.
prophet ['prɒfɪt] *n* profeta.
proportion [prə'pɔ:ʃən] *n*
proporción. • **out of proportion** desproporcionado,-a.
proposal [prə'pəʊzəl] *n* propuesta.
propose [prə'pəʊz] *vt* **1** proponer (*sugerencia*). **2** pensar,
tener la intención de. ▶ *vi*
pedir la mano, declararse.
propriety [prə'praɪətɪ] *n* **1** corrección. **2** conveniencia.
propulsion [prə'pʌlʃən] *n* propulsión.
prose [prəʊz] *n* prosa.
prosecute ['prɒsɪkju:t] *vt* procesar.
prosecution [prɒsɪ'kju:ʃən] *n*
1 proceso, juicio. **2** la acusación.

prosecutor ['prɒsɪkjuːtə'] *n* fiscal.

prospect ['prɒspekt] *n* **1** perspectiva. **2** probabilidad.

prospectus [prə'spektəs] *n* prospecto.

prosperous ['prɒspərəs] *adj* próspero,-a.

prostate ['prɒsteɪt] *n* próstata.

prostitute ['prɒstɪtjuːt] *n* prostituta.

protect [prə'tekt] *vt* proteger.

protection [prə'tekʃən] *n* protección.

protein ['prəʊtiːn] *n* proteína.

protest [(n) 'prəʊtest, (vb) prə'test] *n* protesta. ► *vt-vi* protestar.

protocol ['prəʊtəkɒl] *n* protocolo.

prototype ['prəʊtətaɪp] *n* prototipo.

protrude [prə'truːd] *vi* sobresalir.

proud [praʊd] *adj* orgulloso,-a.

prove [pruːv] *vt* probar, demostrar. ► *vi* resultar. • **to prove SB right** demostrar que ALGN tiene razón; **to prove SB wrong** demostrar que ALGN está equivocado,-a.

proverb ['prɒvɜːb] *n* proverbio.

provide [prə'vaɪd] *vt* proporcionar, suministrar.

provided [prə'vaɪdɪd] *conj.* **provided (that)** siempre que.

province ['prɒvɪns] *n* provincia.

provision [prə'vɪʒən] *n* **1** suministro, provisión. **2** disposición.

provisional [prə'vɪʒənəl] *adj* provisional.

provoke [prə'vəʊk] *vt* provocar.

prow [praʊ] *n* proa.

proxy ['prɒksɪ] *n* representante, apoderado,-a. • **by proxy** por poderes.

prudent ['pruːdənt] *adj* prudente.

prudish ['pruːdɪʃ] *adj* remilgado,-a.

prune¹ [pruːn] *n* ciruela pasa.

prune² [pruːn] *vt* podar.

psychiatry [saɪ'kaɪətrɪ] *n* psiquiatría.

psychology [saɪ'kɒledʒɪ] *n* psicología.

pub [pʌb] *n* bar, pub.

puberty ['pjuːbətɪ] *n* pubertad.

public ['pʌblɪk] *adj* público,-a. ► *n* público. ▪ **public holiday** fiesta nacional; **public school** colegio privado *(en GB)*, colegio público *(en EEUU)*; **public servant** funcionario,-a.

publicity [pʌ'blɪsɪtɪ] *n* publicidad.

publish ['pʌblɪʃ] *vt* publicar.

publisher ['pʌblɪʃə'] *n* **1** editor,-ra. **2** editorial.

pudding ['pʊdɪŋ] *n* **1** budín, pudín. **2** GB postre.

puddle ['pʌdəl] n charco.

pull [pul] n 1 tirón. 2 atracción. ► vt tirar de. ► vi tirar.

pulley ['puli] n polea.

pullover ['puləuvəʳ] n jersey.

pulp [pʌlp] n pulpa.

pulse [pʌls] n 1 pulsación. 2 pulso.

pumice stone ['pʌmɪsstəun] n piedra pómez.

pump [pʌmp] n 1 bomba (de aire, líquido). 2 surtidor (de gasolina). ► vt bombear.

pumpkin ['pʌmpkɪn] n calabaza.

pun [pʌn] n juego de palabras.

punch[1] [pʌntʃ] n puñetazo.

punch[2] [pʌntʃ] n ponche.

punch[3] [pʌntʃ] vt 1 perforar. 2 picar (billete).

punctual ['pʌŋktjuəl] adj puntual.

punctuation [pʌŋktjʊ'eɪʃən] n puntuación. ▪ **punctuation mark** signo de puntuación.

puncture ['pʌŋktʃəʳ] n pinchazo. ► vt-vi pinchar(se).

punish ['pʌnɪʃ] vt castigar.

punishment ['pʌnɪʃmənt] n castigo.

pup [pʌp] n cría, cachorro,-a.

pupil[1] ['pjuːpɪl] n alumno,-a.

pupil[2] ['pjuːpɪl] n pupila.

puppet ['pʌpɪt] n títere.

puppy ['pʌpɪ] n cachorro,-a.

purchase ['pɜːtʃəs] n compra. ► vt comprar.

pure ['pjuəʳ] adj puro,-a.

purée ['pjuəreɪ] n puré.

purity ['pjuərɪtɪ] n pureza.

purple ['pɜːpəl] adj púrpura.

purpose ['pɜːpəs] n propósito. ● **on purpose** a propósito.

purr [pɜːʳ] n ronroneo.

purse [pɜːs] n 1 GB monedero. 2 US bolso.

pursue [pə'sjuː] vt 1 perseguir. 2 proseguir.

pursuit [pə'sjuːt] n persecución.

purveyor [pɜː'veɪəʳ] n proveedor,-ra.

pus [pʌs] n pus.

push [puʃ] n empujón. ► vt-vi empujar. ► vt pulsar, apretar (botón).

pushchair ['puʃtʃeəʳ] n cochecito de niño.

put [put] vt poner, colocar.

to put aside vt 1 ahorrar, guardar (dinero). 2 dejar a un lado (trabajo).

to put away vt guardar.

to put forward vt 1 proponer (plan). 2 adelantar (reloj).

to put off vt aplazar.

to put on vt 1 encender (luz, radio). 2 ponerse (ropa). 3 ganar (peso, velocidad).

to put out vt apagar.

to put up vt 1 levantar (mano). 2 armar (tienda de campaña). 4 construir.

puzzle ['pʌzəl] n rompecabezas.

pyjamas [pə'dʒɑːməz] *npl* GB pijama.

pylon ['paɪlən] *n* torre *(de tendido eléctrico)*.

pyramid ['pɪrəmɪd] *n* pirámide.

Q

quail [kweɪl] *n* codorniz.

quaint [kweɪnt] *adj* pintoresco,-a.

quake [kweɪk] *n fam* terremoto.

qualification [kwɒlɪfɪ'keɪʃən] *n* **1** requisito *(para empleo)*. **2** diploma, título.

qualified ['kwɒlɪfaɪd] *adj* cualificado,-a.

qualify ['kwɒlɪfaɪ] *vt* capacitar. ► *vi* **1** obtener el título. **2** clasificarse.

quality ['kwɒlɪti] *n* **1** calidad. **2** cualidad.

quantity ['kwɒntɪti] *n* cantidad.

quarantine ['kwɒrəntiːn] *n* cuarentena.

quarrel ['kwɒrəl] *n* riña, pelea. ► *vi* reñir, pelear.

quarter ['kwɔːtəʳ] *n* **1** cuarto, cuarta parte: *a quarter past five*, las cinco y cuarto.

quarterfinal [kwɔːtə'faɪnəl] *n* cuarto de final.

quartz [kwɔːts] *n* cuarzo.

quay [kiː] *n* muelle.

queen [kwiːn] *n* reina.

quench [kwentʃ] *vt* **1** saciar *(sed)*. **2** apagar *(fuego)*.

query ['kwɪərɪ] *n* pregunta.

quest [kwest] *n* búsqueda.

question ['kwestʃən] *n* **1** pregunta. **2** cuestión, problema. ► *vt* **1** hacer preguntas a, interrogar. **2** cuestionar. ■ **question mark** interrogante.

questionnaire [kwestʃə'neəʳ] *n* cuestionario.

queue [kjuː] *n* cola. ► *vi* hacer cola.

quick [kwɪk] *adj* rápido,-a. ► *adv* rápido, rápidamente.

quiet ['kwaɪət] *adj* **1** callado,-a: *be quiet!*, ¡cállate! **2** tranquilo,-a *(lugar)*.

quilt [kwɪlt] *n* edredón.

quince [kwɪns] *n* membrillo.

quirk [kwɜːk] *n* manía.

quit [kwɪt] *vt* dejar.

quite [kwaɪt] *adv* **1** bastante. **2** completamente.

quiver ['kwɪvəʳ] *n* temblor.

quiz [kwɪz] *n* concurso *(televisivo, etc)*.

quota ['kwəʊtə] *n* cuota.

quotation [kwəʊ'teɪʃən] *n* **1** cita *(de libro)*. **2** cotización. ■ **quotation marks** comillas.

quote [kwəʊt] *n* cita. ► *vt* **1** citar. **2** cotizar.

quotient ['kwəʊʃənt] *n* cociente.

R

rabbit ['ræbɪt] *n* conejo.

rabies ['reɪbiːz] *n* rabia.

raccoon [rə'kuːn] *n* mapache.

race[1] [reɪs] *n* raza.

race[2] [reɪs] *n* carrera.

racecourse ['reɪskɔːs] (US **racetrack**) *n* hipódromo.

racist ['reɪsɪst] *adj-n* racista.

rack [ræk] *n* **1** estante. **2** baca *(de coche)*. **3** rejilla *(en tren)*. **4** escurreplatos.

racket[1] ['rækɪt] *n* raqueta.

racket[2] ['rækɪt] *n* alboroto.

radar ['reɪdɑːʳ] *n* radar.

radiation [reɪdɪ'eɪʃən] *n* radiación.

radiator ['reɪdɪeɪtəʳ] *n* radiador.

radical ['rædɪkəl] *adj-n* radical.

radio ['reɪdɪəʊ] *n* radio.

radioactive [reɪdɪəʊ'æktɪv] *adj* radiactivo,-a.

radish ['rædɪʃ] *n* rábano.

radius ['reɪdɪəs] *n* radio.

raffle ['ræfəl] *n* rifa. ► *vt-vi* rifar, sortear.

raft [rɑːft] *n* balsa.

rafter ['rɑːftəʳ] *n* viga.

rag [ræg] *n* **1** harapo. **2** trapo.

rage [reɪdʒ] *n* rabia. ► *vi* **1** rabiar. • **to be all the rage** hacer furor.

raid [reɪd] *n* **1** incursión, razia. **2** redada. **3** atraco, asalto.

rail [reɪl] *n* **1** barra. **2** barandilla. **3** raíl, carril, riel. • **by rail** por ferrocarril.

railings ['reɪlɪŋz] *npl* verja.

railway ['reɪlweɪ] (US **railroad**) *n* ferrocarril. ■ **railway line** vía férrea; **railway station** estación de ferrocarril.

rain [reɪn] *n* lluvia. ► *vi* llover. ■ **rain forest** selva tropical.

rainbow ['reɪnbəʊ] *n* arco iris.

raincoat ['reɪnkəʊt] *n* impermeable.

raindrop ['reɪndrɒp] *n* gota de lluvia.

rainy ['reɪnɪ] *adj* lluvioso,-a.

raise [reɪz] *vt* **1** levantar. **2** subir, aumentar *(precios, temperatura)*. **3** criar, educar *(niños)*. **4** plantear *(asunto, problema)*. **5** recaudar, conseguir *(fondos)*.

raisin ['reɪzən] *n* pasa.

rake [reɪk] *n* rastrillo.

rally ['rælɪ] *n* **1** POL mitin. **2** rally.

ram [ræm] *n* carnero.

ramble ['ræmbəl] *n* excursión.

ramp [ræmp] *n* rampa.

ran [ræn] *pt* → run.

ranch [rɑːntʃ] *n* rancho.

rancid ['rænsɪd] *adj* rancio,-a.

random ['rændəm] *adj* fortuito,-a. • **at random** al azar.

rang [ræŋ] *pp* → ring.

range [reɪndʒ] *n* **1** gama, surtido. **2** alcance *(de misil, telescopio)*. **3** cordillera, sierra.

rank [ræŋk] *n* **1** fila. **2** grado *(militar)*. **3** categoría

ranking ['ræŋkɪŋ] *n* ranking.

ransom ['rænsəm] *n* rescate. ► *vt* rescatar.

rap [ræp] *n* rap *(música)*.

rape[1] [reɪp] *n* violación. ► *vt* violar.

rape[2] [reɪp] *n* colza.

rapid ['ræpɪd] *adj* rápido,-a.

rare [reəʳ] *adj* **1** raro,-a. **2** poco hecho,-a *(carne)*.

rascal ['rɑːskəl] *n* pillo.

rash[1] [ræʃ] *n* sarpullido.

rash[2] [ræʃ] *adj* imprudente.

rasher ['ræʃəʳ] *n* loncha.

raspberry ['rɑːzbərɪ] *n* frambuesa.

rat [ræt] *n* rata.

rate [reɪt] *n* **1** tasa, índice, tipo. **2** velocidad, ritmo. **3** tarifa, precio. • **at any rate** de todos modos. ▪ **rate of exchange** tipo de cambio.

rather ['rɑːðəʳ] *adv* bastante. • **I would rather** preferiría; **rather than** en vez de, mejor que.

ratings ['reɪtɪŋs] *npl* índice de audiencia.

ratio ['reɪʃɪəʊ] *n* razón, relación.

ration ['ræʃən] *n* ración.

rational ['ræʃənəl] *adj* racional.

rattle ['rætəl] *n* **1** sonajero. **2** traqueteo.

rattlesnake ['rætəlsneɪk] *n* serpiente de cascabel.

rave [reɪv] *n* juerga.

raven ['reɪvən] *n* cuervo.

ravine [rə'viːn] *n* barranco.

raw [rɔː] *adj* **1** crudo,-a. **2** bruto,-a. ▪ **raw material** materia prima.

ray[1] [reɪ] *n* rayo *(de luz)*.

ray[2] [reɪ] *n* raya *(pez)*.

razor ['reɪzəʳ] *n* **1** navaja de afeitar. **2** maquinilla de afeitar. ▪ **razor blade** cuchilla de afeitar.

reach [riːtʃ] *n* alcance. ► *vt* **1** alcanzar, llegar a. **2** contactar. ► *vi* llegar. • **within reach of** al alcance de; **out of reach** fuera del alcance.

react [rɪ'ækt] *vi* reaccionar.

reaction [rɪ'ækʃən] *n* reacción.

read [riːd] *vt* **1** leer. **2** estudiar *(en universidad)*. ► *vi* **1** poner *(cartel, anuncio)*. • **to read back** volver a leer, releer; **to read out** leer en voz alta.

reader ['riːdəʳ] *n* lector,-ra.

reading ['riːdɪŋ] *n* lectura.

ready ['redɪ] *adj* preparado,-a.

ready-made [redɪ'meɪd] *adj* hecho,-a, confeccionado,-a.

real [rɪəl] *adj* real. ► *adv fam* muy. ▪ **real estate** bienes inmuebles.

reality [rɪ'ælɪtɪ] *n* realidad.

realize ['rɪəlaɪz] *vt* **1** darse cuenta de. **2** realizar.

reap [riːp] *vt* cosechar.

rear [rɪəʳ] *adj* trasero,-a, de atrás. ► *n* parte de atrás.

rearrange [riːəˈreɪndʒ] vt 1 colocar de otra manera. 2 volver a concertar *(reunión)*.

rear-view [ˈrɪəvjuː] adj. ■ **rear-view mirror** retrovisor.

reason [ˈriːzən] n razón. ▶ vi razonar.

reasonable [ˈriːzənəbəl] adj razonable.

reassure [riːəˈʃʊəʳ] vt tranquilizar.

rebate [ˈriːbeɪt] n devolución, reembolso.

rebel [(adj-n) ˈrebəl, (vb) rɪˈbel] adj-n rebelde. ▶ vi rebelarse.

rebellion [rɪˈbelɪən] n rebelión.

reboot [riːˈbuːt] vt reiniciar.

rebound [(n) ˈriːbaʊnd, (vb) rɪˈbaʊnd] n rebote. ▶ vi rebotar.

rebuild [riːˈbɪld] vt reconstruir.

rebuke [rɪˈbjuːk] vt reprender.

recall [rɪˈkɔːl] vt recordar.

receipt [rɪˈsiːt] n recibo. ▶ npl **receipts** recaudación *(en taquilla)*.

receive [rɪˈsiːv] vt recibir.

receiver [rɪˈsiːvəʳ] n 1 receptor. 2 auricular *(de teléfono)*.

recent [ˈriːsənt] adj reciente.

reception [rɪˈsepʃən] n recepción. ■ **reception desk** recepción.

receptionist [rɪˈsepʃənɪst] n recepcionista.

recess [ˈriːses] n 1 hueco. 2 descanso.

recession [rɪˈseʃən] n recesión.

rechargeable [riːˈtʃɑːdʒəbəl] adj recargable.

recipe [ˈresəpɪ] n receta.

reciprocal [rɪˈsɪprəkəl] adj recíproco,-a.

recital [rɪˈsaɪtəl] n recital.

reckless [ˈrekləs] adj 1 precipitado,-a. 2 temerario,-a.

reckon [ˈrekən] vt-vi 1 considerar. 2 calcular. 3 *fam* creer. ▶ vt creer, considerar.

reclaim [rɪˈkleɪm] vt reclamar.

recline [rɪˈklaɪn] vt-vi reclinar(se).

recognize [ˈrekəgnaɪz] vt reconocer.

recollect [rekəˈlekt] vt recordar.

recommend [rekəˈmend] vt recomendar.

reconsider [riːkənˈsɪdəʳ] vt reconsiderar.

reconstruct [riːkənsˈtrʌkt] vt reconstruir.

record [(n) ˈrekɔːd, (vb) rɪˈkɔːd] n 1 registro, documento. 2 historial, expediente. 3 disco *(música)*. 4 récord, marca. ▶ vt 1 hacer constar. 2 anotar. 3 grabar. ● **off the record** confidencialmente; **to beat the record** batir el récord. ■ **record player** tocadiscos.

recorder [rɪˈkɔːdəʳ] n flauta dulce.

recount [ˈriːkaʊnt] n recuento.

recover [rɪˈkʌvəʳ] vt-vi recuperar(se).

recovery [rɪˈkʌvərɪ] n recuperación.

recruit [rɪ'kruːt] n recluta. ► vt reclutar.

rectangle ['rektæŋgəl] n rectángulo.

rectify ['rektɪfaɪ] vt rectificar.

recycle [riː'saɪkəl] vt reciclar.

red [red] adj **1** rojo,-a. **2** pelirrojo,-a *(pelo)*. ► n rojo. ● **to be in the red** estar en números rojos. ▪ **red tape** papeleo burocrático; **red wine** vino tinto.

redeem [rɪ'diːm] vt rescatar.

reduce [rɪ'djuːs] vt-vi reducir(se).

redundancy [rɪ'dʌndənsɪ] n despido.

redundant [rɪ'dʌndənt] adj **1** redundante. **2** despedido,-a. ● **to be made redundant** ser despedido,-a.

reed [riːd] n **1** caña, junco. **2** lengüeta *(de instrumento)*.

reef [riːf] n arrecife.

reek [riːk] vi apestar.

reel [riːl] n carrete.

refer [rɪ'fɜːʳ] vi **1** referirse. **2** consultar.

referee [refə'riː] n árbitro.

reference ['refərəns] n referencia. ▪ **reference book** libro de consulta.

referendum [refə'rendəm] n referéndum.

refill [(n) 'riːfɪl, (vb) riː'fɪl] n recambio. ► vt rellenar.

refine [rɪ'faɪn] vt refinar.

refinery [rɪ'faɪnərɪ] n refinería.

reflect [rɪ'flekt] vt reflejar. ► vi reflexionar.

reflection [rɪ'flekʃən] n **1** reflejo. **2** reflexión.

reflex ['riːfleks] adj reflejo,-a.

reflexive [rɪ'fleksɪv] adj reflexivo,-a.

reform [rɪ'fɔːm] n reforma. ► vt reformar.

refrain [rɪ'freɪn] n estribillo.

refresh [rɪ'freʃ] vt refrescar.

refreshment [rɪ'freʃmənt] n refresco, refrigerio.

refrigerator [rɪ'frɪdʒəreɪtəʳ] n frigorífico, nevera.

refuge ['refjuːdʒ] n refugio.

refugee [refjuː'dʒiː] n refugiado,-a.

refund [(n) 'riːfʌnd, (vb) riː'fʌnd] n reembolso. ► vt reembolsar.

refusal [rɪ'fjuːzəl] n negativa.

refuse¹ ['refjuːs] n basura.

refuse² [rɪ'fjuːz] vi negarse.

regain [rɪ'geɪn] vt recobrar.

regard [rɪ'gɑːd] vt considerar. ► n respeto. ► npl **regards** recuerdos. ● **as regards...** en lo que se refiere a...; **with regard to** con respecto a.

regarding [rɪ'gɑːdɪŋ] prep respecto a, en relación con.

regime [reɪ'ʒiːm] n régimen.

regiment ['redʒɪmənt] n regimiento.

region ['riːdʒən] n región.

register ['redʒɪstəʳ] n registro, lista. ► vi **1** registrarse *(en ho-*

tel). **2** matricularse *(para clases)*. **3** inscribirse. ► *vt* **1** certificar *(carta)*. **2** inscribir en el registro *(boda, nacimiento)*. ■ **registered post** (US **mail**) correo certificado.

registration [redʒɪs'treɪʃən] *n* **1** registro. **2** matriculación. ■ **registration number** matrícula.

regret [rɪ'gret] *n* pesar. ► *vt* **1** lamentar. **2** arrepentirse de.

regular ['regjʊlə'] *adj* **1** regular. **2** habitual *(cliente)*. **3** normal.

regulate ['regjʊleɪt] *vt* regular.

rehearsal [rɪ'hɜːsəl] *n* ensayo.

rehearse [rɪ'hɜːs] *vt* ensayar.

reign [reɪn] *n* reinado. ► *vi* reinar.

reimburse [riːɪm'bɜːs] *vt* reembolsar.

rein [reɪn] *n* rienda.

reindeer ['reɪndɪə'] *n* reno.

reinforce [riːɪn'fɔːs] *vt* reforzar. ■ **reinforced concrete** hormigón armado.

reinstate [riːɪn'steɪt] *vt* readmitir.

reject [rɪ'dʒekt] *vt* rechazar.

relapse [rɪ'læps] *n* **1** recaída. **2** reincidencia. ► *vi* **1** recaer. **2** reincidir.

relate [rɪ'leɪt] *vt* **1** relatar, contar. **2** relacionar. ► *vi* **1** estar relacionado,-a. **2** identificarse, entenderse.

relation [rɪ'leɪʃən] *n* **1** relación. **2** pariente,-a.

relationship [rɪ'leɪʃənʃɪp] *n* relación.

relative ['relətɪv] *adj* relativo, -a. ► *n* pariente,-a.

relax [rɪ'læks] *vt-vi* relajar(se).

relay ['riːleɪ] *n* **1** relevo. **2** relé.

release [rɪ'liːs] *n* **1** liberación. **2** estreno *(de película)*. **3** disco recién salido. ► *vt* **1** poner en libertad. **2** estrenar *(película)*. **3** sacar *(disco)*.

relevant ['reləvənt] *adj* pertinente.

reliable [rɪ'laɪəbəl] *adj* **1** de fiar *(persona)*. **2** fidedigno,-a *(noticia)*. **3** seguro,-a *(máquina)*.

relieve [rɪ'liːv] *vt* aliviar.

religion [rɪ'lɪdʒən] *n* religión.

reluctant [rɪ'lʌktənt] *adj* reacio,-a.

rely [rɪ'laɪ] *vi* **rely on** confiar en, contar con.

remain [rɪ'meɪn] *vi* quedar(se). ► *npl* **remains** restos.

remark [rɪ'mɑːk] *n* comentario. ► *vt* comentar.

remarkable [rɪ'mɑːkəbəl] *adj* notable, extraordinario,-a.

remedy ['remədɪ] *n* remedio. ► *vt* remediar.

remember [rɪ'membə'] *vt* recordar, acordarse de.

remind [rɪ'maɪnd] *vt* recordar.

remit [rɪ'mɪt] *vt* remitir.

remittance [rɪ'mɪtəns] *n* giro.

remorse [rɪ'mɔːs] *n* remordimiento.

remote [rɪ'məʊt] *adj* remoto,-a.

■ **remote control** mando a distancia.
remove [rɪ'muːv] vt quitar. ► vi trasladarse, mudarse.
renew [rɪ'njuː] vt renovar.
renovate ['renəveɪt] vt reformar.
renown [rɪ'naʊn] n fama.
rent¹ [rent] n alquiler. ► vt alquilar.
rental ['rentəl] n alquiler.
repair [rɪ'peəʳ] n reparación. ► vt reparar, arreglar.
repayment [riː'peɪmənt] n devolución, reembolso.
repeat [rɪ'piːt] n repetición. ► vt repetir.
repetition [repə'tɪʃən] n repetición.
replace [rɪ'pleɪs] vt 1 devolver a su sitio. 2 reemplazar.
replay [(n) 'riːpleɪ, (vb) riː'pleɪ] n 1 repetición. 2 partido de desempate. ► vt repetir.
reply [rɪ'plaɪ] n respuesta. ► vi responder.
report [rɪ'pɔːt] n informe. ► vt informar sobre. ► vi presentarse.
reporter [rɪ'pɔːtəʳ] n reportero,-a, periodista.
represent [reprɪ'zent] vt representar.
repression [rɪ'preʃən] n represión.
repressive [rɪ'presɪv] adj represivo,-a.
reprieve [rɪ'priːv] n indulto. ► vt indultar.

reprimand ['reprɪmɑːnd] vt reprender.
reprisal [rɪ'praɪzəl] n represalia.
reproach [rɪ'prəʊtʃ] n reproche. ► vt reprochar.
reproduce [riːprə'djuːs] vt-vi reproducir(se).
reproduction [riːprə'dʌkʃən] n reproducción.
reptile ['reptaɪl] n reptil.
republic [rɪ'pʌblɪk] n república.
reputable ['repjʊtəbəl] adj 1 acreditado,-a. 2 de confianza.
reputation [repjʊ'teɪʃən] n reputación.
request [rɪ'kwest] n solicitud, petición. ► vt pedir, solicitar.
require [rɪ'kwaɪəʳ] vt requerir.
requirement [rɪ'kwaɪəmənt] n requisito.
rescue ['reskjuː] n rescate. ► vt rescatar.
research [rɪ'sɜːtʃ] n investigación. ► vt-vi investigar.
resemble [rɪ'zembəl] vt parecerse a.
resent [rɪ'zent] vt 1 tener celos de. 2 molestar: *I resent that*, eso me molesta.
reservation [rezə'veɪʃən] n reserva.
reserve [rɪ'zɜːv] n reserva. ► vt reservar.
reservoir ['rezəvwɑːʳ] n embalse.
residence ['rezɪdəns] n residencia.

resident ['rezɪdənt] *adj-n* residente.

residential [resɪ'denʃəl] *adj* residencial.

residue ['rezɪdjuː] *n* residuo.

resign [rɪ'zaɪn] *vt-vi* dimitir. • **to resign oneself to** STH resignarse a algo.

resignation [rezɪg'neɪʃən] *n* **1** dimisión. **2** resignación.

resin ['rezɪn] *n* resina.

resist [rɪ'zɪst] *vt* resistir.

resistance [rɪ'zɪstəns] *n* resistencia.

resistant [rɪ'zɪstənt] *adj* resistente.

resolution [rezə'luːʃən] *n* resolución.

resolve [rɪ'zɒlv] *vt* resolver.

resort [rɪ'zɔːt] *n* lugar de vacaciones.

resource [rɪ'zɔːs] *n* recurso.

respect [rɪ'spekt] *n* respeto. ▶ *vt* respetar.

respective [rɪ'spektɪv] *adj* respectivo,-a.

respond [rɪ'spɒnd] *vi* responder.

response [rɪ'spɒns] *n* respuesta.

responsibility [rɪspɒnsɪ'bɪlɪti] *n* responsabilidad.

rest[1] [rest] *n* descanso. ▶ *vt-vi* **1** descansar. **2** apoyar(se).

rest[2] [rest] *n* resto.

restaurant ['restərɒnt] *n* restaurante.

restore [rɪ'stɔːʳ] *vt* restaurar.

restrain [rɪ'streɪn] *vt* contener.

restrict [rɪ'strɪkt] *vt* restringir.

restriction [rɪ'strɪkʃən] *n* restricción.

result [rɪ'zʌlt] *n* resultado.

to result in *vt* tener como resultado.

resume [rɪ'zjuːm] *vt-vi* reanudar(se).

résumé ['rezjuːmeɪ] *n* **1** resumen. **2** US currículum.

retail ['riːteɪl] *n* venta al por menor. • **retail price** precio de venta al público.

retailer ['riːteɪləʳ] *n* detallista.

retain [rɪ'teɪn] *vt* retener.

retaliation [rɪtælɪ'eɪʃən] *n* represalias.

retch [retʃ] *vi* tener arcadas.

retina ['retɪnə] *n* retina.

retire [rɪ'taɪəʳ] *vt* jubilar. ▶ *vi* **1** jubilarse. **2** retirarse.

retired [rɪ'taɪəd] *adj* jubilado,-a.

retirement [rɪ'taɪəmənt] *n* jubilación.

retort [rɪ'tɔːt] *n* réplica.

retreat [rɪ'triːt] *n* retirada. ▶ *vi* retirarse.

retrieve [rɪ'triːv] *vt* recuperar.

return [rɪ'tɜːn] *n* **1** vuelta, regreso. **2** devolución. ▶ *vi* volver, regresar. ▶ *vt* devolver. • **in return for** a cambio de. ■ **return ticket** GB billete de ida y vuelta.

reunite [riːjuː'naɪt] *vt-vi* reunir(se).

reveal [rɪ'viːl] *vt* revelar.

revenge [rɪ'vendʒ] *n* venganza. ► *vt* vengar.

revenue ['revənjuː] *n* ingresos.

reverence ['revərəns] *n* reverencia.

reverse [rɪ'vɜːs] *adj* inverso,-a. ► *n* **1** reverso *(de moneda)*. **2** revés. **3** marcha atrás. ► *vt* **1** invertir. **2** volver al revés. **3** revocar *(decisión)*. ► *vi* dar marcha atrás. ■ **reverse gear** marcha atrás.

review [rɪ'vjuː] *n* **1** revista. **2** examen. **3** crítica. ► *vt* **1** pasar revista a *(tropas)*. **2** examinar. **3** hacer una crítica de *(libro, película)*.

reviewer [rɪ'vjuːə'] *n* crítico,-a.

revise [rɪ'vaɪz] *vt* **1** revisar. **2** corregir. ► *vt-vi* repasar.

revision [rɪ'vɪʒən] *n* **1** revisión. **2** repaso *(para examen)*.

revival [rɪ'vaɪvəl] *n* reestreno, reposición.

revolt [rɪ'vəʊlt] *n* revuelta. ► *vi* sublevarse. ► *vt* repugnar.

revolting [rɪ'vəʊltɪŋ] *adj* repugnante.

revolution [revə'luːʃən] *n* revolución.

reward [rɪ'wɔːd] *n* recompensa. ► *vt* recompensar.

rewind [riː'waɪnd] *vt* rebobinar.

rheumatism ['ruːmətɪzəm] *n* reumatismo, reuma.

rhinoceros [raɪ'nɒsərəs] *n* rinoceronte.

rhyme [raɪm] *n* rima.

rhythm ['rɪðəm] *n* ritmo.

rib [rɪb] *n* costilla.

ribbon ['rɪbən] *n* cinta.

rice [raɪs] *n* arroz. ■ **rice pudding** arroz con leche.

rich [rɪtʃ] *adj* **1** rico,-a. **2** fuerte, pesado,-a *(comida)*.

ricochet ['rɪkəʃeɪ] *n* rebote. ► *vi* rebotar.

rid [rɪd] *vt* librar. • **to get rid of** deshacerse de.

ridden ['rɪdən] *pp* → ride.

riddle ['rɪdəl] *n* **1** acertijo, adivinanza. **2** enigma.

ride [raɪd] *n* paseo, vuelta. ► *vi* montar a caballo. ► *vt* montar *(a caballo, en moto, bicicleta)*.

rider ['raɪdə'] *n* **1** jinete, amazona. **2** ciclista. **3** motorista.

ridiculous [rɪ'dɪkjʊləs] *adj* ridículo,-a.

riding ['raɪdɪŋ] *n* equitación.

rife [raɪf] *adj* extendido.

rifle ['raɪfəl] *n* rifle, fusil.

rig [rɪg] *n* plataforma petrolífera.

right [raɪt] *adj* **1** derecho,-a *(mano)*. **2** correcto,-a. **3** justo,-a. ► *adv* **1** a la derecha, hacia la derecha. **2** bien: *he spelt her name right*, escribió bien su nombre. **3** inmediatamente. ► *n* **1** derecha. **2** derecho. **3** bien.. • **all right!** ¡bien!, ¡vale!; **right away** enseguida; **right now** ahora mismo; **to be right** tener razón. ■ **right angle** ángulo recto.

right-hand ['raɪthænd] *adj* derecho,-a.

rigid ['rɪdʒɪd] *adj* rígido,-a.

rigour ['rɪgə'] (US **rigor**) *n* rigor.

rim [rɪm] *n* **1** borde, canto. **2** llanta.

rind [raɪnd] *n* corteza.

ring¹ [rɪŋ] *n* **1** anillo. **2** anilla. **3** círculo *(de personas)*. **4** pista. **5** ring, cuadrilátero. ■ **ring road** carretera de circunvalación.

ring² [rɪŋ] *n* **1** tañido; toque *(de campana)*. **2** llamada *(de teléfono, al timbre)*. ► *vi* **1** tañer, repicar *(campana)*. **2** sonar *(teléfono, timbre)*. ► *vt* **1** llamar *(por teléfono)*. **2** tocar *(timbre)*.

rink [rɪŋk] *n* pista de patinaje.

rinse [rɪns] *vt* aclarar.

riot ['raɪət] *n* **1** disturbio. **2** motín. ► *vi* amotinarse.

rip [rɪp] *n* rasgadura. ► *vt-vi* rasgar(se).

ripe [raɪp] *adj* maduro,-a.

rip-off ['rɪpɒf] *n fam* timo.

rise [raɪz] *n* **1** ascenso, subida. **2** aumento *(de sueldo)*. **3** subida, cuesta *(en montaña)*. ► *vi* **1** ascender, subir. **2** aumentar *(precios)*. **3** levantarse *(de la cama)*. **4** salir *(sol, luna)*. **5** alzarse *(voz)*. ● **to give rise to** dar origen a.

risen ['rɪzən] *pp* → rise.

risk [rɪsk] *n* riesgo, peligro. ► *vt* arriesgar.

risky ['rɪskɪ] *adj* arriesgado,-a.

rite [raɪt] *n* rito.

ritual ['rɪtjʊəl] *adj-n* ritual.

rival ['raɪvəl] *adj-n* competidor,-ra, rival. ► *vt* competir con, rivalizar con.

rivalry ['raɪvəlrɪ] *n* rivalidad.

river ['rɪvə'] *n* río.

riverside ['rɪvəsaɪd] *n* ribera.

rivet ['rɪvɪt] *n* remache. ► *vt* remachar.

road [rəʊd] *n* **1** carretera. **2** camino. ■ **road sign** señal de tráfico.

roadway ['rəʊdweɪ] *n* calzada.

roam [rəʊm] *vi* vagar.

roar [rɔː'] *n* **1** bramido. **2** rugido *(de león)*. **3** estruendo *(de tráfico)*. ► *vi* rugir, bramar.

roast [rəʊst] *adj* asado,-a. ► *n* asado. ► *vt* **1** asar *(carne)*. **2** tostar *(café, cacahuetes)*.

rob [rɒb] *vt* **1** robar. **2** atracar *(banco)*.

robber ['rɒbə'] *n* **1** ladrón,-ona. **2** atracador,-ra *(de banco)*.

robbery ['rɒbərɪ] *n* **1** robo. **2** atraco *(de banco)*.

robe [rəʊb] *n* bata.

robot ['rəʊbɒt] *n* robot.

rock [rɒk] *n* **1** roca. **2** rock *(música)*. ► *vt-vi* mecer(se). ● **on the rocks** con hielo *(bebida)*.

rocker ['rɒkə'] *n* balancín.

rocket ['rɒkɪt] *n* cohete.

rocking-chair ['rɒkɪŋtʃeə'] *n* mecedora.

rod [rɒd] *n* **1** vara. **2** barra.

rub out

rode [rəʊd] *pt* → ride.

role [rəʊl] *n* papel.

roll [rəʊl] *n* **1** rollo. **2** lista. **3** bollo, panecillo. ► *vt* **1** hacer rodar. **2** enroscar. **3** liar *(cigarrillo)*. ► *vi* **1** rodar. **2** enroscarse.

roller ['rəʊləʳ] *n* **1** rodillo. **2** rulo. ■ **roller coaster** montaña rusa; **roller skating** patinaje sobre ruedas.

roller-skate ['rəʊləskeɪt] *vi* patinar sobre ruedas.

romance [rəʊ'mæns] *n* **1** romanticismo. **2** romance.

romantic [rəʊ'mæntɪk] *adj* romántico,-a.

roof [ru:f] *n* **1** tejado. **2** cielo *(de boca)*. **3** techo *(de coche)*.

roof-rack ['ru:fræk] *n* baca.

rook [rʊk] *n* **1** grajo. **2** torre *(en ajedrez)*.

room [ru:m] *n* **1** cuarto, habitación. **2** espacio, sitio. ● **to take up room** ocupar sitio.

roomy ['ru:mɪ] *adj* espacioso,-a, amplio,-a.

rooster ['ru:stəʳ] *n* gallo.

root [ru:t] *n* raíz.

rope [rəʊp] *n* cuerda.

rosary ['rəʊzərɪ] *n* rosario.

rose¹ [rəʊz] *n* rosa.

rose² [rəʊz] *pt* → rise.

rosé ['rəʊzeɪ] *n* vino rosado.

rosemary ['rəʊzmərɪ] *n* romero.

rot [rɒt] *vt-vi* pudrir(se).

rotate [rəʊ'teɪt] *vi* girar. ► *vt-vi* *fig* alternar.

rotten ['rɒtən] *adj* podrido,-a

rouge [ru:ʒ] *n* colorete.

rough [rʌf] *adj* **1** áspero,-a, basto,-a *(superficie)*. **2** desigual *(suelo)*. **3** agitado,-a *(mar)*. **4** rudo,-a, tosco,-a *(persona, modales)*. **5** aproximado,-a *(presupuesto)*. ■ **rough copy** borrador; **rough sea** marejada; **rough version** borrador.

roughly ['rʌflɪ] *adv* aproximadamente.

roulette [ru:'let] *n* ruleta.

round [raʊnd] *adj* redondo,-a. ► *n* **1** círculo. **2** ronda. **3** asalto *(de boxeo)*. ► *adv* por ahí. ► *prep* **1** alrededor de. **2** a la vuelta de.

roundabout ['raʊndəbaʊt] *adj* indirecto,-a. ► *n* **1** tiovivo. **2** GB rotonda.

rouse [raʊz] *vt-vi* despertar(se). ► *vt* provocar.

route [ru:t, US raʊt] *n* ruta.

routine [ru:'ti:n] *n* rutina.

row¹ [raʊ] *n* **1** riña, pelea. **2** jaleo, ruido

row² [rəʊ] *n* fila, hilera. ● **in a row** en fila.

row³ [rəʊ] *vt-vi* remar.

rowing ['rəʊɪŋ] *n* remo.

royal ['rɔɪəl] *adj* real.

royalty ['rɔɪəltɪ] *n* realeza. ► *npl* **royalties** derechos.

rub [rʌb] *vt* frotar, restregar. ► *vi* rozar.

to rub out *vt* borrar.

rubber ['rʌbə'] n 1 caucho, goma. 2 goma de borrar. ■ **rubber ring** flotador.
rubbish ['rʌbɪʃ] n basura.
rubble ['rʌbəl] n escombros.
rubella [ruː'belə] n rubeola, rubéola.
ruby ['ruːbɪ] n rubí.
rucksack ['rʌksæk] n mochila.
rudder ['rʌdə'] n timón.
rude [ruːd] adj maleducado,-a.
rug [rʌg] n alfombrilla.
rugby ['rʌgbɪ] n rugby.
ruin [ruːɪn] n ruina. ► vt 1 arruinar. 2 estropear.
rule [ruːl] n 1 regla, norma. 2 gobierno. 3 reinado. ► vt-vi 1 gobernar. 2 reinar.
ruler ['ruːlə'] n 1 gobernante. 2 regla.
rum [rʌm] n ron.
ruminant ['ruːmɪnənt] adj-n rumiante.
rumour ['ruːmə'] (US **rumor**) n rumor. ► vt rumorear.
rump [rʌmp] n ancas.
rumpus ['rʌmpəs] n fam jaleo, escándalo.
run [rʌn] vi 1 correr. 2 funcionar (aparato, organización). 3 presentarse (a elecciones). 4 durar. 5 circular (autobús, tren). 6 desteñirse (color). ► vt 1 correr en. 2 llevar (en coche, moto). 3 dirigir (organización). 4 hacer funcionar (aparato). 5 ejecutar (macro, programa). ► n 1 carrera. 2 viaje, paseo.
3 racha. 4 pista (de esquí). 5 carrera (en media). • **in the long run** a la larga.
to run after vt perseguir.
to run away vi escaparse.
to run into vt 1 chocar con (coche). 2 tropezar con (persona).
to run out vi acabarse.
runaway ['rʌnəweɪ] adj-n fugitivo,-a.
rung [rʌŋ] n escalón. ► pp → ring.
runner ['rʌnə'] n corredor,-ra.
runner-up [rʌnər'ʌp] n subcampeón,-ona.
running ['rʌnɪŋ] n 1 atletismo. 2 gestión, dirección. ► adj 1 corriente (agua). 2 continuo, -a. ■ **running costs** gastos de mantenimiento.
runny ['rʌnɪ] adj blando,-a, líquido,-a.
run-of-the-mill [rʌnəvðə'mɪl] adj corriente y moliente.
runway ['rʌnweɪ] n pista de aterrizaje.
rupture ['rʌptʃə'] n ruptura.
rural ['ruərəl] adj rural.
rush [rʌʃ] n prisa. ► vt 1 apresurar, dar prisa a. 2 llevar rápidamente. ► vi apresurarse. ■ **rush hour** hora punta.
rust [rʌst] n óxido. ► vt-vi oxidar(se).
rustic ['rʌstɪk] adj rústico,-a.
rut [rʌt] n surco.
rye [raɪ] n centeno.

S

sabotage ['sæbətɑːʒ] *n* sabotaje. ► *vt* sabotear.

sack [sæk] *n* saco. ► *vt fam* despedir a. • **to get the sack** *fam* ser despedido,-a.

sacred ['seɪkrəd] *adj* sagrado,-a.

sacrifice ['sækrɪfaɪs] *n* sacrificio. ► *vt* sacrificar.

sad [sæd] *adj* triste.

saddle ['sædəl] *n* **1** silla (*de montar*). **2** sillín (*de bicicleta*).

sadness ['sædnəs] *n* tristeza.

safe [seɪf] *adj* **1** a salvo. **2** seguro,-a. ► *n* caja fuerte.

safety ['seɪftɪ] *n* seguridad. ■ **safety belt** cinturón de seguridad; **safety pin** imperdible.

said [sed] *pt-pp* → say.

sail [seɪl] *n* vela. ► *vi* navegar. • **to set sail** zarpar.

sailing ['seɪlɪŋ] *n* vela (*deporte*). ■ **sailing boat** velero.

sailor ['seɪləʳ] *n* marinero.

saint [seɪnt] *n* san, santo,-a.

sake [seɪk] *n* bien. • **for the sake of** por, por el bien de.

salad ['sæləd] *n* ensalada. ■ **salad bowl** ensaladera; **salad dressing** aliño, aderezo.

salary ['sælərɪ] *n* salario.

sale [seɪl] *n* **1** venta. **2** liquidación, rebajas. **3** subasta. • **for sale** en venta; **on sale 1** a la venta. **2** rebajado,-a.

salesclerk ['seɪlzklɑːk] *n* dependiente,-a.

salesman ['seɪlzmən] *n* **1** vendedor. **2** dependiente. **3** representante, viajante.

saleswoman ['seɪlzwʊmən] *n* **1** vendedora. **2** dependienta. **3** representante, viajante.

saliva [sə'laɪvə] *n* saliva.

salmon ['sæmən] *n* salmón.

salon ['sælɒn] *n* salón.

salt [sɔːlt] *n* sal. ■ **salt beef** cecina; **salt pork** tocino.

salty ['sɔːltɪ] *adj* salado,-a.

salute [sə'luːt] *n* saludo.

same [seɪm] *adj* mismo,-a. ► *pron* **the same** lo mismo. ► *adv* igual, del mismo modo. • **all the same** a pesar de todo.

sample ['sɑːmpəl] *n* muestra. ► *vt* probar, catar (*vino*).

sanction ['sæŋkʃən] *n* sanción. ► *vt* sancionar.

sanctuary ['sæŋktjʊərɪ] *n* santuario.

sand [sænd] *n* arena. ■ **sand dune** duna.

sandal ['sændəl] *n* sandalia.

sandpaper ['sændpeɪpəʳ] *n* papel de lija. ► *vt* lijar.

sandwich ['sænwɪdʒ] *n* sandwich, emparedado.

sang [sæŋ] *pt* → sing.

sanitary ['sænɪtərɪ] *adj* **1** sanitario,-a. **2** higiénico,-a. ■ **sanitary towel** compresa.

sank [sæŋk] *pt* → sink.

sap [sæp] *n* savia.

sapphire ['sæfaɪəʳ] *n* zafiro.

sardine [sɑːˈdiːn] *n* sardina.

sash [sæʃ] *n* faja.

sat [sæt] *pt-pp* → sit.

satchel ['sætʃəl] *n* cartera.

satellite ['sætəlaɪt] *n* satélite. ▪ **satellite dish aerial** antena parabólica.

satisfaction [sætɪsˈfækʃən] *n* satisfacción.

satisfy ['sætɪsfaɪ] *vt* satisfacer.

Saturday ['sætədɪ] *n* sábado.

sauce [sɔːs] *n* salsa. ▪ **sauce boat** salsera.

saucepan ['sɔːspən] *n* **1** cazo, cacerola. **2** olla.

saucer ['sɔːsəʳ] *n* platillo.

sauna ['sɔːnə] *n* sauna.

sausage ['sɒsɪdʒ] *n* salchicha.

savage ['sævɪdʒ] *adj-n* salvaje.

save [seɪv] *vt* **1** salvar *(vida)*. **2** guardar *(comida, fuerzas)*. **3** ahorrar *(dinero)*. **4** archivar *(en ordenador)*. **5** evitar. **6** parar *(pelota)*. ▶ *vi* ahorrar.

saving ['seɪvɪŋ] *n* ahorro. ▶ *npl* **savings** ahorros. ▪ **savings account** cuenta de ahorros; **savings bank** caja de ahorros.

savour ['seɪvəʳ] (US **savor**) *n* sabor. ▶ *vt* saborear.

savoury ['seɪvərɪ] (US **savory**) *adj* salado,-a. ▶ *n* canapé, entremés.

saw[1] [sɔː] *n* sierra. ▶ *vt-vi* serrar.

saw[2] [sɔː] *pt* → see.

sawdust ['sɔːdʌst] *n* serrín.

sawn [sɔːn] *pp* → saw.

saxophone ['sæksəfəʊn] *n* saxofón.

say [seɪ] *vt* decir. ● **it is said that ...** dicen que ..., se dice que ...; **that is to say** es decir.

saying ['seɪɪŋ] *n* dicho, decir.

scab [skæb] *n* costra.

scaffold ['skæfəʊld] *n* **1** andamio. **2** patíbulo.

scald [skɔːld] *vt* escaldar.

scale[1] [skeɪl] *n* escama.

scale[2] [skeɪl] *n* balanza.

scale[3] [skeɪl] *n* escala. ▪ **scale model** maqueta.

scalp [skælp] *n* cuero cabelludo.

scalpel ['skælpəl] *n* bisturí.

scampi ['skæmpɪ] *n* gambas a la gabardina.

scan [skæn] *vt* examinar. ▶ *n* ecografía.

scandal ['skændəl] *n* escándalo.

scar [skɑːʳ] *n* cicatriz.

scarce [skeəs] *adj* escaso,-a.

scarcely ['skeəslɪ] *adv* apenas.

scare [skeəʳ] *vt-vi* asustar(se).

scarecrow ['skeəkrəʊ] *n* espantapájaros.

scarf [skɑːf] *n* **1** pañuelo. **2** bufanda.

scarlet ['skɑːlət] *adj-n* escarlata. ▪ **scarlet fever** escarlatina.

scary ['skeərɪ] *adj* espeluznante.

scatter ['skætə^r] *vt-vi* **1** dispersar(se). **2** esparcir(se).

scenario [sɪ'nɑːrɪəʊ] *n* **1** guion. **2** perspectiva, panorama.

scene [siːn] *n* **1** escena. **2** escenario. **3** vista, panorama. • **behind the scenes** entre bastidores.

scent [sent] *n* **1** olor, fragancia. **2** perfume. **3** pista, rastro.

schedule ['ʃedjuːl, 'skedjuːl] *n* **1** programa. **2** lista. **3** US horario. ► *vt* programar, fijar. • **on schedule** a la hora prevista. ▪ **scheduled flight** vuelo regular.

scheme [skiːm] *n* **1** plan, programa. **2** intriga, ardid.

scholarship ['skɒləʃɪp] *n* beca.

school [skuːl] *n* escuela, colegio, instituto. ▪ **school book** libro de texto.

science ['saɪəns] *n* ciencia. ▪ **science fiction** ciencia ficción.

scientific [saɪən'tɪfɪk] *adj* científico,-a.

scientist ['saɪəntɪst] *n* científico,-a.

scissors ['sɪzəz] *npl* tijeras.

scoff[1] [skɒf] *vi* mofarse.

scoff[2] [skɒf] *vt fam* zamparse.

scold [skəʊld] *vt* reñir.

scoop [skuːp] *n* exclusiva.

scooter ['skuːtə^r] *n* Vespa®.

scope [skəʊp] *n* **1** alcance. **2** posibilidades.

scorch [skɔːtʃ] *vt* chamuscar.

score [skɔː^r] *n* **1** tanteo, puntuación *(en golf, naipes)*. **2** resultado. **3** partitura, música *(de película)*. ► *vt-vi* marcar *(gol, etc)*. ► *vi* obtener una puntuación. ► *vt* lograr, conseguir.

scoreboard ['skɔːbɔːd] *n* marcador.

scorn [skɔːn] *n* desprecio. ► *vt* despreciar.

scorpion ['skɔːpɪən] *n* escorpión.

scoundrel ['skaʊndrəl] *n* canalla.

scout [skaʊt] *n* explorador,-ra.

scowl [skaʊl] *n* ceño fruncido. ► *vi* fruncir el ceño.

scramble ['skræmbəl] *n* lucha. ► *vi* **1** trepar. **2** pelearse. ► *vt* revolver, mezclar. ▪ **scrambled eggs** huevos revueltos.

scrap [skræp] *vt* desechar. ► *n* trozo, pedazo. ► *npl* **scraps** restos, sobras *(de comida)*. ▪ **scrap metal** chatarra; **scrap paper** papel usado.

scrape [skreɪp] *vt* **1** rascar. **2** rasparse.

scratch [skrætʃ] *n* rasguño, arañazo. ► *vt* **1** arañar. **2** rascar.

scream [skriːm] *n* grito. ► *vt-vi* gritar, chillar.

screen [skriːn] *n* **1** biombo. **2** pantalla *(de cine, televisión)*. ► *vt* **1** proteger. **2** examinar. **3** proyectar *(película)*. ▪ **screen saver** protector de pantalla.

screw [skru:] *n* tornillo. ► *vt* atornillar.

screwdriver ['skru:draɪvəʳ] *n* destornillador.

scribble ['skrɪbəl] *n* garabatos. ► *vt-vi* garabatear.

script [skrɪpt] *n* guion.

scrounge [skraʊndʒ] *vi* gorronear. ► *vt* gorronear.

scrub [skrʌb] *n* 1 maleza. 2 fregado. ► *vt* fregar.

scruff [skrʌf] *n* cogote.

scruffy ['skrʌfɪ] *adj* desaliñado,-a.

scrupulous ['skru:pjʊləs] *adj* escrupuloso,-a.

scrutinize ['skru:tɪnaɪz] *vt* escudriñar.

scuba diving ['sku:bədaɪvɪŋ] *n* submarinismo.

sculptor ['skʌlptəʳ] *n* escultor,-ra.

sculptress ['skʌlptrəs] *n* escultora.

sculpture ['skʌlptʃəʳ] *n* escultura.

scum [skʌm] *n* espuma.

sea [si:] *n* mar. ■ **sea lion** león marino; **sea trout** trucha de mar, reo.

seafood ['si:fu:d] *n* marisco.

seafront ['si:frʌnt] *n* paseo marítimo.

seagull ['si:gʌl] *n* gaviota.

sea-horse ['si:hɔ:s] *n* caballito de mar.

seal¹ [si:l] *n* foca.

seal² [si:l] *n* sello. ► *vt* sellar.

seam [si:m] *n* 1 costura. 2 juntura, junta.

search [sɜ:tʃ] *n* 1 búsqueda. 2 registro *(de edificio, persona)*. ► *vi* buscar. ► *vt* registrar. ■ **search engine** buscador; **search warrant** orden de registro.

seasick ['si:sɪk] *adj* mareado,-a.

seaside ['si:saɪd] *n* playa, costa. ■ **seaside resort** centro turístico en la costa.

season ['si:zən] *n* 1 estación *(del año)*. 2 temporada *(para deporte, etc)*. ► *vt* sazonar. • **in season** 1 en sazón *(fruta)*. 2 en celo *(animal)*. 3 en temporada alta *(turismo)*; **out of season** 1 fuera de temporada *(fruta)*. 2 en temporada baja *(turismo)*. ■ **season ticket** abono.

seat [si:t] *n* 1 asiento. 2 localidad *(en teatro, etc)*. 3 escaño. ► *vt* sentar(se). • **to take a seat** sentarse. ■ **seat belt** cinturón de seguridad.

seaweed ['si:wi:d] *n* alga.

second¹ ['sekənd] *adj-n* segundo,-a. ► *adv* segundo. ► *vt* secundar. ► *npl* **seconds** artículos defectuosos. ■ **second name** apellido.

second² ['sekənd] *n* segundo.

secondary ['sekəndərɪ] *adj* secundario,-a. ■ **secondary school** escuela de enseñanza secundaria.

second-hand ['sekəndhænd] *adj* de segunda mano.

secret ['siːkrət] *adj* secreto,-a. ▶ *n* secreto.

secretary ['sekrətərɪ] *n* secretario,-a. ■ **Secretary of State 1** ministro,-a con cartera *(en GB)*. **2** ministro,-a de Estado *(en EEUU)*.

secrete [sɪ'kriːt] *vt* secretar.

sect [sekt] *n* secta.

section ['sekʃən] *n* sección.

sector ['sektə'] *n* sector.

secure [sɪ'kjʊə'] *adj* seguro,-a.

security [sɪ'kjʊərɪtɪ] *n* seguridad. ▶ *npl* **securities** COMM valores.

sedative ['sedətɪv] *adj-n* sedante.

seduce [sɪ'djuːs] *vt* seducir.

see[1] [siː] *vt-vi* **1** ver. **2** procurar. **3** acompañar. **4** entender. ● **let's see** a ver, vamos a ver; **see you later!** ¡hasta luego!

to see off *vt* despedirse de.

to see out *vt* acompañar hasta la puerta.

seed [siːd] *n* **1** semilla *(de planta)*. **2** pepita *(de fruta)*. **3** cabeza de serie *(tenis)*.

seek [siːk] *vt* **1** buscar. **2** solicitar.

seem [siːm] *vi* parecer.

seen [siːn] *pp* → see.

seesaw ['siːsɔː] *n* balancín.

see-through ['siːθruː] *adj* transparente.

segment ['segmənt] *n* segmento.

seize [siːz] *vt* **1** agarrar, coger. **2** incautar, embargar. **3** tomar, apoderarse de.

seldom ['seldəm] *adv* rara vez.

select [sɪ'lekt] *vt* seleccionar. ▶ *adj* selecto,-a.

selection [sɪ'lekʃən] *n* selección.

self [self] *n* yo.

self-conscious [self'kɒnʃəs] *adj* cohibido,-a, tímido,-a.

self-defence [selfdɪ'fens] *n* autodefensa. ● **in self-defence** en defensa propia.

self-employed [selfɪm'plɔɪd] *adj* autónomo,-a.

selfish ['selfɪʃ] *adj* egoísta.

self-portrait [self'pɔːtreɪt] *n* autorretrato.

self-service [self'sɜːvɪs] *n* autoservicio.

sell [sel] *vt-vi* vender.

to sell off *vt* liquidar.

to sell out *vt* agotarse.

sell-by date ['selbaɪdeɪt] *n* fecha de caducidad.

seller ['selə'] *n* vendedor,-ra.

Sellotape® ['seləteɪp] *n* Celo®, cinta adhesiva.

semester [sɪ'mestə'] *n* semestre.

semicolon [semɪ'kəʊlən] *n* punto y coma.

semidetached [semɪdɪ'tætʃt] *adj* adosado,-a. ▶ *n* casa adosada.

semifinal [semɪ'faɪnəl] *n* semifinal.

senate ['senət] *n* senado.

senator ['senətə'] *n* senador,-ra.

send [send] *vt* enviar, mandar.

sender ['sendə'] *n* remitente.

senior ['si:nɪə'] *adj* **1** mayor *(por edad)*. **2** superior *(por rango)*. ► *n* **1** mayor *(por edad)*. **2** superior *(por rango)*. ■ **senior citizen** persona de la tercera edad.

sensation [sen'seɪʃən] *n* sensación.

sense [sens] *n* sentido. ► *vt* sentir, percibir. ● **to make sense** tener sentido, ser sensato,-a.

sensibility [sensɪ'bɪlɪtɪ] *n* sensibilidad.

sensible ['sensɪbəl] *adj* sensato,-a.

sensitive ['sensɪtɪv] *adj* **1** sensible. **2** confidencial.

sent [sent] *pt-pp* → send.

sentence ['sentəns] *n* **1** frase. **2** sentencia, fallo. ► *vt* condenar.

sentry ['sentrɪ] *n* centinela.

separate [*(vb)* 'sepəreɪt, *(adj)* 'sepərət] *vt-vi* separar(se). ► *adj* **1** separado,-a. **2** distinto,-a.

September [sep'tembə'] *n* septiembre, setiembre.

sequence ['si:kwəns] *n* **1** secuencia. **2** sucesión, serie.

serene [sə'ri:n] *adj* sereno,-a.

sergeant ['sɑ:dʒənt] *n* sargento.

serial ['sɪərɪəl] *n* serial. ■ **serial number** número de serie.

series ['sɪərɪːz] *n* serie.

serious ['sɪərɪəs] *adj* **1** serio,-a. **2** grave *(accidente)*.

servant ['sɜːvənt] *n* criado,-a.

serve [sɜːv] *vt-vi* servir. ► *vt* cumplir *(condena)*. ► *n* saque *(en tenis)*.

service ['sɜːvɪs] *n* **1** servicio. **2** revisión, puesta a punto *(de coche)*. **3** oficio *(religioso)*. ● **in service** en funcionamiento; **out of service** fuera de servicio. ■ **service station** estación de servicio.

serviette [sɜːvɪ'et] *n* GB servilleta.

session ['seʃən] *n* sesión.

set[1] [set] *n* **1** juego. **2** conjunto. **3** set *(tenis)*. **4** aparato *(televisor, radio)*.

set[2] [set] *n* plató *(de televisión)*. ► *adj* **1** fijo,-a *(cantidad)*. **2** listo,-a. ► *vt* **1** poner, colocar,. **2** fijar *(fecha)*. **3** marcar *(pelo)*. ► *vi* **1** ponerse *(sol)*. **2** cuajar *(líquido)*. **3** endurecerse *(cemento)*. ● **to set (oneself) up** establecerse. ■ **set lunch** menú del día.

to set back *vt* **1** atrasar, retrasar. **2** *fam* costar.

to set off *vi* salir, ponerse en camino. ► *vt* **1** hacer estallar *(bomba)*. **2** hacer saltar *(alarma)*.

to set out *vi* **1** partir, salir. **2** proponerse, pretender. ► *vt* disponer, exponer.

to set up *vt* **1** levantar *(monumento)*. **2** montar *(tienda de campaña, negocio)*. **3** planear, convocar.

setback ['setbæk] *n* revés.

settee [se'tiː] *n* sofá.

setting ['setɪŋ] *n* **1** escenario *(de película)*. **2** ajuste *(de máquina)*.

settle ['setəl] *vt* **1** acordar *(precio)*. **2** resolver *(disputa)*. ► *vi* **1** posarse *(pájaro)*; depositarse *(polvo)*. **2** afincarse, establecerse. **3** calmarse.

to settle down *vi* **1** instalarse, afincarse. **2** sentar la cabeza. **3** tranquilizarse.

settlement ['setəlmənt] *n* **1** poblado, colonia. **2** acuerdo. **3** pago.

seven ['sevən] *num* siete.

seventeen [sevən'tiːn] *num* diecisiete.

seventeenth [sevən'tiːnθ] *adj* decimoséptimo,-a.

seventh ['sevənθ] *adj-n* séptimo,-a.

seventy ['sevəntɪ] *num* setenta.

several ['sevərəl] *adj-pron* varios,-as.

severe [sɪ'vɪəʳ] *adj* **1** severo, -a. **2** grave *(enfermedad)*.

sew [səʊ] *vt-vi* coser.

sewage ['sjuːɪdʒ] *n* aguas residuales.

sewer [sjʊəʳ] *n* alcantarilla.

sewing ['səʊɪŋ] *n* costura. ■ **sewing machine** máquina de coser.

sewn [səʊn] *pp* → sew.

sex [seks] *n* sexo.

shabby ['ʃæbɪ] *adj* raído,-a.

shack [ʃæk] *n* choza.

shade [ʃeɪd] *n* **1** sombra. **2** pantalla *(de lámpara)*. **3** tono *(de color)*. ► *vt* dar sombra.

shadow ['ʃædəʊ] *n* sombra.

shady ['ʃeɪdɪ] *adj* **1** a la sombra *(lugar)*. **2** *fam* sospechoso,-a *(persona)*.

shaft [ʃɑːft] *n* **1** mango. **2** eje.

shake [ʃeɪk] *n* **1** sacudida. **2** batido *(bebida)*. ► *vt* sacudir. ► *vi* temblar.

shall [ʃæl, unstressed ʃəl] *aux* **1** *indica un tiempo futuro*: **I shall go tomorrow**, iré mañana. **2** *indica ofrecimiento*: **shall I close the window?**, ¿cierro la ventana? **3** *indica una sugerencia*: **shall we go to the cinema?**, ¿vamos al cine? **4** *indica una promesa*: **you shall have everything you want, my dear**, tendrás todo lo que desees, cariño. **5** *uso enfático, una orden*: **you shall stop work immediately**, debes parar de trabajar enseguida.

shallow ['ʃæləʊ] *adj* poco profundo,-a.

shame [ʃeɪm] n 1 vergüenza. 2 lástima, pena.

shampoo [ʃæm'puː] n champú.

shandy ['ʃændɪ] n GB clara.

shape [ʃeɪp] n forma, figura. ► vt modelar.• **out of shape** en baja forma.

share [ʃeəʳ] n 1 parte. 2 acción (en bolsa). ► vt-vi compartir. ► vt repartir.

shareholder ['ʃeəhəʊldəʳ] n accionista.

shark [ʃɑːk] n tiburón.

sharp [ʃɑːp] adj 1 afilado,-a (cuchillo). 2 puntiagudo,-a (palo). 3 agudo,-a (dolor, persona). 4 cerrado,-a (curva). ► adv en punto.

sharpen ['ʃɑːpən] vt 1 afilar (cuchillo). 2 sacar punta a (lápiz).

sharpener ['ʃɑːpənəʳ] n sacapuntas.

shatter ['ʃætəʳ] vi romperse, hacerse añicos.

shave [ʃeɪv] n afeitado. ► vt-vi afeitar(se).

shaver ['ʃeɪvəʳ] n máquina de afeitar.

shaving ['ʃeɪvɪŋ] n afeitado. ■ **shaving brush** brocha de afeitar; **shaving foam** espuma de afeitar.

shawl [ʃɔːl] n chal.

she [ʃiː] pron ella.

shear [ʃɪəʳ] vt esquilar.

shed[1] [ʃed] n cobertizo.

shed[2] [ʃed] vt1 derramar (lágrimas). 2 quitarse (ropa).

sheep [ʃiːp] n oveja.

sheet [ʃiːt] n 1 sábana. 2 hoja (de papel). 3 lámina (de metal).

shelf [ʃelf] n estante. ► npl **shelves** estantería.

shell [ʃel] n 1 cáscara (de huevo, nuez). 2 vaina (de guisante). 3 caparazón (de tortuga). 4 concha (de caracola). 5 obús, proyectil.

shellfish ['ʃelfɪʃ] n marisco.

shelter ['ʃeltəʳ] n refugio. ► vt proteger.

shepherd ['ʃepəd] n pastor.

sherry ['ʃerɪ] n jerez.

shield [ʃiːld] n escudo.

shift [ʃɪft] n 1 cambio. 2 turno (de trabajo). ► vt-vi cambiar(se) de sitio.

shilling ['ʃɪlɪŋ] n chelín.

shin [ʃɪn] n espinilla.

shine [ʃaɪn] n brillo, lustre. ► vi brillar.

shingles ['ʃɪŋgəlz] npl herpes.

shiny ['ʃaɪnɪ] adj brillante.

ship [ʃɪp] n barco, buque.

shipwreck ['ʃɪprek] n naufragio.

shipyard ['ʃɪpjɑːd] n astillero.

shirt [ʃɜːt] n camisa.

shit [ʃɪt] n vulg mierda.

shiver ['ʃɪvəʳ] n escalofrío. ► vi 1 tiritar. 2 temblar.

shock [ʃɒk] n 1 choque. 2 golpe, conmoción. 3 susto. 4 shock. ► vt escandalizar.

shocking ['ʃɒkɪŋ] *adj* escandaloso,-a, chocante.

shoe [ʃuː] *n* **1** zapato. **2** herradura. ▪ **shoe polish** betún; **shoe shop** zapatería.

shoehorn ['ʃuːhɔːn] *n* calzador.

shoelace ['ʃuːleɪs] *n* cordón.

shoemaker ['ʃuːmeɪkəʳ] *n* zapatero,-a.

shone [ʃɒn] *pt-pp* → shine.

shook [ʃʊk] *pt* → shake.

shoot [ʃuːt] *n* **1** brote, retoño. **2** rodaje *(de película)*. ▶ *vt* **1** pegar un tiro a. **2** disparar. **3** rodar *(película)*. **4** chutar *(pelota)*. ▶ *vi* disparar. ▪ **shooting star** estrella fugaz.

to shoot down *vt* **1** derribar. **2** matar a tiros.

shop [ʃɒp] *n* tienda. ▶ *vi* hacer compras, ir de compras. ▪ **shop assistant** dependiente,-a; **shop window** escaparate.

shoplifting ['ʃɒplɪftɪŋ] *n* hurto *(en tiendas)*.

shopping ['ʃɒpɪŋ] *n* compras. ▪ **shopping arcade** galerías comerciales; **shopping centre** GB centro comercial.

shore [ʃɔːʳ] *n* orilla, costa.

shorn [ʃɔːn] *pp* → shear.

short [ʃɔːt] *adj* **1** corto,-a. **2** bajo,-a *(estatura, persona)*. **3** seco,-a, brusco,-a *(modales)*. ▶ *n* cortometraje. ▶ *npl* **shorts** pantalón corto. • **in short** en pocas palabras; **for short** para abreviar; **to be short of** andar mal de. ▪ **short circuit** cortocircuito; **short cut** atajo; **short story** cuento, relato.

shortage ['ʃɔːtɪdʒ] *n* escasez.

shorten ['ʃɔːtən] *vt-vi* acortar(se).

shortly ['ʃɔːtlɪ] *adv* en breve. • **shortly after** poco después; **shortly before** poco antes.

short-sighted [ʃɔːt'saɪtɪd] *adj* miope.

shot¹ [ʃɒt] *n* **1** tiro, disparo. **2** intento. **3** trago. **4** foto. **5** toma *(en cine)*.

shot² [ʃɒt] *pt-pp* → shoot.

shotgun ['ʃɒtgʌn] *n* escopeta.

should [ʃʊd] *aux* **1** debe. **2** deber de.

shoulder ['ʃəʊldəʳ] *n* **1** hombro *(de persona)*. **2** espalda *(de carne)*. ▪ **shoulder blade** omoplato, omóplato.

shout [ʃaʊt] *n* grito. ▶ *vt-vi* gritar.

shove [ʃʌv] *n* empujón. ▶ *vt-vi* empujar.

shovel ['ʃʌvəl] *n* pala.

show [ʃəʊ] *n* **1** espectáculo, función. **2** programa *(televisivo, de radio)*. **3** exposición, feria. **4** demostración, muestra. ▶ *vt* **1** mostrar. **2** exponer. **3** indicar, marcar, señalar. **4** demostrar. ▶ *vt-vi* poner *(película)*. ▪ **show business** el mundo del espectáculo.

to show off *vi* presumir.

to show up *vi fam* presentarse, aparecer.
shower ['ʃauəʳ] *n* **1** ducha. **2** chaparrón. ► *vi* ducharse.
shown [ʃəun] *pp* → show.
showroom ['ʃəurum] *n* sala de exposición.
shrank [ʃræŋk] *pt* → shrink.
shrapnel ['ʃræpnəl] *n* metralla.
shred [ʃred] *n* jirón.
shrimp [ʃrɪmp] *n* GB camarón; US gamba.
shrink [ʃrɪŋk] *vt-vi* encoger(se).
shrivel ['ʃrɪvəl] *vi* marchitarse.
shroud [ʃraud] *n* mortaja.
shrub [ʃrʌb] *n* arbusto.
shrug [ʃrʌg] *vi* encogerse de hombros.
shrunk [ʃrʌŋk] *pp* → shrink.
shuffle ['ʃʌfəl] *vt* barajar. ► *vi* andar arrastrando los pies.
shut [ʃʌt] *vt-vi* cerrar(se).
to shut down *vt-vi* cerrar(se).
to shut up *vi fam* callar(se).
shutdown ['ʃʌtdaun] *n* cierre.
shutter ['ʃʌtəʳ] *n* **1** postigo, contraventana. **2** obturador.
shuttle ['ʃʌtəl] *n* **1** puente aéreo *(de avión)*. **2** servicio regular *(de bus, tren)*. **3** transbordador espacial.
shy [ʃaɪ] *adj* tímido,-a.
shyness ['ʃaɪnəs] *n* timidez.
sick [sɪk] *adj* **1** enfermo,-a. **2** mareado,-a. ■ **sick leave** baja por enfermedad.

sickness ['sɪknəs] *n* **1** enfermedad. **2** náusea, mareo.
side [saɪd] *n* **1** lado. **2** costado *(de persona)*. ● **side by side** juntos,-as. ■ **side effect** efecto secundario; **side street** calle lateral, travesía.
sideboard ['saɪdbɔːd] *n* aparador.
sideburns ['saɪdbɜːnz] *npl* patillas.
sidelight ['saɪdlaɪt] *n* luz de posición.
sideline ['saɪdlaɪn] *n* línea de banda.
sidewalk ['saɪdwɔːk] *n* US acera.
sideways ['saɪdweɪz] *adj* **1** lateral *(movimiento)*. **2** de soslayo *(mirada)*. ► *adv* **1** de lado *(movimiento)*. **2** de soslayo *(mirada)*.
siege [siːdʒ] *n* sitio.
sieve [sɪv] *n* **1** tamiz *(para harina)*. **2** criba *(para granos)*. **3** colador *(para líquidos)*.
sigh [saɪ] *n* suspiro. ► *vi* suspirar.
sight [saɪt] *n* **1** vista. **2** mira *(de escopeta)*. ► *npl* **sights** atracciones. ● **at first sight** a primera vista.
sightseeing ['saɪtsiːɪŋ] *n* visita turística, turismo.
sign [saɪn] *n* **1** signo. **2** señal, gesto. **3** letrero. ► *vt-vi* firmar.
to sign in *vi* firmar el registro.

signal ['sɪgnəl] *n* señal.

signature ['sɪgnɪtʃəʳ] *n* firma.

significant [sɪg'nɪfɪkənt] *adj* significativo,-a.

signpost ['saɪnpəʊst] *n* señal indicadora, poste indicador.

silence ['saɪləns] *n* silencio.

silent ['saɪlənt] *adj* silencioso,-a.

silhouette [sɪluː'et] *n* silueta.

silk [sɪlk] *n* seda.

silkworm ['sɪlkwɜːm] *n* gusano de la seda.

sill [sɪl] *n* alféizar, antepecho.

silly ['sɪlɪ] *adj* tonto,-a.

silver ['sɪlvəʳ] *n* plata. ▪ **silver foil** papel de plata.

similar ['sɪmɪləʳ] *adj* similar.

simmer ['sɪməʳ] *vt-vi* cocer(se) a fuego lento.

simple ['sɪmpəl] *adj* simple.

simplify ['sɪmplɪfaɪ] *vt* simplificar.

sin [sɪn] *n* pecado. ▶ *vi* pecar.

since [sɪns] *adv* desde entonces. ▶ *prep* desde. ▶ *conj* **1** desde que. **2** ya que, puesto que.

sincere [sɪn'sɪəʳ] *adj* sincero,-a.

sincerely [sɪn'sɪəlɪ] *adv* sinceramente. ● **yours sincerely** atentamente *(en carta)*.

sing [sɪŋ] *vt-vi* cantar..

singer ['sɪŋəʳ] *n* cantante.

single ['sɪŋgəl] *adj* **1** solo,-a. **2** único,-a. **3** individual *(cama)*. **4** soltero,-a. ▶ *n* **1** GB billete de ida. **2** single *(disco)*. ▶ *npl*

singles individuales. ▪ **single bed** cama individual; **single parent** madre soltera, padre soltero; **single room** habitación individual.

singular ['sɪŋgjʊləʳ] *adj-n* singular.

sinister ['sɪnɪstəʳ] *adj* siniestro,-a.

sink [sɪŋk] *n* **1** fregadero. **2** US lavabo. ▶ *vt* hundir. ▶ *vi* **1** hundirse *(barco)*. **2** ponerse *(sol, luna)*. **3** bajar, descender.

sinner ['sɪnəʳ] *n* pecador,-ra.

sip [sɪp] *n* sorbo.

sir [sɜːʳ] *n* **1** *fml* señor. **2** sir. ● **Dear Sir** muy señor mío.

siren ['saɪərən] *n* sirena.

sirloin ['sɜːlɔɪn] *n* solomillo.

sister ['sɪstəʳ] *n* hermana.

sister-in-law ['sɪstərɪnlɔː] *n* cuñada.

sit [sɪt] *vi* sentarse.

to sit down *vi* sentarse.

site [saɪt] *n* emplazamiento.

situation [sɪtjʊ'eɪʃən] *n* situación. ▪ **"Situations vacant"** "Ofertas de trabajo".

six [sɪks] *num* seis.

sixteen [sɪks'tiːn] *num* dieciséis.

sixteenth [sɪks'tiːnθ] *adj-n* decimosexto,-a.

sixth [sɪksθ] *adj-n* sexto,-a.

sixty ['sɪkstɪ] *num* sesenta.

size [saɪz] *n* **1** tamaño. **2** talla *(de prenda)*. **3** número *(de zapatos)*.

skate [skeɪt] n patín. ▶ vi patinar.

skateboard ['skeɪtbɔːd] n monopatín.

skating ['skeɪtɪŋ] n patinaje. ■ **skating rink** pista de patinaje.

skeleton ['skelɪtən] n esqueleto. ■ **skeleton key** llave maestra.

sketch [sketʃ] n 1 boceto. 2 esquema. 3 sketch. ▶ vt bosquejar.

ski [skiː] n esquí. ▶ vi esquiar. ■ **ski lift** telesquí, telesilla; **ski resort** estación de esquí.

skid [skɪd] n patinazo. ▶ vi patinar.

skier ['skɪə'] n esquiador,-ra.

skiing ['skiːɪŋ] n esquí.

skill [skɪl] n habilidad.

skilled [skɪld] adj 1 especializado,-a. 2 hábil.

skim [skɪm] vt desnatar.

skin [skɪn] n piel. ▶ vt 1 pelar. 2 despellejar.

skip[1] [skɪp] n salto. ▶ vi saltar. ■ **skipping rope** comba.

skip[2] [skɪp] n contenedor.

skirt [skɜːt] n falda. ■ **skirting board** GB zócalo, rodapié.

skittle ['skɪtəl] n bolo. ▶ npl **skittles** bolos.

skull [skʌl] n cráneo.

sky [skaɪ] n cielo.

skylight ['skaɪlaɪt] n tragaluz.

skyscraper ['skaɪskreɪpə'] n rascacielos.

slack [slæk] adj flojo,-a.

slacken ['slækən] vi 1 aflojarse. 2 reducirse, disminuir.

slam [slæm] n portazo. ▶ vt cerrar de golpe.

slang [slæŋ] n argot, jerga.

slap [slæp] n 1 palmadita (en la espalda). 2 bofetada.

slash [slæʃ] n 1 tajo. 2 cuchillada, navajazo. 3 barra oblicua.

slate [sleɪt] n pizarra.

slaughter ['slɔːtə'] n matanza. ▶ vt masacrar.

slave [sleɪv] n esclavo,-a.

sledge [sledʒ] n trineo.

sleep [sliːp] n sueño. ▶ vt-vi dormir.● **to go to sleep** irse a dormir.

sleeping ['sliːpɪŋ] adj. ■ **sleeping bag** saco de dormir; **sleeping car** coche-cama.

sleepwalker ['sliːpwɔːkə'] n sonámbulo,-a.

sleet [sliːt] n aguanieve. ▶ vi caer aguanieve.

sleeve [sliːv] n 1 manga. 2 funda (de disco).

sleigh [sleɪ] n trineo.

slice [slaɪs] n 1 rebanada (de pan). 2 loncha (de jamón). 3 tajada (de carne). 4 rodaja (de limón). 5 porción (de pastel). ▶ vt cortar a rebanadas/lonchas etc.

slide [slaɪd] n 1 resbalón. 2 tobogán. 3 diapositiva. 4 portaobjetos (de microscopio). ▶ vi 1 deslizarse. 2 resbalar.

snap

slight [slaɪt] *adj* ligero,-a.
slightly ['slaɪtlɪ] *adv* un poco.
slim [slɪm] *adj* **1** delgado,-a. ► *vi* adelgazar.
sling [slɪŋ] *n* cabestrillo.
slip¹ [slɪp] *n* **1** resbalón. **2** combinación *(prenda femenina).* ► *vi* esbalar.
slip² [slɪp] *n* **1** papelito. **2** ficha.
slipper ['slɪpəʳ] *n* zapatilla.
slippery ['slɪpərɪ] *adj* resbaladizo,-a
slit [slɪt] *n* abertura.
slogan ['sləʊɡən] *n* eslogan.
slope [sləʊp] *n* cuesta *(de montaña).* ► *vi* inclinarse.
slot [slɒt] *n* **1** abertura. **2** ranura. **3** muesca. ∎ **slot machine 1** máquina expendedora. **2** tragaperras.
slow [sləʊ] *adj* **1** lento,-a. **2** atrasado,-a *(reloj).*
to slow down *vi* reducir la velocidad.
slug [slʌɡ] *n* babosa.
slum [slʌm] *n* **1** barrio bajo. **2** chabola, tugurio.
slump [slʌmp] *n* crisis económica.
sly [slaɪ] *adj* **1** astuto,-a,. **2** furtivo,-a *(mirada).*
smack [smæk] *n* bofetada, cachete. ► *vt* dar una bofetada a.
small [smɔːl] *adj* pequeño,-a. ∎ **small ads** anuncios por palabras; **small change** cambio, suelto.

smallpox ['smɔːlpɒks] *n* viruela.
smart [smɑːt] *adj* **1** elegante. **2** listo,-a.
smash [smæʃ] *n* smash, mate *(en tenis).* ► *vt* romper. ∎ **smash hit** gran éxito, exitazo.
smashing ['smæʃɪŋ] *adj* GB *fam* fenomenal.
smear [smɪəʳ] *n* mancha. ► *vt* **1** untar. **2** manchar.
smell [smel] *n* **1** olfato. **2** olor. ► *vt-vi* oler.
smelt¹ [smelt] *vt* fundir.
smelt² [smelt] *pt-pp* → smell.
smile [smaɪl] *n* sonrisa. ► *vi* sonreír.
smog [smɒɡ] *n* smog.
smoke [sməʊk] *n* humo. ► *vt-vi* fumar. ► *vt* ahumar. • **"No smoking"** "Prohibido fumar".
smoked [sməʊkt] *adj* ahumado,-a.
smoker ['sməʊkəʳ] *n* fumador,-ra.
smooth [smuːð] *adj* **1** liso,-a, llano,-a. **2** sin grumos *(líquido).* **3** suave *(vino).* ► *vt* alisar.
snack [snæk] *n* tentempié. • **to have a snack** picar algo. ∎ **snack bar** cafetería, bar.
snail [sneɪl] *n* caracol.
snake [sneɪk] *n* serpiente.
snap [snæp] *n* foto. ► *vt* **1** partir *(en dos).* **2** chasquear *(los dedos).*

snapshot ['snæpʃʊt] *n* foto instantánea.

sneakers ['sni:krz] *npl* US zapatillas de deporte.

sneeze [sni:z] *n* estornudo. ► *vi* estornudar.

sniff [snɪf] *vt-vi* oler, olfatear.

snip [snɪp] *vt* cortar.

sniper ['snaɪpəʳ] *n* francotirador,-ra.

snob [snɒb] *n* esnob, snob.

snore [snɔːʳ] *n* ronquido. ► *vi* roncar.

snorkel ['snɔːkəl] *n* tubo de bucear.

snout [snaʊt] *n* hocico.

snow [snəʊ] *n* nieve. ► *vi* nevar.

snowfall ['snəʊfɔːl] *n* nevada.

snowflake ['snəʊfleɪk] *n* copo de nieve.

snowman ['snəʊmæn] *n* muñeco de nieve.

so [səʊ] *adv* 1 tan, tanto,-a: *she's so tired that...*, está tan cansada que... 2 mucho: *I miss you so*, te echo mucho de menos. 3 así: *It's Mary –So it is*, Es Mary –Así es. 4 que sí, que no: *I guess so*, supongo que sí; *I don't think so*, creo que no. 5 también: *I went to the demonstration and so did David*, fui a la manifestación y David también. ► *conj* 1 así que, por lo tanto. 2 para. • **and so on** y así suce-sivamente; **if so** en ese caso; **not so... as...** no tan... como...; **or so** más o menos; **so that...** para que...; **so what?** *fam* ¿y qué?

soak [səʊk] *vt* 1 poner en remojo. 2 empapar.

soap [səʊp] *n* jabón. ► *vt* enjabonar. ■ **soap opera** telenovela, culebrón.

sob [sɒb] *n* sollozo. ► *vi* sollozar.

sober ['səʊbəʳ] *adj* sobrio,-a.

so-called ['səʊkɔːld] *adj* llamado,-a.

soccer ['sɒkəʳ] *n* fútbol.

sociable ['səʊʃəbəl] *adj* sociable.

social ['səʊʃəl] *adj* social. ■ **social security** seguridad social; **social worker** asistente,-a social.

socialism ['səʊʃəlɪzəm] *n* socialismo.

socialize ['səʊʃəlaɪz] *vi* relacionarse, alternar.

society [sə'saɪətɪ] *n* sociedad.

sociology [səʊsɪ'ɒlədʒɪ] *n* sociología.

sock [sɒk] *n* calcetín.

socket ['sɒkɪt] *n* 1 cuenca *(del ojo)*. 2 enchufe.

soda ['səʊdə] *n* soda. ■ **soda water** soda, sifón.

sofa ['səʊfə] *n* sofá.

soft [sɒft] *adj* 1 blando,-a *(cojín)*. 2 suave *(música)*. ■ **soft drink** refresco.

soften ['sɒfən] vt-vi **1** ablandar(se). **2** suavizar(se).

software ['sɒftweə'] n software.

soil [sɔil] n tierra. ► vt ensuciar, manchar.

solar ['səʊlə'] adj solar.

sold [səʊld] pt-pp → sell.

solder ['sɒldə'] n soldadura. ► vt soldar.

soldier ['səʊldʒə'] n soldado.

sole[1] [səʊl] n **1** planta (del pie). **2** suela (de zapato).

sole[2] [səʊl] n lenguado.

sole[3] [səʊl] adj único,-a.

solicitor [sə'lɪsɪtə'] n **1** abogado,-a. **2** notario,-a.

solid ['sɒlɪd] adj **1** sólido,-a. **2** macizo,-a. ► n sólido.

solidarity [sɒlɪ'dærɪtɪ] n solidaridad.

solitary ['sɒlɪtərɪ] adj **1** solitario,-a. **2** solo,-a.

solitude ['sɒlɪtjuːd] n soledad.

solo ['səʊləʊ] n solo.

solution [sə'luːʃən] n solución.

solve [sɒlv] vt resolver.

some [sʌm] adj **1** unos,-as, algunos,-as (con sust pl). **2** un poco (de) (con sust sing). **3** cierto,-a, alguno,-a. **4** bastante. ► pron **1** algunos,-as, unos,-as. **2** algo, un poco.

somebody ['sʌmbədɪ] pron alguien.

somehow ['sʌmhaʊ] adv **1** de algún modo. **2** por alguna razón.

someone ['sʌmwʌn] pron → somebody.

something ['sʌmθɪŋ] n algo.

sometime ['sʌmtaɪm] adv un día, algún día. ► adj antiguo, -a, ex-.

sometimes ['sʌmtaɪmz] adv a veces, de vez en cuando.

somewhat ['sʌmwɒt] adv algo, un tanto.

somewhere ['sʌmweə'] adv en alguna parte, a alguna parte. ► pron en un lugar, un sitio.

son [sʌn] n hijo.

song [sɒŋ] n canción.

son-in-law ['sʌnɪnlɔː] n yerno.

soon [suːn] adv pronto. • **as soon as** en cuanto; **soon afterwards** poco después.

sooner ['suːnə'] adv más temprano. • **no sooner...** nada más...; **sooner or later** tarde o temprano; **the sooner the better** cuanto antes mejor.

soot [sʊt] n hollín.

soothe [suːð] vt **1** calmar (nervios). **2** aliviar (dolor).

soprano [sə'prɑːnəʊ] n soprano.

sore [sɔː'] adj **1** dolorido,-a. **2** fam enfadado,-a. ► n llaga.

sorrow ['sɒrəʊ] n pena, pesar.

sorry ['sɒrɪ] interj ¡perdón!, ¡disculpe! • **to be sorry** sentirlo.

sort [sɔːt] n clase, tipo. ► vt clasificar. • **all sorts of** todo tipo de.

so-so ['səʊsəʊ] *adv fam* así así.

sought [sɔːt] *pt-pp* → seek.

soul [səʊl] *n* alma.

sound[1] [saʊnd] *n* sonido. ► *vi* sonar.

sound[2] [saʊnd] *adj* **1** sano,-a. **2** en buen estado. **3** razonable. **4** robusto,-a.

soundproof ['saʊndpruːf] *adj* insonorizado,-a.

soundtrack ['saʊndtræk] *n* banda sonora.

soup [suːp] *n* **1** sopa, caldo. ■ **soup plate** plato hondo, plato sopero; **soup spoon** cuchara sopera.

sour ['saʊə'] *adj* ácido,-a, agrio,-a.

source [sɔːs] *n* fuente.

south [saʊθ] *n* sur. ► *adj* del sur. ► *adv* hacia el sur, al sur.

southern ['sʌðən] *adj* del sur.

souvenir [suːvə'nɪə'] *n* recuerdo.

sovereign ['sɒvrɪn] *adj-n* soberano,-a.

sow[1] [saʊ] *n* cerda, puerca.

sow[2] [səʊ] *vt* sembrar.

space [speɪs] *n* espacio. ■ **space shuttle** transbordador espacial.

spacecraft ['speɪskrɑːft] *n* nave espacial.

spaceship ['speɪsʃɪp] *n* nave espacial.

spacious ['speɪʃəs] *adj* espacioso,-a, amplio,-a.

spade[1] [speɪd] *n* pala.

spade[2] [speɪd] *n* pica *(naipes)*.

span [spæn] *n* **1** lapso *(de tiempo)*. **2** envergadura *(de alas)*. **3** luz *(de arco)*.

spank [spæŋk] *vt* zurrar.

spanner ['spænə'] *n* llave de tuerca.

spare [speə'] *adj* **1** de sobra, libre. **2** de recambio, de repuesto. ► *n* recambio. ■ **spare room** habitación de invitados; **spare time** tiempo libre.

spark [spɑːk] *n* chispa. ■ **spark plug** bujía.

sparrow ['spærəʊ] *n* gorrión.

spasm ['spæzəm] *n* espasmo.

spat [spæt] *pt-pp* → spit.

speak [spiːk] *vi-vt* hablar. ► *vt* decir. • **so to speak** por así decirlo.

to speak out *vi* hablar claro.

speaker ['spiːkə'] *n* **1** persona que habla. **2** interlocutor,-ra. **3** conferenciante. **4** altavoz.

spear [spɪə'] *n* **1** lanza. **2** arpón.

special ['speʃəl] *adj* especial. ■ **special delivery** correo urgente.

specialist ['speʃəlɪst] *n* especialista.

species ['spiːʃiːz] *n* especie.

specific [spə'sɪfɪk] *adj* específico,-a.

specify ['spesɪfaɪ] *vt* especificar.

specimen ['spesɪmən] *n* espécimen, muestra, ejemplar.

speck [spek] *n* **1** mota *(de polvo)*. **2** pizca.

spectacle ['spektəkəl] *n* espectáculo. ► *npl* **spectacles** gafas.

spectacular [spek'tækjʊlə'] *adj* espectacular.

spectator [spek'teɪtə'] *n* espectador,-ra.

speculate ['spekjʊleɪt] *vi* especular.

sped [sped] *pt-pp* → speed.

speech [spiːtʃ] *n* **1** habla. **2** pronunciación. **3** discurso

speed [spiːd] *n* velocidad. ► *vi* **1** ir corriendo. **2** exceder el límite de velocidad. ■ **speed limit** límite de velocidad.

to speed up *vt-vi* acelerar.

speedometer [spɪ'dɒmɪtə'] *n* velocímetro.

spell[1] [spel] *n* hechizo.

spell[2] [spel] *n* período, temporada.

spell[3] [spel] *vt-vi* deletrear. ► *vt fig* significar.

spelling ['spelɪŋ] *n* ortografía. ■ **spelling mistake** falta de ortografía.

spelt [spelt] *pt-pp* → spell.

spend [spend] *vt* **1** gastar *(dinero)*. **2** pasar.

spent [spent] *pt-pp* → spend.

sperm [spɜːm] *n* esperma.

sphere [sfɪə'] *n* esfera.

spice [spaɪs] *n* especia. ► *vt* sazonar, condimentar.

spicy ['spaɪsɪ] *adj* picante.

spider ['spaɪdə'] *n* araña. ■ **spider's web** telaraña.

spike [spaɪk] *n* **1** punta. **2** pincho. **3** clavo.

spill [spɪl] *n* derrame. ► *vt-vi* derramar(se), verter(se).

spin [spɪn] *n* **1** vuelta. **2** centrifugado *(de lavadora)*. **3** efecto *(de pelota)*. ► *vt* **1** dar vueltas (a). **2** centrifugar.

spinach ['spɪnɪdʒ] *n* espinacas.

spin-dryer [spɪn'draɪə'] *n* secadora.

spine [spaɪn] *n* **1** espina dorsal. **2** lomo *(de libro)*.

spiral ['spaɪərəl] *n* espiral. ■ **spiral staircase** escalera de caracol.

spire ['spaɪə'] *n* aguja.

spirit[1] ['spɪrɪt] *n* alcohol. ► *npl* **spirits** licores.

spirit[2] ['spɪrɪt] *n* espíritu. ► *npl* **spirits** humor, moral. • **to be in high spirits** estar animado,-a; **to be in low spirits** estar desanimado,-a.

spit[1] [spɪt] *n* asador, espetón.

spit[2] [spɪt] *n* esputo. ► *vt-vi* escupir.

spite [spaɪt] *n* despecho. • **in spite of** a pesar de.

splash [splæʃ] *n* **1** chapoteo. **2** salpicadura. ► *vt* salpicar, rociar. ► *vi* chapotear.

splendid ['splendɪd] *adj* espléndido.

splinter ['splɪntə'] *n* astilla.

split [splɪt] *n* **1** grieta *(en madera)*. **2** desgarrón *(en tela)*. **3** división. ► *adj* **1** partido,-a. **2** dividido,-a. ► *vt-vi* **1** agrietar(se). **2** partir(se). **3** rajar(se), rasgar(se).

to split up *vt* partir, dividir. ► *vi* separarse *(pareja)*.

spoil [spɔɪl] *vt* **1** echar a perder. **2** malcriar.

spoke[1] [spəʊk] *pt* → speak.

spoke[2] [spəʊk] *n* radio *(de rueda)*.

spoken [ˈspəʊkən] *pp* → speak.

spokesman [ˈspəʊksmən] *n* portavoz.

sponge [spʌndʒ] *n* esponja. ■ **sponge cake** bizcocho.

sponsor [ˈspɒnsəʳ] *n* patrocinador,-ra. ► *vt* patrocinar.

spontaneous [spɒnˈteɪnɪəs] *adj* espontáneo,-a.

spool [spuːl] *n* carrete, bobina.

spoon [spuːn] *n* cuchara.

spoonful [ˈspuːnfʊl] *n* cucharada.

sport [spɔːt] *n* deporte.

sportsman [ˈspɔːtsmən] *n* deportista.

sportswear [ˈspɔːtsweəʳ] *n* ropa deportiva.

sportswoman [ˈspɔːtswʊmən] *n* deportista.

spot [spɒt] *n* **1** lunar. **2** mancha. **3** grano *(en cara)*. **4** sitio, lugar. **5** aprieto, apuro. **6** spot *(publicitario)*. ► *vt* **1** darse cuenta de. **2** notar.

spotlight [ˈspɒtlaɪt] *n* foco.

spouse [spaʊz] *n* cónyuge.

spout [spaʊt] *n* **1** pico *(de jarra)*. **2** surtidor *(de fuente)*.

sprain [spreɪn] *n* torcedura. ► *vt* torcerse.

sprang [spræŋ] *pt* → spring.

spray [spreɪ] *n* **1** espuma *(del mar)*. **2** spray. ■ **spray can** aerosol.

spread [spred] ► *vt-vi* **1** extender(se). **2** desplegar(se) *(alas)*. **3** propagar(se). ► *vt* untar *(mantequilla)*.

spreadsheet [ˈspredʃiːt] *n* hoja de cálculo.

spree [spriː] *n* juerga.

spring [sprɪŋ] *n* **1** primavera. **2** manantial, fuente. **3** muelle. **4** ballesta *(de coche)*. ► *vi* saltar. ■ **spring onion** cebolleta; **spring roll** rollito de primavera.

springboard [ˈsprɪŋbɔːd] *n* trampolín.

sprinkle [ˈsprɪŋkəl] *vt* rociar.

sprinkler [ˈsprɪŋkələʳ] *n* aspersor.

sprint [sprɪnt] *n* esprin. ► *vi* esprintar.

sprout [spraʊt] *n* brote. ► *vi* brotar.

sprung [sprʌŋ] *pp* → spring.

spun [spʌn] *pt-pp* → spin.

spur [spɜːʳ] *n* espuela.

spurt [spɜːt] *n* chorro.

spy [spaɪ] *n* espía. ► *vi* espiar.

squad [skwɒd] *n* brigada.

squadron ['skwɒdrən] *n* escuadrón.

square [skweəʳ] *n* **1** cuadrado. **2** cuadro *(en tela)*. **3** casilla *(en tablero)*. **4** plaza. ► *adj* cuadrado,-a. ► *vt-vi* cuadrar. ► *vt* elevar al cuadrado. ■ **square brackets** corchetes.

squash¹ [skuɒʃ] *n* **1** zumo. **2** squash. ► *vt* aplastar.

squash² [skuɒʃ] *n* calabaza.

squat [skwɒt] *adj* rechoncho,-a. ► *vi* **1** agacharse. **2** ocupar ilegalmente.

squatter ['skwɒtəʳ] *n* okupa.

squeak [skwiːk] *n* **1** chillido *(de animal)*. **2** chirrido *(de neumático)*. ► *vi* **1** chillar *(animal)*. **2** chirriar *(neumático)*.

squeeze [skwiːz] *n* **1** apretón *(de manos)*. **2** aprieto. ► *vt* **1** apretar. **2** exprimir *(limón)*.

squid [skwɪd] *n* calamar.

squint [skwɪnt] *n* bizquera.

squirrel ['skwɪrəl] *n* ardilla.

stab [stæb] *n* puñalada. ► *vt-vi* apuñalar. ■ **stab of pain** punzada de dolor.

stability [stəˈbɪlɪtɪ] *n* estabilidad.

stable¹ ['steɪbəl] *adj* estable.

stable² ['steɪbəl] *n* cuadra, establo.

stack [stæk] *n* montón, pila.

stadium ['steɪdɪəm] *n* estadio.

staff [stɑːf] *n* personal.

stage [steɪdʒ] *n* **1** etapa. **2** escenario. • **on stage** en escena.

stagger ['stægəʳ] *vi* tambalearse.

stain [steɪn] *n* mancha. ► *vt-vi* manchar(se). ■ **stain remover** quitamanchas.

stainless ['steɪnləs] *adj* inoxidable. ■ **stainless steel** acero inoxidable.

stair [steəʳ] *n* escalón, peldaño. ► *npl* **stairs** escalera.

staircase ['steəkeɪs] *n* escalera.

stake¹ [steɪk] *n* **1** apuesta. **2** intereses. ► *vt* apostar.

stake² [steɪk] *n* estaca, palo.

stalemate ['steɪlmeɪt] *n* tablas *(en ajedrez)*.

stalk¹ [stɔːk] *n* **1** tallo *(de planta)*. **2** rabillo *(de fruta)*.

stalk² [stɔːk] *vt* acechar.

stall [stɔːl] *n* **1** puesto *(de mercado)*. **2** caseta *(de feria)*. ► *npl* **stalls** platea.

stammer ['stæməʳ] *n* tartamudeo. ► *vi* tartamudear.

stamp [stæmp] *n* **1** sello, timbre. **2** tampón. ► *vt* sellar.

stand [stænd] *n* **1** postura. **2** pie *(de lámpara)*. **3** puesto *(de mercado)*. **4** stand *(de feria)*. **5** plataforma. **6** tribuna. ► *vi* **1** estar de pie, ponerse de pie. **2** estar, encontrarse. **3** seguir en pie *(oferta)*. **4** estar. ► *vt fam* aguantar: *I can't stand him*, no lo aguanto.

to stand for *vt* **1** significar. **2** defender, representar.

to stand out *vi* destacar.

to stand up *vi* ponerse de pie.

standard ['stændəd] *n* **1** nivel. **2** criterio. **3** norma. **4** patrón. ► *adj* normal, estándar.

standby ['stændbaɪ] *n* sustituto,-a. • **to be on standby** estar en lista de espera.

stank [stæŋk] *pt* → stink.

staple[1] ['steɪpəl] *n* producto básico.

staple[2] ['steɪpəl] *n* grapa.

stapler ['steɪplə'] *n* grapadora.

star [stɑː'] *n* estrella. ► *adj* estelar. ► *vi* protagonizar.

starboard ['stɑːbəd] *n* estribor.

starch [stɑːtʃ] *n* almidón, fécula.

stare [steə'] *n* mirada fija. ► *vi* mirar fijamente.

starfish ['stɑːfɪʃ] *n* estrella de mar.

start [stɑːt] *n* **1** principio. **2** salida *(de carrera)*. ► *vt-vi* **1** empezar. **2** arrancar *(coche)*.

to start up *vt-vi* arrancar.

starter ['stɑːtə'] *n* **1** juez de salida. **2** motor de arranque. • **for starters 1** para empezar. **2** como primer plato.

starvation [stɑːˈveɪʃən] *n* hambre, inanición.

starve [stɑːv] *vi* **1** pasar hambre. **2** tener mucha hambre.

state [steɪt] *n* estado. ► *vt* exponer.

statement ['steɪtmənt] *n* declaración, afirmación.

statesman ['steɪtsmən] *n* estadista, hombre de Estado.

station ['steɪʃən] *n* **1** estación *(de autobuses, tren)*. **2** emisora *(de radio)*. **3** canal *(de TV)*.

stationery ['steɪʃənərɪ] *n* artículos de escritorio.

statistics [stəˈtɪstɪks] *n* estadística.

statue ['stætjuː] *n* estatua.

status ['steɪtəs] *n* **1** estado. **2** estatus.

stave [steɪv] *n* pentagrama.

stay [steɪ] *n* estancia. ► *vi* **1** quedarse, permanecer. **2** alojarse *(en hotel)*.

to stay in *vi* quedarse en casa.

to stay on *vi* quedarse.

to stay up *vi* no acostarse.

steady ['stedɪ] *adj* **1** firme, estable. **2** constante *(movimiento)*.

steak [steɪk] *n* bistec, filete.

steal [stiːl] *vt-vi* robar.

steam [stiːm] *n* vapor. ► *vt* cocer al vapor. ▪ **steam engine** máquina de vapor; **steam iron** plancha de vapor.

steamer ['stiːmə'] *n* → steamship.

steamroller ['stiːmrəʊlə'] *n* apisonadora.

steamship ['stiːmʃɪp] *n* buque de vapor.

steel [stiːl] *n* acero. ▪ **steel wool** estropajo de aluminio.

steep[1] [stiːp] *adj* **1** empinado,-a, escarpado,-a *(colina)*. **2** *fig* excesivo,-a *(precio)*.

stock

steep² [stiːp] *vt* remojar.
steeple [ˈstiːpəl] *n* aguja.
steer [stɪəʳ] *vt* conducir.
steering [ˈstɪərɪŋ] *n* dirección.
 ▪ **steering wheel** volante.
stem [stem] *n* **1** tallo *(de planta)*. **2** pie *(de vaso)*.
step [step] *n* **1** paso. **2** escalón, peldaño. ▸ *vi* dar un paso, andar.
to step aside *vi* apartarse.
stepbrother [ˈstepbrʌðəʳ] *n* hermanastro.
stepchild [ˈsteptʃaɪld] *n* hijastro,-a.
stepdaughter [ˈstepdɔːtəʳ] *n* hijastra.
stepfather [ˈstepfɑːðəʳ] *n* padrastro.
stepladder [ˈsteplædəʳ] *n* escalera de mano.
stepmother [ˈstepmʌðəʳ] *n* madrastra.
stepsister [ˈstepsɪstəʳ] *n* hermanastra.
stepson [ˈstepsʌn] *n* hijastro.
stereo [ˈsterɪəʊ] *adj* estereofónico,-a.
sterile [ˈsteraɪl] *adj* estéril, esterilizado,-a.
sterling [ˈstɜːlɪŋ] *n* libra esterlina.
stern [stɜːn] *n* popa.
stew [stjuː] *n* estofado, guisado. ▸ *vt* estofar, guisar.
steward [ˈstjuːəd] *n* **1** camarero *(de barco)*. **2** auxiliar de vuelo *(de avión)*.

stewardess [ˈstjuːədes] *n* **1** camarera *(de barco)*. **2** azafata *(de avión)*.
stick¹ [stɪk] *n* **1** palo. **2** bastón *(para caminar)*.
stick² [stɪk] *vt* **1** clavar, hincar *(punta)*. **2** pegar *(con pegamento)*. ▸ *vi* atrancarse.
sticker [ˈstɪkəʳ] *n* **1** etiqueta adhesiva. **2** pegatina.
stiff [stɪf] *adj* rígido,-a, tieso,-a.
 • **to feel stiff** tener agujetas.
still [stɪl] *adj* **1** quieto,-a. **2** tranquilo,-a *(lago)*. **3** sin gas *(agua)*. ▸ *adv* **1** todavía, aún. **2** aun así. **3** sin embargo. ▪ **still life** ART naturaleza muerta, bodegón.
stimulate [ˈstɪmjʊleɪt] *vt* estimular.
stimulus [ˈstɪmjʊləs] *n* estímulo.
sting [stɪŋ] *n* **1** aguijón *(de avispa)*. **2** picadura *(herida)*. ▸ *vt-vi* picar.
stingy [ˈstɪndʒɪ] *adj* tacaño,-a.
stink [stɪŋk] *n* peste, hedor. ▸ *vi* apestar, heder.
stipulate [ˈstɪpjʊleɪt] *vt* estipular.
stir [stɜːʳ] *vt* remover .
stirrup [ˈstɪrəp] *n* estribo.
stitch [stɪtʃ] *n* **1** puntada *(al coser)*. **2** punto. ▸ *vt* **1** coser. **2** suturar.
stock [stɒk] *n* **1** reserva. **2** COMM existencias. **3** capital social. **4** ganado. **5** caldo. • **to**

be out of stock estar agotado,-a. ■ **stock exchange** bolsa; **stock market** bolsa de valores.

stockbroker ['stɒkbrəʊkə'] *n* corredor,-ra de bolsa.

stocking ['stɒkɪŋ] *n* media.

stole[1] [stəʊl] *pt* → steal.

stole[2] [stəʊl] *n* estola.

stolen ['stəʊlən] *pp* → steal.

stomach ['stʌmək] *n* estómago.

stone [stəʊn] *n* **1** piedra. **2** GB hueso *(de cereza, aceituna).*

stood [stʊd] *pt-pp* → stand.

stool [stuːl] *n* taburete.

stop [stɒp] *n* **1** parada, alto. **2** punto *(signo de puntuación).* ► *vt* **1** parar. **2** impedir, evitar. **3** poner fin a *(injusticia).* **4** dejar de: *stop smoking!,* ¡deja de fumar! ► *vi* **1** pararse. **2** terminar. ► *interj* ¡pare!, ¡alto! ■ **stop sign** señal de stop.

stopover ['stɒpəʊvə'] *n* escala *(de avión).*

stopper ['stɒpə'] *n* tapón.

stopwatch ['stɒpwɒtʃ] *n* cronómetro.

storage ['stɔːrɪdʒ] *n* almacenamiento.

store [stɔː'] *n* tienda, almacén. ► *vt* almacenar.

storey ['stɔːrɪ] *n* piso, planta.

stork [stɔːk] *n* cigüeña.

storm [stɔːm] *n* tormenta.

story ['stɔːrɪ] *n* historia, cuento.

stout [staʊt] *n* cerveza negra.

stove [stəʊv] *n* **1** estufa. **2** cocina, hornillo.

straight [streɪt] *adj* **1** recto,-a. **2** liso,-a *(pelo).* **3** seguido,-a. **4** solo,-a *(bebida).* ► *adv* **1** en línea recta. **2** directamente.► *n* recta *(en carrera).* ● **straight ahead** todo recto.

straightaway [streɪtə'weɪ] *adv* en seguida.

straightforward [streɪt'fɔːwəd] *adj* **1** franco,-a. **2** sencillo,-a.

strain [streɪn] *n* **1** presión, tensión. **2** torcedura. ► *vt* **1** estirar *(cuerda).* **2** torcerse *(músculo).* **3** forzar *(vista, voz).*

strait [streɪt] *n* GEOG estrecho.

strand [strænd] *n* **1** hebra, hilo. **2** mechón.

strange [streɪndʒ] *adj* extraño,-a.

stranger ['streɪndʒə'] *n* extraño,-a.

strangle ['stræŋgəl] *vt* estrangular.

strap [stræp] *n* **1** correa *(de reloj).* **2** tirante *(de vestido).*

strategy ['strætədʒɪ] *n* estrategia.

straw [strɔː] *n* paja.

strawberry ['strɔːbərɪ] *n* fresa.

stray [streɪ] *vi* perderse.

streak ['striːk] *n* **1** raya, lista. **2** *fig* racha *(de suerte).*

stream [striːm] *n* **1** arroyo. **2** corriente. ► *vi* **1** manar. **2** *fig* desfilar *(gente).*

streamer ['stri:mə'] n serpentina.

street [stri:t] n calle.

streetlamp ['stri:tlæmp] n farola.

strength [streŋθ] n fuerza. ■ **strength of will** fuerza de voluntad.

strengthen ['streŋθən] vt-vi fortalecer(se)

stress [stres] n 1 estrés. 2 acento. ► vt 1 recalcar, subrayar. 2 acentuar.

stretch [stretʃ] n 1 extensión. 2 tramo (de terreno). 3 intervalo (de tiempo). ► vt-vi 1 extender(se) (terreno). 2 estirar(se).

to stretch out vt 1 estirar (piernas). 2 alargar (mano). ► vi 1 estirarse. 2 alargarse.

stretcher ['stretʃə'] n camilla.

strict [strikt] adj estricto,-a.

stride [straid] n zancada.

strike [straik] n huelga. ► vt 1 pegar, golpear. 2 chocar contra. ► vi 1 atacar. 2 hacer huelga. 3 dar la hora. ● **to be on strike** estar en huelga.

striker ['straikə'] n 1 huelguista. 2 delantero,-a (en fútbol).

string [striŋ] n 1 cuerda, cordón. 2 ristra (de ajos, mentiras). 3 serie (de acontecimientos).

strip[1] [strip] n 1 tira. 2 franja (de tierra).

strip[2] [strip] vi desnudarse.

stripe [straip] n raya.

stroke [strəuk] n 1 golpe. 2 brazada (en natación). 3 campanada. ► vt acariciar.

stroll [strəul] n paseo. ► vi pasear, dar un paseo.

strong [strɒŋ] adj fuerte. ► adv fuerte.

struck [strʌk] pt-pp → strike.

structure ['strʌktʃə'] n estructura. ► vt estructurar.

struggle ['strʌgəl] n lucha. ► vi luchar.

stub [stʌb] n 1 colilla (de cigarrillo). 2 resguardo.

stubble ['stʌbəl] n 1 rastrojo. 2 barba (incipiente).

stubborn ['stʌbən] adj terco,-a.

stuck [stʌk] pt-pp → stick.

stud[1] [stʌd] n tachuela.

stud[2] [stʌd] n semental.

student ['stju:dənt] n estudiante.

studio ['stju:diəu] n estudio. ■ **studio flat** estudio.

study ['stʌdi] n estudio. ► vt-vi-vt estudiar.

stuff [stʌf] n 1 fam cosas, trastos. 2 cosa. ► vt rellenar. 1 disecar. 2 atiborrar. ● **to stuff oneself** fam hartarse de comida.

stuffing ['stʌfiŋ] n relleno.

stuffy ['stʌfi] adj cargado,-a, mal ventilado,-a.

stumble ['stʌmbəl] vi tropezar.

stun [stʌn] vt aturdir.

stung [stʌŋ] pt-pp → sting.

stunk [stʌŋk] *pt-pp* → stink.

stunning ['stʌnɪŋ] *adj* **1** pasmoso. **2** estupendo,-a.

stuntman ['stʌntmæn] *n* doble, especialista.

stuntwoman ['stʌntwʊmən] *n* doble, especialista.

stupid ['stjuːpɪd] *adj-n* tonto,-a.

stutter ['stʌtəʳ] *n* tartamudeo. ▶ *vi* tartamudear.

style [staɪl] *n* estilo.

stylish ['staɪlɪʃ] *adj* elegante.

subdue [səb'djuː] *vt* someter, dominar.

subject [(*n-adj*) 'sʌbdʒekt, (*vb*) səb'dʒekt] *n* **1** tema. **2** asignatura. **3** súbdito. **4** sujeto. ▶ *adj* sujeto,-a. ▶ *vt* someter.

subjunctive [səb'dʒʌŋktɪv] *adj* subjuntivo,-a. ▶ *n* subjuntivo.

sublet [sʌb'let] *vt-vi* realquilar.

submarine [sʌbmə'riːn] *n* submarino.

submerge [səb'mɜːdʒ] *vt-vi* sumergir(se).

submit [səb'mɪt] *vt* someter. ▶ *vi* someterse.

subordinate [(*adj-n*) sə'bɔːdɪnət, (*vb*) sə'bɔːdɪneɪt] *adj-n* subordinado,-a. ▶ *vt* subordinar.

subscribe [səb'skraɪb] *vi* **1** subscribirse *(a revista)*. **2** suscribir *(opinión)*.

subscriber [səb'scraɪbəʳ] *n* **1** subscriptor,-ra *(de revista)*. **2** abonado,-a *(de servicio)*.

subscription [səb'skrɪpʃən] *n* **1** subscripción *(de revista)*. **2** abono *(de servicio)*.

subsidize ['sʌbsɪdaɪz] *vt* subvencionar.

subsidy ['sʌbsɪdɪ] *n* subsidio.

substance ['sʌbstəns] *n* sustancia.

substitute ['sʌbstɪtjuːt] *n* substituto,-a. ▶ *vt* sustituir.

subtle ['sʌtəl] *adj* sutil.

subtract [səb'trækt] *vt* restar.

suburb ['sʌbɜːb] *n* barrio periférico, barrio residencial. ■ **the suburbs** las afueras.

subway ['sʌbweɪ] *n* **1** GB paso subterráneo. **2** US metro.

succeed [sək'siːd] *vi* tener éxito.

success [sək'ses] *n* éxito.

successful [sək'sesfʊl] *adj* que tiene éxito.

successive [sək'sesɪv] *adj* sucesivo,-a.

such [sʌtʃ] *adj* **1** tal, semejante. **2** tan... como, tanto, -a... que. ▶ *adv* muy, mucho, tan, tanto,-a.

suck [sʌk] *n vt-vi* chupar.

sudden ['sʌdən] *adj* repentino,-a.

suddenly ['sʌdənlɪ] *adv* de repente, de pronto.

sue [suː] *vt-vi* demandar.

suede [sweɪd] *n* ante, gamuza.

suffer ['sʌfəʳ] *vt-vi* sufrir.

sufficient [sə'fɪʃənt] *adj* suficiente.

suffix ['sʌfɪks] n sufijo.

suffocate ['sʌfəkeɪt] vt-vi asfixiar(se).

sugar ['ʃʊgəʳ] n azúcar. ∎ **sugar bowl** azucarero.

sugarbeet ['ʃʊgəbiːt] n remolacha azucarera.

suggest [sə'dʒest] vt **1** sugerir. **2** implicar.

suggestion [sə'dʒestʃən] n sugerencia.

suicide ['sjuːɪsaɪd] n suicidio. • **to commit suicide** suicidarse.

suit [sjuːt] n **1** traje. **2** pleito. **3** palo (de naipes). ▶ vt **1** convenir a. **2** sentar bien.

suitable ['sjuːtəbəl] adj **1** apropiado,-a. **2** conveniente.

suitcase ['suːtkeɪs] n maleta.

suite [swiːt] n suite.

sultry ['sʌltrɪ] adj bochornoso,-a.

sum [sʌm] n suma.

summarize ['sʌməraɪz] vt resumir.

summary ['sʌmərɪ] n resumen.

summer ['sʌməʳ] n verano.

summit ['sʌmɪt] n cumbre.

sun [sʌn] n sol.

sunbathe ['sʌnbeɪð] vi tomar el sol.

Sunday ['sʌndeɪ] n domingo.

sunflower ['sʌnflaʊəʳ] n girasol.

sung [sʌŋ] pp → sing.

sunglasses ['sʌnglɑːsɪz] npl gafas de sol.

sunk [sʌŋk] pp → sink.

sunlight ['sʌnlaɪt] n luz del sol.

sunny ['sʌnɪ] adj soleado,-a.

sunrise ['sʌnraɪz] n salida del sol, amanecer.

sunset ['sʌnset] n puesta del sol.

sunshine ['sʌnʃaɪn] n luz del sol.

sunstroke ['sʌnstrəʊk] n insolación.

suntan ['sʌntæn] n bronceado.

superb [suː'pɜːb] adj estupendo,-a.

superficial [suːpə'fɪʃəl] adj superficial.

superintendent [suːpərɪn'tendənt] n inspector,-ra.

superior [suː'pɪərɪəʳ] adj superior. ▶ n superior,-ra.

superlative [suː'pɜːlətɪv] adj superlativo,-a. ▶ n superlativo.

supermarket [suːpə'mɑːkɪt] n supermercado.

supernatural [suːpə'nætʃərəl] adj sobrenatural.

superstitious [sjuːpə'stɪʃəs] adj supersticioso,-a.

supervise ['suːpəvaɪz] vt supervisar.

supper ['sʌpəʳ] n cena.

supplement ['sʌplɪmənt] n suplemento.

supplier [sə'plaɪəʳ] n proveedor,-ra.

supply [sə'plaɪ] vt **1** suministrar, abastecer. ▶ n suministro.

▶ *npl* **supplies** provisiones. • **supply and demand** la oferta y la demanda.

support [sə'pɔːt] *n* apoyo. ▶ *vt* **1** sostener *(peso)*. **2** apoyar *(causa)*.

supporter [sə'pɔːtəʳ] *n* **1** POL partidiario,-a. **2** seguidor,-ra.

suppose [sə'pəʊz] *vt* suponer. • **I suppose so/not** supongo que sí/no.

suppository [sə'pɒzɪtərɪ] *n* supositorio.

suppress [sə'pres] *vt* **1** suprimir *(texto)*. **2** reprimir *(sentimientos, revuelta)*.

supreme [suː'priːm] *adj* supremo,-a.

surcharge ['sɜːtʃɑːdʒ] *n* recargo.

sure [ʃʊəʳ] *adj* seguro,-a. ▶ *adv* **1** claro. **2** seguro. **3** de verdad.

surf [sɜːf] *n* **1** oleaje. **2** espuma. ▶ *vi* hacer surf. • **to surf the Net** navegar por Internet.

surface ['sɜːfəs] *n* superficie.

surgeon ['sɜːdʒən] *n* cirujano,-a.

surgery ['sɜːdʒərɪ] *n* **1** cirugía. **2** GB consultorio, consulta.

surname ['sɜːneɪm] *n* apellido.

surplus ['sɜːpləs] ▶ *n* **1** excedente. **2** superávit.

surprise [sə'praɪz] *n* sorpresa. ▶ *vt* sorprender.

surprising [sə'praɪzɪŋ] *adj* sorprendente.

surrender [sə'rendəʳ] *n* rendición. ▶ *vt-vi* rendir(se).

surround [sə'raʊnd] *vt* rodear.

surroundings [sə'raʊndɪŋs] *npl* alrededores.

survey ['sɜːveɪ] *n* **1** sondeo *(de opinión)*. **2** encuesta, estudio *(de tendencias)*.

survive [sə'vaɪv] *vt-vi* sobrevivir (a).

survivor [sə'vaɪvəʳ] *n* superviviente.

suspect [*(adj-n)* 'sʌspekt, *(vb)* sə'spekt] *adj-n* sospechoso,-a. ▶ *vt* sospechar.

suspend [sə'spend] *vt* suspender *(partido)*.

suspender [sə'spendəʳ] *n* liga. ▶ *npl* **suspenders** tirantes.

suspense [səs'spens] *n* suspense.

suspension [sə'spenʃən] *n* suspensión *(de partido)*, expulsión *(de alumno)*.

suspicion [sə'spɪʃən] *n* sospecha.

suspicious [sə'spɪʃəs] *adj* **1** sospechoso,-a. **2** desconfiado,-a.

sustain [sə'steɪn] *vt* sostener.

swallow¹ ['swɒləʊ] *n* **1** trago *(de bebida)*. **2** bocado *(de comida)*. ▶ *vt-vi* tragar(se).

swallow² ['swɒləʊ] *n* golondrina *(ave)*.

swam [swæm] *pt* → swim.

swamp [swɒmp] *n* pantano, ciénaga.

swan [swɒn] *n* cisne.

swap [swɒp] *vt-vi fam* intercambiar, cambiar.

swarm [swɔːm] *n* enjambre.

swear [sweəʳ] *vt-vi* jurar. ► *vi* decir palabrotas.

swearword ['sweəwɜːd] *n* palabrota, taco.

sweat [swet] *n* sudor. ► *vt-vi* sudar.

sweater ['swetəʳ] *n* suéter.

sweep [swiːp] *n* 1 barrido. 2 redada *(de policía)*. ► *vt-vi* barrer.

sweeper ['swiːpəʳ] *n* barrendero,-a.

sweet [swiːt] *adj* dulce. ► *n* 1 caramelo, golosina. 2 postre. ■ **sweet potato** boniato.

sweeten ['swiːtən] *vt* endulzar.

swelling ['swelɪŋ] *n* hinchazón.

swept [swept] *pt-pp* → sweep.

swim [swɪm] *n* baño. ► *vi* nadar.

swimmer ['swɪməʳ] *n* nadador,-ra.

swimming ['swɪmɪŋ] *n* natación. ■ **swimming baths** piscina *(pública)*; **swimming costume** bañador; **swimming pool** piscina; **swimming trunks** bañador.

swimsuit ['swɪmsuːt] *n* bañador, traje de baño.

swindle ['swɪndəl] *n* estafa, timo. ► *vt* estafar, timar.

swing [swɪŋ] *n* columpio. ► *vt-vi* 1 balancear(se). 2 columpiar(se).

switch [swɪtʃ] *n* interruptor. ► *vt* cambiar, intercambiar.

to switch off *vt* apagar.

to switch on *vt* encender.

sword [sɔːd] *n* espada.

swordfish ['sɔːdfɪʃ] *n* pez espada.

swore [swɔːʳ] *pt* → swear.

sworn [swɔːn] *pp* → swear.

swum [swʌm] *pp* → swim.

swung [swʌŋ] *pt-pp* → swing.

syllable ['sɪləbəl] *n* sílaba.

syllabus ['sɪləbəs] *n* plan de estudios.

symbol ['sɪmbəl] *n* símbolo.

sympathize ['sɪmpəθaɪz] *vi* 1 compadecerse. 2 comprender.

sympathy ['sɪmpəθɪ] *n* 1 compasión. 2 pésame. 3 comprensión.

symphony ['sɪmfənɪ] *n* sinfonía.

symptom ['sɪmptəm] *n* síntoma.

synonym ['sɪnənɪm] *n* sinónimo.

syntax ['sɪntæks] *n* sintaxis.

synthesis ['sɪnθəsɪs] *n* síntesis.

synthetic [sɪnθetɪk] *adj* sintético,-a.

syringe [sɪrɪndʒ] *n* jeringuilla.

syrup ['sɪrəp] *n* 1 jarabe. 2 almíbar.

system ['sɪstəm] *n* sistema.

tab 194

T

tab [tæb] *n* **1** lengüeta. **2** etiqueta *(en ropa)*.

table ['teɪbəl] *n* **1** mesa. **2** tabla, cuadro. ▪ **table football** futbolín; **table tennis** tenis de mesa.

tablecloth ['teɪbəlklɒθ] *n* mantel.

tablespoon ['teɪbəlspuːn] *n* cuchara de servir.

tablet ['tæblət] *n* pastilla.

tabloid ['tæblɔɪd] *n* periódico.

tact [tækt] *n* tacto.

tactics ['tæktɪks] *npl* táctica.

tadpole ['tædpəʊl] *n* renacuajo.

tag [tæg] *n* etiqueta.

tail [teɪl] *vt* seguir. ▶ *n* cola. ▶ *npl* **tails** cruz *(de moneda)*.

tailor ['teɪlə'] *n* sastre,-a.

take [teɪk] *vt* **1** tomar, coger. **2** llevar. **3** requerir, necesitar. **4** apuntar, anotar. **5** ocupar. **6** llevar, tardar.

to take away *vt* **1** llevarse. **2** quitar, sacar. **3** restar.

to take back *vt* **1** devolver. **2** retractarse.

to take down *vt* apuntar.

to take off *vt* quitarse *(ropa)*. ▶ *vi* despegar *(avión)*.

to take out *vt* invitar a salir.

takeaway ['teɪkəweɪ] *n* establecimiento que vende comida para llevar.

taken ['teɪkən] *pp* → take.

takeoff ['teɪkɒf] *n* despegue.

talcum powder ['tælkəm-paʊdə'] *n* polvos de talco.

tale [teɪl] *n* cuento.

talent ['tælənt] *n* talento. ▪ **talent scout** cazatalentos.

talk [tɔːk] *vt-vi* hablar. ▶ *n* conversación. ▪ **talk show** programa de entrevistas.

talkative ['tɔːkətɪv] *adj* hablador,-ra.

tall [tɔːl] *adj* alto,-a.

tambourine [tæmbə'riːn] *n* pandereta.

tame [teɪm] *vt* domar.

tampon ['tæmpɒn] *n* tampón.

tan [tæn] *n* bronceado. ▶ *vi* ponerse moreno,-a.

tangent ['tændʒənt] *n* tangente.

tangerine [tændʒə'riːn] *n* mandarina.

tank [tæŋk] *n* **1** depósito. **2** tanque.

tanker ['tæŋkə'] *n* **1** buque cisterna. **2** petrolero. **3** camión cisterna.

tantrum ['tæntrəm] *n* rabieta.

tap[1] [tæp] *n* grifo.

tap[2] [tæp] *n* golpecito.

tape [teɪp] *n* cinta. ▶ *vt* grabar. ▪ **tape measure** cinta métrica; **tape recorder** magnetófono, grabadora.

tapestry ['tæpəstrɪ] *n* tapiz.

tar [tɑː'] *n* alquitrán.

target ['tɑːgɪt] *n* blanco, objetivo.

tariff ['tærɪf] n tarifa.

tarmac ['tɑːmæk] n asfalto.

tart [tɑːt] n tarta, pastel.

task [tɑːsk] n tarea, labor.

taste [teɪst] n sabor, gusto. ► vt 1 probar (comida). 2 catar (vino). ► vi saber.

tasteless ['teɪstləs] adj 1 de mal gusto. 2 insípido,-a, soso,-a.

tattoo [təˈtuː] n tatuaje. ► vt tatuar.

taught [tɔːt] pt-pp → teach.

tavern ['tævən] n taberna.

tax [tæks] n impuesto. ► vt gravar. ■ **tax free** libre de impuestos; **tax return** declaración de la renta.

taxi ['tæksɪ] n taxi. ■ **taxi driver** taxista.

taxpayer ['tækspeɪə'] n contribuyente.

tea [tiː] n 1 té. 2 merienda. 3 cena.

teach [tiːtʃ] vt 1 enseñar. 2 dar clases de (asignatura).

teacher ['tiːtʃə'] n maestro,-a, profesor,-ra.

teaching ['tiːtʃɪŋ] n enseñanza.

teacup ['tiːkʌp] n taza de té.

team [tiːm] n equipo.

teapot ['tiːpɒt] n tetera.

tear[1] [tɪə'] n lágrima. ■ **tear gas** gas lacrimógeno.

tear[2] [teə'] n rotura, siete. ► vt rasgar.

tease [tiːz] vt burlarse de.

teaspoon ['tiːspuːn] n cucharilla.

teat [tiːt] n 1 teta. 2 tetina (de botella).

technical ['teknɪkəl] adj técnico,-a.

technique [tekˈniːk] n técnica.

technology [tekˈnɒlədʒɪ] n tecnología.

teddy bear ['tedɪbeə'] n osito de peluche.

teenager ['tiːneɪdʒə'] n adolescente (de 13 a 19 años).

tee-shirt ['tiːʃɜːt] n camiseta.

teeth [tiːθ] npl → tooth.

teetotaller [tiːˈtəʊtlə'] n abstemio,-a.

telegram ['telɪɡræm] n telegrama.

telegraph ['telɪɡrɑːf] n telégrafo.

telephone ['telɪfəʊn] n teléfono. ► vt-vi llamar por teléfono. ■ **telephone box** cabina telefónica; **telephone directory** guía telefónica; **telephone operator** telefonista.

telephoto lens [telɪfəʊtəʊˈlenz] n teleobjetivo.

telescope ['telɪskəʊp] n telescopio.

television ['telɪvɪʒən] n televisión. ■ **television set** televisor.

telex ['teleks] n télex.

tell [tel] vt 1 decir. 2 contar (historia). ► vi saber.

to tell off vt echar una bronca a, reñir.

teller ['telə'] n cajero,-a.

telling-off [telɪŋ'ɒf] *n fam* bronca.

telly ['telɪ] *n fam* tele.

temper ['tempəʳ] *n* temperamento. ► *vt* templar. ● **to lose one's temper** enfadarse.

temperature ['temprətʃəʳ] *n* temperatura. ● **to have a temperature** tener fiebre.

tempest ['tempəst] *n* tempestad.

temple ['tempəl] *n* 1 templo. 2 sien.

temporary ['tempərərɪ] *adj* temporal.

tempt [tempt] *vt* tentar.

temptation [temp'teɪʃən] *n* tentación.

ten [ten] *num* diez.

tenacity [tə'næsɪtɪ] *n* tenacidad.

tenant ['tenənt] *n* inquilino,-a.

tend [tend] *vi* tender a, tener tendencia a. ► *vt* cuidar.

tendency ['tendənsɪ] *n* tendencia.

tender[1] ['tendəʳ] *adj* tierno,-a.

tender[2] ['tendəʳ] *n* oferta.

tendon ['tendən] *n* tendón.

tenement ['tenəmənt] *n* bloque de pisos.

tennis ['tenɪs] *n* tenis. ■ **tennis court** pista de tenis.

tenor ['tenəʳ] *n* tenor.

tense [tens] *adj* tenso,-a. ► *n* tiempo *(de verbo)*.

tension ['tenʃən] *n* tensión.

tent [tent] *n* tienda de campaña.

tentacle ['tentəkəl] *n* tentáculo.

tenth [tenθ] *adj-n* décimo,-a.

tepid ['tepɪd] *adj* tibio,-a.

term [tɜːm] *vt* calificar de. ► *n* 1 trimestre. 2 período, plazo. 3 término. ► *npl* **terms** 1 condiciones. 2 relaciones.

terminal ['tɜːmɪnəl] *adj-n* terminal.

terminate ['tɜːmɪneɪt] *vt-vi* terminar.

terminus ['tɜːmɪnəs] *n* terminal.

termite ['tɜːmaɪt] *n* termita.

terrace ['terəs] *n* terraza.

terrain [tə'reɪn] *n* terreno.

terrible ['terɪbəl] *adj* terrible.

terrific [tə'rɪfɪk] *adj* fabuloso,-a.

terrify ['terɪfaɪ] *vt* aterrar.

territory ['terɪtərɪ] *n* territorio.

terror ['terəʳ] *n* terror.

terrorism ['terərɪzəm] *n* terrorismo.

test [test] *n* 1 prueba. 2 examen, test. ► *vt* probar, poner a prueba. ■ **test tube** tubo de ensayo.

testament ['testəmənt] *n* testamento.

testicle ['testɪkəl] *n* testículo.

testify ['testɪfaɪ] *vt-vi* testificar.

testimony ['testɪmənɪ] *n* testimonio.

tetanus ['tetənəs] *n* tétanos.

text [tekst] *n* texto.

textbook ['tekstbʊk] *n* libro de texto.

textile ['tekstaɪl] *adj* textil. ► *n* textil, tejido.

texture ['tekstʃə'] *n* textura.
than [ðæn] *conj* **1** que. **2** de.
thank [θæŋk] *vt* agradecer. ► *npl* **thanks** gracias. • **thanks to** gracias a; **thank you** gracias.
thankful ['θæŋkfʊl] *adj* agradecido,-a.
that [ðæt] *adj* ese, esa, aquel, aquella. ► *pron* **1** ése, ésa, aquél, aquélla. **2** eso, aquello. **3** que *(relativo)*. ► *conj* que. • **that is** es decir.
thaw [θɔ:] *n* deshielo. ► *vt-vi* deshelar(se).
the [ðə] *det* el, la, los, las.
theatre ['θɪətə'] (US **theater**) *n* **1** teatro. **2** quirófano.
theft [θeft] *n* robo, hurto.
their [ðeə'] *adj* su, sus.
theirs [ðeəz] *pron* (el) suyo, (la) suya, (los) suyos, (las) suyas.
them [ðem, *unstressed* ðəm] *pron* **1** los, las *(comp directo)*. **2** les *(comp indirecto)*. **3** ellos, ellas *(con preposisición)*.
theme [θi:m] *n* tema. ■ **theme park** parque temático.
themselves [ðəm'selvz] *pron* **1** ellos mismos, ellas mismas. **2** se.
then [ðen] *adv* **1** entonces. **2** luego, después. **3** en ese caso. • **then again** también.
theology [θɪ'ɒlədʒɪ] *n* teología.
theory ['θɪərɪ] *n* teoría.
therapy ['θerəpɪ] *n* terapia.

there [ðeə'] *adv* allí, allá, ahí. • **there is/are** hay; **there was/were** había; **there you are** ahí tienes.
thereabouts [ðeərə'baʊts] *adv* por ahí.
thereafter [ðeə'rɑːftə'] *adv* a partir de entonces.
thereby ['ðeəbaɪ] *adv* de ese modo.
therefore ['ðeəfɔː'] *adv* por lo tanto.
thermal ['θɜːməl] *adj* termal.
thermometer [θə'mɒmɪtə'] *n* termómetro.
thermos® ['θɜːmɒs] *n* termo. También **thermos flask**.
these [ði:z] *adj* estos,-as. ► *pron* éstos,-as.
thesis ['θi:sɪs] *n* tesis.
they [ðeɪ] *pron* ellos,-as.
thick [θɪk] *adj* **1** grueso,-a. **2** espeso,-a. **3** poblado,-a *(barba)*.
thief [θi:f] *n* ladrón,-ona.
thigh [θaɪ] *n* muslo.
thimble ['θɪmbəl] *n* dedal.
thin [θɪn] *adj* **1** delgado,-a, flaco,-a *(persona)*. **2** fino,-a *(rebanada, material)*. **3** ralo,-a *(pelo, vegetación)*. **4** claro,-a, poco espeso,-a *(líquido)*.
thing [θɪŋ] *n* cosa. • **the thing is...** el caso es que...
think [θɪŋk] *vt - vi* pensar.
third [θɜːd] *adj* tercero,-a. ■ **Third World** Tercer Mundo.
thirst [θɜːst] *n* sed.

thirsty ['θɜːstɪ] *adj* sediento,-a.
• **to be thirsty** tener sed.
thirteen [θɜːˈtiːn] *num* trece.
thirteenth [θɜːˈtiːnθ] *adj - n* decimotercero,-a.
thirty ['θɜːtɪ] *num* treinta.
this [ðɪs] *adj* este, esta. ► *pron* éste, ésta, esto.
thistle ['θɪsəl] *n* cardo.
thong [θɒŋ] *n* correa.
thorn [θɔːn] *n* espina, pincho.
thorough ['θʌrə] *adj* **1** a fondo *(investigación)*. **2** cuidadoso,-a, minucioso,-a *(persona)*.
those [ðəʊz] *adj* esos,-as, aquellos,-as. ► *pron* ésos,-as, aquéllos,-as.
though [ðəʊ] *conj* **1** aunque, si bien. **2** pero. ► *adv* sin embargo.
thought [θɔːt] *ptpp* → think. ► *n* **1** pensamiento. **2** idea.
thoughtful ['θɔːtful] *adj* **1** pensativo,-a. **2** considerado,-a.
thousand ['θaʊzənd] *num* mil.
thrash [θræʃ] *vt* dar una paliza a.
thread [θred] *n* **1** hilo. **2** rosca *(de tornillo)*. ► *vt* **1** enhebrar *(aguja)*. **2** ensartar *(cuentas)*.
threat [θret] *n* amenaza.
threaten ['θretən] *vt - vi* amenazar.
three [θriː] *num* tres.
threshold ['θreʃəʊld] *n* umbral.
threw [θruː] *pt* → throw.
thrifty ['θrɪftɪ] *adj* frugal.

thrill [θrɪl] *n* emoción.
thriller ['θrɪləʳ] *n* novela de suspense, película de suspense.
thrive [θraɪv] *vi* **1** crecer *(planta)*. **2** prosperar *(industria)*.
throat [θrəʊt] *n* garganta.
throb [θrɒb] *n* latido, palpitación. ► *vi* latir, palpitar.
throne [θrəʊn] *n* trono.
through [θruː] *prep* **1** por. **2** durante todo,-a. **3** hasta el final de. ► *adv* **1** de un lado a otro. **2** hasta el final. ► *adj* directo,-a. • **to be through with** haber acabado con.
throughout [θruːˈaʊt] *prep* **1** por, en todo,-a. **2** durante todo,-a, a lo largo de. ► *adv* **1** por todas partes, en todas partes. **2** completamente. **3** todo el tiempo.
throve [θrəʊv] *pt* → thrive.
throw [θrəʊ] *n* lanzamiento. ► *vt* tirar, lanzar.
to throw away *vt* **1** tirar *(basura)*. **2** desaprovechar *(oportunidad)*
to throw up *vi* vomitar.
thru [θruː] *prep-adv* US → through.
thrush [θrʌʃ] *n* tordo.
thrust [θrʌst] *n* **1** empuje. **2** estocada *(de espada)*.
thumb [θʌm] *n* pulgar.
thumbtack ['θʌmtæk] *n* US chincheta.
thump [θʌmp] *n* golpe. ► *vt* golpear.

thunder ['θʌndə'] n trueno. ►
vi tronar.

thunderstorm ['θʌndəstɔːm]
n tormenta.

Thursday ['θɜːzdɪ] n jueves.

thus [ðʌs] adv así.

thyme [taɪm] n tomillo.

tic [tɪk] n tic.

tick[1] [tɪk] n garrapata.

tick[2] [tɪk] n 1 tictac (ruido). 2
marca, señal.

to tick off vt marcar.

ticket ['tɪkɪt] n 1 billete (de bus,
etc). 2 entrada (de cine, etc). 3
etiqueta, resguardo. 4 fam multa. ▪ **ticket collector** revisor,
-ra; **ticket machine** máquina
expendedora de billetes; **ticket office** taquilla.

tickle ['tɪkəl] vt hacer cosquillas a. ► vi tener cosquillas.

tide [taɪd] n marea.

tidy ['taɪdɪ] adj ordenado,-a
(habitación, persona). 2 arreglado,-a (aspecto).

to tidy up vt 1 ordenar, arreglar (habitación). 2 arreglar,
acicalar (persona).

tie [taɪ] n 1 corbata. 2 lazo,
vínculo. 3 empate. ► vt atar,
hacer (nudo). ► vi empatar.

tier [tɪə'] n 1 grada, fila (de
asientos). 2 piso (de pastel).

tiger ['taɪgə'] n tigre.

tight [taɪt] adj 1 apretado,-a.
2 tenso,-a (cuerda). 3 ajustado,-a, ceñido,-a (ropa). ► adv
con fuerza.

tighten ['taɪtən] vt 1 apretar.
2 tensar (cuerda).

tightrope ['taɪtrəʊp] n cuerda
floja.

tights [taɪts] npl 1 panties,
medias. 2 leotardos.

tile [taɪl] n 1 azulejo (de pared).
2 baldosa (de suelo). 3 teja (de
tejado).

till [tɪl] prep hasta. ► conj hasta
que. ► n caja registradora.

tilt [tɪlt] n inclinación, ladeo.
► vt-vi inclinar(se).

timber ['tɪmbə'] n 1 madera
(de construcción). 2 viga.

time [taɪm] n 1 tiempo. 2 rato. 3 hora: **what time is it?**,
¿qué hora es? 4 vez: **two at a
time**, de dos en dos. ► vt 1
cronometrar. 2 fijar la hora
de. ► prep **times** por, multi-
plicado por. • **at any time** en
cualquier momento; **at times**
a veces; **for the time being**
de momento; **from time to
time** de vez en cuando; **it's
about time** ya va siendo hora; **on time** puntualmente;
to have a good time divertirse, pasarlo bien; **to tell
the time** decir la hora.

timetable ['taɪmteɪbəl] n horario.

timid ['tɪmɪd] adj tímido,-a.

tin [tɪn] n 1 estaño. 2 lata,
bote. ▪ **tin opener** abrelatas.

tinkle ['tɪŋkəl] n tintineo.

tiny ['taɪnɪ] adj diminuto,-a.

tip[1] [tɪp] *n* extremo, punta.

tip[2] [tɪp] *n* **1** propina. **2** consejo. ► *vt* dar una propina a.

tiptoe ['tɪptəʊ] *vi* ir de puntillas. • **on tiptoe** de puntillas.

tire[1] ['taɪə'] *vt-vi* cansar(se).

tire[2] ['taɪə'] *n* US neumático.

tired ['taɪəd] *adj* cansado,-a.

tireless ['taɪələs] *adj* incansable.

tissue ['tɪʃuː] *n* pañuelo de papel.

title ['taɪtəl] *n* título.

to [tʊ, unstressed tə] *prep* **1** a. **2** hacia, a. **3** a, hasta. **4** menos. **5** para, a fin de.

toad [təʊd] *n* sapo.

toadstool ['təʊdstuːl] *n* seta venenosa.

toast [təʊst] *n* **1** pan tostado: *a piece of toast*, una tostada. **2** brindis. ► *vt* **1** tostar *(pan)*. **2** brindar por. • **to drink a toast to** hacer un brindis por, brindar por.

toaster ['təʊstə'] *n* tostador.

tobacco [tə'bækəʊ] *n* tabaco.

tobacconist [tə'bækənɪst] *n* estanquero,-a. ■ **tobacconist's** estanco.

today [tə'deɪ] *n* hoy. ► *adv* **1** hoy. **2** hoy en día.

toe [təʊ] *n* dedo del pie.

together [tə'geðə'] *adv* junto, juntos,-as. • **all together** todos,-as juntos,-as; **together with** junto con.

toilet ['tɔɪlət] *n* **1** váter, lavabo *(en casa)*. **2** servicios *(públicos)*. **3** aseo, arreglo personal. ■ **toilet bag** neceser; **toilet paper** papel higiénico.

token ['təʊkən] *n* ficha.

told [təʊld] *ptpp* → tell.

tolerate ['tɒləreɪt] *vt* tolerar.

toll [təʊl] *n* **1** peaje. **2** número.

tomato [tə'mɑːtəʊ, US tə'meɪtəʊ] *n* tomate.

tomb [tuːm] *n* tumba.

tombstone ['tuːmstəʊn] *n* lápida.

tomorrow [tə'mɒrəʊ] *adv-n* mañana.

ton [tʌn] *n* tonelada.

tone [təʊn] *n* tono.

tongs [tɒnz] *npl* pinzas.

tongue [tʌn] *n* lengua. ■ **tongue twister** trabalenguas.

tonic ['tɒnɪk] *adj* tónico,-a.

tonight [tə'naɪt] *adv-n* esta noche.

tonne [tʌn] *n* tonelada.

tonsil ['tɒnsəl] *n* amígdala.

too [tuː] *adv* **1** demasiado, mucho. **2** también. • **too many** demasiados,-as; **too much** demasiado,-a.

took [tʊk] *pt* → take.

tool [tuːl] *n* herramienta.

tooth [tuːθ] *n* diente, muela.

toothache ['tuːθeɪk] *n* dolor de muelas.

toothbrush ['tuːθbrʌʃ] *n* cepillo de dientes.

toothpaste ['tuːθpeɪst] *n* pasta de dientes.

top [tɒp] n **1** parte superior, parte de arriba. **2** tapón *(de botella)*. **3** top, blusa. ► *adj* de arriba, superior, más alto,-a.

topic ['tɒpɪk] n tema, asunto.

topical ['tɒpɪkəl] adj de actualidad.

torch [tɔːtʃ] n **1** antorcha. **2** linterna.

tore [tɔːʳ] pt → tear.

torn [tɔːn] pp → tear.

tornado [tɔːˈneɪdəʊ] n tornado.

torpedo [tɔːˈpiːdəʊ] n torpedo.

tortoise ['tɔːtəs] n tortuga.

torture ['tɔːtʃə] n tortura. ► vt torturar.

total ['təʊtəl] adj - n total. ► vt-vi sumar.

touch [tʌtʃ] n **1** toque. **2** tacto. ► vt-vi tocar(se). ► vt conmover. • **to get in touch with** ponerse en contacto con; **to keep in touch** mantenerse en contacto.

touchdown ['tʌtʃdaʊn] n **1** aterrizaje. **2** amerizaje. **3** ensayo *(en rugby)*.

tough [tʌf] adj **1** fuerte *(persona)*. **2** duro,-a. ■ **tough luck** mala suerte.

toupee ['tuːpeɪ] n peluquín.

tour [tʊəʳ] n **1** viaje. **2** visita *(de edificio)*. **3** gira. ► vt **1** recorrer *(país)*. **2** visitar *(edificio)*.

tourism ['tʊərɪzəm] n turismo.

tourist ['tʊərɪst] n turista. ■ **tourist office** oficina de turismo.

tournament ['tʊənəmənt] n torneo.

tow [təʊ] vt remolcar.

towards [təˈwɔːdz] prep **1** hacia. **2** para con *(actitud, responsabilidad)*. **3** para. También **toward**.

towel ['taʊəl] n toalla.

tower ['taʊəʳ] n torre.

town [taʊn] n **1** ciudad. **2** pueblo. ■ **town council** ayuntamiento; **town hall** ayuntamiento.

toxic ['tɒksɪk] n tóxico,-a.

toy [tɔɪ] n juguete.

toyshop ['tɔɪʃɒp] n juguetería.

trace [treɪs] n indicio, rastro.

track [træk] n **1** pista, huellas. **2** camino, senda. **3** pista, calle *(atletismo)*. **4** circuito *(de carreras)*. **5** vía *(de ferrocarril)*. ► vt seguir la pista de.

tracksuit ['træksuːt] n chándal.

tractor ['træktəʳ] n tractor.

trade [treɪd] n **1** oficio. **2** negocio. **3** comercio. ► vi comerciar. ► vt cambiar. ■ **trade union** sindicato obrero.

trademark ['treɪdmɑːk] n marca registrada.

trading ['treɪdɪŋ] n comercio. ■ **trading estate** polígono comercial.

tradition [trəˈdɪʃən] n tradición.

traffic ['træfɪk] n tráfico. ► vi traficar. ■ **traffic jam** embotellamiento, atasco; **traffic light** semáforo.

tragedy ['trædʒədɪ] n tragedia.
tragic ['trædʒɪk] adj trágico,-a.
trail [treɪl] n 1 rastro, pista. 2 camino, sendero. 3 estela.
trailer ['treɪlə'] n 1 remolque. 2 tráiler, avance (película).
train [treɪn] n 1 tren. 2 cola (de vestido). ▶ vt-vi 1 entrenar(se). 2 formar(se). ■ **train station** estación de tren.
trainee [treɪ'niː] n aprendiz,-za.
trainer ['treɪnə'] n 1 entrenador,-ra. 2 zapatilla (de deporte).
training ['treɪnɪŋ] n 1 formación. 2 entrenamiento.
traitor ['treɪtə'] n traidor,-ra.
tram [træm] n tranvía.
tramp [træmp] n vagabundo,-a.
trampoline ['træmpəliːn] n cama elástica.
trance [trɑːns] n trance.
transatlantic [trænzət'læntɪk] adj transatlántico,-a.
transcript ['trænskrɪpt] n transcripción.
transfer [(n) 'trænsfɜː', (vb) træns'fɜː'] n 1 transferencia (de dinero). 2 traslado (de empleado). 3 traspaso (de bienes, poderes). ▶ vt 1 transferir (dinero). 2 traspasar (bienes, poderes). ▶ vi hacer trasbordo.
transform [træns'fɔːm] vt-vi transformar(se).
transfusion [træns'fjuːʒən] n transfusión.
transitive ['trænsɪtɪv] adj transitivo,-a.

translate [træns'leɪt] vt traducir.
translation [træns'leɪʃən] n traducción.
translator [træns'leɪtə'] n traductor,-ra.
transmit [trænz'mɪt] vt transmitir.
transparent [træns'peərənt] adj transparente.
transplant ['trænsplɑːnt] n trasplante.
transport [(n) 'trænspɔːt, (vb) træns'pɔːt] n transporte. ▶ vt transportar.
trap [træp] n trampa. ▶ vt atrapar.
trash [træʃ] n US basura.
travel ['trævəl] n viajes. ▶ vi 1 viajar. 2 ir, circular. ■ **travel agency** agencia de viajes.
traveller ['trævələ'] n 1 viajero,-a. 2 viajante. ■ **traveller's cheque** cheque de viaje.
travel-sick ['trævəlsɪk] adj mareado,-a.
tray [treɪ] n bandeja.
treacherous ['tretʃərəs] adj 1 traidor,-ra, traicionero,-a. 2 muy peligroso,-a.
treason ['triːzən] n traición.
treasure ['treʒə'] n tesoro.
treat [triːt] vt 1 tratar. 2 convidar, invitar. 3 darse el gusto, permitirse el lujo.
treatment ['triːtmənt] n 1 tratamiento. 2 trato, conducta.
treaty ['triːtɪ] n tratado.
tree [triː] n árbol.

trek [trek] *n* **1** viaje. **2** caminata *(a pie)*. ▶ *vi* caminar.

tremble ['trembəl] *vi* temblar, estremecerse.

trench [trentʃ] *n* **1** zanja. **2** trinchera.

trend [trend] *n* tendencia.

trespass ['trespəs] *vi* entrar ilegalmente. • **"No trespassing"** "Prohibido el paso".

trestle ['tresəl] *n* caballete.

trial ['traɪəl] *n* **1** proceso, juicio. **2** prueba. • **on trial** a prueba. ▪ **trial run** ensayo.

triangle ['traɪæŋgəl] *n* triángulo.

tribe [traɪb] *n* tribu.

tribunal [traɪˈbjuːnəl] *n* tribunal.

tributary ['trɪbjʊtəri] *n* afluente.

trick [trɪk] *n* truco. ▶ *vt* engañar.

trill [trɪl] *n* trino. ▶ *vt - vi* trinar.

trim [trɪm] *adj* bien arreglado, -a. ▶ *n* recorte *(de pelo)*. ▶ *vt* **1** recortar *(pelo, bigote)*. **2** decorar.

trinket ['trɪŋkɪt] *n* baratija.

trip [trɪp] *n* **1** viaje. **2** excursión. ▶ *vi* tropezar.

tripe [traɪp] *n* callos *(plato)*.

triple ['trɪpəl] *adj* triple.

tripod ['traɪpɒd] *n* trípode.

triumph ['traɪəmf] *n* triunfo. ▶ *vi* triunfar.

trivial ['trɪvɪəl] *adj* trivial.

trolley ['trɒli] *n* carro, carrito.

trombone [trɒmˈbəʊn] *n* trombón.

troop [truːp] *n* grupo, banda *(de gente)*. ▶ *npl* **troops** tropas.

trophy ['trəʊfi] *n* trofeo.

tropic ['trɒpɪk] *n* trópico.

tropical ['trɒpɪkəl] *adj* tropical.

trot [trɒt] *n* trote. ▶ *vi* trotar.

trotter ['trɒtəʳ] *n* manita *(de cerdo)*.

trouble ['trʌbəl] *n* **1** problema. **2** preocupación. **3** molestia. ▶ *vt* **1** preocupar. **2** molestar. ▶ *vi* molestarse.

trough [trɒf] *n* abrevadero.

trousers ['traʊzəz] *npl* pantalón.

trousseau ['truːsəʊ] *n* ajuar.

trout [traʊt] *n* trucha.

truant ['truːənt] *phr.* • **to play truant** hacer novillos.

truce [truːs] *n* tregua.

truck [trʌk] *n* **1** GB vagón. **2** US camión.

true [truː] *adj* verdadero,-a. • **it's true** es verdad.

truffle ['trʌfəl] *n* trufa.

truly ['truːli] *adv* verdaderamente. • **yours truly** atentamente.

trumpet ['trʌmpɪt] *n* trompeta.

truncheon ['trʌntʃən] *n* porra.

trunk [trʌŋk] *n* **1** tronco. **2** baúl. **3** trompa. **4** US maletero. ▶ *npl* **trunks** bañador. ▪ **trunk call** llamada interurbana.

trust [trʌst] *n* confianza, fe. ▶ *vt* confiar en, fiarse de.

truth [truːθ] *n* verdad.

try [traɪ] *n* **1** intento. **2** ensayo *(en rugby)*. ► *vt* - *vi* intentar. ► *vt* probar *(comida)*.

T-shirt [ˈtiːʃɜːt] *n* camiseta.

tub [tʌb] *n* **1** tina. **2** bañera, baño. **3** tarrina.

tube [tjuːb] *n* **1** tubo. **2** GB metro.

Tuesday [ˈtjuːzdɪ] *n* martes.

tuft [tʌft] *n* **1** mechón. **2** mata.

tug [tʌg] *vt* tirar de.

tuition [tjuˈɪʃən] *n* enseñanza.

tulip [ˈtjuːlɪp] *n* tulipán.

tumble [ˈtʌmbəl] *n*. ■ **tumble dryer** secadora.

tumbler [ˈtʌmbələʳ] *n* vaso.

tumour [ˈtjuːməʳ] (US **tumor**) *n* tumor.

tuna [ˈtjuːnə] *n* atún, bonito.

tundra [ˈtʌndrə] *n* tundra.

tune [tjuːn] *n* melodía. ► *vt* **1** afinar *(piano, etc)*. **2** poner a punto *(motor)*. **3** sintonizar *(radio, etc)*. ● **in tune** afinado,-a; **out of tune** desafinado,-a.

tunnel [ˈtʌnəl] *n* túnel.

turbot [ˈtɜːbət] *n* rodaballo.

tureen [tjʊˈriːn] *n* sopera.

turf [tɜːf] *n* césped.

turkey [ˈtɜːkɪ] *n* pavo.

turn [tɜːn] *n* **1** vuelta. **2** curva. **3** turno. ► *vt* **1** girar, dar la vuelta a. **2** doblar *(esquina)*. **3** pasar *(página)*. ► *vi* **1** girar, dar vueltas. **2** volverse, dar la vuelta *(persona)*. **3** torcer. **4** hacerse, ponerse, volverse.

to turn back *vi* volver(se).

to turn down *vt* bajar *(radio, etc)*.

to turn into *vt* convertir.

to turn off *vt* **1** desconectar *(electricidad)*. **2** apagar *(luz, gas)*. **3** cerrar *(agua)*. **4** parar *(máquina)*.

to turn on *vt* **1** conectar *(electricidad)*. **2** encender *(luz)*. **3** abrir *(gas, grifo)*. **4** poner en marcha *(máquina)*.

to turn up *vi* aparecer.

turnip [ˈtɜːnɪp] *n* nabo.

turnover [ˈtɜːnəʊvəʳ] *n* volumen de negocio.

turnpike [ˈtɜːnpaɪk] *n* US autopista de peaje.

turpentine [ˈtɜːpəntaɪn] *n* trementina, aguarrás.

turtle [ˈtɜːtəl] *n* tortuga.

tusk [tʌsk] *n* colmillo.

tutor [ˈtjuːtəʳ] *n* **1** profesor,-ra particular. **2** tutor,-ra.

tuxedo [tʌkˈsiːdəʊ] *n* US esmoquin.

twelfth [twelfθ] *adj* - *n* duodécimo,-a.

twelve [twelv] *num* doce.

twentieth [ˈtwentɪəθ] *adj* - *n* vigésimo,-a.

twenty [ˈtwentɪ] *num* veinte.

twice [twaɪs] *adv* dos veces.

twilight [ˈtwaɪlaɪt] *n* crepúsculo.

twin [twɪn] *n* gemelo,-a. ■ **twin room** habitación con dos camas.

twist [twɪst] *n* **1** recodo, vuelta *(de carretera)*. **2** torcedura. **3** twist *(baile)*. ▸ *vt* **1** torcer. **2** girar *(tapa)*. ▸ *vi* torcerse *(tobillo)*.

two [tuː] *num* dos.

type [taɪp] *n* **1** tipo, clase. **2** letra, carácter.

typewriter ['taɪpraɪtəʳ] *n* máquina de escribir.

typhoon [taɪ'fuːn] *n* tifón.

typical ['tɪpɪkəl] *adj* típico,-a.

typist ['taɪpɪst] *n* mecanógrafo,-a.

tyranny ['tɪrənɪ] *n* tiranía.

tyrant ['taɪərənt] *n* tirano,-a.

tyre ['taɪəʳ] (US **tire**) *n* neumático, llanta.

U

udder ['ʌdəʳ] *n* ubre.

ugly ['ʌglɪ] *adj* feo,-a.

ulcer ['ʌlsəʳ] *n* úlcera.

umbrella [ʌm'brelə] *n* paraguas.

umpire ['ʌmpaɪəʳ] *n* árbitro. ▸ *vt* arbitrar.

unable [ʌn'eɪbəl] *adj* incapaz.

unanimous [juː'nænɪməs] *adj* unánime.

unavailable [ʌnə'veɪləbəl] *adj* no disponible.

unaware [ʌnə'weəʳ] *adj* inconsciente.

unbalanced [ʌn'bælənst] *adj* desequilibrado,-a.

unbeatable [ʌn'biːtəbəl] *adj* **1** invencible, insuperable *(rival)*. **2** inmejorable *(precio)*.

unbelievable [ʌnbɪ'liːvəbəl] *adj* increíble.

unbiassed [ʌn'baɪəst] *adj* imparcial.

unbutton [ʌn'bʌtən] *vt* desabrochar, desbotonar.

uncertain [ʌn'sɜːtən] *adj* **1** incierto,-a, dudoso,-a *(futuro)*. **2** indeciso,-a *(persona)*.

uncle ['ʌnkəl] *n* tío.

uncommon [ʌn'kɒmən] *adj* **1** poco común. **2** insólito,-a.

unconscious [ʌn'kɒnʃəs] *adj* inconsciente.

uncouth [ʌn'kuːθ] *adj* tosco,-a.

uncover [ʌn'kʌvəʳ] *vt* **1** destapar, descubrir. **2** revelar.

under ['ʌndəʳ] *prep* **1** bajo, debajo de. **2** menos de. ▸ *adv* abajo, debajo.

underclothes ['ʌndəkləʊðz] *npl* ropa interior.

undercoat ['ʌndəkəʊt] *n* primera mano *(de pintura)*.

undercover [ʌndə'kʌvəʳ] *adj* clandestino,-a, secreto,-a.

underdeveloped [ʌndədɪ'veləpt] *adj* subdesarrollado,-a.

underdone [ʌndə'dʌn] *adj* poco hecho,-a.

underestimate [ʌndər'estɪmeɪt] *vt* subestimar, infravalorar.

undergo [ʌndə'gəʊ] vt 1 experimentar, sufrir (cambio, dificultades). 2 someterse a (operación).

undergraduate [ʌndə'grædjʊət] n estudiante universitario,-a no licenciado,-a.

underground [(adj-n) 'ʌndəgraʊnd, (adv) ʌndə'graʊnd] adj 1 subterráneo. 2 fig clandestino, -a. ▶ n 1 metro. 2 resistencia, movimiento clandestino. ▶ adv 1 bajo tierra. 2 en secreto.

undergrowth ['ʌndəgrəʊθ] n maleza.

underline [ʌndə'laɪn] vt subrayar.

underneath [ʌndə'niːθ] prep debajo de. ▶ adv debajo. ▶ n parte inferior.

underpants ['ʌndəpænts] npl calzoncillos, eslip.

underpass ['ʌndəpæs] n paso subterráneo.

underskirt ['ʌndəskɜːt] n enaguas.

understand [ʌndə'stænd] vt entender, comprender.

understanding [ʌndə'stændɪŋ] n 1 entendimiento, comprensión. 2 acuerdo, arreglo.

understood [ʌndə'stʊd] pt-pp → understand.

undertake [ʌndə'teɪk] vt 1 emprender. 2 asumir. 3 comprometerse.

undertook [ʌndə'tʊk] pt → undertake.

underwater [ʌndə'wɔːtəʳ] adj submarino,-a.

underwear ['ʌndəwɜːəʳ] n ropa interior.

underwent [ʌndə'went] pt → undergo.

undid [ʌn'dɪd] pt → undo.

undo [ʌn'duː] vt 1 deshacer (nudo). 2 desabrochar (botón). 3 abrir (paquete).

undress [ʌn'dres] vt-vi desnudar(se), desvestir(se).

uneasy [ʌn'iːzɪ] adj intranquilo,-a, inquieto,-a.

unemployed [ʌnɪm'plɔɪd] adj desempleado,-a.

unemployment [ʌnɪm'plɔɪmənt] n paro, desempleo. ■ **unemployment benefit** subsidio de desempleo.

unequal [ʌn'iːkwəl] adj desigual.

uneven [ʌn'iːvən] adj 1 desigual. 2 irregular (superficie). 3 lleno,-a de baches (carretera).

unexpected [ʌnɪk'spektɪd] adj inesperado,-a.

unfamiliar [ʌnfə'mɪlɪəʳ] adj desconocido,-a.

unfasten [ʌn'fɑːsən] vt 1 desabrochar (botón). 2 desatar (nudo). 3 abrir (puerta).

unfit [ʌn'fɪt] adj 1 inadecuado,-a. 2 desentrenado,-a.

unfold [ʌn'fəʊld] vt-vi desplegar(se), abrir(se).

unforeseen [ʌnfɔː'siːn] adj imprevisto,-a.

unhappy [ʌn'hæpɪ] *adj* infeliz, triste.

unhurt [ʌn'hɜːt] *adj* ileso,-a.

unidentified [ʌnaɪ'dentɪfaɪd] *adj* no identificado,-a.

unification [juːnɪfɪ'keɪʃən] *n* unificación.

uniform ['juːnɪfɔːm] *adj-n* uniforme.

unify ['juːnɪfaɪ] *vt* unificar.

union ['juːnɪən] *n* 1 unión. 2 sindicato.

unique [juː'niːk] *adj* único,-a.

unisex ['juːnɪseks] *adj* unisex.

unit ['juːnɪt] *n* unidad.

unite [juː'naɪt] *vt-vi* unir(se).

universe ['juːnɪvɜːs] *n* universo.

university [juːnɪ'vɜːsɪtɪ] *n* universidad.

unjust [ʌn'dʒʌst] *adj* injusto,-a.

unkind [ʌn'kaɪnd] *adj* 1 poco amable *(persona)*. 2 cruel.

unknown [ʌn'nəʊn] *adj* desconocido,-a.

unless [ən'les] *conj* a menos que, a no ser que, si no.

unlike [ʌn'laɪk] *adj* diferente. ► *prep* a diferencia de.

unlikely [ʌn'laɪklɪ] *adj* improbable, poco probable.

unload [ʌn'ləʊd] *vt* descargar.

unlock [ʌn'lɒk] *vt* abrir.

unmanned [ʌn'mænd] *adj* no tripulado,-a.

unnoticed [ʌn'nəʊtɪst] *adj* inadvertido,-a, desapercibido,-a.

unoccupied [ʌn'ɒkjʊpaɪd] *adj* 1 deshabitado,-a *(casa)*. 2 de-

socupado,-a *(persona)*. 3 vacante *(empleo)*.

unofficial [ʌnə'fɪʃəl] *adj* extraoficial, oficioso,-a.

unpack [ʌn'pæk] *vt* 1 desempaquetar, desembalar. 2 deshacer *(maleta)*.

unpleasant [ʌn'plezənt] *adj* desagradable.

unplug [ʌn'plʌg] *vt* desenchufar.

unpublished [ʌn'pʌblɪʃt] *adj* inédito,-a.

unreadable [ʌn'riːdəbəl] *adj* 1 ilegible. 2 imposible de leer.

unreal [ʌn'rɪəl] *adj* irreal.

unreasonable [ʌn'riːzənəbəl] *adj* 1 poco razonable. 2 desmesurado,-a, excesivo,-a.

unreliable [ʌnrɪ'laɪəbəl] *adj* 1 de poca confianza *(persona)*. 2 poco fiable *(máquina)*.

unrest [ʌn'rest] *n* 1 malestar, intranquilidad. 2 disturbios.

unripe [ʌn'raɪp] *adj* verde *(fruta)*.

unroll [ʌn'rəʊl] *vt-vi* desenrollar(se).

unsafe [ʌn'seɪf] *adj* inseguro,-a.

unscrew [ʌn'skruː] *vt* 1 desatornillar. 2 desenroscar.

unskilled [ʌn'skɪld] *adj* 1 no cualificado,-a *(obrero)*. 2 no especializado,-a *(trabajo)*.

unspeakable [ʌn'spiːkəbəl] *adj* indecible.

unstable [ʌn'steɪbəl] *adj* inestable.

unsteady [ʌn'stedɪ] *adj* inseguro,-a, inestable.

unsuccessful [ʌnsək'sesfʊl] *adj* fracasado,-a, sin éxito.

unsuitable [ʌn'suːtəbəl] *adj* 1 poco apropiado,-a *(persona)*. 2 inoportuno, inconveniente.

untidy [ʌn'taɪdɪ] *adj* 1 desordenado,-a *(habitación)*. 2 desaliñado,-a *(persona)*.

untie [ʌn'taɪ] *vt* desatar.

until [ən'tɪl] *prep* hasta. ► *conj* hasta que.

untrue [ʌn'truː] *adj* 1 falso,-a. 2 infiel.

unveil [ʌn'veɪl] *vt* revelar.

unwell [ʌn'wel] *adj* indispuesto,-a.

unwilling [ʌn'wɪlɪŋ] *adj* reacio,-a, poco dispuesto,-a.

unwind [ʌn'waɪnd] *vt* desenrollar(se).

unwise [ʌn'waɪz] *adj* imprudente, poco aconsejable.

unworthy [ʌn'wɜːðɪ] *adj* indigno,-a.

unwound [ʌn'waʊnd] *pt-pp* → unwind.

unwrap [ʌn'ræp] *vt* desenvolver, abrir.

up [ʌp] *adv* 1 arriba, hacia arriba. 2 levantado,-a. 3 hacia. 4 más alto,-a. 5 acabado,-a.► *prep* 1 *to go up the stairs*, subir la escalera. 2 en lo alto de: *up a tree*, en lo alto de un árbol. ► *vt fam* subir, aumentar. • **up to** hasta; **it's up**

to you *fam* es cosa tuya; **up and down** de arriba a abajo, de un lado al otro. ■ **ups and downs** altibajos.

update [*(n)* 'ʌpdeɪt, *(vb)* ʌp'deɪt] *n* actualización. ► *vt* actualizar.

upgrade [ʌp'greɪd] *vt* 1 ascender *(persona)*. 2 mejorar. 3 actualizar. ► *n* actualización.

uphill [ʌp'hɪl] *adv* cuesta arriba.

upholstery [ʌp'həʊlstərɪ] *n* tapicería, tapizado.

upkeep ['ʌpkiːp] *n* mantenimiento.

upon [ə'pɒn] *prep* → on.

upper ['ʌpəʳ] *adj* superior, de arriba. ■ **upper case** mayúsculas, caja alta; **upper class** clase alta.

uppermost ['ʌpəməʊst] *adj* 1 más alto,-a. 2 *fig* principal.

upright ['ʌpraɪt] *adj* derecho, -a, vertical.

uprising [ʌp'raɪzɪŋ] *n* sublevación, rebelión.

upset [ʌp'set] *adj* disgustado,-a, ofendido,-a. ► *vt* 1 disgustar. 2 desbaratar *(planes)*. 3 volcar *(barco)*. 4 derramar *(recipiente)*. ► *n* revés.

upside down [ʌpsaɪd'daʊn] *adv* al revés.

upstairs [*(adv)* ʌp'steəz, *(n)* 'ʌpsteəz] *adv* 1 en el piso de arriba *(situación)*. 2 al piso de arriba *(movimiento)*. ► *n* piso de arriba. ► *adj* de arriba.

up-to-date [ʌptə'deɪt] *adj* al día, actualizado,-a.

upward ['ʌpwəd] *adj* hacia arriba, ascendente. ► *adv* hacia arriba.

upwards ['ʌpwədz] *adv* hacia arriba.

urban ['ɜːbən] *adj* urbano,-a.

urge [ɜːdʒ] ► *vt* encarecer.

urgency ['ɜːdʒənsɪ] *n* urgencia.

urgent ['ɜːdʒənt] *adj* urgente.

urn [ɜːn] *n* urna.

us [ʌs, unstressed əz] *pron* nos, nosotros,-as.

usage ['juːzɪdʒ] *n* uso.

use [(n) juːs, (vb) juːz] *n* uso. ► *vt* usar, utilizar. • **used to** soler, acostumbrar *(se refiere solo al pasado)*: **he used to get up early**, solía levantarse temprano. • **"Not in use"** "No funciona"; **out of use** en desuso; **what's the use of...?** ¿de qué sirve...?

used [juːst] *adj* usado,-a. • **to be used to** STH estar acostumbrado,-a a algo; **to get used to** STH acostumbrarse a algo.

useful ['juːsfʊl] *adj* útil.

useless ['juːsləs] *adj* inútil.

user ['juːzəʳ] *n* usuario,-a.

usher ['ʌʃəʳ] *n* **1** ujier. **2** acomodador,-ra.

usual ['juːʒʊəl] *adj* usual, habitual, normal. • **as usual** como de costumbre, como siempre.

usually ['juːʒʊəlɪ] *adv* normalmente.

utensil [juː'tensəl] *n* utensilio. • **kitchen utensils** batería de cocina.

utility [juː'tɪlɪtɪ] *n* **1** utilidad. **2** empresa de servicio público.

utilize ['juːtɪlaɪz] *vt* utilizar.

utmost ['ʌtməʊst] *adj* sumo,-a.

utopia [juː'təʊpɪə] *n* utopía.

utter ['ʌtəʳ] *adj* absoluto,-a, total. ► *vt* pronunciar, articular.

U-turn ['juːtɜːn] *n* cambio de sentido, giro de 180 grados.

V

vacancy ['veɪkənsɪ] *n* **1** vacante *(puesto de trabajo)*. **2** habitación libre. • **"No vacancies"** "Completo".

vacant ['veɪkənt] *adj* **1** vacío. **2** vacante. **3** libre.

vacate [və'keɪt] *vt* **1** dejar vacante. **2** desocupar.

vacation [və'keɪʃən] *n* vacaciones.

vaccinate ['væksɪneɪt] *vt* vacunar.

vaccine ['væksiːn] *n* vacuna.

vacuum ['vækjʊəm] *n* vacío. ► *vt* pasar la aspiradora por. ■ **vacuum cleaner** aspiradora; **vacuum flask** termo.

vacuum-packed ['vækjuəm-pækt] *adj* envasado,-a al vacío.

vagina [və'dʒaɪnə] *n* vagina.

vague [veɪg] *adj* vago,-a, indefinido,-a.

valid ['vælɪd] *adj* **1** válido,-a.

valley ['vælɪ] *n* valle.

valuable ['væljuəbəl] *adj* valioso,-a. ► *npl* **valuables** objetos de valor.

value ['vælju:] *n* valor. ► *vt* **1** valorar.

valve [vælv] *n* válvula.

vampire ['væmpaɪəʳ] *n* vampiro.

van [væn] *n* **1** camioneta, furgoneta. **2** GB furgón.

vandalism ['vændəlɪzəm] *n* vandalismo.

vanguard ['vængɑːd] *n* vanguardia.

vanish ['vænɪʃ] *vi* desaparecer.

vanity ['vænɪtɪ] *n* vanidad.

vapour ['veɪpəʳ] (US **vapor**) *n* vapor, vaho.

variable ['veərɪəbəl] *adj-n* variable.

variation [veərɪ'eɪʃən] *n* variación.

varied ['veərɪd] *adj* variado,-a.

variety [və'raɪətɪ] *n* variedad. ■ **variety show** espectáculo de variedades.

various ['veərɪəs] *adj* varios, -as.

varnish ['vɑːnɪʃ] *n* barniz. ► *vt* barnizar.

vary ['veərɪ] *vt-vi* variar.

vase [vɑːz] *n* jarrón, florero.

vast [vɑːst] *adj* vasto,-a, inmenso,-a.

vat [væt] *n* tina, cuba.

VAT [væt, ˌviː'eɪ'tiː] *abbr* **(value added tax)** IVA.

vault [vɔːlt] *n* **1** bóveda. **2** cámara acorazada *(de banco)*. **3** panteón, cripta *(de iglesia)*.

veal [viːl] *n* ternera.

vegetable ['vedʒɪtəbəl] *adj* vegetal. ► *n* hortaliza, verdura, legumbre.

vegetarian [vedʒɪ'teərɪən] *adj-n* vegetariano,-a.

vegetation [vedʒɪ'teɪʃən] *n* vegetación.

vehicle ['viːəkəl] *n* vehículo.

veil [veɪl] *n* velo.

vein [veɪn] *n* vena.

velocity [və'lɒsɪtɪ] *n* velocidad.

velvet ['velvɪt] *n* terciopelo.

vending machine ['vendɪŋ-məʃiːn] *n* máquina expendedora.

vengeance ['vendʒəns] *n* venganza.

vent [vent] *n* abertura, respiradero.

ventilate ['ventɪleɪt] *vt* ventilar.

ventilator ['ventɪleɪtəʳ] *n* ventilador.

venture ['ventʃəʳ] *n* empresa arriesgada, aventura. ► *vt-vi* arriesgar(se).

venue ['venjuː] *n* lugar.

veranda [və'rændə] *n* veranda, terraza.

vinyl

verb [vɜːb] *n* verbo.

verge [vɜːdʒ] *n* borde, margen.

verify ['verɪfaɪ] *vt* verificar.

vermin ['vɜːmɪn] *n* **1** alimaña. **2** bichos, sabandijas.

verruca [vəˈruːkə] *n* verruga.

versatile ['vɜːsətaɪl] *adj* versátil.

verse [vɜːs] *n* **1** estrofa, versículo. **2** verso, poesía.

version [vɜːʒən] *n* versión.

versus ['vɜːsəs] *prep* contra.

vertebra [vɜːtɪbrə] *n* vértebra.

vertical ['vɜːtɪkəl] *adj* vertical.

vertigo ['vɜːtɪɡəʊ] *n* vértigo.

very ['verɪ] *adv* **1** muy. **2** mucho.

vessel ['vesəl] *n* nave.

vest [vest] *n* **1** camiseta *(interior)*. **2** US chaleco.

vet [vet] *n fam* veterinario,-a. ► *vt* GB investigar, examinar.

veteran ['vetərən] *adj-n* veterano,-a.

veterinarian [vetərɪˈneərɪən] *n* US veterinario,-a.

veterinary ['vetərɪnərɪ] *adj* veterinario,-a.

veto ['viːtəʊ] *n* veto. ► *vt* vetar.

via ['vaɪə] *prep* vía, por vía de, por.

viaduct ['vaɪədʌkt] *n* viaducto.

vibrate [vaɪˈbreɪt] *vi* vibrar.

vice [vaɪs] *n* vicio.

vice versa [vaɪsˈvɜːsə] *adv* viceversa.

vicinity [vɪˈsɪnɪtɪ] *n* cercanías.

vicious ['vɪʃəs] *adj* **1** cruel. **2** violento,-a, brutal.

victim ['vɪktɪm] *n* víctima.

victory ['vɪktərɪ] *n* victoria.

video ['vɪdɪəʊ] *n* vídeo. ■ **video camera** videocámara; **video cassette** videocasete; **video game** videojuego; **video shop** videoclub; **video recorder** vídeo.

videotape ['vɪdɪəʊteɪp] *vt* grabar en vídeo. ► *n* cinta de vídeo.

view [vjuː] *n* **1** vista, panorama. **2** parecer, opinión. ► *vt* mirar, ver. ● **in my view** en mi opinión; **in view of** en vista de.

viewer ['vjuːəʳ] *n* telespectador,-ra.

viewpoint ['vjuːpɔɪnt] *n* punto de vista.

vigour ['vɪɡəʳ] (US **vigor**) *n* vigor.

villa ['vɪlə] *n* chalet.

village ['vɪlɪdʒ] *n* pueblo.

villain ['vɪlən] *n* malo,-a.

vinaigrette [vɪnəˈɡret] *n* vinagreta.

vindicate ['vɪndɪkeɪt] *vt* reivindicar.

vine [vaɪn] *n* vid, parra.

vinegar ['vɪnɪɡəʳ] *n* vinagre.

vineyard ['vɪnjɑːd] *n* viña, viñedo.

vintage ['vɪntɪdʒ] *n* cosecha. ■ **vintage car** coche antiguo.

vinyl ['vaɪnəl] *n* vinilo.

violate ['vaɪəleɪt] *vt* violar.

violence ['vaɪələns] *n* violencia.

violent ['vaɪələnt] *adj* violento,-a.

violet ['vaɪələt] *n* violeta.

violin [vaɪə'lɪn] *n* violín.

viper ['vaɪpəʳ] *n* víbora.

virgin ['vɜːdʒɪn] *adj-n* virgen.

virtual ['vɜːtjʊəl] *adj* virtual. ▪ **virtual reality** realidad virtual.

virtue ['vɜːtjuː] *n* virtud.

virus ['vaɪərəs] *n* virus. ▪ **virus checker** antivirus.

visa ['viːzə] *n* visado.

visible ['vɪzɪbəl] *adj* visible.

vision ['vɪʒən] *n* visión, vista.

visit ['vɪzɪt] *n* visita. ► *vt* visitar. • **to pay a visit** visitar.

visitor ['vɪzɪtəʳ] *n* **1** visita. **2** visitante.

visor ['vaɪzəʳ] *n* visera.

visual ['vɪzjʊəl] *adj* visual. ▪ **visual display unit** pantalla.

vital ['vaɪtəl] *adj* vital.

vitality [vaɪ'tælɪtɪ] *n* vitalidad.

vitamin ['vɪtəmɪn] *n* vitamina.

vivid ['vɪvɪd] *adj* **1** vivo,-a, intenso,-a. **2** gráfico,-a.

vixen ['vɪksən] *n* zorra.

vocabulary [vəˈkæbjʊlərɪ] *n* vocabulario.

vocal ['vəʊkəl] *adj* vocal.

vocation [vəʊˈkeɪʃən] *n* vocación.

vodka ['vɒdkə] *n* vodka.

vogue [vəʊg] *n* boga, moda. •

to be in vogue estar de moda.

voice [vɔɪs] *n* voz. ▪ **voice mail** buzón de voz.

volcano [vɒlˈkeɪnəʊ] *n* volcán.

volley ['vɒlɪ] *n* volea. ► *vi* volear.

volleyball ['vɒlɪbɔːl] *n* balonvolea, voleibol.

volt [vəʊlt] *n* voltio.

voltage ['vəʊltɪdʒ] *n* voltaje.

voluble ['vɒljʊbəl] *adj* locuaz, hablador,-ra.

volume ['vɒljuːm] *n* volumen.

voluntary ['vɒləntərɪ] *adj* voluntario,-a. ▪ **voluntary organization** organización benéfica.

volunteer [vɒlənˈtɪəʳ] *n* **1** voluntario,-a. **2** cooperante. ► *vt-vi* ofrecerse *(voluntario)* para hacer algo.

vomit ['vɒmɪt] *n* vómito. ► *vt-vi* vomitar.

vote [vəʊt] *n* **1** voto. **2** votación. ► *vt-vi* votar.

voter ['vəʊtəʳ] *n* votante.

voucher ['vaʊtʃəʳ] *n* vale, bono.

vow [vaʊ] *n* promesa solemne, voto.

vowel ['vaʊəl] *n* vocal.

voyage ['vɔɪɪdʒ] *n* viaje.

voyager ['vɔɪədʒəʳ] *n* viajero,-a.

vulgar ['vʌlgəʳ] *adj* vulgar.

vulnerable ['vʌlnərəbəl] *adj* vulnerable.

vulture ['vʌltʃəʳ] *n* buitre.

vulva ['vʌlvə] *n* vulva.

W

wafer ['weɪfəʳ] n **1** barquillo, galleta, oblea. **2** hostia.

waffle ['wɒfəl] n gofre.

wag [wæg] n meneo. ► vt-vi menear(se).

wage [weɪdʒ] n sueldo.

wager ['weɪdʒəʳ] n apuesta.

wagon ['wægən] n **1** carro, carromato. **2** vagón (de tren).

waist [weɪst] n cintura, talle.

waistcoat ['weɪskəʊt] n chaleco.

wait [weɪt] n espera. ► vi esperar.

waiter ['weɪtəʳ] n camarero.

waiting ['weɪtɪŋ] n espera. ■ **waiting list** lista de espera; **waiting room** sala de espera.

waitress ['weɪtrəs] n camarera.

wake [weɪk] n velatorio. ► vt despertar.

to wake up vt-vi despertar(se).

waken ['weɪkən] vt-vi despertar(se).

walk [wɔːk] n paseo, caminata. ► vi andar, caminar. ► vt **1** pasear (perro). **2** acompañar (persona). ● **to go for a walk** dar un paseo.

to walk out vi **1** marcharse. **2** ir a la huelga.

walkie-talkie [wɔːkɪ'tɔːkɪ] n walkie-talkie.

walking stick ['wɔːkɪŋstɪk] n bastón.

Walkman® ['wɔːkmən] n Walkman®.

wall [wɔːl] n **1** muro (exterior). **2** pared (interior).

wallet ['wɒlɪt] n cartera.

wallpaper ['wɔːlpeɪpəʳ] n papel pintado. ► vt empapelar.

wally ['wɒlɪ] n fam inútil, imbécil.

walnut ['wɔːlnʌt] n nuez. ■ **walnut tree** nogal.

walrus ['wɔːlrəs] n morsa.

waltz [wɔːls] n vals.

wand [wɒnd] n varita.

wander ['wɒndəʳ] vi vagar.

want [wɒnt] vt **1** querer. **2** fam necesitar.

wanted ['wɒntɪd] adj **1** necesario,-a: *"Boy wanted"*, "Se necesita chico". **2** buscado,-a: *"Wanted"*, "Se busca".

war [wɔːʳ] n guerra.

ward [wɔːd] n **1** sala (de hospital). **2** GB distrito electoral.

warden ['wɔːdən] n vigilante, guardián,-ana.

wardrobe ['wɔːdrəʊb] n **1** armario (ropero), guardarropa. **2** vestuario.

warehouse ['weəhaʊs] n almacén.

warfare ['wɔːfeəʳ] n guerra.

warm [wɔːm] adj **1** caliente. **2** tibio,-a, templado,-a. **3** cálido,-a (clima). **4** de abrigo (ropa). ► vt calentar.

to warm up *vt* calentar. ► *vi*
1 calentarse. **2** hacer ejercicios de calentamiento.

warmth [wɔːmθ] *n* calor.

warn [wɔːn] *vt* avisar, advertir, prevenir.

warning [wɔːnɪŋ] *n* aviso, advertencia.

warrant [wɒrənt] *n* orden judicial. ► *vt* justificar.

warranty [wɒrənti] *n* garantía.

warrior [wɒrɪəʳ] *n* guerrero,-a.

wart [wɔːt] *n* verruga.

was [wɒz] *pt* → be.

wash [wɒʃ] *vt-vi* lavar(se).

to wash up *vt-vi* fregar *(platos)*.

washbasin [wɒʃbeɪsən] *n* lavabo.

washer [wɒʃəʳ] *n* **1** arandela, junta. **2** lavadora.

washing [wɒʃɪŋ] *n* **1** lavado. **2** colada. • **to do the washing** hacer la colada. ▪ **washing machine** lavadora.

washing-up [wɒʃɪŋ'ʌp] *n* **1** fregado. **2** platos. • **to do the washing up** fregar los platos, lavar los platos. ▪ **washing-up liquid** lavavajillas.

washroom [wɒʃruːm] *n* US servicios, lavabo.

wasp [wɒsp] *n* avispa.

waste [weɪst] *n* **1** desperdicio. **2** derroche *(de dinero)*. **3** desechos. ► *vt* **1** desperdiciar, malgastar *(comida, oportunidad)*. **2** despilfarrar, derrochar *(dinero)*.

watch [wɒtʃ] *n* reloj *(de pulsera)*. ► *vt* **1** mirar, ver *(televisión, película)*. **2** observar. **3** vigilar. **4** tener cuidado con. • **watch out!** ¡ojo!, ¡cuidado!

watchdog [wɒtʃdɒg] *n* perro guardián.

watchman [wɒtʃmən] *n* vigilante.

water [wɔːtəʳ] *n* agua. ► *vt* regar. ► *vi* **1** llorar *(ojos)*. **2** hacerse agua *(boca)*. ▪ **water bottle** cantimplora; **water lily** nenúfar; **water polo** waterpolo.

to water down *vt* aguar.

watercolour [wɔːtəkʌləʳ] (US **watercolor**) *n* acuarela.

watercress [wɔːtəkres] *n* berros.

waterfall [wɔːtəfɔːl] *n* cascada.

watermelon [wɔːtəmelən] *n* sandía.

watermill [wɔːtəmɪl] *n* molino de agua.

waterproof [wɔːtəpruːf] *adj* impermeable.

water-skiing [wɔːtəskiːɪŋ] *n* esquí acuático.

watertight [wɔːtətaɪt] *adj* hermético,-a.

wave [weɪv] *n* **1** ola *(de mar)*. **2** onda. ► *vt* **1** agitar. **2** marcar, ondular *(pelo)*.

wavelength [weɪvleŋθ] *n* longitud de onda.

wavy [weɪvi] *adj* ondulado,-a.

well

wax [wæks] *n* cera. ▶ *vt* encerar.

way [weɪ] *n* **1** camino. **2** dirección. **3** manera, modo. • **by the way** a propósito; **on the way** por el camino; **the right way round** bien puesto; **the wrong way round** al revés; **to get out of the way** apartarse del camino, quitarse de en medio; **to give way** ceder el paso; **to lose one's way** perderse; **to stand in the way of** obstruir el paso de.

we [wiː, unstressed wɪ] *pron* nosotros,-as.

weak [wiːk] *adj* débil.

weakness ['wiːknəs] *n* debilidad.

wealth [welθ] *n* riqueza.

wealthy ['welθɪ] *adj* rico,-a.

weapon ['wepən] *n* arma.

wear [weəʳ] *n* **1** uso. **2** desgaste, deterioro. **3** ropa. ▶ *vt* **1** llevar puesto,-a. **2** vestir, ponerse *(ropa)*. **3** calzar *(zapatos)*. **4** desgastar.

weary ['wɪərɪ] *adj* cansado,-a.

weasel ['wiːzəl] *n* comadreja.

weather ['weðəʳ] *n* tiempo. ▪ **weather forecast** pronóstico del tiempo.

weathercock ['weðəkɒk] *n* veleta.

weave [wiːv] *n* tejido. ▶ *vt-vi* tejer.

web [web] *n* **1** telaraña. **2** *fig* red. **3** Internet. ▪ **web page** página web.

website ['websaɪt] *n* sitio web.

wedding ['wedɪŋ] *n* boda. ▪ **wedding dress** vestido de novia; **wedding ring** alianza.

wedge [wedʒ] *n* cuña, calce.

Wednesday ['wenzdɪ] *n* miércoles.

week [wiːk] *n* semana.

weekday ['wiːkdeɪ] *n* día laborable.

weekend ['wiːkend] *n* fin de semana.

weekly ['wiːklɪ] *adj* semanal. ▶ *adv* semanalmente. ▶ *n* semanario.

weep [wiːp] *vi* llorar.

weigh [weɪ] *vt* pesar.

weight [weɪt] *n* **1** peso. **2** pesa. • **to lose weight** perder peso; **to put on weight** engordar.

weightlifting ['weɪtlɪftɪŋ] *n* halterofilia.

weir [wɪəʳ] *n* presa *(de río)*.

weird [wɪəd] *adj* raro,-a.

welcome ['welkəm] *adj* bienvenido,-a. ▶ *n* bienvenida. ▶ *vt* dar la bienvenida a. • **you're welcome** de nada, no hay de qué.

weld [weld] *n* soldadura. ▶ *vt* soldar.

welfare ['welfeəʳ] *n* bienestar.

well[1] [wel] *adj-adv* bien. ▶ *interj* bueno • **as well** también; **as well as** además de; **just as well** menos mal; **pretty well 1** bastante bien. **2** casi.

well[2] [wel] *n* pozo.

well-being [wel'biːɪŋ] *n* bien-estar.

well-built [wel'bɪlt] *adj* forni-do,-a.

wellington ['welɪŋtən] *n* bo-ta de goma.

well-known [wel'nəʊn] *adj* conocido,-a, famoso,-a.

well-meaning [wel'miːnɪŋ] *adj* bien intencionado,-a.

well-off [wel'ɒf] *adj* rico,-a.

well-timed [wel'taɪmd] *adj* oportuno,-a.

well-to-do [weltə'duː] *adj* acomodado,-a.

went [went] *pt* → go.

wept [wept] *pt-pp* → weep.

were [wɜːʳ] *pt* → be.

west [west] *n* oeste, occiden-te. ► *adj* del oeste, occidental. ► *adv* al oeste, hacia el oeste.

western ['westən] *adj* del oeste. ► *n* western,.

wet [wet] *adj* **1** mojado,-a. **2** húmedo,-a. **3** lluvioso,-a *(tiem-po)*. ► *vt* humedecer. • **"Wet paint"** "Recién pintado".

whale [weɪl] *n* ballena.

wharf [wɔːf] *n* muelle.

what [wɒt] *adj* **1** qué *(pregun-tas)*. **2** qué, menudo *(exclama-ciones)*. ► *pron* **1** qué *(preguntas)*. **2** lo que *(subordinadas)*: *that's what he said*, eso es lo que dijo.

whatever [wɒt'evəʳ] *adj* **1** cualquiera que. **2** en absolu-to. ► *pron* (todo) lo que.

whatsoever [wɒtsəʊ'evəʳ] *adj* → whatever.

wheat [wiːt] *n* trigo.

wheel [wiːl] *n* **1** rueda. **2** volante.■ **wheel clamp** cepo.

wheelbarrow ['wiːlbærəʊ] *n* carretilla de mano.

wheelchair ['wiːltʃeəʳ] *n* silla de ruedas.

when [wen] *adv* cuándo. ► *conj* cuando.

whenever [wen'evəʳ] *conj* cuando quiera que, siempre que. ► *adv* **1** cuando sea. **2** cuándo.

where [weəʳ] *adv* dónde, adónde. ► *conj* **1** donde. **2** mientras que.

whereabouts [*(n)* 'weərə-baʊts, *(adv)* weərə'baʊts] *n* pa-radero. ► *adv* dónde, adónde.

whereas [weər'æz] *conj* mien-tras que.

whereby [weə'baɪ] *adv* por el/la/lo cual.

wherever [weər'evəʳ] *adv* dónde, adónde. ► *conj* don-dequiera que.

whether ['weðəʳ] *conj* si.

which [wɪtʃ] *adj* qué. ► *pron* **1** cuál, cuáles *(en interrogativas)*. **2** que *(en subordinadas)*. **3** el/la/lo que, el/la/lo cual *(con preposición)*, los/las que, los/las cuales. **4** el/la cual, los/las cuales. **5** lo que/cual.

whichever [wɪtʃ'evəʳ] *adj* (no importa) el/la/los/las que. ►

pron cualquiera, el/la/los/las que.

while [waɪl] *n* rato, tiempo. ► *conj* **1** mientras. **2** aunque. **3** mientras que. • **for a while** un rato; **once in a while** de vez en cuando.

whilst [waɪlst] *conj* → while.

whim [wɪm] *n* antojo.

whip [wɪp] *n* látigo, fusta. ► *vt* **1** azotar. **2** batir, montar *(nata, etc).* ▪ **whipped cream** nata montada.

whirlpool [ˈwɜːlpuːl] *n* remolino.

whisk [wɪsk] *n* **1** batidor. **2** batidora *(eléctrica).* ► *vt* montar *(nata, claras).*

whisker [ˈwɪskə^r] *n* pelo *(de bigote).* ► *npl* **whiskers 1** patillas *(de persona).* **2** bigotes *(de gato).*

whiskey [ˈwɪskɪ] *n* whisky, güisqui *(irlandés).*

whisky [ˈwɪskɪ] *n* whisky, güisqui.

whisper [ˈwɪspə^r] *n* susurro. ► *vt-vi* susurrar.

whistle [ˈwɪsəl] *n* **1** silbato. **2** silbido, pitido. ► *vt-vi* silbar.

white [waɪt] *adj* blanco,-a. ► *n* **1** blanco *(color).* **2** clara *(de huevo).* ▪ **white coffee** café con leche.

white-collar [waɪtˈkɒlə^r] *adj* administrativo,-a.

whitewash [ˈwaɪtwɒʃ] *n* cal. ► *vt* encalar.

who [huː] *pron* **1** quién, quiénes *(en interrogativas directas e indirectas).* **2** que *(en subordinadas-objeto).*

whoever [huːˈevə^r] *pron* **1** quien. **2** quienquiera que, cualquiera que.

whole [həʊl] *adj* **1** entero,-a. **2** intacto,-a. ► *n* conjunto, todo. • **as a whole** en conjunto.

wholemeal [ˈhəʊlmiːl] *adj* integral.

wholesale [ˈhəʊlseɪl] *adj-adv* COMM al por mayor.

whom [huːm] *pron* **1** *fml* a quién, a quiénes *(en interrogativas).* **2** a quien, a quienes *(en subordinadas).*

whose [huːz] *pron* de quién, de quiénes. ► *adj* **1** de quién, de quiénes. **2** cuyo,-a, cuyos,-as.

why [waɪ] *adv* por qué.

wick [wɪk] *n* pábilo.

wicked [ˈwɪkɪd] *adj* malo,-a.

wicker [ˈwɪkə^r] *n* mimbre.

wide [waɪd] *adj* **1** ancho,-a. **2** amplio,-a. • **wide open** abierto,-a de par en par.

widow [ˈwɪdəʊ] *n* viuda.

widower [ˈwɪdəʊə^r] *n* viudo.

width [wɪdθ] *n* ancho.

wife [waɪf] *n* esposa, mujer.

wig [wɪg] *n* peluca.

wild [waɪld] *adj* **1** salvaje. **2** silvestre, campestre *(planta).*

wildcat [ˈwaɪldkæt] *n* gato montés.

wildlife ['waɪldlaɪf] *n* fauna.

will[1] [wɪl] *aux* **1** *se usa para formar el futuro de los verbos*: *she will be here tomorrow*, estará aquí mañana. **2** *indica voluntad*: *the car won't start*, el coche no arranca. **3** *indica insistencia*: *he will leave the door open*, es que no hay manera de que cierre la puerta. **4** *poder*: *this phone will accept credit cards*, este teléfono acepta tarjetas de crédito. **5** *indica una suposición*: *that will be the postman*, debe de ser el cartero.

will[2] [wɪl] *n* **1** voluntad. **2** testamento.

willing ['wɪlɪŋ] *adj* complaciente. • **willing to do** STH dispuesto,-a a hacer algo.

willow[1] ['wɪləʊ] *n* sauce.

willpower ['wɪlpaʊər] *n* fuerza de voluntad.

win [wɪn] *n* victoria, triunfo. ▶ *vt-vi* ganar.

wind[1] [wɪnd] *n* **1** viento, aire. **2** gases, flato. ▪ **wind instrument** instrumento de viento; **wind power** energía eólica.

wind[2] [waɪnd] *vt* **1** envolver. **2** arrollar, enrollar. **3** dar cuerda a *(reloj)*. **4** dar vueltas a *(palanca)*. ▶ *vi* serpentear.

to wind up ['waɪnd'ʌp] *vt* dar cuerda a *(reloj)*.

windmill ['wɪndmɪl] *n* molino de viento.

window ['wɪndəʊ] *n* **1** ventana. **2** ventanilla *(de vehículo)*. **3** escaparate *(de tienda)*.

windpipe ['wɪndpaɪp] *n* tráquea.

windscreen ['wɪndskriːn] *n* GB parabrisas.

wind-shield ['wɪndʃiːld] *n* US parabrisas.

wine [waɪn] *n* vino.

wing [wɪŋ] *n* **1** ala. **2** aleta *(de coche)*. **3** banda *(fútbol)*. ▶ *npl* **wings** bastidores.

wink [wɪŋk] *n* guiño.

winner ['wɪnər] *n* ganador,-ra.

winning ['wɪnɪŋ] *adj* ganador, -ra. ▶ *npl* **winnings** ganancias.

winter ['wɪntər] *n* invierno.

wipe [waɪp] *vt* **1** limpiar, pasar un trapo a. **2** secar.

to wipe out *vt* borrar.

wiper ['waɪpər] *n* limpiaparabrisas.

wire ['waɪər] *n* **1** alambre. **2** cable. **3** US telegrama.

wisdom ['wɪzdəm] *n* **1** sabiduría. **2** prudencia, juicio. ▪ **wisdom tooth** muela del juicio.

wise [waɪz] *adj* **1** sabio,-a. **2** prudente.

wish [wɪʃ] *n* deseo. ▶ *vt-vi* desear. • **I wish to…** quisiera…; **(with) best wishes** muchos recuerdos.

wit [wɪt] *n* agudeza, ingenio.

witch [wɪtʃ] *n* bruja. ▪ **witch doctor** hechicero.

with [wɪð] *prep* con.

withdraw [wɪðˈdrɔː] *vt-vi* retirar(se).

withdrawal [wɪðˈdrɔːəl] *n* **1** retirada. **2** reintegro.

withdrawn [wɪðˈdrɔːn] *pp* → withdraw.

withdrew [wɪðˈdruː] *pt* → withdraw.

wither [ˈwɪðəʳ] *vt-vi* marchitar(se).

within [wɪˈðɪn] *prep* **1** dentro de. **2** al alcance de. **3** a menos de. **4** antes de. ► *adv* dentro.

without [wɪˈðaut] *prep* sin.

withstand [wɪðˈstænd] *vt* resistir, aguantar.

witness [ˈwɪtnəs] *n* testigo. ► *vt* presenciar.

witty [ˈwɪtɪ] *adj* ingenioso,-a.

wizard [ˈwɪzəd] *n* brujo.

woke [wəuk] *pt* → wake.

woken [ˈwəukən] *pp* → wake.

wolf [wulf] *n* lobo.

woman [ˈwumən] *n* mujer.

womb [wuːm] *n* útero.

won [wʌn] *pt-pp* → win.

wonder [ˈwʌndəʳ] *n* **1** maravilla. **2** admiración, asombro. ► *vi* preguntarse.

wonderful [ˈwʌndəful] *adj* maravilloso,-a.

wood [wud] *n* **1** madera. **2** bosque.

wooden [ˈwudən] *adj* de madera.

woodpecker [ˈwudpekəʳ] *n* pájaro carpintero.

woodwork [ˈwudwɜːk] *n* carpintería.

wool [wul] *n* lana.

woollen [ˈwulən] *adj* de lana.

word [wɜːd] *n* palabra. • **in a word** en pocas palabras; **in other words** en otras palabras, o sea; **to have words with SB** discutir con ALGN. ■ **word processor** procesador de textos.

wore [wɔːʳ] *pt* → wear.

work [wɜːk] *vt-vi* trabajar. ► *vi* **1** funcionar *(máquina, plan)*. **2** surtir efecto *(medicamento)*. ► *n* **1** trabajo. **2** obra. • **out of work** parado,-a. ■ **work of art** obra de arte.

to work out *vt* **1** calcular. **2** planear *(plan)*. **3** solucionar *(problema)*. ► *vi* salir bien.

worker [ˈwɜːkəʳ] *n* trabajador,-ra.

workforce [ˈwɜːkfɔːs] *n* mano de obra.

working [ˈwɜːkɪŋ] *adj* de trabajo, laboral.

workout [ˈwɜːkaut] *n* entrenamiento.

works [wɜːks] *n* fábrica.

workshop [ˈwɜːkʃɒp] *n* taller.

worktop [ˈwɜːktɒp] *n* encimera.

world [wɜːld] *n* mundo.

worldwide [ˈwɜːldwaɪd] *adj* mundial, universal.

worm [wɜːm] *n* gusano, lombriz.

worn [wɔːn] pp → wear.
worn-out [wɔːn'aʊt] adj **1** gastado,-a (ropa, neumático). **2** rendido,-a (persona).
worried ['wʌrɪd] adj preocupado,-a.
worry ['wʌrɪ] n preocupación. ► vt-vi preocupar(se).
worse [wɜːs] adj-adv peor. ► n lo peor. • **to get worse** empeorar.
worst [wɜːst] adj-adv peor. ► n lo peor.
worth [wɜːθ] n valor. ► adj que vale. • **to be worth** valer.
worthless ['wɜːθləs] adj **1** sin valor (objeto). **2** despreciable (persona).
worthwhile [wɜːθ'waɪl] adj que vale la pena.
worthy ['wɜːðɪ] adj digno,-a.
would [wʊd] aux **1** (condicional): **she would tell you if she knew**, te lo diría si lo supiese. **2** (disponibilidad): **he wouldn't help me**, se negó a ayudarme. **3** (suposición): **that would have been Jim**, ese debió de ser Jim. **4** soler: **we would often go out together**, solíamos salir juntos. • **would like** querer.
wound[1] [wuːnd] n herida. ► vt herir.
wound[2] [waʊnd] pt-pp → wind.
wounded ['wuːndɪd] adj herido,-a.

wove [wəʊv] pt → weave.
woven ['wəʊvən] pp → weave.
wrap [ræp] vt envolver.
wrapping ['ræpɪŋ] n envoltorio. ▪ **wrapping paper** papel de envolver.
wreath [riːθ] n corona.
wreck [rek] n **1** naufragio. **2** barco naufragado. **3** restos (de coche).
wrench [rentʃ] n llave inglesa.
wrestle ['resəl] vi luchar.
wrestler ['reslə'] n luchador,-ra.
wrestling ['reslɪŋ] n lucha.
wretched ['retʃɪd] adj **1** desgraciado,-a. **2** fam horrible.
wrinkle ['rɪŋkəl] n arruga. ► vt-vi arrugar(se).
wrist [rɪst] n muñeca.
wristwatch ['rɪstwɒtʃ] n reloj de pulsera.
write [raɪt] vt-vi escribir. ► vt extender (cheque).
to write back vi contestar.
to write down vt anotar.
writer ['raɪtə'] n escritor,-ra.
writing ['raɪtɪŋ] n **1** escritura. **2** letra. ► npl **writings** obras. ▪ **writing desk** escritorio; **writing paper** papel de cartas.
written ['rɪtən] pp → write. ► adj escrito,-a.
wrong [rɒŋ] adj **1** equivocado,-a. **2** malo,-a. ► adv mal. • **to be in the wrong** no tener razón, tener la culpa; **to be wrong** estar equivocado,-a,

yours

equivocarse; **to go wrong 1** equivocarse *(persona)*. **2** estropearse *(máquina)*.
wrote [rəʊt] *pt* → write.
wrought [rɔːt] *adj* forjado,-a.

X

xenophobia [zenə'fəʊbɪə] *n* xenofobia.
X-ray ['eksreɪ] *n* **1** rayo X. **2** radiografía. ► *vt* radiografiar.
xylophone ['zaɪləfəʊn] *n* xilófono.

Y

yacht [jɒt] *n* yate.
yard [jɑːd] *n* **1** patio. **2** US jardín. **3** yarda.
yarn [jɑːn] *n* hilo.
yawn [jɔːn] *n* bostezo. ► *vi* bostezar.
yeah [jeə] *adv fam* sí.
year [jɪəʳ] *n* **1** año. **2** curso.
yeast [jiːst] *n* levadura.
yell [jel] *n* grito, alarido. ► *vi* gritar, dar alaridos.
yellow ['jeləʊ] *adj* amarillo,-a. ► *n* amarillo. ■ **yellow press** prensa amarilla.

yes [jes] *adv* sí. ► *n* sí.
yesterday ['jestədɪ] *adv* ayer.
yet [jet] *adv* **1** todavía, aún: *the taxi hasn't arrived yet*, aún no ha llegado el taxi. **2** ya: *has the taxi arrived yet?*, ¿ya ha llegado el taxi? ► *conj* no obstante, sin embargo.
yew [juː] *n* tejo.
yield [jiːld] *n* **1** rendimiento. **2** cosecha. ► *vt* **1** producir, dar. **2** rendir. ► *vi* rendirse, ceder.
yoga ['jəʊgə] *n* yoga.
yoghurt ['jɒgət] *n* yogur.
yoke [jəʊk] *n* yugo. ► *vt* uncir.
yolk [jəʊk] *n* yema.
you [juː] *pron* **1** tú, vosotros, -as. **2** usted, ustedes. **3** se *(sujeto - impersonal)*. **4** ti *(complemento)*. **5** te *(antes del verbo)*. **6** vosotros,-as *(plural)*. **7** os *(antes del verbo)*. **8** usted *(complemento)*. **9** le *(antes del verbo)*. **10** ustedes *(plural)*. **11** les *(antes del verbo)*. **12** *(complemento - impersonal)*: *you never know*, nunca se sabe.
young [jʌŋ] *adj* joven.
your [jɔːʳ] *adj* **1** tu, tus, vuestro,-a, vuestros,-as. **2** su, sus.
yours [jɔːz] *pron* **1** (el) tuyo, (la) tuya, (los) tuyos, (las) tuyas, (el) vuestro, (la) vuestra, (los) vuestros, (las) vuestras. **2** (el) suyo, (la) suya, (los) suyos, (las) suyas.

yourself [jɔː'self] *pron* **1** te, tú mismo,-a. **2** se, usted mismo,-a.

yourselves [jɔː'selvz] *pron* **1** os, vosotros,-as mismos,-as. **2** se, ustedes mismos,-as.

youth [juːθ] *n* **1** juventud. **2** joven. ▪ **youth hostel** albergue de juventud.

yo-yo® [ˈjəʊjəʊ] *n* yoyo, yoyó.

Z

zeal [ziːl] *n* celo, entusiasmo.

zealous [ˈzeləs] *adj* celoso,-a, entusiasta.

zebra [ˈziːbrə, ˈzebrə] *n* cebra. ▪ **zebra crossing** paso de peatones, paso de cebra.

zenith [ˈzenɪθ] *n* cenit.

zeppelin [ˈzepəlɪn] *n* zepelín.

zero [ˈzɪərəʊ] *n* cero.

zest [zest] *n* entusiasmo.

zigzag [ˈzɪgzæg] *n* zigzag. ▶ *vt* zigzaguear.

zip [zɪp] *n* cremallera. ▶ *vi* ir como un rayo. ▪ **zip code** US código postal.

to zip up *vt* cerrar con cremallera.

zipper [ˈzɪpr] *n* US cremallera.

zodiac [ˈzəʊdɪæk] *n* zodiaco, zodíaco.

zombie [ˈzɒmbɪ] *n* zombi.

zone [zəʊn] *n* zona.

zoo [zuː] *n* zoo, zoológico.

zoological [zʊəˈlɒdʒɪkəl] *adj* zoológico,-a.

zoology [zʊˈblədʒɪ] *n* zoología.

zoom [zuːm] *n* **1** zumbido. **2** zoom, teleobjetivo. ▶ *vt-vi* pasar zumbando. ▪ **zoom lens** teleobjetivo.

Phrasal verbs

Verbos españoles con preposición

Phrasal verbs

A

to abide by *vt (promise)* cumplir con; *(rules, decision)* acatar.

to account for *vi* explicar.

to add to *vt* aumentar, incrementar: *the rain only added to our problems,* la lluvia no hizo más que agravar nuestros problemas.

to add up 1 *vt - vi* sumar: *it adds up to a total of 2500 euros,* suma un total de 2500 euros. **2** *vi fig* cuadrar: *I don't understand it, it doesn't add up,* no lo entiendo, no cuadra.

to aim at *vt* apuntar a.

to aim to *vt* tener la intención de.

to alight on *vt* posarse en.

to allow for *vt* tener en cuenta.

to amount to *vt* ascender a; *fig* equivaler a.

to answer back *vt - vi* replicar.

to answer for *vt* responder por, responder de.

to approve of *vt* aprobar.

to ask after *vt* preguntar por.

to ask back *vt* invitar a casa.

to ask for *vt* pedir.

to ask out *vt* invitar a salir.

to attend to 1 *vt* ocuparse de. **2** *vt (in shop)* despachar.

B

to back away *vi* retirarse.

to back down *vi* claudicar.

to back out *vi* volverse atrás.

to back up *vt* COMPUT hacer una copia de seguridad de.

to bail out 1 *vt* JUR conseguir la libertad de alguien bajo fianza. **2** *vt fig* sacar de un apuro. **3** *vt* MAR achicar.

to bandy about *vt* difundir.

to bank on *vt* contar con.

to bargain for *vt* contar con.

to bear out *vt* confirmar.

to bear up *vi* mantenerse firme.

to bear with *vt* tener paciencia con.

to beat up *vt* dar una paliza a.

to belt along *vi* ir a todo gas.

to belt up 1 *vi* GB *fam (stop talking)* callarse. **2** *vi* GB *fam (put belt on)* abrocharse el cinturón.

to bend down *vi* agacharse.

to bend over *vi* inclinarse.

to black out *vt* apagar las luces de. **2** *vi (faint)* desmayarse.

to blare out *vi* sonar muy fuerte.

to blot out 1 *vt (hide)* ocultar. **2** *vt (memory)* borrar.

to blow out 1 *vt* apagar. **2** *vi* apagarse.

to blow over 1 *vi (storm)* amainar. **2** *vi (scandal)* olvidarse.

to blow up 1 *vt (explode)* hacer explotar. **2** *vt (inflate)* hinchar. **3** *vt (photograph)* ampliar. **4** *vi (explode)* explotar. **5** *vi (lose one's temper)* salirse de sus casillas.

to boil down to *vt* reducirse a.

to boot out *vt* echar, echar a patadas.

to border on *vt* lindar con; *fig* rayar en.

to boss around *vt* mangonear.

to break down 1 vt derribar. **2** vt (analyse) desglosar. **3** vi (car) averiarse; (driver) tener una avería. **4** vi (appliance) estropearse.

to break in vt domar.

to break into vt (house) entrar por la fuerza en; (safe) forzar.

to break out 1 vi (prisoners) escaparse. **2** vi (war, etc.) estallar.

to break up 1 vt (crowd) disolver. **2** vi (crowd) disolverse. **3** vi (marriage) fracasar; (couple) separarse. **4** vi (school) empezar las vacaciones.

to brighten up 1 vi (weather) despejarse. **2** vi (person) animarse. **3** vt animar, hacer más alegre.

to bring about vt provocar, causar.

to bring back 1 vt (return) devolver. **2** vt (reintroduce) volver a introducir: **to bring back memories of,** hacer recordar.

to bring down 1 vt (cause to fall) derribar. **2** vt (reduce) hacer bajar.

to bring forward vt adelantar.

to bring in 1 vt (introduce) introducir. **2** vt (yield) producir. **3** vt JUR (verdict) emitir.

to bring off vt conseguir, lograr.

to bring on vt (illness) provocar.

to bring out vt sacar; (book, etc.) publicar.

to bring round 1 vt (persuade) persuadir, convencer. **2** vt (revive) hacer volver en sí.

to bring to vt hacer volver en sí.

to bring up 1 vt (educate) criar, educar. **2** vt (mention) plantear. **3** vt (vomit) devolver.

to bristle with vt fig estar lleno,-a de.

to brush up vt refrescar, repasar.

to buck up 1 vt fam: **buck your ideas up!,** ¡espabílate!. **2** vi animarse.

to bugger about vi vulg hacer el gilipollas.

to bugger off vi vulg largarse.

to bugger up vt vulg joder.

to build up 1 vt acumular. **2** vi acumularse.

to bump into vt encontrar por casualidad, tropezar con.

to bump off vt matar.

to burn down 1 vt incendiar. **2** vi incendiarse.

to burn out 1 vi (fire) extinguirse. **2** vi (person, machine) gastarse.

to bustle about vi ir y venir, no parar.

to butt in vi entrometerse.

to butter up vt fam dar coba a.

C

to call for 1 vt (pick up) pasar a buscar. **2** vt (demand) exigir. **3** vt (need) necesitar: **this calls for a celebration,** esto hay que celebrarlo.

to call off vt (suspend) suspender.

to call on 1 vt (visit) visitar. **2** vt fml (urge) instar: **he called on them to negotiate,** les instó a negociar.

to call out 1 vt (troops) sacar a la calle. **2** vt (doctor) hacer venir. **3** vt (workers) llamar a la huelga. **4** vt – vi gritar.

to call up 1 vt MIL llamar a filas. **2** vt (telephone) llamar.

to calm down vt tranquilizar, calmar.

to care for 1 vt (look after) cuidar. **2** vt (like) gustar, interesar.

to carry forward vt llevar a la columna siguiente, llevar a la página siguiente.

to carry off 1 vt realizar con éxito. **2** vt (prize) llevarse.

to carry on vt seguir, continuar.

to carry on with vt estar liado,-a con.

to carry out vt llevar a cabo, realizar; (order) cumplir.

to cast off 1 vt desechar. **2** vi MAR soltar amarras.

to catch on 1 vi caer en la cuenta. **2** vi (become popular) hacerse popular.

to catch out vt pillar, sorprender.

to catch up 1 vt atrapar, alcanzar. **2** vt (with news) ponerse al día.

to cave in vi hundirse, derrumbarse.

to chalk up vt fam apuntarse.

to chat up vt fam intentar ligar con.

to check in 1 vi (at airport) facturar. **2** vi (at hotel) registrarse.

to cheer up 1 vt animar, alegrar. **2** vi animarse, alegrarse.

to chicken out vi fam rajarse.

to choke back vt contener.

to chop down vt talar.

to chop up 1 vt cortar en trozos. **2** vt CULIN picar.

to chuck out 1 vt (person) echar. **2** vt (thing) tirar.

to churn out vt producir en serie.

to clam up vi fam cerrar el pico.

to clamp down on vt poner freno a.

to clean out 1 vt limpiar a fondo. **2** vt fam dejar sin blanca a.

to clean up vt limpiar.

to clear away vt quitar.

to clear off vi fam largarse.

to clear out 1 vi largarse. **2** vt (room, etc.) vaciar. **3** vt (old things) tirar.

to clear up 1 vt (solve) aclarar. **2** vt (tidy) ordenar. **3** vt (weather) mejorar.

to climb down 1 vi bajarse. **2** vi fig ceder.

to clock on vi fichar a la entrada.

to clock off vi fichar a la salida.

to clock up vt (miles) recorrer.

to close down vt - vi cerrar definitivamente.

to close in 1 vi (days) acortarse. **2** vi (night) caer. **3** vi (get nearer) acercarse.

to cloud over vi nublarse.

to clown about/around vi hacer el payaso.

to club together vi hacer una recolecta.

to clutch at vt intentar agarrar.

to cobble together vt amañar, apañar.

to cock up vt GB fam fastidiar.

to come about vi ocurrir, suceder.

to come across 1 vt encontrar por casualidad. **2** vi causar una impresión: *to come across badly,* causar mala impresión; *to come across well,* causar buena impresión.

to come along 1 vi progresar, avanzar. **2** vi (arrive) presentarse.

to come apart vi romperse, partirse.

to come at vt atacar.

to come back vi volver, regresar.

to come before 1 vt (in time) preceder. **2** vt fig ser más importante que.

to come by vt conseguir.

to come down 1 vi (plane) caer. **2** vi (prices) bajar.

to come down with vt fam (illness) coger (una enfermedad).

to come forward 1 vi avanzar. **2** vi (volunteer) ofrecerse, presentarse.

to come from vt ser de.

to come in 1 vi entrar: *come in!,* ¡adelante!. **2** vi (train) llegar.

to come in for vt ser objeto de.

to come into vt (inherit) heredar.

to come off 1 vi (happen) tener lugar. **2** vi (be successful) tener éxito. **3** vi (break off) desprenderse.

to come on 1 vi progresar, avanzar. **2** vi fam (start) empezar.

to come out 1 vi salir: *when the sun comes out,* cuando salga el sol. **2** vi (stain) quitarse. **3** vi GB (on strike) declararse en huelga. **4** vi (photograph) salir.

to come out with vt soltar.

to come round 1 vi (regain consciousness) volver en sí. **2** vi (be persuaded) dejarse convencer, ceder. **3** vi (visit) visitar.

to come through 1 vi (arrive) llegar. **2** vt (survive) sobrevivir.

to come to 1 vi (regain consciousness) volver en sí. **2** vt (total) subir a, ascender a.

to come up 1 vi (arise) surgir. **2** vi (approach) acercarse. **3** vi (sun) salir.

to come up against vt topar con.

to come up to vt llegar a: *the water came up to my waist,* el agua me llegaba a la cintura.

to come up with vt (idea) tener; (solution) encontrar.

to come upon vt encontrar.

to conjure up vt (memories) evocar.

to cook up 1 vt (plan) tramar. **2** vt (excuse) inventar.

to cool down 1 vt (food) enfriar; (person) calmar. **2** vi (food) enfriarse; (person) calmarse.

to coop up vt encerrar.

to cop out vi fam rajarse.

to cope with vt (work) poder con; (problem) hacer frente a.

to cotton on vi caer en la cuenta.

to cough up 1 vt (bring up) soltar. 2 vt fam (pay) desembolsar, aflojar la pasta.

to count in vt fam incluir, contar con.

to count on vt contar con.

to count out 1 vt ir contando. 2 vt fam no contar con.

to cover up 1 vt (put STH over) cubrir. 2 vt (hide) encubrir. 3 vi cubrirse, taparse.

to crop up vi fam surgir.

to cross off vt borrar, tachar.

to cross out vt borrar, tachar.

to cross over vt pasar, atravesar.

to cry out vi gritar: *to cry out for STH*, pedir algo a gritos.

to cut down 1 vt talar, cortar. 2 vt fig *to cut down on*, reducir.

to cut in vi interrumpir.

to cut off vt cortar; (isolate) aislar: *after the storm, the town was cut off*, tras la tormenta, la ciudad quedó incomunicada.

to cut out 1 vt recortar; (dress) cortar. 2 vt (exclude) eliminar, suprimir.

D

to dash off 1 vt escribir deprisa y corriendo. 2 vi salir corriendo.

to deal with 1 vt COMM tratar con. 2 vt (manage) abordar, ocuparse de. 3 vt (treat) tratar de.

to depend on 1 vt (trust) confiar en, fiarse de. 2 vt (vary, be supported by) depender de.

to descend on/upon 1 vt atacar. 2 vt fig visitar: *they descended on us at supper time*, se dejaron caer por casa a la hora de cenar.

to descend to vt rebajarse a.

to die away vi desvanecerse.

to die down 1 vi extinguirse. 2 vi fig disminuir.

to die off vi morir uno por uno.

to die out vi perderse, desaparecer.

to dig out/up vt desenterrar.

to dip into 1 vt (glance through) hojear. 2 vt (savings, etc.) echar mano de.

to dish out vt fam repartir.

to dish up vt servir.

to dispense with vt prescindir de, pasar sin.

to dispose of vt (rubbish) tirar; (object) deshacerse de.

to do away with 1 vt abolir. 2 vt fam acabar con, eliminar.

to do in 1 vt fam (kill) matar, cargarse. 2 vt (tire) agotar: *I'm done in*, estoy hecho,-a polvo.

to do up 1 vt fam (fasten, belt) abrocharse; (laces) atar. 2 vt (wrap) envolver. 3 vt (dress up) arreglar; (decorate) renovar.

to do with vt (need): *I could do with a rest*, un descanso me vendría muy bien.

to do without vt pasar sin.

to dole out vt repartir.

to double up 1 vt retorcer. 2 vi doblarse. 3 vt (share) compartir.

to doze off vi quedarse dormido,-a.

to drag on vi prolongarse.

to drag out vt alargar, prolongar.

to drag up vt fam (revive) sacar a relucir.

to draw back 1 vi retroceder. 2 vi (pull out) echarse para atrás.

to draw in vi apartarse, echarse a un lado.

to draw on vt recurrir a.

to draw out vt (lengthen) alargar.

to draw up 1 vt (contract) preparar; (plan) esbozar. 2 vi (arrive) llegar.

to dream up vt fam pej inventarse.

to dress down vt (scold) regañar.

to dress up 1 vi (child) disfrazarse (as, de); (formal) ponerse de tiros largos. 2 vt fig disfrazar.

to drink in vt (scene, etc.) apreciar.

to drive at vt fam insinuar.

to drop away vi disminuir.

to drop by/in/round vi dejarse caer, pasar.

to drop off 1 vt fam quedarse dormido, -a. 2 vi (lessen) disminuir.

to drop out vi (of school) dejar los estudios; (match) retirarse.

to dwell on/upon *vt* insistir en.

E

to ease off *vi* disminuir.
to eat away *vt* desgastar; *(metal)* corroer.
to eat into *vt fig* consumir.
to eat out *vi* comer fuera.
to eat up *vt* comerse (todo).
to edge forward *vi* avanzar lentamente.
to egg on *vt* animar.
to end up *vi* acabar, terminar.
to enlarge upon *vt* extenderse sobre.
to enter into 1 *vt (negotiations)* iniciar. **2** *vt (contract)* firmar. **3** *vt (conversation)* entablar.
to even out *vt - vi* igualar.
to expand on *vt* ampliar.

F

to face up to *vt* hacer cara a, afrontar.
to fade away *vi* desvanecerse.
to fall back *vi* retroceder.
to fall back on *vt* recurrir a, echar mano de.
to fall behind *vi* retrasarse.
to fall for 1 *vt (be tricked)* dejarse engañar por. **2** *vt fam (in love)* enamorarse de.
to fall off *vi* caer, caerse.
to fall out *vi* reñir *(with,* con).
to fall through *vi* fracasar.
to fan out *vi* abrirse en abanico.
to fawn on *vt* adular, lisonjear.
to feel for *vt (have sympathy for)* compadecer a, compadecerse de.
to fence off *vt* separar mediante cercas.
to fend off *vt* parar, desviar; *fig* esquivar.
to ferret out *vt* descubrir.
to fiddle about/around *vi fam* perder el tiempo.
to fight back *vi* resistir, defenderse.

to fight off 1 *vt* rechazar. **2** *vt fig (illness)* librarse de, cortar.
to figure out *vt fam* comprender, explicarse.
to fill in 1 *vt (space, form)* rellenar. **2** *vt (inform)* poner al corriente *(on,* de).
to fill in for *vt* sustituir a.
to fill out 1 *vi* llenarse *(with,* de). **2** *vi* engordar.
to fill up *vt - vi* llenar(se).
to find out 1 *vt - vi* averiguar. **2** *vi (discover)* enterarse *(about,* de).
to finish with 1 *vt* acabar con. **2** *vt (person)* romper con.
to fit in 1 *vi (adapt)* encajar. **2** *vi (match)* cuadrar. **3** *vt* encontrar un hueco para.
to fit out *vt* equipar.
to fix on *vt* decidir, optar por.
to fix up *vt* proveer *(with,* de).
to fizzle out *vi* ir perdiendo fuerza hasta quedarse en nada.
to flare up *vi* estallar.
to flounce in *vi* entrar airadamente.
to fluff out/up 1 *vt (hair, etc.)* encrespar, erizar. **2** *vi* encresparse, erizarse.
to follow out *vt* ejecutar.
to follow through *vt* llevar a cabo.
to follow up *vt* seguir de cerca, profundizar en.
to fool about/around *vi* hacer el tonto.
to fork out *vt fam (money)* soltar, aflojar.
to foul up *vt fam* estropear.
to freak out *vt - vi sl* flipar, alucinar.
to freshen up 1 *vt* asear. **2** *vi* asearse.
to fret for *vt* añorar.
to frighten away/off *vt* ahuyentar.
to fritter away *vi pej* malgastar.
to frown upon *vt fig* desaprobar, censurar.

G

to gang up on *vt* unirse contra.
to get about *vi (move about)* moverse; *(travel)* viajar.

to get across 1 *vt (cross)* cruzar. **2** *vt (communicate)* comunicar.

to get ahead *vi* adelantar, progresar.

to get along 1 *vi (manage)* arreglárselas. **2** *vi (leave)* marcharse.

to get along with *vt* llevarse (bien) con.

to get around *vi (move about)* moverse; *(travel)* viajar.

to get around to *vt* encontrar el tiempo para.

to get at 1 *vt (reach)* alcanzar, llegar a. **2** *vt (insinuate)* insinuar: *what are you getting at?*, ¿qué insinúas? **3** *vt (criticize)* meterse con.

to get away *vi* escaparse.

to get away with *vt* salir impune de.

to get back 1 *vt (return)* volver, regresar. **2** *vt (recover)* recuperar.

to get behind *vi* atrasarse.

to get by 1 *vi (manage)* arreglárselas. **2** *vi (pass)* pasar.

to get down 1 *vt (depress)* deprimir. **2** *vi (descend)* bajarse.

to get down to *vt* ponerse a.

to get in 1 *vt (arrive)* llegar. **2** *vt (enter)* entrar; *(car)* subir.

to get into 1 *vt (arrive)* llegar a. **2** *vt (enter)* entrar en; *(car)* subir a.

to get off 1 *vt (remove)* quitar. **2** *vt (vehicle, horse, etc.)* bajar de. **3** *vi (from vehicle, horse, etc.)* bajarse. **4** *vi (start journey)* salir. **5** *vi (begin)* comenzar. **6** *vi (escape)* escaparse, librarse.

to get off with *vt (partner)* ligar.

to get on 1 *vt (vehicle)* subir a, subirse a; *(bicycle, horse, etc.)* montar. **2** *vi (make progress)* progresar, avanzar; *(succeed)* tener éxito. **3** *vi (be friendly)* llevarse bien, avenirse. **4** *vi (continue)* seguir: *get on with your work!*, ¡seguid con vuestro trabajo! **5** *vi (grow old)* envejecerse; *(grow late)* hacerse tarde.

to get on for *vt* ser casi: *it's getting on for 5 o'clock*, son casi las cinco.

to get onto 1 *vt (person)* ponerse en contacto con. **2** *vt (subject)* empezar a hablar de. **3** *vt (vehicle, horse)* subirse a.

to get out 1 *vt (thing)* sacar; *(stain)* quitar. **2** *vi (leave)* salir. **3** *vi (escape)* escapar.

to get out of *vt (avoid)* librarse de.

to get over 1 *vt (illness)* recuperarse de. **2** *vt (loss)* sobreponerse a. **3** *vt (obstacle)* salvar; *(difficulty)* vencer. **4** *vt (idea)* comunicar.

to get over with *vt* acabar con.

to get round 1 *vt (obstacle)* salvar; *(law)* soslayar. **2** *vt (person)* convencer.

to get round to *vt* encontrar el tiempo para.

to get through 1 *vi (on telephone)* conseguir hablar *(to,* con). **2** *vi (arrive)* llegar. **3** *vt (finish)* acabar; *(consume)* consumir; *(money)* gastar; *(drink)* beber. **4** *vt (exam)* aprobar. **5** *vt (make understand)* hacer entender.

to get together *vi* reunirse, juntarse.

to get up 1 *vi* levantarse. **2** *vt* levantar.

to get up to *vt* hacer.

to give away 1 *vt (as a gift)* regalar. **2** *vt (betray)* delatar, traicionar.

to give back *vt* devolver.

to give in 1 *vi (yield)* ceder, rendirse. **2** *vt (hand in)* entregar.

to give off *vt (send out)* desprender.

to give out 1 *vt (distribute)* repartir. **2** *vt (announce)* anunciar. **3** *vi (run out)* acabarse, agotarse.

to give over 1 *vi (stop)* parar. **2** *vt (hand over)* entregar.

to give up 1 *vt* dejar: *to give up smoking*, dejar de fumar. **2** *vi (surrender)* rendirse; *(to police, etc.)* entregarse.

to gloss over *vt* omitir, pasar por alto.

to go after *vt (chase)* perseguir.

to go along with 1 *vt (agree)* estar de acuerdo con. **2** *vt (accompany)* acompañar.

to go around *vi* ➤ go round.

to go away *vi* marcharse.

to go back *vi* volver.

to go back on *vt* romper.

to go by *vi* pasar.

to go down 1 *vi (prices, etc.)* bajar; *(tyre)* deshincharse. **2** *vi (be received)* ser acogido,-a.

to go down with *vt (illness)* coger, pillar.

to go for 1 *vt (attack)* atacar. **2** *vt (fetch)* ir a buscar. **3** *vt fam (like)* gustar: **I don't go for flamenco much,** el flamenco no me gusta mucho. **4** *vt fam (be valid)* valer para: **that goes for me too!,** ¡eso vale para mí también!.

to go in for *vt* dedicarse a: **I don't go in for that sort of thing,** eso tipo de cosas no me va.

to go into 1 *vt (investigate)* investigar. **2** *vt (crash)* chocar contra.

to go off 1 *vi (bomb)* estallar; *(alarm)* sonar; *(gun)* dispararse. **2** *vi (food)* estropearse. **3** *vt* perder el gusto por, perder el interés por.

to go on 1 *vi (continue)* seguir. **2** *vi (happen)* pasar. **3** *vi (complain)* quejarse *(about, de)*.

to go out 1 *vi (gen)* salir. **2** *vi (fire, light)* apagarse.

to go over *vt (check, revise)* revisar.

to go over to *vt* pasarse a.

to go round 1 *vi* dar vueltas, girar. **2** *vi (be enough)* haber bastante: **I don't think the beer will go round,** no creo que haya bastante cerveza para todos. **3** *vi (spend time)* salir, estar: **he goes round with a funny crowd,** se le ve con gente extraña. **4** *vi (rumour)* circular, correr.

to go through 1 *vt (undergo)* sufrir, padecer. **2** *vt (examine)* examinar; *(search)* registrar. **3** *vi* ser aprobado,-a.

to go through with *vt* llevar a cabo.

to go under *vi* hundirse; *fig* fracasar.

to go up 1 *vi (rise, increase)* subir. **2** *vi (explode)* estallar.

to go without *vt* pasar sin, prescindir de.

to gravitate towards *vt* sentirse atraído,-a por.

to grow into *vt* convertirse en.

to grow on *vt* llegar a gustar.

to grow up *vi* hacerse mayor.

to gun down *vt* matar a tiros.

H

to hand back *vt* devolver.

to hand in *vt* entregar, presentar.

to hand out *vt* repartir.

to hand over *vt* entregar.

to hand round *vt* ofrecer.

to hang about, hang around 1 *vi (wait)* esperar. **2** *vi (waste time)* perder el tiempo.

to hang back *vi* quedarse atrás.

to hang out 1 *vt* tender. **2** *vi fam* frecuentar: **he hangs out in sleazy bars,** frecuenta baretos sórdidos.

to hang up *vt - vi* colgar.

to harp on about *vt* insistir en.

to have on 1 *vt (wear)* llevar puesto,-a. **2** *vt (tease)* tomar el pelo.

to have out *vt (tooth)* sacarse; *(appendix)* operarse de.

to head for *vt* dirigirse hacia.

to hem in *vt* cercar, rodear.

to hold back 1 *vt* retener. **2** *vt (information)* ocultar.

to hold forth *vi* hablar largo y tendido.

to hold on 1 *vi* agarrar fuerte. **2** *vi (wait)* esperar; *(on telephone)* no colgar.

to hold out 1 *vt (hand)* tender. **2** *vi* durar; *(person)* resistir.

to hold over *vt* aplazar.

to hold up 1 *vt (rob)* atracar, asaltar. **2** *vt (delay)* retrasar. **3** *vt (raise)* levantar. **4** *vt (support)* aguantar, sostener.

to hold with *vt* estar de acuerdo con.

to hook up *vt* conectar.

I

to ice over/up *vi* helarse.

to idle away *vt* desperdiciar.

to improve on *vt* mejorar respecto a.

J

to jazz up vt animar, alegrar.
to jerk off vi vulg hacerse una paja.
to join in vi participar.
to jump at vt aceptar sin pensarlo.

K

to keel over vi (ship) zozobrar; (person) desplomarse.
to keep away vt mantener a distancia.
to keep back 1 vt (money) reservar, guardar; (information) ocultar. 2 vt (enemy) tener a raya.
keep back from vi mantenerse lejos de.
to keep down vt (oppress) oprimir.
to keep in vt no dejar salir.
to keep on 1 vi (go on) seguir, continuar. 2 vt (clothes) no quitarse.
to keep out 1 vt no dejar entrar. 2 vi no entrar.
to keep up 1 vt mantener. 2 vt (from sleeping) mantener despierto,-a, tener en vela.
to key in vt COMPUT introducir, entrar.
to kick out vt echar.
to kill off vt exterminar.
to knock back vt beber de un trago.
to knock down 1 vt (building) derribar. 2 vt (with a car) atropellar.
to knock off 1 vt tirar. 2 vt fam (steal) birlar, mangar. 3 vt fam (kill) liquidar a. 4 vt (price) rebajar. 5 vi (stop work) acabar, salir del trabajo.
to knock out vt dejar sin conocimiento; (boxing) dejar fuera de combate.
to knock over vt (object) volcar; (with a car) atropellar.
to knock up 1 vt GB fam despertar. 2 vt US fam dejar preñada. 3 vi (tennis, etc.) pelotear.
to knuckle down vi fam ponerse a trabajar en serio.
to knuckle under vi pasar por el aro.

L

to lark about/around vi hacer tonterías, hacer el indio.
to lash out 1 vi repartir golpes a diestro y siniestro. 2 vi (spend) despilfarrar.
to lash out at vt criticar.
to lash out on vt gastar mucho dinero en.
to lay down 1 vt (tools) dejar; (arms) deponer. 2 vt (wine) guardar (en bodega).
to lay in vt proveerse de.
to lay into vt atacar.
to lay off 1 vt (worker) despedir. 2 vt fam dejar en paz.
to lay on vt proveer.
to lay out 1 vt tender, extender. 2 vt (town, etc.) hacer el trazado de; (garden) diseñar. 3 vt fam (knock down) dejar fuera de combate.
to lay up vt almacenar.
to leave out vt (omit) omitir.
to let down 1 vt (deflate) deshinchar. 2 vt (lengthen) alargar. 3 vt (disappoint) defraudar.
to let in vt dejar entrar, dejar pasar.
to let off 1 vt (bomb) hacer explotar; (firework) hacer estallar. 2 vt (forgive) perdonar.
to let on vi fam descubrir el pastel: you won't let on, will you?, no dirás nada, ¿verdad?
to let out 1 vt dejar salir; (release) soltar. 2 vt (rent) alquilar. 3 vt (utter) soltar.
to let through vt dejar pasar.
to let up vi cesar.
to lie back vi recostarse.
to lie down vi acostarse, tumbarse.
to line up 1 vt poner en fila. 2 vt fam preparar, organizar. 3 vi (get in line) ponerse en fila.
to live down vt lograr que se olvide.
to log in/log on vi COMPUT entrar (en sistema).
to log off/log out vi COMPUT salir (del sistema).
to look after 1 vt (deal with) ocuparse de. 2 vt (take care of) cuidar.
to look ahead vi mirar al futuro.

to look at vt mirar.
to look down on vt despreciar.
to look for vt buscar.
to look forward to vt esperar (con ansia).
to look into vt investigar.
to look like vt parecer.
to look on 1 vt considerar. 2 vi mirar.
to look onto vt dar a.
to look out vi vigilar, ir con cuidado.
to look round 1 vt volver la cabeza. 2 vi (in shop) mirar. 3 vt (town) visitar.
to look through vt examinar, revisar; (book, quickly) hojear.
to look up 1 vi mejorar. 2 vt buscar. 3 vt (visit) ir a visitar.
to lump together vt juntar.
to lust after vt codiciar.

M

to make for 1 vt (move towards) dirigirse hacia. 2 vt (result in) contribuir a.
to make out 1 vt (write - list, receipt) hacer; (- cheque) extender. 2 vt (see) distinguir; (writing) descifrar. 3 vt (understand) entender. 4 vt (pretend) pretender. 5 vi (manage) arreglárselas.
to make up 1 vt (invent) inventar. 2 vt (put together) hacer; (package) empaquetar. 3 vt (complete) completar. 4 vt (constitute) componer, formar. 5 vt (cosmetics) maquillar. 6 vi (cosmetics) maquillarse.
to make up for vt compensar.
to map out vt (plan) proyectar, planear.
to march past vi desfilar.
to mark down 1 vt (lower prices) rebajar. 2 vt (lower marks) bajar la nota. 3 vt (write) anotar, apuntar.
to mark out 1 vt (area) delimitar. 2 vt (person) destinar (for, a).
to measure up vi estar a la altura (to, de).
to meet up vi fam (by arrangement) quedar.
to meet with 1 vt (difficulty) tropezar con; (success) tener. 2 vt (person) reunirse con, encontrarse con.

to melt away 1 vi (ice, snow) derretirse. 2 vi (money, people) desaparecer. 3 vi (feeling) desvanecerse.
to mess about/around 1 vi (idle) gandulear. 2 vi (act the fool) hacer el tonto. 3 vt fastidiar.
to mess up 1 vt fam (make untidy) desordenar. 2 vt (spoil) estropear. 3 vt (dirty) ensuciar.
to mill about/around vi arremolinarse.
to miss out vt (omit) saltarse.
to miss out on vi dejar pasar, perderse.
to mist over/up 1 vi (window) empañarse. 2 vi (countryside) cubrirse de neblina.
to mix up 1 vt mezclar. 2 vt (confuse) confundir. 3 vt (mess up) revolver.
to mop up 1 vt (clean) enjuagar, limpiar. 2 vt (beat) acabar con.
to mount up vi subir, aumentar.
to move along vi avanzar.
to move away 1 vi apartarse. 2 vi (change house) mudarse de casa, trasladarse.
to move forward 1 vt - vi avanzar. 2 vt (clock) adelantar.
to move in 1 vi (into new home) instalarse. 2 vi (go into action) intervenir.
to move on 1 vi (continue a journey) circular, seguir. 2 vi (change to) pasar a.
to move over vt - vi correr.
to muck about/around vi perder el tiempo.
to muck in vi fam echar una mano.
to muck up 1 vt (dirty) ensuciar. 2 vt (spoil, ruin) echar a perder.
to muddle through vi ingeniárselas.

N

to narrow down vt reducir.
to nod off vi dormirse.

O

to own up vi confesar.

P

to pack up 1 *vi (finish work)* terminar de trabajar. **2** *vi (machine)* estropearse.

to pair off *vi* formar pareja *(with,* con).

to pair up 1 *vt* emparejar. **2** *vi* emparejarse.

to parcel out *vt* repartir.

to parcel up *vt* empaquetar.

to part with *vt* separarse de.

to pass away *vi* pasar a mejor vida.

to pass by *vi* pasar, pasar cerca.

to pass off 1 *vi (happen)* transcurrir. **2** *vi (disappear)* desaparecer. **3** *vt (succeed in presenting)* hacer pasar por.

to pass on 1 *vt* pasar: *he passed on the information to his colleagues,* pasó la información a sus colegas; *I'll pass you on to her secretary,* le paso con su secretaria. **2** *vi (die)* pasar a mejor vida.

to pass out *vi* desmayarse.

to pass over *vt* hacer caso omiso de.

to pass through *vi* estar de paso.

to pass up *vt* dejar pasar.

to pay back *vt* devolver.

to pay in *vt* ingresar.

to pay off 1 *vt (debt)* saldar. **2** *vt (mortgage)* acabar de pagar. **3** *vt (worker)* dar el finiquito a. **4** *vi (be successful)* salir bien.

to perk up *vi* animarse, reanimarse.

to phase in *vt* introducir progresivamente.

to phase out *vt* retirar progresivamente.

to pick off *vt* matar uno a uno.

to pick on *vt* meterse con.

to pick out 1 *vt (choose)* escoger. **2** *vt (see)* distinguir.

to pick up 1 *vt (take)* coger; *(from floor)* recoger. **2** *vt (acquire)* conseguir. **3** *vt (go and get)* ir a buscar. **4** *vt (on radio)* captar. **5** *vt (learn)* aprender. **6** *vt fam (sex partner)* ligarse.

to piece together *vt* reconstruir.

to pile up *vt - vi* amontonarse.

to pin down *vt (identify)* definir, precisar. **2** *vt (prevent from)* inmovilizar.

to pipe down *vi* callarse.

to piss off 1 *vi sl* largarse. **2** *vt sl* cabrear, poner de mala leche.

to pitch into 1 *vt* atacar: *he pitched into his work,* se puso a trabajar.

to play along *vi* seguir la corriente.

to play down *vt* quitar importancia a.

to play on *vt* aprovecharse de.

to play up 1 *vt* causar problemas a. **2** *vi (machine)* no funcionar bien. **3** *vi (child)* dar guerra.

to plug in 1 *vt* enchufar. **2** *vi* enchufarse.

to plump for *vt* optar por.

to point out *vt* señalar.

to polish off 1 *vt (work)* despachar. **2** *vt (food)* zamparse.

to pop in *vi* entrar un momento.

to pop out *vi* salir un momento.

to pop up *vi* aparecer.

to pore over *vt* estudiar detenidamente.

to portion out *vt* repartir.

to potter about/around *vi* entretenerse.

to press ahead/on *vi* seguir adelante.

to press for *vt* exigir, reclamar.

to prey on 1 *vt (to live off)* alimentarse de. **2** *vt (trouble)* atormentar: *fear preyed on his mind,* el miedo hizo presa en él.

to print out *vt* COMPUT imprimir.

to prop up 1 *vt (roof)* apuntalar. **2** *vt (person)* apoyar, sostener.

to provide for 1 *vt (family)* mantener. **2** *vt (future event)* prevenir.

to puff up 1 *vt* hinchar. **2** *vi* hincharse.

to pull apart *vt (machine)* desmontar.

to pull away *vi (vehicle)* alejarse.

to pull down *vt (gen)* bajar; *(building)* derribar.

to pull in 1 *vt (customer)* atraer. **2** *vi (train)* entrar en la estación.

to pull off 1 *vt (achieve)* llevar a cabo. **2** *vt (remove)* quitar, sacar.

to pull out 1 *vt (gen)* sacar; *(tooth)* arrancar. **2** *vi (train)* salir de la estación. **3** *vi (withdraw)* retirarse.

to pull through *vi* reponerse.

to pull together *vi (cooperate)* trabajar como equipo.

to pull up 1 *vt (sock)* subir. **2** *vt (plant)* arrancar. **3** *vi* detenerse.

to push around vt dar órdenes a.

to push off vi fam largarse.

to push on vi seguir, continuar.

to put across vt comunicar.

to put aside 1 vt (money) ahorrar, guardar. **2** vt (work) dejar a un lado.

to put away 1 vt (thing) guardar. **2** vt (person) encerrar.

to put back 1 vt (postpone) aplazar, retrasar. **2** vt (reset) atrasar. **3** vt (replace) devolver a su sitio.

to put down 1 vt (lay down) dejar. **2** vt (rebellion) sofocar. **3** vt (animal) sacrificar. **4** vt (write) apuntar, escribir. **5** vt fam (humble) humillar.

to put down to vt atribuir a.

to put forward 1 vt (plan) proponer. **2** vt (clock) adelantar.

to put in 1 vt (time) dedicar. **2** vt (claim) presentar.

to put in for vt solicitar.

to put off 1 vt (postpone) aplazar. **2** vt (distract) distraer. **3** vt (discourage) desanimar, quitar las ganas a uno.

to put on 1 vt (gen) poner. **2** vt (clothes, glasses, etc.) ponerse. **3** vt (weight, speed) ganar. **4** vt (play, show) montar.

to put out 1 vt (fire, light) apagar. **2** vt (cause trouble to) molestar.

to put over vt comunicar, transmitir.

to put through 1 vt (on phone) conectar (to, con). **2** vt (cause to suffer) someter.

to put to vt proponer.

to put together 1 vt (gather) reunir, juntar. **2** vt (assemble) montar.

to put up 1 vt (raise) levantar. **2** vt (lodge) alojar. **3** vt (tent) armar. **4** vt (building) construir. **5** vt (painting) colgar. **6** vt (prices, taxes) aumentar, subir.

to put up with vt soportar, aguantar.

to puzzle out vt descifrar, resolver.

R

to rally round vi unirse.

to rattle off vt (speaking) decir a toda prisa; (writing) escribir a toda prisa.

to rattle on vi hablar sin parar.

to rattle through vt despachar rápidamente.

to read up on vt investigar, buscar datos sobre.

to reckon on vt contar con.

to reckon with 1 vt tener en cuenta. **2** vt (deal with) vérselas con.

to reflect on vt perjudicar.

to rest with vi corresponder a, depender de.

to result in vt producir, causar.

to ride on vt depender de.

to ride out vt aguantar hasta el final de.

to rig up vt improvisar.

to rip off 1 vi arrancar. **2** vt fam timar.

to roll out vt (pastry) extender.

to roll up 1 vt enrollar. **2** vi enrollarse. **3** vt (into a ball) enroscar. **4** vi (into a ball) enroscarse.

to rope in vt fam enganchar.

to round off vt completar, acabar.

to round up 1 vt (number) redondear. **2** vt (cattle) acorralar. **3** vt (people) reunir.

to rub out vt borrar.

to rule out vt excluir, descartar.

to run after vt perseguir.

to run along vi irse.

to run away vi escaparse.

to run down 1 vt (knock down) atropellar. **2** vt (criticize) criticar. **3** vt (battery) agotar. **4** vi (battery) agotarse. **5** vi (clock) pararse.

to run in 1 vt (car) rodar. **2** vt (criminal) detener.

to run into 1 vt (car) chocar con. **2** vt (meet) tropezar con.

to run off 1 vi (escape) escaparse. **2** vt (print) imprimir.

to run off with vt escaparse con.

to run out vi acabarse: *I've run out of sugar*, se me ha acabado el azúcar.

to run over 1 vt (knock down) atropellar. **2** vi (overflow) rebosar. **3** vi (spill) derramar.

to run through 1 vt ensayar. **2** vt (read) echar un vistazo a.

to run up 1 vt (debts) acumular. **2** vt (flag) izar.

S

to scale down vt reducir.

to scale up vt ampliar.

to scare away/off vt espantar, ahuyentar.

to scoop out vt sacar con pala, sacar con cucharón.

to scrape along vi ir tirando.

to scrape through vt (exam) aprobar por los pelos.

to screw up 1 vt (twist) arrugar; (face) hacer una mueca. **2** vt sl (ruin) jorobar, fastidiar.

to scurry away/off vi escabullirse.

to scuttle away/off vi escabullirse.

to seal off 1 vt (close) cerrar. **2** vt (block) cerrar el acceso a.

to see about vt ocuparse de.

to see off vt despedirse de.

to see out 1 vt (last) durar. **2** vt (go to door with) acompañar hasta la puerta.

to see through vt calar a, verle el plumero a.

to see to vt ocuparse de.

to seek out vt buscar.

to seize up vi agarrotarse.

to sell off 1 vt (cheaply) liquidar. **2** vi venderse.

to sell out 1 vi (be disloyal) claudicar, venderse. **2** vt agotarse: *the tickets are sold out,* las localidades están agotadas.

to sell up vi venderlo todo.

to send away vt despachar.

to send away for vt pedir algo por correo.

to send back 1 vt (goods, etc.) devolver. **2** vt (person) hacer volver.

to send for 1 vt (person) mandar llamar a. **2** vt (thing, by post) pedir por correo.

to send in 1 vt (post) mandar, enviar. **2** vt (visitor) hacer pasar.

to send off 1 vt (post) enviar. **2** vt (football) expulsar.

to send on 1 vt (letter) hacer seguir. **2** vt (luggage) mandar por adelantado.

to set about 1 vt empezar a: *they set about cleaning the house,* se pusieron a limpiar la casa.

to set aside 1 vt (save) guardar, reservar. **2** vt (disregard) dejar de lado.

to set back 1 vt (at a distance) apartar: *the house is set back from the road,* la casa está apartada de la carretera. **2** vt (make late) retrasar. **3** vt fam (cost) costar.

to set down 1 vt (write) poner por escrito. **2** vt GB (leave off) dejar.

to set in 1 vi (bad weather) comenzar; (problems, etc.) surgir.

to set off 1 vi salir, ponerse en camino. **2** vt (bomb) hacer estallar; (alarm) hacer sonar, convocar. **3** vt hacer saltar.

to set out 1 vi partir, salir (for, para). **2** vi (intend) proponerse (to, -), pretender (to, -). **3** vt disponer, exponer.

to set up 1 vt (raise) levantar; (tent, stall) montar. **2** vt (found) crear, montar. **3** vt (arrange) planear, convocar.

to settle down 1 vi (in place) instalarse, afincarse. **2** vi (live a quiet life) sentar la cabeza. **3** vi (adapt) adaptarse.

to settle for vt conformarse con.

to settle in 1 vi (in job) adaptarse; (in home) instalarse.

to settle on vt decidirse por.

to shake off 1 vt (get rid) sacudirse. **2** vt (elude) quitarse de encima.

to shake up 1 vt (liquid) agitar. **2** vt (shock) conmocionar. **3** vt (rearrange) reorganizar.

to shell out vt fam soltar, pagar.

to shoot down vt (aircraft) derribar.

to shoot out vi salir disparado,-a.

to shoot past vi pasar volando.

to shoot up 1 vi (flames) salir; (prices) dispararse; (plant, child) crecer rápidamente. **2** vt sl (heroin, etc.) chutarse.

shore up vt (building) apuntalar.

to shout down vt hacer callar a gritos.

to shove off vi fam largarse.

to show off vi fardar, fanfarronear.

to show up 1 vt (reveal) hacer resaltar, destacar. **2** vt (embarrass) dejar en ridículo. **3** vi fam (arrive) presentarse, aparecer.

to shrink away from vi retroceder, echarse atrás.

to shrug off vt quitar importancia a.

to shut away 1 vt (person) encerrar. **2** vt (papers) guardar bajo llave.

to shut down 1 vt cerrar. **2** vi cerrarse.

to shut off 1 vt (interrupt) cortar, cerrar. **2** vt (isolate) aislar (from, de).

to shut up 1 vt (close) cerrar. **2** vt (quieten) hacer callar. **3** vi fam (stop talking) callar, callarse.

to sign away vt ceder.

to sign in vi firmar el registro.

to sign on/up vt (worker) contratar; (player) fichar.

to single out 1 vt (choose) escoger. **2** vt (distinguish) destacar.

to sink in 1 vi caer en la cuenta de. **2** vi fig causar impresión.

to sit about/around vi fam hacer el vago.

to sit down vi sentarse.

to sit in for vt sustituir a.

to sit on 1 vt (be member of) formar parte de. **2** vt fam (delay) retener, no tramitar.

to sit out/through vt aguantar (hasta el final).

to sit up 1 vi (in bed) incorporarse. **2** vi (stay up late) quedarse levantado,-a.

to size up vt evaluar.

to sleep in vi quedarse en la cama, dormir hasta tarde.

to sleep through vt no oír, no despertarse con.

to slice off/through vt cortar.

to slink away / off vi escabullirse.

to slip away/by vi pasar volando.

to slip into/on vt (clothes) ponerse rápidamente.

to slip off vt (clothes) quitarse.

to slip up vi cometer un desliz, equivocarse.

to slow down vi (gen) ir más despacio; (vehicle) reducir la velocidad.

to smack of vt fig oler a.

to smooth back/down/out vt alisar.

to snap up vt no dejar escapar.

to sneak away/off vi escabullirse.

to sneak in vi entrar a hurtadillas.

to sneak out vi salir a hurtadillas.

to sneak up vt acercarse sigilosamente (on, a).

to snip off vt cortar con tijeras.

to snuff out vt sofocar.

to soak through vi penetrar, calar.

to soak up vt absorber.

to sober up vi pasársele a uno la borrachera.

to sort out 1 vt clasificar, ordenar. **2** vt (solve) arreglar, solucionar.

to spark off vt provocar.

to speak out vi hablar claro.

to speak up vi hablar más fuerte.

to speak (up) for vi salir en defensa de.

to speed past vi pasar volando.

to speed up 1 vt (car) acelerar; (person) apresurar. **2** vi (car) acelerar; (person) apresurarse.

to spill over vt desbordarse.

to spin out vt prolongar.

to spirit away/off vt llevarse como por arte de magia.

to spit out vt escupir.

to splash out vi fam derrochar dinero.

to split up 1 vt partir, dividir. **2** vi dispersarse; (couple) separarse.

to sponge off vt pej vivir a costa de.

to spring up vi aparecer, surgir.

to square up vi fam ajustar las cuentas.

to squeeze in 1 vt meter con dificultad. **2** vi meterse con dificultad.

to squirt out vi salir a chorro.

to stake out vt delimitar.

to stamp out vt fig acabar con.

to stand back vi apartarse, alejarse (from, de).

to stand by 1 vi (remain inactive) quedarse sin hacer nada. **2** vi (be ready) estar preparado,-a. **3** vt (person) respaldar a; (decision, etc.) atenerse a.

to stand for 1 vt (signify) significar. **2** vt (put up with) tolerar. **3** vt (support) defender.

to stand in for vt sustituir a.

to stand out vi destacar.

to stand up 1 *vi* ponerse de pie. **2** *vt fam* dejar plantado,-a.

to stand up for *vt fig* defender.

to start back *vi* emprender la vuelta.

to start off/out 1 *vi (begin)* empezar. **2** *vi (leave)* salir, partir.

to start up *vt - vi (car, etc.)* arrancar.

to stave off 1 *vt (avoid)* evitar. **2** *vt (delay)* aplazar.

to stay in *vi* quedarse en casa, no salir.

to stay on *vi* quedarse.

to stay out *vi* quedarse fuera.

to stay up *vi* no acostarse: *to stay up late*, acostarse tarde.

to steal away *vi* escabullirse.

to steam up *vi* empañarse.

to stem from *vi* derivarse de.

to step aside *vi* apartarse.

to step back 1 *vi (move back)* retroceder, dar un paso atrás. **2** *vi (become detached)* distanciarse.

to step down *vi* renunciar *(from,* a).

to step in *vi* intervenir.

to step out *vi* salir.

to step up *vt fam* aumentar.

to stick around *vi fam* quedarse.

to stick at *vt* seguir con.

to stick by *vt fam (friend)* apoyar; *(promise)* cumplir con.

to stick out 1 *vi (protrude)* sobresalir. **2** *vi fam (be obvious)* saltar a la vista. **3** *vt* sacar.

to stick to 1 *vt (keep to)* atenerse a. **2** *vt (carry out)* cumplir con.

to stick up 1 *vi (project)* salir, sobresalir; *(hair)* estar de punta. **2** *vt (raise)* levantar.

to stick up for *vt fam* defender.

to stir up 1 *vt (cause)* provocar. **2** *vt (water, mud)* remover.

to stock up *vi* abastecerse *(on/with,* de).

to stoke up *vi fig* atiborrarse *(on,* de).

to stoop to *vt fig* rebajarse a.

to stop by *vi fam* pasar *(at,* por).

to stop off *vi* hacer una parada *(at/in,* en).

to stop up *vt* tapar, taponar.

to store up *vt* acumular.

to straighten out 1 *vt* resolver. **2** *vi* resolverse.

to straighten up 1 *vt (tidy)* ordenar. **2** *vt (make straight)* poner derecho,-a. **3** *vi* ponerse derecho,-a.

to stretch out 1 *vt* estirar. **2** *vt (lengthen)* alargar. **3** *vi* estirarse; *(lie down)* tumbarse. **4** *vi (lengthen)* alargarse.

to strike back *vi* devolver el golpe.

to strike down *vt* abatir.

to strike off 1 *vt* tachar. **2** *vt* JUR suspender.

to strike up *vt* entablar.

to string along *vi* seguir la corriente *(with,* a).

to strip down *vt* desmontar.

to strip off *vi* desnudarse.

to sum up *vt* resumir.

to swap round *vt* cambiar de sitio.

to swear by *vt fam* tener entera confianza en.

to sweep aside *vt fig* rechazar.

to switch off *vt (radio, TV, etc.)* apagar; *(current)* cortar.

to switch on *vt (light)* encender; *(radio, TV)* poner.

to switch over *vi* cambiar.

T

to tag on *vt* añadir.

to take after *vt* parecerse a.

to take away 1 *vt (carry away)* llevarse. **2** *vt (remove)* quitar. **3** *vt* MATH restar.

to take back 1 *vt (return)* devolver. **2** *vt (one's word)* retractarse: *he took back what he said,* se retractó de lo dicho.

to take down 1 *vt (remove)* desmontar. **2** *vt (coat, etc.)* descolgar. **3** *vt (write)* apuntar.

to take in 1 *vt (shelter)* dar cobijo a. **2** *vt (deceive)* engañar. **3** *vt (grasp)* asimilar. **4** *vt (include)* incluir. **5** *vt (clothes)* meter.

to take off 1 *vt (clothes)* quitarse. **2** *vt (imitate)* imitar. **3** *vi (plane)* despegar.

to take on 1 *vt (job)* hacerse cargo de, aceptar. **2** *vt (worker)* contratar, emplear.

to take out 1 *vt (remove)* sacar. **2** *vt (person)* invitar a salir. **3** *vt (insurance)* hacer.

to take over 1 *vt (country)* apoderarse de. **2** *vi* tomar el poder.

to take over from *vt* relevar.

to take to 1 *vt (person)* tomar cariño a. **2** *vt (vice)* darse a. **3** *vt (start to do)* empezar a.

to take up 1 *vt (time, space)* ocupar. **2** *vt (continue)* continuar. **3** *vt (offer)* aceptar. **4** *vt (start to do)* empezar a.

to talk over *vt* discutir.

to talk round *vt* convencer.

to tangle with *vt* meterse con.

to tear down *vt* derribar.

to tear into *vt* arremeter contra.

to tear up *vt* romper en pedazos.

to tell apart *vt* distinguir.

to tell off *vt* echar una bronca a, reñir.

to tell on 1 *vt (have effect)* afectar a. **2** *vt (tell tales)* chivar.

to thin down 1 *vt* aclarar. **2** *vi* adelgazar.

to think back 1 *vi* recordar, hacer memoria.

to think over *vt* meditar, reflexionar.

to think up *vt* inventar, idear.

to throw away 1 *vt (discard)* tirar. **2** *vt (chance)* desaprovechar.

to throw back *vt* devolver.

to throw in *vt fam* incluir (gratis).

to throw off *vt* librarse de.

to throw out 1 *vt (kick out)* echar. **2** *vt (reject)* rechazar.

to throw up *vi* vomitar.

to tick off 1 *vt (mark off)* marcar. **2** *vt (scold)* regañar.

to tide over *vt* ayudar, sacar de un apuro.

to tidy up 1 *vt (room)* ordenar, arreglar; *(person)* arreglar, acicalar: **tidy yourself up a bit,** arréglate un poco. **2** *vi* poner las cosas en orden, recoger.

to tie down *vt* sujetar.

to tie up *vt* atar.

to tip off *vt* dar un soplo a.

to tip over/up 1 *vt* volcar. **2** *vi* volcarse.

to tire out *vt* agotar, cansar.

to tone down *vt* atenuar, suavizar.

to top up *vt* llenar hasta arriba.

to toss up for *vt* echar a cara y cruz.

to tot up *vt* sumar.

to touch down 1 *vi (plane)* aterrizar. **2** *vi* SP hacer un ensayo.

to touch off *vt* provocar.

to touch up *vt* retocar.

to tower above/over *vt* destacar sobre.

to toy with 1 *vt (thing)* juguetear. **2** *vt (idea)* contemplar, darle vueltas a.

to track down *vt* localizar, encontrar.

to trigger off *vt* provocar, desencadenar.

to trip over *vt - vi* tropezar (y caerse).

to trump up *vt* inventar.

to try on *vt* probarse.

to try out *vt* probar.

to tuck in 1 *vi* comer con apetito. **2** *vt (sheets, clothes, etc.)* meter. **3** *vt (person)* arropar.

to tune in to *vt* RAD sintonizar.

to turf out *vt fam* poner de patitas en la calle.

to turn away 1 *vt* no dejar entrar. **2** *vi* apartarse.

to turn back 1 *vt* hacer retroceder. **2** *vi* volver, volverse.

to turn down 1 *vt (reject)* rechazar. **2** *vt (radio, etc.)* bajar.

to turn in 1 *vt* entregar a la policía. **2** *vi fam* acostarse.

to turn into *vt* convertir, transformar: **they turned the bedroom into an office,** convirtieron el dormitorio en un despacho.

to turn off 1 *vt (electricity)* desconectar; *(light, gas)* apagar; *(water)* cerrar; *(machine)* parar. **2** *vt (off road)* salir de.

to turn on *vt (electricity)* conectar; *(light)* encender; *(gas, tap)* abrir; *(machine)* poner en marcha. **2** *vt (attack)* atacar. **3** *vt fam* excitar.

to turn out 1 *vt (gas, light)* apagar. **2** *vt (produce)* producir. **3** *vt (empty)* vaciar. **4** *vi (prove to be)* salir, resultar. **5** *vi (attend)* acudir. **6** *vi (crowds)* salir a la calle.

to turn over 1 vt *(reverse)* dar la vuelta
a. 2 vt *(idea)* dar vueltas a. 3 vt *(hand over)* entregar. 4 vt COMM facturar. 5 vi darse la vuelta, volcarse.

to turn to 1 vt *(resort)* recurrir. 2 vt *(page)* buscar.

to turn up 1 vi *(be found)* aparecer. 2 vi *(arrive)* presentarse, llegar. 3 vt *(light, gas, etc.)* subir.

U

to usher in vt hacer pasar.

V

to verge on vt rayar en.
to vest with vt conferir a.

W

to wake up 1 vt despertar. 2 vi despertarse.

to walk off with 1 vt *(win)* ganar con facilidad. 2 vt *fam (steal)* mangar, birlar.

to walk out 1 vi *(leave)* marcharse. 2 vi *(strike)* ir a la huelga.

to walk out on vt abandonar.

to ward off 1 vt *(illness)* prevenir, evitar. 2 vt *(blow)* parar.

to warm up 1 vt calentar. 2 vi calentarse. 3 vi SP hacer ejercicios de calentamiento.

to wash out vt *(stain)* quitar lavando.

to wash up 1 vt *(the dishes)* fregar. 2 vt fregar los platos, lavar los platos. 3 vi US *(wash oneself)* lavarse.

to water down 1 vt *(dilute)* aguar. 2 vt fig descafeinar.

to wear away 1 vt erosionar. 2 vi erosionarse.

to wear off vi desaparecer.

to wear out 1 vi gastarse, desgastarse. 2 vt *(person)* agotar; *(clothes, shoes)* gastar.

to weigh down 1 vt sobrecargar. 2 vt fig abrumar, agobiar.

to weigh up vt evaluar.

to whip off vt quitar deprisa.

to wittle away vt ir reduciendo.

to win over/round vt convencer, persuadir.

to wind down 1 vi *(clock)* quedarse sin cuerda. 2 vi *(person)* relajarse. 3 vt AUTO *(window)* bajar.

to wind up 1 vt *(clock)* dar cuerda a. 2 vt - vi concluir. 3 vt fam acabar: **he wound up in jail,** dio con los huesos en la cárcel.

to wipe out 1 vt *(destroy)* aniquilar, exterminar. 2 vt *(erase)* borrar.

to wolf down vt zamparse.

to work out 1 vt *(calculate)* calcular. 2 vt *(plan)* planear, pensar. 3 vt *(solve)* solucionar, resolver. 4 vi *(calculation)* salir. 5 vi *(turn out well)* ir bien, salir bien. 6 vi SP hacer ejercicio.

to work up 1 vt *(excite)* exaltar. 2 vt *(develop)* hacer, desarrollar.

to wrap up vi abrigarse.

to write back vi contestar (por carta).

to write down vt anotar, apuntar.

to write off 1 vt *(debt)* anular. 2 vt *(project)* dar por perdido,-a.

to write off for vt pedir por correo.

to write out 1 vt *(write fully)* escribir (en su forma completa). 2 vt *(cheque, etc.)* extender.

to write up vt redactar, escribir.

Z

to zip up vt cerrar con cremallera.

Verbos españoles con preposición

A

abandonarse a *vpr (entregarse)* to give oneself up (to): *se abandonó a la bebida* he gave himself up to drinking.

abatirse sobre *vpr (ave)* to swoop (down on); *(avión)* to dive (down on).

abdicar en *vi (soberanía)* to abdicate: *abdicó en su hija* he abdicated in favour of his daughter.

abdicar de *vi (ideales, ideas)* to give up.

abogar por *vi (preconizar)* to advocate, propose; *(defender)* to defend; *(luchar por)* to fight (for).

abonarse a *vpr (a revista)* to subscribe (to); *(a teatro, tren, etc.)* to buy a season ticket (for).

abstenerse de *vpr* to abstain (from), refrain (from): *se abstuvieron de votar* they abstained from voting.

aburrirse con, de *vpr* to get bored (with).

abusar de *vi* **1** *(propasarse)* to go too far, abuse: *abusar de alguien* to take unfair advantage of somebody. **2** *(usar mal)* to misuse: *abusar de la bebida* to drink too much.

acabar con 1 *vi (destruir)* to destroy, put an end to: *la revolución acabó con los privilegios de los aristócratas* the revolution put an end to the privileges of the aristocrats; *la caída de la bolsa acabó con su fortuna* the stock market crash ruined him; *¡este chico acabará conmigo!* this boy will be the death of me! **2** *(terminar)* to finish, finish off.

acabar de *vi* (+ *inf*) to have just + *pp*: *no lo toques, acabo de pintarlo ahora mismo* don't touch it, I've just painted it.

acabar por *vi* (+ *inf*) to end up + - *ing*: *acabé por comprar el vestido* I ended up buying the dress.

acertar a *vi* (+ *inf*) to happen to + *inf*: *yo acertaba a estar allí* I happened to be there.

acordarse de *vpr* to remember: *no se acuerda de nada* she can't remember anything.

acostumbrarse a *vpr* to become accustomed, get used.

adaptarse a *vpr (persona)* to adapt oneself; *(cosa)* to fit, adjust.

adelantarse a *vpr (anticiparse)* to get ahead.

adentrarse en 1 *vpr (penetrar)* to penetrate (into), enter deep (into). **2** *vpr fig (profundizar)* to go deeply (into), study thoroughly, delve (into).

admirarse de *vpr (asombrarse)* to be astonished (at), be amazed (at).

adolecer de *vi (padecer)* to suffer (from): *adolece de asma* he suffers from asthma; *adolece del corazón* she has a heart problem.

alcanzar para *vi (ser suficiente)* to be sufficient (for), be enough (for), suffice (for): *eso no alcanza para todos* that's not enough for all of us.

alegrarse de *vpr* to be pleased, be glad (about).

alejarse de *vpr* to go/move away.

aludir a *vi* to allude (to), mention , refer (to).

amenazar con *vt* to threaten: *lo amenazaron con el despido* they threatened to sack him.

amoldarse a *vpr* to adapt, adjust (to): *se amoldó a las costumbres españolas* he adapted himself to Spanish customs.

animar a *vt (alentar)* to encourage.

animarse a *vpr (decidirse)* to make up one's mind: *anímate a venir* say that you'll come.

apiadarse de *vpr* to take pity (on).

apostar por 1 *vt* to bet (on): *te apuesto veinte euros a que no gana* I bet you twenty euros that she won't win; *apostó todo su dinero por Red Rum* he bet all his money on Red Rum. **2** *vi* to bet (on): *apostó por él* she bet on him; *apuesto a que sí llega tarde* I bet he'll be late.

aprender a *vi* to learn: *así aprenderás a no decir mentiras* that'll teach you not to tell lies.

apresurarse a *vpr* to hurry, hurry up.

aprovecharse de *vpr (de alguien)* to take advantage of; *(de algo)* to make the most of.

apuntarse a *vpr fam (participar)* to take part (in): *¿te apuntas?* are you game?

apurarse por *(preocuparse)* to get worried, be worried (about).

arrepentirse de *vpr* **1** to regret: *se arrepintió de haber llegado tarde* he regretted having arrived late. **2** to repent: *se arrepintió de sus pecados* he repented of his sins.

arriesgarse a *vpr* to dare to do something, risk doing something.

ascender a 1 *vi (de categoría)* to be promoted (to). **2** *vi (sumar)* to amount (to).

asistir a *vi* to attend, be present: *la niña asiste a la escuela cada día* the girl goes to school every day; *solo asistieron diez personas* only ten people were present.

asociarse con 1 *vpr (relacionarse)* to be associated (with): *aquella música se asociaba con una época particular* that music was associated with a par-

ticular period. **2** *vpr* to collaborate, form a partnership, become partners.

asomarse a *vpr (una ventana)* to stick one's head out (of), lean out (of): *varios vecinos se asomaron a la ventana para ver qué pasaba* several neighbours stuck their heads out of their windows to see what was happening; *(a un balcón)* to come out (onto).

asombrarse de *vpr* to be astonished, be amazed, be surprised: *nos asombramos de su altura* we were amazed at her height.

aspirar a *vi (desear)* to aspire (to): *aspiraba a convertirse en una estrella de cine* he aspired becoming a film star.

asustarse con, de *vpr* to be frightened, be scared: *mi bebé se asusta del ruido* my baby is frightened of noise.

atenerse a 1 *vpr (ajustarse)* to abide (by), comply (with). **2** *vpr (acogerse)* to rely (on).

aventurarse a *vpr* to venture, dare.

avergonzarse de *vpr* to be ashamed (of), be embarrassed (about).

ayudar a *vi* to help, aid, assist.

ayudarse con, de *vpr (apoyarse)* to make use (of).

B

bastar con *vi* to be enough: *es muy concentrado, basta con una gota* it's highly concentrated, one drop is enough.

brindar (a la salud) de *vi* to toast (to), drink (to): *¡brindemos por el futuro!* let's drink to the future!

brindarse a *vpr* to offer (to), volunteer (to): *se brindó a prestarme ayuda* he offered to help me.

burlarse de *vpr* to mock, make fun (of), laugh (at).

C

cansarse de *vpr fig (hartarse)* to get tired (of), get fed up (with): *me cansé de sus* *chistes y me fui* I got tired of their jokes and I left.

carecer de *vi* to lack: *el pueblo carecía de alumbrado público* the village lacked street lighting, the village had no street lighting.

casarse con *vpr* to get married (to), marry.

ceñirse a 1 *vpr (atenerse)* to keep (to), limit oneself (to): *ceñirse al tema* to keep to the subject. **2** *vpr (ajustarse)* to adhere (to), stick (to), abide (by): *se ciñe a la normativa* she sticks to the rules.

colarse por *vpr (enamorarse)* to fall (for): *se coló por Ana* he fell for Ana.

clamar por *vi* to clamour (*US* clamor) (for), cry out (for): *clamar por la justicia* to cry out for justice.

comenzar a *vi* to begin, start: *comenzó a reír* he began to laugh, he began laughing.

comenzar con *vi* to begin with.

comenzar por (+ *inf*) to begin by +-*ing*: *comenzó por decir que...* he began by saying that ....

comerciar con *vi (hacer negocios)* to do business (with).

complacerse en *vpr* to take pleasure (in): *los señores Solano se complacen en invitarle al enlace matrimonial de su hijo* Mr and Mrs Solano have great pleasure in inviting you to their son's wedding.

comprometerse a *vpr (contraer una obligación)* to commit oneself, pledge: *se comprometió a pagar* she promised to pay.

condenar a *vt JUR (decretar condena)* to sentence (to), condemn (to): *lo condenaron a muerte* he was sentenced to death.

confiar en 1 *vi (tener fe)* to trust, confide (in): *no confiamos en él* we don't trust him. **2** *vi (estar seguro)* to be confident, trust: *confío en que no llegarán tarde* I am confident that they won't be late. **3** *vi (contar)* to count (on), rely (on): *confío en mi inteligencia para resolver el problema* I am counting on my intelligence to solve the problem.

confiarse a 1 *vpr (entregarse)* to entrust oneself: *se confió a los médicos* she put herself in the hands of the doctors. **2** *vpr (confesarse)* to confide (in): *me confiaré a mi mejor amiga* I'll confide in my best friend.

conformarse con *vpr (contentarse)* to resign oneself (to), be content (with), make do (with): *tendré que conformarme con este sueldo* I'll have to content myself with this salary.

consagrarse a *vpr (dedicarse)* to devote oneself (to), dedicate oneself (to).

consentir en *vi (admitir)* to consent (to), agree (to): *el niño no consiente en comer* the child refuses to eat.

consistir en 1 *vi (estribar)* to lie (in), consist (in): *la solución consiste en crear un nuevo archivo* the solution lies in creating a new file. **2** *vi (estar formado)* to consist (of).

contar con 1 *vi (confiar en)* to rely on, count on: *cuento contigo* I'm relying on you; *contamos con tu ayuda* we're relying on your help. **2** *vi (incluir)* to count in: *cuenta conmigo para la fiesta* you can count me in for the party. **3** *vi (tener presente)* to take into account. **4** *vi (estar provisto de)* to have, be provided with: *el coche cuenta con aire acondicionado* the car is equipped with air conditioning.

contribuir a *vi* to contribute (to): *contribuir a los gastos* to contribute to the expenses; *varios factores contribuyen al crecimiento del paro* several factors contribute to the rise in unemployment.

convenir en *vi (acordar)* to agree (on): *convinimos en la fecha* we agreed on the date; *convinieron en que se repartirían el trabajo* they agreed on sharing the work.

convertirse en 1 *vpr (transformarse)* to turn (into), change (into). **2** *vpr (volverse)* to become, turn (into): *se convirtió en una joven preciosa* she turned into a beautiful young woman; *su sueño se convirtió en realidad* his dream came true.

convertirse a *vpr REL* to be converted (to).

convidar a 1 to invite (to): *me convidó a una fiesta* he invited me to a party; *nos ha convidado a comer* she's invited us to lunch. **2** *vt (ofrecer)* to offer: *nos convidó a pastel* he offered us some cake. **3** *vt fig (incitar, mover, animar)* to prompt, inspire, move: *este tiempo convida a pasear* this weather makes you want to go for a walk.

corresponder a *vi (encajar)* to correspond (to), tally (with); *(descripción)* to fit.

cuidar a, de *vt* to look after, take care of, care for.

cuidarse de *vpr (preocuparse)* to worry about, mind: *no se cuida de lo que dicen* she doesn't care what they say.

D

dar a 1 *vi (botón, interruptor)* to press: *dale al botón* press the button. **2** *vi (mirar una cosa hacia una parte)* to look out onto, overlook: *la ventana da a la playa* the window looks out onto the beach; *(ir a parar a una parte)* to lead to, open onto: *esa puerta da a la cocina* this door leads to the kitchen.

dar con *vi (encontrar algo)* to find, discover: *al final dio con la calle* she eventually found the street; *(encontrar a alguien)* to meet, come across, bump into: *al salir de casa dio con mi primo* as he was leaving the house, he bumped into my cousin; *(acertar)* to find: *dio con la solución* he found the solution.

dar de *vi (suministrar)* to give: *les dio de comer/beber* he gave them something to eat/drink; *esto les dará de qué hablar* this'll give them something to talk about; *dar de palos/bofetadas/tortas a alguien* to beat somebody up.

dar en *vi (acertar)* to find, hit on.

dar para *vi (ser suficiente)* to be enough for, be sufficient for: *la sopa da para cuatro* the soup serves four.

darse a *vpr (consagrarse)* to devote oneself to: *se dio al estudio* she devoted herself to study; *(a un vicio)* to take to, abandon oneself to: *se ha dado a la bebida* he has taken to drink.

darse con, contra *(chocar)* to crash (into).

deber de *aux (probabilidad)* must: *deben de ser las seis* it must be six o'clock; *debes de haberlo oído* you must have heard it; *no sé cuántas veces he debido de decírtelo* I don't know how many times I must have told you; *(negativa)* can't: *no deben de haber llegado* they can't have arrived.

deberse a 1 *vpr (ser consecuencia)* to be due (to): *esto se debe a su falta de interés* this is due to his lack of interest. **2** *vpr (tener una obligación)* to have a duty (to): *un soldado se debe a su patria* a soldier has a duty to his country.

decidirse por *vi* to decide on: *se decidió por la falda roja* she decided on the red skirt.

declararse a *vpr (amor)* to declare one's love (for): *le declaró su amor durante la fiesta* he declared his love for her during the party.

dedicarse a *vpr* to devote oneself (to), dedicate oneself (to): *se dedica a la enseñanza* she's a teacher, she teaches; *en verano se dedica a pasear* in summer he spends his time walking; *¿a qué te dedicas?* what do you do for a living?

depender de 1 *vi* to depend (on): *depende de ti* it's up to you; *depende de lo que quieras* it depends on what you want. **2** *vi (estar bajo el mando o autoridad)* to be under, be answerable to: *los vendedores dependen de Juan* the salesmen are answerable to Juan, Juan is in charge of the salesmen; *(necesitar)* to be dependent on: *aún depende de sus padres* she's still dependent on her parents.

desvivirse por 1 *vpr (desvelarse)* to do one's utmost (for), be devoted (to). **2** *vpr (desear)* to be mad (about).

dignarse a *vpr* to deign (to), condescend (to): *no se dignó a hablarnos* he didn't deign to talk to us.

dirigirse a 1 *vpr (ir)* to go (to), make one's way (to), make (for): *nos dirigimos al cine* we made our way to the cinema. **2** *vpr (hablar)* to address, speak (to): *se dirigió a su padre* she addressed her father. **3** *vpr (escribir)* to write: *si quiere más información diríjase a esta dirección* if you want further information write to this address.

disfrutar con *vi (gozar)* to enjoy: *disfruta con el café* she enjoys coffee.

disfrutar de *vi (poseer)* to enjoy, have, possess: *disfruta de buena salud* he enjoys good health; *el caballero disfrutaba de excelente fama en la ciudad* the gentleman had an excellent reputation in the city.

disponer de 1 *vi (tener)* to have: *todas las habitaciones disponen de aire acondicionado* all the rooms are equipped with air conditioning; *no disponemos de tiempo* we haven't got time. **2** *vi (hacer uso)* to make use (of), have the use (of): *dispuso de su dinero* he made use of his money.

disponerse a *vpr (prepararse)* to get ready (to), prepare (to): *me dispongo a salir* I'm getting ready to go out.

distinguirse por *vpr (diferenciarse)* to differ (in), be distinguished: *se distinguen por el color* they differ in colour.

E

echar a *vi (+ inf) (empezar)* to begin (to): *echó a andar* he began to walk; *echó a correr* she ran off.

echarse a *vpr (+ inf) (empezar)* to begin (to): *se echó a reír* he burst out laughing.

empeñarse en *vpr (insistir)* to insist (on): *se empeñó en venir con nosotros* he insisted on coming with us.

empezar a *vi* to begin, start: *empezó a leer* he began to read.

encargarse de *vpr* to take charge (of), look after, see (to), deal (with).

encomendarse a *vpr* to entrust oneself (to).

encontrarse con *vpr* to meet up (with), run (into).

enfadarse con 1 *vpr* to get angry (with), get cross (with): *no te enfades conmigo* don't get angry with me. **2** *vpr (pelearse)* to fall out (with).

enfrentarse a, con 1 *vpr (hacer frente)* to face, confront: *tuvo que enfrentarse con los sindicatos* he had to confront the unions. **2** *vpr DEP* to meet. **3** *vpr (pelearse)* to have an argument (with), fall out (with); *(chocar)* to clash (with).

enojarse con *vpr* to get angry (with), get annoyed (with), lose one's temper (with): *se enojó con su jefe* he got annoyed with his boss.

entender de *vi (tener conocimiento)* to know (about).

entender en *vi (ser autoridad)* to be an expert (in); *(encargarse)* to deal (with).

entenderse con *vpr fam (relación amorosa)* to have an affair (with): *dicen que se entiende con la vecina de al lado* they say he's having an affair with the woman next door.

entregarse a 1 *vpr (rendirse)* to give in (to), surrender: *el enemigo se entregó* the enemy surrendered; *se entregó a las autoridades* he gave himself up to the authorities. **2** *vpr (dedicarse)* to devote oneself (to), be devoted (to): *se entrega plenamente a su trabajo* she's totally devoted to her work. **3** *vpr pey (caer en)* to give oneself over (to), take (to): *se entregó a la bebida* he took to the bottle.

equivaler a 1 *vi (ser igual)* to be equivalent (to), be equal (to). **2** *vi (significar)* to be tantamount (to), amount (to), mean: *eso equivale a una declaración de guerra* this amounts to a declaration of war.

esforzarse en *vpr* to try hard (in); to endeavor (to).

esforzarse por *vpr* to strive (for).

estar a *aux (precio)* to be, sell at; *(fecha)* to be: **están a 20 euros** they're 20 euros; **estamos a 15 de marzo** it's the 15th of March.

estar con *aux (tener)* to have; *(estar de acuerdo)* to agree with: **estoy con gripe** I have the flu; **estoy con Ana** I agree with Ana.

estar en *aux (creer)* to think, believe; *(depender de uno)* to be up to: **estoy en que no vendrán** I don't think they'll come; **está en él decírselo** it's up to him to tell her.

estar para *aux; (estar a punto)* to be about to: **está para marchar** she's about to leave; *(estar acabado)* to be finished, be ready: **estará para las cuatro** it'll be finished by four; *(estar de humor)* to feel like, be in the mood for: **no estoy para bromas** I'm in no mood for jokes.

estar por *aux (no haberse ejecutado)* to remain to be: **está por escribir** it still has to be written; *(estar determinado)* to be for: **estoy por quedarme** I'm for staying; *(ir a)* to be going to: **está por salir** she's going to go out; *(a favor)* to be for: **estamos por este partido** we're for this party.

estar sin *aux (+ inf)* not to have been + *pp*: **el coche está sin lavar** the car hasn't been washed, the car still needs washing.

exponerse a *vpr (arriesgarse)* to expose oneself to, run the risk of: **se ha expuesto a muchos peligros** he has exposed himself to many dangers.

F

fallar a *vi (decepcionar)* to let down: **hasta la fecha no me ha fallado nunca** he's never let me down yet.

familiarizarse con *vpr* to get to know, get used (to), familiarize oneself: **familiarízate con el teclado** get to know the keyboard, get used to the keyboard.

felicitar por *vt* to congratulate (on): **nos felicitó por el acuerdo** he congratulated us on the agreement.

fiarse de *vpr (confiarse)* to trust: **no me fío de él** I don't trust him; **no te fíes, las apariencias engañan** watch out, appearances can be deceptive.

fichar por *vi DEP* to sign up (with): **finalmente fichó por el Barcelona** he finally signed up with Barcelona F.C.

fijarse en *vpr (darse cuenta)* to notice: **¿te fijaste en el color de sus ojos?** did you notice the colour of his eyes?

G

gozar de *vi (poseer, disfrutar)* to enjoy: **goza de extensas propiedades** it has many properties; **goza de muy buena salud** he enjoys very good health.

guardarse de *vpr (precaverse, evitar)* to guard against, avoid, be careful not to: **te guardarás muy bien de revelar nuestro secreto** be very careful not to reveal our secret.

H

haber de *aux (+ infin) (obligación)* to have to, must, should: **has de pedirlo** you have to ask for it; **han de venir** hoy they must come today.

habituarse a *vpr* to become accustomed (to), get used (to).

hacer de *vi (actuar)* to play; *(representar)* to act: **hizo de Peribáñez** he played Peribáñez; **hizo de abuela** she played the grandmother.

hacer por *vpr (+ infin)* to try to, do one's best to: **haz por llegar pronto** try to arrive early.

hacerse a *vpr (acostumbrarse)* to get used (to), become accustomed (to): **se hizo al colegio nuevo** he got used to his new school.

hartarse de *vpr (cansarse)* to get fed up (with), get tired (of): **me harté de esperarla** I got tired of waiting for her.

I

ilusionarse con *vpr (entusiasmarse)* to be excited (about).

incidir en *vi (repercutir en)* to have an effect on, affect: *la crisis ha incidido notablemente en el turismo* the crisis has had a considerable effect on tourism.

incitar a *vt* to incite (to): *incitó a la tropa a la rebelión* he incited the troops to mutiny; *sus escritos incitan al racismo* his writings encourage racism.

inclinarse por *vpr (escoger)* to choose, opt for: *se inclinaron por el candidato más joven* they opted for the youngest candidate.

infiltrarse en *vpr* to infiltrate: *el topo se infiltró en el servicio de inteligencia* the mole infiltrated the intelligence service.

inflarse *vpr fam (hartarse de comer, etc.)* to stuff oneself (with): *nos inflamos de salchichas* we stuffed ourselves with sausages; *este fin de semana me he inflado de leer* I read nonstop all weekend.

influir en *vi* to influence, have an affect (on).

inhibirse de *vpr (abstenerse)* to refrain (from); *(negarse)* to refuse (to).

inspirarse en *vpr* to be inspired (by).

instar a *vi* to urge (to).

interesarse en, por *vpr* to take an interest (in).

intimar con *vi* to become close (to).

invitar a 1 *vt to invite.* **2** *vi (incitar)* to encourage: *esta piscina invita a bañarse* the water is tempting; *(a la violencia)* to incite.

J

jactarse de *vpr* to boast, brag (about).

juntarse con 1 *vpr (relacionarse)* to go out (with), mix (with): *últimamente no se junta con nadie* she hasn't gone out

with anyone lately. **2** *vpr (amancebarse)* to move in (with), start living together.

L

liarse a *vpr* to start + *ger*: *se liaron a patadas/golpes* they started kicking/hitting each other.

liarse con *vpr* to have an affair (with).

librarse de *vpr* to escape (from): *intentaron librarse de sus perseguidores* they tried to throw off their pursuers; *siempre se libra de hacer los trabajos sucios* he always gets out of doing the dirty work.

lidiar con *vt fig (luchar con)* to battle with, struggle against.

limitarse a *vpr (+ inf)* to restrict oneself to + *inf*, do no more than + *inf*: *una persona inteligente no se limita a ver la televisión* an intelligent person does not restrict himself to watching television; *limítate a cumplir ordenes* just obey orders.

llegar a *vi (+ inf) (uso enfático)*: *llegó a llamarme ladrón* he went so far as to call me a thief, he even called me a thief; *si llego a saber que hay huelga, no me levanto* if I'd known there was a strike, I wouldn't have gotten out of bed; *si lo llega a pillar lo mata* if he'd caught him he would have killed him.

llevar a *vi (+ inf) (inducir)* to lead to, make: *esto me lleva a pensar que...* this leads me to think that ...; *¿qué lo llevó a actuar así?* what made him act like that?

M

machacar con *vi (insistir en)* to go on (about), harp on (about).

maravillarse de *vpr* to marvel (at).

medirse con *vpr* to measure oneself (against).

meter en *vt (implicar)* to put (into), get (into), involve (in): *en buen lío nos has* *metido* you've got us into a real mess; *tú me metiste en este asunto* you got me involved in this business.

meterse con *vpr (provocar)* to pick (on): *no te metas con él que es más fuerte que tú* don't pick on him, he's stronger than you.

meterse en 1 *vpr (tomar parte - negocio)* to go (into): *se ha metido en un negocio de compraventa* she's gone into buying and selling; *(involucrarse en)* to get involved (in/with), get mixed up (in/with): *se ha metido en una secta* she's got mixed up with a sect. **2** *vpr (introducirse)* to get involved (in): *se ha metido en la especulación del terreno* he's got involved in property speculation; *se ha metido en el Ayuntamiento* he's on the council; *siempre te estás metiendo donde no te llaman* you're always sticking your nose in where you're not wanted; *me metí totalmente en el papel* I got completely into the role; *se mete a fondo en todo lo que hace* he throws himself into everything he does; *nos vamos a meter en la compra de un piso* we're going to take the plunge and buy a flat *(US apartment)*. **3** *vpr (dedicarse)* to go (into): *quiere meterse en política* he wants to go into politics.

mezclar en *vt (persona)* to involve (in): *le han mezclado en negocios turbios* they've involved him in shady dealings.

mezclarse con *vpr (personas)* to mix (with): *a mí no me gusta la gente con quien te mezclas* I don't like the people you're mixing with.

mezclarse en *vpr (entrometerse)* to interfere (in).

mirar por *vi* to care (about), to worry (about), to think (of).

mojarse en *vpr fam (comprometerse)* to commit oneself, get involved.

molestarse en *vpr (tomarse la molestia)* to bother: *no se moleste en venir, ya se lo mandaremos a casa* don't bother coming, we'll send it round to you; *ni se molestó en decir adiós* he didn't even bother to say goodbye.

morir de *vi* to die (of, from): *murieron de hipotermia* they died of hypothermia; *murió de vejez* she died of old age.

morirse por *vpr (+ inf)* to be dying to + *inf*: *se muere por verla* he's dying to see her.

N

nacer de *vi (idea, sentimiento)* to originate (from), spring (from), stem (from): *el miedo nace de la ignorancia* fear stems from ignorance.

nacer para *vi* to be born to be something: *nació para ser estrella* she was born to be a star.

negarse a *vpr* to refuse (to): *se negó a devolverme el dinero* he refused to give me my money back.

nutrirse de 1 *vpr (alimentarse)* to receive nourishment (from). **2** *vpr fig (abastecerse)* to draw (on).

O

obedecer a 1 *vi (responder)* to respond (to). **2** *vi (tener por causa)* to be due (to): *¿a qué obedece su visita?* what is the reason for your visit?

obligar a *vt* to force (to).

obsesionarse con *vpr* to get obsessed (with).

obstinarse en *vpr* to persist (in), insist (on).

ocuparse de *vpr (encargarse de)* to take care (of); *(tratar)* to deal (with).

ofenderse por *vpr* to get offended (by): *se ofendió conmigo por lo que le dije* what I said offended him.

ofrecerse a *vpr (prestarse)* to offer (to), volunteer: *se ofreció a llevarme* he offered to give me a lift.

oler a *vi* to smell (of, like): *huele a gas* it smells of gas in here.

olvidarse de *vpr* to forget: *se olvidó de cerrar la puerta* he forgot to close the door; *me olvidé de que venías hoy* I forgot you were coming today.

operar a *vt* to operate (on): *¿a ti quién te operó?* who operated on you?

opinar de *vi* to think (about): *¿qué opinas de esta cuestión?* what do you think about this matter?; *aquí todos tenemos derecho a opinar* we all have the right to give our opinion here.

oponerse a 1 *vpr (estar en contra)* to oppose, be against: *se opusieron a nuestra boda* they were against our wedding. **2** *vpr (ser contrario)* to be in opposition (to), contradict.

optar a *vi (aspirar)* to apply (for).

optar entre *vi (elegir)* to choose (from): *puede optar entre tres modelos diferentes* you have three different models to choose from.

optar por *vi* to opt (for), to decide: *opté por no decir nada* I decided not to say anything.

P

parar de *vi* to stop + ing: *¡para de gritar!* stop shouting!

pararse a *vpr* to stop (to).

parecerse a *vpr* to be alike, look like: *el pequeño se parece mucho a su padre* the little one looks just like his father.

pasar a *vi* to pass (to), proceed (to).

pasar de 1 *vi (límite)* to exceed. **2** *vi fam* not to be bothered about something: *paso de hacer cola* I can't be bothered to queue up; *pasa de todo* he couldn't care less about anything, he doesn't give a damn about anything.

pasar sin *vi* to do without.

pasarse de *vpr fam (excederse)* to overdo it; *(ir demasiado lejos)* to go too far: *te has pasado de sincero* you were too honest.

pasar(se) por *vi/vpr (ir)* to go (by), call in (at): *pásate por casa cuando quieras* pop in any time.

pensar de *vi (opinar)* to think (about).

pensar en 1 *vi* to think (of/about): *estuvo pensando en sus amigos* he was thinking about his friends. **2** *vi (considerar)* to consider, think (about).

percatarse de *vpr* to notice, realice.

perfilarse como *vpr* to take shape: *Torres se perfila como ganador* Torres is beginning to look like the winner.

persistir en *vi (mantenerse firme)* to persist, persevere.

poner de *vt* to call somebody something: *lo puso de ladrón y de mentiroso* she called him a thief and a liar.

ponerse a *vpr (+ inf)* to start + to + inf + -ing: *se puso a cantar* he started to sing, he started singing.

preciarse de *vpr* to be proud (of).

prendarse de *vpr* to fall in love (with): *se quedó prendado de la camisa en cuanto la vio* he fell in love with the shirt the minute he saw it.

preocuparse de *vpr* to mind: *tú preocúpate de lo tuyo* mind your own business.

preocuparse por *vpr (sentir preocupación)* to worry (about), get worried (about).

prescindir de *vi (pasar sin)* to do without: *prescindamos de formalismos* let's cut out the formalities; *(no contar con)* to leave out: *prescindieron de él para la organización del viaje* they left him out of the arrangements for the trip.

prestarse a *vpr (ofrecerse)* to lend oneself.

presumir de *vi (vanagloriarse)* to boast (about), show off (about): *siempre está presumiendo de sus hijos* she's always boasting about her children; *presume de habilidoso* he likes to think he is a handyman.

primar sobre *vi* to be more important (than).

privar(se) de *vt (despojar)* to deprive (of).

proceder contra *vi JUR* to start proceedings (against).

profundizar en *vi (tema, cuestión)* to look deeply (into), analyse (*US* analyze) in depth.

Q

quedar con *vi* to meet.

quedar en *vi (convenir)* to agree to: *quedamos en volver más tarde* we agreed to come back later; *quedamos en que la película no era buena* we agreed that it wasn't a good film.

quedar por *vi (+ inf)* not to have been + *pp*: *la cama quedó por hacer* the bed had not been made, the bed was left unmade; *quedan esos platos por lavar* there are still those dishes to be washed up; *queda por ver si llegarán a algún acuerdo* it remains to be seen whether they will come to some agreement.

quedarse a *vpr* to stay (to), remain (to).

quedarse con 1 *vpr (retener algo)* to keep: *quédese con el cambio* keep the change. **2** *fam* to make a fool of somebody, have somebody on.

quedarse sin *vpr* to run out (of).

quejarse de *vpr (del descontento)* to complain (about): *¡no te quejes!* stop complaining!

quitarse de *vpr (del juego, bebida, etc.)* to give up: *se quitó de fumar* she gave up smoking.

R

rabiar de *vi fig (padecer)* to suffer (from): *rabiar de hambre* to be dying of hunger; *rabiar de dolor* to writhe in pain.

rabiar por *vi* to be dying (for), long (for): *rabiaba por tener un coche nuevo* she was dying for a new car.

radicar en 1 *vi (encontrarse)* to be (in), be situated (in): *el documento radica en la notaría* the document is in the notary's office. **2** *vi fig (consistir)* to lie (in), stem (from): *el problema radica*

en la falta de solidaridad the problem lies in the lack of solidarity.

rebajarse a *vpr* to stoop (to), lower oneself (to).

recaer en, sobre *vi* to fall (on): *el premio recayó sobre Teresa* the prize went to Teresa.

recelar de *vi (desconfiar)* to be suspicious (of): *recela de todos* he is suspicious of everybody.

recochinearse de *vpr fam* to make fun (of), laugh (at).

recrearse con, en *vpr* to take pleasure in, take delight in.

recuperarse de 1 *vpr (disgusto, emoción, etc.)* to get over, recover (from). **2** *vpr (enfermedad)* to recover (from), recuperate (from).

recurrir a *vi (acogerse - a algo)* to resort (to); *(- a alguien)* to turn (to): *recurrió a la mentira* he resorted to lies; *recurrió a sus padres* she turned to her parents.

reducirse a *vpr (resultar)* to come down (to): *todo se redujo a una equivocación* it all came down to a mistake.

redundar en *vi (resultar)* to redound (to): *redundó en nuestro beneficio* it was to our advantage.

regalarse con *vpr (deleitarse)* to treat oneself (to): *se regaló con una copa de champaña* he treated himself to a glass of champagne.

regirse por *vpr (guiarse)* to follow, abide (by), go (by): *se rige por la opinión de su padre* he goes by his father's opinion.

reírse de 1 *vpr* to laugh (at): *¿de qué te ríes?* what are you laughing at? **2** *(burlarse)* to laugh (at), make fun (of).

relacionarse con 1 *vpr (estar conectado)* to be related (to), be connected (with). **2** *vpr (alternar)* to get acquainted (with), mix (with), meet.

renegar de *vi (gen)* to renounce *renegar de su fe* to renounce one's faith; *(familia)* to disow: *el padre renegó de él* his father disowned him.

renunciar a 1 *vi (abandonar)* to give up, abandon: *renunció a la compra* he decided not to buy; *renunció al tabaco* she gave up smoking. **2** *vi* to renounce, relinquish: **renunció a su fe** she renounced her faith; **renunció a la herencia** he relinquished the inheritance.

reparar en *vi (darse cuenta)* to realize: **no reparé en lo que estaba haciendo** I didn't realize what I was doing.

resentirse de *vpr (sentirse)* to suffer (from), feel the effects (of): **me resiento del tobillo** my ankle hurts, I have a sore ankle.

reservarse para *vpr (conservarse)* to save oneself (for): **resérvate para después** save yourself for later.

resignarse a *vpr* to resign oneself (to): **se resignó a perder el partido** he resigned himself to losing the match.

resistirse a *vpr (negarse)* to refuse: **me resisto a opinar** I refuse to give my opinion.

residir en 1 *vi* to reside (in), live (in). **2** *vi fig* to lie (in): **ahí reside el problema** the problem lies there.

resolverse a *vpr (decidirse)* to resolve, make up one's mind, decide: **se resolvió a cantar** he decided to sing.

responder por *vi* to vouch (for), act as a guarantor (for).

reunirse con *vpr* to meet, get together, have a meeting with: **me reuní con Juan** I met Juan.

revestir de *vt (recubrir)* to cover (with), coat (with), line (with).

revertir en *vi (resultar)* to result (in).

romper a *vi (+ inf) fig (empezar)* to burst out: **romper a reír** to burst out laughing.

romper con *vi* to break up (with).

S

saber a *vi (tener sabor)* to taste (of, like).

saber de *vi (de alguien)* to have heard (from): **¿qué sabes de Pedro?** have you heard from Pedro?; *(de algo)* to know (of): **sé de un lugar...** I know of a place ....

salir a 1 *vi (parecerse)* to take after: **ha salido a su padre** she takes after her

father. **2** *vi (dar a)* to open (onto), come out (at): **esta calle sale a la avenida** this street comes out at the avenue.

salir con 1 *vi* to go out (with), date. **2** *vi (decir inesperadamente)* to come out (with): **¡ahora me sales con eso!** now you come out with this!

salir de 1 *vi (ir hacia afuera)* to go out (of): **salir de casa** to go out of the house. **2** *vi (proceder)* to come (from): **de la aceituna sale el aceite** olive oil comes from olives. **3** *vi (librarse)* to get out (of).

salirse de *vpr (la carretera)* to go off (the road).

ser de 1 *vi (pertenecer)* to be, belong (to): **estas sillas son de ellos** these chairs are theirs; **el coche es de Ana** the car belongs to Ana; **¿de quién es este libro?** whose book is this? **2** *vi (ser propio)* to be like: **es muy de Pilar** it's just like Pilar. **3** *vi (suceder)* to happen (to): **¿qué fue de Iván?** what happened to Iván? **4** *vi (proceder)* to be from, come from: **Santi es de Cáceres** Santi is from Cáceres. **5** *vi (+ inf) (ser digno)* to be worth: **es de ver** it's worth seeing; **es de admirar** she's to be admired.

servir de *vi* to serve as; *(persona)* to act as: **sirvió de mediador** he acted as mediator; **si sirve de algo** for what it's worth.

servir para *vpr* to be used for, be for: **sirve para dormir** it's used for sleeping on; **también sirve para abrir latas** it's also used for opening tins (*US* cans).

servirse de *vpr (usar)* to use, make use (of); to take advantage (of).

soltarse a *vpr (+ inf)* to begin + inf, start + inf/ -ing: **ya se suelta a caminar** he's beginning to walk.

someterse a 1 *vpr (rendirse)* to surrender (to). **2** *vpr (tratamiento, etc.)* to undergo.

sonar a *vi (tener apariencia)* to look (like), sound (like), seem (like): **el proyecto sonaba a estafa** the project sounded like a con.

soñar con 1 *vi (al dormir)* to dream (about/of): **soñé contigo** I dreamt about you. **2** *vi fig (fantasear)* to daydream (about), dream (about/of).

soprenderse de *vpr fig* to be surprised (at).

subir a *vi fig (cuenta)* to come (to): *la deuda sube a dos mil euros* the debt comes to two thousand euros.

subirse a 1 *vpr (piso, escalera, etc.)* to go up. **2** *vpr (árbol, muro, etc.)* to climb up. **3** *vpr (en un vehículo - coche)* to get in; *(autobús)* to get on; *(avión, barco, tren, etc.)* to get on, get onto: *¡súbete, súbete al coche!* get in, get into the car! **4** *vpr (en animales, bicicleta, etc.)* to get on, mount.

suceder a *vi (seguir)* to follow, succeed: *sucedió a su padre en el puesto* he succeeded his father in the job.

sumirse en *vpr fig* to immerse oneself (in), lose oneself (in).

supeditar a 1 *vt (subordinar)* to subordinate (to). **2** *vt (condicionar)* to subject (to).

T

tardar en 1 *vi* to take *(time)* (to). **2** *vi (demorar)* to take a long time: *tardó mucho en contestar* he took a long time to answer.

tender a *vi (tener tendencia)* to tend (to), have a tendency (to): *tiende al aburrimiento* it tends to be boring.

tenerse por *vpr* to consider oneself, think oneself: *se tiene por guapo* he thinks he's handsome.

terminar con 1 *vi (eliminar)* to put an end (to): *quieren terminar con la violencia* they want to put an end to violence. **2** *vi (estropear)* to damage, ruin: *la lluvia terminó con la cosecha* the rain damaged the crops. **3** *vi (reñir)* to break up (with): *ha terminado con su novio* she's broken up with her boyfriend.

terminar de *vi* to finish (+ ing).

terminar por *vi* to end up (+ ing).

tirar a 1 *vi fig (inclinarse)* to be attracted (to), be drawn (to): *esta chica tira hacia las artes* this girl is drawn to the arts. **2** *vi fig (parecerse)* to take after: *tira a su padre* she takes after her father.

tirar de 1 *vi (cuerda, puerta)* to pull. **2** *vi (carreta, carro)* to draw. **3** *vi fam* to use: *cuando no tiene dinero tira de tarjeta* when he hasn't got any money he uses his credit card.

tirarse a *vpr arg (fornicar)* to lay.

tirarse sobre *vpr (abalanzarse)* to rush (at), jump (on).

toparse con 1 *vpr (encontrarse alguien)* to meet, bump into: *me topé con tu amigo* I bumped into your friend. **2** *vpr fig (dificultades, etc.)* to meet with, encounter, run into.

trabajar de *vi* to be, work as: *trabaja de profesor* he's a teacher.

tratar con 1 *vi (relacionarse)* to be acquainted (with), know. **2** *vi (tener tratos)* to deal (with). **3** *vi (negociar)* to negotiate (with).

tratar de 1 *vi (intentar)* to try (to): *trata de hacerlo* try to do it. **2** *vi (versar)* to be about: *trata de los espías* it's about the spies.

tratar(se) con *vi (relacionarse)* to be acquainted (with), know.

tratarse de *vpr (referirse)* to be about: *se trataba de un atraco* it was about a robbery; *se trata de...* it's a question of ..., it's a matter of ...: *se trata de averiguar cómo lo hicieron* it's a question of working out how they did it.

tropezar con 1 *vi (tropicar)* to trip (over), stumble (over): *tropezó con mi pie* he tripped over my foot. **2** *vi fig (encontrar a alguien)* to come (across), bump (into). **3** *vi fig (encontrar dificultades, etc.)* to come up (against), run (into). **4** *vi fig (estar en desacuerdo)* to disagree (with).

U

untarse de *vpr* to get something all over one: *se había untado de grasa* he'd gotten grease all over him.

usar de *vi* to use: *usó de sus encantos para conseguir el trabajo* he used his charm to get the job.

V

valerse de *vpr (utilizar)* to use, make use (of): *se valió de un bastón* he used a stick.

velar por *vi fig (cuidar)* to watch (over), look (after): *velaron por él* they looked after him.

venir a *aux (+ inf) (aproximación)* to be about: *viene a hacer dos metros de alto* it's about two metres high; *(alcanzar, llegar a)* to arrive at; *(terminar por)* to end up: *finalmente vinimos a coincidir* we finally agreed; *vino a parar a la cárcel* he ended up in jail.

verse en *vpr (en una situación, etc.)* to find oneself, be: *se vio en un apuro* he was in a fix.

vestirse de *vpr (ir vestido)* to wear, dress (in); *(disfrazarse)* to disguise oneself (as), dress up (as): *se vistió de policía* he dressed up as a policeman.

vivir de *vi* to live (on): *viven de su pensión* they live on his pension.

vivir para *vi* to live (for): *vive para la música* he lives for music, music is his whole life.

volcarse en *vpr fig (entregarse)* to do one's utmost.

volver a *vi (hacer otra vez)* to do again: *volver a leer* to read again.

Y

yacer con *vi lit (dormir)* to be lying; *(acostarse)* to lie (with).

Z

zafarse de *vpr* to get away (from), free oneself (from), escape (from): *logró zafarse de la policía* he managed to get away from the police.

Key to Pronunciation in Spanish

VOWELS

Letter	Approximate sound
a	Like *a* in English *far, father*, e.g., **casa, mano**.
e	When stressed, like *a* in English *pay*, e.g., **dedo**. When unstressed, it has a shorter sound like in English *bet, net*, e.g., **estado, decidir**.
i	Like *i* in English *machine* or *ee* in *feet*, e.g., **fin**.
o	Like *o* in English *obey*, e.g., **mona, poner**.
u	Like *u* in English *rule* or *oo* in *boot*, e.g., **atún**. It is silent in **gue** and **gui**, e.g., **guerra, guisado**. If it carries a diaeresis (**ü**), it is pronounced (see Diphthongs), e.g., **bilingüe**. It is also silent in **que** and **qui**, e.g., **querer, quinto**.
y	When used as a vowel, it sounds like the Spanish **i**, e.g., **y, rey**.

DIPHTHONGS

Diph.	Approximate sound
ai, ay	Like *i* in English *light*, e.g., **caigo, hay**.
au	Like *ou* in English *sound*, e.g., **cauto, paular**.
ei, ey	Like *ey* in English *they* or *a* in *ale*, e.g., **reina, ley**.
eu	Like the *a* in English *pay* combined with the sound of *ew* in English *knew*, e.g., **deuda, feudal**.
oi, oy	Like *oy* in English *toy*, e.g., **oiga, soy**.
ia, ya	Like *ya* in English *yarn*, e.g., **rabia, raya**.
ua	Like *wa* in English *wand*, e.g., **cuatro, cual**.
ie, ye	Like *ye* in English *yet*, e.g., **bien, yeso**.
ue	Like *wa* in English *wake*, e.g., **buena, fue**.
io, yo	Like *yo* in English *yoke*, without the following sound of *w* in this word, e.g., **región, yodo**.

Diph.	Approximate sound
uo	Like *uo* in English *quote*, e.g., **cuota, oblicuo.**
iu, yu	Like *yu* in English *Yule*, e.g., **ciudad, triunfo.**
ui	Like *wee* in English *week*, e.g., **ruido.**

TRIPHTHONGS

Triph.	Approximate sound
iai	Like *ya* in English *yard* combined with the *i* in *fight*, e.g., **estudiáis.**
iei	Like the English word *yea*, e.g., **estudiéis.**
uai, uay	Like *wi* in English *wide*, e.g., **averiguáis, guay.**
uei, uey	Like *wei* in English *weigh*, e.g., **amortigüéis.**

CONSONANTS

Letter	Approximate sound
b	Generally like the English *b* in *boat, bring, obsolete*, when it is at the beginning of a word or preceded by *m*, e.g., **baile, bomba.** Between two vowels and when followed by *l* or *r*, it has a softer sound, almost like the English *v* but formed by pressing both lips together, e.g., **acaba, haber, cable.**
c	Before *a, o, u*, or a consonant, it sounds like the English *c* in *coal*, e.g., **casa, saco.** Before *e* or *i*, it is pronounced like the English *s* in *six* in American Spanish and like the English *th* in *thin* in Castillian Spanish, e.g., **cerdo, cine.** If a word contains two *c*s, the first is pronounced like *c* in *coal*, and the second like *s* or *th* accordingly, e.g., **acción.**
ch	Like *ch* in English *cheese* or *such*, e.g., **chato.**
d	Generally like *d* in English *dog* or *th* in English *this*, e.g., **dedo, digo.** When ending a syllable, it is pronounced like the English *th*, e.g., **usted.**
f	Like *f* in English *fine, life*, e.g., **final.**

Letter	Approximate sound
g	Before *a, o,* and *u;* the groups *ue* and *ui;* or a consonant, it sounds like *g* in English *gain,* e.g., **gato, guitar, digno.** Before *e* or *i,* like a strongly aspirated English *h,* e.g., **general.**
h	Always silent, e.g., **hoyo, historia.**
j	Like *h* in English *hat,* e.g., **joven, reja.**
k	Like *c* in English *coal,* e.g., **kilo.** It is found only in words of foreign origin.
l	Like *l* in English *lion,* e.g., **libro, límite.**
ll	In some parts of Spain and Spanish America, like the English *y* in *yet;* generally in Castillian Spanish, like the *lli* in English *million;* e.g., **castillo, silla.**
m	Like *m* in English *map,* e.g., **moneda, tomo.**
n	Like *n* in English *nine,* e.g., **nuevo, canto.**
ñ	Like *ni* in English *onion* or *ny* in English *canyon,* e.g., **cañón, paño.**
p	Like *p* in English *parent,* e.g., **pipa, pollo.**
q	Like *c* in English *coal.* This letter is only used in the combinations *que* and *qui* in which the *u* is silent, e.g., **queso, aquí.**
r	At the beginning of a word and when preceded by *l, n,* or *s,* it is strongly trilled, e.g., **roca.** In all other positions, it is pronounced with a single tap of the tongue, e.g., **era, padre.**
rr	Strongly trilled, e.g., **carro, arriba.**
s	Like *s* in English *so,* e.g., **cosa, das.**
t	Like *t* in English *tip* but generally softer, e.g., **toma.**
v	Like *v* in English *mauve,* but in many parts of Spain and the Americas, like the Spanish b, e.g., **variar.**
x	Generally like *x* in English *expand,* e.g., **examen.** Before a consonant, it is sometimes pronounced like *s* in English *so,* e.g., **excepción, extensión.** In the word **México,** and in other place names of that country, it is pronounced like the Spanish j.

Letter	Approximate sound
y	When used as a consonant between vowels or at the beginning of a word, like the y in English *yet*, e.g., **yate**, **yeso**, **hoyo**.
z	Like Spanish c when it precedes e or i, e.g., **azul**.

Español - Inglés

A

a *prep* **1** *(dirección)* to: **girar a la derecha**, to turn (to the) right. **2** *(destino)* to, towards. **3** *(distancia)* away. **4** *(lugar)* at, on. **5** *(tiempo)* at: **a los tres días**, three days later; **estamos a 30 de mayo**, it's the thirtieth of May. **6** *(modo, manera)*: **a ciegas**, blindly; **a pie**, on foot. **7** *(instrumento)*: **escrito a mano**, handwritten; **escrito a máquina**, typewritten. **8** *(precio)* a: **a 3 euros el kilo**, three euros a kilo. **9** *(medida)* at. **10** *(complemento directo, no se traduce)*: **vi a Juana**, I saw Juana. **11** *(complemento indirecto)* to: **te lo di a ti**, I gave it to you. **12** *verbo + a + inf*: **aprender a nadar**, to learn (how) to swim.

abadía *nf (edificio)* abbey.

abajo *adv* **1** *(situación)* below, down. **2** *(en una casa)* downstairs. **3** *(dirección)* down, downwards. • **hacia abajo** downwards.

abandonar *vt* **1** *(desamparar)* to abandon. **2** *(lugar)* to leave.

abanico *nm* fan.

abarrotado,-a *adj* packed.

abastecer *vt* to supply.

abastecimiento *nm* supply.

abatir *vt* **1** *(derribar)* to bring down. **2** *(matar)* to shoot.

abdomen *nm* abdomen.

abecedario *nm* alphabet.

abedul *nm* birch tree.

abeja *nf* bee.

abeto *nm* fir tree.

abierto,-a *adj* **1** *(puerta, boca, ojos)* open. **2** *(grifo)* on, running. **3** *(sincero)* frank.

abismo *nm* abyss.

abogado,-a *nm,f* lawyer.

abollar *vt* to dent.

abonado,-a *nm,f (a teléfono, revista)* subscriber; *(a teatro etc)* season-ticket holder.

abonar *vt* **1** *(pagar)* to pay. **2** *(tierra)* to fertilize. ▶ *vpr* **abonarse** *(a revista)* to subscribe; *(a teatro)* to buy a season ticket.

abono *nm* **1** *(pago)* payment. **2** *(para tierra)* fertilizer. **3** *(a revista)* subscription; *(a teatro, tren, etc)* season ticket.

aborrecer *vt* to abhor, hate.

aborto *nm (voluntario)* abortion; *(espontáneo)* miscarriage.

abrasar *vt (quemar)* to burn. ▶ *vi (comida, etc)* to be boiling hot.

abrazar *vt* to embrace.

abrazo *nm* hug, embrace.

abrebotellas *nm* bottle opener.

abrelatas *nm* GB tin opener; US can opener.

abreviatura *nf* abbreviation.
abridor *nm* opener.
abrigarse *vpr* to wrap oneself up.
abrigo *nm* coat, overcoat.
abril *nm* April.
abrir *vt* 1 *(gen)* to open. 2 *(luz)* to switch on, turn on. 3 *(grifo, gas)* to turn on.
abrochar(se) *vt-vpr* to do up, fasten: *abróchense los cinturones*, please fasten your seatbelts.
ábside *nm* apse.
absoluto,-a *adj* absolute. ● **en absoluto** not at all.
absolver *vt* to acquit.
absorber *vt* to absorb.
abstemio,-a *nm,f* teetotaller.
abstenerse *vpr* 1 *(en votación)* to abstain. 2 *(de hacer algo)* to refrain *(de,* from).
abstracto,-a *adj* abstract.
absurdo,-a *adj* absurd.
abuchear *vt* to boo.
abuela *nf* grandmother.
abuelo *nm* grandfather. ► *nm pl* **abuelos** grandparents.
abultar *vi* to be bulky.
abundancia *nf* abundance, plenty.
abundante *adj* abundant, plentiful.
aburrido,-a *adj* 1 *(con ser)* boring, tedious: *es un libro muy aburrido*, it's a very boring book. 2 *(con estar)* bored: *estoy aburrido*, I'm bored.

aburrir *vt* to bore. ► *vpr* **aburrirse** to get bored.
abusar *vi* **abusar de** 1 *(persona)* to take advantage of; *(autoridad, paciencia)* to abuse. 2 *(sexualmente)* to sexually abuse.
abuso *nm* 1 *(uso excesivo)* abuse, misuse. 2 *(injusticia)* injustice.
acá *adv (lugar)* here, over here: *de acá para allá*, to and fro, up and down.
acabar *vt* 1 *(gen)* to finish. 2 *(consumir)* to use up, run out of. ► *vi* **acabar por** + *inf* **acabar** + *ger* to end up: *acabarás comprando el vestido*, you'll end up buying the dress. ► *vpr* **acabarse** *(terminarse)* to end, finish; *(no quedar)* to run out. ● **acabar con** to destroy, put an end to; **acabar de** to have just.
acacia *nf* acacia.
academia *nf* 1 *(institución)* academy. 2 *(escuela)* school.
acampada *nf* camping.
acampar *vi* to camp.
acantilado *nm* cliff.
acariciar *vt (persona)* to caress, fondle; *(animal)* to stroke.
acaso *adv* 1 *(en preguntas)*: *¿acaso no me crees?*, don't you believe me? 2 *fml (quizá)* perhaps, maybe: *acaso necesite tu ayuda*, I might need your help. ● **por si acaso** just in case.

acatarrarse *vpr* to catch a cold.

acceder *vi* **1** *(consentir)* to consent, agree. **2** *(tener entrada)* to enter. **3** INFORM to access.

acceso *nm* **1** *(entrada)* access, entry. **2** *(carretera)* approach road.

accesorio *nm* accessory.

accidentado,-a *nm,f* casualty, accident victim.

accidente *nm* **1** *(percance)* accident. **2** *(geográfico)* feature. ▪ **accidente aéreo** plane crash; **accidente de coche** car crash.

acción *nf* **1** *(gen)* action. **2** *(acto)* act, deed. **3** *(en bolsa)* share.

accionar *vt* **1** *(manivela)* to pull. **2** *(pieza mecánica)* to operate; *(alarma etc)* to set off.

accionista *nmf* shareholder, stockholder.

acecho ▪ **al acecho** in wait.

aceite *nm* oil. ▪ **aceite de oliva** olive oil.

aceitera *nf* oil bottle.

aceituna *nf* olive. ▪ **aceituna rellena** stuffed olive.

acelerador *nm* accelerator.

acelerar *vt* to accelerate.

acelga *nf* chard.

acento *nm* **1** *(gráfico)* accent, written accent; *(tónico)* stress. **2** *(regional, etc)* accent.

acentuar *vt* **1** *(palabra, letra)* to accent. **2** *(resaltar)* to emphasize, stress.

aceptable *adj* acceptable.

aceptar *vt* to accept, receive.

acequia *nf* irrigation ditch.

acera *nf* GB pavement; US sidewalk.

acerca de *prep* about, concerning.

acercar *vt* to bring closer. ▶ *vpr* **acercarse** to come closer.

acero *nm* steel.

acertante *nmf* winner.

acertar *vt* **1** *(repuesta)* to get right. **2** *(adivinanza)* to guess.

achaque *nm* ailment.

acidez *nf* *(de fruta, vinagre)* sourness; *(en química)* acidity. ▪ **acidez de estómago** heartburn.

ácido,-a *adj* **1** *(sabor)* sharp, tart. **2** acidic. ▶ *nm* **ácido** acid.

acierto *nm* **1** *(solución correcta)* right answer. **2** *(decisión adecuada)* wise decision.

aclaración *nf* explanation.

aclarar *vt* **1** *(cabello, color)* to lighten. **2** *(enjuagar)* to rinse. **3** *(explicar)* to explain.

acogedor,-ra *adj* *(lugar)* cosy, warm.

acoger *vt* *(recibir)* to receive; *(invitado)* to welcome.

acomodador,-ra *nm,f* *(hombre)* usher; *(mujer)* usherette.

acomodarse *vpr* to make oneself comfortable.

acompañamiento *nm* *(guarnición)* accompaniment.

acompañante *nmf* companion.

acompañar *vt* (*ir con*) to go with, come with. • **le acompaño en el sentimiento** please accept my condolences.

aconsejar *vt* to advise.

acontecimiento *nm* event, happening.

acordar *vt* to agree. ► *vpr* **acordarse** to remember.

acordeón *nm* accordion.

acortar *vt* to shorten.

acostar *vpr* to go to bed.

acostumbrado,-a *adj* (*persona*) accustomed, used to. **2** (*hecho*) usual, customary.

acostumbrar(se) *vi-vpr*. • **acostumbrar a hacer algo** to be in the habit of doing STH. • **acostumbrarse a algo** to get used to STH.

acreedor,-ra *nm,f* creditor.

acrílico,-a *adj* acrylic.

acróbata *nmf* acrobat.

acta *nf* **1** (*de reunión*) minutes. **2** (*certificado*) certificate.

actitud *nf* attitude.

activar *vt* to activate.

actividad *nf* activity.

activo,-a *adj* active. ► *nm* **activo** assets.

acto *nm* **1** (*acción*) act. **2** (*ceremonia*) ceremony. **3** (*de obra teatral*) act. • **acto seguido** immediately afterwards; **en el acto** at once.

actor *nm* actor.

actriz *nf* actress.

actuación *nf* **1** (*interpretación*) performance. **2** (*comportamiento*) GB behaviour; US behavior.

actual *adj* **1** (*de este momento*) present, current. **2** (*moderno*) up-to-date.

actualidad *nf* **1** (*momento presente*) present time, present. **2** (*hechos*) current affairs.

actualizar *vt* **1** (*poner al día*) to bring up to date. **2** (*programa*) to upgrade; (*página de Internet*) to refresh.

actualmente *adv* (*hoy en día*) nowadays; (*ahora*) at present.

actuar *vi* (*gen*) to act; (*cantante, bailarín*) to perform.

acuarela *nf* GB watercolour; US watercolor.

acuario *nm* aquarium.

acuático,-a *adj* aquatic, water.

acudir *vi* (*ir*) to go; (*venir*) to come.

acueducto *nm* aqueduct.

acuerdo *nm* agreement. • **¡de acuerdo!** all right!, O.K.!; **estar de acuerdo** to agree.

acusación *nf* (*inculpación*) accusation; (*en derecho*) charge.

acusar *vt* (*culpar*) to accuse; (*en derecho*) to charge.

acústico,-a *adj* acoustic.

adaptación *nf* adaptation.

adaptar(se) *vt-vpr* to adapt.

adecuado,-a *adj* adequate, suitable.

adelantado,-a *adj* **1** *(desarrollado)* developed. **2** *(reloj)* fast. • **por adelantado** in advance.

adelantamiento *nm* overtaking.

adelantar *vt* **1** *(mover adelante)* to move forward. **2** *(reloj)* to put forward. **3** *(pasar adelante)* to pass; *(vehículo)* to overtake. **4** *(dinero)* to pay in advance. ▶ *vi (reloj)* to be fast. ▶ *vpr* **adelantarse 1** *(llegar temprano)* to be early. **2** *(reloj)* to gain, be fast.

adelante *adv* forward. ▶ *interj* come in! • **en adelante** from now on; **hacia adelante** forwards; **más adelante** later on.

adelanto *nm* **1** *(avance)* advance. **2** advance.

adelgazar *vi (perder peso)* to lose weight; *(con régimen)* to slim.

además *adv* **1** *(por añadidura)* besides. **2** *(también)* also. • **además de** besides.

adentro *adv* inside.

aderezar *vt (condimentar)* to season; *(ensalada)* to dress.

adicto,-a *nm,f* addict.

adiós *nm* goodbye.

adivinanza *nf* riddle.

adivinar *vt* to guess.

adjetivo *nm* adjective.

adjudicar *vt* to award. ▶ *vpr* **adjudicarse** *(victoria)* to win.

administración *nf* **1** *(de empresa)* administration, management. **2** *(de medicamento)* administering. ■ **administración de lotería** lottery office.

administrar *vt* **1** *(organizar)* to manage. **2** *(proporcionar)* to give.

administrativo,-a *nm,f (funcionario)* official; *(de empresa, banco)* office worker.

admirable *adj* admirable.

admiración *nf* **1** *(estima)* admiration. **2** *(signo)* exclamation mark.

admirar *vt* **1** *(estimar)* to admire. **2** *(sorprender)* to amaze, surprise.

admisión *nf* admission. • **"Reservado el derecho de admisión"** "The management reserves the right to refuse admission".

admitir *vt* **1** *(dar entrada a, reconocer)* to admit. **2** *(aceptar)* to accept.

adobar *vt* to marinate.

adolescente *adj-nmf* adolescent.

adonde *adv* where.

adónde *adv* where.

adoptar *vt* to adopt.

adoquín *nm (piedra redonda)* cobble; *(piedra cuadrada)* paving stone.

adorar *vt* to adore, worship.

adornar *vt* to decorate.

adorno *nm* decoration. • **de adorno** decorative.

adosado,-a *adj:* **casas adosadas**, semidetached houses.

adquirir *vt (comprar)* to buy, get.

adrede *adv* on purpose.

aduana *nf* customs *pl*.

aduanero,-a *nm,f* customs officer.

adulto,-a *adj-nm,f* adult.

adverbio *nm* adverb.

adversario,-a *nm,f* adversary, opponent.

advertencia *nf* 1 *(aviso)* warning. 2 *(consejo)* piece of advice.

advertir *vt* 1 *(avisar)* to warn. 2 *(aconsejar)* to advise.

aéreo,-a *adj* 1 *(vista, fotografía)* aerial. 2 *(tráfico)* air.

aeropuerto *nm* airport.

aerosol *nm* aerosol, spray.

afán *nm* 1 *(anhelo)* eagerness. 2 *(esfuerzo)* hard work.

afección *nf (enfermedad)* complaint, illness.

afectar *vt* 1 *(concernir)* to affect. 2 *(impresionar)* to move.

afecto *nm* affection.

afeitado *nm* shave, shaving.

afeitar(se) *vt-vpr* to shave.

afición *nf* 1 *(inclinación)* liking. 2 *(pasatiempo)* hobby.

aficionado,-a *adj* 1 *(entusiasta)* keen, fond. 2 *(no profesional)* amateur. ▶ *nm,f* 1 *(entusiasta)*, fan, enthusiast. 2 *(no profesional)* amateur.

aficionarse *vpr* to become fond *(de, of)*.

afilar *vt* to sharpen.

afinar *vt* 1 *(piano, etc)* to tune. 2 *(puntería)* to sharpen.

afirmación *nf* statement, assertion.

afirmar *vt (aseverar)* to state, say.

aflojar *vt (soltar)* to loosen.

afluente *nm* tributary.

afonía *nf* loss of voice.

afónico,-a *adj* hoarse. • **estar afónico,-a** to have lost one's voice.

afortunado,-a *adj* lucky, fortunate.

África *nf* Africa.

africano,-a *adj-nm,f* African.

afrontar *vt* to face up to.

afuera *adv* outside. ▶ *nf pl* **afueras** outskirts.

agacharse *vpr* 1 *(acuclillarse)* to crouch down; *(inclinarse)* to bend down.

agallas *nf (de pez)* gills.

agarrado,-a *adj* stingy. • **bailar agarrado** to dance cheek to cheek.

agarrar *vt (coger fuerte)* to grab; *(sujetar)* to hold. ▶ *vpr* **agarrarse** to hold on, cling *(a, to)*.

agencia *nf* agency. ▪ **agencia de viajes** travel agency; **agencia inmobiliaria** estate agent's.

agenda *nf* 1 *(libro)* diary. 2 *(de direcciones)* address book.

agente *nmf* agent. ■ **agente de policía** police officer.

ágil *adj* agile.

agitar *vt (líquido)* to shake.

aglomeración *nf (acumulación)* agglomeration; *(de gente)* crowd.

agobiar *vt* to overwhelm. ► *vpr* **agobiarse** to get worked up.

agonía *nf (sufrimiento)* agony, grief; *(de moribundo)* death throes.

agosto *nm* August.

agotado,-a *adj* **1** *(cansado)* exhausted. **2** *(libro)* out of print; *(mercancía)* sold out.

agotar *vt* to exhaust. ► *vpr* **agotarse** **1** *(cansarse)* to become exhausted. **2** *(acabarse)* to run out; *(existencias)* to be sold out.

agradable *adj* nice, pleasant.

agradar *vi* to please.

agradecer *vt* to thank.

agradecimiento *nm* gratitude, thankfulness.

agrandar *vt* to enlarge.

agravante *nm & nf* **1** *(gen)* added difficulty. **2** JUR aggravating circumstance.

agravarse *vpr* to get worse.

agredir *vt* to attack.

agregar *vt* to add.

agresión *nf* aggression.

agresivo,-a *adj* aggressive.

agresor,-ra *nm,f* aggressor.

agrícola *adj* agricultural.

agricultor,-ra *nm,f* farmer.

agricultura *nf* agriculture, farming.

agridulce *adj* **1** *(gen)* bittersweet. **2** *(salsa)* sweet and sour.

agrio,-a *adj* sour.

agruparse *vpr* **1** *(congregarse)* to group together. **2** *(asociarse)* to associate.

agua *nf* water. ■ **agua con gas** sparkling water; **agua dulce** fresh water; **agua mineral** mineral water; **agua oxigenada** hydrogen peroxide; **agua potable** drinking water; **agua salada** salt water; **agua sin gas** still water; **aguas termales** thermal waters.

aguacate *nm* avocado, avocado pear.

aguacero *nm* downpour.

aguantar *vt* **1** *(sostener)* to hold; *(peso)* to support, bear. **2** *(sufrir - frases afirmativas)* to put up with; *(- frases negativas)* to stand: **no sé cómo aguanta a su marido**, I don't know how she puts up with her husband; **no aguanto a gente como él**, I can't stand people like him. **3** *(contener - respiración)* to hold; *(- risa, lágrimas)* to hold back. ► *vpr* **aguantarse** *(resignarse)*: **tendrás que aguantarte**, you'll have to put up with it.

aguardar vt-vi to wait (for), await.

aguardiente nm liquor, brandy.

aguarrás nm turpentine.

agudo,-a adj 1 (afilado) sharp. 2 (dolor, acento, ángulo) acute. 3 (ingenioso) witty. 4 (voz) high-pitched.

aguijón nm 1 (de animal) sting. 2 (de planta) thorn, prickle.

águila nf eagle.

aguja nf 1 (de coser, jeringuilla) needle. 2 (de reloj) hand. 3 (de tocadiscos) stylus. 4 (de torre, iglesia) spire, steeple. 5 (de tren) GB point; US switch.

agujero nm hole.

agujetas nf pl stiffness.

ahí adv there. • **por ahí** 1 (lugar) round there. 2 (aproximadamente) more or less.

ahogar vt to drown. ▶ vpr **ahogarse** 1 (en agua) to be drowned. 2 (asfixiarse) to choke.

ahora adv 1 (en este momento) now. 2 (hace un momento) a moment ago. 3 (dentro de un momento) in a minute, shortly. • **ahora bien** however; **ahora mismo** 1 (en este momento) right now. 2 (enseguida) right away; **de ahora en adelante** from now on; **hasta ahora** until now, so far; **por ahora** for the time being.

ahorcar vt to hang.

ahorrar vt to save.

ahorros nm pl savings.

ahumado,-a adj smoked; (bacon) smoky.

aire nm 1 (fluido) air. 2 (viento) wind. 3 (aspecto) air, appearance. • **al aire libre** in the open air, outdoors; **tomar el aire** to get some fresh air. ▪ **aire acondicionado** air conditioning.

aislamiento nm 1 (acción, estado) isolation. 2 (eléctrica) insulation.

aislante adj insulating. ▶ nm insulator.

aislar vt 1 (apartar) to isolate. 2 (eléctricamente) to insulate.

ajedrez nm (juego) chess; (tablero y piezas) chess set.

ajeno,-a adj (de otro) another's.

ajillo • **al ajillo** with garlic.

ajo nm garlic.

ajustado,-a adj 1 (ropa) tight, close-fitting. 2 (resultado, victoria) close.

ajustar vt (adaptar) to adjust; (uso técnico) to fit.

al contr → a.

ala nf wing. ▪ **ala delta** hang glider.

alabar vt to praise.

alacrán nm scorpion.

alambre nm wire.

alameda nf 1 (bosque) poplar grove. 2 (paseo) avenue.

álamo nm poplar.

alargar vt 1 (prenda) to lengthen; *(cuerda)* to stretch. **2** *(prolongar)* to prolong, extend. **3** *(brazo, mano)* to stretch out.

alarma *nf* alarm. ■ **alarma antirrobo 1** *(para casa)* burglar alarm. **2** *(para coche)* car alarm; **alarma contra incendios** fire alarm.

alba *nf* dawn, daybreak.

albañil *nm* bricklayer.

albaricoque *nm* apricot.

albergar *vt* **1** *(alojar)* to put up. **2** *(esperanzas)* to cherish. **3** *(duda)* GB to harbour; US to harbour.

albergue *nm* hostel. ■ **albergue juvenil** youth hostel.

albóndiga *nf* meatball.

albornoz *nm* bathrobe.

alborotar *vt* **1** *(agitar)* to agitate, excite. **2** *(sublevar)* to incite to rebel.

albufera *nf* lagoon.

álbum *nm* album.

alcachofa *nf* artichoke.

alcalde *nm* mayor.

alcaldesa *nf* mayoress.

alcaldía *nf* **1** *(cargo)* mayorship. **2** *(oficina)* mayor's office.

alcance *nm* **1** *(de persona)* reach: *fuera del alcance de los niños,* out of children's reach. **2** *(de arma, emisora)* range. **3** *(trascendencia)* scope, importance.

alcantarilla *nf* *(cloaca)* sewer; *(boca)* drain.

alcanzar *vt* **1** *(lugar, edad, temperatura)* to reach; *(persona)* to catch up with. **2** *(conseguir)* to attain, achieve.

alcaparra *nf* caper.

alcázar *nm* fortress.

alcoba *nf* bedroom.

alcohol *nm* alcohol. ● **sin alcohol** non-alcoholic.

alcohólico,-a *adj-nm,f* alcoholic.

alcornoque *nm* cork oak.

aldaba *nf* **1** *(llamador)* knocker. **2** *(pestillo)* latch.

aldea *nf* hamlet, small village.

aleación *nf* alloy.

alegrar *vt* to make happy. ► *vpr* **alegrarse** to be happy, be pleased.

alegre *adj* **1** *(persona - contenta)* happy; *(- borracha)* tipsy. **2** *(color)* bright.

alegría *nf* happiness.

alejar *vt* to move away. ► *vpr* **alejarse** to go away, move away.

alemán,-ana *adj-nm,f* German. ► *nm* **alemán** *(idioma)* German.

Alemania *nf* Germany.

alergia *nf* allergy.

alérgico,-a *adj* allergic.

alero *nm* **1** *(del tejado)* eaves. **2** *(de baloncesto)* forward.

alerta *adv* on the alert. ► *nf* alert.

aleta *nf* fin.

alfabeto *nm* alphabet.
alfalfa *nf* alfalfa, lucerne.
alfarería *nf* pottery.
alfil *nm* bishop.
alfiler *nm* **1** *(en costura)* pin. **2** *(joya)* brooch.
alfombra *nf (grande)* carpet; *(pequeña)* rug.
alga *nf* alga; *(marina)* seaweed; *(de agua dulce)* weed.
álgebra *nf* algebra.
algo *pron (en frases afirmativas)* something; *(en frases interrogativas)* anything: *vamos a tomar algo*, let's have something to drink; *¿hay algo que no entiendas?*, is there anything you don't understand? ► *adv (un poco)* a bit, a little.
• **algo es algo** something is better than nothing.
algodón *nm* cotton. ■ **algodón hidrófilo** cotton wool.
alguien *pron (en frases afirmativas)* somebody, someone; *(en frases interrogativas y negativas)* anybody, anyone: *alguien se lo habrá olvidado*, somebody must have left it behind; *¿conoces alguien que hable japonés?*, do you know anyone who speaks Japanese?
algún *adj* → alguno,-a.
alguno,-a *adj (en frases afirmativas)* some; *(en frases interrogativas)* any; *(en frases negativas)* no, not ... any: *me he*

comprado *algunos libros*, I've bought some books; *¿tienes alguna idea mejor?*, do you have any better idea?; *sin éxito alguno*, with no success at all; *no vino persona alguna*, nobody came. ► *pron (en frases afirmativas)* someone, somebody; *(en frases interrogativas)* anybody: *hubo alguno que se quejó*, there was somebody who complained; *puedes quedarte con alguna de estas fotos*, you can keep some of those pictures; *¿alguno sabe la respuesta?*, does anyone know the answer?
alhaja *nf* jewel.
aliado,-a *nm,f* ally.
alianza *nf* **1** *(pacto)* alliance. **2** *(anillo)* wedding ring.
aliarse *vpr* to form an alliance.
alicates *nm pl* pliers.
aliciente *nm* incentive, inducement.
aliento *nm* breath. • **sin aliento** breathless.
alimentación *nf* **1** *(acción)* feeding. **2** *(comida)* food; *(dieta)* diet.
alimentar *vt* to feed. ► *vi (servir de alimento)* to be nutritious, be nourishing. ► *vpr* **alimentarse de** to live on.
alimento *nm* food.
aliñar *vt (ensalada)* to dress; *(guiso)* to season.

aliño *nm* *(de ensalada)* dressing; *(de guiso)* seasoning.

alisar *vt* to smooth.

alistarse *vpr* to enlist.

aliviar *vt* 1 *(enfermedad, dolor)* to relieve. 2 *(consolar)* to comfort.

alivio *nm* relief.

allá *adv* there.

allí *adv* there. • **por allí** that way.

alma *nf* soul.

almacén *nm* warehouse. ► *nm pl* **(grandes) almacenes** department store.

almacenar *vt* to store.

almeja *nf* clam.

almendra *nf* almond. ■ **almendra garapiñada** sugared almond.

almendro *nm* almond tree.

almíbar *nm* syrup.

almidón *nm* starch.

almirante *nm* admiral.

almohada *nf* pillow.

almohadón *nm* cushion.

almorzar *vi* to have lunch.

almuerzo *nm* lunch.

alojamiento *nm* lodging, accommodation.

alojarse *vpr* to stay.

alpargata *nf* rope-soled sandal, espadrille.

alpinismo *nm* mountaineering.

alpinista *nmf* mountaineer, mountain climber.

alpiste *nm* birdseed.

alquilar *vt* 1 *(dar en alquiler - casa)* to rent out, GB let; *(- coche, bicicleta)* to hire, rent; *(- aparato)* to rent. 2 *(tomar en alquiler - casa)* to rent; *(- coche, bicicleta)* to hire, rent.

alquiler *nm* 1 *(cesión - de casa)* renting; GB letting; *(- de coche etc.)* hire, rental; *(- de aparato)* rental. 2 *(cuota - de casa)* rent; *(- de coche etc.)* hire charge; *(- de aparato)* rental.

alquitrán *nm* tar.

alrededor *adv* *(gen)* around; *(cantidad)* around, about: *alrededor de veinte*, about twenty. ► *nm pl* **alrededores** surrounding area *sing*.

alta *nf* *(a un enfermo)* discharge.

altar *nm* altar.

altavoz *nm* loudspeaker.

alterar *vt* to alter, change. ► *vpr* **alterarse** *(enfadarse)* to lose one's temper.

altercado *nm* 1 *(discusión)* argument. 2 *(disturbio)* disturbance.

alternar *vt-vi* *(sucederse)* to alternate. ► *vi* *(relacionarse)* to socialize, mix.

alternativo,-a *adj* alternative.

alteza *nf* Highness.

altibajos *nm pl* ups and downs.

altillo *nm* *(armario)* cupboard.

altitud *nf* height, altitude.

alto,-a *adj* 1 *(gen)* high. 2 *(persona, edificio, árbol)* tall. 3 *(so-*

nido, voz) loud ► *nm* **alto 1**
(*altura*): **Pepe mide dos metros
de alto**, Pepe's two metres tall.
2 (*elevación*) height, hillock.
3 (*parada*) halt, stop. ► *adv* **1**
(*volar, subir*) high. **2** (*hablar*)
loud, loudly.
altura *nf* **1** (*gen*) height. **2**
(*persona*) tall: **mide dos metros de altura**, he's two metres tall. **3** (*cosa*) high: **mide
dos metros de altura**, it's two
metres high. **4** (*altitud*) altitude. • **a la altura de** next to: *a
la altura de la catedral*, next
to the cathedral.
alubia *nf* bean.
alud *nm* avalanche.
alumbrado *nm* lighting.
alumbrar *vt* (*iluminar - calles,
habitación*) to light; (*- monumento, estadio*) to light up, illuminate.
aluminio *nm* GB aluminium;
US aluminum.
alumno,-a *nm,f* (*de colegio*)
pupil; (*de universidad*) student.
alza *nf* rise, increase.
alzar *vt* (*levantar - mano, cabeza*) to raise, lift; (*voz*) to raise.
ama *nf*. ▪ **ama de casa** housewife.
amabilidad *nf* kindness.
amable *adj* kind, nice.
amainar *vi* to die down.
amanecer *vi* **1** (*hacerse de día*)
to dawn. **2** (*clarear*) to get
light. ► *nm* dawn, daybreak.

amante *nmf* lover.
amapola *nf* poppy.
amar *vt* to love.
amargo,-a *adj* bitter.
amarillo,-a *adj* yellow. ► *nm*
amarillo yellow.
amarra *nf* mooring cable. •
soltar amarras to cast off.
amasar *vt* **1** (*masa*) to knead;
(*cemento*) to mix. **2** (*dinero*) to
amass.
amazona *nf* horsewoman.
ámbar *nm* amber.
ambición *nf* ambition.
ambicioso,-a *adj* ambitious.
ambiental *adj* **1** (*contaminación, impacto*) environmental.
2 (*música*) background.
ambiente *nm* **1** (*aire*) air,
atmosphere. **2** (*entorno*) environment; (*de casa, ciudad, época*) atmosphere. **3** (*animación*)
life, atmosphere.
ambiguo,-a *adj* ambiguous.
ambos,-as *adj-pron* both.
ambulancia *nf* ambulance.
ambulante *adj* itinerant, travelling.
ambulatorio *nm* surgery,
clinic.
amenaza *nf* threat. ▪ **amenaza de bomba** bomb scare.
amenazar *vt-vi* to threaten.
ameno,-a *adj* (*agradable*)
pleasant; (*entretenido*) entertaining.
América *nf* America.
americana *nf* jacket.

americano,-a *adj-nm,f* American.

ametralladora *nf* machine gun.

amígdala *nf* tonsil.

amigo,-a *nm,f* friend.

amistad *nf* friendship.

amnesia *nf* amnesia.

amo *nm* 1 *(señor)* master. 2 *(dueño)* owner.

amoniaco *nm* ammonia.

amontonar *vt* to pile up.

amor *nm* love. • **hacer el amor** to make love. ■ **amor propio** self-esteem.

amortiguador *nm* shock absorber.

amparar *vt* to protect, shelter. ► *vpr* **ampararse en** *(una ley)* to seek protection in.

ampliación *nf* 1 *(de edificio, plazo)* extension. 2 *(de negocio, mercado)* expansion. 3 *(de fotografía)* enlargement.

ampliar *vt* 1 *(edificio, plazo)* to extend. 2 *(negocio, mercado)* to expand. 3 *(fotografía)* to enlarge, blow up.

amplio,-a *adj* 1 *(espacioso)* roomy, spacious. 2 *(margen, gama)* wide; *(mayoría)* large.

ampolla *nf (en la piel)* blister.

amueblar *vt* to furnish.

amuleto *nm* charm, amulet.

analfabeto,-a *adj-nm,f* illiterate.

analgésico,-a *adj* analgesic. ► *nm* **analgésico** analgesic.

análisis *nm* analysis. ■ **análisis de sangre** blood test.

analizar *vt* GB to analyse; US analyze.

anarquía *nf* anarchy.

anatomía *nf* anatomy.

anca *nf* haunch.

ancho,-a *adj* 1 *(calle, cama, habitación)* wide; *(espalda, cara)* broad. 2 *(prenda)* loose, loose-fitting. ► *nm* **ancho** breadth, width. • **de ancho**: *tres metros de ancho*, three metres wide.

anchoa *nf* anchovy.

anchura *nf* breadth, width.

anciano,-a *nm,f (hombre)* elderly man; *(mujer)* elderly woman.

ancla *nf* anchor.

anclar *vi* to anchor.

andamio *nm* scaffolding.

andar *vi* 1 *(caminar)* to walk. 2 *(funcionar)* to work, go.

andén *nm* platform.

anécdota *nf* anecdote.

anemia *nf* GB anaemia; US anemia.

anestesia *nf* GB anaesthesia; US anesthesia.

anfibio *nm* amphibian.

anfitrión,-ona *nm,f (hombre)* host; *(mujer)* hostess.

ángel *nm* angel.

angina *nf* angina. • **tener anginas** to have a sore throat. ■ **angina de pecho** angina pectoris.

anguila *nf* eel.

angula *nf* elver.

ángulo *nm* 1 (*geometría*) angle. 2 (*rincón*) corner.

angustia *nf* anguish, distress.

anilla *nf* ring.

anillo *nm* ring.

animación *nf* liveliness.

animado,-a *adj* 1 (*persona*) cheerful. 2 (*situación*) animated, lively. 3 (*calle*) full of people.

animal *adj* animal. ► *nm* 1 (*ser vivo*) animal. 2 (*persona bruta*) blockhead. ■ **animal doméstico** 1 (*de granja*) domestic animal. 2 (*de compañía*) pet.

animar *vt* 1 (*alentar*) to encourage. 2 (*alegrar - persona*) to cheer up; (*- fiesta, reunión*) to liven up. ► *vpr* **animarse** 1 (*alegrarse - persona*) to cheer up; (*- fiesta, reunión*) to liven up. 2 (*decidirse*) to make up one's mind.

ánimo *nm* 1 (*estado emocional*) spirits. 2 (*aliento*) encouragement.

anís *nm* 1 (*planta*) anise. 2 (*bebida*) anisette.

aniversario *nm* anniversary.

ano *nm* anus.

anoche *adv* last night.

anochecer *vi* to get dark. ► *nm* nightfall, dusk.

anónimo,-a *adj* anonymous.

anorak *nm* anorak.

anormal *adj* abnormal.

anotar *vt* (*apuntar*) to make a note of, take down.

ansia *nf* (*deseo*) longing.

ansiedad *nf* anxiety.

ante¹ *prep* 1 (*delante de*) before. 2 (*frente a*) in the face of. ● **ante todo** 1 (*primero*) first of all. 2 (*por encima de*) above all.

ante² *nm* (*piel*) suede.

anteayer *adv* the day before yesterday.

antebrazo *nm* forearm.

antelación *nf*. ● **con antelación** in advance.

antemano *adv*. ● **de antemano** beforehand, in advance.

antena *nf* 1 (*de aparato*) aerial. 2 (*de animal*) antenna. ■ **antena parabólica** satellite dish.

antepasado *nm* ancestor.

anterior *adj* previous.

antes *adv* 1 (*en el tiempo - previamente*) before; (*- más temprano*) earlier: **te lo he dicho antes**, I told you earlier. 2 (*en el espacio*) before. ● **antes de** before.

antibiótico *nm* antibiotic.

anticiclón *nm* anticyclone, high pressure area.

anticiparse *vpr* 1 (*suceder antes*) to be early. 2 (*adelantarse*) to beat to it.

anticipo *nm* advance.

anticonceptivo *nm* contraceptive.

anticongelante *adj-nm* antifreeze.

anticuario *nm* antiquary, antiques dealer.

antídoto *nm* antidote.

antigüedad *nf* 1 *(período)* antiquity. 2 *(edad)*: *una ciudad de tres mil años de antigüedad*, a city which is three thousand years old. ▶ *nf pl* **antigüedades** antiques.

antiguo,-a *adj* 1 *(muy viejo)* ancient. 2 *(viejo)* old. 3 *(anterior)* old, former: *mi antiguo jefe*, my former boss.

antipatía *nf* antipathy, dislike.

antipático,-a *adj* unpleasant.

antirrobo *adj* antitheft.

antivirus *nm* antivirus system.

antojo *nm* 1 *(capricho)* whim; *(de embarazada)* craving. 2 *(en la piel)* birthmark.

antorcha *nf* torch.

anual *adj* annual, yearly.

anular¹ *nm* ring finger.

anular² *vt* to annul, cancel.

anunciar *vt* 1 *(notificar)* to announce. 2 *(hacer publicidad de)* to advertise.

anuncio *nm* 1 *(en periódico)* advertisement, advert, ad; *(en televisión, radio)* advertisement, advert, commercial. 2 *(notificación)* announcement.

anzuelo *nm* hook.

añadir *vt* to add.

añejo,-a *adj (vino)* old.

año *nm* year. • **tener… años** to be… years old: *¿cuántos años tienes?*, how old are you? ■ **Año Nuevo** New Year.

aorta *nf* aorta.

apagar *vt* 1 *(fuego)* to extinguish, put out. 2 *(luz)* to turn off. 3 *(aparato)* to turn off, switch off. ▶ *vpr* **apagarse** *(luz)* to go out.

apagón *nm* power cut, blackout.

aparato *nm* 1 *(máquina)* machine; *(dispositivo)* device. 2 *(electrodoméstico)* appliance; *(televisor, radio)* set. 3 *(de gimnasio)* piece of apparatus. 4 *(para los dientes)* brace; *(audífono)* hearing aid. 5 *(conjunto de órganos)* system.

aparcamiento *nm* 1 *(acción)* parking. 2 *(lugar)* GB car park; US parking lot; *(en la calle)* place to park.

aparcar *vt-vi* to park.

aparecer *vi* 1 *(gen)* to appear; *(objeto perdido)* to turn up. 2 *(dejarse ver)* to show up, turn up.

apariencia *nf* appearance.

apartado,-a *adj* 1 *(lejano)* distant. 2 *(aislado)* isolated, remote. ▶ *nm* **apartado** section. ■ **apartado de correos** post office box.

apartamento *nm* apartment.

apartar vt 1 (alejar) to move away. 2 (poner a un lado) to set aside. ► vpr **apartarse** (de un lugar) to move away.

aparte adv 1 (a un lado) aside, to one side; (por separado) apart, separately. 2 (además) besides.

apasionante adj exciting, fascinating.

apasionar vt to excite, fascinate.

apeadero nm (de trenes) halt.

apearse vpr (de caballo) to dismount; (de vehículo) to get off.

apellidarse vpr to be called: *¿cómo se apellida usted?*, what's your surname?

apellido nm surname, family name.

apenas adv 1 (casi no) hardly, scarcely. 2 (casi nunca) hardly ever.

apéndice nm appendix.

apendicitis nf appendicitis.

aperitivo nm 1 (bebida) aperitif. 2 (comida) appetizer.

apertura nf (gen) opening; (de temporada, curso académico) start, beginning.

apetecer vi: *me apetece un café*, I feel like a coffee, I fancy a coffee; *¿te apetece ir a la playa?*, do you fancy going to the beach?

apetito nm appetite.

apetitoso,-a adj appetizing.

apio nm celery.

apisonadora nf steamroller.

aplanar vt to level, make even.

aplastar vt to squash, flatten.

aplaudir vt to clap, applaud.

aplauso nm applause.

aplazar vt (reunión, acto) to postpone, put off; (pago) to defer.

aplicación nf application.

aplicado,-a adj 1 (ciencia) applied. 2 (estudiante) studious, diligent.

aplicar vt 1 (extender) to apply. 2 (poner en práctica) to put into practice.

apoderarse vpr to take possession.

apodo nm nickname.

aportar vt to contribute.

aposento nm 1 (cuarto) room. 2 (hospedaje) lodgings.

aposta adv on purpose.

apostar vt-vi to bet.

apóstol nm apostle.

apoyar vt 1 (reclinar) to rest, lean. 2 (basar) to base, found. 3 (defender) to back, support. ► vpr **apoyarse** (basarse) to be based.

apoyo nm support.

apreciar vt 1 (sentir aprecio por) to regard highly. 2 (valorar) to appreciate.

aprecio nm esteem, regard.

aprender vt-vi to learn.

aprendizaje nm learning.

apresurar(se) *vt-vpr* to hurry.
apretar *vt* **1** *(estrechar)* to squeeze. **2** *(tornillo, nudo)* to tighten. **3** *(pulsar - botón)* to press; *(- gatillo)* to pull.
aprieto *nm* fix, awkward situation.
aprisa *adv* quickly.
aprobación *nf (gen)* approval; *(de ley)* passing.
aprobado *nm* pass.
aprobar *vt* **1** *(decisión, plan, préstamo)* to approve. **2** *(comportamiento)* to approve of. **3** *(examen, ley)* to pass.
aprovechar *vt* **1** *(sacar provecho de)* to make good use of. **2** *(emplear)* to use. ▶ *vpr* **aprovecharse** to take advantage. • **¡que aproveche!** enjoy your meal!
aproximarse *vpr* to approach, draw near.
apto,-a *adj* **1** *(apropiado)* suitable. **2** *(capaz)* capable, able. • **apta para todos los públicos** GB U-certificate; US rated G; **no apta** for adults only.
apuesta *nf* bet.
apuesto,-a *adj* good-looking.
apuntar *vt* **1** *(señalar)* to point at. **2** *(arma)* to aim. **3** *(anotar)* to note down, make a note of. ▶ *vt-vpr* **apuntar(se)** *(inscribir - en curso)* GB to enrol; US to enroll; *(- en lista)* to put down.
apuntes *nm pl (de clase)* notes.
apuñalar *vt* to stab.

apurar *vt (terminar)* to finish up. ▶ *vpr* **apurarse** to worry.
apuro *nm* tight spot.
aquel,-lla *adj* that.
aquél,-lla *pron* that one.
aquello *pron*: **aquello fue lo que más me gustó**, that was what I liked the most; **¿te acuerdas de aquello que me dijiste?**, do you remember what you told me?
aquí *adv* **1** *(lugar)* here. **2** *(tiempo)* now. • **por aquí por favor** this way please.
árabe *adj (gen)* Arab; *(de Arabia)* Arabian; *(alfabeto, número)* Arabic. ▶ *nmf (persona)* Arab; *(de Arabia)* Arabian. ▶ *nm (idioma)* Arabic.
arado *nm* GB plough; US plow.
araña *nf (animal)* spider.
arañar(se) *vt-vpr* to scratch.
arañazo *nm* scratch.
arar *vt* GB to plough; US to plow.
arbitrar *vt (fútbol, rugby, boxeo)* to referee; *(tenis)* to umpire.
árbitro *nm (en fútbol, rugby, boxeo)* referee; *(en tenis)* umpire.
árbol *nm* tree.
arbusto *nm* shrub, bush.
arca *nf* chest.
arcada *nf* **1** *(de puente)* arcade. **2** *(al vomitar)*: **me dieron arcadas**, I retched.
arcaico,-a *adj* archaic.
archipiélago *nm* archipelago.

archivar vt 1 (ordenar) to file.
2 INFORM to save.

archivo nm 1 (documento) file.
2 (lugar) archive. ■ **archivo
adjunto** INFORM attachment.

arcilla nf clay.

arco nm 1 ARQ arch. 2 MAT arc.
3 (de violín, flecha) bow. ■ **arco
iris** rainbow.

arder vi 1 (quemarse) to burn.
2 (estar muy caliente) to be
boiling hot.

ardilla nf squirrel.

ardor nm GB ardour; US ardor.
■ **ardor de estómago** heartburn.

área nf 1 (zona, medida) area.
2 (en fútbol) penalty area.

arena nf sand. ■ **arenas mo-
vedizas** quicksand.

arenque nm herring.

Argentina nf Argentina, the
Argentine.

argentino,-a adj-nm,f Argen-
tinian.

argot nm 1 (popular) slang. 2
(técnico) jargon.

argumento nm 1 (razón) argument. 2 (de novela, obra,
etc) plot.

árido,-a adj 1 (tierra) arid, dry.
2 (texto, tema) dry.

arista nf edge.

aristócrata nmf aristocrat.

aritmética nf arithmetic.

arma nf weapon, arm. ■ **arma
blanca** knife; **arma de fuego**
firearm.

armada nf navy.

armadura nf 1 (defensa) GB armour; US armor. 2 (armazón)
framework.

armamento nm armament.

armar vt (proveer de armas)
to arm. 2 (ruido, alboroto) to
make.

armario nm (de cocina) cupboard; (de ropa) GB wardrobe;
US closet.

armonía nf harmony.

armónica nf harmonica,
mouth organ.

aro nm hoop, ring.

aroma nm aroma; (del vino)
bouquet.

arpa nf harp.

arpón nm harpoon.

arqueología nf GB archaeology; US archeology.

arquitecto,-a nm,f architect.

arquitectura nf architecture.

arrancar vt 1 (planta) to up-
root, pull up. 2 (página) to tear
out. ► vi 1 (coche) to start. 2
(ordenador) to boot.

arranque nm 1 (de motor) starting mechanism: **el motor de
arranque**, the starter motor. 2
(arrebato) fit.

arrasar vt to raze, demolish.
► vi to sweep the board.

arrastrar vt (llevar por el suelo)
to drag (along), pull (along).
► vpr **arrastrarse** (reptar) to
crawl.

arrebato nm fit, outburst.

arrecife *nm* reef.

arreglar *vt* 1 (*resolver - conflicto*) to settle; (*- asunto*) to sort out. 2 (*ordenar*) to tidy, tidy up. 3 (*reparar*) to mend, fix up. ▶ *vpr* **arreglarse** (*componerse*) to get ready; (*cabello*) to do.

arreglo *nm* 1 (*reparación*) repair. 2 (*acuerdo*) agreement. • **con arreglo a** according to.

arrepentirse *vpr* to regret, be sorry.

arrestar *vt* to arrest.

arresto *nm* arrest.

arriar *vt* 1 (*velas*) to lower. 2 (*bandera*) to strike.

arriba *adv* 1 (*dirección*) up; (*encima*) on (the) top. 2 (*situación*) above. 3 (*piso*) upstairs. ▶ *interj* up! • **hacia arriba** upwards.

arriesgado,-a *adj* risky, dangerous.

arriesgar(se) *vt-vpr* to risk.

arrimarse *vpr* to come closer, come nearer.

arrodillarse *vpr* to kneel down.

arrojar *vt* 1 (*tirar*) to throw. 2 (*resultado*) to show.

arroyo *nm* (*río*) stream.

arroz *nm* rice. ▪ **arroz con leche** rice pudding; **arroz integral** brown rice.

arruga *nf* (*en la piel*) wrinkle; (*en la ropa*) crease.

arrugar(se) *vt-vpr* 1 (*piel*) to wrinkle. 2 (*ropa*) to crease. 3 (*papel*) to crumple.

arruinar *vt* to bankrupt, ruin. ▶ *vpr* **arruinarse** to be bankrupt, be ruined.

arsenal *nm* arsenal.

arte *nm* 1 (*gen*) art: *bellas artes*, fine arts. 2 (*habilidad*) craft, skill. ▪ **arte dramático** drama.

artefacto *nm* device.

arteria *nf* artery.

artesanía *nf* 1 (*actividad*) craftsmanship. 2 (*productos*) handicrafts.

artesano,-a *nm,f* craftsman, artisan.

articulación *nf* joint.

artículo *nm* article.

artificial *adj* artificial.

artillería *nf* artillery.

artista *nmf* artist.

artístico,-a *adj* artistic.

artritis *nf* arthritis.

as *nm* ace.

asa *nf* handle.

asado,-a *adj* (*carne*) roast; (*pescado, patata*) baked. ▶ *nm* **asado** roast.

asaltante *nmf* attacker.

asaltar *vt* 1 (*atacar*) to assault, attack. 2 (*robar - banco*) to rob, raid; (*- persona*) to mug.

asalto *nm* 1 (*ataque*) assault, attack. 2 (*robo - de banco*) raid, robbery; (*- a persona*) mugging. 3 (*en boxeo*) round.

asamblea *nf* 1 (*en parlamento*) assembly. 2 (*reunión*) meeting.

asar vt (carne) to roast; (pescado, patata) to bake.

ascender vi 1 (subir) to climb. 2 (sumar) to amount.

ascenso nm 1 (subida - de temperatura, precio) rise; (- de montaña) ascent. 2 (- de empleado, equipo) promotion.

ascensor nm GB lift; US elevator.

asco nm disgust. • dar asco to be disgusting.

asearse vpr to wash.

asegurado,-a nm,f policy holder.

aseguradora nf insurance company.

asegurar vt 1 (coche, casa) to insure. 2 (garantizar) to ensure, guarantee. 4 (afirmar) to assure. ▶ vpr **asegurarse** 1 (cerciorarse) to make sure. 2 (tomar un seguro) to insure oneself.

aseo nm 1 (limpieza) cleanliness, tidying up. 2 (cuarto) bathroom, toilet.

asequible adj accessible: a un precio asequible, at a reasonable price.

asesinar vt to kill, murder.

asesinato nm killing, murder.

asesino,-a nm,f killer.

asesorar vt to advise, give advice.

asesor,-ra nm,f adviser, consultant.

asfalto nm asphalt.

asfixia nf asphyxia, suffocation.

asfixiarse vpr to suffocate.

así adv 1 (de esta manera) like that, like this, in this way. 2 (de esa manera) that way. ▶ adj such: **un hombre así**, a man like that, such a man. • **así así** so-so; **así que 1** (de manera que) so, therefore. 2 (tan pronto como) as soon as; **aun así 1** even so. 2 (por así decirlo) so to speak.

Asia nf Asia.

asiático,-a adj-nm,f Asian.

asiento nm (silla etc) seat; (de bicicleta) saddle.

asignatura nf subject.

asilo nm (amparo) asylum; (residencia) home.

asimilar vt to assimilate.

asimismo adv 1 (también) also. 2 (de esta manera) likewise.

asistencia nf 1 (presencia) attendance. 2 (público) audience, public. 3 (ayuda) assistance. ■ **asistencia médica** medical care.

asistente adj attending. ▶ nmf assistant.

asistir vi to attend, be present. ▶ vt 1 (ayudar) to assist, help. 2 (cuidar) to treat.

asma nf asthma.

asmático,-a adj-nm,f asthmatic.

asno *nm* ass, donkey.

asociación *nf* association.

asociar *vt* to associate. ► *vpr* **asociarse** to form a partnership.

asomar *vi* to appear, show. ► *vpr* **asomarse** *(a ventana)* to lean out; *(a balcón)* to come out. • **"Prohibido asomarse por la ventanilla"** "Do not lean out of the window".

asombrar *vt* to amaze, astonish. ► *vpr* **asombrarse** to be amazed, be astonished.

asombroso,-a *adj* amazing, astonishing.

aspa *nf* 1 *(cruz)* X-shaped cross. 2 *(de molino)* arm; *(de ventilador)* blade.

aspecto *nm* 1 *(apariencia)* look, appearance. 2 *(faceta)* aspect.

áspero,-a *adj* rough, coarse.

aspiración *nf* 1 *(al respirar)* inhalation. 2 *(ambición)* aspiration, ambition.

aspiradora *nf* vacuum cleaner, GB hoover.

aspirante *nmf* candidate.

aspirar *vt* to inhale, breathe in. ► *vi* to aspire to.

aspirina® *nf* aspirin®.

asqueroso,-a *adj* 1 *(sucio)* dirty, filthy. 2 *(desagradable)* disgusting.

asta *nf* 1 *(de bandera)* flagpole. 2 *(cuerno)* horn.

asterisco *nm* asterisk.

astilla *nf* splinter.

astillero *nm* shipyard, dockyard.

astro *nm* star.

astrología *nf* astrology.

astronauta *nmf* astronaut.

astronomía *nf* astronomy.

astucia *nf* *(sagacidad)* astuteness, shrewdness; *(malicia)* cunning.

astuto,-a *adj* *(sagaz)* astute, shrewd; *(malicioso)* cunning.

asumir *vt* 1 *(gen)* to assume, take part on. 2 *(aceptar)* to come to term with, accept.

asunto *nm* 1 *(cuestión)* matter, subject. 2 *(ocupación)* affair, business.

asustar *vt* to frighten. ► *vpr* **asustarse** to be frightened.

atacar *vt* to attack.

atajo *nm* short cut.

atalaya *nf* watchtower.

ataque *nm* 1 *(gen)* attack. 2 *(acceso)* fit. ■ **ataque cardíaco** heart attack; **ataque de nervios** nervous breakdown.

atar *vt* to tie, fasten. ► *vpr* **atarse** to tie up, do up.

atardecer *vi* to get dark, grow dark. ► *nm* evening, dusk.

atascar *vt* to block, obstruct. ► *vpr* **atascarse** 1 *(obstruirse)* to get blocked. 2 *(mecanismo)* to jam.

atasco *nm* traffic jam.

ataúd *nm* coffin.

ateísmo *nm* atheism.

atención *nf* attention. • **prestar atención** to pay attention. ▪ **atención al cliente** customer service.

atender *vt* 1 *(cliente)* to attend to; *(bar, tienda)* to serve: *¿ya la atienden?*, are you being served? 2 *(enfermo)* to take care of, look after. 3 *(llamada)* to answer. ▶ *vi* to pay attention.

atentado *nm* attack, assault.

atentamente *adv (en carta)* sincerely, faithfully.

atentar *vi.* • **atentar contra ALGN** to make an attempt on SB's life.

atento,-a *adj* 1 *(pendiente)* attentive. 2 *(amable)* polite, courteous.

ateo,-a *adj-nm,f* atheist.

aterrizaje *nm* landing.

aterrizar *vt* to land.

ático *nm (buhardilla)* attic; *(piso - último)* top floor; *(- lujoso)* penthouse.

atlántico,-a *adj* Atlantic. • **el (océano) Atlántico** the Atlantic *(Ocean).*

atlas *nm* atlas.

atleta *nmf* athlete.

atletismo *nm* athletics.

atmósfera *nf* atmosphere.

atmosférico,-a *adj* atmospheric.

atómico,-a *adj* atomic.

átomo *nm* atom.

atracador,-ra *nm,f (de banco)* bank robber; *(en la calle)* mugger.

atracar *vt (robar - banco)* to hold up, rob; *(- persona)* to mug. ▶ *vi (amarrar)* to tie up.

atracción *nf* attraction.

atraco *nm (de banco)* hold-up, robbery; *(de persona)* mugging.

atractivo,-a *adj* attractive. ▶ *nm* **atractivo** *(de persona)* attractiveness, charm; *(de cosa)* attraction.

atraer *vt* to attract.

atragantarse *vpr* to choke.

atrapar *vt* to capture, catch.

atrás *adv* 1 *(posición)* back. 2 *(tiempo)* ago. • **hacia atrás** backwards.

atrasar *vt* 1 *(salida)* to delay. 2 *(reloj)* to put back. ▶ *vi (reloj)* to be slow. ▶ *vpr* **atrasarse** 1 *(tren etc)* to be late. 2 *(quedarse atrás)* to stay behind.

atraso *nm* 1 *(retraso)* delay. 2 *(de reloj)* slowness. 3 *(de país)* backwardness.

atravesar *vt* 1 *(cruzar)* to cross. 2 *(crisis, situación)* to go through.

atreverse *vpr* to dare.

atrevido,-a *adj* 1 *(osado)* daring, bold. 2 *(indecoroso)* risqué.

atribuir *vt* to attribute, ascribe.

atributo *nm* attribute, quality.

atril *nm* lectern.

atrio *nm* **1** *(patio)* atrium. **2** *(vestíbulo)* vestibule.

atropellar *vt* to knock down, run over.

atropello *nm* **1** *(accidente)*: **ha habido un atropello**, someone has been run over. **2** *(abuso)* outrage, abuse.

ATS *abr (ayudante técnico sanitario)* medical auxiliary.

atún *nm* tuna.

audaz *adj* audacious, bold.

audición *nf* **1** *(acción)* hearing. **2** *(para obra etc)* audition.

audiencia *nf* **1** *(recepción, público)* audience. **2** *(tribunal)* court.

audífono *nm* hearing aid.

audiovisual *adj* audio-visual.

auditorio *nm* **1** *(público)* audience. **2** *(lugar)* auditorium.

auge *nm* **1** *(del mercado)* boom. **2** *(subida)* rise. **3** *(crecimiento)* growth.

aula *nf (en escuela)* classroom; *(en universidad)* lecture hall.

aullido *nm* howl.

aumentar *vt* **1** *(incrementar)* to increase, raise. **2** *(fotos)* to enlarge.

aumento *nm* **1** *(incremento)* rise, increase. **2** *(de foto)* enlargement.

aun *adv* even. • **aun así** even so; **aun cuando** although.

aún *adv* **1** *(en afirmativas, interrogativas)* still: **aún la estoy esperando**, I'm still waiting for her. **2** *(en negativas)* yet: **aún no ha llegado**, he hasn't arrived yet. **3** *(en comparaciones)* even: **dicen que aún hará más frío**, they say it's going to get even colder.

aunque *conj* **1** *(a pesar de que)* although, even though. **2** *(incluso)* even if. **3** *(pero)* although, though.

auricular *nm (de teléfono)* receiver, earpiece. ► *nm pl* **auriculares** headphones.

aurora *nf* dawn.

auscultar *vt* to sound.

ausencia *nf* absence.

ausente *adj* absent.

austero,-a *adj* austere.

Australia *nf* Australia.

australiano,-a *adj-nm,f* Australian.

Austria *nf* Austria.

austríaco,-a *adj-nm,f* Austrian.

auténtico,-a *adj (cuadro)* authentic, genuine; *(persona, afecto)* genuine; *(piel, joya)* real.

auto *nm (coche)* car.

autobús *nm* bus.

autocar *nm* coach.

autoescuela *nf* driving school.

autógrafo *nm* autograph.

automático,-a *adj* automatic.

automóvil *nm* car; US automobile.

automovilismo *nm* motoring.

automovilista *nmf* motorist.
autonomía *nf* **1** *(independencia)* autonomy. **2** *(comunidad)* autonomous region.
autónomo,-a *adj* **1** POL autonomous, self-governing. **2** *(trabajador)* self-employed; *(traductor etc)* freelance.
autopista *nf* GB motorway; US expressway; US freeway.
autor, -ra *nm,f* **1** *(de libro)* author, writer; *(de canción)* writer. **3** *(de crimen)* perpetrator.
autoridad *nf* authority.
autorización *nf* authorization.
autorizar *vt* to authorize.
autoservicio *nm* self-service restaurant.
autostop *nm* hitch-hiking. • **hacer autostop** to hitch-hike.
autovía *nf* GB dual-carriageway; US highway.
auxiliar *vt* to help, assist. ▸ *nmf* assistant. ▪ **auxiliar de vuelo** flight attendant.
auxilio *nm* help, assistance.
avalancha *nf* avalanche.
avance *nm* **1** *(progreso, movimiento)* advance. **2** *(pago)* advance payment.
avanzar *vt* to advance, move forward. ▸ *vi* **1** *(ir hacia adelante)* to advance, to move forward. **2** *(progresar)* to make progress.
avaro,-a *nm,f* miser.

ave *nf* bird.
AVE *abr (Alta Velocidad Española) Spanish high-speed train.*
avellana *nf* hazelnut.
avena *nf* oats.
avenida *nf* avenue.
aventura *nf* **1** *(suceso)* adventure. **2** *(riesgo)* venture. **3** *(relación amorosa)* affair, love affair.
avergonzarse *vpr* **1** *(por mala acción)* to be ashamed. **2** *(por situación bochornosa)* to be embarrassed.
avería *nf* **1** *(en coche)* breakdown. **2** *(en máquina)* fault.
averiado,-a *adj* **1** *(aparato)* faulty, not working. **2** *(coche)* broken down. • **"Averiado"** "Out of order".
averiarse *vpr* **1** *(coche)* to break down. **2** *(máquina)* to malfunction.
averiguar *vt* to find out.
avestruz *nm* ostrich.
avión *nm* plane; GB aeroplane; US airplane.
avioneta *nf* light aircraft.
avisar *vt* **1** *(informar)* to tell. **2** *(advertir)* to warn. **3** *(mandar llamar)* to call for.
aviso *nm* **1** *(información)* notice. **2** *(advertencia)* warning.
avispa *nf* wasp.
axila *nf* armpit.
ayer *adv* yesterday.
ayuda *nf* help, assistance.
ayudante *nmf* assistant.
ayudar *vt* to help, aid, assist.

ayunas *nm pl.* • **en ayunas** without having eaten breakfast.

ayuntamiento *nm* **1** *(corporación)* GB town council; US city council. **2** *(edificio)* GB town hall; US city hall.

azada *nf* hoe.

azafata *nf* **1** *(de avión)* flight attendant. **2** *(de congresos)* hostess.

azafrán *nm* saffron.

azar *nm* chance. • **al azar** at random; **por azar** by chance.

azotar *vt* **1** *(con látigo)* to whip. **2** *(golpear)* to beat.

azotea *nf* flat roof.

azúcar *nm & nf* sugar.

azucarero *nm* sugar bowl.

azul *adj-nm* blue.

azulejo *nm* tile.

B

baba *nf (de adulto)* spittle; *(de niño)* dribble.

babero *nm* bib.

babor *nm* port, port side.

bacalao *nm* cod.

bache *nm* **1** *(en carretera)* pothole. **2** *(en el aire)* air pocket. **3** *fig (mal momento)* bad patch.

bacon *nm* bacon.

bacteria *nf* bacterium.

bahía *nf* bay.

bailar *vt-vi* to dance. • **sacar a ALGN a bailar** to ask SB to dance.

bailarín,-ina *nm,f* dancer.

baile *nm* **1** *(danza, fiesta)* dance. **2** *(de etiqueta)* ball.

baja *nf* **1** *(descenso)* fall, drop. **2** *(en guerra)* casualty. **3** *(por enfermedad)* sick leave: **está de baja**, he's off sick. • **darse de baja 1** *(de un club)* to resign. **2** *(en una suscripción)* to cancel one's subscription.

bajada *nf* **1** *(acción)* descent. **2** *(en carretera etc)* slope. **3** *(de temperatura)* fall, drop.

bajamar *nf* low tide.

bajar *vt* **1** *(de un lugar alto)* to bring down, take down. **2** *(mover abajo)* to lower. **3** *(recorrer de arriba abajo)* to come down, go down. **4** *(voz, radio, volumen)* to lower. **5** *(precios)* to reduce. **6** INFORM *(de la red)* to download. ▶ *vi* **1** *(ir abajo - acercándose)* to come down; *(- alejándose)* to go down. **2** *(apearse - de coche)* to get out; *(- de bicicleta, caballo, avión, tren)* to get off. **3** *(reducirse)* to fall, drop, come down. ▶ *vpr* **bajarse 1** *(ir abajo - acercándose)* to come down; *(- alejándose)* to go down. **2** *(apearse - de coche)* to get out; *(- de bicicleta, caballo, avión, tren)* to get off. **3** *(pantalones, falda)* to pull down.

bajo,-a *adj* **1** *(de poca altura)* low. **2** *(persona)* short. **3** *(inferior)* poor, low: *la clase baja*, the lower classes; *los bajos fondos*, the underworld. ▶ *adv* **bajo 1** *(volar)* low. **2** *(hablar)* softly, quietly. ▶ *prep (gen)* under; *(con temperaturas)* below. ▶ *nm* **bajo 1** *(piso)* GB ground floor; US first floor. **2** *(instrumento)* bass. ▶ *nm pl* **bajos** GB ground floor; US first floor. • **por lo bajo 1** *(disimuladamente)* on the sly. **2** *(en voz baja)* in a low voice.

bala *nf* bullet: *un disparo de bala*, a gunshot. • **como una bala** *fam* like a shot.

balance *nm* **1** balance, balance sheet. **2** *(resultado)* result.

balancear(se) *vi-vpr (mecerse)* to rock; *(en columpio)* to swing; *(barco)* to roll.

balanza *nf* **1** *(para pesar)* scales. **2** balance.

balar *vi* to bleat.

balcón *nm* balcony.

balda *nf* shelf.

balde *nm (cubo)* bucket, pail. • **de balde** free, for nothing; **en balde** in vain.

baldosa *nf* floor tile.

balear *adj* ▪ **Islas Baleares** Balearic Islands.

ballena *nf* whale.

ballet *nm* ballet.

balneario *nm* spa, health resort.

balón *nm* ball.

baloncesto *nm* basketball.

balonmano *nm* handball.

balonvolea *nf* volleyball.

balsa *nf (barca)* raft.

bálsamo *nm* balsam, balm.

bambú *nm* bamboo.

banana *nf* banana.

banca *nf (sector)* banking; *(los bancos)* the banks.

bancarrota *nf* bankruptcy.

banco *nm* **1** *(institución financiera)* bank. **2** *(asiento)* bench. ▪ **banco de datos** data bank.

banda[1] *nf* **1** *(de gala)* sash. **2** *(lado)* side. ▪ **banda magnética** magnetic srip; **banda sonora** sound track.

banda[2] *nf* **1** *(de ladrones)* gang. **2** *(musical)* band.

bandeja *nf* tray.

bandera *nf* flag.

bandido,-a *nm,f* bandit.

bando *nm (facción)* faction, party.

banqueta *nf (taburete)* stool, footstool.

banquete *nm* banquet, feast. ▪ **banquete de boda** wedding reception.

banquillo *nm* **1** *(de acusados)* dock. **2** *(en deporte)* bench.

bañador *nm (de mujer)* bathing costume, swimming costume; *(de hombre)* swimming trunks.

bañar *vt* **1** *(en bañera)* to bath. **2** *(con salsa)* to coat. **3** *(con* *licor)* to soak. ► *vpr* **bañarse** *(en bañera)* to have a bath, take a bath; *(en el mar, piscina)* to swim • **"Prohibido bañarse"** "No swimming".

bañera *nf* bath, bathtub.

baño *nm* **1** *(acción)* bath. **2** *(bañera)* bath, bathtub. **3** *(capa)* coat, coating. **4** *(sala de baño)* bathroom. **5** *(wáter)* toilet. ► *nm pl* **baños** *(balneario)* spa *sing*. ■ **baño María** bain-marie.

bar *nm (cafetería)* café, snack bar; *(de bebidas alcohólicas)* bar.

baraja *nf* pack, deck.

barajar *vt (naipes)* to shuffle.

barandilla *nf* handrail, banister.

barato,-a *adj* cheap. ► *adv* **barato** cheaply, cheap.

barba *nf* beard. • **dejarse la barba** to grow a beard; **por barba** each, a head.

barbaridad *nf* **1** *(crueldad)* cruelty. **2** *(disparate)* piece of nonsense: ***cuesta una barbaridad***, it costs a fortune.

bárbaro,-a *adj* **1** HIST barbarian. **2** *(cruel)* cruel. **3** *fam (grande)* enormous. **4** *fam (espléndido)* tremendous, terrific.

barbería *nf* barber's.

barbilla *nf* chin.

barca *nf* boat.

barco *nm* boat, vessel, ship. ■ **barco de vela** GB sailing boat; US sailboat.

barómetro *nm* barometer.

barón *nm* baron.

barquero,-a *nm,f (hombre)* boatman; *(mujer)* boatwoman.

barquillo *nm* wafer.

barra *nf* **1** *(de hierro)* bar. **2** *(de pan)* loaf. **3** *(de bar, cafetería)* bar. ■ **barra de labios** lipstick; **barra libre** free bar.

barraca *nf* **1** *(chabola)* shanty. **2** *(de feria)* stall.

barranco *nm* **1** *(precipicio)* precipice. **2** *(entre montañas)* gully.

barrendero,-a *nm,f* street sweeper.

barrer *vt* to sweep.

barrera *nf* barrier. ■ **barrera de coral** coral reef.

barricada *nf* barricade.

barriga *nf* belly.

barril *nm* barrel, keg.

barrio *nm* GB district, area; US neighborhood. ■ **barrio bajo** seedy area; **barrio residencial** residential area.

barro *nm* **1** *(lodo)* mud. **2** *(arcilla)* clay.

barroco,-a *adj* baroque. ► *nm* **barroco** baroque.

barrote *nm* **1** *(de celda)* bar. **2** *(de escalera, silla)* rung.

basar *vt* to base. ► *vpr* **basarse** to be based.

báscula *nf* scales.

base *nf* **1** *(superficie)* base. **2** *(fundamento)* basis. **3** *(componente principal)*: ***la base de su***

dieta es la carne, his diet is meat-based; *la base del éxito*, the key to success. • **a base de**: *un postre hecho a base de leche y huevos*, a pudding made of milk and eggs; *a base de mucho trabajo*, by working hard. ■ **base de datos** database.

básico,-a *adj* basic.

basílica *nf* basilica.

bastante *adj-pron* **1** *(suficiente)* enough, sufficient. **2** *(abundante)* quite a lot. ► *adv* **1** enough. **2** *(un poco)* fairly, quite.

bastar *vi* to be sufficient, be enough.

basto,-a *adj* **1** *(grosero)* coarse, rough. **2** *(sin pulimentar)* rough, unpolished.

bastón *nm* stick, walking stick.

basura *nf* GB rubbish; US garbage. • **tirar algo a la basura** to throw STH away, throw STH in the bin; **sacar la basura** to take out the rubbish (US garbage).

bata *nf* **1** *(de casa)* dressing gown. **2** *(de trabajo)* overall; *(de médicos etc)* white coat. **3** *(de colegial)* child's overall.

batalla *nf* battle. • **de batalla** *fam* ordinary, everyday: *zapatos de batalla*, everyday shoes.

bate *nm* bat.

batería *nf* **1** *(de coche)* battery. **2** *(cañones)* battery. **3** *(de conjunto)* drums. ► *nmf* drummer. • **en batería** *(coches)* at an angle to the kerb (US curb). ■ **batería de cocina** set of pots and pans.

batido *nm* milk shake.

batir *vt* **1** *(huevos)* to beat; *(nata, claras)* to whip. **2** *(alas)* to flap. **5** *(vencer)* to beat, defeat. **6** *(récord)* to break. ► *vpr* **batirse** to fight.

batuta *nf* baton.

baúl *nm* trunk.

bautismo *nm* baptism, christening.

bautizar *vt* **1** to baptize, christen. **2** *(poner nombre a)* to name.

bautizo *nm* **1** *(sacramento)* baptism, christening. **2** *(fiesta)* christening party.

baya *nf* berry.

bayeta *nf* cloth.

bazar *nm* bazaar.

bazo *nm* spleen.

bebé *nm* baby.

beber *vt* to drink.

bebida *nf* drink, beverage. ■ **bebida alcohólica** alcoholic drink.

beca *nf* **1** *(ayuda)* grant. **2** *(por méritos)* scholarship.

becerro *nm* calf.

bechamel *nf* béchamel sauce.

béisbol *nm* baseball.

belén *nm* nativity scene, crib.

belga *adj-nmf* Belgian.
Bélgica *nf* Belgium.
belleza *nf* beauty.
bello,-a *adj* beautiful.
bellota *nf* acorn.
bendecir *vt* to bless.
bendición *nf* blessing.
beneficiar *vt* to benefit. ▶
vpr **beneficiarse** to benefit
from.
beneficio *nm* profit.
beneficioso,-a *adj* beneficial,
useful.
benéfico,-a *adj* charitable:
función benéfica, charity performance.
bengala *nf* flare.
benigno,-a *adj* **1** *(tumor)* benign. **2** *(clima)* mild.
berberecho *nm* cockle.
berenjena *nf* GB aubergine;
US eggplant.
bermudas *nf pl* Bermuda
shorts.
berro *nm* watercress, cress.
berza *nf* cabbage.
besamel *nf* bechamel sauce.
besar *vt* to kiss. ▶ *vpr* **be-
sarse** to kiss one another.
beso *nm* kiss.
bestia *nf* *(animal)* beast. ▶ *nmf*
(persona) brute.
besugo *nm* **1** *(pez)* sea bream.
2 *(persona)* idiot.
betún *nm* shoe polish.
biberón *nm* baby bottle.
Biblia *nf* Bible.
bíblico,-a *adj* biblical.

bibliografía *nf* **1** *(en libro)* bibli-
ography. **2** *(de curso)* reading
list.
biblioteca *nf* **1** *(edificio)* library. **2** *(mueble)* bookcase,
bookshelf.
bicarbonato *nm* bicarbonate.
bíceps *nm* biceps.
bicho *nm* **1** *(insecto)* bug. **2**
(persona) nasty character: *es
un bicho raro*, he's a weirdo.
bici *nf fam* bike.
bicicleta *nf* bicycle: *ir en bicicleta*, to cycle. ▪ **bicicleta de
carreras** racing bicycle; **bicicleta de montaña** mountain
bike; **bicicleta estática** exercise bike.
bidé *nm* bidet.
bidón *nm* **1** *(pequeño)* can. **2**
(grande) drum.
bien *adv* **1** *(de manera satisfac-
toria)* well. **2** *(correctamente)*
right, correctly. **3** *(debida-
mente)* properly: *¡pórtate bi-
en!*, behave yourself! **4** *(de
acuerdo)*: *¡muy bien!*, O.K.,
all right. **5** *(mucho)* very; *(bastante)* quite: *es bien sencillo*,
it's very simple; *bien tarde*,
pretty late. ▶ *nm* good: *el
bien y el mal*, good and
evil. ▶ *adj* well-to-do: *gente
bien*, the upper classes. ▶
nm pl **bienes** property, pos-
sessions. ● **bien que** althoug;
más bien rather; **si bien** although.

bienestar *nm* well-being, comfort.

bienvenida *nf* welcome. • **dar la bienvenida a** ALGN to welcome SB.

bigote *nm* 1 *(de persona)* GB moustache; US mustache. 2 *(de gato)* whiskers.

bikini *nm* bikini.

bilingüe *adj* bilingual.

bilis *nf* bile.

billar *nm* 1 *(juego)* billiards. 2 *(mesa)* billiard table.

billete *nm* 1 *(de banco)* GB note; US bill. 2 *(de tren, autobús, sorteo, etc)* ticket: *sacar un billete,* to buy a ticket. ▪ **billete de ida** one-way ticket; **billete de ida y vuelta** GB return ticket; US round-trip ticket.

billetero *nm* wallet.

billón *nm* trillion; GB *(antiguamente)* billion; .

bingo *nm* 1 *(juego)* bingo. 2 *(sala)* bingo hall.

biografía *nf* biography.

biología *nf* biology.

biológico,-a *adj* 1 *(ciclo, madre)* biological. 2 *(alimento)* organic.

biombo *nm* folding screen.

biquini *nm* bikini.

bisagra *nf* hinge.

bisiesto *adj*: *año bisiesto,* leap year.

bisté *nm* steak.

bistec *nm* steak.

bisturí *nm* scalpel.

bisutería *nf* GB imitation jewellery; US imitation jewelry.

bit *nm* bit.

bizco,-a *adj* cross-eyed.

bizcocho *nm* sponge cake.

blanco,-a *adj* white. ▶ *nm* **blanco** 1 *(color)* white. 2 *(objetivo físico)* target. 3 *(hueco)* blank, gap. • **dar en el blanco** 1 *(diana)* to hit the mark. 2 *(acertar)* to hit the nail on the head; **quedarse en blanco** *(olvidar)* to forget everything.

blando,-a *adj* 1 *(superficie, madera, queso)* soft; *(carne)* tender. 2 *(persona)* soft.

blanquear *vt* 1 *(poner blanco)* to whiten. 2 *(con cal)* to whitewash. 3 *fam (dinero)* to launder.

bloc *nm* pad, notepad.

bloque *nm* 1 *(de piedra)* block. 2 *(de papel)* notepad. 3 POL bloc. ▪ **bloque de pisos** block of flats.

bloquear *vt* 1 *(camino, entrada)* to block. 2 *(puerto, país)* to blockade. ▶ *vpr* **bloquearse** 1 *(quedarse paralizado)* to freeze. 2 *(quedarse en blanco)* to have a blank. 3 *(mecanismo)* to jam.

blusa *nf* blouse.

boa *nf* boa.

bobina *nf* 1 *(carrete)* reel, bobbin. 2 *(eléctrica)* coil.

bobo,-a *adj* silly, foolish. ▶ *nm,f* fool, dunce.

boca *nf* **1** mouth. **2** *(abertura)* entrance, opening. • **boca abajo** face down; **boca arriba** face up. ▪ **boca a boca** mouth to mouth resuscitation; **boca del estómago** pit of the stomach.

bocacalle *nf* side street: *la primera bocacalle a la izquierda*, the first turn to the left.

bocadillo *nm* **1** *(de pan de molde)* sandwich. **2** *(en barra)* roll. **3** *(en cómics)* speech balloon.

bocata *nm* **1** *fam (de pan de molde)* sandwich. **2** *(en barra)* roll.

bochorno *nm* **1** *(calor)* sultry weather, close weather. **2** *(vergüenza)* embarrassment, shame.

bocina *nf* horn.

boda *nf* **1** *(ceremonia)* marriage, wedding. **2** *(fiesta)* reception.

bodega *nf* **1** *(de vinos)* cellar, wine cellar. **2** *(tienda)* wine shop. **3** *(de barco, avión)* hold.

bodegón *nm* still-life painting.

bofetada *nf* slap in the face.

boicot *nm* boycott.

boina *nf* beret.

bol *nm* bowl.

bola *nf* **1** *(cuerpo esférico)* ball. **2** *(de helado)* scoop. **3** *fam (mentira)* fib, lie.

bolera *nf* bowling alley.

boleto *nm* *(de lotería)* ticket; *(de quiniela)* coupon.

boli *nm* *fam* ballpen, Biro®.

bolígrafo *nm* ballpoint pen, Biro®.

Bolivia *nf* Bolivia.

boliviano,-a *adj-nm,f* Bolivian.

bollo *nm* **1** *(dulce)* bun. **2** *(de pan)* roll.

bolo *nm* skittle, ninepin: *jugar a los bolos*, to go bowling.

bolsa[1] *nf* bag. ▪ **bolsa de basura** bin liner; **bolsa de viaje** travel bag.

bolsa[2] *nf* stock exchange.

bolsillo *nm* pocket.

bolso *nm* GB handbag; US purse.

bomba[1] *nf* *(explosivo)* bomb. • **pasarlo bomba** to have a ball.

bomba[2] *nf* *(para bombear)* pump.

bombero,-a *nm,f* *(hombre)* firefighter, fireman; *(mujer)* firefighter, firewoman.

bombilla *nf* light bulb, bulb.

bombo *nm* **1** bass drum. **2** *(para sorteo)* drum.

bombón *nm* chocolate.

bombona *nf* cylinder, bottle. ▪ **bombona de butano** butane cylinder.

bondad *nf* **1** *(cualidad)* goodness. **2** *(afabilidad)* kindness: *tenga la bondad de contestar*, be so good as to reply.

bonito,-a *adj* nice, pretty. ▶ *nm* **bonito** *(pez)* tuna, bonito.

bono *nm* **1** bond. **2** *(vale)* voucher. **3** *(para transporte)* pass.

bonobús *nm* bus pass.

boquerón *nm* anchovy.

borda *nf* gunwale. • **arrojar por la borda** to throw overboard.

bordado *nm* embroidering, embroidery.

bordar *vt* to embroider.

borde¹ *adj fam* nasty.

borde² *nm (extremo)* edge; *(de prenda)* hem; *(de camino)* side; *(de vaso, taza)* rim: *al borde del mar*, beside the sea.

bordillo *nm* kerb.

bordo *nm* board. • **a bordo** on board.

borrachera *nf* • **pillar una borrachera** to ger drunk.

borracho,-a *adj* drunk. ▶ *nm,f* drunkard.

borrador *nm* **1** *(de texto)* rough copy, first draft. **2** *(de pizarra)* duster.

borrar *vt* **1** *(con goma etc.)* to erase, rub out. **2** INFORM to delete.

borrasca *nf* area of low pressure.

borrego,-a *nm,f (animal)* lamb.

borroso,-a *adj* blurred, hazy.

bosque *nm* wood; *(grande)* forest.

bostezar *vi* to yawn.

bostezo *nm* yawn.

bota¹ *nf (calzado)* boot. • **ponerse las botas** *(al comer)* to stuff oneself.

bota² *nf (de vino)* wineskin.

botánico,-a *adj* botanical.

botar *vt* **1** *(pelota)* to bounce. **2** *(barco)* to launch. ▶ *vi (saltar)* to jump.

bote¹ *nm* small boat. ▪ **bote salvavidas** lifeboat.

bote² *nm (salto)* bounce.

bote³ *nm* **1** *(recipiente)* tin, can; *(para propinas)* box for tips. **2** *(de lotería)* jackpot.

bote⁴ • **estar de bote en bote** to be jam-packed.

botella *nf* bottle.

botellín *nm* small bottle.

botijo *nm* drinking jug.

botín *nm* **1** *(de guerra)* booty. **2** *(de ladrones)* loot.

botiquín *nm* **1** *(de medicinas)* first-aid kit. **2** *(enfermería)* sick bag.

botón *nm* **1** *(de camisa)* button. **2** *(tecla)* button. ▪ **botón de arranque** starter; **botón de muestra** sample.

botones *nm (de hotel)* GB bellboy; US bellhop.

bóveda *nf* vault.

boxeador,-a *nm* boxer.

boxear *vi* to box.

boxeo *nm* boxing.

boya *nf* **1** buoy. **2** *(corcho de pesca)* float.

bragas *nf pl* panties, knickers.

bragueta *nf* fly, flies.

brasa *nf* live coal. • **a la brasa** barbecued.

Brasil *nm* Brazil.

brasileño,-a *adj-nm,f* Brazilian.

bravo,-a *adj* 1 *(valiente)* brave, courageous. 2 *(fiero)* fierce, ferocious. ► *interj* well done!, bravo!

braza *nf (en natación)* breast stroke.

brazo *nm* 1 *(de persona, sillón)* arm. 2 *(de animal)* foreleg.

brecha *nf* 1 *(abertura)* break, opening. 2 *(herida)* gash.

Bretaña *nf* Brittany. ■ **Gran Bretaña** Great Britain.

breve *adj* short, brief. • **en breve** soon, shortly.

bricolaje *nm* do-it-yourself, DIY.

brida *nf* bridle.

brillante *adj* 1 *(luz, color)* bright; *(pelo, calzado)* shiny. 2 *(destacado)* brilliant. ► *nm (diamante)* diamond.

brillar *vi* 1 *(sol, luz, ojos, oro)* to shine. 2 *(sobresalir)* to shine, be outstanding.

brillo *nm* 1 *(resplandor)* shine. 2 *(de estrella)* brightness, brilliance.

brincar *vi* to jump, leap.

brindar *vi* to toast. ► *vt (proporcionar)* to offer: *me brindó su apoyo*, she gave me her support.

brindis *nm* toast.

brisa *nf* breeze.

británico,-a *adj* British. ► *nm,f (hombre)* British man, Briton; *(mujer)* British woman, Briton.

brocha *nf* paintbrush. ■ **brocha de afeitar** shaving brush.

broche *nm* 1 *(cierre)* fastener. 2 *(joya)* brooch.

broma *nf* joke. • **gastar una broma a ALGN** to play a joke on SB. ■ **broma pesada** practical joke.

bronca *nf* row, quarrel. • **armar una bronca** to kick up a fuss; **echar una bronca a ALGN** to come down on SB.

bronce *nm* bronze.

bronceado *nm* tan, suntan.

bronceador *nm* suntan lotion.

bronquios *nm pl* bronchial tubes.

bronquitis *nf* bronchitis.

brotar *vi* 1 *(planta)* to sprout, bud. 2 *(hoja)* to sprout, come out. 3 *(agua)* to spring.

brote *nm* 1 *(de planta)* bud, sprout. 2 *(de conflicto, epidemia)* outbreak.

bruja *nf* 1 *(hechicera)* witch, sorceress. 2 *fam (harpía)* old hag.

brujo *nm* wizard, sorcerer.

brújula *nf* compass.

bruma *nf* mist, fog.

brusco,-a *adj* 1 *(persona)* brusque, abrupt. 2 *(movimiento)* sudden.

bruto,-a *adj* **1** *(necio)* stupid, ignorant. **2** *(tosco)* rough, coarse. **3** *(montante, peso)* gross. **4** *(petróleo)* crude.

bucear *vi* to swim under water.

budista *adj-nmf* Buddhist.

buen *adj* → bueno,-a.

bueno,-a *adj* **1** *(gen)* good. **2** *(persona - amable)* kind; *(- agradable)* nice, polite. **3** *(apropiado)* right, suitable. **4** *(grande)* big; *(considerable)* considerable: *un buen número de participantes*, quite a few participants. • **de buenas a primeras** *fam* from the very start; **por las buenas** willingly.

buey *nm* ox.

búfalo *nm* buffalo.

bufanda *nf* scarf.

bufé *nm* buffet. ■ **bufé libre** self-service buffet.

bufete *nm* **1** *(mesa)* writing desk. **2** *(de abogado)* lawyer's office.

buhardilla *nf* attic.

búho *nm* owl.

buitre *nm* vulture.

bujía *nf* spark plug.

bulevar *nm* boulevard.

bulto *nm* **1** *(tamaño)* size, bulk. **2** *(hinchazón)* swelling, lump. **3** *(fardo)* bundle, pack: *¿cuántos bultos lleva?*, how many pieces of luggage do you have?

buñuelo *nm* **1** *(dulce)* doughnut. **2** *(de bacalao etc)* fritter.

buque *nm* ship, vessel.

burbuja *nf* bubble.

burla *nf* mockery, gibe.

burlar *vt* **1** *(engañar)* to deceive, trick. **2** *(eludir)* to dodge, evade. ▶ *vpr* **burlarse** to mock. • **burlarse de ALGN** to make fun of SB, laugh at SB.

burocracia *nf* bureaucracy.

burro,-a *nm,f* **1** *(asno)* donkey. **2** *(ignorante)* idiot. **3** *(bruto)* brute.

busca *nf* search.

buscador *nm* INFORM search engine.

buscar *vt* *(gen)* to look for, search for; *(en diccionario)* to look up: *ir a buscar algo*, to go and get STH; *vinieron a buscarme a la estación*, they came to pick me up from the station.

búsqueda *nf* search.

busto *nm* bust.

butaca *nf* **1** *(sillón)* armchair. **2** *(en teatro)* seat.

butano *nm* butane.

butifarra *nf* pork sausage.

buzo *nm* diver.

buzón *nm* **1** *(en casa)* GB letterbox; US mailbox. **2** *(en calle)* GB post box; US mailbox. **3** INFORM mailbox. • **echar una carta al buzón** to post a letter. ■ **buzón de voz** voicemail.

byte *nm* byte.

C

caballa *nf* mackerel.

caballero *nm* **1** *(señor)* gentleman. **2** HIST knight.

caballo *nm* **1** horse. **2** *(en ajedrez)* knight. • **a caballo** on horseback; **montar a caballo** to ride.

cabaña *nf* cabin, hut.

cabecera *nf* **1** *(de periódico)* headline. **2** *(de cama)* bedhead.

cabello *nm* hair. ■ **cabello de ángel** sweet pumpkin preserve.

caber *vi* to fit: *en esta lata caben diez litros*, this can holds ten litres; *no caben más*, there is no room for any more. • **dentro de lo que cabe** all things considered; **no cabe duda** there is no doubt.

cabestrillo *nm*. • **en cabestrillo** in a sling.

cabeza *nf* head. • **cabeza abajo** upside down; **cabeza arriba** the right way up; **por cabeza** a head, per person. ■ **cabeza de ajo** head of garlic; **cabeza rapada** skinhead.

cabida *nf* capacity, room.

cabina *nf* cabin, booth. ■ **cabina telefónica** phone box.

cable *nm* cable.

cabo *nm* **1** *(gen)* end: *al cabo de un mes*, in a month. **2** *(cuerda)* strand. **3** GEOG cape.

4 *(militar)* corporal. • **de cabo a rabo** from head to tail; **llevar a cabo** to carry out.

cabra *nf* goat.

cabrito *nm* kid.

caca *nf* **1** *fam* poo; US poop. **2** *(cosa sucia)* dirty thing. **3** *(basura)* load of rubbish.

cacahuete *nm* peanut.

cacao *nm* **1** *(planta)* cacao. **2** *(polvo, bebida)* cocoa.

cacarear *vi* **1** *(gallina)* to cluck. **2** *(gallo)* to crow.

cacerola *nf* saucepan.

cachalote *nm* cachalot, sperm whale.

cacharro *nm* **1** *(de cocina)* pot. **2** *fam (cosa)* thing, piece of junk.

caché *nm* cache memory.

cachear *vt* to search, frisk.

cacho *nm fam* bit, piece.

cachorro,-a *nm,f (de perro)* puppy; *(de león, tigre)* cub.

cacto *nm* cactus.

cactus *nm* cactus.

cada *adj* **1** *(para individualizar)* each: *tres caramelos para cada uno*, three sweets for each; *cada cual, cada uno*, each one, every one. **2** *(con números, tiempo)* every: *cada cuatro años hay un año bisiesto*, there's a leap year every four years. **3** *(uso enfático)*: *¡dice cada tontería!*, he says such stupid things! • **cada vez más** more and more;

cada vez que whenever, every time that.

cadáver *nm* corpse, body.

cadena *nf* **1** *(de eslabones, establecimientos)* chain. **2** *(industrial)* line. **3** *(montañosa)* range. **4** *(musical)* music centre. **5** *(de televisión)* channel. **6** *(de radio)* station. ► *nf pl* **cadenas** *(de nieve)* tyre (US tire) chains. • **tirar de la cadena del wáter** to flush the toilet.

cadera *nf* hip.

caducar *vi* to expire: *¿cuándo caduca la leche?*, what's the sell-by date on the milk?

caducidad *nf* **1** *(de documento)* expiration, loss of validity. **2** *(de alimento)* best before date.

caer *vi* **1** *(gen)* to fall. **2** *(coincidir fechas)* to be: *el día cuatro cae en jueves*, the fourth is a Thursday. ► *vpr* **caerse** to fall. • **caer bien**: *me cae bien*, I like her; **caer mal**: *me cae mal*, I don't like him; **caer enfermo,-a** to fall ill; **dejar caer** to drop; **estar al caer** to be about to arrive.

café *nm* **1** *(bebida)* coffee. **2** *(cafetería)* café. ■ **café con leche** white coffee; **café descafeinado** decaffeinated coffee; **café exprés** expresso; **café solo** black coffee.

cafeína *nf* caffeine.

cafetera *nf* coffeepot.

cafetería *nf* cafeteria, café.

caída *nf* **1** *(gen)* fall. **2** *(de tejidos)* body, hang.

caimán *nm* alligator.

caja *nf* **1** *(gen)* box; *(de madera)* chest; *(grande)* crate. **2** *(de bebidas)* case. **3** *(en tienda, bar)* cash desk; *(en supermercado)* checkout; *(en banco)* cashier's desk. ■ **caja de ahorros** savings bank; **caja de cambios** gearbox; **caja fuerte** safe; **caja negra** black box; **caja registradora** cash register.

cajero,-a *nm,f* cashier. ■ **cajero automático** cash dispenser.

cajetilla *nf* packet *(of cigarettes)*.

cajón *nm* drawer.

cal *nf* lime.

cala *nf* cove.

calabacín *nm* GB courgette; US zucchini.

calabaza *nf* pumpkin.

calabozo *nm* **1** *(prisión)* jail. **2** *(celda)* cell.

calado,-a *adj fam* soaked.

calamar *nm* squid. ■ **calamares a la romana** squid fried in batter.

calambre *nm* **1** *(muscular)* cramp. **2** *(eléctrico)* shock, electric shock.

calamidad *nf* calamity, disaster.

calar *vt* **1** *(mojar)* to soak, drench. **2** *fam (intención)* to rumble. ► *vpr* **calarse** *(con* *agua)* to get soaked. **2** *(motor)* to stop, stall.

calavera *nf* skull.

calcetín *nm* sock.

calcio *nm* calcium.

calculadora *nf* calculator.

calcular *vt* to calculate, work out.

cálculo *nm* **1** *(de cantidad, presupuesto)* calculation. **2** *(del riñón, etc)* stone.

caldera *nf* boiler.

calderilla *nf* small change.

caldero *nm* cauldron.

caldo *nm* **1** *(sopa)* broth. **2** *(para cocinar)* stock. ▪ **caldo de cultivo** culture medium.

calefacción *nf* heating. ▪ **calefacción central** central heating.

calendario *nm* calendar.

calentador *nm* heater.

calentar *vt-vi (gen)* to warm up; *(agua, horno, etc)* to heat, heat up.

calidad *nf* quality. ● **en calidad de** as.

cálido,-a *adj* warm.

caliente *adj (ardiendo)* hot; *(templado)* warm.

calificar *vt* **1** *(etiquetar)* to describe. **2** *(dar nota)* to mark, grade.

callado,-a *adj* silent, quiet.

callar(se) *vi-vpr (dejar de hablar)* to stop talking; *(no hablar)* to say nothing, remain silent: *¡cállate!*, shut up!

calle *nf* **1** street, road. **2** *(en atletismo)* lane. ▪ **calle mayor** high street, main street; **calle peatonal** pedestrian street.

callejero *nm* street directory.

callejón *nm*. ▪ **callejón sin salida** cul-de-sac, dead end.

callo *nm (en mano, planta del pie)* callus; *(en dedo del pie)* corn. ▶ *nm pl* **callos** tripe.

calma *nf* calm.

calmante *adj* soothing. ▶ *nm* painkiller.

calmar *vt* **1** *(nervios)* to calm; *(persona)* to calm down. **2** *(dolor)* to relieve, soothe. ▶ *vt-vpr* **calmar(se)** to calm down.

calor *nm (sensación)* heat: *hace calor*, it is hot; *tengo calor*, I feel warm, I feel hot.

caloría *nf* calorie.

caluroso,-a *adj (tiempo)* hot, warm.

calva *nf* bald patch.

calvo,-a *adj (persona)* bald. ▶ *nm,f* bald person.

calzada *nf* road, roadway.

calzado *nm* footwear, shoes.

calzador *nm* shoehorn.

calzarse *vpr* to put one's shoes on. ● *¿qué número calzas?* what size shoes do you take?

calzoncillos *nm pl* underpants, pants.

cama *nf* bed. ▪ **cama de matrimonio** double bed; **cama individual** single bed.

camaleón *nm* chameleon.

cámara *nf* **1** *(fotográfica)* camera. **2** *(del parlamento)* house. **3** *(de rueda)* inner tube. • **a cámara lenta** in slow motion.

camarada *nmf* **1** *(colega)* colleague; *(de colegio)* schoolmate. **2** POL comrade.

camarero,-a *nm,f* **1** *(en bar - hombre)* waiter; *(- mujer)* waitress. **2** *(en barco, - hombre)* steward; *(- mujer)* stewardess.

camarón *nm* shrimp.

camarote *nm* cabin.

cambiar *vt* **1** *(gen)* to change. **2** *(intercambiar)* to exchange, swap. ► *vi* to change. ► *vpr* **cambiarse** to change: *cambiarse de ropa*, to get changed. • **cambiar de** to change: *cambiar de trabajo*, to change jobs.

cambio *nm* **1** *(gen)* change. **2** *(canje)* exchange. **3** *(de divisas)* exchange rate. **4** *(de tren)* switch. **5** *(de marchas)* gear change. • **a cambio de** in exchange for; **en cambio 1** *(por otro lado)* on the other hand. **2** *(en lugar de)* instead. ▪ **cambio automático** *(de coche)* automatic transmission; **cambio de marchas** gearshift.

camello *nm* camel.

camerino *nm* dressing room.

camilla *nf* stretcher.

caminar *vt-vi* to walk.

camino *nm* **1** *(sendero)* path, track. **2** *(ruta)* way.

camión *nm* GB lorry; US truck.

camioneta *nf* van.

camisa *nf* shirt.

camiseta *nf* **1** *(interior)* vest. **2** *(exterior)* T-shirt. **3** *(de deportes)* shirt.

camisón *nm* nightdress, nightgown, nightie.

campamento *nm* camp.

campana *nf* bell. ▪ **campana extractora** cooker hood.

campanario *nm* belfry, bell tower.

campanilla *nf* *(úvula)* uvula.

campaña *nf* campaign.

campeonato *nm* championship.

campeón,-ona *nm,f* champion.

campesino,-a *nm,f* *(que vive en el campo)* country person; *(que trabaja en el campo)* farm worker.

camping *nm* camping site. • **ir de camping** to go camping.

campo *nm* **1** *(gen)* field. **2** *(campiña)* country, countryside; *(paisaje)* countryside. • **ir campo a través** to cut across the fields. ▪ **campo de concentración** concentration camp; **campo de fútbol** football pitch; US soccerfield; **campo de golf** golf course.

cana *nf* grey hair; US gray hair.

canal *nm* **1** *(artificial)* canal. **2** *(natural, de televisión)* channel.

canapé *nm* *(comida)* canapé.

Canarias *nf pl.* ▪ **islas Canarias** Canary Islands.

canario *nm* *(pájaro)* canary.

canasta *nf* basket.

cancelar *vt* **1** *(anular)* to cancel. **2** *(deuda)* to pay off, settle.

cáncer *nm* **1** *(tumor)* cancer. **2** *(signo)* Cancer.

cancha *nf* court.

canción *nf* song.

candado *nm* padlock.

candidato,-a *nm,f* candidate.

canela *nf* cinnamon.

canelones *nm pl* cannelloni.

cangrejo *nm* crab. ▪ **cangrejo (de río)** crayfish.

canguro *nm* kangaroo. ▶ *nmf* baby-sitter.

canoa *nf* canoe.

cansado,-a *adj* **1** *(fatigado, harto)* tired. **2** *(trabajo, viaje)* tiring, boring.

cansancio *nm* tiredness.

cansar *vt* **1** *(fatigar)* to tire, tire out. **2** *(molestar)* to annoy: *me cansan sus discursos*, I'm fed up with his speeches. ▶ *vi* to be tiring. ▶ *vpr* **cansarse** to get tired.

cantante *nmf* singer.

cantar *vt-vi* *(gen)* to sing; *(gallo)* to crow.

cante *nm.* ▪ **cante hondo** flamenco.

cantidad *nf* **1** *(volumen)* quantity, amount. **2** *(de dinero)* sum, amount. ▶ *adv fam* a lot: *me gusta cantidad*, I love it.

cantimplora *nf* water bottle.

cantina *nf* **1** *(en fábrica, colegio)* canteen. **2** *(en estación)* buffet, cafeteria.

canto¹ *nm* *(arte)* singing.

canto² *nm* **1** *(borde)* edge. **2** *(piedra)* stone. • **de canto** sideways.

caña *nf* **1** *(planta)* reed. **2** *(tallo)* cane. **3** *(de pescar)* fishing rod. **4** *(de cerveza)* beer, glass of beer. ▪ **caña de azúcar** sugar cane.

cañería *nf* pipe.

cañón *nm* **1** *(de artillería)* cannon. **2** *(de arma)* barrel. **3** GEOG canyon.

caoba *nf* mahogany.

caos *nm* chaos.

capa *nf* **1** *(prenda)* cloak, cape. **2** *(baño)* coat. **3** *(estrato)* layer.

capacidad *nf* **1** *(cabida)* capacity. **2** *(habilidad)* capability, ability.

capaz *adj* capable, able.

capilla *nf* *(de iglesia)* chapel. ▪ **capilla ardiente** funeral chapel.

capital *nm* *(dinero)* capital. ▶ *nf* *(ciudad)* capital.

capitán,-ana *nm,f* captain.

capitel *nm* capital.

capítulo *nm* *(de libro)* chapter; *(de serie televisiva)* episode.

capó *nm* GB bonnet; US hood.
capote *nm (de torero)* cape.
capricho *nm* whim, caprice.
capricornio *nm* Capricorn.
cápsula *nf* capsule.
captar *vt* **1** *(atraer interés, atención)* to capture; *(adeptos)* to attract. **2** *(comprender)* to understand.
capturar *vt (persona, animal)* to capture; *(alijo)* to seize.
capucha *nf* hood.
capullo *nm* **1** *(de insectos)* cocoon. **2** *(de flor)* bud.
caqui *nm (fruta)* persimmon.
cara *nf* **1** face. **2** *(lado)* side. **3** *(descaro)* cheek, nerve. • **cara a cara** face to face; **cara o cruz** heads or tails; **dar la cara** to take responsibility; **de cara a** opposite, facing; **tener buena cara** to look well; **tener cara de + *adj*** to look + *adj*; **tener mala cara** to look ill.
caracol *nm* **1** *(de tierra)* snail; *(de mar)* winkle. **2** *(del oído)* cochlea.
caracola *nf* conch.
carácter *nm* **1** *(personalidad, genio)* character: *tiene mucho carácter*, he's got a strong personality. **2** *(condición)* nature: *el proyecto tiene carácter científico*, this project is of a scientific nature. **3** *(de imprenta)* letter. • **tener buen carácter** to be good-natured;

tener mal carácter to be bad-tempered.
característico,-a *adj* characteristic.
carambola *nf (billar)* GB cannon; US carom.
caramelo *nm* **1** *(golosina)* GB sweet; US candy. **2** *(azúcar quemado)* caramel.
caravana *nf* **1** *(vehículo)* caravan. **2** *(atasco)* GB tailback; US backup.
carbón *nm (mineral)* coal. ■ **carbón vegetal** charcoal.
carbono *nm* carbon.
carburador *nm* GB carburettor; US carburetor.
carburante *nm* fuel.
carcajada *nf* burst of laughter, guffaw.
cárcel *nf* prison, jail.
cardenal[1] *nm (de la iglesia)* cardinal.
cardenal[2] *nm (hematoma)* bruise.
cardíaco,-a *adj* cardiac, heart.
cardo *nm (planta)* thistle
carecer *vi*. • **carecer de algo** to lack STH.
carga *nf* **1** *(mercancías)* load. **2** *(peso)* burden. **3** *(flete)* cargo, freight. **4** *(obligación)* duty. **5** *(explosiva, eléctrica, militar)* charge. **6** *(de pluma, bolígrafo)* refill.
cargamento *nm (de tren, camión)* load; *(de avión, barco)* cargo.

cargar vt 1 *(vehículo, arma, mercancías)* to load. 2 *(pluma, encendedor)* to fill. 3 *(pila)* to charge. ► vpr **cargarse** fam *(destrozar)* to smash, ruin. • **cargar con** 1 *(peso)* to carry. 2 *(responsabilidad)* to take.

cargo nm 1 *(puesto)* post, position. 2 *(gobierno, custodia)* charge, responsibility. 3 JUR charge, accusation. • **hacerse cargo de** 1 *(responsabilizarse de)* to take charge of. 2 *(entender)* to take into consideration, realize.

caricatura nf caricature.

caricia nf 1 *(a persona)* caress, stroke. 2 *(a animal)* stroke.

caridad nf charity.

caries nf tooth decay, caries.

cariño nm 1 *(afecto)* love, affection, fondness. 2 *(apelativo)* darling.

carnaval nm carnival.

carne nf 1 meat. 2 *(de persona, fruta)* flesh. • **en carne viva** raw; **ser de carne y hueso** to be only human. ■ **carne asada** roasted meat; **carne de buey** beef; **carne de gallina** goose flesh, goose bumps; **carne picada** GB mincemeat; US ground beef.

carné nm card. ■ **carné de conducir** GB driving licence; US driver's license; **carné de identidad** identity card.

carnet nm → **carné**.

carnicería nf *(tienda)* butcher's.

caro,-a adj expensive, dear. ► adv **caro** at a high price.

carpa[1] nf *(pez)* carp.

carpa[2] nf *(toldo)* marquee; *(de circo)* big top.

carpeta nf folder, file.

carpintería nf 1 *(labor)* carpentry. 2 *(taller)* carpenter's shop.

carrera nf 1 *(competición)* race. 2 *(estudios)* university education. 3 *(profesión)* career. 4 *(trayecto)* route. 5 *(en las medias)* ladder.

carreta nf cart.

carrete nm 1 *(de película)* roll of film, film. 2 *(de hilo, pesca)* reel.

carretera nf road. ■ **carretera nacional** GB A road, main road; US state highway.

carril nm lane. ■ **carril bici** GB cycle lane; US bikeway.

carro nm 1 *(carreta)* cart. 2 *(militar)* tank. 3 *(en supermercado, aeropuerto)* GB trolley; US cart.

carrocería nf bodywork.

carroza nf 1 *(de caballos)* coach, carriage. 2 *(de carnaval)* float.

carruaje nm carriage, coach.

carta nf 1 *(documento)* letter. 2 *(naipe)* card. 3 *(en restaurante)* menu. ■ **carta certificada** registered letter.

cartel nm poster.

cartelera nf 1 *(para carteles)* GB hoarding; US billboard. 2

(en periódicos) entertainment guide.

cartera *nf* **1** *(monedero)* wallet. **2** *(de colegial)* satchel, schoolbag. **3** *(de ejecutivo)* briefcase; *(sin asa)* portfolio.

carterista *nmf* pickpocket.

cartero,-a *nm,f (hombre)* GB postman; US mailman; *(mujer)* GB postwoman; US mailwoman.

cartilla *nf.* ▪ **cartilla de ahorros** savings book; **cartilla del seguro** social security card.

cartón *nm* **1** *(material)* cardboard. **2** *(de cigarrillos, leche)* carton.

casa *nf* **1** *(edificio)* house. **2** *(hogar)* home. ▪ **casa adosada** terraced house; **casa de campo** country house; **casa de huéspedes** guesthouse, boarding house; **casa de socorro** first aid post; **casa pareada** semi-detached house.

casarse *vpr* to get married.

cascada *nf* waterfall, cascade.

cascanueces *nm* nutcracker.

cáscara *nf* **1** *(de huevo, nuez)* shell. **2** *(de plátano)* skin. **3** *(de naranja, limón)* peel, rind. **4** *(de grano)* husk.

casco *nm* **1** *(protector)* helmet. **2** *(envase)* empty bottle. **3** *(de barco)* hull. **4** *(de caballo)* hoof. ▶ *nm pl* **cascos** *(auriculares)* headphones. ▪ **casco antiguo** old town; **casco azul** blue beret; **casco urbano** city centre; US downtown area.

caserío *nm* country house.

casero,-a *adj (productos)* homemade. ▶ *nm,f (dueño - hombre)* landlord; *(- mujer)* landlady.

caseta *nf* **1** *(de feria)* stall. **2** *(de bañistas)* GB bathing hut; US bath house. **3** *(de perro)* kennel.

casete *nm (aparato)* cassette player, cassette recorder. ▶ *nf (cinta)* cassette *(tape)*.

casi *adv* **1** *(gen)* almost, nearly. **2** *(en frases negativas)* hardly: *casi nunca*, hardly ever.

casilla *nf* **1** *(de casillero)* pigeonhole. **2** *(cuadrícula)* square. **3** *(de formulario)* box.

casino *nm* casino.

caso *nm* case. • **en caso de que** if; **en ese caso** in that case; **en todo caso** anyhow, at any rate.

caspa *nf* dandruff.

castaña *nf (fruto)* chestnut.

castaño,-a *adj* chestnut-coloured; *(pelo)* brown. ▶ *nm* **castaño** *(árbol)* chestnut tree.

castañuela *nf* castanet.

castellano,-a *adj-nm,f* Castilian. ▶ *nm* **castellano** *(idioma)* Castilian, Spanish.

castigar *vt* to punish.

castigo *nm* punishment.

castillo *nm* castle.

castor *nm* beaver.

casualidad *nf* chance, coincidence. • **por casualidad** by chance.

catalán,-ana *adj-nm,f* Catalan, Catalonian. ▸ *nm* **catalán** *(idioma)* Catalan.

catálogo *nm* catalogue.

catarata *nf* 1 *(de agua)* waterfall. 2 *(en ojo)* cataract.

catarro *nm* cold.

catástrofe *nf* catastrophe.

catedral *nf* cathedral.

catedrático,-a *nm,f (de universidad)* professor; *(de instituto)* head of department.

categoría *nf* 1 *(rango)* category. 2 *(nivel)* level.

católico,-a *adj-nm,f* Catholic.

catorce *num* fourteen; *(en fechas)* fourteenth.

cauce *nm* 1 *(de río)* river bed. 2 *(canal)* channel.

caucho *nm* rubber.

caudal *nm* 1 *(de río)* volume of water. 2 *(riqueza)* fortune, wealth.

causa *nf* 1 *(motivo, ideal)* cause. 2 *(proceso)* lawsuit. • **a causa de** because of, on account of.

causar *vt* to cause, bring about.

cautiverio *nm* captivity.

cauto,-a *adj* cautious.

cava *nm (bebida)* cava. ▸ *nf (bodega)* wine cellar.

cavar *vt* to dig.

caverna *nf* cavern, cave.

caviar *nm* caviar.

cavidad *nf* cavity.

caza *nf* 1 *(acción)* hunting. 2 *(animales)* game. ▸ *nm (avión)* fighter.

cazadora *nf (chaqueta)* jacket.

cazador,-ra *nm,f* hunter.

cazar *vt* to hunt.

cazo *nm* 1 *(cucharón)* ladle. 2 *(cacerola)* saucepan.

cazuela *nf* casserole.

CD-ROM *nm* CD-ROM.

cebada *nf* barley.

cebo *nm* 1 *(para animales)* food. 2 *(para pescar)* bait.

cebolla *nf* onion.

cebolleta *nf* 1 *(hierba)* chive. 2 *(cebolla)* spring onion.

cebra *nf* zebra.

ceder *vt (dar)* to give. ▸ *vi* 1 *(rendirse)* to give in yield: **cedió a mis peticiones**, she gave in to my requests. 2 *(caerse)* to fall, give way: **las paredes cedieron**, the walls caved in. • **ceder el paso** GB to give way; US to yield.

cedro *nm* cedar.

ceguera *nf* blindness.

ceja *nf* eyebrow.

celda *nf* cell.

celebración *nf* 1 *(fiesta)* celebration. 2 *(de reunión, congreso, etc)* holding.

celebrar *vt* 1 *(festejar)* to celebrate. 2 *(reunión, congreso, etc)* to hold. 3 *(misa)* to say. ▸ *vpr* **celebrarse** to take place, be held.

célebre *adj* well-known, famous.

celo[1] *nm* **1** *(entusiasmo)* zeal. **2** *(cuidado)* care. ► *nm pl* **celos** jealousy. • **estar en celo** to be on heat, be in season; **tener celos** to be jealous.

celo[®2] *nm* GB Sellotape®; US Scotch tape®.

celofán *nm* Cellophane®.

célula *nf* cell.

cementerio *nm* cemetery.

cemento *nm* cement. ▪ **cemento armado** reinforced concrete.

cena *nf* dinner, supper.

cenar *vi* to have dinner, have supper. ► *vt* to have for dinner, have for supper.

cenicero *nm* ashtray.

ceniza *nf* ash.

censo *nm* census. ▪ **censo electoral** electoral roll.

centeno *nm* rye.

centígrado,-a *adj* centigrade.

centímetro *nm* GB centimetre; US centimeter.

céntimo *nm* cent, centime.

centollo *nm* spider crab.

central *adj* central. ► *nf* **1** *(oficina principal)* head office, headquarters. **2** *(eléctrica)* power station.

centralita *nf* switchboard.

céntrico,-a *adj* central: *una calle céntrica*, a street in the centre (US center) of town.

centro *nm* **1** *(gen)* GB centre; US center. **2** *(de la ciudad)* town centre; US downtown. ▪ **centro comercial** GB shopping centre; US mall.

cepa *nf* *(de vid)* vine.

cepillar(se) *vt-vpr* *(pelo, zapato, etc)* to brush.

cepillo *nm* brush. ▪ **cepillo de dientes** toothbrush.

cera *nf* *(gen)* wax; *(de abeja)* beeswax; *(de oreja)* earwax.

cerámica *nf* ceramics, pottery.

cerca[1] *nf* *(valla)* fence.

cerca[2] *adv* near, close. • **cerca de 1** *(cercano a)* near. **2** *(casi)* nearly; **de cerca** close up.

cercano,-a *adj* **1** *(lugar)* nearby. **2** *(tiempo)* near. **3** *(pariente, amigo)* close.

cerda *nf* *(animal)* sow.

cerdo *nm* **1** *(animal)* pig. **2** *(carne)* pork.

cereal *adj-nm* cereal.

cerebro *nm* brain.

ceremonia *nf* ceremony.

cereza *nf* cherry.

cerilla *nf* match.

cero *nm* **1** zero, nought. **2** nil: *ganamos tres a cero*, we won three-nil. • **bajo cero** below zero.

cerrado,-a *adj* **1** *(gen)* shut, closed. **2** *(con llave)* locked. **3** *(acento)* broad. **4** *(curva)* sharp.

cerradura *nf* lock.

cerrajero *nm* locksmith.

cerrar vt **1** to close, shut. **2** (con llave) to lock. **3** (grifo, gas) to turn off. **4** (luz) to switch off. **5** (cremallera) to zip (up).

cerrojo nm bolt.

certamen nm competition, contest.

certeza nf certainty.

certificado,-a adj **1** (documento) certified. **2** (envío) registered. ► nm **certificado** (documento) certificate.

cerveza nf beer. ■ **cerveza de barril** GB draught beer; US draft beer.

cesar vi (parar) to cease, stop. ● **sin cesar** nonstop.

césped nm lawn, grass. ● "Prohibido pisar el césped" "Keep off the grass".

cesta nf basket.

cesto nm basket.

chabola nf shack.

chacal nm jackal.

chal nm shawl.

chalé nm **1** (gen) house. **2** (en campo, playa) villa.

chaleco nm GB waistcoat; US vest. ■ **chaleco salvavidas** life jacket.

chalet nm chalé.

champán nm champagne.

champiñón nm mushroom.

champú nm shampoo.

chancleta nf GB flip-flop; US thong.

chándal nm tracksuit, jogging suit.

chantaje nm blackmail.

chapa nf **1** (de metal) sheet. **2** (de madera) board. **3** (tapón) bottle top. **4** (de coche) bodywork.

chaparrón nm downpour, heavy shower.

chapuzón nm dip.

chaqué nm morning coat.

chaqueta nf jacket.

chaquetón nm short coat.

charanga nf brass band.

charca nf pool, pond.

charco nm (de lluvia) puddle; (de sangre, etc.) pool.

charcutería nf pork butcher's shop, delicatessen.

charlar vi to chat, talk.

chárter adj-nm charter.

chasis nm chassis.

chatarra nf **1** (metal) scrap metal. **2** fam (monedas) small change.

chatear vi to chat.

chato,-a adj **1** (nariz) snub. **2** (persona) snub-nosed. **3** (objeto) flat. ► nm **chato** (vaso) small glass.

chaval,-la nm,f kid, youngster; (chico) lad; (chica) lass.

cheque nm GB cheque; US check. ● **extender un cheque** to issue a cheque. ■ **cheque al portador** cheque payable to bearer; **cheque de viaje** traveller's cheque; **cheque en blanco** blank cheque; **cheque sin fondos** dud cheque.

chequeo *nm* checkup.

chichón *nm* bump, lump.

chicle *nm* chewing gum.

chico,-a *nm,f* **1** *(niño)* kid; *(niña)* girl. **2** *(muchacho)* boy, guy; *(muchacha)* girl.

Chile *nm* Chile.

chileno,-a *adj-nm,f* Chilean.

chillar *vi (persona)* to scream, yell; *(gritar)* to shout.

chillido *nm* **1** *(de persona)* scream, yell. **2** *(de animal)* screech, squeal.

chimenea *nf* **1** *(exterior)* chimney. **2** *(hogar)* fireplace. **3** *(de barco)* funnel.

chimpancé *nm* chimpanzee.

chincheta *nf* GB drawing pin; US thumbtack.

chino,-a *adj* Chinese.

chip *nm* INFORM chip.

chipirón *nm* baby squid.

chiquito,-a *adj* tiny, very small. ► *nm* **chiquito** small glass of wine.

chiringuito *nm fam (en playa)* bar, restaurant; *(en carretera)* roadside snack bar.

chispa *nf* **1** *(de fuego)* spark. **2** *fig (ingenio)* wit.

chiste *nm* joke. ▪ **chiste verde** blue joke, dirty joke.

chistera *nf* top hat.

chivato,-a *nm,f fam (delator)* informer, GB grass; *(acusica)* GB telltale; US tattletale. ► *nm* **chivato** *(piloto)* warning light.

chocar *vi* **1** *(colisionar)* to collide, crash. **2** *fig (sorprender)* to surprise. **4** *(escandalizar)* to shock. ► *vt (manos)* to shake.

chocolate *nm* chocolate. ▪ **chocolate a la taza** drinking chocolate; **chocolate con leche** milk chocolate.

chocolatina *nf* chocolate bar.

chófer *nm (particular)* chauffeur; *(de autocar etc)* driver.

chopo *nm* poplar.

choque *nm* collision, crash.

chorizo *nm* spicy pork sausage.

chorro *nm* **1** *(de líquido)* stream, jet. **2** *(de vapor)* jet.

choza *nf* hut.

christmas *nm* Christmas card.

chubasco *nm* heavy shower.

chubasquero *nm* raincoat.

chufa *nf* tiger nut.

chuleta *nf (de carne)* chop.

chulo,-a *adj* **1** *(engreído)* cocky. **2** *fam (bonito)* nice. ► *nm,f (presuntuoso)* show-off.

chupar *vt* **1** *(succionar)* to suck. **2** *(lamer)* to lick. **3** *(absorber)* to absorb, soak up.

chupete *nm* GB dummy; US pacifier.

churrería *nf* fritter shop.

churro *nm* **1** *(comida)* fritter. **2** *fam (chapuza)* botch.

chutar *vi* to shoot.

cibercafé *nm* Internet café, cybercafé.

ciberespacio *nm* cyberspace.

cibernética *nf* cybernetics.

cicatriz *nf* scar.

cicatrizar(se) *vt-vpr* to heal.

ciclismo *nm* cycling.

ciclista *nmf* cyclist.

ciclo *nm* **1** *(gen)* cycle. **2** *(de conferencias)* series. **3** *(de películas)* season.

ciclón *nm* cyclone.

ciego,-a *adj (persona)* blind. ▶ *nm,f (persona)* blind person.

cielo *nm* **1** *(gen)* sky. **2** REL heaven. **3** *(apelativo)* darling.

ciempiés *nm* centipede.

cien *num* a hundred, one hundred. • **cien por cien** a hundred per cent.

ciencia *nf* science. • **a ciencia cierta** with certainty. ▪ **ciencia ficción** science fiction.

científico,-a *adj* scientific. ▶ *nm,f* scientist.

ciento *num* a hundred, one hundred. • **por ciento** per cent.

cierre *nm* **1** *(de prenda)* fastener. **2** *(de collar, pulsera)* clasp. **3** *(de fábrica)* closure; *(de tienda)* closing-down. ▪ **cierre centralizado** central locking.

cierto,-a *adj* **1** *(seguro)* certain, sure. **2** *(verdadero)* true. **3** *(algún)* (a) certain, some: *cierto día*, one day. ▶ *adv* **cierto** certainly. • **estar en lo cierto** to be right; **por cierto** by the way.

ciervo *nm* deer.

cifra *nf* figure.

cigala *nf* Dublin Bay prawn.

cigarrillo *nm* cigarette.

cigarro *nm* **1** *(cigarrillo)* cigarette. **2** *(puro)* cigar.

cigüeña *nf (ave)* stork.

cilindro *nm* cylinder.

cima *nf* summit, peak.

cimiento *nf* foundation.

cinc *nm* zinc.

cinco *num* five; *(en fechas)* fifth.

cincuenta *num* fifty.

cine *nm* **1** *(lugar)* GB cinema; US movie theater. **2** *(arte)* cinema. ▪ **cine mudo** silent films; **cine negro** film noir.

cinta *nf* **1** *(casete, vídeo)* tape. **2** *(tira)* tape, band; *(decorativa)* ribbon. ▪ **cinta adhesiva** sticky tape; **cinta aislante** insulating tape; **cinta métrica** tape measure; **cinta transportadora** conveyor belt; **cinta virgen** blank tape.

cintura *nf* waist.

cinturón *nm* belt. ▪ **cinturón de seguridad** seat belt, safety belt.

ciprés *nm* cypress.

circo *nm* circus.

circuito *nm* circuit.

circulación *nf* **1** *(de sangre, dinero)* circulation. **2** *(de vehículos)* traffic.

circular *adj* circular. ▶ *nf (carta)* circular letter. ▶ *vi* **1** *(sangre)* to circulate. **2** *(trenes, autobuses)* to run; *(coches)* to drive; *(peatones)* to walk.

círculo *nm* circle.
circunferencia *nf* circumference.
circunstancia *nf* circumstance.
ciruela *nf* plum. ▪ **ciruela claudia** greengage; **ciruela pasa** prune.
cirugía *nf* surgery.
cirujano,-a *nm,f* surgeon.
cisne *nm* swan.
cisterna *nf* cistern, tank.
cita *nf* 1 *(para negocios, médico, etc)* appointment. 2 *(con novio, novia)* date. 3 *(mención)* quotation.
citar *vt* 1 *(convocar)* to arrange to meet. 2 *(mencionar)* to quote.
cítricos *nm pl* citrus fruits.
ciudad *nf (grande)* city; *(más pequeña)* town.
ciudadano,-a *nm,f* citizen.
civil *adj* civil.
civilización *nf* civilization.
clandestino,-a *adj* 1 *(actividad, reunión)* clandestine, secret. 2 *(periódico, asociación)* underground.
clara *nf* 1 *(de huevo)* egg white. 2 *(bebida)* shandy.
claridad *nf* clarity, clearness.
clarinete *nm* clarinet. ► *nmf* clarinettist.
claro,-a *adj* 1 *(gen)* clear. 2 *(color)* light. 3 *(salsa)* thin. ► *adv* **claro** clearly. ► *nm (de bosque)* clearing. ► *interj* ¡**cla-**

ro! of course! ● **claro que no** of course not; **claro que sí** of course; **estar claro** to be clear.
clase *nf* 1 *(alumnos)* class. 2 *(lección)* lesson, class. 3 *(aula)* classroom. 4 *(tipo)* type, sort. ● **dar clase** to teach. ▪ **clase alta** upper class; **clase baja** lower class; **clase media** middle class; **clase obrera** working class; **clase particular** private class.
clásico,-a *adj* classical.
clasificación *nf* 1 *(ordenación)* classification, sorting. 2 *(deportiva)* league, table.
clasificar *vt* 1 *(ordenar)* to class, classify. 2 *(documentos, cartas)* to sort. ► *vpr* **clasificarse** *(deportista)* to qualify.
claustro *nm (de iglesia)* cloister.
cláusula *nf* clause.
clavar *vt* 1 *(sujetar)* to nail. 2 *(a golpes)* to hammer. 3 *(aguja, cuchillo)* to stick.
clave *nf* 1 *(gen)* key. 2 *(de signos)* code.
clavel *nm* carnation.
clavícula *nf* collarbone, clavicle.
clavija *nf (enchufe macho)* plug; *(pata de enchufe)* pin.
clavo *nm* 1 *(de metal)* nail. 2 *(especia)* clove.
claxon *nm* horn, hooter.
cliente *nmf* 1 *(de empresa)* client. 2 *(de tienda)* customer.

clientela *nf* **1** *(de empresa)* clients. **2** *(de tienda)* customers. **3** *(de restaurante)* clientele.

clima *nm* climate.

climatizado,-a *adj* air-conditioned.

clínica *nf* clinic, private hospital.

clip *nm* *(para papel)* paper clip.

clon *nm* clone.

cloro *nm* chlorine.

club *nm* club.

coartada *nf* alibi.

cobarde *nmf* coward.

cobra *nf* cobra.

cobrador,-ra *nm,f (de autobús - hombre)* conductor; *(- mujer)* conductress.

cobrar *vt (fijar precio por)* to charge; *(cheques)* to cash; *(salario)* to earn. ► *vi* to be paid.

cobre *nm* copper.

cobro *nm* cashing, collection. ▪ **cobro revertido** reverse charge.

cocción *nf (acción de guisar)* cooking; *(en agua)* boiling; *(en horno)* baking.

cocer(se) *vt-vpr (guisar)* to cook; *(hervir)* to boil; *(hornear)* to bake.

coche *nm* **1** *(automóvil)* GB car; US car, automobile. **2** *(de tren, de caballos)* carriage, coach. ▪ **coche cama** sleeping car; **coche de alquiler** hire car.

cochinillo *nm* sucking pig.

cochino,-a *adj (sucio)* filthy. ► *nm,f* **1** *(animal)* pig. **2** *fam (persona)* dirty person.

cocido,-a *adj* cooked; *(en agua)* boiled. ► *nm* **cocido** *(plato)* stew.

cocina *nf* **1** *(lugar)* kitchen. **2** *(gastronomía)* cooking, cuisine. **3** *(aparato)* GB cooker; US stove. ▪ **cocina casera** home cooking; **cocina de mercado** food in season.

cocinar *vt* to cook.

cocinero,-a *nm,f* cook.

coco *nm* coconut.

cocodrilo *nm* crocodile.

cocotero *nm* coconut palm.

cóctel *nm* **1** *(bebida)* cocktail. **2** *(fiesta)* cocktail party.

código *nm* code. ▪ **código de barras** bar code; **código de circulación** highway code; **código postal** GB postcode; US zipcode.

codo *nm* elbow.

codorniz *nf* quail.

cofre *nm* trunk, chest.

coger *vt* **1** *(gen)* to catch. **2** *(tomar)* to take. **3** *(fruta, flor)* to pick.

cogollo *nm* **1** *(de lechuga etc)* heart. **2** *(brote)* shoot.

coherente *adj* coherent.

cohete *nm* rocket.

coincidencia *nf* coincidence.

coincidir *vi* **1** *(fechas, resultados)* to coincide. **2** *(estar de* *acuerdo)* to agree. **3** *(encontrarse)* to meet.

cojear *vi* to limp, hobble.

cojo,-a *adj* lame.

col *nf* cabbage. ▪ **col de Bruselas** Brussels sprout.

cola¹ *nf* **1** *(de animal)* tail. **2** *(fila)* GB queue; US line. ● **hacer cola** GB to queue up; US to stand in line.

cola² *nf (pegamento)* glue.

colaborar *vi* **1** *(en tarea)* to collaborate. **2** *(en prensa)* to contribute.

colada *nf* washing.

colador *nm* **1** *(de té, café)* strainer. **2** *(de alimentos)* colander.

colar *vt (filtrar)* to strain, filter. ▶ *vpr* **colarse 1** *(en un lugar)* to sneak in. **2** *(en una cola)* to push in.

colcha *nf* bedspread.

colchón *nm* mattress.

colchoneta *nf* **1** *(de gimnasio)* mat. **2** *(de playa)* air bed.

colección *nf* collection.

colectivo,-a *adj* collective.

colega *nmf* **1** *(de trabajo)* colleague. **2** *fam (amigo)* GB mate; US buddy.

colegio *nm (escuela)* school. ▪ **colegio electoral** polling station; **colegio mayor** hall of residence; **colegio privado** private school; **colegio público** state school.

cólera¹ *nf (furia)* anger, rage.

cólera² *nm (enfermedad)* cholera.

coleta *nf* pigtail.

colgador *nm* hanger.

colgar *vt* **1** *(cuadro)* to hang, put up; *(colada)* to hang out; *(abrigo)* to hang up. **2** *(teléfono)* to put down.

colibrí *nm* humming bird.

cólico *nm* colic.

coliflor *nf* cauliflower.

colilla *nf* cigarette end, cigarette butt.

colina *nf* hill.

colirio *nm* eyewash.

collar *nm* **1** *(joya)* necklace. **2** *(de animal)* collar.

colmena *nf* beehive.

colmillo *nm* **1** *(de persona)* eye tooth, canine tooth. **2** *(de elefante)* tusk.

colocación *nf* **1** *(acto)* placing. **2** *(situación)* situation. **3** *(empleo)* employment.

colocar *vt* **1** *(situar)* to place, put. **2** *(emplear)* to give a job to.

Colombia *nf* Colombia.

colombiano,-a *adj-nm,f* Colombian.

colon *nm* colon.

colonia¹ *nf (grupo, territorio)* colony. ▶ *nf pl* summer camp.

colonia² *nf (perfume)* cologne.

color *nm* GB colour; US color.

colorete *nm* rouge.

columna *nf* column. ▪ **columna vertebral** spine, spinal column.

columpio *nm* swing.

coma[1] *nf (signo)* comma.

coma[2] *nm* MED coma.

comandante *nm* **1** *(oficial)* commander, commanding officer. **2** *(graduación)* major.

comando *nm* **1** *(de combate)* commando. **2** INFORM command.

comarca *nf* area, region.

combate *nm* **1** *(lucha)* combat, battle. **2** *(en boxeo)* fight.

combinar *vt (ingredientes, esfuerzos)* to combine. ▶ *vi (colores)* to match, go with.

combustible *adj* combustible. ▶ *nm* fuel.

comedia *nf* comedy.

comedor *nm* **1** *(de casa)* dining room. **2** *(de fábrica)* canteen. **3** *(de colegio)* dining hall.

comentar *vt* **1** *(por escrito)* to comment on; *(oralmente)* to talk about, discuss. **2** *(decir)* to tell.

comentario *nm* remark, comment. • **sin comentarios** no comment.

comenzar *vt-vi* to begin, start.

comer *vt* to eat. ▶ *vi* **1** *(alimentarse)* to eat. **2** *(al mediodía)* to have lunch.

comercial *adj* commercial.

comerciante *nmf* **1** *(tendero)* GB shop-keeper; US storekeeper. **2** *(negociante)* trader, dealer.

comerciar *vi* to trade, deal.

comercio *nm* **1** *(ocupación)* commerce, trade. **2** *(tienda)* GB shop; US store. ■ **comercio electrónico** e-commerce.

comestible *adj* edible. ▶ *nm pl* **comestibles** groceries, food.

cometa *nm (astro)* comet. ▶ *nf (juguete)* kite.

cometer *vt (crimen)* to commit; *(falta, error)* to make.

cómic *nm* comic.

cómico,-a *adj* comic.

comida *nf* **1** *(comestibles)* food. **2** *(a cualquier hora)* meal. **3** *(a mediodía)* lunch.

comienzo *nm* start, beginning.

comillas *nf pl* inverted commas.

comino *nm* cumin.

comisaría *nf* police station.

comisario *nm* GB superintendent; US captain.

comisión *nf* **1** *(retribución)* commission. **2** *(comité)* committee.

comité *nm* committee.

como *adv* **1** *(lo mismo que)* as: *negro como el tizón*, as dark as night. **2** *(de tal modo)* like: *hablas como un político*, you talk like a politician. **3** *(según)* as: *como dice tu amigo*, as your friend says. **4** *(en calidad de)* as: *como invitado*, as a guest. ▶ *conj* **1** *(así que)* as soon as. **2** *(si)* if: *como lo* *vuelvas a hacer ...*, if you do it again ... **3** *(porque)* as, since: *como llegamos tarde no pudimos entrar*, since we arrived late we couldn't get in. • **como quiera que** since, as, given that; **como sea** whatever happens, no matter what.

cómo *adv* **1** *(de qué modo)* how: *¿cómo se hace?*, how do you do it? **2** *(por qué)* why: *¿cómo no viniste?*, why didn't you come? • **¿cómo está usted? 1** *(al conocerse)* how do you do? **2** *(de salud)* how are you?; **¡cómo no!** but of course!, certainly!

comodidad *nf* **1** *(confort)* comfort. **2** *(facilidad)* convenience.

comodín *nm* joker.

cómodo,-a *adj* comfortable, cosy.

compact disc *nm* compact disc.

compacto *adj* compact. ▶ *nm* compact disc.

compañero,-a *nm,f* **1** *(de trabajo)* colleague. **2** *(pareja)* partner.

compañía *nf* company.

comparación *nf* comparison.

comparar *vt* to compare.

compartimento *nm* compartment.

compartir *vt* to share.

compás *nm* **1** *(instrumento)* compass, a pair of compasses. **2** *(ritmo)* beat.

compatible *adj* compatible.

compatriota *nmf* compatriot.

competencia *nf* **1** *(rivalidad)* competition. **2** *(competidores)* competitors. **3** *(habilidad)* competence, ability.

competente *adj* competent, capable.

competición *nf* competition.

competir *vi* to compete.

complejo,-a *adj* complex. ▶ *nm* **complejo** complex.

complemento *nm* complement. ▶ *nm pl* **complementos** accessories.

completar *vt* to complete, finish.

completo,-a *adj* **1** *(entero, total)* complete. **2** *(lleno)* full. • **al completo 1** *(lleno)* full up, filled to capacity. **2** *(la totalidad de)* the whole, all of; **por completo** completely.

complicado,-a *adj* complicated, complex.

complicar *vt* to complicate.

cómplice *nmf* accomplice.

componente *adj-nm* component.

componer *vt* **1** *(formar)* to make up. **2** *(música)* to compose; *(poema)* to write, compose.

comportamiento *nm* GB behaviour; US behavior.

comportarse *vpr* to behave.

composición *nf* composition.

compositor,-ra *nm,f* composer.

compota *nf* compote.

compra *nf* purchase, buy. • **hacer la compra** to do the shopping; **ir de compras** to go shopping.

comprador,-ra *nm,f* buyer.

comprar *vt* to buy.

comprender *vt* **1** *(entender)* to understand. **2** *(contener)* to comprise, include.

compresa *nf* **1** *(higiénica)* sanitary towel. **2** *(venda)* compress.

comprimido *nm* tablet.

comprobante *nm* receipt, voucher.

comprobar *vt* to check.

comprometerse *vpr* **1** *(prometer)* to commit oneself. **2** *(novios)* to get engaged.

compromiso *nm* **1** *(obligación)* commitment. **2** *(acuerdo)* agreement. **3** *(cita)* engagement.

compuesto,-a *adj* compound.

computadora *nf* computer.

comulgar *vi* to receive Holy Communion.

común *adj* common. • **por lo común** generally.

comunicación *nf* **1** *(relación)* communication. **2** *(telefónica)* connection.

comunicado *nm* comuniqué. ▪ **comunicado de prensa** press release.

comunicar *vi* *(teléfono)* GB to be engaged; US to be busy. ▶ *vt* **1** *(hacer saber)* to inform. **2** *(unir)* to connect, link.

comunidad *nf* community.

comunión *nf* communion.

comunismo *nm* communism.

comunista *adj-nmf* communist.

con *prep* **1** *(compañía, instrumento, medio)* with: *hay que comerlo con una cuchara*, you have to eat it with a spoon. **2** *(modo, circunstancia)* in, with: *¿vas a salir con ese frío?*, are you going out in this cold?. **3** *(relación)* to: *sé amable con ella*, be kind to her.

conceder *vt* *(dar - préstamo, deseo)* to grant; *(- premio)* to award.

concentración *nf* concentration.

concentrar(se) *vt-vpr* to concentrate.

concepto *nm* concept. • **bajo ningún concepto** under no circumstances; **en concepto de** by way of.

concertar *vt* *(entrevista, cita)* to arrange.

concesión *nf* **1** *(en negociación)* concession. **2** *(de premio)* awarding.

concesionario *nm* dealer.

concha *nf* shell.

conciencia *nf* **1** *(moral)* conscience. **2** *(conocimiento)* awareness. • **a conciencia** conscientiously.

concierto *nm* *(espectáculo)* concert; *(obra)* concerto.

conclusión *nf* conclusion.

concretar *vt* *(precisar)* to specify: *concretar una hora*, to fix a time, set a time.

concreto,-a *adj* **1** *(real)* concrete. **2** *(particular)* specific, definite. • **en concreto 1** *(en particular)* in particular. **2** *(para ser exacto)* to be precise.

concurrido,-a *adj* busy, crowded.

concursante *nmf* contestant, participant.

concursar *vi* to compete.

concurso *nm* *(competición - gen)* competition; *(- de belleza, deportivo)* contest; *(- en televisión)* quiz show.

conde *nm* count.

condecoración *nf* decoration, medal.

condena *nf* sentence.

condenar *vt* **1** *(declarar culpable)* to convict. **2** *(sentenciar)* to sentence.

condesa *nf* countess.

condición *nf* condition. • **a condición de que** on condition that, provided (that).

condimentar *vt* to season, GB flavour; US flavor.

condimento *nm* seasoning, GB flavouring; US flavoring.

conducir *vt* *(guiar)* to lead; *(coche, animales)* to drive; *(moto)* to ride. ► *vi* **1** *(dirigir un vehículo)* to drive. **2** *(llevar)* to lead: *esta carretera conduce a Teruel*, this road leads to Teruel.

conducta *nf* conduct.

conducto *nm* **1** *(tubería)* pipe, conduit. **2** *(del cuerpo)* duct.

conductor,-ra *nm,f* driver.

conectar *vt* **1** *(unir)* to connect. **2** *(aparato, luz, etc.)* to switch on, turn on.

conejo *nm* rabbit.

conexión *nf* connection.

confección *nf* **1** *(de prendas)* dressmaking. **2** *(elaboración)* making.

conferencia *nf* **1** *(charla)* talk, lecture. **2** *(congreso)* conference. **3** *(llamada telefónica)* long-distance call.

conferenciante *nmf* lecturer.

confesar(se) *vt-vpr* to confess.

confesión *nf* confession.

confianza *nf* **1** *(seguridad)* confidence. **2** *(fe)* trust. **3** *(familiaridad)* familiarity.

confiar *vi* **1 confiar en** ALGN/**algo** *(tener fe)* to trust SB/STH. **2 confiar en + inf** *(estar seguro)* to be confident that, be sure that: *confío en aprobar el examen*, I'm confident that I'll pass the exam.

configuración *nf* INFORM configuration. ▪ **configuración por defecto** default settings.

confirmar *vt* to confirm.

confitería *nf (bombonería)* GB sweet shop; US candy shop; *(pastelería)* cake shop.

conflicto *nm* conflict.

conformarse *vpr* to resign oneself, be content.

conforme *adj* 1 *(de acuerdo)*: **estar conforme**, to agree. 2 *(satisfecho)* satisfied, happy.

confortable *adj* comfortable.

confundir *vt* 1 *(mezclar)* to mix up. 2 *(desconcertar)* to confuse. 3 *(no reconocer)* to mistake. ▶ *vpr* **confundirse** *(equivocarse)* to be mistaken, make a mistake.

confusión *nf* 1 *(desorden)* confusion. 2 *(equivocación)* mistake.

congelado,-a *adj* frozen.

congelador *nm* freezer.

congelar(se) *vt-vpr* to freeze.

congestión *nf* congestion.

congreso *nm* conference, congress.

congrio *nm* conger eel.

conífera *nf* conifer.

conjugación *nf* conjugation.

conjunción *nf* conjunction.

conjuntivitis *nf* conjunctivitis.

conjunto *nm* 1 *(grupo)* group, collection. 2 *(todo)* whole. 3 *(de música - pop)* band, group; *(- clásica)* ensemble. 4 *(prenda)* outfit.

conmigo *pron* with me.

conmoción *nf (cerebral)* concussion.

cono *nm* cone.

conocer *vt* 1 *(gen)* to know; *(persona por primera vez)* to meet. 2 *(país, lugar)* to have been to.

conocido,-a *adj* 1 *(reconocible)* familiar. 2 *(famoso)* well-known. ▶ *nm,f* acquaintance.

conocimiento *nm* 1 *(saber)* knowledge. 2 *(conciencia)* consciousness.

conquista *nf* conquest.

conquistador,-ra *nm,f* conqueror.

conquistar *vt* 1 *(con armas)* to conquer. 2 *(victoria, título)* to win. 3 *(ligar con)* to win over.

consciente *adj* conscious.

consecuencia *nf* consequence, result.

conseguir *vt (cosa)* to obtain, get; *(objetivo)* to attain, get. ● **conseguir + inf** to manage to + *inf*.

consejero,-a *nm,f* 1 *(asesor)* adviser. 2 POL counsellor.

consejo *nm (recomendación)* advice: *te daré un consejo*, I'll give you a piece of advice. ▪ **consejo de administración** board of directors; **consejo de ministros** cabinet.

consentir vt 1 (permitir) to allow, permit, tolerate. 2 (a un niño) to spoil.

conserje nmf 1 (de hotel, oficina) porter. 2 (de escuela) caretaker.

conservas nf pl tinned food, canned food.

conservación nf 1 (de naturaleza, especie) conservation. 2 (de alimentos) preservation.

conservante nm preservative.

conservar vt 1 (alimentos) to preserve. 2 (calor) retain. 3 (guardar) to keep.

consideración nf 1 (deliberación, atención) consideración. 2 (respeto) regard.

considerar vt 1 (reflexionar) to consider, think over. 2 (juzgar) to consider.

consigna nf (en estación etc) GB left-luggage office; US checkroom.

consigo pron (con él) with him; (con ella) with her; (con usted, ustedes, vosotros,-as) with you; (con ellos,-as) with them; (con uno mismo) with oneself.

consiguiente adj consequent. ▪ **por consiguiente** therefore, consequently.

consistir vi to consist (en, of).

consola nf INFORM console.

consolar vt to console, comfort.

consomé nm consommé, clear soup.

consonante adj-nf consonant.

conspiración nf conspiracy, plot.

constante adj 1 (invariable) constant. 2 (persona) persevering. ▪ **constantes vitales** vital signs.

constar vi 1 (consistir en) to consist (de, of). 2 (ser cierto): **me consta que ha llegado**, I am absolutely certain that he has arrived.

constipado nm cold.

constitución nf constitution.

constituir vt to constitute.

construcción nf 1 (acción) construction, building. 2 (edificio) building.

construir vt to build, construct.

consuelo nm consolation, comfort.

cónsul nmf consul.

consulado nm 1 (oficina) consulate. 2 (cargo) consulship.

consulta nf 1 (pregunta) consultation. 2 (de médico) GB surgery; US office.

consultar vt (persona) to consult; (libro) to look it up in.

consumición nf (bebida) drink.

consumidor,-ra nm,f consumer.

consumir vt to consume.

contabilidad *nf* **1** *(profesión)* accountancy. **2** *(ciencia)* accountancy, book-keeping.

contacto *nm* **1** *(entre personas, cosas)* contact. **2** *(de coche)* ignition.

contagiar *vt* **1** *(enfermedad)* to transmit, pass on. **2** *(persona)* to infect.

contagioso,-a *adj* contagious.

contaminación *nf* *(de agua, radiactiva)* contamination; *(atmosférica)* pollution.

contar *vt* **1** *(calcular)* to count. **2** *(explicar)* to tell. ▶ *vi* to count. • **contar con** ALGN *(confiar)* to count on SB, rely on SB; **contar con algo** *(esperar)* to expect STH.

contemplar *vt-vi* to contemplate.

contener *vt* **1** *(tener dentro)* to contain, hold. **2** *(reprimir)* to contain, hold back.

contenido *nm* content, contents.

contento,-a *adj* happy.

contestación *nf* *(respuesta)* answer, reply.

contestador *nm.* • **contestador automático** answering machine.

contestar *vt* to answer.

contigo *pron* with you.

contiguo,-a *adj* contiguous, adjoining.

continental *adj* continental.

continente *nm* continent.

continuación *nf* continuation. • **a continuación** next.

continuar *vt-vi* to continue, carry on.

contra *prep* against. • **en contra** against.

contrabando *nm* **1** *(actividad)* smuggling. **2** *(mercancía)* contraband.

contraer *vt* **1** *(gen)* to contract. **2** *(enfermedad)* to catch.

contrario,-a *adj* **1** *(dirección, sentido)* contrary, opposite. **2** *(opinión)* contrary. **3** *(rival)* opposing. ▶ *nm,f* opponent. • **al contrario** on the contrary.

contrarreloj *adj* against the clock. ▶ *nf* time trial.

contraseña *nf* password.

contratar *vt* **1** *(servicio etc)* to sign a contract for. **2** *(empleado)* to hire, take on.

contrato *nm* contract. ▪ **contrato de alquiler** lease, leasing agreement.

contraventana *nf* shutter.

contribución *nf* **1** *(aportación)* contribution. **2** *(impuesto)* tax.

contribuir *vt-vi* to contribute.

contrincante *nm* opponent.

control *nm* **1** *(dominio)* control. **2** *(verificación)* examination, inspection. ▪ **control remoto** remote control; **control de pasaportes** passport control; **control de policía** police checkpoint.

controlador,-ra *nm,f.* • **controlador,-ra aéreo,-a** air traffic controller.

controlar *vt* to control.

convencer *vt* to convince.

conveniente *adj* **1** *(cómodo)* convenient. **2** *(ventajoso)* advantageous. **3** *(aconsejable)* advisable.

convenio *nm* agreement.

convenir *vi* **1** *(ser oportuno)* to suit. **2** *(ser aconsejable)*: *te conviene descansar*, you should get some rest.

convento *nm* *(de monjas)* convent; *(de monjes)* monastery.

conversación *nf* conversation.

conversar *vi* to talk.

convertir *vt* to turn into.

convivir *vi* to live together.

convocar *vt* to call.

convocatoria *nf* **1** *(llamamiento)* call. **2** *(examen)* examination, sitting.

coñac *nm* cognac, brandy.

cooperación *nf* cooperation.

cooperar *vi* to cooperate.

coordinación *nf* coordination.

coordinar *vt* to coordinate.

copa *nf* **1** *(recipiente)* glass. **2** *(bebida)* drink. **3** *(de árbol)* top. • **ir de copas** to go (out) drinking; **tomar una copa** to have a drink.

copia *nf* copy. ▪ **copia de seguridad** backup.

copiar *vt* to copy.

copo *nm* *(de cereal)* flake; *(de nieve)* snowflake.

coral¹ *adj* choral. ▶ *nf* choir.

coral² *nm* coral.

corazón *nm* heart.

corbata *nf* tie.

corcho *nm* cork.

cordero,-a *nm,f* lamb.

cordial *adj* cordial, friendly.

cordillera *nf* mountain range.

cordón *nm* *(cuerda)* cord, string; *(de zapatos)* lace, shoelace. ▪ **cordón policial** police cordon; **cordón umbilical** umbilical cord.

coreografía *nf* choreography.

córnea *nf* cornea.

córner *nm* corner.

corneta *nf* bugle.

coro *nm* *(grupo)* choir.

corona *nf* **1** *(de rey)* crown. **2** *(de flores etc)* wreath.

coronel *nm* colonel.

corporación *nf* corporation.

corral *nm* *(de aves)* yard.

correa *nf* **1** *(de piel)* strap. **2** *(cinturón)* belt. **3** *(de perro)* lead. **4** *(de máquina)* belt.

correcto,-a *adj* **1** *(exacto, adecuado)* correct. **2** *(educado)* polite, courteous.

corredor,-ra *nm,f* **1** *(atleta)* runner. **2** *(ciclista)* cyclist. ▶ *nm* **corredor** corridor.

corregir *vt* to correct.

correo *nm* GB post; US mail. ▶ *nm pl* **correos** *(oficina)* post office. • **echar al correo** GB to post; US to mail; **mandar por correo** GB to post; US to mail. ▪ **correo certificado** GB registered post; US registered mail; **correo electrónico** e-mail, electronic mail: *envíamelo por correo electrónico*, e-mail it to me; **correo urgente** express mail.

correr *vi* **1** *(persona, animal)* to run. **2** *(agua)* to flow. **3** *(tiempo)* to pass. **4** *(darse prisa)* to hurry. ► *vt* **1** *(carrera)* to run. **2** *(deslizar)* to close; *(cortina)* to draw.

correspondencia *nf* **1** *(relación)* correspondence. **2** *(cartas)* GB post; US mail. **3** *(de trenes etc)* connection.

corresponder *vi* **1** *(equivaler)* to correspond. **2** *(pertenecer)* to belong, pertain. **3** *(devolver)* to return.

correspondiente *adj* **1** *(perteneciente)* corresponding. **2** *(respectivo)* respective.

corrida *nf*. ▪ **corrida de toros** bullfight.

corriente *adj* **1** *(frecuente)* common. **2** *(no especial)* ordinary. **3** *(agua)* running. ► *nf* **1** *(masa de agua)* current, stream. **2** *(de aire)* GB draught; US draft. **3** *(eléctrica)* current. **4** *(de arte etc)* current, trend. • **al corriente** up to date; **estar al corriente de algo** to know about STH.

corrupción *nf* corruption.

cortado *nm* coffee with a dash of milk.

cortar *vt* **1** *(gen)* to cut. **2** *(interrumpir)* to cut off, interrupt. **3** *(calle, carretera)* to close. ► *vpr* **cortarse 1** *(herirse)* to cut. **2** *(pelo - por otro)* to have one's hair cut; *(- uno mismo)* to cut one's hair. **3** *(leche)* to curdle.

cortaúñas *nm* nail clippers.

corte[1] *nf* court.

corte[2] *nm* *(herida, interrupción)* cut. ▪ **corte de pelo** haircut.

cortés *adj* courteous, polite.

cortesía *nf* courtesy.

corteza *nf* **1** *(de árbol)* bark. **2** *(de pan)* crust. **3** *(de queso)* rind. ▪ **corteza terrestre** earth's crust.

cortina *nf* curtain.

corto,-a *adj* short.

cortocircuito *nm* short circuit.

cortometraje *nm* short (film).

cosa *nf* thing. • **¿alguna cosa más?** anything else?

cosecha *nf* **1** *(acción)* harvest. **2** *(producto)* crop. **3** *(año del vino)* vintage.

cosechar *vt-vi* *(recoger - cosecha)* to harvest, gather; *(- éxitos etc)* to reap.

coser *vt* **1** *(gen)* to sew. **2** *(herida)* to stitch up.

cosmético,-a *adj* cosmetic. ► *nm* **cosmético** cosmetic.

cosquillas *nf pl* • **tener cosquillas** to be ticklish.

cosquilleo *nm* tickling.

costa[1] *nf* coast.

costa[2]. • **a costa de** at the expense of; **a toda costa** at all costs.

costado *nm* side.

costar *vt* 1 *(valer)* to cost. 2 *(esfuerzo, tiempo)* to take. ► *vi* 1 *(al comprar)* to cost. 2 *(ser difícil)* to be difficult.

coste *nm* cost.

costero,-a *adj* coastal.

costilla *nf* 1 *(de persona, animal)* rib. 2 *(como comida)* chop.

costo *nm* *(precio)* cost.

costumbre *nf* 1 *(hábito)* habit. 2 *(tradición)* custom.

costura *nf* 1 *(cosido)* sewing. 2 *(línea de puntadas)* seam.

cotidiano,-a *adj* daily, everyday.

coto *nm*. ▪ **coto de caza** game preserve.

cotorra *nf* *(animal)* parrot.

coyote *nm* coyote.

coz *nf* kick.

cráneo *nm* skull, cranium.

cráter *nm* crater.

creación *nf* creation.

crear *vt* 1 *(producir)* to create. 2 *(fundar)* to found, establish.

crecer *vi* 1 *(gen)* to grow. 2 *(corriente, marea)* to rise.

creciente *adj* *(luna)* crescent.

crecimiento *nm* growth, increase.

crédito *nm* 1 *(al comprar)* credit. 2 *(préstamo)* loan.

creencia *nf* belief.

creer *vi* 1 *(tener fe)* to believe *(en,* in). 2 *(pensar)* to think. ► *vt* 1 *(gen)* to believe. 2 *(pensar)* to think, suppose. • **creo que sí** I think so; **creo que no** I don't think so.

crema *nf* 1 *(nata)* cream. 2 *(natillas)* custard.

cremallera *nf* 1 *(de vestido)* GB zip; US zipper. 2 *(de máquina)* rack.

cremoso,-a *adj* creamy.

cresta *nf* 1 *(de ola)* crest. 2 *(de gallo)* comb.

cría *nf* *(cachorro)* baby.

criar *vt* 1 *(educar)* to bring up. 2 *(dar el pecho)* to nurse. 3 *(animales)* to breed; *(plantas)* to grow.

crimen *nm* 1 *(delito)* crime. 2 *(asesinato)* murder.

criminal *adj-nmf* criminal.

crin *nf* mane.

crisis *nf* 1 *(mal momento)* crisis. 2 *(ataque)* fit, attack.

cristal *nm* glass.

cristalino *nm* crystalline lens.

cristiano,-a *adj-nm,f* Christian.

criterio *nm* 1 *(norma)* criterion. 2 *(juicio)* judgement. 3 *(opinión)* opinion.

crítica *nf* 1 *(juicio, censura)* criticism. 2 *(reseña)* review.

criticar *vt* to criticize.

crítico,-a *adj* critical. ▶ *nm,f* critic.

croar *vi* to croak.

croissant *nm* croissant.

crol *nm* crawl.

cromo *nm* 1 *(metal)* chromium. 2 *(estampa)* picture card.

crónica *nf (en periódico)* article.

crónico,-a *adj* chronic.

cronómetro *nm* stopwatch.

croqueta *nf* croquette.

cross *nm* cross-country race.

cruce *nm* 1 *(acción)* crossing. 2 *(de calles)* crossroads. 3 *(de carreteras)* junction.

crucero *nm* 1 *(buque)* cruiser. 2 *(viaje)* cruise. 3 *(de templo)* transept.

crucifijo *nm* crucifix.

crucigrama *nm* crossword.

crudo,-a *adj* 1 *(sin cocer)* raw; *(poco hecho)* underdone. 2 *(color)* off-white. ▶ *nm* **crudo** *(petróleo)* crude.

cruel *adj* cruel.

crujiente *adj* crunchy.

crujir *vi (puerta)* to creak.

crustáceo *nm* crustacean.

cruz *nf* 1 *(figura)* cross. 2 *(de moneda)* tails.

cruzar *vt* 1 *(río, piernas, animales)* to cross. 2 *(miradas, palabras)* to exchange. ▶ *vpr* **cruzarse** to pass each other.

cuaderno *nm* 1 *(de notas)* notebook. 2 *(escolar)* exercise book.

cuadra *nf* stable.

cuadrado,-a *adj* square: *diez metros cuadrados*, ten square meters. ▶ *nm* **cuadrado** square.

cuadrilátero *nm* ring.

cuadro *nm* 1 *(pintura)* painting. 2 *(cuadrado)* square. 3 *(diagrama)* chart. • **a cuadros** 1 *(estampado)* checkered. 2 *(camisa)* checked, check.

cual *pron (precedido de artículo - persona)* who, whom; *(- cosa)* which: *la gente a la cual preguntamos dijo que...*, the people whom we asked said that... • **cada cual** everyone, everybody; **con lo cual** with the result that.

cuál *pron* which one, what.

cualidad *nf* quality.

cualificado,-a *adj* qualified, skilled.

cualquier *adj* → cualquiera.

cualquiera *adj* any. ▶ *pron (persona indeterminada)* anybody, anyone; *(cosa indeterminada)* any, any one: *cualquiera te lo puede decir* anyone can tell you. • **cualquier cosa** anything; **cualquier otro** anyone else; **cualquiera que** whatever, whichever.

cuando *adv* when. ▶ *conj* 1 *(temporal)* when: *cuando deje de llover*, when it stops raining. 2 *(condicional)* if: *cuando ella lo dice...*, if she says so... • **de (vez en) cuando** now and then.

cuándo *adv* when.

cuanto,-a *adj (singular)* as much as; *(plural)* as many as. ▶ *pron (singular)* everything, all; *(plural)* all who, everybody who. • **cuanto antes** as soon as possible; **en cuanto** as soon as; **en cuanto a** as far as; **unos,-as cuantos,-as** some, a few.

cuánto,-a *adj* 1 *(interrogativo - singular)* how much; *(- plural)* how many. 2 *(exclamativo)* what a lot of. ▶ *pron (singular)* how much; *(plural)* how many. ▶ *adv* how, how much: *¡cuánto me alegro!*, I'm so glad!

cuarenta *num* forty.

cuartel *nm* barracks. ▪ **cuartel general** headquarters.

cuarto,-a *num* fourth. ▶ *nm* **cuarto** 1 *(parte)* quarter. 2 *(habitación)* room. ▪ **cuarto creciente** first quarter; **cuarto menguante** last quarter; **cuarto de baño** bathroom; **cuarto de estar** living room.

cuarzo *nm* quartz.

cuatro *num* four; *(en fechas)* fourth. ▪ **cuatro por cuatro** four-wheel drive.

cuatrocientos,-as *num* four hundred.

cuba *nf* cask, barrel.

cubalibre *nm (de ron)* rum and coke; *(de ginebra)* gin and coke.

cubano,-a *adj-nm,f* Cuban.

cúbico,-a *adj* cubic.

cubierta *nf* 1 *(tapa)* covering. 2 *(de libro)* jacket. 3 *(de neumático)* GB tyre; US tire. 5 *(de barco)* deck.

cubierto,-a *adj* 1 covered. 2 *(cielo)* overcast. ▶ *nm* **cubierto** 1 *(en la mesa)* place setting. 2 *(menú)* set menu.

cubito *nm.* ▪ **cubito (de hielo)** ice cube.

cubo¹ *nm* 1 *(recipiente)* bucket. 2 *(de rueda)* hub. ▪ **cubo de la basura** GB dustbin; US garbage can.

cubo² *nm (figura)* cube.

cubrir *vt* 1 *(tapar)* to cover. 2 *(puesto, vacante)* to fill.

cucaracha *nf* cockroach.

cuchara *nf* spoon.

cucharilla *nf* teaspoon.

cuchilla *nf* blade. ▪ **cuchilla de afeitar** razor blade.

cuchillo *nm* knife.

cucurucho *nm* 1 *(de papel)* cone. 2 *(helado)* cornet, cone.

cuello *nm* 1 *(de persona, animal)* neck. 2 *(de prenda)* collar. 3 *(de botella)* neck. ▪ **cuello alto** GB polo neck; US turtleneck; **cuello de pico** V-neck.

cuenta *nf* 1 *(bancaria)* account. 2 *(factura)* GB bill; US check. • **darse cuenta de algo** to realize STH; **tener en cuenta** to take into account. ▪ **cuenta atrás** countdown.

cuentagotas *nm* dropper.

cuentakilómetros *nm* GB mileometer; US odometer.

cuento *nm* short story, tale.

cuerda *nf* 1 *(soga)* rope; *(cordel, de guitarra)* string. 2 *(de reloj)* spring. • **dar cuerda a un reloj** to wind up a watch.

cuerno *nm (de toro)* horn; *(de ciervo)* antler.

cuero *nm* 1 *(de animal)* skin, hide. 2 *(curtido)* leather.

cuerpo *nm* body. • **a cuerpo** without a coat.

cuervo *nm* raven.

cuesta *nf* slope. • **a cuestas** on one's back, on one's shoulders; **cuesta abajo** downhill; **cuesta arriba** uphill.

cuestión *nf* question.

cuestionario *nm* questionnaire.

cueva *nf* cave.

cuidado *nm* 1 *(atención)* care. 2 *(recelo)* worry. ► *interj* **¡cuidado!** look out!, watch out! • **"Cuidado con el perro"** "Beware of the dog"; **tener cuidado** to be careful. ■ **cuidados intensivos** intensive care.

cuidar *vt-vi* to look after, take care of.

culebra *nf* snake.

culinario,-a *adj* culinary.

culo *nm* 1 *(trasero)* bottom, backside, GB bum; US butt. 2 *(de recipiente)* bottom.

culpa *nf* 1 *(culpabilidad)* guilt, blame. 2 *(falta)* fault.

culpabilidad *nf* guilt, culpabililty.

culpable *adj* guilty. ► *nmf* offender, culprit.

cultivar *vt* 1 *(terreno)* to cultivate, farm. 2 *(plantas)* to grow.

culto,-a *adj* 1 *(con cultura)* cultured, educated. 2 *(estilo)* refined. ► *nm* **culto** worship.

cultura *nf* culture.

cumbre *nf (de montaña)* summit, top. 2 *(reunión)* summit.

cumpleaños *nm* birthday.

cumplir *vt* 1 *(orden)* to carry out. 2 *(compromiso, obligación)* to fulfil. 3 *(promesa)* to keep. 4 *(condena)* to serve. 5 *(años)*: *mañana cumplo veinte años*, I'll be twenty tomorrow.

cuna *nf* GB cot; US crib, cradle.

cuneta *nf* ditch.

cuñado,-a *nm,f (hombre)* brother-in-law; *(mujer)* sister-in-law.

cuota *nf* 1 *(pago)* membership fee, dues. 2 *(porción)* quota, share.

cúpula *nf* cupola, dome.

cura *nm (párroco)* priest. ► *nf (curación)* cure.

curación *nf* cure, healing.

curar *vt* 1 *(sanar)* to cure. 2 *(herida)* to dress; *(enfermedad)* to treat. ► *vpr* **curarse** *(recuperarse)* to recover, get well.

curiosidad *nf* curiosity.

curioso,-a adj 1 (interesado) curious, inquisitive. 2 (indiscreto) nosy. 3 (extraño) strange: **iqué curioso!**, how strange!

currículum nm curriculum (vitae), CV.

curso nm 1 (gen) course. 2 (académico) year. • **en curso** current.

cursor nm cursor.

curva nf 1 curve. 2 (de carretera) bend.

cutis nm skin, complexion.

cuyo,-a pron whose, of which. •**en cuyo caso** in which case.

D

dado nm die.

dama nf 1 (señora) lady. 2 (en ajedrez) queen; (en damas) king. ► nf pl **damas** GB draughts; US checkers. ■ **dama de honor** bridesmaid.

danza nf dance.

dañar vt (cosa) to damage; (persona) to harm.

daño nm 1 (en cosas) damage. 2 (en personas) harm. • **hacer daño** 1 (doler) to hurt. 2 (perjudicar) to do harm; **hacerse daño** to hurt oneself. ■ **daños y perjuicios** damages.

dar vt 1 (gen) to give. 2 (las horas) to strike. 3 (película) to show; (obra de teatro) to perform. ► vi (mirar a) to look out.

dardo nm dart.

dátil nm date.

dato nm piece of information. ► nm pl **datos** (información) information; (informáticos) data. ■ **datos personales** personal details.

de prep 1 (gen) of. 2 (posesión) 's, s': **el coche de María**, María's car; **los libros de los chicos**, the boys' books. 3 (materia, tema): **una profesora de inglés**, an English teacher. 4 (origen, procedencia) from: **es de Navarra**, he's from Navarre. 5 (descripción) with, in: **la chica del pelo largo**, the girl with long hair; **el hombre de negro**, the man in black. 6 (agente) by: **un libro de Dickens**, a book by Dickens. 7 **de** + inf if: **de seguir así, acabarás en la cárcel**, if you continue like this, you'll end up in prison.

debajo adv underneath, below. • **debajo de** under.

debate nm debate.

deber nm (obligación) duty. ► vt (dinero) to owe. ► aux 1 **deber** + inf (obligación) must, to have to; (recomendación) should: **debo irme**, I must go; **de-**

berías ir al médico, you should see the doctor. **2 deber de** *(conjetura)* must: **deben de ser las seis**, it must be six o'clock. ▶ *nm pl* **deberes** homework.

debido,-a *adj.* • **como es debido** properly; **debido,-a** a due to, owing to.

débil *adj* **1** *(persona)* weak. **2** *(ruido)* faint. **3** *(luz)* dim.

década *nf* decade.

decadencia *nf* decadence.

decente *adj* **1** *(decoroso)* decent. **2** *(honesto)* honest.

decepcionar *vt* to disappoint.

decidir *vt-vi* to decide. ▶ *vpr* **decidirse** to make up one's mind.

décima *nf* tenth.

decimal *adj-nm* decimal.

décimo,-a *num* tenth. ▶ *nm* **décimo** lottery ticket.

decir *vt* **1** *(gen)* to say: *dijo que vendría mañana*, he said he'd come tomorrow. **2** *(a alguien)* to tell: *dime lo que piensas*, tell me what you think. • **es decir** that is to say; **querer decir** to mean.

decisión *nf* decision.

declaración *nf* **1** *(afirmación)* statement. **2** *(de guerra, amor)* declaration. • **prestar declaración** *(en juicio)* to give evidence. ▪ **declaración de la renta** income tax return.

declarar *vt* **1** *(gen)* to declare: *¿no tiene nada que declarar?*, do you have anything to declare? **2** *(considerar)* to find. ▶ *vi (dar testimonio)* to testify. ▶ *vpr* **declararse** *(fuego, guerra)* to start, break out.

decoración *nf* decoration.

decorado *nm* scenery, set.

decorar *vt* to decorate.

decreto *nm* decree.

dedal *nm* thimble.

dedicar *vt* to dedicate. ▶ *vpr* **dedicarse** to devote oneself: *¿a qué te dedicas?*, what do you do?

dedo *nm (de la mano)* finger; *(del pie)* toe. • **hacer dedo** to hitchhike. ▪ **dedo del corazón** middle finger; **dedo gordo** thumb.

deducir *vt* **1** *(inferir)* to deduce. **2** *(descontar)* to deduct.

defecto *nm* defect, fault.

defectuoso,-a *adj* defective, faulty.

defender *vt* to defend.

defensa *nf* GB defence; US defense. ▶ *nmf (jugador)* defender.

defensor,-ra *adj* defending. ▶ *nm,f* defender.

déficit *nm* deficit.

definición *nf* definition.

definir *vt* to define.

definitivo,-a *adj* definitive, final.

deformar *vt* to deform.

defraudar vt 1 *(decepcionar)* to disappoint. 2 *(estafar)* to defraud; *(robar)* to steal.

dejar vt 1 *(gen)* to leave. 2 *(permitir)* to let: *déjame entrar*, let me in. 3 *(prestar)* to lend: *¿me dejas tu bici?*, will you lend me your bike?, can I borrow your bike? ► *aux* 1 **dejar de** + *inf* to stop: *deja de gritar*, stop shouting. 2 **no dejar de** + *inf*: *no dejaron de bailar*, they went on dancing. ► *vpr* **dejarse** *(olvidar)* to forget.

delantal nm apron.

delante adv in front. ► prep **delante de** in front of. ● **de delante** front; **hacia delante** forward; **por delante** ahead.

delantero,-a adj *(rueda)* front; *(pata)* fore. ► nm **delantero** *(deportista)* forward. ■ **delantero centro** centre forward.

delegación nf 1 *(personas)* delegation. 2 *(sucursal)* branch.

delegar vt to delegate.

deletrear vt to spell.

delfín nm *(animal)* dolphin.

delgado,-a adj thin.

delicado,-a adj 1 *(gen)* delicate. 2 *(sensible)* sensitive; *(tiquismiquis)* hard to please.

delicioso,-a adj delicious.

delincuente adj-nmf delinquent.

delito nm offence, crime.

demanda nf 1 *(de producto)* demand. 2 *(legal)* lawsuit.

demandar vt JUR to sue.

demás adj other. ► pron the others, the rest. ● **por lo demás** otherwise.

demasiado,-a adj *(singular)* too much; *(plural)* too many. ► adv **demasiado** *(después de verbo)* too much; *(delante de adjetivo)* too.

democracia nf democracy.

democrático,-a adj democratic.

demonio nm demon, devil.

demostración nf 1 *(muestra)* demonstration. 2 *(prueba)* proof.

demostrar vt 1 *(mostrar)* to demonstrate. 2 *(probar)* to prove.

denegar vt to refuse.

denominación nf denomination.

denominar vt to denominate, name.

denso,-a adj dense.

dentadura nf teeth. ■ **dentadura postiza** false teeth.

dentífrico nm toothpaste.

dentista nmf dentist.

dentro adv *(gen)* inside; *(de edificio)* indoors. ► prep **dentro de** in. ● **por dentro** inside.

denuncia nf report, complaint. ● **presentar una denuncia** to lodge a complaint.

denunciar vt (situación) to condemn; (delito) to report.

departamento nm department.

dependencia nf 1 (de persona, drogas) dependence, dependency. 2 (en edificio) outbuilding.

depender vi to depend.

dependiente,-a nm,f sales assistant.

depilar vt (con cera) to wax.

deporte nm sport.

deportista nmf (hombre) sportsman; (mujer) sportswoman.

depositar vt to deposit.

depósito nm 1 (gen) deposit. 2 (almacén) store. 3 (receptáculo) tank. ▪ **depósito de gasolina** GB petrol tank; US gas tank.

depresión nf depression.

deprisa adv quickly.

derecha nf 1 (dirección) right. 2 (mano) right hand; (pierna) right leg. 3 POL right wing. • **a la derecha** to the right: *girar a la derecha*, to turn right.

derecho,-a adj 1 (diestro) right. 2 (recto) straight. ▶ nm **derecho** 1 (poder, oportunidad) right. 2 (ley) law. ▪ **derechos de autor** copyright.

derramar vt 1 (leche, vino) to spill. 2 (sangre, lágrimas) to shed.

derrapar vi to skid.

derretir(se) vt-vpr to melt.

derribar vt 1 (edificio) to demolish. 2 (avión) to shoot down.

derrochar vt to squander.

derrota nf defeat.

derrotar vt to defeat.

derrumbarse vpr (edificio, techo) to collapse.

desabrochar vt to undo, unfasten.

desacuerdo nm disagreement.

desafiar vt to defy.

desafinar vi to be out of tune.

desafío nm 1 (reto) challenge. 2 (duelo) duel.

desagradable adj unpleasant.

desagüe nm drain.

desalojar vt 1 (persona) to remove. 2 (inquilino) to evict. 3 (ciudad) to evacuate. 4 (edificio) to clear.

desangrarse vpr to bleed to death.

desanimado,-a adj despondent.

desapacible adj unpleasant.

desaparecer vi to disappear.

desaparición nf disappearance.

desaprovechar vt to waste.

desarmar vt 1 (quitar armas) to disarm. 2 (desmontar) to dismantle.

desarrollar vt 1 (gen) to develop. 2 (realizar) to carry

out. ► *vpr* **desarrollarse 1**
(crecer) to develop. **2** *(ocurrir)*
to take place.
desarrollo *nm* development.
• **en vías de desarrollo** developing.
desastre *nm* disaster.
desatar *vt* to untie.
desatascar *vt* to unblock.
desatornillar *vt* to unscrew.
desayunar *vt* to have for
breakfast. ► *vi* to have breakfast.
desayuno *nm* breakfast.
desbordar *vt* *(sobrepasar)* to
surpass. ► *vpr* **desbordarse**
(río) to overflow.
descafeinado,-a *adj* *(café)*
decaffeinated.
descalificar *vt* **1** *(de un concurso)* to disqualify. **2** *(des-
prestigiar)* to dismiss.
descalzo,-a *adj* barefoot.
descampado *nm* piece of open
ground.
descansar *vi* **1** *(reposar)* to
have a rest. **2** *(apoyarse)* to
rest.
descansillo *nm* landing.
descanso *nm* **1** *(reposo)* rest;
(en el trabajo) break. **2** *(en encuentro deportivo)* half time.
descapotable *adj-nm* convertible.
descarga *nf* **1** *(de electricidad)*
discharge. **2** *(de fuego)* discharge, volley. **3** *(en ordenador)*
download.

descargar *vt* **1** *(mercancías)* to
unload. **2** *(en ordenador)* to
download. ► *vpr* **descargar-
se** *(batería)* to go flat.
descarrilar *vi* to be derailed.
descartar *vt* to rule out.
descendencia *nf* offspring,
children.
descender *vi* **1** *(ir abajo)* to go
down, come down. **2** *(temperatura, índice)* to drop, fall.
descendiente *nmf* descendant.
descenso *nm* **1** *(de escalera,
cumbre)* descent. **2** *(de temperatura, índice)* fall.
descolgar *vt* **1** *(cuadro, cortina)* to take down. **2** *(teléfono)*
to pick up.
descomposición *nf* **1** *(putre-
facción)* decomposition, de-
cay. **2** *(diarrea)* GB diarrhoea;
US diarrhea.
desconectar *vt* to disconnect.
desconfiar *vi* to be distrust-
ful.
descongelar *vt* **1** *(comida)* to
thaw. **2** *(nevera)* to defrost.
desconocido,-a *adj* **1** *(no
conocido)* unknown. **2** *(extraño)* strange, unfamiliar. ►
nm,f stranger.
descontento *nm* dissatisfac-
tion.
descorchar *vt* to uncork.
descosido *nm* split seam.
descremado,-a *adj* skimmed.
describir *vt* to describe.

descripción *nf* description.

descubierto,-a *adj* 1 *(sin cubrir)* uncovered; *(sin sombrero)* bareheaded. 2 *(piscina)* outdoor.

descubrimiento *nm* discovery.

descubrir *vt* 1 *(encontrar)* to discover. 2 *(revelar)* to make known. 3 *(averiguar)* to find out.

descuento *nm* discount.

descuido *nm* 1 *(negligencia)* carelessness. 2 *(desliz)* slip, error.

desde *prep* 1 *(lugar)* from: *desde aquí no se ve*, you can't see it from here. 2 *(tiempo)* since: *salen juntos desde junio*, they've been going out together since June. • **desde ahora** from now on; **desde entonces** since then; **desde hace** for: *vivo aquí desde hace cinco años*, I've lived here for five years; **desde luego** of course; **desde que** ever since.

desdoblar *vt* to unfold.

desear *vt* to want.

desechable *adj* disposable.

desechos *nm pl* 1 *(basura)* waste *sing*. 2 *(sobras)* leftovers.

desembarcar *vi* to land.

desembocadura *nf* mouth.

desembocar *vi* 1 *(río)* to flow. 2 *(calle, acontecimiento)* to lead.

desempate *nm* breakthrough.

desempeñar *vt* 1 *(obligación)* to discharge. 2 *(cargo)* to hold.

desempleo *nm* unemployment.

desencadenar *vt (crisis, debate)* to spark off. ▶ *vpr* **desencadenarse** *(tormenta, guerra)* to break out

desenchufar *vt* to unplug.

desenfocado,-a *adj* out of focus.

desengaño *nm* disappointment.

desenlace *nm* 1 *(de aventura)* outcome. 2 *(de libro, película)* ending.

desenterrar *vt* 1 *(objeto escondido)* to unearth. 2 *(cadáver)* to dig up.

desenvolver *vt* to unwrap. ▶ *vpr* **desenvolverse** 1 *(transcurrir)* to develop. 2 *(espabilarse)* to manage.

deseo *nm* 1 *(anhelo)* wish. 2 *(apetito sexual)* desire.

desequilibrio *nm* imbalance.

desertar *vi (soldado)* to desert.

desértico,-a *adj (clima, zona)* desert.

desesperación *nf* 1 *(irritación)* exasperation. 2 *(angustia)* desperation.

desesperar *vt* 1 *(irritar)* to exasperate. 2 *(angustiar)* to drive to despair. ▶ *vi-vpr* **desesperar(se)** 1 *(irritarse)* to be exasperated. 2 *(angustiarse)* to despair.

desfallecer *vi* to faint.

desfiladero *nm* **1** *(barranco)* gorge. **2** *(paso)* narrow pass.

desfile *nm* parade.

desgracia *nf (mala suerte)* misfortune. **2** *(accidente)* mishap. • **por desgracia** unfortunately.

deshacer *vt* **1** *(gen)* to undo. **2** *(disolver)* to dissolve; *(fundir)* to melt. ► *vpr* **deshacerse 1** *(costura, nudo)* to come undone. **2** *(disolverse)* to dissolve; *(fundirse)* to melt.

deshidratarse *vpr* to get dehydrated.

deshielo *nm* thaw.

deshinchar *vt* to deflate.

desierto *nm* desert.

designar *vt* **1** *(nombrar)* to appoint. **2** *(fijar)* to designate.

desigualdad *nf* **1** *(diferencia)* inequality. **2** *(irregularidad)* unevenness.

desilusión *nf* disappointment.

desinfectante *adj-nm* disinfectant.

desinflar(se) *vt-vpr* to deflate.

desinterés *nm* lack of interest.

deslizar *vt-vi* to slide. ► *vpr* **deslizarse** *(resbalar)* to slip; *(sobre agua)* to glide.

desmayarse *vpr* to faint.

desmayo *nm* fainting fit.

desmontar *vt* *(mueble)* to dismantle. ► *vi* *(del caballo)* to dismount.

desnatado,-a *adj (leche)* skimmed; *(yogur)* low-fat.

desnivel *nm* **1** *(desigualdad)* unevenness. **2** *(distancia vertical)* drop.

desnudarse *vpr* to get undressed.

desnudo,-a *adj* naked.

desobedecer *vt* to disobey.

desocupado,-a *adj* **1** *(libre)* free. **2** *(ocioso)* unoccupied. **3** *(desempleado)* unemployed.

desodorante *adj-nm* deodorant.

desorden *nm* disorder.

despachar *vt* **1** *(enviar)* to dispatch. **2** *(despedir)* to sack. **3** *(en tienda)* to serve; *(vender)* to sell.

despacho *nm (en oficina)* office; *(en casa)* study.

despacio *adv* slowly.

despedida *nf* goodbye.

despedir *vt* **1** *(lanzar)* to throw. **2** *(del trabajo)* to dismiss. **3** *(decir adiós a)* to say goodbye to. ► *vpr* **despedirse** to say goodbye.

despegar *vt (desenganchar)* to detach. ► *vi (avión)* to take off.

despegue *nm* takeoff.

despejado,-a *adj* clear.

despejar *vt (habitación, calle)* to clear. ► *vi* to clear up. ► *vpr* **despejarse 1** *(tiempo, cielo)* to clear up. **2** *(persona)* to clear one's head.

despensa *nf* pantry.

desperdiciar *vt* to waste.

desperdicios *nm pl* scraps.

desperfecto *nm* slight damage.

despertador *nm* alarm clock.

despertar(se) *vt-vpr* to wake up.

despido *nm* dismissal.

despierto,-a *adj* **1** *(no dormido)* awake. **2** *(espabilado)* sharp.

despistado,-a *adj* absent-minded.

despistar *vt* *(desorientar)* to confuse. ► *vpr* **despistarse 1** *(perderse)* to get lost. **2** *(distraerse)* to get distracted.

desplazar *vt* to move. ► *vpr* **desplazarse** to travel.

desplegar *vt* **1** *(mapa)* to unfold. **2** *(alas)* to spread. **3** *(actividad, cualidad)* to display. **4** *(tropas, armas)* to deploy.

despreciar *vt* **1** *(menospreciar)* to despise. **2** *(rechazar)* to reject.

desprecio *nm* contempt.

desprenderse *vpr* **1** *(soltarse)* to come off. **2** *(deducirse)* to emerge.

desprevenido,-a *adj* unprepared.

después *adv* **1** *(más tarde)* afterwards, later. **2** *(entonces)* then: *y después dijo que sí,* and then he said yes. ► *prep* **después de** *(tras)* after. • **después de todo** after all; **poco después** soon after.

destacar *vt* **1** *(tropas)* to detach. **2** *(resaltar)* to emphasize.

destapar *vt* **1** *(olla, caja)* to take the lid off. **2** *(botella)* to open.

destierro *nm* exile.

destinar *vt* **1** *(asignar)* to allocate. **2** *(a un puesto)* to post.

destinatario,-a *nm,f* **1** *(de carta)* addressee. **2** *(de mercancías)* consignee.

destino *nm* **1** *(sino)* destiny, fate. **2** *(lugar)* destination. **3** *(empleo)* post. • **con destino a** bound for: *el tren con destino a Bilbao,* the train to Bilbao.

destituir *vt* to dismiss.

destornillador *nm* screwdriver.

destreza *nf* skill.

destrozar *vt* *(edificio, enemigo)* to destroy; *(mueble, cristalera)* to smash; *(planes, vida)* to ruin; *(corazón)* to break.

destrucción *nf* destruction.

destruir *vt* to destroy.

desván *nm* loft, attic.

desventaja *nf* disadvantage.

desvestirse *vpr* to undress.

desviar *vt* **1** *(trayectoria)* to deviate. **2** *(carretera)* to divert. ► *vpr* **desviarse** *(de un camino)* to go off course; *(coche)* to take a detour.

desvío *nm* diversion.

detalle *nm* **1** *(pormenor)* detail. **2** *(delicadeza)* gesture.

detectar *vt* to detect.

detective *nmf* detective.

detener *vt* 1 *(parar)* to stop. 2 *(arrestar)* to arrest. ► *vpr* **detenerse** to stop.

detenido,-a *nm,f* prisoner.

detergente *adj-nm* detergent.

deteriorar *vt* to damage. ► *vpr* **deteriorarse** to deteriorate.

determinación *nf* 1 *(valor)* determination. 2 *(decisión)* decision. 3 *(firmeza)* firmness.

determinar *vt* 1 *(decidir)* to decide. 2 *(fijar)* to determine.

detestar *vt* to detest.

detrás *adv (gen)* behind. ► *prep* **detrás de** behind.

deuda *nf* debt.

devolución *nf* 1 *(de dinero pagado)* refund. 2 *(de artículo comprado)* return.

devolver *vt* 1 to give back. 2 *(vomitar)* to vomit.

día *nm* 1 *(gen)* day. 2 *(horas de luz)* daylight. • ¡**buenos días**! good morning!; **hoy en día** today, now, nowadays. ■ **día festivo** holiday; **día laborable** working day; **día libre** day off.

diabetes *nf* diabetes.

diabético,-a *adj-nm,f* diabetic.

diablo *nm* devil.

diagnosticar *vt* to diagnose.

diagnóstico *nm* diagnosis.

diagonal *adj-nf* diagonal.

diagrama *nm* diagram.

diálogo *nm* dialogue.

diamante *nm* diamond.

diámetro *nm* diameter.

diana *nf (blanco de tiro)* target; *(para dardos)* dartboard.

diapositiva *nf* slide.

diario,-a *adj* daily. ► *nm* **diario** 1 *(prensa)* newspaper. 2 *(íntimo)* diary, journal. • **a diario** every day.

diarrea *nf* GB diarrhoea; US diarrhea.

dibujar *vt* to draw.

dibujo *nm* 1 *(gen)* drawing. 2 *(estampado)* pattern. ■ **dibujos animados** cartoons.

diccionario *nm* dictionary.

dicho,-a *adj* said. • **mejor dicho** or rather.

diciembre *nm* December.

dictado *nm* dictation.

dictador *nm* dictator.

dictadura *nf* dictatorship.

dictar *vt* to dictate.

diecinueve *num* nineteen; *(en fechas)* nineteenth.

dieciocho *num* eighteen; *(en fechas)* eighteenth.

dieciséis *num* sixteen; *(en fechas)* sixteenth.

diecisiete *num* seventeen; *(en fechas)* seventeenth.

diente *nm* 1 *(de la boca)* tooth. 2 *(de ajo)* clove.

diestro,-a *adj (mano)* right; *(persona)* right-handed. ► *nm* **diestro** bullfighter.

dieta *nf (régimen)* diet.

dietas *nf pl* expense allowance.

diez *num* ten; *(en fechas)* tenth.

diferencia *nf* difference.

diferente *adj* different.

diferido,-a *adj* recorded.

difícil *adj* **1** *(costoso)* difficult. **2** *(improbable)* unlikely.

dificultad *nf* difficulty.

difunto,-a *nm,f* deceased.

difusión *nf* **1** *(de luz)* diffusion. **2** *(de noticia)* spreading. **3** *(por radio, televisión)* broadcast.

digerir *vt* to digest.

digestión *nf* digestion.

digital *adj* digital.

digno,-a *adj* **1** *(merecedor)* worthy. **2** *(adecuado)* fitting. **3** *(respetable)* respectable.

diluvio *nm* flood.

dimensión *nf* **1** *(magnitud física)* dimension. **2** *(tamaño)* size.

diminuto,-a *adj* tiny.

dimisión *nf* resignation.

dimitir *vt* to resign.

Dinamarca *nf* Denmark.

dinero *nm* money. ▪ **dinero en efectivo** cash.

dinosaurio *nm* dinosaur.

dintel *nm* lintel.

dioptría *nf* GB dioptre; US diopter.

dios *nm* god.

diosa *nf* goddess.

dióxido *nm* dioxide.

diploma *nm* diploma.

diplomático,-a *adj* diplomatic. ▶ *nm,f* diplomat.

diputado,-a *nm,f* deputy.

dirección *nf* **1** *(rumbo)* direction; *(sentido)* way. **2** *(en empresa)* management. **3** *(domicilio)* address. **4** *(de coche)* steering. ▪ **dirección electrónica** e-mail address.

directo,-a *adj* direct. ● **en directo** *(transmisión)* live.

director,-ra *nm,f* *(gerente)* manager; *(de orquesta)* conductor.

dirigente *adj* *(clase, élite)* ruling. ▶ *nm,f* leader.

dirigir *vt* **1** *(orientar)* to direct. **2** *(negocio)* to manage. **3** *(orquesta)* to conduct. ▶ *vpr* **dirigirse 1** *(ir)* to go. **2** *(hablar)* to address, speak to.

disciplina *nf* discipline.

disco *nm* **1** *(de música)* record. **2** *(en deporte)* discus. **3** *(de ordenador)* disk. ▪ **disco compacto** compact disc; **disco duro** hard disk.

discoteca *nf* nightclub.

discreto,-a *adj* **1** *(callado)* discreet. **2** *(sobrio)* sober.

discriminación *nf* discrimination.

disculpa *nf* apology.

discurso *nm* speech.

discusión *nf* **1** *(disputa)* argument. **2** *(debate)* discussion.

discutir *vt-vi* **1** *(debatir)* to discuss. **2** *(disputar)* to argue.

diseño *nm* design.

disfraz *nm* **1** *(para engañar)* disguise. **2** *(para fiesta)* costume.

disfrutar *vt* to enjoy.

disgusto *nm* upset. • **a disgusto** unwillingly.

disimular *vt* (*ocultar*) to hide. ► *vi* (*fingir*) to pretend.

disminuir *vt* to reduce. ► *vi* to decrease, fall.

disparar *vt* **1** (*arma*) to fire. **2** (*balón*) to drive.

disparo *nm* shot.

disponer *vt-vi* (*colocar*) to arrange. ► *vt* (*ordenar*) to order. ► *vi* (*poseer*) to have. ► *vpr* **disponerse** (*prepararse*) to get ready to.

disposición *nf* **1** (*actitud*) disposition. **2** (*colocación*) arrangement. • **a su disposición** at your disposal.

dispositivo *nm* device.

disputar *vt* **1** (*discutir*) to dispute. **2** (*partido*) to play.

disquete *nm* diskette.

disquetera *nf* disk drive.

distancia *nf* distance.

distinguir *vt* **1** (*diferenciar*) to distinguish. **2** (*ver*) to see.

distinto,-a *adj* different.

distracción *nf* **1** (*divertimiento*) amusement. **2** (*despiste*) distraction.

distraer *vt* **1** (*divertir*) to keep amused. **2** (*atención*) to distract. ► *vpr* **distraerse 1** (*divertirse*) to amuse oneself . **2** (*despistarse*) to get distracted.

distribución *nf* **1** (*reparto*) distribution. **2** (*colocación*) arrangement.

distribuir *vt* **1** (*repartir*) to distribute. **2** (*colocar*) to arrange.

diurno,-a *adj* **1** (*curso, autobús*) daytime. **2** (*animal*) diurnal.

diversidad *nf* diversity.

diversión *nf* (*gozo*) fun; (*pasatiempo*) pastime.

diversos,-as *adj pl* several, various.

divertir *vt* to amuse. ► *vpr* **divertirse** to enjoy oneself.

dividir *vt* to divide.

divino,-a *adj* divine.

divisa *nf* currency.

divisar *vt* make out.

división *nf* division.

divorcio *nm* divorce.

divulgar *vt* **1** (*dar a conocer*) to make public. **2** (*propagar*) to spread.

doblar *vt* **1** (*duplicar*) to double. **2** (*plegar*) to fold. **3** (*esquina*) to turn. **4** (*película*) to dub.

doble *adj-nm* double.

doce *num* twelve; (*en fechas*) twelfth.

docena *nf* dozen.

doctor,-ra *nm,f* doctor.

documentación *nf* documentation.

documento *nm* document.

dólar *nm* dollar.

doler *vi* to hurt: *me duele la cabeza*, I've got a headache.

dolor *nm* (*físico, moral*) pain; (*sordo*) ache. ■ **dolor de cabeza** headache; **dolor de es-**

tómago stomachache; **dolor de garganta** sore throat; **dolor de muelas** toothache.

doméstico,-a *adj* domestic.

domicilio *nm* address.

dominar *vt* 1 *(gen)* to dominate. 2 *(tema)* to master.

domingo *nm* Sunday.

dominical *nm* Sunday newspaper.

dominio *nm* 1 *(poder)* control. 2 *(de tema)* mastery. 3 INFORM domain.

dominó *nm* *(ficha)* domino; *(juego)* dominoes *pl.*

don *nm* *(título)* don.

donante *nmf* donor.

donde *conj* where.

dónde *adv* where.

dondequiera *adv* wherever.

dorado,-a *adj* *(gen)* gold; *(color)* golden.

dormir *vi* to sleep. ► *vpr* **dormirse** to go to sleep. • **dormir la siesta** to have a nap.

dormitorio *nm* bedroom.

dorso *nm* back.

dos *num* two; *(en fechas)* second. • **de dos en dos** in twos; **dos puntos** colon.

doscientos,-as *num* two hundred.

dosis *nf* dose.

drama *nm* drama.

dramático,-a *adj* dramatic.

droga *nf* drug. ▪ **droga blanda** soft drug; **droga dura** hard drug.

drogadicto,-a *nm,f* drug addict.

droguería *nf* hardware and household goods shop.

dromedario *nm* dromedary.

ducha *nf* shower. • **darse una ducha** to have a shower.

ducharse *vpr* to have a shower.

duda *nf* doubt. • **sin duda** undoubtedly.

dudar *vi* to hesitate. ► *vt* to doubt.

duelo *nm* duel.

duende *nm* elf.

dueño,-a *nm,f* 1 *(propietario)* owner. 2 *(de casa alquilada - hombre)* landlord; *(- mujer)* landlady.

dulce *adj* *(comida, bebida)* sweet.► *nm (caramelo)* sweet.

duna *nf* dune.

dúo *nm* 1 *(pareja)* duo. 2 *(composición)* duet.

duodécimo,-a *num* twelfth.

dúplex *adj-nm* duplex.

duque *nm* duke.

duquesa *nf* duchess.

duración *nf* duration.

durante *adv* 1 *(a lo largo de un período)* for: *durante todo el día*, all day long. 2 *(dentro de un período)* during, in: *durante la noche*, during the night, in the night.

durar *vi* to last.

duro,-a *adj* *(gen)* hard; *(carne)* tough.

E

ébano *nm* ebony.
ebrio,-a *adj* drunk.
eccema *nm* eczema.
echar *vt* 1 *(lanzar)* to throw. 2 *(del trabajo)* to sack. 3 *(correo)* GB to post; US to mail. ▶ *vi-vpr* **echar(se) a** + *inf* to begin to: *echar a correr*, to run off. ▶ *vpr* **echarse** *(tenderse)* to lie down. • **echar algo a perder** to spoil STH; **echar de menos** to miss; **echarse atrás** 1 *(inclinarse)* to lean back. 2 *(desdecirse)* to back out.
eclipse *nm* eclipse.
eco *nm* echo.
ecología *nf* ecology.
ecológico,-a *adj* 1 *(gen)* ecological. 2 *(cultivo)* organic.
ecologista *nmf* environmentalist.
economía *nf* 1 *(de un país)* economy. 2 *(ciencia)* economics.
económico,-a *adj* 1 *(de la economía)* economic. 2 *(barato)* economical.
ecosistema *nm* ecosystem.
ecuación *nf* equation.
ecuador *nm* equator.
ecuatorial *adj* equatorial.
edad *nf* age: *¿qué edad tiene usted?*, how old are you? ▪ **la tercera edad** 1 *(etapa de la vida)* old age. 2 *(gente mayor)* senior citizens.

edición *nf* 1 *(tirada)* edition. 2 *(publicación)* publication. ▪ **edición electrónica** electronic publishing.
edificio *nm* building.
editor,-ra *nm,f* 1 *(que publica)* publisher. 2 *(que prepara)* editor. ▪ **editor de texto** text editor.
editorial *nm* *(artículo)* editorial, leading article. ▶ *nf* publishing house, publisher.
edredón *nm* quilt. ▪ **edredón nórdico** duvet.
educación *nf* 1 *(enseñanza)* education. 2 *(crianza)* upbringing. 3 *(cortesía)* manners.
educado,-a *adj* polite.
educar *vt* *(enseñar)* to educate.
efectivo,-a *adj* *(eficaz)* effective. ▶ *nm* **efectivo** cash. ▶ *nm pl* **efectivos** forces.
efecto *nm* 1 *(gen)* effect. 2 *(impresión)* impression. 3 *(pelota)* spin. • **en efecto** indeed; **hacer efecto** to take effect. ▪ **efecto invernadero** greenhouse effect; **efectos especiales** special effects; **efectos personales** personal belongings.
efectuar *vt* 1 *(maniobra, investigación, etc.)* to carry out. 2 *(pago, viaje, etc.)* to make.
efervescente *adj* 1 *(pastilla)* effervescent. 2 *(bebida)* fizzy.
eficaz *adj* 1 *(que surte efecto)* effective. 2 *(eficiente)* efficient.

eficiente *adj* efficient.

egoísta *adj* selfish, egoistic. ► *nmf* egoist.

eje *nm* 1 (*en geometría, astronomía*) axis. 2 (*de motor*) shaft. 3 (*de ruedas*) axle.

ejecución *nf* execution.

ejecutar *vt* 1 (*orden*) to carry out. 2 (*programa informático*) to run. 3 (*ajusticiar*) to execute.

ejecutivo,-a *adj-nm,f* executive.

ejemplar *nm* 1 (*obra*) copy. 2 (*espécimen*) specimen.

ejemplo *nm* example. • **por ejemplo** for example, for instance.

ejercer *vt* 1 (*profesión etc*) to practise. 2 (*derecho, poder*) to exercise. 3 (*influencia*) to exert.

ejercicio *nm* 1 (*gen*) exercise. 2 (*financiero*) year. • **hacer ejercicio** to exercise.

ejército *nm* army.

el *det* 1 the: *el coche*, the car. 2 **el + de** the one: *el de tu amigo*, your friend's. 3 **el + que** the one: *el que vino ayer*, the one who came yesterday.

él *pron* 1 (*sujeto - persona*) he; (*- cosa, animal*) it. 2 (*después de preposición - persona*) him; (*- cosa, animal*) it. • **de él** (*posesivo*) his: *es de él*, it's his; **él mismo** himself.

elaborar *vt* to make, manufacture.

elástico,-a *adj* elastic.

elección *nf* 1 (*nombramiento*) election. 2 (*opción*) choice. ► *nf pl* **elecciones** elections.

electricidad *nf* electricity.

eléctrico,-a *adj* electric.

electrocutarse *vpr* to be electrocuted.

electrodoméstico *nm* electrical appliance.

electrónico,-a *adj* electronic.

elefante *nm* elephant.

elegante *adj* elegant.

elegir *vt* 1 (*escoger*) to chose. 2 (*por votación*) to elect.

elemental *adj* elementary.

elemento *nm* element.

elevado,-a *adj* (*edificio*) tall; (*montaña, número*) high.

elevar *vt* to raise. ► *vpr* **elevarse** (*ascender - avión*) to climb; (*- globo*) to rise.

eliminación *nf* elimination.

eliminar *vt* 1 (*gen*) to eliminate. 2 (*obstáculo, mancha*) to remove.

ella *pron* 1 (*sujeto - persona*) she; (*- cosa, animal*) it. 2 (*después de preposición - persona*) her; (*- cosa, animal*) it. • **de ella** hers.

ello *pron* it.

ellos,-as *pron* 1 (*sujeto*) they. 2 (*complemento*) them. • **de ellos** theirs: *es de ellas*, it's theirs.

elogio *nm* praise.

embajada *nf* embassy.

embajador,-ra *nm,f* ambassador.

embalaje *nm* packing.
embalar *vt* to pack.
embalse *nm* reservoir.
embarazada *nf* pregnant woman.
embarazo *nm* (*preñez*) pregnancy.
embarcación *nf* boat.
embarcadero *nm* jetty.
embarcar(se) *vt-vpr* to embark.
embargo *nm* 1 (*incautación de bienes*) seizure. 2 (*prohibición de comercio*) embargo. • **sin embargo** however.
embarque *nm* (*de personas*) boarding.
emblema *nm* emblem.
emborrachar *vt* to make drunk. ▶ *vpr* **emborracharse** to get drunk.
emboscada *nf* ambush.
embotellamiento *nm* (*de tráfico*) traffic jam.
embrague *nm* clutch.
embrión *nm* embryo.
embudo *nm* funnel.
embustero,-a *nm,f* liar.
embutido *nm* cold meat.
emergencia *nf* emergency.
emigración *nf* emigration.
emigrante *adj-nmf* emigrant.
emisión *nf* 1 (*de energía, gas*) emission. 2 (*de bonos, acciones*) issue. 3 (*en radio, TV*) broadcast.
emisor *nm* radio transmitter.
emisora *nf* radio station.

emitir *vt* 1 (*sonido, luz, calor*) to emit. 2 (*bonos, acciones*) to issue. 3 (*programa de radio, TV*) to broadcast.
emoción *nf* 1 (*sentimiento*) emotion. 2 (*excitación*) excitement.
emocionante *adj* 1 (*conmovedor*) moving. 2 (*excitante*) exciting.
emocionar *vt* 1 (*conmover*) to move. 2 (*excitar*) to excite. ▶ *vpr* **emocionarse** (*conmoverse*) to be moved.
empacho *nm* indigestion.
empalagoso,-a *adj* (*dulces*) sickly.
empalme *nm* 1 (*de tuberías, cables*) connection. 2 (*de carreteras, vías*) junction.
empanada *nf* pasty.
empanadilla *nf* pasty.
empañarse *vpr* (*cristal*) to steam up.
empapar *vt* to soak.
empaquetar *vt* to pack.
emparedado *nm* sandwich.
empaste *nm* filling.
empatar *vi* (*acabar igualados*) to draw; (*igualar*) to equalize.
empate *nm* tie, draw.
empeine *nm* instep.
empeñar *vt* (*objeto*) to pawn. ▶ *vpr* **empeñarse** (*insistir*) to insist.
empeño *nm* (*insistencia*) determination. •

emperador *nm* emperor.
emperatriz *nf* empress.
empezar *vt-vi* to begin, start.
empinado,-a *adj* steep.
empleado,-a *nm,f (gen)* employee; *(oficinista)* clerk. ▪ **empleada de hogar** maid.
emplear *vt* to employ.
empleo *nm* 1 *(puesto)* job. 2 *(trabajo)* employment.
empotrado,-a *adj* built-in.
emprender *vt* to undertake.
empresa *nf (compañía)* firm, company.
empresario,-a *nm,f* 1 *(hombre)* businessman; *(mujer)* businesswoman. 2 *(patrón)* employer.
empujar *vt* to push.
empujón *nm* push, shove.
en *prep* 1 *(lugar - gen)* in, at; *(- en el interior)* in, inside; *(- sobre)* on: **en casa**, at home; **en Valencia**, in Valencia; **en el cajón**, in the drawer; **en la mesa**, on the table. 2 *(tiempo - año, mes, estación)* in; *(- día)* on: **en 2004**, in 2004; **en viernes**, on Friday. 3 *(dirección)* into: **entró en su casa**, he went into his house. 4 *(transporte)* by, in: **ir en coche**, to go by car. 5 *(tema, materia)* at, in: **es experto en política**, he's an expert in politics. 6 *(modo)* in: **en voz baja**, in a low voice. ● **en seguida** at once, straight away.

enamorado,-a *adj* in love. ▶ *nm,f* lover.
enamorarse *vpr* to fall in love.
enano,-a *adj-nm,f* dwarf.
encabezar *vt* 1 *(en escrito)* to head. 2 *(ser líder)* to lead.
encadenar *vt* 1 *(poner cadenas a)* to chain. 2 *(enlazar)* to link.
encajar *vt-vi* to fit.
encaje *nm (tejido)* lace.
encallar *vi* to run aground.
encaminarse *vpr* to head.
encantado,-a *adj (contento)* delighted. ● **encantado,-a de conocerle** *fml* pleased to meet you.
encantador,-ra *adj* charming.
encantar *vi*: **me encanta la natación**, I love swimming.
encanto *nm (atractivo)* charm.
encarcelar *vt* to imprison.
encargado,-a *nm,f (responsable)* person in charge; *(de negocio - hombre)* manager; *(- mujer)* manageress.
encargar *vt* 1 *(encomendar)* to entrust. 2 *(solicitar)* to order. ▶ *vpr* **encargarse** to take charge.
encargo *nm* 1 *(recado)* errand; *(tarea)* job. 2 *(de productos)* order. ● **por encargo** to order.
encendedor *nm* lighter.
encender *vt* 1 *(fuego, vela, cigarro)* to light; *(cerilla)* to strike.

2 *(luz, radio, tele)* to turn on, switch on.

encerrar *vt* **1** *(persona - en habitación)* to shut in; *(- en cárcel)* to lock up. **2** *fig (contener)* to contain.

encestar *vi* to score (a basket).

enchufar *vt (aparato)* to plug in.

enchufe *nm (de aparato - hembra)* socket; *(- macho)* plug.

encía *nf* gum.

encierro *nm* **1** *(protesta)* sit-in. **2** *(de toros)* bullpen.

encima *adv* **1** *(más arriba)* above; *(sobre)* on top. **2** *(consigo)* on me/you/him *etc*: *¿llevas cambio encima?*, do you have any change on you? **3** *(además)* in addition. ■ **encima de** on; **por encima 1** *(a más altura)* above. **2** *(de pasada)* superficially; **por encima de** above.

encina *nf* evergreen oak.

encoger(se) *vt-vi-vpr* to shrink.

encontrar *vt* **1** *(hallar)* to find. **2** *(creer)* to think. ► *vpr* **encontrarse 1** *(hallarse)* to be. **2** *(personas)* to meet. **3** *(sentirse)* to feel: *me encuentro bien,* I feel fine; *me encuentro mal,* I feel ill.

encubrir *vt (delito)* to cover up.

encuentro *nm* **1** *(coincidencia)* encounter. **2** *(reunión)* meeting. **3** *(en deporte)* match.

encuesta *nf* survey.

endibia *nf* endive.

endulzar *vt (hacer dulce)* to sweeten.

endurecer(se) *vt-vpr* to harden.

enemigo,-a *adj-nm,f* enemy.

energía *nf* energy. ■ **energía atómica** atomic power; **energía eléctrica** electric power; **energía nuclear** nuclear power; **energía solar** solar energy.

enero *nm* January.

enfadado,-a *adj* angry.

enfadarse *vpr* to get angry.

enfado *nm* anger.

enfermedad *nf (estado de enfermo)* illness; *(patología específica)* disease.

enfermería *nf* **1** *(profesión)* nursing. **2** *(lugar)* infirmary.

enfermero,-a *nm,f (hombre)* (male) nurse; *(mujer)* nurse.

enfermo,-a *adj* ill, sick. ► *nm,f* sick person.

enfocar *vt* **1** *(con cámara)* to focus on. **2** *(problema etc)* to approach.

enfrentarse *vpr* **1** *(encararse)* to face up. **2** *(pelearse)* to have a confrontation.

enfrente *adv* opposite. ● **enfrente de** opposite.

enfriarse *vpr* **1** *(algo caliente)* to cool down. **2** *(acatarrarse)* catch a cold.

enfurecerse *vpr* to get furious.

enganchar vt (gen) to hook; (animales) to hitch; (vagones) to couple.

engañar vt 1 (gen) to deceive. 2 (mentir) to lie to. 3 (a la pareja) to be unfaithful to.

engaño nm deceit.

engordar vi 1 (persona) to put on weight: *he engordado cinco kilos*, I've put on five kilos. 2 (alimento) to be fattening.

engrasar vt (gen) to lubricate; (con grasa) to grease; (con aceite) to oil.

enhorabuena nf congratulations. • **dar la enhorabuena a ALGN** to congratulate SB.

enigma nm enigma, puzzle.

enjabonar vt to soap.

enjuagar(se) vt-vpr to rinse.

enlace nm 1 (conexión) link. 2 (boda) marriage. 3 (en internet) link.

enlazar vi to connect.

enmienda nf 1 (de error) correction; (de daño) repair. 2 (de texto, ley) amendment.

enojado,-a adj (enfadado) angry; (molesto) annoyed.

enojarse vpr (enfadarse) to get angry; (molestarse) to get annoyed.

enorgullecerse vpr to be proud, feel proud.

enorme adj enormous, huge.

enredadera nf creeper, climbing plant.

enredar vt 1 (enmarañar) to tangle. 2 (dificultar) to complicate. ▶ vi (hacer travesuras) to get up to mischief. ▶ vpr **enredarse** (cuerda, pelo) to get tangled.

enriquecerse vpr to get rich.

enrollado,-a adj fam (persona) cool.

enrollar vt to roll up. ▶ vpr **enrollarse** fam (hablar) to go on and on. • **enrollarse con ALGN** to get off with SB.

ensalada nf salad.

ensaladera nf salad bowl.

ensaladilla nf. ■ **ensaladilla rusa** Russian salad.

ensanchar vt (agrandar) to widen; (prenda) to let out

ensanche nm 1 (de carretera) widening. 2 (de ciudad) new development.

ensayar vt (obra de teatro) to rehearse; (música) to practise.

ensayo nm 1 (de obra de teatro) rehearsal; (de música) practice. 2 (prueba) test, trial. 3 (literario) essay. ■ **ensayo general** dress rehearsal.

enseguida adv at once, straight away.

enseñanza nf 1 (educación) education. 2 (docencia) teaching.

enseñar vt 1 (en escuela etc) to teach. 2 (mostrar) to show.

ensuciar(se) vt-vpr to get dirty.

entablar *vt (conversación)* to start; *(amistad)* to strike up.

entender *vt* **1** *(comprender)* to understand. **2** *(opinar)* to consider. ► *vi* to know: *¿tú entiendes de motores?*, do you know anything about engines? ► *vpr* **entenderse** *fam (llevarse bien)* to get along well together. • **dar a entender que...** to imply that...

entendido,-a *nm,f* expert.

enterarse *vpr* **1** *(averiguar)* to find out. **2** *(darse cuenta)* to notice. **3** *(comprender)* to understand.

entero,-a *adj (completo)* whole.

enterrar *vt* to bury.

entidad *nf* **1** *(organismo)* body. **2** *(ente, ser)* entity. ■ **entidad bancaria** bank.

entierro *nm* **1** *(acto)* burial. **2** *(ceremonia)* funeral.

entonación *nf* intonation.

entonces *adv* then.

entorno *nm* environment.

entorpecer *vt (dificultar)* to obstruct, hinder.

entrada *nf* **1** *(acción)* entrance, entry. **2** *(lugar)* entrance. **3** *(en espectáculo - billete)* ticket; *(admisión)* admission. **4** *(pago inicial)* down payment. ► *nf pl* **entradas** receding hairline. • **"Prohibida la entrada"** "No admittance".

entrañable *adj* beloved.

entrañas *nf pl* entrails.

entrar *vi* **1** *(ir adentro)* to come in, go in. **2** *(en una sociedad etc.)* to join. **3** *(encajar)* to fit. **4** *(en fase, etapa)* to enter. **5** *(venir)*: *me entraron ganas de llorar*, I felt like crying.

entre *prep* **1** *(dos términos)* between; *(más de dos términos)* among. **2** *(sumando)* counting: *entre niños y adultos somos doce*, counting children and adults, there are twelve of us. • **entre tanto** meanwhile.

entreacto *nm* interval.

entrecot *nm* entrecôte.

entrega *nf (acción)* handing over; *(de mercancía)* delivery.

entregar *vt* **1** *(dar)* to hand over; *(deberes, solicitud)* to hand in. **2** *(mercancía)* to deliver.

entremés *nm* hors d'oeuvre.

entrenador,-ra *nm,f* trainer, coach.

entrenamiento *nm (acción)* training; *(sesión)* training session.

entrenar(se) *vt-vpr* to train.

entresuelo *nm* mezzanine.

entretanto *adv* meanwhile.

entretener *vt* **1** *(divertir)* to entertain. **2** *(distraer)* to distract. ► *vpr* **entretenerse 1** *(retrasarse)* to be late. **2** *(divertirse)* keep oneself amused.

entretenido,-a *adj* **1** *(divertido)* entertaining. **2** *(complicado)* timeconsuming.

entretenimiento *nm* entertainment.

entrevista *nf* interview.

entusiasmar *vt* to excite: *me entusiasma la ópera*, I love opera. ▶ *vpr* **entusiasmarse** to get enthusiastic.

entusiasmo *nm* enthusiasm.

enumerar *vt* to enumerate.

enunciado *nm* statement.

envasar *vt* (*en paquete*) to pack; (*en botella*) to bottle; (*en lata*) to can, tin. • **envasado,-a al vacío** vacuum-packed.

envase *nm* (*recipiente*) container; (*botella*) bottle.

envejecer *vt* (*dar aspecto viejo*) to make look older. ▶ *vi* (*hacerse viejo*) to grow old.

envenenamiento *nm* poisoning.

envenenarse *vpr* to poison oneself.

enviado,-a *nm,f.* ■ **enviado,-a especial** special correspondent.

enviar *vt* to send.

envidia *nf* envy.

envío *nm* **1** (*acción*) sending. **2** (*remesa*) consignment; (*de mercancía*) dispatch, shipment. ■ **envío contra reembolso** cash on delivery.

envolver *vt* **1** (*cubrir*) to wrap. **2** (*rodear*) to surround. **3** (*implicar*) to involve.

enyesar *vt* (*pierna, brazo*) to put in plaster.

epidemia *nf* epidemic.

episodio *nm* episode.

época *nf* **1** (*período*) time, period. **2** (*del año*) season.

equilibrio *nm* balance. • **mantener el equilibrio** to keep one's balance; **perder el equilibrio** to lose one's balance.

equipaje *nm* luggage, baggage. • **hacer el equipaje** to pack, do the packing. ■ **equipaje de mano** hand luggage.

equipo *nm* **1** (*de personas, jugadores*) team. **2** (*equipamiento*) equipment. **3** (*ordenador*) machine.

equivalente *adj-nm* equivalent.

equivaler *vi* **1** (*ser igual*) to be equivalent. **2** (*significar*) to be tantamount.

equivocación *nf* mistake, error.

equivocarse *vpr* **1** (*no tener razón*) to be mistaken, be wrong. **2** (*cometer un error*) to make a mistake.

era *nf* (*período*) era, age.

erguirse *vpr* to straighten up.

erigir *vt* to erect. ▶ *vpr* **erigirse** to set oneself up.

erizo *nm* hedgehog. ■ **erizo de mar** sea urchin.

ermita *nf* (*capilla*) chapel.

erosión *nf* erosion.

erótico,-a *adj* erotic.

errar *vt* (*objetivo, disparo*) to miss; (*pronóstico*) to get wrong.

error *nm* mistake, error. • **por error** by mistake.

eructo *nm* belch.

erupción *nf* 1 *(volcánica)* eruption. 2 *(cutánea)* rash.

esbozo *nm (dibujo)* sketch.

escabeche *nm* pickle.

escafandra *nf* diving suit.

escala *nf* scale. • **a escala** scale; **hacer escala 1** *(avión)* to stop over. 2 *(barco)* to put in.

escalador,-ra *nm,f* climber.

escalar *vt* to climb.

escalera *nf* 1 *(de edificio)* stairs. 2 *(portátil)* ladder. 3 *(naipes)* run. ▪ **escalera de caracol** spiral staircase; **escalera mecánica** escalator.

escalerilla *nf (de barco)* gangway; *(de avión)* steps.

escalofrío *nm* shiver.

escalón *nm (peldaño)* step.

escalope *nm* escalope.

escama *nf* scale.

escándalo *nm* 1 *(acto inmoral)* scandal. 2 *(alboroto)* racket.

escanear *vt* to scan.

escáner *nm* scanner.

escapada *nf* 1 *fam (viaje)* quick trip. 2 *(en ciclismo)* breakaway.

escapar(se) *vi-vpr (lograr salir)* to escape; *(irse corriendo)* to run away. ▶ *vpr* **escaparse 1** *(gas etc)* to leak out. 2 *(autobús etc.)* to miss.

escaparate *nm* shop window.

escape *nm* 1 *(huida)* escape. 2 *(de gas etc)* leak. 3 *(de coche)* exhaust.

escarabajo *nm* beetle.

escarcha *nf* frost.

escarola *nf* GB curly endive; US escarole.

escaso,-a *adj* scarce, scant.

escayola *nf* plaster.

escayolar *vt* to put in plaster.

escena *nf* 1 *(gen)* scene. 2 *(escenario)* stage.

escenario *nm* 1 *(en teatro)* stage. 2 *(de suceso)* scene.

escéptico,-a *adj* GB sceptical; US skeptical.

esclavo,-a *nm,f* slave.

esclusa *nf (de canal)* lock; *(compuerta)* sluice gate.

escoba *nf* broom.

escobilla *nf* 1 *(gen)* brush. 2 *(de coche)* windscreen (US windshield) wiper blade.

escocer *vi (herida)* to smart.

escocés,-a *adj* Scottish. ▶ *nm,f (persona)* Scot.

Escocia *nf* Scotland.

escoger *vt* to choose.

escolar *adj* school.

escolta *nmf* escort.

escombros *nm pl* rubble.

esconder(se) *vt-vpr* to hide.

escopeta *nf* shotgun.

escorpión *nm* scorpion.

escote[1] *nm (de vestido)* neckline.

escote[2]. • **pagar a escote** to share the expenses.

escotilla *nf* hatchway.

escozor *nm (picor)* irritation, smarting.

escribir *vt-vi* to write. ► *vpr* **escribirse 1** *(dos personas)* to write to each other. **2** *(palabra)* to spell: *se escribe con "j"*, it's spelt with a "j".

escrito,-a *adj* written.• **por escrito** in writing.

escritor,-ra *nm,f* writer.

escritorio *nm* **1** *(mueble)* writing desk. **2** INFORM desktop.

escrupuloso,-a *adj* **1** *(cuidadoso)* scrupulous. **2** *(aprensivo)* finicky, fussy.

escuadra *nf* **1** *(instrumento)* square. **2** *(de soldados)* squad.

escuchar *vt* **1** *(atender)* to listen to. **2** *(oír)* to hear.

escudo *nm* shield.

escuela *nf* school.

escultor,-ra *nm,f (hombre)* sculptor; *(mujer)* sculptress.

escultura *nf* sculpture.

escupir *vi* to spit.

escurridor *nm* **1** *(colador)* colander. **2** *(de platos)* dish rack.

escurrir *vt (platos)* to drain; *(ropa)* to wring out. ► *vpr* **escurrirse** *(resbalarse)* to slip.

ese,-a *adj* that.

ése,-a *pron* that one.

esencial *adj* essential.

esfera *nf* **1** *(figura)* sphere. **2** *(de reloj)* face.

esforzarse *vpr* to try hard.

esfuerzo *nm* effort.

esgrima *nf* fencing.

esguince *nm* sprain.

eslabón *nm* link.

eslip *nm* briefs, underpants.

eslogan *nm* slogan.

esmalte *nm* enamel. ▪ **esmalte de uñas** nail polish, nail varnish.

esmeralda *nf* emerald.

esmerarse *vpr* to do one's best.

esmoquin *nf* GB dinner jacket; US tuxedo.

eso *pron* that.

esófago *nm* GB oesophagus; US esophagus.

espacial *adj (cohete etc)* space; *(en física)* spatial.

espacio *nm* **1** *(sitio)* space. **2** *(de tiempo)* period. **3** *(en radio, televisión)* programme. ▪ **espacio aéreo** air space.

espada *nf* sword.

espaguetis *nm pl* spaghetti.

espalda *nf* **1** *(parte del cuerpo)* back. **2** *(en natación)* backstroke.

espantapájaros *nm* scarecrow.

espantar *vt* **1** *(asustar)* to frighten, scare. **2** *(ahuyentar)* to frighten away.

espantoso,-a *adj* **1** *(terrible)* frightful, dreadful. **2** *(muy feo)* hideous, frightful.

español,-la *adj* Spanish. ► *nm,f (persona)* Spaniard. ► *nm* **español** *(idioma)* Spanish.

esparadrapo *nm* GB sticking plaster; US Band-Aid®.
espárrago *nm* asparagus.
esparto *nm* esparto grass.
especia *nf* spice.
especial *adj* special.
especialidad *nf* GB speciality; US specialty.
especie *nf* 1 *(de animales, plantas)* species. 2 *(tipo)* kind, sort.
específico,-a *adj* specific.
espectáculo *nm* 1 *(escena)* spectacle, sight. 2 *(de TV, radio etc)* show.
espectador,-ra *nm,f* 1 *(en un estadio)* spectator. 2 *(en teatro, cine)* member of the audience; *(de televisión)* viewer.
espejo *nm* mirror. ■ **espejo retrovisor** rear-view mirror.
espera *nf* wait.
esperanza *nf* hope. • **perder la esperanza** to lose hope. ■ **esperanza de vida** life expectancy.
esperar *vt* 1 *(aguardar)* to wait for, await. 2 *(confiar)* to hope for, expect: *espero que sí,* I hope so. 3 *(bebé)* to expect. ► *vi* to wait.
esperma *nm* sperm.
espeso,-a *adj* thick.
espía *nmf* spy.
espiga *nf* *(de trigo)* ear; *(de flor)* spike.
espina *nf* 1 *(de planta)* thorn. 2 *(de pez)* fishbone. ■ **espina dorsal** spine, backbone.

espinacas *nf pl* spinach *sing.*
espinilla *nf* 1 *(tibia)* shinbone. 2 *(grano)* blackhead.
espiral *adj-nf* spiral.
espíritu *nm* spirit.
espléndido,-a *adj* 1 *(magnífico)* splendid, magnificent. 2 *(generoso)* lavish.
esponja *nf* sponge.
espontáneo,-a *adj* spontaneous.
esposas *nf pl* handcuffs.
esposo,-a *nm,f* spouse; *(hombre)* husband; *(mujer)* wife.
espuela *nf* spur.
espuma *nf* *(de mar)* foam; *(de olas)* surf; *(de jabón)* lather; *(de cerveza)* froth. ■ **espuma de afeitar** shaving foam.
espumadera *nf* skimmer.
espumoso,-a *adj* *(vino)* sparkling.
esquela *nf* death notice.
esqueleto *nm* skeleton.
esquema *nm* *(plan)* outline; *(gráfica)* diagram.
esquí *nm* 1 *(tabla)* ski. 2 *(deporte)* skiing. ■ **esquí acuático** water-skiing.
esquiar *vi* to ski.
esquimal *adj-nmf* Eskimo.
esquina *nf* corner. • **a la vuelta de la esquina** just around the corner; **doblar la esquina** to turn the corner.
esquivar *vt* 1 *(persona)* to avoid. 2 *(golpe)* to dodge.
estable *adj* stable, steady.

establecer vt to establish. ►
vpr **establecerse** to settle.

establecimiento nm (local)
establishment; (tienda) shop.

establo nm stable.

estación nf 1 (del año)
season. 2 (de tren) station. ■
estación de esquí ski resort; **estación de servicio**
service station.

estacionarse vt-vpr to park.

estadio nm stadium.

estadística nf statistics.

estado nm 1 (gen) state. 2
(médico) condition. • **estar
en mal estado 1** (alimento)
to be off. 2 (carretera) to be in
poor condition; **estar en estado** to be pregnant. ■ **estado civil** marital status.

estafar vt 1 (timar) to swindle. 2 (defraudar) to defraud.

estalactita nf stalactite.

estalagmita nf stalagmite.

estallar vi 1 (bomba) to explode. 2 (neumático, globo)
to burst. 3 (rebelión, guerra) to
break out.

estancarse vpr 1 (líquido) to
stagnate. 2 (proceso) to come
to a standstill.

estancia nf 1 (permanencia)
stay. 2 (aposento) room.

estanco nm tobacconist's.

estándar adj-nm standard.

estanque nm pool, pond.

estante nm (gen) shelf; (para
libros) bookcase.

estantería nf shelves.

estaño nm tin.

estar vi to be. ► aux estar +
inf to be: **estar comiendo**, to
be eating.

estatua nf statue.

estatura nf height.

este adj-nm east.

este,-a adj this.

éste,-a pron this one.

estela nf (de barco) wake; (de
avión) GB vapour trail; US vapor trail.

estelar adj 1 (sideral) stellar.
2 (actuación, elenco) star.

estepa nf steppe.

estéreo adj stereo.

estéril adj sterile.

esternón nm sternum.

esteticista nmf beautician.

estético,-a adj GB aesthetic;
US esthetic.

estetoscopio nm stethoscope.

estilo nm 1 (gen) style. 2 (en
natación) stroke. • **estilo de
vida** way of life, lifestyle.

estilográfica nf fountain pen.

estimado,-a adj 1 (aprecia-
do) esteemed. 2 (valorado)
valued. • **estimada señora**
(en carta) Dear Madam; **estimado señor** (en carta) Dear
Sir.

estimar vt 1 (apreciar) to esteem; (objeto) to value. 2 (juzgar) to consider.

estímulo nm 1 stimulus. 2
(aliciente) encouragement.

estirar(se) *vt-vpr* to stretch.
estival *adj* summer.
esto *pron* this.
estofado *nm* stew.
estómago *nm* stomach.
estorbar *vt* 1 *(dificultar)* to hinder. 2 *(molestar)* to annoy. ► *vi* to get in the way.
estornudo *nm* sneeze.
estos,-as *adj pl* these.
éstos,-as *pron* these.
estragón *nm* tarragon.
estrangular *vt* to strangle.
estrategia *nf* strategy.
estrechar *vt* 1 *(calle)* to narrow; *(vestido)* to take in. 2 *(abrazar)* to embrace. • **estrechar la mano** to shake hands.
estrecho,-a *adj* 1 *(gen)* narrow; *(vestido, zapatos)* tight. 2 *(amistad etc)* close. ► *nm* **estrecho** straits, strait.
estrella *nf* star. ■ **estrella de mar** starfish.
estrellarse *vpr* to crash, smash.
estrenar *vt* 1 *(gen)* to use for the first time; *(ropa)* to wear for the first time. 2 *(obra de teatro)* to open; *(película)* to release.
estreno *nm* 1 *(de cosa)* first use. 2 *(de obra de teatro)* first night, opening night; *(de película)* premiere.
estreñimiento *nm* constipation.

estrés *nm* stress.
estribillo *nm* *(de canción)* chorus.
estribo *nm* stirrup. • **perder los estribos** to lose one's head.
estribor *nm* starboard.
estricto,-a *adj* strict.
estrofa *nf* stanza.
estropajo *nm* scourer.
estropear *vt* 1 *(máquina)* to damage, break. 2 *(plan etc)* to spoil, ruin. ► *vpr* **estropearse** 1 *(máquina)* to break down. 2 *(comida)* to go off.
estructura *nf* structure.
estruendo *nm* great noise, din.
estuario *nm* estuary.
estuche *nm* case, box.
estudiante *nmf* student.
estudiar *vt-vi* to study.
estudio *nm* 1 *(gen)* study. 2 *(apartamento, oficina; de cine, televisión)* studio. ► *nm pl* **estudios** studies, education.
estufa *nf* heater
estupendo,-a *adj* wonderful.
estúpido,-a *adj* stupid. ► *nm,f* idiot.
etapa *nf* 1 *(gen)* stage. 2 *(en competición)* leg, stage.
eterno,-a *adj* eternal, everlasting.
ético,-a *adj* ethical.
etiqueta *nf* 1 *(rótulo)* label. 2 *(formalidad)* etiquette.

eucalipto *nm* eucalyptus.

euforia *nf* euphoria, elation.

euro *nm* euro.

Europa *nf* Europe.

europeo,-a *adj-nm,f* European.

evacuar *vt* to evacuate.

evadir *vt (capital)* to evade. ▶ *vpr* **evadirse** *(escaparse)* to escape.

evaluar *vt* to evaluate, assess.

evaporar(se) *vt-vpr* to evaporate.

evasión *nf* escape.

eventual *nmf* casual worker, temporary worker.

evidencia *nf* obviousness.

evidente *adj* evident, obvious.

evitar *vt* to avoid.

evolución *nf (gen)* evolution; *(de enfermedad)* development; *(de enfermo)* progress.

evolucionar *vi (gen)* to evolve; *(enfermedad)* to develop; *(enfermo)* progress.

exacto,-a *adj* exact, accurate.

exagerar *vt-vi* to exaggerate.

examen *nm* exam, examination. ■ **examen de conducir** driving test; **examen médico** check-up, medical.

examinar *vt* **1** *(estudiante)* to examine. **2** *(considerar)* to look into, consider.

excavar *vt (gen)* to dig; *(en arqueología)* to excavate.

excelente *adj* excellent.

excepción *nf* exception.

excepcional *adj* exceptional.

excepto *adv* except, apart from.

exceso *nm (demasía)* excess; *(de mercancía)* surplus. ■ **exceso de equipaje** excess baggage; **exceso de velocidad** speeding.

excitar *vt* **1** *(gen)* to excite. **2** *(emociones)* to stir up.

exclamación *nf* exclamation.

exclusivo,-a *adj* exclusive.

excursión *nf* excursion, outing.

excursionista *nmf (turista)* tripper; *(a pie)* hiker.

excusa *nf* excuse.

exhaustivo,-a *adj* exhaustive, thorough.

exhibición *nf* **1** *(exposición)* exhibition. **2** *(de película)* showing.

exhibir *vt (mostrar)* to exhibit, put on, show.

exigente *adj* demanding.

exigir *vt (pedir)* to demand; *(necesitar)* to require, demand.

exilio *nm* exile.

existencia *nf* existence. ▶ *nf pl* **existencias** inventory, stocks. ● **en existencia** in stock.

existir *vi* **1** *(ser real)* to exist. **2** *(haber)* to be.

éxito *nm* success. ● **tener éxito** to be successful.

exótico,-a *adj* exotic.
expedición *nf* 1 *(viaje, grupo)* expedition. 2 *(envío)* shipping.
expedir *vt* 1 *(documento)* to issue. 2 *(carta, paquete)* to dispatch.
experiencia *nf* experience.
experimentar *vt* 1 *(probar)* to test. 2 *(sentir)* to experience; *(cambio)* to undergo.
experimento *nm* experiment.
experto,-a *adj-nm,f* expert.
explicación *nf* explanation.
explicar *vt* to explain.
explorador,-ra *nm,f* explorer.
explorar *vt* to explore.
explosión *nf* explosion.
explosivo *nm* explosive.
explotación *nf* exploitation.
explotar *vt* *(sacar provecho de)* to exploit; *(mina)* to work; *(tierra)* to cultivate. ► *vi* *(explosionar)* to explode.
exponer *vt* 1 *(explicar)* to explain. 2 *(mostrar)* to show.
exportación *nf* export.
exportar *vt* to export.
exposición *nf* 1 *(de arte)* exhibition. 2 *(de fotografía)* exposure.
expresar(se) *vt-vpr* to express (oneself).
expresión *nf* expression.
expreso *nm* *(tren)* express train, express.
exprimir *vt* to squeeze.
expulsar *vt* 1 *(gen)* to expel. 2 *(jugador)* to send off.

expulsión *nf* 1 *(gen)* expulsion. 2 *(de jugador)* sending off.
exquisito,-a *adj* delicious.
extender *vt* 1 *(gen)* to extend. 2 *(cheque)* to make out. 3 *(mantequilla, pintura)* to spread.
extensión *nf* 1 *(gen)* extension. 2 *(dimensión)* extent.
exterior *adj* 1 *(de fuera)* exterior, outer. 2 *(extranjero)* foreign. ► *nm* exterior, outside.
externo,-a *adj* external, outward. • **"Para uso externo"** "External use only".
extinción *nf* extinction.
extintor *nm* fire extinguisher.
extra *adj* 1 *(adicional)* extra. 2 *(superior)* top. ► *nmf* *(actor)* extra. ► *nm* 1 *(gasto)* extra expense. 2 *(plus)* bonus.
extracto *nm* 1 *(substancia)* extract. 2 *(resumen)* summary. ▪ **extracto de cuenta** statement of account.
extraer *vt* to extract.
extranjero,-a *adj* foreign. ► *nm,f* foreigner. • **vivir en el extranjero** to live abroad.
extraño,-a *adj* 1 *(raro)* strange. 2 *(desconocido)* alien, foreign.
extraordinario,-a *adj* extraordinary.
extraviado,-a *adj* missing, lost.
extremo,-a *adj* extreme. ► *nm* **extremo** 1 *(límite)* extreme; *(punta)* end. 2 *(en deporte)* wing.

F

fa *nf (nota)* F.
fábrica *nf* factory.
fabricar *vt (crear)* to make; *(en fábrica)* to manufacture.
fabuloso,-a *adj* fabulous.
fachada *nf* façade, front.
fácil *adj* easy.
facilitar *vt* **1** *(simplificar)* to make easy. **2** *(proporcionar)* to provide.
factor *nm* factor.
factura *nf* bill.
facturar *vt* **1** *(cobrar)* to invoice; *(vender)* to have a turnover of. **2** *(equipaje)* to check in.
facultad *nf* **1** *(capacidad)* faculty. **2** *(de universidad)* faculty.
faena *nf* **1** *(tarea)* job. **2** *fam (mala pasada)* dirty trick.
faisán *nm* pheasant.
faja *nf (de mujer)* girdle.
fajo *nm (de billetes)* wad.
falda *nf* **1** *(prenda)* skirt. **2** *(regazo)* lap. **3** *(ladera)* slope. ▪ **falda pantalón** culottes.
fallar[1] *vt (tiro, penalty)* to miss. ▶ *vi (no funcionar)* to fail
fallar[2] *vt (premio)* to award.
fallecimiento *nm* death.
fallo[1] *nm* **1** *(error)* mistake; *(fracaso)* failure. **2** *(defecto)* fault.
fallo[2] *nm* **1** *(de tribunal)* judgement. **2** *(premio)* awarding.

falsedad *nf* **1** *(hipocresía)* falseness. **2** *(mentira)* falsehood.
falsificar *vt* to forge.
falso,-a *adj* false, untrue.
falta *nf* **1** *(carencia)* lack, shortage. **2** *(ausencia)* absence. **3** *(error)* mistake: **falta de ortografía**, spelling mistake. **4** *(delito menor)* GB misdemeanour; US misdemeanor. **5** *(en fútbol)* foul; *(en tenis)* fault. • **hacer falta** to be necessary: *no hace falta preguntar*, there is no need to ask; **sin falta** without fail. ▪ **falta de educación** bad manners.
faltar *vi* **1** *(cosa)* to be missing; *(persona)* to be absent. **2** *(haber poco)* to be needed: *me falta azúcar*, I haven't got enough sugar. **3** *(no acudir)* to miss. **4** *(quedar)* to be left: *faltan dos semanas para el examen*, there are two weeks to go till the exam. • **¡no faltaba más!** *(por supuesto)* of course!
fama *nf (renombre)* fame, renown. • **tener buena fama** to have a good name; **tener mala fama** to have a bad name.
familia *nf* **1** *(parientes)* family. **2** *(prole)* children.
famoso,-a *adj* famous.
fan *nmf* fan.
fanático,-a *adj-nm,f* fanatic.
fango *nm (barro)* mud.
fantasía *nf* fantasy.

fantasma *nm (espectro)* ghost.
fantástico,-a *adj* fantastic.
faringe *nf* pharynx.
farmacéutico,-a *adj* pharmaceutical. ► *nm,f (de farmacia)* GB chemist; US druggist, pharmacist.
farmacia *nf (tienda)* GB chemist's; US drugstore, pharmacy.
faro *nm* 1 *(torre)* lighthouse. 2 *(en coche)* headlight.
farol *nm (de luz)* lantern; *(farola)* streetlamp, streetlight.
farola *nf* streetlight, streetlamp.
fascículo *nm* part, GB instalment; US installment.
fascinante *adj* fascinating.
fase *nf* 1 *(etapa)* stage. 2 *(en física)* phase.
fastidiar *vt* 1 *(molestar)* to annoy, bother. 2 *(dañar)* to hurt. ► *vpr* **fastidiarse** *(aguantarse)* to put up with: *si no le gusta que se fastidie*, if he doesn't like it that's tough.
fatal *adj* 1 *(inexorable)* fateful. 2 *(mortal)* deadly, fatal. 3 *fam (muy malo)* awful, terrible. ► *adv fam* badly, terribly: *me siento fatal*, I feel awful.
fatiga *nf (cansancio)* fatigue.
fauna *nf* fauna.
favor *nm* GB favour; US favor. • *por favor* please;
favorable *adj* GB favourable; US favorable; *(condiciones)* suitable.

favorecer *vt* 1 *(ayudar)* GB to favour; US to favor. 2 *(agraciar)* to suit.
favorito,-a *adj-nm,f* GB favourite; US favorite.
fax *nm* fax. • **enviar por fax** to fax.
fe *nf* faith. • **de buena fe** in good faith.
febrero *nm* February.
fecha *nf* 1 *(día, mes, etc)* date. 2 *(día)* day. • **hasta la fecha** to date. ■ **fecha de caducidad** best before date: *"Fecha de caducidad..."*, "Best before...".
fecundación *nf* fertilization. ■ **fecundación in vitro** in vitro fertilization.
federación *nf* federation.
felicidad *nf* happiness. • **¡felicidades!** congratulations!
felicitación *nf (tarjeta)* greetings card.
felicitar *vt* to congratulate.
feliz *adj* 1 *(contento)* happy. 2 *(acertado)* fortunate.
felpa *nf* felt.
felpudo *nm* doormat.
femenino,-a *adj (gen)* feminine; *(sexo)* female.
fenomenal *adj* 1 *(extraordinario)* phenomenal. 2 *fam (fantástico)* fantastic, terrific.
fenómeno *nm* 1 *(hecho)* phenomenon. 2 *(prodigio)* genius.
feo,-a *adj* ugly.
féretro *nm* coffin.

feria nf 1 (exhibición) fair. 2 (fiesta) fair, festival. ▪ **feria de muestras** trade fair.

fermentar vi to ferment.

feroz adj fierce, ferocious.

ferretería nf (tienda) GB ironmonger's; US hardware store.

ferrocarril nm GB railway; US railroad.

fértil adj fertile.

fertilizante nm fertilizer.

festejo nm (celebración) celebration.

festival nm festival.

festivo,-a adj 1 (alegre) festive. 2 (agudo) witty.

fiable adj reliable.

fiambre nm cold meat.

fiambrera nf lunch box.

fianza nf 1 (depósito) deposit, security. 2 (para acusado) bail. • **bajo fianza** on bail.

fiar vt to sell on credit. ▶ vpr **fiarse** to trust.

fibra nf GB fibre; US fiber.

ficción nf fiction.

ficha nf 1 (tarjeta) index card; (datos) file. 2 (de máquina) token. 3 (en juegos) counter; (de ajedrez) piece, man; (de dominó) domino.

fichar vt 1 (anotar) to put on an index card, put on a file. 2 (futbolista etc) to sign up. ▶ vi (al entrar) to clock in; (al salir) to clock out. • **estar fichado,-a por la policía** to have a police record.

fichero nm 1 (de ordenador) file. 2 (archivo) card index.

fidelidad nf 1 (lealtad) fidelity. 2 (exactitud) accuracy.

fideo nm noodle.

fiebre nf fever. • **tener fiebre** GB to have a temperature; US to have a fever.

fiel adj 1 (leal) faithful. 2 (exacto) accurate.

fieltro nm felt.

fiera nf 1 (animal) wild animal. 2 (persona) beast, brute. 3 (genio) wizard.

fiesta nf 1 (día festivo) holiday. 2 (celebración) party. ▪ **la fiesta nacional** bullfighting.

figura nf figure.

figurarse vpr (imaginarse) to imagine.

fijador nm (laca) hair-spray; (gomina) hair gel.

fijar vt 1 (sujetar) to fix, fasten. 2 (pegar) to stick. 3 (establecer) to set. ▶ vpr **fijarse** 1 (darse cuenta) to notice. 2 (poner atención) to pay attention.

fijo,-a adj 1 (sujeto) fixed, fastened. 2 (permanente) fixed, permanent.

fila nf 1 (línea) line. 2 (en cine, clase) row. • **en fila india** in single file.

filete nm (de carne, pescado) fillet; (solomillo) sirloin.

filial adj-nf (empresa) subsidiary.

filmar vt (gen) to film; (escena, película) to shoot.

filo *nm* edge.

filosofía *nf* philosophy.

filósofo,-a *nm,f* philosopher.

filtro *nm* filter.

fin *nm* 1 *(final)* end. 2 *(objetivo)* purpose, aim. ● **a fin de** in order to; **a fin de que** so that; **al fin y al cabo** when all's said and done; **en fin** anyway; **¡por fin!** at last! ■ **fin de año** New Year's Eve; **fin de semana** weekend.

final *adj* final. ► *nm (conclusión)* end. ► *nf (en competición)* final.

finalizar *vt-vi* to end, finish.

financiar *vt* to finance.

finanzas *nm pl* finances.

finca *nf* property, estate. ■ **finca urbana** building.

fingir *vt* to feign.

fino,-a *adj* 1 *(gen)* fine. 2 *(alimento)* fine, choice. 3 *(educado)* refined, polite. ► *nm* **fino** *(vino)* dry sherry. ● **no estar fino** *(de salud)* 1 not to be feeling well. 2 *(agudo, centrado)* not to be on the ball.

firma *nf* 1 *(autógrafo)* signature. 2 *(acto)* signing. 3 *(empresa)* firm.

firmar *vt* to sign.

firme *adj* firm, steady.

fiscal *adj* fiscal. ► *nmf* GB public prosecutor; US district attorney.

física *nf* physics.

físico,-a *adj* physical.

flaco,-a *adj* skinny.

flan *nm* caramel custard, crème caramel.

flash *nm* flash.

flato *nm* stitch.

flauta *nf* flute. ■ **flauta dulce** recorder.

flecha *nf* arrow.

flemón *nm* gumboil, abscess.

flequillo *nm* GB fringe; US bangs *pl*.

flexible *adj* flexible.

flexo *nm* desk lamp.

flojo,-a *adj* 1 *(suelto)* loose. 2 *(débil)* weak.

flor *nf* flower.

floreciente *adj* flourishing.

florero *nm* vase.

floristería *nf* florist's.

flota *nf* fleet.

flotador *nm* 1 *(para pescar)* float. 2 *(de niño)* rubber ring.

flotar *vi* to float.

flote *nm*. ● **salir a flote** 1 *(recuperarse)* to get back on one's feet. 2 *(descubrirse)* to emerge.

fluido,-a *adj* 1 *(sustancia)* fluid. 2 *(lenguaje)* fluent. ► *nm* **fluido** fluid. ■ **fluido eléctrico** current.

flúor *nm* fluorine.

fluorescente *adj* fluorescent. ► *nm* fluorescent light.

foca *nf (animal)* seal.

foco *nm* 1 *(centro)* centre, focal point. 2 *(en fotografía, física)* focus. 3 *(en teatro)* spotlight; *(en estadio)* floodlight.

folleto *nm (prospecto)* leaflet; *(explicativo)* instruction leaflet; *(turístico)* brochure.

fomentar *vt (industria, turismo)* to promote; *(desarrollo, ahorro)* to encourage.

fonda *nf* 1 *(para comer)* restaurant. 2 *(para alojarse)* guest house.

fondo *nm* 1 *(parte más baja)* bottom. 2 *(parte más lejana)* end, back. 3 *(segundo término)* background. ▶ *nm pl* **fondos** *(dinero)* funds. • **a fondo** thoroughly; **en el fondo** deep down, at heart. ▪ **fondo del mar** sea bed.

fontanero,-a *nm,f* plumber.

footing *nm* jogging.

forestal *adj* forest.

forma *nf* 1 *(figura)* form, shape. 2 *(manera)* way. 3 *(condiciones físicas)* form. • **de forma que** so that; **de todas formas** anyway; **estar en forma** to be fit. ▪ **forma de pago** method of payment; **forma física** physical fitness.

formación *nf* 1 *(gen)* formation. 2 *(educación)* training.

formal *adj* 1 *(serio)* serious. 2 *(cumplidor)* reliable, dependable.

formalidad *nf (trámite)* formality.

formar *vt* 1 *(gen)* to form. 2 *(educar)* to educate; *(en técnicas)* to train.

formatear *vt* to format.

formidable *adj (maravilloso)* wonderful.

fórmula *nf* formula.

formulario *nm (documento)* form.

forofo,-a *nm,f* fan.

forrar *vt* 1 *(por dentro)* to line. 2 *(por fuera)* to cover. ▶ *vpr* **forrarse** *fam (de dinero)* to make a packet.

forro *nm* 1 *(interior)* lining. 2 *(funda)* cover.

fortaleza *nf* 1 *(vigor)* strength. 2 *(castillo)* fortress.

fortuna *nf* 1 *(suerte)* luck. 2 *(capital)* fortune.

forzar *vt* to force.

fosa *nf* 1 *(sepultura)* grave. 2 *(hoyo)* pit. ▪ **fosas nasales** nostrils.

fósforo *nm* 1 *(elemento)* phosphorus. 2 *(cerilla)* match.

fósil *nm* fossil.

foso *nm (gen)* pit; *(de castillo etc.)* moat.

foto *nf fam* photo. • **hacer una foto** to take a photo.

fotocopia *nf* photocopy.

fotografía *nf* 1 *(proceso)* photography. 2 *(retrato)* photograph.

fotógrafo,-a *nm,f* photographer.

fracaso *nm* failure.

fractura *nf* fracture.

frágil *adj* 1 *(delicado)* fragile. 2 *(débil)* frail.

fragmento *nm* **1** *(pedazo)* fragment. **2** *(literario)* passage.

fraile *nm* friar.

frambuesa *nf* raspberry.

francés,-esa *adj* French. ► *nm,f (persona)* French person. ► *nm* **francés** *(idioma)* French.

Francia *nf* France.

franela *nf* flannel.

franja *nf* band, strip.

franquear *vt (carta)* to frank. • **a franquear en destino** postage paid.

franqueo *nm* postage.

frasco *nm* flask.

frase *nf* **1** *(oración)* sentence. **2** *(expresión)* phrase.

fraterno,-a *adj* fraternal, brotherly.

fraude *nm* fraud. ▪ **fraude fiscal** tax evasion.

frecuencia *nf* frequency.

frecuente *adj* **1** *(repetido)* frequent. **2** *(usual)* common.

fregadero *nm* kitchen sink.

fregar *vt* **1** *(lavar)* to wash. **2** *(frotar)* to scrub. **3** *(suelo)* to mop. • **fregar los platos** to do the washing up.

fregona *nf (utensilio)* mop.

freidora *nf* fryer.

freír *vt* to fry.

frenar *vt-vi* to brake.

freno *nm* **1** *(de vehículo)* brake. **2** *(de caballería)* bit.

frente *nm* front. ► *nf* forehead. ► *adv* **frente a** in front of, opposite. • **al frente de**

at the head of; **frente a frente** face to face.

fresa *nf* strawberry.

fresco,-a *adj* **1** *(gen)* cool. **2** *(comida)* fresh. **3** *(desvergonzado)* cheeky, shameless. ► *nm*

fresco 1 *(frescor)* fresh air. **2** *(pintura)* fresco. • **hacer fresco** to be chilly.

fresno *nm* ash tree.

fresón *nm* large strawberry.

frialdad *nf* coldness.

fricción *nf* **1** *(gen)* friction. **2** *(friega)* rubbing.

frigorífico *nm* refrigerator, fridge.

frío,-a *adj* cold. ► *nm* **frío** cold. • **hacer frío** to be cold; **tener frío, pasar frío** to be cold.

frito,-a *adj (comida)* fried. ► *nm pl* **fritos** fried food *sing*.

frontal *adj* **1** *(choque)* head-on. **2** *(oposición)* direct.

frontera *nf (geográfica)* frontier; *(entre países)* border.

frotar *vt* to rub.

frustración *nf* frustration.

fruta *nf* fruit. ▪ **fruta del tiempo** seasonal fruit.

frutal *nm* fruit tree.

frutería *nf* fruit shop.

frutero *nm* fruit bowl.

fruto *nm* fruit. ▪ **frutos secos 1** *(almendras etc)* nuts. **2** *(pasas etc)* dried fruit.

fuego *nm* **1** *(gen)* fire. **2** *(lumbre)* light. **3** *(fogón de cocina)* burner, ring. • **a fuego lento 1** *(cocinar)* on a low flame. **2** *(al horno)* in a slow oven. • **¿me da fuego?** have you got a light? ▪ **fuegos artificiales** fireworks.

fuente *nf* **1** *(manantial)* spring. **2** *(artificial)* fountain. **3** *(recipiente)* serving dish. **4** *(de información)* source.

fuera *adv* **1** *(gen)* out, outside. **2** *(en otro lugar)* away; *(en el extranjero)* abroad. • **fuera de combate** knocked out. ▪ **fuera de juego** offside.

fuerte *adj* **1** *(gen)* strong. **2** *(intenso)* severe. **3** *(sonido)* loud. **4** *(golpe)* heavy. ► *nm* *(fortificación)* fort.

fuerza *nf* strength. • **a la fuerza** by force. ▪ **fuerza de voluntad** willpower **fuerzas del orden** police force.

fuga *nf* **1** *(escapada)* escape. **2** *(de gas, líquido)* leak.

fugarse *vpr* to flee, escape.

fumador,-ra *adj* smoking. ► *nm,f* smoker.

fumar(se) *vt-vi-vpr* to smoke. • **"No fumar"** "No smoking".

función *nf* **1** *(gen)* function. **2** *(espectáculo)* performance. • **en función de** according to.

funcionamiento *nm* operation, working.

funcionar *vi* to work. • **"No funciona"** "Out of order".

funcionario,-a *nm,f* civil servant.

funda *nf* **1** *(flexible)* cover. **2** *(rígida)* case. ▪ **funda de almohada** pillowcase.

fundación *nf* foundation.

fundador,-ra *nm,f* founder.

fundamental *adj* fundamental.

fundamento *nm* basis, grounds.

fundar *vt* **1** *(crear)* to found; *(erigir)* to raise. **2** *(basar)* to base, found.

fundir *vt* **1** *(un sólido)* to melt. **2** *(metal)* to cast; *(hierro)* to smelt. **3** *(bombilla, plomos)* to blow.

funeral *nm* **1** *(entierro)* funeral. **2** *(ceremonia)* memorial service.

funicular *nm* funicular railway.

furgoneta *nf* van.

furioso,-a *adj* furious.

fusible *nm* fuse.

fusil *nm* rifle.

fusilar *vt* *(ejecutar)* to shoot.

fusión *nf* **1** *(de metales)* fusion; *(de hielo)* thawing. **2** *(de empresas)* merger.

fútbol *nm* soccer; GB football.

futbolín *nm* GB table football, US table soccer.

futbolista *nmf* soccer player; GB footballer, football player.

futuro,-a *adj* future. ► *nm* **futuro** future.

G

gabardina *nf* raincoat.

gafas *nf pl* glasses. ▪ **gafas de sol** sunglasses.

gai *adj-nmf* gay.

gaita *nf* bagpipes *pl*.

gajo *nm (de naranja)* section.

gala *nf (espectáculo)* show: *cena de gala*, gala dinner; *traje de gala*, evening dress.

galardón *nm* award.

galaxia *nf* galaxy.

galería *nf* gallery. ▪ **galería de arte** art gallery; **galerías comerciales** GB shopping arcade *sing*; US mall.

Gales (País de) *nm* Wales.

galés,-a *adj* Welsh. ► *nm,f (hombre)* Welshman; *(mujer)* Welshwoman. ► *nm* **galés** *(idioma)* Welsh.

galgo *nm* greyhound.

gallego,-a *adj-nm,f* Galician. ► *nm* **gallego** *(idioma)* Galician.

galleta *nf* GB biscuit; US cookie. ▪ **galleta salada** cracker.

gallina *nf (ave)* hen.

gallinero *nm* **1** *(corral)* henhouse. **2** *(en teatro)* the gods.

gallo *nm* **1** *(ave)* cock, rooster. **2** *(nota falsa)* false note.

galón *nm (distintivo)* stripe.

galopar *vi* to gallop.

gama *nf (variedad)* range.

gamba *nf* GB prawn; US shrimp.

gamberro,-a *nm,f* hooligan.

gamo *nm* fallow deer.

gana *nf* wish, desire: *el equipo jugó sin ganas*, the team played half-heartedly. • **de buena gana** willingly; **de mala gana** reluctantly; **dar la gana** to want: *no me da la gana*, I don't want to; **tener ganas de** to want, feel like.

ganadería *nf* **1** *(cría)* livestock farming. **2** *(ganado)* livestock.

ganado *nm* livestock.

ganador,-ra *nm,f* winner.

ganancia *nf* gain, profit.

ganar *vt* **1** *(premio, concurso)* to win. **2** *(dinero)* to earn. **3** *(a un contrincante)* to beat. • **salir ganando** to do well.

gancho *nm* hook.

ganga *nf* bargain.

gangrena *nf* gangrene.

gángster *nm* gangster.

ganso *nm* goose; *(macho)* gander.

garaje *nm* garage.

garantía *nf* guarantee.

garbanzo *nm* chickpea.

garganta *nf* **1** throat. **2** *(desfiladero)* gorge.

garra *nf (de león, oso, etc.)* claw; *(de águila, halcón, etc.)* talon.

garrafa *nf* container.

gas *nm* gas.

gasa *nf* gauze.

gaseosa *nf* fizzy lemonade.

gaseoso,-a *adj* **1** *(estado)* gaseous. **2** *(bebida)* carbonated, fizzy.

gasoil *nm* diesel, diesel oil.

gasóleo *nm* diesel, diesel oil.

gasolina *nf* GB petrol; US gas, gasoline. • **echar gasolina** to put some petrol in. ■ **gasolina normal** two-star petrol; **gasolina sin plomo** lead-free petrol; **gasolina súper** four-star petrol.

gasolinera *nf* GB petrol station; US gas station.

gastar *vt* **1** *(dinero)* to spend. **2** *(usar)* to use.

gasto *nm* **1** *(de dinero)* expenditure, expense. **2** *(de agua, luz)* consumption. • **con todos los gastos pagados** all expenses paid.

gastronomía *nf* gastronomy.

gatear *vi* to crawl.

gatillo *nm* *(de arma)* trigger.

gato,-a *nm,f* *(animal)* cat. ▶ *nm* **gato** *(de coche)* jack. • **a gatas** on all fours.

gaviota *nf* gull.

gazpacho *nm* cold tomato soup.

gel *nm* gel.

gelatina *nf* **1** *(sustancia)* gelatine. **2** *(de fruta)* jelly.

gemelo,-a *adj-nm,f (hermano)* twin. ▶ *nm* **gemelo** *(músculo)* calf muscle. ▶ *nm pl* **geme-**

los 1 *(de camisa)* cufflinks. **2** *(prismáticos)* binoculars.

gen *nm* gene.

generación *nf* generation.

general *adj* general. ▶ *nm (oficial)* general. • **en general** in general; **por lo general** generally.

generar *vt* to generate.

género *nm* **1** *(clase)* sort: *es único en su género*, it's unique of its kind. **2** *(gramatical)* gender. **3** *(especie)* genus. **4** *(en literatura)* genre. **5** *(tela)* cloth. **6** *(producto)* merchandise. ■ **géneros de punto** knitwear.

generoso,-a *adj* generous.

genético,-a *adj* genetic.

genial *adj* brilliant.

genio *nm* **1** *(carácter)* temper: *tiene mal genio*, he's bad tempered. **2** *(persona)* genius. **3** *(criatura imaginaria)* genie.

gente *nf* people.

gentileza *nf* **1** *(elegancia)* grace. **2** *(cortesía)* politeness. • **por gentileza de** by courtesy of.

gentío *nm* crowd.

genuino,-a *adj* genuine, real.

geografía *nf* geography.

geología *nf* geology.

geometría *nf* geometry.

geranio *nm* geranium.

gerente *nmf (hombre)* manager; *(mujer)* manager, manageress.

germen *nm* germ.

gerundio *nm* gerund.

gesticular *vi* to gesticulate.

gestión *nf* **1** *(negociación)* negotiation. **2** *(de negocio)* administration, management. **3** *(trámite)* step.

gesto *nm* **1** *(gen)* gesture. **2** *(con la cara)* expression.

gestor,-ra *nm,f* agent.

gestoría *nf* business agency.

gigante,-a *adj-nm,f* giant.

gimnasia *nf* gymnastics. • **hacer gimnasia** to exercise, work out. ▪ **gimnasia rítmica** rhythmic gymnastics.

gimnasio *nm* gym(nasium).

ginebra *nf* gin.

ginecólogo,-a *nm,f* GB gynaecologist; US gynecologist.

gira *nf* *(artística)* tour.

girar *vi* **1** *(dar vueltas)* to rotate, revolve; *(rápidamente)* to spin. **2** *(torcer)* to turn. **3** *(conversación)* GB to centre around; US to center round.

girasol *nm* sunflower.

giro *nm* **1** *(vuelta)* turn. **2** *(de dinero, postal)* money order. **3** *(frase idiomática)* turn of phrase.

gitano,-a *adj-nm,f* gypsy.

glaciar *nm* glacier.

glándula *nf* gland.

global *adj* total.

globo *nm* **1** *(esfera)* globe, sphere. **2** *(de aire)* balloon. ▪ **globo ocular** eyeball; **globo terráqueo** globe.

glóbulo *nm* **1** globule. **2** *(en sangre)* corpuscle.

gloria *nf* **1** *(triunfo, honor)* glory. **2** *(fama)* fame.

glorieta *nf* **1** *(rotonda)* GB roundabout; US traffic circle. **2** *(en jardín)* arbour, bower.

glorioso,-a *adj* glorious.

glucosa *nf* glucose.

gobernar *vt* *(país)* to govern.

gobierno *nm* *(de país)* government.

gol *nm* goal. • **marcar un gol** to score a goal.

golf *nm* golf.

golfo *nm* *(bahía)* gulf.

golondrina *nf* swallow.

golosinas *nf* GB sweets; US candy *sing.*

goloso,-a *adj* sweet-toothed.

golpe *nm* **1** *(porrazo)* blow, knock. **2** *(ruido)* knock, bang. **3** *(en coche)* bump. **4** *(desgracia)* blow. • **de golpe** suddenly; **no dar golpe** not to do a thing. ▪ **golpe de Estado** coup d'état.

golpear *vt* to hit.

goma *nf* **1** *(material)* rubber. **2** *(de borrar)* GB rubber; US eraser. **3** *(tira elástica)* elastic band.

gomina *nf* hair gel.

gordo,-a *adj* **1** *(persona, cara)* fat. **2** *(libro, jersey)* thick. **3** *(accidente, problema)* serious. ▶ *nm* **gordo** *(en lotería)* first prize, jackpot.

gorila *nm* gorilla.

gorra *nf* *(con visera)* cap; *(de bebé)* bonnet. • **de gorra** *fam* free.

grave

gorrión *nm* sparrow.
gorro *nm* **1** *(de lana)* hat. **2** *(de bebé)* bonnet.
gota *nf* **1** *(de líquido)* drop. **2** *(enfermedad)* gout.
gotera *nf* leak.
gótico,-a *adj* Gothic.
gozar *vi* to enjoy oneself.
grabación *nf* recording.
grabado *nm* **1** *(técnica)* engraving. **2** *(ilustración)* engraving, print.
grabadora *nf* recorder.
grabar *vt* **1** *(en piedra)* to engrave. **2** *(sonido, imagen)* to record. **3** INFORM to save.
gracia *nf* **1** *(donaire)* gracefulness. **2** *(encanto)* charm. **3** *(chiste)* joke. • **dar las gracias a ALGN** to thank SB; **gracias a** thanks to; **hacer gracia** to be funny; **¡muchas gracias!** thank you very much!
gracioso,-a *adj* funny.
grada *nf* **1** *(peldaño)* step. **2** *(asiento)* row of seats.
grado *nm* degree.
graduable *adj* adjustable.
graduación *nf* **1** *(acción)* adjustment. **2** *(militar)* rank.
graduar *vt* **1** *(regular)* to adjust. **2** *(ordenar)* to grade. • **graduarse la vista** to have one's eyes tested.
gráfico,-a *adj* graphic. ▶ *nm* **gráfico** graph. ▪ **gráfico de barras** bar chart.
gragea *nf* pill.

gramática *nf* grammar.
gramo *nm* gram, gramme.
gran *adj* → grande.
granada *nf* **1** *(fruta)* pomegranate. **2** *(bomba)* grenade.
granate *adj-nm* *(color)* maroon.
grande *adj* **1** *(de tamaño)* big, large. **2** *(de número, cantidad)* large. **3** *(de importancia)* great.
granel *adv.* **a granel** *(sólidos)* loose, in bulk; *(líquidos)* in bulk.
granero *nm* granary, barn.
granizada *nf* hailstorm.
granizado *nm* slush.
granizar *vi* to hail.
granizo *nm* hail.
granja *nf* farm.
granjero,-a *nm,f* farmer.
grano *nm* **1** *(de arroz)* grain; *(de café)* bean. **2** *(en la piel)* spot, pimple.
grapa *nf* **1** *(para papel)* staple. **2** *(bebida)* grappa.
grapadora *nf* stapler.
grasa *nf* **1** *(comestible)* fat. **2** *(lubricante, suciedad)* grease.
gratinar *vt* to brown under the grill.
gratis *adv* free.
gratuito,-a *adj* free.
grava *nf* **1** *(piedras)* gravel. **2** *(piedra machacada)* broken stone.
grave *adj* **1** *(accidente, enfermedad)* serious: **está muy grave**, she's very seriously ill. **2** *(situación)* difficult. **3** *(voz)* deep, low.

gravedad *nf* **1** *(de la Tierra)* gravity. **2** *(importancia)* seriousness.

Grecia *nf* Greece.

griego,-a *adj-nm,f* Greek. ► *nm* **griego** *(idoma)* Greek.

grieta *nf* crack, crevice.

grifo *nm* GB tap; US faucet.

grillo *nm* *(insecto)* cricket.

gripe *nf* flu, influenza.

gris *adj-nm* GB grey; US gray.

gritar *vi* *(gen)* to shout; *(chillar)* to cry out, scream.

grito *nm* **1** *(gen)* shout. **2** *(de dolor)* cry. **3** *(de miedo)* scream. • **ser el último grito** to be the latest fashion.

grosella *nf* redcurrant. ■ **grosella silvestre** gooseberry.

grosero,-a *adj* **1** *(vulgar)* coarse, rough. **2** *(maleducado)* rude.

grosor *nm* thickness.

grúa *nf* **1** crane. **2** *(para averías)* breakdown van; *(por mal aparcamiento)* tow truck. • **"No aparcar, se avisa grúa"** "Any vehicles parked here will be towed away".

grueso,-a *adj* **1** *(objeto)* thick. **2** *(persona)* fat, stout.

grumete *nm* cabin boy.

grumo *nm* **1** *(de salsa)* lump. **2** *(de sangre)* clot.

gruñido *nm* **1** *(de cerdo)* grunt. **2** *(de perro)* growl.

grupo *nm* group. ■ **grupo de noticias** newsgroup.

gruta *nf* cave.

guante *nm* glove.

guantera *nf* glove compartment.

guapo,-a *adj* *(hombre)* good-looking; *(mujer)* pretty, beautiful.

guarda *nmf* *(vigilante)* guard; *(de zoo)* keeper. ■ **guarda de seguridad** security guard; **guarda jurado** armed security guard.

guardabarros *nm* mudguard.

guardabosque *nmf* forest ranger.

guardaespaldas *nm* bodyguard.

guardameta *nmf* goalkeeper.

guardar *vt* **1** *(en su sitio)* to put away. **2** *(mantener)* to keep. **3** *(para otra ocasión)* to save. **4** INFORM to save. • **guardar cama** to stay in bed; **guardar silencio** to remain silent.

guardarropa *nm* *(en museo, discoteca)* cloakroom.

guardería *nf* crèche, nursery.

guardia *nmf* *(vigilante)* guard. ► *nf* **1** *(servicio)* turn of duty. **2** *(tropa)* guard. • **estar de guardia** to be on duty. ■ **guardia urbana** local police.

guarida *nf* **1** *(de animales)* den. **2** *(de personas)* hideout.

guarnición *nf* **1** *filete con guarnición de patatas fritas*, steak with chips. **2** *(militar)* garrison.

guarro,-a *adj* **1** *(sucio)* dirty, filthy. **2** *(indecente)* disgusting, revolting.

guay *adj fam* GB cool; US neat.

guerra *nf* war.

guerrillero,-a *nm,f* guerrilla.

guía *nmf (persona)* guide. ► *nf (libro)* guidebook: *una guía de Madrid*, a guide to Madrid. ■ **guía telefónica** telephone directory.

guiar *vt (instruir, orientar)* to guide, lead: *nos guió por la ciudad*, he took us round the city.

guinda *nf* cherry.

guindilla *nf* (chilli) pepper.

guiñar *vt* to wink.

guiñol *nm* puppet theatre.

guion o **guión** *nm* **1** hyphen. **2** *(de discurso)* notes. **3** *(de película)* script.

guionista *nmf* scriptwriter.

guiri *nmf arg* foreigner.

guisado,-a *adj* cooked, prepared. ► *nm* **guisado** stew.

guisante *nm* pea.

guisar *vt (cocinar)* to cook; *(carne, pescado)* to stew.

guiso *nm* stew.

güisqui *nm* whisky.

guitarra *nf* guitar. ■ **guitarra eléctrica** electric guitar.

guitarrista *nmf* guitarist.

gusano *nm (de tierra)* worm; *(de mariposa)* caterpillar. ■ **gusano de seda** silkworm.

gustar *vi* to like: *me gusta*, I like it; *le gusta leer*, she likes reading. • **gustar más** to prefer: *¿cuál te gusta más?* which do you prefer?; **cuando guste** *fml* whenever you want.

gusto *nm* **1** *(sentido)* taste. **2** *(sabor)* GB flavour; US flavor: *no le noto el gusto* I can't taste it. **3** *(placer)* pleasure: *tenemos el gusto de invitarles a la boda*, we are pleased to invite you to the wedding. • **con mucho gusto** with pleasure; **dar gusto** to be nice; **estar a gusto** to feel comfortable; **tanto gusto** pleased to meet you.

H

haba *nf* broad bean.

haber *aux* to have. ► *nm* **1** *(cuenta corriente)* credit. **2** *(posesiones)* property. • **haber de** to have to, must: *he de salir*, I have to go out; **hay** there is/there are: *hay dos habitaciones*, there are two bedrooms; **hay que** you have to: *hay que tener mucho cuidado*, you have to be very careful.

hábil *adj* **1** *(diestro)* skilful. **2** *(despabilado)* clever.

habilidad *nf* skill.

habitación *nf* **1** *(cuarto)* room. **2** *(dormitorio)* bedroom.

habitante *nmf* inhabitant.

hábito *nm* habit.

habitual *adj* **1** *(normal)* usual. **2** *(cliente, visitante)* regular.

habla *nf* **1** *(facultad)* speech. **2** *(idioma)* language.

hablar *vi* **1** *(gen)* to talk. **2** *(en situaciones formales)* to speak. ► *vt (idioma)* to speak. • **¡ni hablar!** certainly not!

hacer *vt* **1** *(crear, producir, causar)* to make: **hacer la comida**, to make lunch. **2** *(actividad, estudios, trayecto)* to do: **hacer los deberes**, to do one's homework; **hicimos 250 km**, we did 250 km. ► *vi (tiempo meteorológico)* to be: **hace calor**, it's hot. ► *vpr* **hacerse** *(convertirse en)* to become, turn, get. • **hace 1** *(tiempo pasado)* ago: **compré la bici hace tres años**, I bought the bike three years ago. **2** *(tiempo que dura)* for: **tengo la bici desde hace tres años**, I've had the bike for three years.

hacha *nf* axe.

hacia *prep* **1** *(dirección)* towards. **2** *(tiempo)* about, around.

hacienda *nf (finca)* estate. ■ **hacienda pública** public funds, public finances.

hada *nf* fairy. ■ **hada madrina** fairy godmother.

halcón *nm* falcon.

hallar *vt* to find. ► *vpr* **hallarse** *(estar)* to be.

hamaca *nf* hammock.

hambre *nf* **1** *(apetito)* hunger. **2** *(escasez)* famine. • **tener hambre** to be hungry.

hamburguesa *nf* hamburger.

harina *nf* flour.

harto,-a *adj* **1** *(repleto)* full. **2** *fam (cansado)* fed up.

hasta *prep* **1** *(tiempo)* until, till: **hasta ahora**, until now. **2** *(lugar)* as far as: **te acompañaré hasta la iglesia**, I'll go with you as far as the church. ► *conj* even: **hasta mi hermano pequeño podría hacerlo**, even my little brother could do it. • **¡hasta luego!** see you later!; **hasta que** until.

haya *nf (árbol)* beech.

hazaña *nf* deed, exploit.

hebilla *nf* buckle.

hechizo *nm* spell, charm.

hecho,-a *adj (manufacturado)* made. ► *nm* **hecho 1** *(realidad)* fact. **2** *(suceso)* event. • **bien hecho** *(bistec)* well done; **de hecho** in fact.

hectárea *nf* hectare.

helada *nf* frost.

heladería *nf* GB ice-cream parlour; US ice-cream parlor.

helado *nm* ice cream.

helar *vi* to freeze.

helecho *nm* fern.

hélice *nf* propeller.

helicóptero *nm* helicopter.

hembra *nf* female.
hemisferio *nm* hemisphere.
hemorragia *nf* GB haemorrhage; US hemorrhage.
heredar *vt* to inherit.
hereditario,-a *adj* hereditary.
herencia *nf* 1 *(bienes)* inheritance. 2 *(genética)* heredity.
herida *nf* *(con arma)* wound; *(en accidente)* injury.
herido,-a *adj* *(con arma)* wounded; *(en accidente)* injured.
herir *vt* *(con arma)* to wound; *(en accidente)* to injure.
hermano,-a *nm,f* *(hombre)* brother; *(mujer)* sister.
hermoso,-a *adj* beautiful.
hernia *nf* hernia, rupture.
héroe *nm* hero.
heroína *nf* 1 *(mujer)* heroine. 2 *(droga)* heroin.
herradura *nf* horseshoe.
herramienta *nf* tool.
herrero *nm* blacksmith.
hervir *vt-vi* to boil.
hidratante *adj* moisturizing.
hidroavión *nm* seaplane.
hidrógeno *nm* hydrogen.
hiedra *nf* ivy.
hielo *nm* ice.
hiena *nf* hyena.
hierba *nf* 1 *(césped, pasto)* grass. 2 *(para cocinar)* herb.
hierbabuena *nf* mint.
hierro *nm* iron. ■ **hierro colado** cast iron; **hierro forjado** wrought iron.

hígado *nm* liver.
higiene *nf* hygiene.
higo *nm* fig. ■ **higo chumbo** prickly pear.
higuera *nf* fig tree.
hijo,-a *nm,f* *(chico)* son; *(chica)* daughter; *(sin especificar)* child.
hilera *nf* row.
hilo *nm* 1 *(de coser)* thread. 2 *(lino)* linen. 3 *(telefónico)* wire. ■ **hilo musical** piped music.
himno *nm* hymn. ■ **himno nacional** national anthem.
hincar *vt* to drive in.
hincha *nmf* fan, supporter.
hinchar *vt* to inflate, blow up.
hinchazón *nf* swelling.
hipermercado *nm* hypermarket.
hípico,-a *adj* *(club)* riding.
hipo *nm* hiccups.
hipócrita *nmf* hypocrite.
hipódromo *nm* racetrack, racecourse.
hipopótamo *nm* hippopotamus.
hipoteca *nf* mortgage.
hispano,-a *adj* 1 *(de España)* Spanish, Hispanic. 2 *(de América)* Spanish-American. ► *nm,f* *(de América)* Spanish American; US Hispanic.
hispanoamericano,-a *adj* Spanish American.
histérico,-a *adj* hysterical.
historia *nf* 1 *(estudio del pasado)* history. 2 *(relato)* story.
historial *nm* *(médico)* record.

histórico,-a *adj* historical.
hobby *nm* hobby.
hockey *nm* hockey. ▪ **hockey sobre hielo** ice hockey; **hockey sobre hierba** hockey.
hogar *nm* home. • **sin hogar** homeless.
hoguera *nf* bonfire.
hoja *nf* 1 *(de planta)* leaf. 2 *(de papel, metal)* sheet. 3 *(de libro)* page. 4 *(de cuchillo)* blade. ▪ **hoja de afeitar** razor blade.
hojalata *nf* tin.
hojaldre *nm & nf* puff pastry.
hola *interj* hello!, hi!
Holanda *nf* Holland.
holandés,-esa *adj* Dutch. ▶ *nm,f* Dutch person. ▶ *nm* **holandés** *(idioma)* Dutch.
hombre *nm* man. ▪ **hombre de negocios** businessman.
hombro *nm* shoulder.
homenaje *nm* tribute, homage.
homicidio *nm* homicide, murder.
homogéneo,-a *adj* homogeneous.
homosexual *adj-nmf* homosexual.
hondo,-a *adj* deep.
honesto,-a *adj* honest.
hongo *nm* *(planta)* fungus; *(como comida)* mushroom.
honor *nm* GB honour; US honor.
honrado,-a *adj* honest.
hora *nf* 1 *(60 minutos)* hour. 2 *(tiempo)* time: *¿qué hora es?*,

what time is it?; *¿tiene hora, por favor?*, have you got the time? 3 *(cita)* appointment: *mañana tengo hora con el dentista*, I have an appointment with the dentist for tomorrow. • **de última hora** last-minute: *noticias de última hora*, breaking news. ▪ **hora punta** 1 *(tráfico)* rush hour. 2 *(electricidad, teléfonos)* peak time; **horas de oficina** business hours; **horas extras** overtime.
horario *nm* 1 *(de trenes, clases)* timetable. 2 *(de trabajo, consulta)* hours. ▪ **horario de atención al público** opening hours.
horca *nf* gallows.
horizontal *adj* horizontal.
horizonte *nm* horizon.
hormiga *nf* ant.
hormigón *nm* concrete. ▪ **hormigón armado** reinforced concrete.
hormigueo *nm* prickling sensation.
hormona *nf* hormone.
horno *nm* 1 *(de cocina)* oven. 2 *(de fábrica)* furnace. • **al horno** 1 *(manzana, patata, pescado)* baked. 2 *(pollo)* roast.
horóscopo *nm* horoscope.
horquilla *nf* hairgrip.
horrible *adj* horrible, dreadful.
horror *nm* 1 *(miedo)* horror. 2 *fam (muchísimo)* an awful lot.

horroroso,-a *adj* **1** *(atroz)* horrible. **2** *(malísimo)* dreadful.

hortalizas *nf pl* vegetables.

hortensia *nf* hydrangea.

hospedarse *vpr* to stay.

hospital *nm* hospital.

hospitalidad *nf* hospitality.

hostal *nm* small hotel.

hostelería *nf* hotel and catering industry.

hostia *nf* **1** *(oblea)* host. **2** *fam (golpe)* thump. ▶ *interj* **¡hostia!** *fam (enfado)* damn it!, bugger!; *(sorpresa)* bloody hell!

hotel *nm* hotel.

hoy *adv* **1** *(día)* today. **2** *(actualmente)* now. • **hoy en día** nowadays; **hoy por hoy** at the present time.

hoyo *nm* hole.

hoz *nf* sickle.

hucha *nf* money box.

hueco *nm* hollow.

huelga *nf* strike. ▪ **huelga de celo** work-to-rule.

huella *nf* **1** *(de pie)* footprint; *(de animal, máquina)* track. **2** *(vestigio)* trace, sign. ▪ **huella dactilar** fingerprint.

huérfano,-a *adj-nm,f* orphan.

huerta *nf (de verduras)* vegetable garden; *(de frutales)* orchard.

huerto *nm (de verduras)* vegetable garden; *(de frutales)* orchard.

hueso *nm* **1** *(del cuerpo)* bone. **2** *(de aceituna, cereza)* GB stone; US pit.

huésped,-da *nm,f* guest.

huevo *nm* egg. ▪ **huevo duro** hard-boiled egg; **huevo escalfado** poached egg; **huevo estrellado** fried egg; **huevo frito** fried egg; **huevo pasado por agua** soft-boiled egg; **huevos revueltos** scrambled eggs.

huida *nf* escape, flight.

huir *vi* **1** *(escapar)* to escape, flee. **2** *(evitar)* to avoid: **huir de algo,** to avoid STH.

humanidad *nf* humanity.

humanitario,-a *adj* humanitarian.

humano,-a *adj* human.

humedad *nf* **1** *(en la atmósfera)* humidity. **2** *(en pared, suelo)* damp.

húmedo,-a *adj* **1** *(tiempo, clima)* humid. **2** *(pelo, tierra)* damp.

humilde *adj* humble.

humillar *vt* to humiliate.

humo *nm* smoke.

humor *nm* **1** *(ánimo)* mood. **2** *(gracia)* GB humour; US humor. ▪ **humor negro** black comedy.

hundir *vt* **1** *(gen)* to sink. **2** *(mano, puñal)* to plunge. ▶ *vpr* **hundirse 1** *(gen)* to sink. **2** *(edificio)* to collapse. **3** *(empresa)* to go under. **4** *(bolsa, precio)* to plummet.

huracán *nm* hurricane.

I

ida *nf.* • **billete de ida** GB single; US one-way ticket; **billete de ida y vuelta** GB return ticket; US round-trip ticket.
idea *nf* idea.
ideal *adj-nm* ideal.
idéntico,-a *adj* identical.
identificar *vt* to identify.
ideología *nf* ideology.
idioma *nm* language.
idiota *nmf* idiot.
ídolo *nm* idol.
idóneo,-a *adj* suitable, fit.
iglesia *nf* church.
ignorancia *nf* ignorance.
ignorar *vt (no saber)* not to know, be ignorant of.
igual *adj* 1 *(idéntico)* the same. 2 *(en jerarquía)* equal. ► *nm (signo)* equals sign. ► *adv* 1 *(quizá)* maybe: **igual no vienen**, they may not come. 2 *(de la misma manera)* the same: **piensan igual**, they think the same. • **dar igual** not to matter; **es igual** it doesn't matter; **igual de...** as... as: **soy igual de alto que tú**, I'm as tall as you.
ilegal *adj* illegal.
ileso,-a *adj* unharmed, unhurt.
iluminación *nf* lighting.
iluminar *vt* to light up, illuminate.

ilusión *nf* 1 *(esperanza)* hope. 2 *(imagen falsa)* illusion. • **hacerle ilusión algo a** ALGN: **me hace mucha ilusión que vengas**, I'm really looking forward to you coming.
ilustración *nf* illustration.
ilustre *adj* illustrious, distinguished.
imagen *nf* 1 *(gen)* image. 2 *(en televisión)* picture.
imaginación *nf* imagination.
imaginar(se) *vt-vpr* to imagine.
imán *nm* magnet.
imbécil *nmf* idiot, imbecile.
imitación *nf* 1 *(copia)* imitation. 2 *(parodia)* impression.
imitar *vt* 1 *(copiar)* to imitate, copy. 2 *(gestos)* to mimic; *(como diversión)* to do an impression of, GB take off.
impaciente *adj* impatient.
impar *adj* odd.
imparcial *adj* impartial.
impasible *adj* impassive.
impedir *vt* 1 *(imposibilitar)* to prevent. 2 *(dificultar)* to impede, hinder.
imperativo *nm* imperative.
imperdible *nm* safety pin.
imperfecto,-a *adj (defectuoso)* flawed, imperfect. ► *nm* **imperfecto** imperfect, imperfect tense.
imperio *nm* empire.
impermeable *adj* waterproof. ► *nm* raincoat.

impersonal *adj* impersonal.
implantar *vt* **1** *(corazón, cabello)* to implant. **2** *(reforma)* to introduce.
implicar *vt (conllevar)* to imply.
imponer *vt* **1** *(castigo, tarea)* to impose. **2** *(respeto, miedo)* to inspire. ▶ *vpr* **imponerse 1** *(hacerse obedecer)* to impose one's authority. **2** *(vencer)* to win.
importación *nf* import. • **de importación** imported.
importancia *nf* importance.
importante *adj* important.
importar *vi* **1** *(tener importancia)* to matter: *no me importa*, I don't care. **2** *(molestar)* to mind: *¿te importaría cerrar la ventana?*, would you mind closing the window? ▶ *vt* to import. • **no importa** it doesn't matter.
importe *nm* **1** *(coste)* cost. **2** *(cantidad)* amount.
imposible *adj* impossible.
impotente *adj* impotent.
imprenta *nf* **1** *(arte)* printing. **2** *(taller)* printer's, printing house.
imprescindible *adj* essential, indispensable.
impresión *nf* **1** *(sensación)* impression. **2** *(de texto)* printing.
impresionante *adj* impressive, striking.
impresionar *vt* **1** *(causar admiración a)* to impress. **2** *(conmover)* to touch, move.

impreso,-a *adj* printed. ▶ *nm* **impreso** *(formulario)* form.
impresora *nf* printer. ▪ **impresora de chorro de tinta** inkjet printer; **impresora láser** laser printer.
imprevisto,-a *adj* unforeseen, unexpected.
imprimir *vt* to print.
improbable *adj* improbable.
improvisar *vt-vi* to improvise.
imprudente *adj (irreflexivo)* imprudent, rash; *(al conducir)* careless, reckless.
impuesto *nm* tax, duty. ▪ **impuesto sobre el valor añadido (IVA)** value added tax *(VAT)*; **impuesto sobre la renta** income tax.
impulso *nm* **1** *(deseo súbito)* impulse, urge. **2** *(fuerza, velocidad)* momentum. **3** *(estímulo)* boost.
inadmisible *adj* unacceptable.
inaguantable *adj* intolerable, unbearable.
inalámbrico,-a *adj* cordless.
inauguración *nf* opening, inauguration.
inaugurar *vt* to open, inaugurate.
incapaz *adj* **1** *(no capaz)* incapable. **2** *(incompetente)* incompetent.
incendiar *vt* to set on fire, set fire to. ▶ *vpr* **incendiarse** to catch fire.

incendio *nm* fire. ■ **incendio provocado** arson.

incentivo *nm* incentive.

incesante *adj* incessant, unceasing.

incidente *nm* incident.

incierto,-a *adj* 1 *(dudoso)* uncertain, doubtful. 2 *(desconocido)* unknown.

incinerar *vt (basura)* to incinerate; *(cadáver)* to cremate.

incisivo *nm (diente)* incisor.

incitar *vt* to incite.

inclinación *nf* 1 *(pendiente)* slant, slope. 2 *(tendencia)* inclination.

inclinar *vt (ladear)* to tilt; *(cuerpo)* to bow; *(cabeza)* to nod.

incluir *vt* to include.

incluso *adv-conj-prep* even.

incógnita *nf* 1 unknown quantity. 2 *(misterio)* mystery.

incoherencia *nf* incoherence.

incoloro,-a *adj* colourless.

incómodo,-a *adj* 1 *(gen)* uncomfortable. 2 *(molesto)* awkward.

incomunicado,-a *adj* 1 *(aislado)* isolated; *(por la nieve)* cut off. 2 *(preso)* in solitary confinement.

inconfundible *adj* unmistakable.

inconsciente *adj* unconscious.

inconveniente *nm (desventaja)* drawback; *(dificultad)* problem.

incorporar *vt* to incorporate. ▶ *vpr* **incorporarse** 1 *(levantarse)* to sit up. 2 *(a puesto, regimiento)* to join.

incorrecto,-a *adj* incorrect.

increíble *adj* incredible.

incremento *nm* increase.

incubadora *nf* incubator.

incurable *adj* incurable.

indecente *adj* indecent.

indeciso,-a *adj* indecisive.

indefenso,-a *adj* GB defenceless; US defenseless.

indefinido,-a *adj* 1 *(impreciso)* undefined, vague. 2 *(ilimitado)* indefinite.

indemnización *nf* 1 *(acción)* indemnification. 2 *(compensación)* compensation, indemnity.

independencia *nf* independence.

independiente *adj* independent.

indicación *nf* 1 *(señal)* sign. 2 *(observación)* hint.

indicador *nm (gen)* indicator; *(uso técnico)* gauge.

indicar *vt* to indicate, show.

indicativo,-a *adj-nm* indicative.

índice *nm* 1 *(gen)* index. 2 *(dedo)* index finger, forefinger. ■ **índice de precios al consumo** retail price index.

indicio *nm* sign, indication.

indiferente *adj* indifferent.

indígena *adj-nmf* native.

indigente *nmf* destitute person.

indigestión *nf* indigestion.

indignar *vt* to infuriate, make angry. ▶ *vpr* **indignarse** to get angry.

indio,-a *adj-nm,f* Indian.

indiscreto,-a *adj* **1** *(falto de discreción)* indiscreet. **2** *(falto de tacto)* tactless.

indispensable *adj* indispensable, essential.

indispuesto,-a *adj* indisposed, unwell.

individual *adj* *(gen)* individual; *(habitación, cama)* single.

individuo *nm* person, individual.

indulto *nm* pardon.

indumentaria *nf* clothing, clothes.

industria *nf* industry.

industrial *adj* industrial.

inercia *nf* inertia.

inesperado,-a *adj* unexpected.

inevitable *adj* inevitable, unavoidable.

infalible *adj* infallible.

infancia *nf* childhood.

infantería *nf* infantry. ▪ **infantería de marina** marines.

infantil *adj* **1** *(libro, enfermedad)* children's. **2** *(educación, población)* child.

infarto *nm* heart attack.

infección *nf* infection.

infeccioso,-a *adj* infectious.

infectar *vt* to infect.

infeliz *adj* unhappy.

inferior *adj* **1** *(gen)* lower. **2** *(en calidad)* inferior.

infierno *nm* hell.

infinitivo *nm* infinitive.

infinito,-a *adj* infinite.

inflación *nf* inflation.

inflamable *adj* inflammable.

inflamación *nf* inflammation.

inflar *vt* **1** *(globo, neumático)* to inflate, blow up. **2** *(hechos, noticias)* to exaggerate.

influencia *nf* influence.

influir *vi* to influence.

información *nf* **1** *(datos)* information. **2** *(oficina)* information desk. **3** *(noticias)* news.

informal *adj* **1** *(ambiente, reunión)* informal. **2** *(ropa)* casual.

informar *vt* to inform.

informática *nf* computer science, computing.

informático,-a *adj* computer, computing. ▶ *nm,f* computer expert.

informativo,-a *adj* informative. ▶ *nm* **informativo** news bulletin.

informe *nm* report.

infracción *nf* *(fiscal, de circulación)* GB offence; US offense; *(de ley)* infringement.

infusión *nf* infusion: *infusión de manzanilla*, camomile tea; *infusión de menta*, mint tea.

ingeniero,-a *nm,f* engineer.

ingenioso,-a *adj (inteligente)* ingenious, clever; *(con chispa)* witty.

ingenuo,-a *adj* naïve, ingenuous.

ingerir *vt* to consume, ingest.

Inglaterra *nf* England.

ingle *nf* groin.

inglés,-esa *adj* English. ► *nm,f (persona)* English person. ► *nm* **inglés** *(idioma)* English.

ingrediente *nm* ingredient.

ingresar *vt* 1 *(dinero)* to deposit, pay in. 2 *(paciente)* to admit. ► *vi (en colegio)* to enter; *(en club etc)* to become a member; *(en hospital)* to be admitted to.

ingreso *nm* 1 *(en organización)* entry. 2 *(en hospital, club, etc)* admission. 3 *(en cuenta bancaria)* deposit. ► *nm pl* **ingresos** income.

inicial *adj-nf* initial.

iniciar *vt* 1 *(introducir)* to initiate. 2 *(empezar)* to begin.

iniciativa *nf* initiative.

inicio *nm* beginning, start.

injusto,-a *adj* unjust, unfair.

inmediato,-a *adj (reacción, respuesta)* immediate. • **inmediato,-a** next to, near.

inmenso,-a *adj* immense.

inmigrante *adj-nmf* immigrant.

inmigrar *vi* to immigrate.

inmobiliaria *nf* GB estate agency; US real estate agency.

inmóvil *adj* still, motionless.

inmueble *nm* building.

inmunidad *nf* immunity.

innovación *nf* innovation.

inocente *adj* 1 *(libre de culpa)* innocent. 2 *(ingenuo)* naïve. 3 *(no culpable)* not guilty, innocent. ► *nmf (no culpable)* innocent person.

inodoro *nm* toilet.

inofensivo,-a *adj* inoffensive, harmless.

inoxidable *adj (gen)* rustproof; *(acero)* stainless.

inquietar(se) *vt-vpr* to worry.

inquieto,-a *adj* 1 *(agitado)* restless. 2 *(preocupado)* worried, anxious.

inquilino,-a *nm,f* tenant.

inscribirse *vpr* 1 *(en colegio)* to enrol. 2 *(en club, organización)* to join. 3 *(en concurso)* to enter.

inscripción *nf* 1 *(grabado)* inscription. 2 *(registro)* enrolment, registration.

insecticida *adj-nm* insecticide.

insecto *nm* insect.

inseguro,-a *adj* 1 *(falto de confianza)* insecure. 2 *(peligroso)* unsafe.

insertar *vt* to insert.

inservible *adj* useless, unusable.

insignia *nf (distintivo)* badge.

insignificante *adj* insignificant.

insinuar *vt* to insinuate, hint.

insípido,-a *adj* insipid.

insistir *vi* to insist.

insolación *nf* sunstroke.

insólito,-a *adj* unusual.

insomnio *nm* insomnia.

inspección *nf* inspection.

inspector,-ra *nm,f* inspector.

inspiración *nf* inspiration.

inspirar *vt* 1 *(aspirar)* to inhale, breathe in. 2 *(infundir)* to inspire.

instalación *nf* installation. ► *nf pl* **instalaciones** *(recinto)* installations; *(servicios)* facilities.

instalar *vt* to install. ► *vpr* **instalarse** to settle.

instantánea *nf* snapshot.

instantáneo,-a *adj* 1 *(repuesta, reacción)* instantaneous. 2 *(éxito, resultado, café)* instant.

instante *nm* moment, instant. • **al instante** immediately.

instinto *nm* instinct.

institución *nf* institution, establishment.

instituto *nm* 1 *(organismo)* institute. 2 *(de enseñanza)* GB secondary school; US high school. ■ **instituto de belleza** beauty salon.

instrucción *nf* education. ► *nf pl* **instrucciones** instructions.

instrumento *nm* instrument.

insuficiencia *nf* lack, shortage. ■ **insuficiencia cardíaca** heart failure; **insuficien-**

cia respiratoria respiratory failure.

insultar *vt* to insult.

insulto *nm* insult.

intacto,-a *adj* intact.

integración *nf* integration.

integral *adj* 1 *(total)* comprehensive. 2 *(sin refinar - pan, harina)* wholemeal; *(- arroz)* brown.

íntegro,-a *adj* 1 *(completo)* whole, entire. 2 *(honrado)* honest, upright.

intelectual *adj-nmf* intellectual.

inteligencia *nf* intelligence.

inteligente *adj* intelligent, clever.

intención *nf* intention.

intensidad *nf (gen)* intensity; *(de viento)* force.

intenso,-a *adj (gen)* intense; *(dolor)* acute.

intentar *vt* to try, attempt.

intento *nm* attempt, try.

intercambio *nm* exchange.

interés *nm* interest.

interesante *adj* interesting.

interesar *vi* to interest.

interferencia *nf* interference.

interfono *nm* intercom.

interior *adj* 1 *(jardín, patio)* interior. 2 *(estancia, piso)* inner. 3 *(bolsillo)* inside. 4 *(comercio, política)* domestic, internal. 5 *(mar, desierto)* inland. ► *nm* 1 *(parte interna)* inside, inner part. 2 *(de país)* interior.

interjección *nf* interjection.
intermedio,-a *adj* **1** *(nivel)* intermediate. **2** *(tamaño)* medium. ▶ *nm* **intermedio** intermission, interval.
intermitente *nm* GB indicator; US turn signal.
internacional *adj* international.
internauta *nmf* Net user.
interno,-a *adj* internal.
interpretación *nf* **1** *(explicación)* interpretation. **2** *(actuación)* performance. **3** *(traducción)* interpreting.
interpretar *vt (obra, pieza)* to perform; *(papel)* to play; *(canción)* to sing.
intérprete *nmf* **1** *(traductor)* interpreter. **2** *(actor, músico)* performer.
interrogación *nf (signo)* question mark.
interrogar *vt* **1** *(testigo)* to question. **2** *(sospechoso)* to interrogate, question.
interrumpir *vt* to interrupt.
interruptor *nm* switch.
interurbano,-a *adj (transporte)* intercity; *(llamada)* long-distance.
intervalo *nm* **1** *(de tiempo)* interval. **2** *(de espacio)* gap.
intervención *nf* **1** *(gen)* intervention. **2** *(operación)* operation. **3** *(discurso)* speech.
intervenir *vi* to take part. ▶ *vt (paciente)* to operate on.

intestino *nm* intestine.
íntimo,-a *adj* **1** *(secreto, ambiente)* intimate. **2** *(vida)* private. **3** *(amistad)* close.
intoxicación *nf* poisoning.
intranet *nm* intranet.
intriga *nf* **1** *(maquinación)* intrigue. **2** *(de película etc)* plot.
introducción *nf* introduction.
introducir *vt (meter)* to put in, insert. ▶ *vpr* **introducirse** to enter, get in.
intruso,-a *nm,f* intruder.
intuición *nf* intuition.
inundación *nf* flood.
inútil *adj* useless.
invadir *vt* to invade.
inválido,-a *adj (persona)* disabled, handicapped.
invasión *nf* invasion.
invención *nf* invention.
inventar *vt* to invent.
invento *nm* invention.
invernadero *nm* greenhouse, hothouse.
invernal *adj* wintry, winter.
inversión *nf (de dinero, tiempo)* investment.
inverso,-a *adj* inverse.
invertir *vt* **1** *(orden)* to invert. **2** *(dinero, tiempo)* to invest.
investigación *nf* **1** *(policial, judicial)* investigation, inquiry. **2** *(científica, académica)* research.
investigar *vt* **1** *(indagar)* to investigate. **2** *(estudiar)* to do research on.

invierno *nm* winter.
invisible *adj* invisible.
invitación *nf* invitation.
invitado,-a *nm,f* guest.
invitar *vt* to invite: *déjame que te invite a un café*, let me buy you a coffee.
inyección *nf* injection.
ir *vi* 1 *(gen)* to go. 2 *(camino etc)* to lead. 3 *(funcionar)* to work. ▶ *aux* 1 **ir** + **a** + *infin*: *voy a salir*, I'm going out. 2 **ir** + *ger*: *vas mejorando*, you're getting better; *fuimos corriendo*, we ran. ▶ *vpr* **irse** *(marcharse)* to go away, leave.
ira *nf* anger, rage, wrath.
iris *nm* iris.
Irlanda *nf* Ireland. ▪ **Irlanda del Norte** Northern Ireland.
irlandés,-esa *adj* Irish. ▶ *nm,f (hombre)* Irishman; *(mujer)* Irish woman. ▶ *nm* **irlandés** *(idioma)* Irish.
irónico,-a *adj* ironic.
irregular *adj* irregular.
irritar *vt* to irritate, annoy.
isla *nf* island.
islámico,-a *adj* Islamic.
Italia *nf* Italy.
italiano,-a *adj-nm,f* Italian.
itinerario *nm* itinerary, route.
izar *vt* to hoist.
izquierda *nf* 1 *(dirección)* left: *gira a la izquierda*, turn left. 2 *(mano)* left hand; *(pierna)* left leg. 3 POL left wing.
izquierdo,-a *adj* left.

J

jabalí *nm* wild boar.
jabón *nm* soap.
jabonera *nf* soapdish.
jacinto *nm* hyacinth.
jaleo *nm (alboroto)* racket, din.
jamás *adv* never; *(con superlativos)* ever: *jamás he escrito un libro*, I have never written a book; *el mejor libro que jamás se haya escrito*, the best book ever written.
jamón *nm* ham. ▪ **jamón de York** boiled ham; **jamón serrano** cured ham.
jaque *nm* check. ▪ **jaque mate** checkmate.
jaqueca *nf* migraine, headache.
jarabe *nm* syrup.
jardín *nm* garden. ▪ **jardín de infancia** nursery school.
jardinero,-a *nm,f* gardener.
jarra *nf* GB jug; US pitcher. ▪ **jarra de cerveza** beer mug.
jarro *nm* GB jug; US pitcher.
jarrón *nm* vase.
jaula *nf* cage.
jefe,-a *nm,f (superior)* boss; *(de departamento)* head; *(de tribu)* chief. ▪ **jefe de estación** station master; **jefe de Estado** Head of State.
jerarquía *nf* 1 *(gradación)* hierarchy. 2 *(categoría)* rank.

jergón *nm* straw mattress.

jeringuilla *nf* syringe.

jeroglífico *nm* **1** *(texto antiguo)* hieroglyph. **2** *(juego)* rebus.

jersey *nm* sweater, pullover, GB jumper.

jilguero *nm* goldfinch.

jinete *nm* rider, horseman.

jirafa *nf* giraffe.

jornada *nf* day.

joroba *nf (deformidad)* hump.

joven *adj* young. ► *nmf (hombre)* youth, young man; *(mujer)* girl, young woman.

joya *nf* jewel.

joyería *nf (tienda)* GB jewellery shop, jeweller's; US jewelry store, jeweler's.

joyero *nm* GB jewellery box; US jewelry box.

juanete *nm* bunion.

jubilación *nf* **1** *(acción)* retirement. **2** *(dinero)* pension.

jubilado,-a *nm,f* retired person.

jubilarse *vpr* to retire.

judía *nf (planta)* bean. ■ **judía blanca** haricot bean; **judía pinta** kidney bean; **judía verde** French bean, green bean.

judicial *adj* judicial.

judío,-a *adj* Jewish. ► *nm,f* Jew.

juego *nm* **1** *(para entretenerse)* game. **2** *(acto)* play. **3** *(en tenis)* game. **4** *(de apuestas)* gambling. **5** *(conjunto de piezas)* set. ● **a juego** matching; **hacer juego** to match.

juerga *nf fam* binge, rave-up.

jueves *nm* Thursday.

juez *nmf* judge. ■ **juez de banda** linesman; **juez de línea** linesman.

jugada *nf (en ajedrez)* move; *(en billar)* shot; *(en dardos)* throw.

jugador,-ra *nm,f* **1** *(en deportes, juegos)* player. **2** *(apostador)* gambler.

jugar *vt-vi* **1** *(gen)* to play. **2** *(apostar)* to bet.

jugo *nm* juice.

juguete *nm* toy.

juguetería *nf* toy shop.

juicio *nm* **1** *(facultad)* judgement. **2** *(sensatez)* reason, common sense. **3** *(proceso)* trial, lawsuit. ● **a mi juicio** in my opinion.

julio *nm* July.

jungla *nf* jungle.

junio *nm* June.

junta *nf* **1** *(reunión)* meeting. **2** *(conjunto de personas)* board, committee.

juntar *vt (unir)* to put together; *(piezas)* to assemble. ► *vpr* **juntarse** *(reunirse)* to get together.

junto,-a *adj* together. ► *adv.* ● **junto a** near, close to; **junto con** together with.

jurado *nm* **1** *(tribunal)* jury. **2** *(en concurso)* panel of judges, jury.

juramento *nm (promesa)* oath.
jurar *vt-vi* to swear.
justicia *nf* justice.
justificar *vt* to justify.
justo,-a *adj* **1** *(con justicia)* fair, just. **2** *(apretado)* tight. **3** *(exacto)* exact: *me dio el dinero justo*, she gave me the right money. **4** *(escaso)*: *me queda el dinero justo*, I've just got enough money left. ▸ *adv* **justo** exactly, precisely.
juvenil *adj-nmf (en deporte)* under 18.
juventud *nf* **1** *(edad)* youth. **2** *(conjunto de jóvenes)* young people, youth.
juzgado *nm* court.
juzgar *vi* **1** *(gen)* to judge. **2** *(en tribunal)* to try.

K

karaoke *nm* karaoke.
kárate *nm* karate.
kart *nm* go-cart.
kilo(gramo) *nm* kilo(gram).
kilométrico *nm* runabout ticket.
kilómetro *nm* kilometre, kilometer.
kiosko *nm* → quiosco.
kiwi *nm* kiwi.
Kleenex® *nm* Kleenex®, tissue.

L

la¹ *det* the.
la² *pron (persona, ella)* her; *(usted)* you; *(cosa, animal)* it.
la³ *nm (nota musical)* la, A.
labio *nm* lip.
labor *nf* **1** *(trabajo)* task. **2** *(de costura)* needlework; *(de punto)* knitting.
laborable *adj* working.
laboratorio *nm* laboratory.
labrador,-ra *nm,f* farm worker.
labrar *vt (tierra, metal)* to work.
laca *nf (para pelo)* hair lacquer, hair spray.
lácteo,-a *adj* dairy, milk.
ladera *nf* slope, hillside.
lado *nm* side. • **al lado** close by, near by; **al lado de** next to, beside.
ladrar *vi* to bark.
ladrillo *nm* brick.
ladrón,-ona *nm,f* thief.
lagartija *nf (wall)* lizard.
lagarto *nm* lizard.
lago *nm* lake.
lágrima *nf* tear.
laguna *nf* pool.
lamentar *vt* to regret, be sorry about.
lamer *vt* to lick.
lámpara *nf* lamp.
lamparón *nm* stain.
lana *nf* wool. • **de lana** woollen.

lancha *nf* launch.
langosta *nf* 1 *(crustáceo)* lobster. 2 *(insecto)* locust.
langostino *nm* GB prawn; US shrimp.
lanza *nf* *(en torneo)* lance; *(arrojadiza)* spear.
lanzadera *nf* shuttle.
lanzamiento *nm* 1 *(de objeto)* throwing. 2 *(de cohete, producto)* launch. ▪ **lanzamiento de disco** the discus; **lanzamiento de jabalina** the javelin.
lanzar *vt* 1 *(tirar)* to throw. 2 *(cohete, nave, producto)* to launch.
lapa *nf* limpet.
lápida *nf* tombstone.
lápiz *nm* pencil. ▪ **lápiz de labios** lipstick.
largo,-a *adj* long. ► *nm* **largo** length: *tiene dos metros de largo*, it's two metres long. • **a lo largo de** along, throughout.
largometraje *nm* feature film, full-length film.
laringe *nf* larynx.
larva *nf* larva.
las *det* the. ► *pron (ellas)* them; *(ustedes)* you.
láser *nm* laser.
lástima *nf* pity, shame.
lastimarse *vpr* to get hurt.
lata *nf* 1 *(envase)* tin, can. 2 *fam (fastidio)* bore, nuisance. • **dar la lata** to annoy; **en lata** canned, tinned.

lateral *adj* lateral, side.
latido *nm* beat.
látigo *nm* whip.
latir *vi* to beat.
latitud *nf* latitude.
latón *nm* brass.
laurel *nm* 1 *(árbol)* bay tree. 2 *(hoja)* bay leaf.
lava *nf* lava.
lavabo *nm* 1 *(pila)* washbasin. 2 *(cuarto de baño)* bathroom. 3 *(público)* toilet.
lavadora *nf* washing machine.
lavandería *nf* laundry. ▪ **lavandería automática** GB launderette; US laundromat.
lavaplatos *nm* → lavavajillas.
lavar *vt* 1 *(manos, ropa)* to wash. 2 *(platos)* to wash up. 3 *(limpiar)* to clean. ► *vpr* **lavarse** to have a wash, get washed.
lavavajillas *nm* 1 *(máquina)* dishwasher. 2 *(líquido)* washing-up liquid.
laxante *adj-nm* laxative.
lazo *nm* 1 *(lazada)* bow. 2 *(nudo)* knot.
le *pron* 1 *(objeto directo)* him; *(usted)* you. 2 *(objeto indirecto - a él)* him; *(- a ella)* her; *(a cosa, animal)* it; *(a usted)* you.
leal *adj* loyal, faithful.
lección *nf* lesson.
leche *nf* milk. ▪ **leche condensada** condensed milk; **le-**

che descremada skimmed milk; **leche en polvo** powdered milk; **leche entera** whole milk.

lechón *nm* sucking pig.

lechuga *nf* lettuce.

lechuza *nf* barn owl.

lector *nm* reader.

lectura *nf* 1 *(acción)* reading. 2 *(textos)* reading matter.

leer *vt* to read.

legal *adj* legal.

legaña *nf* sleep.

legendario,-a *adj* legendary.

legislación *nf* legislation.

legislativo,-a *adj* legislative.

legislatura *nf* term of office.

legítimo,-a *adj* legitimate.

legumbre *nf* pulse.

lejano,-a *adj* distant.

lejía *nf* bleach.

lejos *adv* far, far away.

lencería *nf* 1 *(de mujer)* underwear, lingerie. 2 *(tienda)* lingerie shop.

lengua *nf* 1 *(en la boca)* tongue. 2 *(idioma)* language. 3 *(de tierra)* strip. ▪ **lengua materna** mother tongue.

lenguado *nm* sole.

lenguaje *nm* 1 *(gen)* language. 2 *(habla)* speech.

lengüeta *nf* *(de zapato)* tongue.

lente *nm & nf* lens. ▪ **lentes de contacto** contact lenses.

lenteja *nf* lentil.

lentilla *nf* contact lens.

lento,-a *adj* slow.

leña *nf* firewood.

leñador,-ra *nm,f* woodcutter.

leño *nm* log.

león,-ona *nm,f* *(macho)* lion; *(hembra)* lioness.

leopardo *nm* leopard.

leotardos *nm pl* thick tights.

lepra *nf* leprosy.

les *pron* 1 *(objeto indirecto - a ellos)* them; *(- a ustedes)* you. 2 *(objeto directo - ellos)* them; *(- ustedes)* you.

lesión *nf* injury.

lesionarse *vpr* to injure oneself, get injured.

letra *nf* 1 *(del alfabeto)* letter. 2 *(de imprenta)* type. 3 *(escritura)* handwriting. 4 *(de canción)* lyrics, words. ▪ **letra de cambio** bill of exchange, draft.

letrero *nm* sign, notice.

levadura *nf* yeast.

levantar *vt* 1 *(alzar)* to raise; *(bulto, trampilla)* to lift. 2 *(construir)* to erect, build. 3 *(sanción, embargo)* to lift. ▶ *vpr* **levantarse** 1 *(ponerse de pie)* to rise, stand up. 2 *(de la cama)* to get up, rise.

leve *adj* 1 *(ligero)* light. 2 *(poco importante)* slight, trifling.

léxico,-a *adj* lexical.

ley *nf* *(gen)* law; *(del parlamento)* act, bill.

leyenda *nf* legend.

liar *vt* 1 *(cigarrillo)* to roll. 2 *(confundir)* to confuse.

libélula *nf* dragonfly.

liberación *nf (de país)* liberation; *(de preso, rehén)* freeing, release.

liberar *vt (país)* to liberate; *(preso, rehén)* to free, release.

libertad *nf* freedom, liberty. ▪ **libertad bajo fianza** bail.

libra *nf (moneda, peso)* pound.

libre *adj* free. • **libre de impuestos** tax-free, duty-free.

librería *nf* **1** *(tienda)* GB bookshop; US bookstore. **2** *(estantería)* bookcase.

libreta *nf* notebook.

libro *nm* book. ▪ **libro de bolsillo** paperback; **libro de consulta** reference book; **libro de reclamaciones** complaints book; **libro de texto** textbook.

licencia *nf* **1** *(documento)* permit; GB licence; US license. **2** *(permiso)* permission.

licenciado,-a *nm,f* graduate.

lícito,-a *adj* licit, lawful.

licor *nm* liqueur.

licuadora *nf* liquidizer.

líder *nmf* leader.

lidiar *vt (toros)* to fight.

liebre *nf* hare.

liga *nf* **1** *(para media)* garter. **2** *(en política, deporte)* league.

ligamento *nm* ligament.

ligar *vt (salsa)* to thicken. ▶ *vi fam (conquistar)* to pick up.

ligero,-a *adj* **1** *(liviano)* light. **2** *(leve)* slight. **3** *(frívolo)* flippant, thoughtless. • **a la lige-** ra hastily.

light *adj* **1** *(comida)* low-calorie; *(refresco)* diet. **2** *(tabaco)* light.

lija *nf* sandpaper.

lila *adj-nf* lilac.

lima¹ *nf (utensilio)* file.

lima² *nf (fruta)* lime.

limitar *vt* to limit. ▶ *vi* to border.

límite *nm* **1** *(tope)* limit. **2** *(frontera)* boundary, border.

limón *nm* lemon.

limonada *nf* lemonade.

limosna *nf* alms. • **pedir limosna** to beg.

limpiacristales *nmf-nm* window cleaner.

limpiaparabrisas *nm* GB windscreen wiper; US windshield wiper.

limpiar *vt* **1** *(gen)* to clean. **2** *(con paño)* to wipe.

limpio,-a *adj* **1** *(gen)* clean. **2** *(persona)* neat, tidy.

línea *nf* **1** *(gen)* line. **2** *(tipo)* figure. • **cuidar la línea** to watch one's weight; **en línea** on-line. ▪ **línea aérea** airline; **línea continua** solid white line; **línea férrea** railway line.

lingote *nm* ingot.

lino *nm* **1** *(tela)* linen. **2** *(planta)* flax.

linterna *nf (de pilas)* GB torch; US flashlight.

lío *nm* **1** *(embrollo)* mess, muddle. **2** *(problema)* trouble.

liquidación *nf* **1** *(de deuda)* settlement. **2** *(de mercancías)* clearance sale.

líquido,-a *adj* liquid. ► *nm* **líquido** liquid.

lírico,-a *adj* lyrical.

lirio *nm* iris.

liso,-a *adj* **1** *(superficie)* smooth, even. **2** *(pelo)* straight. **3** *(color)* plain.

lista *nf* list. ▪ **lista de correo** mailing list; **lista de espera 1** *(gen)* waiting list. **2** *(para avión)* standby.

listado *nm* INFORM listing.

listín *nm* telephone directory.

listo,-a *adj* **1** *(preparado)* ready. **2** *(inteligente)* clever, smart.

litera *nf* *(en dormitorio)* bunk bed; *(en barco)* bunk; *(en tren)* couchette.

literatura *nf* literature.

litoral *nm* coast.

litro *nm* GB litre; US liter.

llaga *nf* ulcer, sore.

llama¹ *nf* *(de fuego)* flame. ● **en llamas** ablaze.

llama² *nf* *(animal)* llama.

llamada *nf* **1** *(telefónica)* phone call. **2** *(a la puerta)* knock; *(con timbre)* ring. ▪ **llamada a cobro revertido** GB reverse-charge call; US collect call.

llamar *vt* **1** *(gen)* to call. **2** *(por teléfono)* to phone, call, ring. ► *vi (a la puerta)* to knock; *(al timbre)* to ring. ► *vpr* **llamarse** to be called, be named: *¿có-*

mo te llamas?, what's your name?; *me llamo Juan*, my name is Juan.

llano,-a *adj* *(plano)* flat.

llanta *nf* rim.

llanto *nm* crying, weeping.

llanura *nf* plain.

llave *nf* **1** *(de puerta etc)* key. **2** *(herramienta)* spanner. ● **cerrar con llave** to lock. ▪ **llave de contacto** ignition key; **llave de paso 1** *(del agua)* stopcock. **2** *(del gas)* mains tap; **llave inglesa** adjustable spanner; **llave maestra** master key.

llavero *nm* key ring.

llegada *nf* **1** *(gen)* arrival. **2** *(en deportes)* finishing line.

llegar *vi* **1** *(gen)* to arrive, reach. **2** *(alcanzar)* to reach: *¿llegas al estante?*, can you reach the shelf? **3** *(ser suficiente)* to be enough: *no me llega el dinero*, I haven't got enough money.

llenar *vt* gen) to fill (up); *(formulario)* to fill in. ► *vi* to be filling. ► *vpr* **llenarse** *(de gente)* to get crowded.

lleno,-a *adj* **1** *(gen)* full. **2** *(de gente)* crowded.

llevar *vt* **1** *(transportar)* to carry. **2** *(prenda)* to wear, have on. **3** *(acompañar)* to take; *(conducir, guiar)* to lead: *te llevaré al zoo*, I'll take you to the zoo. **4** *(libros, cuentas)* to keep. **5** *(dirigir)* to be in charge of, manage, run. ▶ *vpr* **llevarse 1** *(coger)* to take. **2** *(premio)* to win. **3** *(estar de moda)* to be fashionable. **4** *(entenderse)* to get on.

llorar *vi* **1** *(persona)* to cry, weep. **2** *(ojos)* to water.

llover *vi* to rain.

llovizna *nf* drizzle.

lluvia *nf* rain.

lo *det* the. ▶ *pron (él)* him; *(usted)* you; *(cosa, animal)* it.

lobo,-a *nm,f (macho)* wolf; *(hembra)* she-wolf.

local *adj* local. ▶ *nm* premises.

localidad *nf* **1** *(pueblo)* village; *(ciudad)* town. **2** *(asiento)* seat. **3** *(entrada)* ticket. • **"No hay localidades"** "Sold out".

loción *nf* lotion.

loco,-a *adj* mad, crazy.

locomotora *nf* engine, locomotive.

locura *nf* madness, insanity.

locutor,-ra *nm,f* announcer.

lodo *nm* mud, mire.

lógico,-a *adj* logical.

lograr *vt* **1** *(trabajo, beca)* to get, obtain. **2** *(objetivo)* to attain, achieve.

lomo *nm* **1** *(de animal)* back. **2** *(de cerdo)* loin. **3** *(de libro)* spine.

lona *nf* canvas.

loncha *nf* slice.

longaniza *nf* pork sausage.

longitud *nf* **1** *(largo)* length. **2** *(geográfica)* longitude.

loro *nm* parrot.

los *det* the. ▶ *pron (ellos)* them; *(ustedes)* you.

lote *nm* **1** *(de productos)* lot. **2** *(en informática)* batch.

lotería *nf* lottery.

lubina *nf* bass.

lucha *nf* **1** *(pelea)* fight, struggle. **2** *(deporte)* wrestling.

luchar *vi* **1** *(pelear)* to fight. **2** *(como deporte)* to wrestle.

luego *adv* **1** *(más tarde)* later. **2** *(después de algo)* then. ▶ *conj* therefore, then.

lugar *nm* **1** *(sitio)* place. **2** *(posición)* position. • **en lugar de** instead of.

lujo *nm* luxury. • **de lujo** luxury.

luna *nf* **1** *(astro)* moon. **2** *(cristal - de ventana)* window pane; *(- de vehículo)* GB windscreen; US windshield. ▪ **luna de miel** honeymoon; **luna llena** full moon.

lunar *adj* lunar. ▶ *nm* **1** *(en la piel)* mole; *(postizo)* beauty spot. **2** *(en tejido)* spot, polkadot.

lunes *nm* Monday.

lupa *nf* magnifying glass.

luto *nm* mourning.

luz *nf* **1** *(gen)* light. **2** *fam (electricidad)* electricity. • **dar a luz** to give birth to. ▪ **luces de carretera** full-beam headlights; **luces de cruce** dipped headlights; **luces de posición** sidelights.

M

macarrones *nm pl* macaroni.

macedonia *nf* fruit salad.

maceta *nf* plant pot, flowerpot.

macho *nm* **1** *(animal)* male. **2** *(pieza)* male piece, male part.

macizo,-a *adj* **1** *(sólido)* solid; *(fuerte)* well-built. ▶ *nm* **macizo** *(montañoso)* massif.

madera *nf* **1** *(gen)* wood; *(para la construcción)* timber.

madre *nf* mother.

madrina *nf* **1** *(de bautizo)* godmother. **2** *(de boda)* matron of honour.

madrugada *nf* **1** *(después de medianoche)* early morning. **2** *(alba)* dawn. • **de madrugada** in the small hours.

madrugar *vi* to get up early.

madurar *vt (fruta)* to ripen. ▶ *vi* to mature.

maduro,-a *adj* **1** *(persona)* mature. **2** *(fruta)* ripe.

maestro,-a *nm,f* teacher.

magdalena *nf* sponge cake.

magia *nf* magic.

magistrado,-a *nm,f* judge.

magnetófono *nm* tape recorder.

magnífico,-a *adj* magnificent, splendid.

mago,-a *nm,f* magician, wizard.

mahonesa *nf* mayonnaise.

maíz *nm* maize; US corn.

majestad *nf* majesty.

mal *adj* **1** *(desagradable, adverso)* bad. **2** *(enfermo)* ill. ▶ *adv* badly, wrong. • **menos mal que…** thank goodness…

maldición *nf* curse.

maldito,-a *adj fam* damned, bloody.

maleducado,-a *adj* rude, bad-mannered.

malentendido *nm* misunderstanding.

malestar *nm* **1** *(incomodidad)* discomfort. **2** *fig (inquietud)* uneasiness.

maleta *nf* suitcase, case. • **hacer la maleta** to pack.

maletero *nm (de coche)* GB boot; US trunk.

maletín *nm* briefcase.

maleza *nf* weeds.

malgastar *vt (tiempo)* to waste; *(dinero)* squander.

malherido,-a *adj* seriously injured.

malhumor *nm* bad temper.

malla *nf* **1** *(red)* mesh. **2** *(prenda)* leotard.

Mallorca *nf* Majorca.

malo,-a *adj* **1** *(perjudicial, imperfecto)* bad. **2** *(malvado)* wicked. • **estar malo,-a** to be ill.

maltratar *vt (animal)* to illtreat, mistreat; *(persona)* to batter.

malva *adj-nm (color)* mauve.
malvado,-a *nm,f* villain.
mama *nf (de mujer)* breast; *(de animal)* udder.
mamá *nf fam* GB mum(my); US mom(my).
mamar *vi (niño)* to suck.
mamífero *nm* mammal.
mampara *nf* screen.
manada *nf (de elefantes)* herd; *(de lobos)* pack.
manantial *nm* spring.
mancha *nf (de sangre, aceite, comida)* stain; *(de bolígrafo)* mark; *(en la piel)* spot.
manchar *vt-vi* to stain. ► *vpr* **mancharse** to get dirty.
manco,-a *adj* one-handed.
mandar *vt* 1 *(ordenar)* to order. 2 *(enviar)* to send.
mandarina *nf* tangerine.
mandíbula *nf* jaw.
mando *nm* 1 *(autoridad)* command. 2 *(para mecanismos)* control. ■ **mando a distancia** remote control.
manecilla *nf (de reloj)* hand.
manejable *adj* manageable, easy-to-handle.
manejar *vt* to handle, operate.
manera *nf* way, manner. ● **de manera que** so that; **de ninguna manera** by no means; **de todas maneras** anyway, in any case. ■ **manera de ser** character, the way SB is.
manga *nf* sleeve.
mango[1] *nm (asa)* handle.

mango[2] *nm (fruta)* mango.
manguera *nf* hose.
manía *nf* 1 *(ojeriza)* dislike. 2 *(obsesión)* mania.
manicomio *nm* mental hospital.
manifestación *nf* 1 *(de protesta, etc.)* demonstration. 2 *(expresión)* manifestation. 3 *(declaración)* statement.
manifestar *vt (opinión)* to express, state; *(sentimiento)* to show. ► *vpr* **manifestarse** *(en la calle)* to demonstrate.
manilla *nf (de reloj)* hand.
manillar *nm* handlebars.
maniobra *nf* GB manoeuvre; US maneuver.
manipular *vt* to manipulate.
maniquí *nm (muñeco)* dummy. ► *nmf (modelo)* model.
manivela *nf* crank.
manjar *nm* delicacy.
mano *nf* 1 *(de persona)* hand. 2 *(de pintura, etc.)* coat. ● **dar la mano** *(saludar)* to shake hands; **de segunda mano** secondhand. ■ **mano de obra** GB labour; US labor.
manojo *nm* bunch.
mansión *nf* mansion.
manso,-a *adj* tame, docile.
manta *nf* 1 *(para abrigarse)* blanket. 2 *(pez)* manta ray. ■ **manta de viaje** travelling rug.
manteca *nf* fat. ■ **manteca de cacao** cocoa butter; **manteca de cerdo** lard.

mantecado *nm* shortbread.

mantel *nm* tablecloth.

mantener *vt* **1** *(conservar)* to keep. **2** *(guardar)* to store. **3** *(sostener)* to support, hold up. **4** *(ideas)* to defend.

mantenimiento *nm* maintenance.

mantequilla *nf* butter.

manual *adj-nm* manual.

manuscrito *nm* manuscript.

manzana *nf* **1** *(fruta)* apple. **2** *(de casas)* block.

manzanilla *nf* **1** *(flor)* camomile. **2** *(infusión)* camomile tea. **3** *(vino)* manzanilla sherry.

manzano *nm* apple tree.

mañana *nf* *(parte del día)* morning. ▶ *nm* *(porvenir)* tomorrow, the future. ▶ *adv* tomorrow. • **hasta mañana** see you tomorrow; **pasado mañana** the day after tomorrow.

mapa *nm* map.

maquillaje *nm* make-up.

máquina *nf* machine. ▪ **máquina de afeitar** razor, shaver; **máquina de escribir** typewriter; **máquina de fotos** camera; **máquina tragaperras** slot machine.

maquinilla *nf.* ▪ **maquinilla de afeitar** razor.

mar *nm & nf* **1** *(gen)* sea. **2** *fam* very, a lot: *lo pasamos la mar de bien*, we had a great time. • **en alta mar** on the high seas;

hacerse a la mar to put to sea. ▪ **mar adentro** out to sea.

maravilloso,-a *adj* wonderful, marvellous.

marca *nf* **1** *(señal)* mark, sign. **2** *(de comestibles, productos del hogar)* brand; *(de otros productos)* make. **3** *(récord)* record. • **de marca** top-quality: *ropa de marca*, designer clothes. ▪ **marca de fábrica** trademark; **marca registrada** registered trademark.

marcador *nm* scoreboard.

marcar *vt* **1** *(señalar)* to mark. **2** *(hacer un tanto)* to score. **3** *(a otro jugador)* to mark. **4** *(pelo)* to set. **5** *(al teléfono)* to dial.

marcha *nf* **1** *(caminar)* march. **2** *(partida)* departure. **3** *(música)* march. • **a marchas forzadas** against the clock; **salir de marcha** to go out. ▪ **marcha atlética** walking race; **marcha atrás** reverse gear.

marcharse *vpr* to leave. • **¡marchando!** coming up!

marchitarse *vt-vpr* to wither.

marco *nm* frame.

marea *nf* tide. ▪ **marea alta** high tide; **marea baja** low tide; **marea negra** oil slick.

mareado,-a *adj* **1** *(con náuseas)* sick. **2** *(aturdido)* dizzy, giddy. **3** *(borracho)* tipsy.

marearse *vpr* *(sentir náuseas)* to get sick; *(sentirse aturdido)* to feel dizzy.

mareo *nm* **1** *(con náuseas)* sickness. **2** *(aturdimiento)* dizziness.

marfil *nm* ivory.

margarina *nf* margarine.

margarita *nf* daisy.

margen *nm & nf* **1** *(gen)* margin. **2** *(extremidad)* border, edge. **3** *(de río)* bank.

marginar *vt* to leave out.

marido *nm* husband.

marinero *nm* sailor.

marino,-a *adj* marine. ► *nm* **marino** seaman.

marioneta *nf* puppet, marionette.

mariposa *nf* butterfly.

mariquita *nf* ladybird.

marisco *nm* shellfish, seafood.

marisma *nf* salt marsh.

marisquería *nf* seafood restaurant.

marítimo,-a *adj* maritime.

mármol *nm* marble.

marrón *adj-nm* brown.

martes *nm* Tuesday.

martillo *nm* hammer.

mártir *nmf* martyr.

marzo *nm* March.

mas *conj* but.

más *adv* **1** *(gen)* more: *más pequeño*, smaller; *más caro*, more expensive, dearer; *¿no quieres más?*, don't you want more? **2** *(superlativo)* most: *el más caro*, the most expensive; *el más pequeño*, the smallest. **3** *(de nuevo)* any-more: *no voy más a ese sitio*, I'm not going there anymore. **4** *(con pronombre)* else: *¿algo más?*, anything else? ► *pron* more. ► *nm (signo)* plus. • **de más** spare, extra; **más bien** rather; **más o menos** more or less; **ni más ni menos** no less; **por más (que)** however much.

masa *nf* **1** *(de volumen)* mass. **2** *(de pan)* dough.

masaje *nm* massage.

máscara *nf* mask.

mascarilla *nf* **1** *(cosmética)* face pack. **2** *(de médico)* face mask.

masculino,-a *adj* **1** *(no femenino)* male. **2** *(para hombres)* men's. **3** *(sustantivo)* masculine.

masticar *vt-vi* to masticate, chew.

mástil *nm* **1** mast. **2** *(de bandera)* flagpole.

mata *nf (arbusto)* bush. ▪ **mata de pelo** mop of hair.

matadero *nm* slaughterhouse, abattoir.

matamoscas *nm (insecticida)* flykiller; *(pala)* flyswatter.

matar *vt-vi* to kill.

matasellos *nm* postmark.

mate *adj (sin brillo)* matt.

matemáticas *nf pl* mathematics.

materia *nf* **1** *(sustancia)* matter. **2** *(asignatura)* subject. ▪ **materia prima** raw material.

material *adj-m* material. ■ **material de oficina** office stationery.

materno,-a *adj* maternal: *leche materna*, mother's milk.

matiz *nm* **1** *(color)* shade, tint. **2** *fig (variación)* nuance.

matorral *nm* bushes, thicket.

matrícula *nf* **1** *(en curso)* registration. **2** *(número)* GB registration number; GB license number; *(placa)* GB number plate; US license plate. ■ **matrícula de honor** honours.

matricular(se) *vt-vpr* to register; GB enrol; US enroll.

matrimonio *nm* **1** *(ceremonia, institución)* marriage. **2** *(pareja)* married couple.

maullido *nm* miaow.

maxilar *adj* maxillary. ► *nm* jaw.

máximo,-a *adj* maximum.

mayo *nm* May.

mayonesa *nf* mayonnaise.

mayor *adj* **1** *(comparativo)* bigger, greater, larger; *(persona)* older; *(hermanos, hijos)* elder. **2** *(superlativo)* biggest, greatest, largest; *(persona)* oldest; *(hermanos, hijos)* eldest. ● **al por mayor** wholesale.

mayordomo *nm* butler.

mayoría *nf* majority, most. ■ **mayoría de edad** adulthood.

mayorista *nmf* wholesaler.

mayúscula *nf* capital letter.

mazapán *nm* marzipan.

mazorca *nf* cob.

me *pron* **1** *(como objeto)* me. **2** *(reflexivo)* myself.

mecánico,-a *adj* mechanical. ► *nm,f* mechanic.

mecanismo *nm* mechanism.

mecanógrafo,-a *nm,f* typist.

mecedora *nf* rocking chair.

mecha *nf* **1** *(de vela)* wick. **2** *(de bomba)* fuse. ► *nf pl* **mechas** *(en el pelo)* highlights.

mechero *nm* lighter.

medalla *nf* medal.

media *nf (promedio)* average. ► *fpl* **medias** *(hasta la cintura)* tights; *(hasta la pierna)* stockings.

mediano,-a *adj* **1** *(de tamaño)* middle-sized. **2** *(de calidad)* average, medium.

medianoche *nf* midnight.

mediante *adj* by means of.

medicamento *nm* medicine.

medicina *nf* medicine.

médico,-a *adj* medical. ► *nm,f* doctor, physician.

medida *nf* **1** *(unidad)* measure. **2** *(disposición)* measure, step. ● **a medida que** as; **hecho a medida** made-to-measure.

medio,-a *adj* **1** *(mitad)* half. **2** *(intermedio)* middle. **3** *(promedio)* average. ► *nm* **medio 1** *(mitad)* half. **2** *(centro)* middle. ► *adv* half. ► *nm pl* **medios** means. ● **a medias 1** *(sin terminar)* half done, half finished. **2** *(entre dos)* between the two: *lo pagamos a medias*, we went halves on it. ■ **media pensión** half board; **medio ambiente** environment; **medio de transporte** means of transport; **medios de comunicación** the mass media.

mediocre *adj* mediocre.

mediodía *nm* **1** *(las doce)* noon, midday. **2** *(hora del almuerzo)* lunchtime.

medir *vt* **1** *(tomar medidas)* to measure. **2** *(calcular)* to gauge.

médula *nf* marrow. ■ **médula espinal** spinal cord.

medusa *nf* jellyfish.

megáfono *nm* megaphone, loudspeaker.

mejilla *nf* cheek.

mejillón *nm* mussel.

mejor *adj-adv* **1** *(comparativo)* better. **2** *(superlativo)* best. ● **a lo mejor** perhaps, maybe; **mejor dicho** rather; **tanto mejor** so much the better.

mejorar *vt* to improve. ▶ *vi-vpr* **mejorar(se) 1** *(reponerse)* to recover, get better. **2** *(el tiempo)* to clear up.

melena *nf* **1** *(de persona)* long hair. **2** *(de león, caballo)* mane.

mellizo,-a *adj-nm,f* twin.

melocotón *nm* peach.

melodía *nf* melody.

melón *nm* melon.

membrana *nf* membrane.

membrete *nm* letterhead.

membrillo *nm* *(fruto)* quince; *(dulce)* quince jelly.

memoria *nf* **1** *(gen)* memory. **2** *(informe)* report. ▶ *nf pl* **memorias** *(biografía)* memoirs. ● **de memoria** by heart.

mencionar *vt* to mention.

mendigo,-a *nm,f* beggar.

mendrugo *nm* hard crust of bread.

menestra *nf* vegetable stew.

menisco *nm* meniscus.

menopausia *nf* menopause.

menor *adj* **1** *(comparativo)* smaller, lesser; *(persona)* younger. **2** *(superlativo)* smallest, least; *(persona)* youngest. ▶ *nmf* **menor (de edad)** minor. ● **al por menor** retail.

Menorca *nf* Minorca.

menos *adj* **1** *(comparativo - con incontables)* less; *(- con contables)* fewer. **2** *(superlativo - con incontables)* the least; *(con contables)* the fewest. ▶ *adv* **1** *(comparativo - con incontables)* less; *(- con contables)* fewer. **2** *(superlativo - con incontables)* the least; *(con contables)* the fewest. **3** *(para hora)* to: *las tres menos cuarto*, a quarter to three. ▶ *prep (excepto)* except, but. ▶ *nm* minus. ● **a menos que** unless; **al menos** at least; **por lo menos** at least.

mensaje *nm* message.

menstruación *nf* menstruation.

mezclar

mensual *adj* monthly.
menta *nf* mint.
mental *adj* mental.
mente *nf* mind.
mentir *vi* to lie, tell lies.
mentira *nf* lie.
mentiroso,-a *nm,f* liar.
mentón *nm* chin.
menú *nm* menu.
menudo,-a *adj* 1 *(pequeño)* small, tiny. 2 fine: *¡menudo lío!*, what a fine mess! • **a menudo** often, frequently.
meñique *nm* little finger.
mercadillo *nf* market, street market.
mercado *nm* market. ■ **mercado de valores** stock-market.
mercancía *nf* goods.
mercería *nf (tienda)* GB haberdasher's; US notions store.
merecer(se) *vt-vi* to deserve.
merendar *vi* to have an afternoon snack, have tea.
merendero *nm* picnic spot.
merengue *nm* meringue.
merienda *nf* afternoon snack.
mérito *nm* merit, worth.
merluza *nf* hake.
mermelada *nf (de cítricos)* marmalade; *(de otras frutas)* jam.
mero *nm* grouper.
mes *nm* month.
mesa *nf (de salón, comedor)* table; *(de despacho)* desk. • **poner la mesa** to set the table;

quitar la mesa to clear the table.
meseta *nf* tableland, plateau.
mesilla *nf* small table. ■ **mesilla de noche** bedside table.
mesón *nm* inn, tavern.
mestizo,-a *adj* of mixed race, half-breed.
meta *nf* 1 *(portería)* goal; *(de carreras)* finishing line. 2 *fig (objetivo)* aim, goal.
metal *nm* metal.
metálico,-a *adj* metallic. • **pagar en metálico** to pay cash.
meter *vt* 1 *(introducir)* to put. 2 *(punto)* to score. ► *vpr* **meterse** 1 *(entrar)* to get in. 2 *(entrometerse)* to interfere, meddle. • **meterse con** ALGN 1 *(burlarse)* to tease SB. 2 *(atacar)* to pick on SB.
método *nm* method.
metralleta *nf* submachine gun.
metro[1] *nm (medida)* GB metre; US meter.
metro[2] *nm (transporte)* GB underground, tube; US subway.
mexicano,-a *adj-nm,f* Mexican.
México *nm* Mexico.
mezcla *nf* 1 *(acción - de razas, colores)* mixing; *(- de cafés, tabacos)* blending. 2 *(producto - de razas, colores)* mixture; *(- de cafés, tabacos)* blend.
mezclar *vt* 1 *(razas, colores)* to mix; *(cafés, tabacos)* blend. 2 *(desordenar)* to mix up.

mezquita *nf* mosque.
mi¹ *adj* my.
mi² *nm (nota)* E.
mí *pron* **1** me. **2** *(mí mismo,-a)* myself.
michelín *nm fam* spare tyre.
microbio *nm* microbe.
micrófono *nm* microphone.
microondas *nm* microwave.
microscopio *nm* microscope.
miedo *nm* fear. • **tener miedo** to be afraid.
miel *nf* honey.
miembro *nm* **1** *(socio)* member. **2** *(extremidad)* limb.
mientras *conj* **1** while. **2** *(condición)* as long as, while. ▶ *adv* meanwhile. • **mientras tanto** meanwhile, in the meantime.
miércoles *nm* Wednesday.
mierda *nf* shit.
miga *nf* crumb.
migración *nf* migration.
migraña *nf* migraine.
mil *num* thousand.
milagro *nm* miracle.
milenio *nm* millenium.
milímetro *nm* GB millimetre; US millimeter.
militar *adj* military. ▶ *nm* military man, soldier. ▶ *vi* POL to be a militant.
milla *nf* mile.
millón *nm* million.
mimar *vt* to spoil.
mimbre *nm* wicker.

mina *nf* **1** *(gen)* mine. **2** *(de lápiz)* lead.
mineral *adj-nm* mineral.
miniatura *nf* miniature.
minifalda *nf* miniskirt.
mínimo,-a *adj (gasto)* minimal; *(cantidad, temperatura)* minimum. • **como mínimo** at least.
ministerio *nm* GB ministry; US department.
ministro,-a *nm,f* GB minister; US secretary.
minoría *nf* minority.
minorista *nmf* retailer.
minúscula *nf* small letter.
minusválido,-a *adj* handicapped, disabled.
minutero *nm* minute hand.
minuto *nm* minute.
mío,-a *adj* my, of mine. ▶ *pron* mine.
miope *adj* short-sighted.
miopía *nf* shortsightedness.
mirada *nf* look.
mirador *nm* viewpoint.
mirar *vi* **1** *(ver)* to look at. **2** *(observar)* to watch.
misa *nf* mass.
miseria *nf* **1** *(desgracia)* misery. **2** *(pobreza)* extreme poverty.
misil *nm* missile.
misión *nf* mission.
mismo,-a *adj* **1** *(igual)* same. **2** *(enfático - propio)* own; *(- uno mismo)* oneself: *lo haré yo mismo*, I'll do it myself. ▶

pron same. ▶ *adv* right: *aquí mismo*, right here.

misterio *nm* mystery.

mitad *nf* **1** half: *la mitad de una botella*, half a bottle. **2** *(en medio)* middle: *en mitad de la carretera*, in the middle of the road.

mitin *nm* rally.

mito *nm* myth.

mocasín *nm* loafer, moccasin.

mochila *nf* rucksack, backpack.

moco *nm* mucus.

moda *nf* fashion. • **pasado de moda** old-fashioned.

modales *nm pl* manners.

modelo *adj-nm* model. ▶ *nmf* fashion model.

módem *nm* modem.

moderar *vt* to moderate.

moderno,-a *adj* modern.

modesto,-a *adj* modest,.

modificar *vt* to modify,.

modista *nmf (que confecciona)* dressmaker; *(que diseña)* fashion designer.

modo *nm* manner, way. • **de cualquier modo** anyway; **de ningún modo** by no means; **de todos modos** anyhow, in any case; **en cierto modo** to a certain extent.

módulo *nm* module.

moflete *nm fam* chubby cheek.

moho *nm* GB mould; US mold.

mojar *vt (empapar)* to wet; *(humedecer)* to dampen.

molde *nm* GB mould; US mold.

moler *vt (café)* to grind.

molestar *vt-vi* to disturb, bother. ▶ *vpr* **molestarse 1** *(tomarse el trabajo)* to bother. **2** *(ofenderse)* to get upset.

molestia *nf* **1** *(incomodidad)* nuisance, bother. **2** *(dolor)* slight pain, discomfort. • **"Rogamos disculpen las molestias"** "We apologize for any inconvenience".

molido,-a *adj (café)* ground.

molinillo *nm* grinder, mill.

molino *nm* mill.

molusco *nm* GB mollusc; US mollusk.

momento *nm* **1** *(gen)* moment, instant. **2** *(época)* time. • **de momento** for the time being; **por el momento** for the time being.

momia *nf* mummy.

monarquía *nf* monarchy.

monasterio *nm* monastery.

mondadientes *nm* toothpick.

moneda *nf* **1** *(unidad monetaria)* currency, money. **2** *(pieza)* coin.

monedero *nm* purse.

monitor,-ra *nm,f (profesor)* instructor. ▶ *nm* **monitor** *(pantalla)* monitor.

monja *nf* nun.

monje *nm* monk.

mono,-a *adj (bonito)* pretty, cute. ▶ *nm* **mono 1** *(animal)* monkey. **2** *(prenda)* overalls.

monopatín *nm* skateboard.

monótono,-a *adj* monotonous.

monstruo *nm* monster.

montacargas *nm* GB goods lift; US freight elevator.

montaje *nm* 1 *(de aparato, mueble)* assembly. 2 *(de película)* cutting, editing. 3 *(de obra teatral)* staging.

montaña *nf* mountain. ▪ **montaña rusa** big dipper.

montañismo *nm* mountain climbing, mountaineering.

montar *vi* 1 *(a vehículo)* to mount, get on. 2 *(caballo, bicicleta)* to ride. ► *vt* 1 *(cabalgar)* to ride. 2 *(nata)* to whip; *(claras)* whisk. 3 *(máquinas)* to assemble. 4 *(negocio, exposición)* to set up. 5 *(película)* to edit, mount. 6 *(obra de teatro)* to stage.

monte *nm* mountain, mount.

montón *nm* 1 *(pila)* heap, pile. 2 *fam (gran cantidad)* loads great, quantity.

montura *nf (de gafas)* frame.

monumento *nm* monument.

moño *nm (de pelo)* bun.

moqueta *nf* fitted carpet.

mora *nf* 1 *(de moral)* mulberry. 2 *(zarzamora)* blackberry.

morado,-a *adj* dark purple. ► *nm* **morado** 1 *(color)* dark purple. 2 *(golpe)* bruise.

moral *adj* moral. ► *nf* 1 *(reglas)* morality, morals. 2 *(ánimo)* morale, spirits.

morcilla *nf* black pudding.

morder *vt-vi* to bite.

mordisco *nm* bite.

moreno,-a *adj* dark. ► *nm* **moreno** suntan. ● **ponerse moreno** to tan.

morir(se) *vi-vpr* to die.

moro,-a *adj* 1 *(norteafricano)* Moorish. 2 *(musulmán)* Muslim.

morro *nm* 1 *fam (de persona)* mouth, lips. 2 *(de animal)* snout, nose.

morsa *nf* walrus.

mortadela *nf* mortadella.

mortal *adj* 1 *(persona)* mortal. 2 *(mortífero)* lethal.

mortero *nm* mortar.

mosaico *nm* mosaic.

mosca *nf* fly.

moscardón *nm* blowfly.

mosquearse *vpr fam (enfadarse)* to get cross.

mosquito *nm* mosquito.

mostaza *nf* mustard.

mosto *nm* grape juice.

mostrador *nm* counter. ▪ **mostrador de facturación** check-in desk.

mostrar *vt (enseñar)* to show. ► *vpr* **mostrarse** to be: *se mostró muy interesado*, he was very interested.

mote *nm* nickname.

motín *nm* riot.

motivar *vt* 1 *(causar)* to cause, give rise to. 2 *(estimular)* to motivate.

motivo *nm* **1** *(causa)* motive, reason. **2** *(de dibujo, música)* motif. ● **con motivo de** on the occasion of.

moto *nf fam* motorbike.

motocicleta *nf* motorbike.

motor,-ra *adj* motor. ► *nm* **motor** *(no eléctrico)* engine; *(eléctrico)* motor. ■ **motor de búsqueda** search engine.

motora *nf* small motorboat.

motorista *nmf* motorcyclist.

mover(se) *vt-vpr* to move.

móvil *adj* movable, mobile. ► *nm* **1** *(teléfono)* mobile (phone), cellular phone. **2** *(motivo)* motive, inducement.

movimiento *nm* movement.

mozo,-a *nm,f (chico)* boy, lad; *(chica)* girl, lass.

muchacho,-a *nm,f (chico)* boy, lad; *(chica)* girl, lass.

muchedumbre *nf* crowd.

mucho,-a *adj* **1** *(frases afirmativas - singular)* a lot of, much; *(- plural)* a lot of, many. **2** *(frases negativas e interrogativas - singular)* much; *(- plural)* many. ► *pron (singular - frases afirmativas)* a lot, much; *(- frases negativas e interrogativas)* much; *(plural)* many. ► *adv* **mucho 1** *(gen)* a lot: *lo siento mucho*, I'm very sorry. **2** *(comparaciones)* much. **3** *(mucho tiempo)* a long time. **4** *(frecuentemente)* often, much.

mudanza *nf* removal.

mudarse *vpr* **1** *(gen)* to change. **2** *(de residencia)* to move.

mudo,-a *adj* dumb.

mueble *nm* piece of furniture.

mueca *nf* grimace

muela *nf* tooth.

muelle[1] *nm (en puerto)* dock.

muelle[2] *nm (resorte)* spring.

muerte *nf* death.

muerto,-a *adj* dead. ► *nm,f* dead person. ● **estar muerto de hambre** to be starving.

muestra *nf* **1** *(ejemplar)* sample. **2** *(señal)* proof, sign.

muestrario *nm* collection of samples.

mujer *nf* **1** woman. **2** *(esposa)* wife. ■ **mujer de la limpieza** cleaning lady.

mulato,-a *adj-nm,f* mulatto.

muleta *nf* crutch.

mulo,-a *nm,f (macho)* mule; *(hembra)* she-mule.

multa *nf* fine.

multinacional *adj-nf* multinational.

múltiple *adj* **1** *(numeroso)* multiple. **2** *(muchos)* many, a number of.

multiplicar(se) *vt-vpr* to multiply.

multitud *nf* multitude, crowd.

mundial *adj* world(wide). ► *nm* world championship.

mundo *nm* world. ● **todo el mundo** everybody.

municipal *adj* municipal.

municipio *nm* municipality.
muñeca *nf* **1** *(del brazo)* wrist. **2** *(juguete)* doll.
muñeco *nm* **1** *(monigote)* dummy. **2** *(juguete)* doll. ▪ **muñeco de nieve** snowman; **muñeco de peluche** soft toy.
mural *adj-nm* mural.
muralla *nf* wall.
murciélago *nm* bat.
murmurar *vi* to murmur.
muro *nm* wall.
muscular *adj* muscular.
músculo *nm* muscle.
museo *nm* museum.
musgo *nm* moss.
música *nf* music. ▪ **música de fondo** background music.
músico,-a *adj* musical. ▶ *nm,f* musician.
muslo *nm* thigh.
musulmán,-ana *adj-nm,f* Muslim, Moslem.
mutuo,-a *adj* mutual.
muy *adv* very.

N-Ñ

nabo *nm* turnip.
nácar *nm* mother-of-pearl.
nacer *vi* **1** *(persona, animal)* to be born. **2** *(río)* to rise.
nacimiento *nm* **1** *(de persona, animal)* birth. **2** *(de río)* source.

nación *nf* nation.
nacional *adj* **1** *(bandera, equipo, seguridad)* national. **2** *(productos, mercados, vuelos)* domestic.
nada *pron* nothing, not... anything. ▶ *adv* not at all: **no es nada fácil**, it isn't at all easy. ● **como si nada** as if nothing had happened; **–de nada** –don't mention it.
nadar *vi* to swim.
nadie *pron* nobody, not... anybody.
naipe *nm* card.
nana *nf* lullaby.
naranja *nf* orange.
naranjada *nf* orangeade.
narcótico *nm* narcotic.
nariz *nf* nose.
narración *nf* **1** *(acción)* narration, account. **2** *(relato)* story.
nata *nf* **1** *(para montar)* cream. **2** *(de leche hervida)* skin.
natación *nf* swimming.
natal *adj* of birth. ▪ **ciudad natal** home town.
natillas *nf pl* custard.
nativo,-a *adj-nm,f* native.
natural *adj* **1** *(color, estado, gesto)* natural. **2** *(fruta, flor)* fresh. **3** *(yogur)* plain.
naturaleza *nf* nature.
naufragio *nm* *(de barco)* shipwreck.
náusea *nf* nausea, sickness. ● **sentir náuseas/tener náuseas** to feel sick.

náutico,-a *adj* nautical.

navaja *nf* **1** *(cuchillo)* pen-knife, pocketknife. **2** *(molus-co)* razor-shell. ▪ **navaja de afeitar** razor.

nave *nf* **1** *(barco)* ship. **2** *(de iglesia)* nave. ▪ **nave espacial** spaceship; **nave industrial** industrial building.

navegador *nm* browser.

navegar *vi* to navigate, sail. • **navegar por Internet** to surf the Net.

Navidad *nf* Christmas: *¡Feliz Navidad!*, Merry Christmas!

necesario,-a *adj* necessary.

neceser *nm* GB toilet bag; US toilet kit.

necesidad *nf* **1** *(falta)* need. **2** *(cosa esencial)* necessity. • **hacer sus necesidades** to relieve oneself.

necesitar *vt* to need. • **"Se necesita camarero"** "Waiter required".

negar *vt* **1** *(acusación, afirmación)* to deny. **2** *(permiso, solicitud)* to refuse. ▶ *vpr* **negarse** to refuse.

negativo,-a *adj* negative.

negociación *nf* negotiation.

negociar *vi* **1** *(comerciar)* to trade, deal. **2** *(hablar)* to negotiate.

negocio *nm* **1** *(comercio, actividad)* business. **2** *(transacción)* deal, transaction.

negro,-a *adj* **1** *(color, raza, pelo)* black. **2** *(tono, ojos, piel)* dark. ▶ *nm* **negro** *(color)* black.

nervio *nm* nerve.

nervioso,-a *adj* nervous.

neto,-a *adj* net.

neumático *nm* GB tyre; US tire.

neutro,-a *adj* **1** *(neutral)* neutral. **2** *(género)* neuter.

nevada *nf* snowfall.

nevar *vi* to snow.

nevera *nf* fridge, refrigerator.

ni *conj* **1** *(en doble negación)* neither… nor: *no tengo tiempo ni dinero*, I have neither time nor money. **2** *(ni siquiera)* not even: *ni por dinero*, not even for money.

nido *nm* nest.

niebla *nf* fog.

nieto,-a *nm,f (gen)* grandchild; *(niño)* grandson; *(niña)* granddaughter.

nieve *nf* snow.

ningún *adj* → ninguno,-a.

ninguno,-a *adj* no, not… any. ▶ *pron* **1** *(hablando de varias personas o cosas)* none: *ninguno de nosotros vio nada*, none of us saw anything. **2** *(hablando de dos personas o cosas)* neither: *ninguno de los dos funciona*, neither of them works. **3** *(nadie)* nobody, no one: *ninguno lo vio*, nobody saw it, no one saw it.

niñera *nf* nursemaid, nanny.

niño,-a *nm,f* *(gen)* child; *(chico)* boy; *(chica)* girl; *(bebé)* baby.

níspero *nm* medlar.

nivel *nm* **1** *(en una escala, jerarquía)* level. **2** *(calidad)* standard.

no *adv* **1** no, not. **2** *(prefijo)* non: *la no violencia*, nonviolence. ► *nm* no. • *..., ¿no?* tag question: *lo viste, ¿no?*, you saw it, didn't you?

noble *adj* noble.

noche *nf* night. • **buenas noches 1** *(saludo)* good evening. **2** *(despedida)* good night; **esta noche** tonight; **por la noche** at night.

nochebuena *nf* Christmas Eve.

nochevieja *nf* New Year's Eve.

noción *nf* notion.

nocivo,-a *adj* harmful.

nogal *nm* walnut tree.

nómada *nmf* nomad.

nombre *nm* **1** *(gen)* name. **2** *(sustantivo)* noun. • **en nombre de** on behalf of. ■ **nombre de pila** first name, Christian name; **nombre y apellidos** full name.

nómina *nf* *(sueldo)* pay.

noria *nf* *(de feria)* big wheel.

norma *nf* rule.

normal *adj* **1** *(común, usual)* normal. **2** *(nada especial)* ordinary.

norte *adj-nm* north.

nos *pron* **1** *(complemento)* us. **2** *(reflexivo)* ourselves. **3** *(recíproco)* each other.

nosotros,-as *pron* **1** *(sujeto)* we. **2** *(complemento, con preposiciones)* us.

nota *nf* **1** *(anotación)* note. **2** *(calificación)* GB mark; US grade. **3** *(cuenta)* GB bill; US check. **4** *(musical)* note.

notar *vt* **1** *(percibir)* to notice. **2** *(sentir)* to feel. • **se nota que...** you can see that....

notario,-a *nm,f* notary.

noticia *nf* news: *una noticia*, a piece of news.

novato,-a *nm,f* novice, beginner.

novecientos,-as *num* nine hundred.

novedad *nf* **1** *(cosa nueva)* novelty. **2** *(cambio)* change.

novela *nf* novel.

noveno,-a *num* ninth.

noventa *num* ninety.

noviazgo *nm* engagement.

noviembre *nm* November.

novio,-a *nm,f* **1** *(chico)* boyfriend; *(chica)* girlfriend. **2** *(prometido - chico)* fiancé; *(- chica)* fiancée. **3** *(en boda - hombre)* bridegroom; *(- mujer)* bride.

nube *nf* cloud.

nublado,-a *adj* cloudy, overcast.

nuboso,-a *adj* cloudy.

nuca *nf* nape of the neck.

nuclear *adj* nuclear.
núcleo *nm* nucleus.
nudillo *nm* knuckle.
nudo *nm* knot.
nuera *nf* daughter-in-law.
nuestro,-a *adj* our, of ours. ► *pron* ours.
nueve *num* nine; *(en fechas)* ninth.
nuevo,-a *adj* new. • **de nuevo** again.
nuez *nf* walnut. ■ **nuez de Adán** Adam's apple; **nuez moscada** nutmeg.
nulo,-a *adj* invalid.
numerar *vt* to number.
número *nm* 1 *(gen)* number. 2 *(de zapatos)* size.
nunca *adv* 1 *(en negativa)* never. 2 *(en interrogativa)* ever. • **casi nunca** hardly ever; **nunca más** never again.
nutria *nf* otter.
nutritivo,-a *adj* nutritious, nourishing.
ñoqui *nm* gnocchi.
ñu *nm* gnu.

O

o *conj* or. • **o... o...** either... or..; **o sea** that is to say.
oasis *nm* oasis.
obedecer *vt* to obey.
obediente *adj* obedient.

obeso,-a *adj* obese.
obispo *nm* bishop.
objetivo,-a *adj* objective. ► *nm* **objetivo** 1 *(fin)* aim, goal. 2 *(de ataque)* target. 3 *(lente)* lens.
objeto *nm* object.
oblicuo,-a *adj* oblique.
obligación *nf* obligation.
obligar *vt* to oblige, force.
obligatorio,-a *adj* compulsory, obligatory.
obra *nf* 1 *(de arte, ingeniería)* work; *(de literatura)* book; *(de teatro)* play. 2 *(acto)* deed. 3 *(edificio en construcción)* building site. ► *nf pl* **obras** *(en casa)* building work; *(en la calle)* roadworks. ■ **obra maestra** masterpiece.
obrero,-a *nm,f* worker.
obsequio *nm* gift.
observación *nf* observation.
observar *vt* 1 *(mirar)* to observe. 2 *(notar)* to notice.
obsesión *nf* obsession.
obstáculo *nm* obstacle, hindrance.
obstante. • **no obstante** however, nevertheless.
obstruirse *vpr* to get blocked up.
obtener *vt* to obtain.
obús *nm* shell.
obvio,-a *adj* obvious.
oca *nf* goose.
ocasión *nf* 1 *(momento)* occasion. 2 *(oportunidad)* opportu-

nity, chance. **3** *(ganga)* bargain. • **de ocasión 1** *(segunda mano)* secondhand. **2** *(barato)* bargain.

ocaso *nm* sunset.

occidental *adj* western.

occidente *nm* the West.

océano *nm* ocean.

ochenta *num* eighty.

ocho *num* eight; *(en fechas)* eighth.

ochocientos,-as *num* eight hundred.

ocio *nm (tiempo libre)* leisure.

octavo,-a *num* eighth.

octubre *nm* October.

oculista *nmf* ophthalmologist.

ocultar *vt* to hide.

ocupación *nf* occupation.

ocupado,-a *adj* **1** *(persona)* busy. **2** *(asiento)* taken; *(aseos, teléfono)* engaged.

ocupar *vt* **1** *(conquistar)* to occupy. **2** *(llenar)* to take up.

ocurrir *vi* to happen, occur. ► *vpr* **ocurrirse**: *no se le ocurrió preguntar*, it didn't occur to her to ask.

odiar *vt* to hate.

odio *nm* hatred.

odontólogo,-a *nm,f* dental surgeon, odontologist.

oeste *nm* west.

ofender *vt* to offend.

ofensiva *nf* offensive.

oferta *nf* **1** *(propuesta, ganga)* offer. **2** *(en concurso)* bid, tender. • **de oferta** on offer.

oficial *adj* official. ► *nm* **1** *(militar)* officer. **2** *(empleado)* clerk. **3** *(obrero)* journeyman.

oficina *nf* office.

oficinista *nmf* office worker.

oficio *nm (trabajo manual especializado)* trade; *(profesión)* profession.

ofimática *nf* office automation.

ofrecer *vt* **1** *(dar - premio, trabajo)* to offer; *(- banquete, fiesta)* to hold. **2** *(presentar - posibilidad)* to give; *(- dificultad)* to present.

oído *nm* **1** *(sentido)* hearing. **2** *(órgano)* ear.

oír *vt* to hear.

ojal *nm* buttonhole.

ojeras *nm pl* bags under the eyes.

ojo *nm* **1** *(órgano)* eye. **2** *(agujero)* hole. • **a ojo** at a rough guess. ■ **ojo de buey** porthole; **ojo de la cerradura** keyhole.

ola *nf* wave.

oleaje *nm* swell.

óleo *nm (material)* oil paint; *(cuadro)* oil painting.

oler *vt-vi* to smell. • **olerse algo** to suspect STH.

olfato *nm* sense of smell.

oliva *nf* olive.

olivo *nm* olive tree.

olla *nf* pot. ■ **olla a presión** pressure cooker.

olmo *nm* elm.

olor *nm* smell.
olvidar *vt* **1** *(gen)* to forget. **2** *(dejar)* to leave.
olvido *nm (lapsus)* oversight.
ombligo *nm* navel.
once *num* eleven; *(en fechas)* eleventh.
onceavo,-a *num* eleventh.
onda *nf* wave.
ondear *vi (bandera)* to flutter.
opaco,-a *adj* opaque.
opción *nf* option.
ópera *nf* opera.
operación *nf* operation.
operador,-ra *nm,f* operator. ▪ **operador turístico** tour operator.
operar *vt* to operate.
opinar *vt* to think. ▶ *vi* to express an opinion.
opinión *nf (juicio)* opinion. • **cambiar de opinión** to change one's mind.
oponer *vt (resistencia)* to offer. ▶ *vpr* **oponerse 1** *(estar en contra)* to oppose. **2** *(ser contrario)* to be opposed.
oportunidad *nf* **1** *(ocasión)* opportunity. **2** *(ganga)* bargain. **3** *(conveniencia)* advisability.
oposición *nf* **1** *(enfrentamiento)* opposition. **2** *(examen)* competitive examination.
oprimir *vt* **1** *(tecla, botón)* to press. **2** *(persona, pueblo)* to oppress.
optativo,-a *adj* optional.

óptica *nf* **1** *(tienda)* optician's. **2** *(ciencia)* optics.
optimismo *nm* optimism.
opuesto,-a *adj* opposite.
oración *nf* **1** *(rezo)* prayer. **2** *(frase)* clause, sentence.
orador,-ra *nm,f* speaker.
oral *adj* oral. • **por vía oral** to be taken orally.
orangután *nm* orang-utan.
órbita *nf* **1** *(de satélite)* orbit. **2** *(de ojo)* socket.
orca *nf* killer whale.
orden *nm (disposición)* order. ▶ *nf* **1** *(mandato, asociación)* order. **2** *(judicial)* warrant. • **del orden de** GB in the order of; US on the order of. ▪ **orden del día** agenda; **orden público** law and order.
ordenado,-a *adj* tidy.
ordenador *nm* computer. ▪ **ordenador portátil** laptop.
ordenar *vt* **1** *(arreglar)* to put in order; *(habitación)* to tidy up. **2** *(mandar)* to order.
ordeñar *vt* to milk.
ordinario,-a *adj* **1** *(corriente)* ordinary. **2** *(grosero)* vulgar, common.
orégano *nm* oregano.
oreja *nf* ear.
organigrama *nm (de empresa)* organization chart; *(de procedimiento, sistema)* flow chart.
organismo *nm* **1** *(ser viviente)* organism. **2** *(entidad pública)* organization, body.

organización *nf* organization.

organizar *vt* to organize.

órgano *nm* organ.

orgullo *nm* pride.

orgulloso,-a *adj* proud.

orientación *nf* 1 *(dirección)* orientation. 2 *(guía)* guidance.

oriental *adj* eastern.

orientar *vt* 1 *(dirigir)* to orientate. 2 *(guiar)* to guide. ► *vpr* **orientarse** 1 *(encontrar el camino)* to find one's way about.

oriente *nm* east.

orificio *nm* orifice.

origen *nm* origin: *de origen español*, of Spanish extraction.

original *adj-nm* original.

orilla *nf* 1 *(borde)* edge. 2 *(del río)* bank; *(del mar)* shore.

orina *nf* urine.

orinal *nm* *(de adulto)* chamber pot; *(de niño)* potty.

oro *nm* gold.

orquesta *nf* 1 *(clásica, sinfónica)* orchestra. 2 *(banda)* dance band.

orquídea *nf* orchid.

ortiga *nf* nettle.

ortografía *nf* spelling.

oruga *nf* caterpillar.

os *pron* 1 *(complemento directo)* you. 2 *(complemento indirecto)* to you. 3 *(reflexivo)* yourselves. 4 *(recíproco)* each other.

oscuridad *nf* darkness.

oscuro,-a *adj* 1 *(lugar, color)* dark. 2 *(origen, explicación)* obscure. • **a oscuras** in the dark.

oso *nm* bear. ■ **oso de peluche** teddy bear; **oso hormiguero** anteater.

ostentar *vt* 1 *(exhibir)* to flaunt. 2 *(poseer)* to hold.

ostra *nf* oyster.

otoño *nm* GB autumn; US fall.

otorgar *vt* *(conceder)* to grant; *(premio)* to award.

otro,-a *adj* 1 *(con sustantivo en singular)* another; *(precedido de determinante o adjetivo posesivo)* other: *vino otra persona en su lugar*, another person came in his place; *la otra silla era más cómoda*, the other chair was more confortable. 2 *(con sustantivo en plural)* other: *entre otras cosas*, amongst other things. ► *pron* 1 *(singular)* another, another one. 2 **el otro, la otra** *(cosa, persona)* the other one. 3 **los otros, las otras** *(cosa)* the other ones, the others; *(personas)* the others. • **otro tanto** as much.

ovación *nf* ovation.

ovalado,-a *adj* oval.

ovario *nm* ovary.

oveja *nf* sheep

óvulo *nm* ovule.

oxidado,-a *adj* rusty.

oxígeno *nm* oxygen.

oyente *nmf* *(de la radio)* listener. ► *nm pl* **oyentes** audience.

ozono *nm* ozone. ■ **capa de ozono** ozone layer.

P

pabellón *nm* **1** *(edificio - aislado)* block, section; *(- anexo en feria)* pavilion. **2** *(de la oreja)* outer ear. ▪ **pabellón deportivo** sports hall.

paciencia *nf* patience.

paciente *adj-nmf* patient.

pacífico,-a *adj* peaceful.

pacto *nm* pact, agreement.

padecer *vt-vi* to suffer.

padre *nm* father.

padrenuestro *nm* Lord's Prayer.

padrino *nm* **1** *(de bautizo)* godfather. **2** *(de boda)* man who gives the bride away.

paella *nf* paella.

paga *nf* pay; *(de niños)* pocket money. ▪ **paga extra** bonus.

pagar *vt (compra, entrada)* to pay for; *(sueldo, alquiler, cuenta)* to pay; *(deuda)* to pay off.

página *nf* page.

pago *nm* payment. ▪ **pago por visión** pay per view.

país *nm* country.

paisaje *nm* **1** *(terreno)* landscape. **2** *(vista)* scenery.

paja *nf* straw.

pajarería *nf* pet shop.

pajarita *nf* **1** *(lazo)* bow tie. **2** *(de papel)* paper bird.

pájaro *nm* bird. ▪ **pájaro carpintero** woodpecker.

pala *nf* **1** *(para cavar)* spade. **2** *(de pelota)* bat.

palabra *nf* word. • **tener la palabra** to have the floor. ▪ **palabra clave** keyword.

palabrota *nf* swearword.

palacio *nm* palace. ▪ **palacio de congresos** conference centre (US center); **palacio de deportes** sports centre (US center).

paladar *nm* palate.

palanca *nf* lever. ▪ **palanca de cambio** gear lever, gearstick.

palangana *nf* washbasin.

palco *nm* box. ▪ **palco de autoridades** royal box.

pálido,-a *adj* pale.

palillo *nm* **1** *(mondadientes)* toothpick. **2** *(de tambor)* drumstick. ▪ **palillos chinos** chopsticks.

paliza *nf* **1** *(zurra)* beating, thrashing. **2** *(derrota)* defeat. **3** *fam (pesadez)* bore.

palma *nf* **1** *(planta)* palm tree. **2** *(de la mano)* palm.

palmera *nf* palm tree.

palo *nm* **1** *(vara)* stick. **2** *(mástil)* mast. • **a palo seco** on its own. ▪ **palo de golf** golf club.

paloma *nf* dove, pigeon.

palomitas *nf pl* popcorn.

palpitación *nf* palpitation.

pamela *nf* sun hat.

pan *nm (alimento)* bread; *(hogaza)* round loaf; *(barra)* French loaf. ▪ **pan de molde** sliced bread; **pan integral** wholemeal bread; **pan rallado** breadcrumbs.

pana *nf* corduroy.

panadería *nf* bakery, baker's.

panal *nm* honeycomb.

pancarta *nf* placard.

páncreas *nm* pancreas.

panda *nm* panda.

pandereta *nf* small tambourine.

panel *nm* panel.

panfleto *nm* pamphlet.

pánico *nm* panic.

panorama *nm* panorama, view.

pantalla *nf* 1 *(gen)* screen. 2 *(de lámpara)* shade.

pantalón *nm* trousers. ▪ **pantalón corto** shorts; **pantalón vaquero** jeans.

pantano *nm* (*ciénaga*) marsh; *(embalse)* reservoir.

pantera *nf* panther.

pantorrilla *nf* calf.

pañal *nm* GB nappy ; US diaper.

paño *nm* 1 *(tela)* cloth, material. 2 *(trapo para polvo)* duster. ▪ **paño de cocina** tea cloth, tea towel.

pañuelo *nm* 1 *(para sonarse)* handkerchief. 2 *(complemento)* scarf. ▪ **pañuelo de papel** tissue.

papa *nm* *(pontífice)* pope.

papá *nm* fam dad, daddy. ▪ **Papá Noel** Father Christmas.

papagayo *nm* parrot.

papel *nm* 1 *(material)* paper. 2 *(hoja)* piece of paper, sheet of paper. 3 *(en obra, película)* role, part. ▪ **papel de aluminio** aluminium foil; **papel de fumar** cigarette paper; **papel de lija** sandpaper; **papel de plata** silver paper, tinfoil; **papel higiénico** toilet paper; **papel pintado** wallpaper.

papelera *nf* 1 *(en oficina)* wastepaper basket. 2 *(en la calle)* GB litter bin; US litter basket.

papelería *nf* stationer's.

paperas *nf pl* mumps.

papilla *nf* 1 *(para enfermo)* pap. 2 *(para bebé)* baby food.

paquete *nm* *(de libros, ropa)* package, parcel; *(de tabaco, folios, galletas)* packet; *(de azúcar, harina)* bag. ▪ **paquete postal** parcel.

par *adj* even. ► *nm (pareja)* pair. ● **a la par** 1 *(al mismo tiempo)* at the same time. 2 *(juntos)* together; **de par en par** wide open; **sin par** matchless.

para *prep* 1 *(finalidad)* for, to, in order to: *para ahorrar dinero*, (in order) to save money. 2 *(dirección)* for, to: *el tren para Toledo*, the train to Toledo; *para adelante*, forwards; *para atrás*, backwards. 3 *(tiempo, fechas límites)* by: *déjalo para luego*, leave it for later. ● **para entonces**

by then; **para que** in order that, so that; **¿para qué?** what for?

parabrisas *nm* GB windscreen; US windshield.

paracaídas *nm* parachute.

parachoques *nm (de coche)* GB bumper; US fender.

parada *nf* 1 *(gen)* stop. 2 DEP save. ▪ **parada de taxis** GB taxi stand; US cab stand.

parado,-a *adj* 1 *(quieto)* still, motionless. 2 *(desempleado)* unemployed. ● **salir bien/mal parado de algo** to come off well/badly out of STH.

parador *nm* hotel.

paraguas *nm* umbrella.

paraíso *nm* paradise. ▪ **paraíso fiscal** tax haven.

paraje *nm* spot, place.

paralelo,-a *adj* parallel.

parálisis *nf* paralysis. ▪ **parálisis cerebral** cerebral palsy.

paralítico,-a *adj-nm,f* paralytic.

paralizarse *vpr* 1 *(miembro)* to be paralysed. 2 *(actividad)* to come to a standstill.

parapente *nm (deporte)* paragliding; *(paracaídas)* paraglider.

parar(se) *vt-vi-vpr (gen)* to stop. ● **ir a parar** to end up; **sin parar** nonstop, without stopping.

pararrayos *nm* lightning conductor.

parásito *nm* parasite.

parche *nm* patch.

parchís *nm* GB ludo; US Parcheesi®.

parcial *adj* partial. ▪ *nm (examen)* mid-term exam.

parecer *vi* 1 *(por cómo se percibe)* to seem; *(por su aspecto externo)* to look. 2 *(opinar)* to think: *si te parece bien...*, if it's all right with you... 3 *(aparentar)* to look as if: *parece que va a llover*, it looks as if it's going to rain. ▪ *vpr* **parecerse** 1 to look alike, be alike: *Hugo y su hermano se parecen*, Hugo and his brother look alike. 2 to look like: *Hugo se parece a su padre*, Hugo looks like his father. ▪ *nm (opinión)* opinion. ● **al parecer** apparently.

parecido,-a *adj* similar.

pared *nf* wall.

pareja *nf* 1 *(gen)* pair. 2 *(de personas)* couple. 3 *(de baile, compañero)* partner. ● **hacer buena pareja** to be two of a kind. ▪ **pareja de hecho** unmarried couple.

parentesco *nm* kinship, relationship.

paréntesis *nm* 1 *(signo)* parenthesis, bracket. 2 *(pausa)* break, interruption. ● **entre paréntesis** in brackets.

pariente,-a *nm,f* relative.

parir *vi* to give birth.

parking *nm (público)* GB carpark; US parking lot; *(particular)* garage: *una plaza de parking,* a parking space.

parlamento *nm* parliament.

paro *nm* 1 *(desempleo)* unemployment. 2 *(interrupción)* stoppage. 3 *(dinero)* unemployment benefit. • **estar en el paro** to be out of work, be unemployed. ■ **paro cardiaco** cardiac arrest.

párpado *nm* eyelid.

parque *nm* park. ■ **parque de atracciones** funfair; **parque infantil** children's playground; **parque natural** nature reserve; **parque temático** theme park.

parqué *nm* parquet.

parra *nf* grapevine.

párrafo *nm* paragraph.

parrilla *nf* grill. • **a la parrilla** grilled. ■ **parrilla de salida** starting grid.

parrillada *nf* mixed grill.

parte *nf* 1 *(gen)* part. 2 *(en contrato)* party. 3 *(de un partido)* half. • **a partes iguales** in equal shares; **de parte de** on behalf of, from; **¿de parte de quién?** who's calling?; **en ninguna parte** nowhere; **por todas partes** everywhere; **por una parte...**, **por otra** on the one hand..., on the other hand... ■ **parte facultativo** medical report;

parte meteorológico weather report.

participación *nf* 1 *(colaboración)* participation. 2 *(de lotería)* share.

participante *nmf* participant.

participar *vi (tomar parte)* to take part, participate. ► *vt (notificar)* to notify, inform.

participio *nm* participle.

partícula *nf* particle.

particular *adj* 1 *(específico)* particular. 2 *(especial)* special. 3 *(privado)* private. • **sin otro particular** yours faithfully.

partida *nf* 1 *(salida)* departure, leave. 2 *(documento)* certificate. 3 *(de juego)* game.

partidario,-a *nm,f* supporter.

partido *nm* 1 *(grupo)* party, group. 2 *(partida)* game, match. • **sacar partido de** to profit from; **tomar partido** to take sides. ■ **partido amistoso** friendly match.

partir *vt* 1 *(separar)* to divide, split. 2 *(romper)* to break, crack. ► *vi (irse)* to leave, set out, set off. ► *vpr* **partirse** to split up, break up. • **a partir de hoy** from today onwards.

partitura *nf* score.

parto *nm* (child)birth, delivery. ■ **parto provocado** induced labour (US labor); **parto sin dolor** painless childbirth.

pasa *nf* raisin.

pasadizo *nm* passage.

pasado,-a *adj* **1** *(anterior)* past, gone by: *el lunes pasado*, last Monday. **2** *(último)* last. **3** *(carne)* overdone. ▸ *nm* **pasado** *(momento anterior)* past; *(de un verbo)* past tense. •**pasadas las...** after...; **las... pasadas** gone...: *son las cuatro pasadas*, it's gone four.

pasaje *nm* **1** *(billete)* ticket. **2** *(pasajeros)* passengers *pl.* **3** *(calle)* passage, alley. **4** *(de texto)* passage.

pasajero,-a *adj* passing. ▸ *nm,f* passenger.

pasamanos *nm* handrail.

pasamontañas *nm* balaclava.

pasaporte *nm* passport.

pasar *vi* **1** *(gen)* to pass. **2** *(entrar)* to come in, go in. **3** *(cesar)* to come to an end. **4** *(límite)* to exceed: *pasa de la edad que piden*, he is over the age they are asking for. **5** *(ocurrir)* to happen. **6** *fam (mostrar poco interés)* not to be bothered. ▸ *vt* **1** *(entregar)* to pass. **2** *(página)* to turn. **3** *(límite)* to go beyond. **4** *(aventajar)* to surpass, beat. **5** *(adelantar)* to overtake. **6** *(tiempo)* to spend. ▸ *vpr* **pasarse 1** *(excederse)* to go too far, exaggerate. **2** *(pudrirse)* to go off. **3** *(ir)* to go by,

walk past. • **pasar por** to be considered; **pasarlo bien/ mal** to have a good/bad time; **¿qué pasa?** what's the matter?, what's wrong?

pasarela *nf (de barco)* walkway; *(de modelos)* catwalk.

pasatiempo *nm* pastime, hobby.

Pascua *nf (cristiana)* Easter; *(judía)* Passover. ▸ *nf pl* **Pascuas** Christmas.

pase *nm* **1** *(gen)* pass, permit. **2** *(de película)* showing.

pasear *vt* to walk. ▸ *vi-vpr* **pasear(se)** to go for a walk.

paseo *nm* **1** *(a pie)* walk, stroll; *(en coche)* drive; *(en bici, a caballo)* ride. **2** *(calle)* avenue, promenade. • **dar un paseo** to go for a walk. ■ **paseo marítimo** sea front, promenade.

pasillo *nm (de casa)* corridor; *(de avión)* aisle.

pasión *nf* passion.

pasivo,-a *adj* passive. ▸ *nm* **pasivo** liabilities.

paso *nm* **1** *(al caminar)* step, footstep. **2** *(camino)* passage, way. • **a dos pasos** just round the corner; **abrirse paso** to force one's way through; **"Ceda el paso"** "Give way"; **de paso 1** on the way: *me pilla de paso al trabajo*, it's on my way to work. **2** in passing: *lo dijo de paso*, he mentioned it in passing; **estar de paso** to be passing through; **"Prohibido el paso"** "No entry". ■ **paso a nivel** GB level crossing; US grade crossing; **paso de cebra** zebra crossing; **paso de peatones** pedestrian crossing; **paso elevado** GB flyover; US overpass; **paso subterráneo** underpass.

pasta *nf* 1 *(masa)* paste; *(de pan)* dough. 2 *(fideos, macarrones, etc.)* pasta. 3 *(pastelito)* cake. 4 *fam (dinero)* dough, money. ■ **pasta dentífrica** toothpaste.

pastar *vt-vi* to pasture, graze.

pastel *nm* 1 *(tipo bizcocho)* cake; *(tipo empanada)* pie, tart. 2 *(colores, etc.)* pastel.

pastelería *nf* cake shop.

pastilla *nf* 1 *(medicamento)* tablet, pill. 2 *(de jabón)* cake, bar.

pasto *nm* pasture.

pastor,-ra *nm,f (hombre)* shepherd; *(mujer)* shepherdess.

pata¹ *nf* 1 *(gen)* leg. 2 *(garra)* paw. 3 *(pezuña)* hoof. ● **a cuatro patas** on all fours; **a la pata coja** hopping; **meter la pata** *fam* to put one's foot in it; **patas arriba** upside down. ■ **patas de gallo** crow's feet.

pata² *nf (ave)* female duck.

patada *nf* kick.

patata *nf* potato. ■ **patatas fritas** 1 *(de bolsa)* GB crisps; US potato chips. 2 *(de sartén)* GB chips; US French fries.

paté *nm* paté.

patente *adj* patent, evident. ▶ *nf* patent.

paterno,-a *adj* paternal.

patín *nm* 1 skate. 2 *(de agua)* pedalo. ■ **patines de ruedas** roller skates; **patines en línea** rollerblades.

patinaje *nm* skating. ■ **patinaje artístico** figure skating; **patinaje sobre hielo** ice skating.

patinar *vi* 1 *(con patines)* to skate. 2 *(vehículo)* to skid.

patinazo *nm (con el coche)* skid.

patinete *nm* scooter.

patio *nm* 1 *(de casa)* patio. 2 *(de escuela)* playground. ■ **patio de butacas** GB stalls; US orchestra.

pato *nm* duck.

patria *nf* homeland.

patrimonio *nm* heritage, patrimony. ■ **patrimonio de la humanidad** world heritage.

patriotismo *nm* patriotism.

patrocinar *vt* to sponsor.

patrón,-ona *nm,f* 1 *(santo)* patron saint. 2 *(jefe)* employer, boss. 3 *(de barco)* skipper. ▶ *nm* **patrón** 1 *(de modista)* pattern. 2 *(modelo)* standard.

patrulla *nf* patrol.

pausa *nf* pause.

pavo *nm* turkey. ■ **pavo real** peacock.

payaso *nm* clown.
paz *nf* peace. • **dejar en paz** to leave alone; **hacer las paces** to make up, make it up.
peaje *nm* toll.
peatón *nm* pedestrian.
peca *nf* freckle.
pecado *nm* sin.
pecera *nf* (redonda) fishbowl; (rectangular) aquarium, fish tank.
pecho *nm* 1 (tórax) chest. 2 (de mujer - busto) bust; (- seno) breast. • **dar el pecho** to breast-feed.
pechuga *nf* breast.
peculiar *adj* peculiar.
pedal *nm* pedal.
pedazo *nm* piece, bit. • **hacer pedazos** to break to pieces.
pedestal *nm* pedestal.
pediatra *nmf* pediatrician.
pedido *nm* order. • **hacer un pedido** to place an order.
pedir *vt* 1 (gen) to ask for. 2 (mendigar) to beg. 3 (mercancías, en restaurante) to order: *¿qué has pedido de postre?*, what did you order for dessert?
pedo *nm fam* (ventosidad) fart. • **estar pedo** *fam* to be drunk.
pega *nf fam* (dificultad) snag.
pegamento *nm* glue.
pegar[1] *vt* 1 (adherir - gen) to stick; (- con pegamento) to glue. 2 (arrimar) to put. ► *vi* (combi-

nar) to match: *ese color no pega en el salón*, that colour doesn't look right in the living room. ► *vpr* **pegarse** (adherirse) to stick.
pegar[2] *vt* 1 (golpear) to hit. 2 (dar) to give: *deja ya de pegar gritos*, stop shouting. ► *vpr* **pegarse** (golpearse) to hit each other.
pegatina *nf* sticker.
peinado *nm* hair style.
peinar *vt* (con peine) to comb; (con cepillo) to brush. ► *vpr* **peinarse** to comb one's hair.
peine *nm* comb.
peladilla *nf* sugared almond.
pelar *vt* 1 (fruta, verdura) to peel. 2 (persona) to cut SB's hair. ► *vpr* **pelarse** 1 (perder piel) to peel. 2 (cortarse el pelo) to get one's hair cut.
peldaño *nm* step.
pelea *nf* fight, quarrel.
pelear(se) *vi-vpr* 1 (gen) to fight, quarrel. 2 (a golpes) to come to blows.
peletería *nf* fur shop, furrier's.
pelícano *nm* pelican.
película *nf* film. ■ **película de acción** adventure film; **película de miedo** horror film; **película de suspense** thriller; **película del oeste** western; **película muda** silent movie.
peligro *nm* danger.

peligroso,-a *adj* dangerous.
pelirrojo,-a *adj* red-haired. ▶ *nm,f* redhead.
pellizco *nm* pinch.
pelo *nm* 1 *(gen)* hair. 2 *(de barba)* whisker. 3 *(de animal)* coat, fur. ● **no tener pelos en la lengua** to speak one's mind; **por los pelos** by the skin of one's teeth; **tomarle el pelo a** ALGN to pull SB's leg; **venir a pelo** to be just what SB needs.
pelota *nf* ball. ● **en pelotas** *fam* naked; **hacer la pelota a** ALGN *fam* to suck up to SB. ▪ **pelota vasca** pelota.
pelotón *nm* squad.
peluca *nf* wig.
peluche *nm* plush.
peluquería *nf* hairdresser's.
peluquín *nm* hairpiece.
pelusa *nf* fluff.
pelvis *nf* pelvis.
pena *nf* 1 *(tristeza)* grief, sorrow. 2 *(lástima)* pity. 3 *(castigo)* penalty, punishment. ● **valer la pena** to be worth while.
penalti *nm* penalty.
pendiente *adj* 1 *(por resolver)* pending. 2 *(deuda)* outstanding. 3 *(atento): estaba pendiente de todos los detalles,* none of the details escaped him, he missed nothing. ▶ *nf* slope. ▶ *nm* earring.
pene *nm* penis.

penetrar *vt* 1 *(atravesar)* to penetrate. 2 *(líquido)* to permeate.
península *nf* peninsula.
pensamiento *nm* 1 *(idea, facultad)* thought. 2 *(mente)* mind. 3 *(flor)* pansy.
pensar *vt-vi* to think. ● **¡ni pensarlo!** no way!, don't even think about it!; **sin pensar** without thinking.
pensión *nf* 1 *(dinero)* pension. 2 *(residencia)* boarding house. ▪ **media pensión** half board; **pensión completa** full board; **pensión de jubilación** retirement pension.
pensionista *nmf* pensioner.
pentágono *nm* pentagon.
pentagrama *nm* stave, staff.
penúltimo,-a *adj-nm,f* penultimate.
peña *nf* *(roca)* rock.
peón *nm* 1 *(trabajador)* unskilled labourer. 2 *(en damas)* man. 3 *(en ajedrez)* pawn.
peor *adj-adv* 1 *(comparativo)* worse. 2 *(superlativo)* worst.
pepinillo *nm* gherkin.
pepino *nm* cucumber.
pepita *nf* 1 *(de fruta)* seed, pip. 2 *(de metal)* nugget.
pequeño,-a *adj* 1 *(de tamaño)* little, small. 2 *(de edad)* young, small: *tengo dos hermanos pequeños,* I have to younger brothers. ● **de pequeño,-a** as a child.

pera *nf* pear.

percance *nm* mishap.

percatarse *vpr* to notice.

percebe *nm* goose barnacle.

percha *nf (individual)* hanger; *(de gancho)* coat hook.

perchero *nm (en la pared)* coat rack; *(de pie)* coat stand.

percibir *vt (notar)* to perceive.

perdedor,-ra *nm,f* loser.

perder *vt* 1 *(gen)* to lose. 2 *(malgastar)* to waste. 3 *(tren, avión etc)* to miss. ► *vi* 1 *(salir derrotado)* to lose. 2 *(empeorar)* to go downhill. ► *vpr* **perderse** 1 *(extraviarse)* to go astray, get lost. 2 *(acontecimiento)* to miss.

pérdida *nf* 1 *(extravío)* loss. 2 *(de tiempo, dinero)* waste. 3 *(escape)* leak. • **no tener pérdida** to be easy to find: *no tiene pérdida*, you can't miss it.

perdido,-a *adj* 1 *(gen)* lost: *objetos perdidos*, lost property. 2 *(desperdiciado)* wasted.

perdigón *nm* pellet.

perdiz *nf* partridge.

perdón *nm* 1 *(indulto)* pardon. 2 *(de pecado)* forgiveness. • **con perdón** if you'll pardon the expression; **pedir perdón** to apologize; **¡perdón!** sorry!; **¿perdón?** pardon?, sorry?

perdonar *vt* 1 *(error, ofensa)* to forgive. 2 *(deuda)* to let off. 3 *(excusar)* to excuse.

perdurar *vt* to last, endure.

peregrino,-a *nm,f* pilgrim.

perejil *nm* parsley.

perenne *adj* perennial, perpetual: *árbol de hoja perenne*, evergreen tree.

pereza *nf* laziness, idleness.

perfección *nf* perfection.

perfecto,-a *adj* 1 *(ideal)* perfect. 2 *(rematado)* complete: *un perfecto desconocido*, a complete stranger.

perfil *nm* profile.

perforar *vt* 1 *(gen)* to perforate. 2 *(uso técnico)* to drill, bore.

perfume *nm* perfume, scent.

perfumería *nf* perfumery, perfume shop.

periferia *nf* 1 *(gen)* periphery. 2 *(afueras)* outskirts.

perilla *nf* goatee.

perímetro *nm* perimeter.

periódico,-a *adj* periodic. ► *nm* **periódico** newspaper.

periodista *nmf* journalist.

periodo *nm* period.

periquito *nm* parakeet; *(australiano)* budgerigar.

periscopio *nm* periscope.

perito *nm* expert.

perjudicar *vt* to damage, harm.

perjudicial *adj* harmful.

perjuicio *nm (moral)* injury; *(material)* damage.

perla *nf (joya)* pearl. ▪ **perla cultivada** cultured pearl.

permanecer *vi* to remain.
permanente *adj* permanent, lasting. ► *nf (del pelo)* perm.
• **hacerse la permanente** to have one's hair permed.
permiso *nm* 1 *(autorización)* permission. 2 *(documento)* permit. 3 *(soldado)* leave. • **con su permiso** if you'll excuse me.
■ **permiso de conducir** driving licence.
permitir *vt* to permit, allow, let. ► *vpr* **permitirse** to take the liberty of.
pero *conj* but.
peroné *nm* fibula.
perpendicular *adj-nf* perpendicular.
perra *nf* bitch.
perro *nm* dog. • **"Cuidado con el perro"** "Beware of the dog". ■ **perro callejero** stray dog; **perro guardián** guard dog.
persecución *nf* 1 *(seguimiento)* pursuit. 2 *(represión)* persecution.
perseguir *vt* 1 *(delincuente, presa)* to pursue, chase. 2 *(pretender)* to be after.
persiana *nf (gen)* blind; *(enrollable)* roller blind; *(de tablas)* shutter.
persistente *adj* persistent.
persona *nf* person: *una persona, dos personas*, one person, two people. ■ **persona mayor** adult, grown-up.

personaje *nm* 1 *(en libro, etc)* character. 2 *(persona famosa)* celebrity.
personal *adj* personal. ► *nm* personnel, staff.
personalidad *nf* 1 *(carácter)* personality. 2 *(persona famosa)* public figure.
perspectiva *nf* 1 *(gen)* perspective. 2 *(posibilidad)* prospect. 3 *(vista)* view.
persuadir *vi* to persuade, convince.
pertenecer *vi* to belong
pertenencias *nf pl* belongings.
pértiga *nf* pole.
perverso,-a *adj* perverse.
pesa *nf* weight: *hacer pesas*, to do weight training.
pesadilla *nf* nightmare.
pesado,-a *adj* 1 *(gen)* heavy. 2 *(aburrido)* dull, tiresome, boring.
pésame *nm* condolences, expression of sympathy. • **dar el pésame** to offer one's condolences.
pesar *vt-vi (gen)* to weigh. ► *vi* 1 *(tener mucho peso)* to be heavy. 2 *(sentir)* to be sorry, regret. ► *nm* 1 *(pena)* sorrow, grief. 2 *(arrepentimiento)* regret. • **a pesar de** in spite of, despite.
pesca *nf* fishing. ■ **pesca de arrastre** trawling; **pesca submarina** underwater fishing.

pescadería *nf* fishmonger's.
pescadilla *nf* small hake.
pescado *nm* fish.
pescador *nm* fisherman.
pescar *vi* to fish.
pesebre *nm* (de Navidad) crib.
pesimista *adj* pessimistic. ▶ *nmf* pessimist.
pésimo,-a *adj* very bad.
peso *nm* 1 (gen) weight. 2 (balanza) scales, balance. 3 DEP shot: *lanzamiento de peso*, shot put; *levantamiento de peso*, weight-lifting.
pestaña *nf* 1 (del ojo) eyelash. 2 (de cartón) flap.
peste *nf* 1 (epidemia) plague. 2 (mal olor) stink, stench.
pestillo *nm* bolt.
pétalo *nm* petal.
petanca *nf* petanque.
petardo *nm* (cohete) banger.
petición *nf* request.
petirrojo *nm* robin.
peto *nm* bib.
petróleo *nm* oil, petroleum.
petrolero *nm* oil tanker.
pez *nm* fish.
pezón *nm* nipple.
pezuña *nf* hoof.
pianista *nmf* pianist.
piano *nm* piano: *yo toco el piano*, I can play the piano. ▪ **piano de cola** grand piano.
piar *vi* to chirp.
piara *nf* herd of pigs.
pica *nf* 1 (lanza) pike. 2 (de toros) goad.

picado,-a *adj* 1 (ajo, cebolla) chopped; (carne) GB minced; US ground. 2 (mar) choppy. 3 (vino) sour. 4 (diente) decayed. 5 *fam* (ofendido) offended. • **caer en picado** to plummet.
picadura *nf* 1 (de mosquito, serpiente) bite; (de abeja, avispa) sting. 2 (tabaco) cut tobacco.
picante *adj* 1 (sabor) hot, spicy. 2 (pícaro) spicy, naughty.
picaporte *nm* 1 (llamador) door knocker. 2 (pomo) door handle.
picar *vt* 1 (mosquito, serpiente) to bite; (abeja, avispa) to sting. 2 (algo de comer) to nibble. 3 (cebolla, patata, etc) to chop; (carne) GB to mince; US to grind; (hielo) to crush. ▶ *vi* 1 (sentir escozor) to itch. 2 (tomar algo de comer) to nibble. 3 (estar picante) to be spicy. ▶ *vpr* **picarse** 1 (fruta) to begin to go rotten. 2 (diente) to begin to decay. 3 (mar) to get choppy. 4 (enfadarse) to take offence (US offense).
pícaro,-a *adj* 1 (malicioso) mischievous. 2 (astuto) sly, crafty.
pichón *nm* young pigeon.
picnic *nm* picnic.
pico *nm* 1 (de ave) beak. 2 (de montaña) peak. 3 (herramienta) pick, pickaxe. 4 (cantidad) small amount: *tres mil y pico*, three thousand odd.

picor *nm* itch.

picotear *vt* **1** *(ave)* to peck at. **2** *(persona)* to nibble.

pie *nm* **1** foot: *fuimos a pie*, we went on foot; *con los pies descalzos*, barefoot. **2** *(de página)* bottom. **3** *(de columna, lámpara)* base, stand. • **al pie de la letra** literally; **dar pie a** to give, rise to; **ponerse de pie** to stand up. ▪ **pie de atleta** athlete's foot; **pies planos** flat feet.

piedad *nf* **1** *(devoción)* piety. **2** *(compasión)* pity, mercy.

piedra *nf* **1** *(gen)* stone. **2** *(de mechero)* flint. ▪ **piedra pómez** pumice stone; **piedra preciosa** precious stone.

piel *nf* **1** *(de persona)* skin. **2** *(de animal - gen)* skin; *(- de vaca, elefante)* hide; *(- de foca, zorro, visón)* fur. **3** *(cuero - tratado)* leather; *(- sin tratar)* pelt. **4** *(de fruta - gen)* skin; *(- de naranja, manzana, patata)* peel. ▪ **piel de gallina** goose pimples.

pienso *nm* fodder.

pierna *nf* leg.

pieza *nf* piece. ▪ **pieza de recambio** spare part.

pigmento *nm* pigment.

pijama *nm* pyjamas.

pila *nf* **1** *(eléctrica)* battery. **2** *(de bautismo)* font.

píldora *nf* pill.

pillar *vt* *(atrapar)* to catch; *(atropellar)* to run over. ▶ *vpr*

pillarse to catch: *me he pillado el dedo con la puerta*, I caught my finger in the door.

pilotar *vt* *(avión)* to pilot; *(coche)* to drive.

piloto *nmf* *(de avión, barco)* pilot; *(de coche)* driver. ▶ *nm (luz - de coche)* tail light, rear light; *(- de aparato)* pilot light. ▶ *adj* pilot: *piso piloto*, show flat. ▪ **piloto automático** automatic pilot.

pimentón *nm* paprika.

pimienta *nf* pepper.

pimiento *nm* pepper. ▪ **pimiento morrón** sweet red pepper.

pinar *nm* pine grove.

pincel *nm* brush, paintbrush.

pinchadiscos *nmf fam* DJ, disc jockey.

pinchar *vt* **1** *(con objeto punzante)* to prick. **2** *(rueda)* to puncture. **3** *(globo, pelota)* to burst. **4** *fam (teléfono)* to tap. ▶ *vpr* **pincharse 1** *(persona)* to prick oneself. **2** *(rueda)* to puncture. **3** *(globo, pelota)* to burst.

pinchazo *nm* **1** *(punzada)* prick. **2** *(de rueda)* puncture, flat.

pincho *nm* **1** *(espina)* thorn, prickle. **2** *(aperitivo)* tapa, bar snack. ▪ **pincho moruno** kebab.

ping-pong® *nm* ping-pong®.

pingüino *nm* penguin.

pino *nm* pine tree.

pintada *nf* piece of graffiti.

pintalabios *nm* lipstick.

pintar *vt* to paint. ► *vpr* **pintarse** to make oneself up.

pintaúñas *nm* nail varnish.

pintor,-ra *nm,f* painter.

pintoresco,-a *adj* picturesque.

pintura *nf* **1** *(arte)* painting. **2** *(color, bote)* paint. **3** *(cuadro)* picture.

pinza *nf* **1** *(de cangrejo)* claw. **2** *(para la ropa)* peg. ► *nf pl* **pinzas** *(de cocina)* tongs; *(de manicura)* tweezers.

piña *nf* **1** *(fruta)* pineapple. **2** *(de pino)* pine cone.

piñón *nm (de pino)* pine nut.

piojo *nm* louse.

pionero,-a *adj* pioneering.

pipa[1] *nf (de tabaco)* pipe.

pipa[2] *nf* **1** *(de fruta)* pip, seed. **2** *(de girasol)* sunflower seed.

piragua *nf* canoe.

pirámide *nf* pyramid.

pirata *nm* pirate.

piropo *nm* compliment.

pirueta *nf* pirouette, caper.

piruleta *nf* lollipop.

pirulí *nm* lollipop.

pisada *nf* **1** *(acción)* footstep. **2** *(huella)* footprint.

pisapapeles *nm* paperweight.

pisar *vt* to tread on, step on.

piscina *nf* swimming-pool.

piso *nm* **1** *(planta, suelo)* floor. **2** *(vivienda)* apartment; GB flat.

pista *nf* **1** *(rastro)* trail, track. **2** *(indicio)* clue. **3** *(de atletismo)* track; *(de tenis)* court; *(de esquí)* slope, ski run. **4** *(de circo)* ring. **5** *(de aterrizaje)* runway. ▪ **pista de baile** dance floor.

pistacho *nm* pistachio.

pistola *nf* pistol.

pistón *nm* piston.

pitar *vi (con silbato)* to blow a whistle; *(con claxon)* to blow one's horn. ► *vt (abuchear)* to boo at.

pitido *nm* whistle.

pitillera *nf* cigarette case.

pitillo *nm* cigarette.

pito *nm* whistle.

pizarra *nf* **1** *(roca)* slate. **2** *(de escuela)* blackboard.

pizca *nf* bit; *(de sal)* pinch.

pizza *nf* pizza.

placa *nf* **1** *(lámina)* plate. **2** *(inscrita)* plaque. **3** *(de policía)* badge. **4** *(de cocinar)* ring.

placer *nm* pleasure.

plaga *nf* plague, pest.

plan *nm* plan, project. ▪ **plan de estudios** syllabus.

plancha *nf* **1** *(de metal)* plate, sheet. **2** *(para planchar)* iron.

planchar *vt (gen)* to iron; *(traje, pantalón)* to press.

planear *vt* to plan. ► *vi (avión)* to glide.

planeta *nm* planet.

planificar *vt* to plan.

plano,-a *adj* flat, even. ► *nm* **plano 1** *(mapa)* plan, map. **2**

(en filmación) shot. ■ **primer plano** *(foto)* close-up.

planta *nf* 1 *(gen)* plant. 2 *(del pie)* sole. 3 *(piso)* floor. ■ **planta baja** GB ground floor; US first floor.

plantación *nf* plantation.

plantar *vt (en tierra)* to plant; *(semilla)* to sow. ● **dejar a ALGN plantado** to stand SB up.

plantear *vt* 1 *(problema)* to set out. 2 *(pregunta)* to pose, raise. ► *vpr* **plantearse** 1 *(pensar)* to think about. 2 *(cuestión)* to arise.

plantilla *nf* 1 *(de zapato)* insole. 2 *(patrón)* model, pattern. 3 *(personal)* staff.

plasma *nm* plasma.

plástico,-a *adj* plastic. ► *nm* **plástico** plastic.

plata *nf* silver.

plataforma *nf* platform. ■ **plataforma de lanzamiento** launchpad; **plataforma petrolífera** oil rig.

plátano *nm* 1 *(fruta)* banana. 2 *(árbol)* plane tree.

platea *nf* stalls.

platillo *nm* 1 *(plato)* saucer. 2 *(de balanza)* pan. 3 *(instrumento)* cymbal. ■ **platillo volante** flying saucer.

plato *nm* 1 *(gen)* dish. 2 *(en comida)* course. ● **fregar los platos** to wahs the dishes; GB to do the washing-up, wash up.

plató *nm* set.

playa *nf* beach.

playeras *nf pl* tennis shoes.

plaza *nf* 1 *(de pueblo, ciudad)* square. 2 *(mercado)* marketplace. 3 *(sitio)* space. 4 *(asiento)* seat. 5 *(empleo)* position, post. ■ **plaza de toros** bullring; **plaza mayor** main square.

plazo *nm* 1 *(de tiempo)* period. 2 *(pago)* GB instalment; US installment.

plegable *adj* folding.

plegar *vt* to fold.

pleito *nm* litigation, lawsuit.

pleno,-a *adj* full, complete.

pliegue *nm* 1 *(doblez)* fold. 2 *(en ropa)* pleat.

plomo *nm* 1 *(metal)* lead. 2 *(de la luz)* fuse: *se fundieron los plomos*, the fuses blew.

pluma *nf* 1 *(de ave)* feather. 2 *(de escribir)* quill pen; *(estilográfica)* fountain pen.

plumero *nm* feather duster.

plural *adj-nm* plural.

población *nf* 1 *(habitantes)* population. 2 *(ciudad)* city, town; *(pueblo)* village. ■ **población activa** working population.

poblado,-a *adj* 1 *(zona)* populated. 2 *(barba)* thick. ► *nm* **poblado** settlement.

pobre *adj* poor.

pobreza *nf* poverty.

pocilga *nf* pigsty.

poco,-a *adj (singular)* little, not much; *(plural)* few, not many. ▶ *pron (singular)* little; *(plural)* not many. ▶ *adv* little, not much. • **dentro de poco** soon; GB presently; **hace poco** not long ago; **poco a poco** little by little; **por poco** nearly.

podar *vt* to prune.

poder *vt* **1** *(gen)* can. **2** *(tener permiso para)* can, may: *¿puedo fumar?*, may I smoke? **3** *(en conjeturas)* may, might: *puede que esté enfermo*, he may be ill, he might be ill. ▶ *nm (capacidad, facultad)* power. • **no poder con** not to be able to cope with; **no poder más** to be unable to do any more; **¿se puede?** may I come in?

podio *nm* podium.

podrido,-a *adj* rotten.

poema *nm* poem.

poesía *nf* **1** *(género)* poetry. **2** *(poema)* poem.

poeta *nmf* poet.

poetisa *nf* poetess.

polar *adj* polar.

polémico,-a *adj* polemic.

polen *nm* pollen.

policía *nf* police. ▶ *nmf (hombre)* policeman; *(mujer)* policewoman.

polideportivo *nm* GB sports centre; US sports center.

polígono *nm* polygon. ▪ **polígono industrial** industrial estate.

polilla *nf* moth.

política *nf* **1** *(ciencia)* politics: *se dedica a la política*, he's in politics. **2** *(método)* policy.

político,-a *adj* political. ▶ *nm,f* politician.

póliza *nf* certificate, policy.

polizón *nm* stowaway.

pollería *nf* poultry shop.

pollo *nm* chicken. ▪ **pollo asado** roast chicken.

polo *nm* **1** *(gen)* pole. **2** *(helado)* GB ice lolly; US Popsicle®. **3** *(jersey)* polo shirt.

polvo *nm* **1** *(en aire, muebles)* dust. **2** *(en farmacia, cosmética)* powder. • **estar hecho polvo** *fam* to be knackered. ▪ **polvos de talco** talcum powder.

pólvora *nf* gunpowder.

polvorón *nm* crumbly shortcake.

pomada *nf* cream.

pomelo *nm* grapefruit.

pomo *nm* knob, handle.

pómulo *nm* cheekbone.

ponche *nm* punch.

poner *vt* **1** *(gen)* to place, put, set. **2** *(instalar)* GB to install; US to instal. **3** *(encender)* to turn on, put on. **4** *(huevos)* to lay. **5** *(estar escrito)* to say: *¿qué pone en ese letrero?*, what does that sign say? **6** *(establecer)* to open: *han puesto un bar*, they've opened a bar. **7** *(programa, película)* to show. **8 poner + adj** to make: *me pone enfermo*, he makes me sick. ► *vpr* **ponerse 1** *(sombrero, ropa)* to put on. **2** *(sol)* to set. **3** *(volverse)* to become, get, turn. **4** *(al teléfono - cogerlo)* to answer the phone; *(- acudir)* to come to the phone: *dígale que se ponga*, tell her to come to the phone. • **ponerse a + inf** to start to + *inf*.

popa *nf* stern.

popular *adj* popular.

por *prep* **1** *(causa)* because of: *llegaron tarde por la nieve*, they were late because of the snow; *lo hice por ti*, I did it for you. **2** *(tiempo)* at, in; *(duración)* for: *por la noche*, at night; *vino por poco tiempo*, he didn't stay for long. **3** *(lugar)* along, in, on, by, up, down: *iremos por la autopista*, we'll go by motorway. **4** *(medio, agente)* by: *por avión*, by air. **5** *(distribución)* per: *cinco por ciento*, five per cent. **6** *(en multiplicación)* times. **7** *(medidas)* by: *mide tres metros por dos*, it measures three metres by two. • *¿por qué?* why?; **por supuesto** of course; **por tanto** therefore.

porcelana *nf* **1** *(material)* porcelain. **2** *(vajilla)* china.

porcentaje *nm* percentage.

porche *nm* porch.

porción *nf* **1** *(parte)* portion, part. **2** *(cuota)* share.

poro *nm* pore.

porque *conj* because.

porquería *nf* dirt, filth.

porra *nf* club; *(de policía)* GB truncheon; US nightstick.

portaaviones *nm* aircraft carrier.

portada *nf* **1** *(de libro)* title page. **2** *(de revista)* cover. **3** *(de periódico)* front page. **4** *(de disco)* sleeve.

portador,-ra *nm,f* bearer; *(de virus)* carrier.

portaequipajes *nm* luggage rack.

portal *nm* **1** *(entrada)* doorway; *(vestíbulo)* entrance hall. **2** *(de Internet)* portal.

portarse *vpr* to behave, act.

portátil *adj* portable. ► *nm* *(ordenador)* laptop, portable.

portavoz *nmf* *(gen)* spokesperson.

portería *nf* **1** *(de edificio)* porter's lodge. **2** *(en fútbol)* goal.

portero,-a *nm,f* **1** *(de edificio)* doorkeeper, porter. **2** *(guardameta)* goalkeeper. ▪ **portero automático** entry phone.

porvenir *nm* future.

posada *nf* lodging-house, inn.

posar *vi* to pose. ► *vpr* **posarse 1** *(pájaro)* to alight, perch, sit. **2** *(sedimento)* to settle.

posdata *nf* postscript.

poseer *vt* to own, possess.

posesión *nf* possession.
posesivo,-a *adj* possessive
posibilidad *nf* possibility.
posible *adj* possible. • **hacer todo lo posible** to do one's best.
posición *nf* position.
positivo,-a *adj* positive.
poso *nm* **1** *(de mineral)* sediment. **2** *(de café, vino)* dregs.
posponer *vt* to postpone, delay, put off.
postal *adj* postal. ► *nf* postcard.
poste *nm* post.
póster *nm* poster.
posterior *adj* **1** *(de atrás)* back, rear. **2** *(más tarde)* later.
postre *nm* dessert.
postura *nf* **1** *(posición)* posture, position. **2** *(actitud)* attitude, stance.
potable *adj* drinkable.
potaje *nm* stew.
potencia *nf* power.
potente *adj* powerful.
potro,-a *nm,f* colt, foal. ► *nm* **potro** *(para gimnasia)* vaulting horse.
pozo *nm* **1** *(de agua, petróleo)* well. **2** *(en mina)* shaft.
práctica *nf* practice. ► *nf pl* **prácticas** training.
practicar *vt* **1** *(idioma, profesión)* GB to practise; US to practice. **2** *(deporte)* to play, do. ► *vi* GB to practise; US to practice.

práctico,-a *adj* practical.
pradera *nf* prairie.
prado *nm* meadow.
precaución *nf* precaution. • **conducir con precaución** to drive carefully.
precedente *adj* preceding, prior, foregoing. ► *nm* precedent. • **sin precedentes** unprecedented.
precinto *nm* seal.
precio *nm* price. ■ **precio de fábrica** factory price; **precio de venta al público** retail price.
precioso,-a *adj* **1** *(valioso)* precious. **2** *(bello)* beautiful.
precipicio *nm* precipice.
precipitación *nf* **1** *(prisa)* rush, haste, hurry. **2** *(lluvia)* precipitation.
precipitarse **1** *(apresurarse)* to be hasty. **2** *(obrar sin reflexión)* to act rashly.
precisión *nf* precision,.
preciso,-a *adj* **1** *(exacto)* precise, exact, accurate. **2** *(necesario)* necessary.
precocinado,-a *adj* precooked.
precoz *adj* **1** *(niño)* precocious. **2** *(envejecimiento, eyaculación)* premature.
predecir *vt* to predict, foretell.
predicar *vt* to preach.
predicción *nf* prediction; *(meteorológica)* forecast.

predominio *nm* predominance.

preferencia *nf* preference. • **tener preferencia** *(al volante)* to have right of way.

preferir *vt* to prefer.

prefijo *nm* prefix; *(telefónico)* code.

pregunta *nf* question.

preguntar *vt* to ask. ▶ *vpr* **preguntarse** to wonder.

prehistoria *nf* prehistory.

prejuicio *nm* prejudice.

prematuro,-a *adj* premature.

premiar *vt* 1 *(otorgar premio a)* to award a prize to. 2 *(recompensar)* to reward.

premio *nm* 1 *(en concurso, sorteo)* prize. 2 *(recompensa)* reward. ■ **premio gordo** jackpot.

prenda *nf* 1 *(de vestir)* garment. 2 *(garantía)* pledge.

prender *vt* 1 *(agarrar)* to seize. 2 *(sujetar)* to attach. ▶ *vi* *(fuego etc)* to catch.

prensa *nf* press. ■ **prensa amarilla** gutter press; **prensa del corazón** gossip magazines.

prensar *vt* to press.

preocupar(se) *vt-vpr* to worry.

preparación *nf* preparation.

preparado,-a *adj* ready, prepared.

preparar *vt* to prepare. ▶ *vpr* **prepararse** to get ready.

preparativos *nm pl* preparations, arrangements.

preposición *nf* preposition.

presa *nf* 1 *(cosa prendida)* prey. 2 *(embalse)* dam.

presencia *nf* presence. ■ **buena presencia** smart appearance.

presenciar *vt* *(asistir)* to be present at; *(contemplar)* to witness.

presentación *nf* 1 *(gen)* presentation. 2 *(de personas)* introduction.

presentador,-ra *nm,f* presenter, host.

presentar *vt* 1 *(gen)* to present. 2 *(mostrar)* to display, show. 3 *(personas)* to introduce. ▶ *vpr* **presentarse** *(comparecer)* to present oneself; *(candidato)* to stand.

presente *adj-nm* present. • **tener presente** to bear in mind.

preservar *vt* *(proteger)* to protect; *(conservar)* to preserve.

preservativo *nm* condom.

presidencia *nf* 1 *(de nación)* presidency. 2 *(en reunión)* chairmanship.

presidente,-a *nm,f* 1 *(de nación, club, etc)* president. 2 *(en reunión - hombre)* chairman; *(- mujer)* chairwoman.

presidir *vt* 1 *(nación)* to be president of. 2 *(reunión)* to chair.

presión *nf* pressure. ■ **presión arterial** blood pressure.

presionar *vt* **1** *(apretar)* to press. **2** *(coaccionar)* to put pressure on.

preso,-a *nm,f* prisoner.

préstamo *nm (acción)* lending; *(dinero)* loan.

prestar *vt* **1** *(dejar prestado)* to lend, loan; *(pedir prestado)* to borrow. **2** *(servicio)* to do, render. **3** *(ayuda)* to give. **4** *(atención)* to pay. ▸ *vpr* **prestarse 1** *(ofrecerse)* to lend oneself. **2** *(dar motivo)* to cause.

prestigio *nm* prestige.

presumir *vi* to be vain.

presupuesto *nm (cálculo anticipado)* estimate; *(coste)* budget.

pretender *vt* **1** *(querer)* to want to. **2** *(intentar)* to try to.

prevenir *vt* **1** *(prever)* to prevent. **2** *(advertir)* to warn.

previo,-a *adj* previous.

previsión *nf* forecast.

previsto,-a *adj: su llegada está prevista para las cinco,* he is expected to arrive at five; *había previsto todo,* she had thought of everything. • **según lo previsto** according to plan.

prima *nf* **1** bonus. **2** → primo, -a.

primavera *nf* spring.

primer *num* → primero,-a.

primera *nf* **1** *(clase)* first class. **2** *(marcha)* first gear

primero,-a *num* first. ▸ *adv* **primero** first. • **a primeros**

de mes at the beginning of the month. ▪ **primeros auxilios** first aid.

primitivo,-a *adj* primitive.

primo,-a *adj* **1** *(materia)* raw. **2** *(número)* prime. ▸ *nm,f* cousin.

princesa *nf* princess.

principal *adj* main, chief. ▸ *nm (piso)* first floor.

príncipe *nm* prince.

principiante,-a *nm,f* beginner.

principio *nm* **1** *(inicio)* beginning, start. **2** *(norma)* principle. • **al principio** at first; **en principio** in principle.

prioridad *nf* priority.

prisa *nf* hurry. • **darse prisa** to hurry, hurry up; **tener prisa** to be in a hurry.

prisión *nf (lugar)* prison, jail. • **en prisión preventiva** remanded in custody.

prisionero,-a *nm,f* prisoner.

prismáticos *nm pl* binoculars.

privado,-a *adj* private.

privar *vt* **1** *(despojar)* to deprive. **2** *(prohibir)* to forbid. ▸ *vpr* **privarse** to do without.

privilegio *nm* privilege.

proa *nf* prow, bow.

probabilidad *nf* probability.

probable *adj* probable, likely.

probador *nm* changing room.

probar *vt* **1** *(demostrar)* to prove. **2** *(comprobar)* to try, test. **3** *(vino, comida)* to taste, try. **4** *(prendas)* to try on.

problema *nm* problem.

procedencia *nf* **1** *(de persona, producto)* origin, source. **2** *(de tren)* point of departure.

proceder *vi (venir de)* to come.

procedimiento *nm* procedure, method.

procesar *vt* **1** *(dato, texto)* to process. **2** JUR to prosecute.

procesión *nf* procession.

proceso *nm* **1** *(gen)* process. **2** JUR trial.

proclamar *vt* to proclaim. ▶ *vpr* **proclamarse**: *se proclamó campeona*, she won the championship.

procurar *vt (intentar)* to try.

producción *nf* production.

producir *vt* **1** *(gen)* to produce. **2** *(causar)* to cause. ▶ *vpr* **producirse** to happen.

productividad *nf* productivity.

producto *nm* product.

productor,-ra *adj* productive. ▶ *nm,f* producer.

profesión *nf* profession.

profesional *adj-nmf* professional.

profesor,-ra *nm,f* teacher; *(de universidad)* lecturer.

profundidad *nf* depth.

profundo,-a *adj* **1** *(agujero, piscina)* deep. **2** *(pensamiento, misterio, etc)* profound.

programa *nm* **1** GB programme; US program. **2** INFORM program.

programación *nf* programming.

programador,-ra *nm,f* INFORM programmer.

programar *vt* **1** GB to programme; US to program. **2** INFORM to program.

progresar *vi* to progress.

progreso *nm* progress.

prohibición *nf* prohibition.

prohibir *vt (gen)* to forbid; *(por ley)* to prohibit, ban.

prolongar *vt (en el tiempo)* to prolong; *(de longitud)* to extend.

promedio *nm* average.

promesa *nf* promise.

prometer *vt* to promise.

prometido,-a *nm,f (hombre)* fiancé; *(mujer)* fiancée. ● **estar prometidos** to be engaged.

promoción *nf* **1** *(gen)* promotion. **2** *(curso)* class, year.

pronombre *nm* pronoun.

pronóstico *nm* **1** *(gen)* forecast. **2** *(médico)* prognosis.

pronto *adv* **1** *(inmediatamente)* soon. **2** *(rápidamente)* quickly. **3** *(temprano)* early. ● **de pronto** suddenly; **¡hasta pronto!** see you soon!; **tan pronto como...** as soon as...

pronunciar *vt* **1** *(palabra)* to pronounce. **2** *(discurso)* to make.

propaganda *nf* **1** POL propaganda. **2** *(anuncios)* advertising.

propiedad *nf* 1 *(derecho)* ownership. 2 *(objeto)* property. • **hablar con propiedad** to speak properly.

propietario,-a *nm,f* owner.

propina *nf* tip.

propio,-a *adj* 1 *(perteneciente)* own: *en defensa propia*, in self-defence. 2 *(indicado)* proper, appropriate. 3 *(particular)* typical, peculiar: *es muy propio de él*, it's very typical of him. 4 *(mismo - él)* himself; *(- ella)* herself; *(- cosa, animal)* itself: *el propio autor*, the author himself.

proponer *vt* to suggest, propose.

proporción *nf* proportion.

proporcionar *vt* to supply, give.

propósito *nm* intention. • **a propósito** *(adrede)* on purpose.

propuesta *nf* proposal.

prórroga *nf* 1 *(de un plazo)* extension. 2 *(en deporte)* GB extra time; US overtime.

prosa *nf* prose.

prospecto *nm* *(de propaganda)* leaflet; *(de medicina)* directions for use.

prosperar *vi* to prosper, thrive.

protagonista *nmf* 1 *(de película)* main character. 2 *(de obra de teatro)* lead.

protección *nf* protection.

proteger *vt* to protect.

proteína *nf* protein.

protesta *nf* protest.

protestar *vi* 1 to protest. 2 *(quejarse)* to complain.

provecho *nm* profit, benefit. • **¡buen provecho!** enjoy your meal!

proveedor,-ra *nm,f* supplier, purveyor.

provenir *vi* to come.

proverbio *nm* proverb, saying.

provincia *nf* province.

provisional *adj* provisional.

provisto,-a *adj* provided.

provocar *vt* 1 *(irritar)* to provoke. 2 *(causar)* to cause.

próximo,-a *adj* 1 *(cercano)* near, close. 2 *(siguiente)* next: *el mes próximo*, next month.

proyección *nf* 1 *(gen)* projection. 2 *(de película)* screening.

proyectil *nm* projectile.

proyecto *nm* 1 *(plan)* plan. 2 *(estudio, esquema)* project. ▪ **proyecto de ley** bill.

prudente *adj* *(sabio)* sensible, wise, prudent; *(cuidadoso)* careful.

prueba *nf* 1 *(demostración)* proof. 2 *(examen)* test. 3 *(deportiva)* event. 4 *(de delito)* piece of evidence. • **hacer la prueba** to try; **poner a prueba** to put to the test. ▪ **prueba de alcoholemia** breath test.

psicología *nf* psychology.

psiquiatra *nmf* psychiatrist.

publicar *vt* to publish.

publicidad *nf* **1** *(difusión)* publicity. **2** *(anuncios)* advertising; *(en televisión)* adverts.

público,-a *adj* public. ► *nm* **público** *(espectadores)* audience.

puchero *nm* cooking pot.

pudrirse *vpr* **1** *(gen)* to rot. **2** *(comida)* to go bad.

pueblo *nm* village, small town.

puente *nm* **1** bridge. **2** *(fiesta)* long weekend. ▪ **puente aéreo** air shuttle; **puente de mando** bridge.

puerro *nm* leek.

puerta *nf* door. ▪ **puerta de embarque** boarding gate.

puerto *nm* **1** *(de mar - pequeño)* harbour; *(- grande)* port. **2** *(de montaña)* mountain pass. **3** INFORM port. ▪ **puerto deportivo** marina.

pues *conj* **1** *(ya que)* since, as. **2** *(por lo tanto)* then, therefore. **3** *(enfático)* well: *pues bien*, well then; *¡pues claro!*, of course!

puesta *nf.* ▪ **puesta a punto** tuning; **puesta de sol** sunset; **puesta en marcha 1** *(de vehículo)* starting. **2** *(de proyecto)* implementation.

puesto *nm* **1** *(lugar)* place. **2** *(de mercado)* stall; *(de feria etc.)* stand. **3** *(empleo)* position, post. • **puesto que** since.

pulga *nf* flea.

pulgar *nm* thumb.

pulmón *nm* lung.

pulmonía *nf* pneumonia.

pulpo *nm* octopus.

pulsar *vt* to press.

pulsera *nf* bracelet.

pulso *nm* pulse. • **echar un pulso** to arm-wrestle; **tener buen pulso** to have a steady hand.

pulverizador *nm* spray, atomizer.

puma *nm* puma.

punta *nf* *(extremo - de dedo, lengua)* tip; *(- de aguja, cuchillo, lápiz)* point. • **sacar punta a** *(lápiz)* to sharpen.

puntería *nf* aim.

punto *nm* **1** *(gen)* point. **2** *(de puntuación)* GB full stop; US period. **3** *(en costura, cirugía)* stitch. • **en punto** sharp, on the dot; **estar en su punto** to be just right; **hasta cierto punto** up to a certain point. ▪ **punto de encuentro** meeting point; **punto de vista** point of view; **punto muerto 1** *(cambio de marchas)* neutral. **2** *(en negociaciones)* impasse, deadlock; **punto y aparte** full stop, new paragraph; **punto y coma** semicolon; **puntos suspensivos** GB dots; US suspension points.

puntuación *nf* **1** *(en ortografía)* punctuation. **2** *(en competición)* scoring; *(total)* score.

puntual *adj* punctual.
puñado *nm* handful.
puñal *nm* dagger.
puñetazo *nm* punch.
puño *nm* 1 *(mano)* fist. 2 *(de prenda)* cuff.
pupila *nf* pupil.
pupitre *nm* desk.
puré *nm* purée. ■ **puré de patatas** mashed potatoes.
puro,-a *adj* 1 *(sin mezclar)* pure. 2 *(mero)* sheer, mere. ► *nm* **puro** cigar.
pus *nm* pus.
puzzle *nm* puzzle.

Q

que[1] *pron* 1 *(sujeto - persona)* who, that; *(- cosa)* that, which. 2 *(complemento - persona)* whom, who; *(cosa)* that, which. 3 *(complemento - de tiempo)* when; *(- de lugar)* where.
que[2] *conj* 1 *(después de verbos)* that. 2 *(con comparativos)* than: *es más alto que su padre*, he is taller than his father.
qué *pron* what? ► *adj* 1 *(en exclamativas)* how, what: *¡qué bonito!*, how nice! 2 *(en interrogativas)* which?
quebrar *vi* to go bankrupt.
quedar *vi* 1 *(faltar)* to remain, be left. 2 *(sentar)* to look: *te queda muy bien*, it suits you. 3 *(estar situado)* to be: *¿por dónde queda tu casa?*, whereabouts is your house? ► *vpr* **quedarse** to remain, stay, be.
queja *nf* 1 *(protesta)* complaint. 2 *(de dolor)* moan, groan.
quejarse *vpr* 1 *(protestar)* to complain. 2 *(gimiendo)* to moan, groan.
quemadura *nf* 1 *(gen)* burn. 2 *(de agua hirviendo)* scald.
quemar *vt* 1 *(gen)* to burn. 2 *(incendiar)* to set on fire. ► *vi* *(estar muy caliente)* to be burning hot. ► *vpr* **quemarse** 1 to burn oneself. 2 *(al sol)* to get burnt.
querer *vt* 1 *(amar)* to love. 2 *(desear)* to want.
querido,-a *adj* dear, beloved.
queso *nm* cheese.
quiebra *nf* bankruptcy.
quien *pron* 1 *(sujeto)* who. 2 *(complemento)* who, whom. 3 *(indefinido)* whoever, anyone who.
quién *pron* 1 *(sujeto)* who. 2 *(complemento)* who, whom. ● *¿de quién?* whose?
quienquiera *pron* whoever.
quieto,-a *adj* still.
quilla *nf* keel.
química *nf* chemistry.
químico,-a *adj* chemical.
quince *num* fifteen; *(en fechas)* fifteenth.

quiniela *nf* football pools.
quinientos,-as *num* five hundred.
quinto,-a *num* fifth.
quiosco *nm* kiosk. ■ **quiosco de periódicos** newspaper stand.
quirófano *nm* GB operating theatre; US operating room.
quiste *nm* cyst.
quitamanchas *nm* stain remover.
quitanieves *nm* GB snowplough; US snowplow.
quitar *vt* to remove, take out, take off. ► *vpr* **quitarse 1** *(apartarse)* to move away. **2** *(desaparecer)* to go away, come out: *se me han quitado las ganas*, I don't feel like it any more. **3** *(ropa)* to take off. ● **de quita y pon** detachable.
quizá *adv* perhaps, maybe.
quizás *adv* perhaps, maybe.

R

rábano *nm* radish.
rabia *nf* **1** *(enfermedad)* rabies. **2** *(enfado)* rage, fury.
rabo *nm* tail
racha *nf* **1** *(de viento)* gust. **2** *(período)*: *una buena racha*, a run of good luck.

racimo *nm* bunch.
ración *nf* **1** *(porción)* portion. **2** *(parte que toca)* share.
racional *adj* rational.
racista *adj-nmf* racist.
radar *nm* radar.
radiactivo,-a *adj* radioactive.
radiador *nm* radiator.
radical *adj-nmf* radical.
radio¹ *nm* **1** *(de círculo)* radius. **2** *(de rueda)* spoke.
radio² *nf* *(medio)* radio.
radio³ *nm* **1** *(hueso)* radius. **2** *(elemento químico)* radium.
radiocasete *nm* radio-cassette.
radiografía *nf* **1** *(técnica)* radiography. **2** *(imagen)* X-ray.
ráfaga *nf* **1** *(de viento)* gust. **2** *(de disparos)* burst.
raíl *nm* rail.
raíz *nf* root. ● **a raíz de** as a result of. ■ **raíz cuadrada** square root.
rallado,-a *adj* grated. ● **pan rallado** breadcrumbs.
rallar *vt* to grate.
rama *nf* branch.
rambla *nf* *(paseo)* boulevard, avenue.
ramo *nm* **1** *(de flores)* bunch. **2** *(ámbito)* field, section.
rampa *nf* ramp.
rana *nf* frog.
rancho *nm* *(granja)* ranch.
rango *nm* rank, class.
ranura *nf* **1** *(canal)* groove. **2** *(para monedas, fichas)* slot.

rapaz *nf (ave)* bird of prey.
rape *nm (pez)* angler fish.
rápido,-a *adj* quick, fast. ▶
nm pl **rápidos** *(del río)* rapids.
raptar *vt* to kidnap.
raqueta *nf* 1 racket. 2 *(para nieve)* snowshoe.
raro,-a *adj* 1 *(poco común)* rare. 2 *(peculiar)* odd, strange. •
raras veces seldom.
rascacielos *nm* skyscraper.
rascar *vt* to scratch.
rasgo *nm* 1 *(línea)* stroke. 2 *(facción)* feature. 3 *(peculiaridad)* characteristic. • **a grandes rasgos** in outline.
rasguño *nm* scratch.
raso *nm (tejido)* satin. • **al raso** in the open air.
raspa *nf (de pescado)* bone.
raspar *vt (rascar)* to scrape; *(quitar rascando)* to scrape off.
rastrillo *nm* rake.
rastro *nm* 1 *(pista)* trail. 2 *(señal)* trace. 3 *(mercado)* flea market.
rata *nf* rat.
ratero,-a *nm,f* pickpocket.
ratificar *vt* to ratify.
rato *nm (momento)* while. •
pasar el rato to kill time.
ratón *nm* mouse.
raya¹ *nf* 1 *(línea)* line. 2 *(de color)* stripe: *a rayas*, striped. 3 *(del pantalón)* crease. 4 *(del pelo)* parting. • **pasarse de la raya** to overstep the mark; **tener a raya** to keep in line.

raya² *nf (pez)* skate.
rayado,-a *adj* 1 *(con rayas)* striped. 2 *(disco)* scratched.
rayar *vt* 1 *(líneas)* to draw lines on, line, rule. 2 *(superficie)* to scratch.
rayo *nm* 1 *(de luz)* ray, beam. 2 *(en el cielo)* flash of lightning. ▪ **rayo de sol** sunbeam.
raza *nf* 1 *(humana)* race. 2 *(animal)* breed.
razón *nf* reason. • **no tener razón** to be wrong; **"Razón aquí"** "Enquire within"; **tener razón** to be right.
razonable *adj* reasonable.
re *nm (nota)* D; *(en solfeo)* re, ray.
reacción *nf* reaction.
reaccionar *vi* to react.
reactor *nm* 1 *(nuclear etc.)* reactor. 2 *(avión)* jet plane.
real¹ *adj (auténtico)* real.
real² *adj (regio)* royal.
realidad *nf* reality. • **en realidad** really, in fact.
realización *nf (de tarea)* carrying out; *(de propósito)* achievement.
realizar *vt* 1 *(propósito, sueño)* to realize. 2 *(tarea)* to accomplish, carry out, do.
reanimar(se) *vt-vpr* to revive.
reanudar *vt* to renew, resume.
rebaja *nf* reduction. ▶ *nf pl* **rebajas** sales.
rebajar *vt* 1 *(precio, coste)* to reduce; *(color)* to tone down. 2 *(nivel)* to lower.

rebanada *nf* slice.
rebaño *nm (de cabras)* herd; *(de ovejas)* flock.
rebasar *vt* to exceed.
rebeca *nf* cardigan.
rebelde *nmf* rebel.
rebelión *nf* rebellion, revolt.
rebobinar *vt* to rewind.
rebotar *vi (balón)* to bounce.
rebote *nm* rebound.
rebozar *vt (con pan rallado)* to coat in breadcrumbs; *(con huevo)* to batter.
rebuznar *vi* to bray.
recado *nm* 1 *(mensaje)* message. 2 *(encargo)* errand.
recaída *nf* relapse.
recambio *nm (de maquinaria)* spare part, spare; *(de pluma, bolígrafo)* refill.
recapacitar *vi* to reflect.
recargable *adj (mechero)* refillable; *(batería)* rechargeable.
recargar *vt* 1 *(arma)* to reload; *(mechero)* to refill; *(batería)* to recharge. 2 *(sobrecargar)* to overload.
recargo *nm* extra charge.
recaudación *nf (dinero)* takings.
recaudar *vt (impuestos)* to collect; *(dinero)* to raise.
recepción *nf* reception.
recepcionista *nmf* receptionist.
receptor *nm* TV receiver.
receta *nf* 1 *(médica)* prescription. 2 *(culinaria)* recipe.

rechazar *vt* to reject, turn down.
rechazo *nm* rejection.
rechoncho,-a *adj* chubby.
recibidor *nm* entrance hall.
recibimiento *nm* reception, welcome.
recibir *vt* 1 *(carta, señal, etc.)* to get, receive. 2 *(persona)* to meet.
recibo *nm* 1 *(resguardo)* receipt. 2 *(factura)* invoice, bill.
reciclable *adj* recyclable.
reciclar *vt* 1 *(materiales)* to recycle. 2 *(profesionales)* to retrain.
recién *adv* recently, newly: *pan recién hecho*, freshly baked bread. • **"Recién pintado"** "Wet paint". ■ **recién casados** newlyweds; **recién nacido** newborn baby.
reciente *adj* recent.
recinto *nm (gen)* premises; *(cerrado)* enclosure.
recipiente *nm* container.
recíproco,-a *adj* reciprocal.
recital *nm* recital.
recitar *vt* to recite.
reclamación *nf* 1 *(demanda)* claim, demand. 2 *(queja)* complaint, protest.
reclamar *vt (pedir)* to demand. ► *vi (quejarse)* to complain.
recluso,-a *nm,f* prisoner.
recluta *nmf* 1 *(voluntario)* recruit. 2 *(obligado)* conscript.
recobrar(se) *vt-vpr* to recover.

recogedor *nm* dustpan.

recoger *vt* 1 *(coger del suelo)* to pick up. 2 *(ordenar)* to tidy up. 3 *(ir a buscar)* to fetch, pick up.

recolectar *vt (cosecha)* to harvest; *(dinero)* to collect.

recomendación *nf* recommendation.

recomendar *vt* to recommend.

recompensa *nf* reward, recompense.

reconocer *vt* 1 *(gen)* to recognize. 2 *(a paciente)* to examine. 3 *(un error)* to admit.

reconocimiento *nm* 1 *(gen)* recognition. 2 *(chequeo médico)* examination, check up

reconstruir *vt* to reconstruct.

récord *adj-nm* record. • **batir un récord** to break a record.

recordar *vt-vi* to remember.

recorrer *vt* to travel round.

recorrido *nm* 1 *(trayecto)* journey. 2 *(distancia)* distance travelled.

recortar *vt* to cut (out).

recorte *nm* 1 *(de periódico)* press clipping. 2 *(de presupuesto)* cut.

recreativo,-a *adj* recreational.

recreo *nm* 1 *(entretenimiento)* recreation, amusement. 2 *(en la escuela)* playtime.

recta *nf* 1 *(línea)* straight line. 2 *(en carretera)* straight (piece of road). ▪ **recta final** final straight.

rectángulo *nm* rectangle.

rectificar *vt* to rectify.

recto,-a *adj* 1 *(derecho)* straight. 2 *(honesto)* just, honest. ▶ *nm* **recto** rectum. ▶ *adv* straight on.

recuadro *nm* box.

recuento *nm* recount.

recuerdo *nm* 1 *(imagen mental)* memory. 2 *(regalo)* souvenir. ▶ *nm pl* **recuerdos** *(saludos)* regards; *(en carta)* best wishes.

recuperar(se) *vt-vpr* to recover.

recurrir *vi (acogerse - a algo)* to resort to; *(- a alguien)* to turn to. ▶ *vt (una sentencia)* to appeal against.

recurso *nm* 1 *(medio)* resort. 2 JUR appeal. ▶ *nm pl* **recursos** resources, means.

red *nf* 1 *(de pesca, Internet)* net. 2 *(sistema)* network.

redacción *nf* 1 *(escrito)* composition. 2 *(oficina)* editorial office. 3 *(redactores)* editorial staff.

redactor,-ra *nm,f* editor.

redada *nf* raid.

redondear *vt (cantidad)* to round off; *(por encima)* to round up; *(por debajo)* to round down.

redondo,-a *adj* 1 *(circular)* round. 2 *(perfecto)* perfect, excellent: *un negocio redondo*, an excellent business deal. ▶ *nm* **redondo** *(de carne)* topside. • **a la redonda** around.

reducir vt (disminuir) to reduce. ► vi (al conducir) to change down.

reembolso nm (pago) reimbursement; (devolución) refund. • **contra reembolso** cash on delivery.

reemplazar vt to replace.

referencia nf reference.

referirse vpr (aludir) to refer: ¿a qué te refieres?, what do you mean?

refinar vt to refine.

reflejar vt to reflect.

reflejo nm 1 (imagen) reflection. 2 (destello) gleam. ► mpl **reflejos** 1 (reacción) reflexes. 2 (en el pelo) highlights.

reflexionar vt to reflect.

reflexivo,-a adj (verbo etc.) reflexive.

reforma nf 1 (cambio) reform. 2 (de edificio) alteration: **"Cerrado por reformas"**, "Closed for alterations".

refrán nm proverb, saying.

refrescar vt 1 (bebida) to cool, chill. 2 (memoria) to refresh. ► vi (tiempo) to turn cool: **por la noche refresca**, the nights are cool. ► vpr **refrescarse** 1 (tomar el fresco) to take a breath of fresh air. 2 (con agua) to freshen up.

refresco nm soft drink.

refrigerador nm fridge.

refuerzos nm pl (tropas) reinforcements.

refugiado,-a adj-nm,f refugee.

refugiarse vpr to take refuge.

refugio nm shelter, refuge.

regadera nf watering can.

regalar vt to give: **me lo han regalado**, I was given it, it was a present.

regaliz nm liquorice.

regalo nm gift, present. • **de regalo** free.

regar vt 1 (plantas) to water. 2 (terreno) to irrigate. 3 (calle) to hose down.

regata nf regatta.

regate nm dribble.

régimen nm 1 (de comida) diet. 2 (político) régime. • **estar a régimen** to be on a diet.

regimiento nm regiment.

región nf region.

registrar vt 1 (inspeccionar) to search, inspect. 2 (datos) to register.

registro nm 1 (inspección) search, inspection. 2 (inscripción) registration. 3 (oficina) registry; (libro) register.

regla nf 1 (norma) rule. 2 (instrumento) ruler. 3 (menstruación) period. • **en regla** in order; **por regla general** as a rule.

reglamento nm regulations.

regresar vi to return, come back, go back.

regreso nm return.

regular adj 1 (habitual) regular. 2 (pasable) so-so, average. ► vt to regulate.

rehén *nmf* hostage.

rehusar *vt* to refuse, decline.

reina *nf* queen.

reinar *vi* to reign.

reincidir *vi* to relapse.

reiniciar *vt* to reboot.

reino *nm* kingdom.

reintegro *nm* **1** *(de dinero de cuenta)* withdrawal. **2** *(de dinero pagado)* reimbursement.

reír(se) *vi-vpr* to laugh.

reivindicar *vt (derecho)* to demand, claim; *(propiedad)* to claim; *(atentado)* to claim responsibility for.

reja *nf* grille.

rejilla *nf* **1** *(de ventilación)* grille. **2** *(de chimenea)* grate.

relación *nf* **1** *(gen)* relation. **2** *(listado)* list. **3** *(de pareja)* relationship. ■ **relaciones públicas** public relations.

relacionar *vt (vincular)* to relate, connect. ► *vpr* **relacionarse** *(tener amistad)* to get acquainted.

relajación *nf* relaxation.

relajarse *vpr* to relax.

relámpago *nm* flash of lightning.

relativo,-a *adj* relative.

relato *nm* story, tale.

relevar *vt (sustituir)* to relieve.

relevo *nm* **1** *(acto, persona)* relief. **2** DEP relay. • **tomar el relevo** to take over.

relieve *nm* relief. • **poner de relieve** to emphasize.

religión *nf* religion.

religioso,-a *adj* religious.

rellano *nm* landing.

rellenar *vt* **1** *(volver a llenar)* to refill. **2** *(cuestionario)* to fill in. **3** *(ave)* to stuff; *(pastel)* to fill.

relleno *nm (de aves)* stuffing; *(de pasteles)* filling.

reloj *nm (de pared, mesa)* clock; *(de pulsera)* watch. • **contra reloj** against the clock. ■ **reloj de arena** hourglass; **reloj de sol** sundial; **reloj despertador** alarm clock; **reloj digital 1** *(de pulsera)* digital watch. **2** *(de pared, mesa)* digital clock.

relojería *nf (tienda)* watchmaker's shop.

remar *vi* to row.

rematar *vt* **1** *(acabar)* to finish off. **2** DEP *(con cabeza)* to head; *(con pie)* to shoot.

remate *nm* **1** *(final)* end. **2** DEP *(con cabeza)* header; *(con pie)* shot.

remedio *nm* **1** *(medicamento)* remedy, cure. **2** *(solución)* solution.

remesa *nf (de mercancías)* consignment, shipment.

remite *nm* sender's name and address.

remitente *nmf* sender.

remitir *vt* **1** *(enviar)* to remit, send. **2** *(tormenta)* to abate; *(fiebre)* to go down.

remo *nm* **1** *(pala)* oar; *(de canoa)* paddle. **2** *(deporte)* rowing.

remojo *nm* soaking. • **poner algo en remojo** to leave STH to soak.

remolacha *nf* beetroot. ▪ **remolacha azucarera** sugar beet.

remolcar *vt* to tow.

remolino *nm* **1** *(de agua)* whirlpool; *(de aire)* whirlwind. **2** *(de pelo)* GB tuft; US cowlick.

remolque *nm* trailer. • **a remolque** in tow.

remontar *vt* **1** *(río)* to go up. **2** *(superar)* to overcome. ▶ *vpr* **remontarse** *(datar)* to go back, date back.

remordimiento *nm* remorse.

remoto,-a *adj* remote.

remover *vt* **1** *(líquido, salsa)* to stir. **2** *(tierra)* to turn over. **3** *(tema)* to bring up again.

renacuajo *nm* tadpole.

rencor *nm* GB rancour; US rancor.

rendido,-a *adj* exhausted.

rendija *nf* crack.

rendimiento *nm* **1** *(de máquina)* output. **2** *(de persona)* performance.

rendir *vt* *(producir)* to yield, produce. ▶ *vt-vi* *(dar fruto)* to pay. ▶ *vpr* **rendirse** to surrender.

reno *nm* reindeer.

renovar *vt* **1** *(contrato, actividad)* to renew. **2** *(casa)* to renovate.

renta *nf* **1** *(ingresos)* income. **2** *(beneficio)* interest. **3** *(alquiler)* rent. ▪ **renta per cápita** per capita income.

rentable *adj* profitable.

renunciar *vt* **1** *(dejar)* to give up; *(abandonar)* to abandon; *(rechazar)* to refuse. **2** *(dimitir)* to resign.

reñir *vi* *(discutir)* to quarrel, argue. ▶ *vt* *(reprender)* to scold.

reparación *nf* *(arreglo)* repair.

reparar *vt* *(arreglar)* to repair, mend.

repartir *vt* **1** *(distribuir)* to deliver. **2** *(entregar)* to give out; *(correo)* to deliver.

reparto *nm* **1** *(gen)* delivery. **2** *(actores)* cast.

repasar *vt* **1** *(lección, texto)* to revise, go over. **2** *(máquina, cuenta)* to check.

repelente *adj* repellent.

repente *nm*. • **de repente** suddenly.

repercusión *nf* repercussion.

repertorio *nm* repertoire.

repetición *nf* repetition.

repetidor *nm* relay, booster station.

repetir *vt-vi* to repeat.

repisa *nf* shelf.

repleto,-a *adj* full up.

réplica *nf* **1** *(respuesta)* answer. **2** *(copia)* replica.

repollo *nm* cabbage.

reportaje *nm* *(en televisión)* report; *(prensa)* feature.

reportero,-a *nm,f* reporter.

reposar *vt-vi* to rest.

reposo *nm* rest. • **dejar en reposo** to leave to stand.

repostar *vi (coche)* to fill up; *(avión)* to refuel.

repostería *nf* confectionery.

representación *nf* 1 *(imagen, sustitución)* representation. 2 *(teatral)* performance. 3 *(delegación)* delegation.

representante *nmf* representative.

representar *vt* 1 *(ilustrar, sustituir)* to represent. 2 *(obra de teatro)* to perform. 3 *(edad)* to look: *no representa esa edad*, she doesn't look that age.

reprimir *vt* to repress.

reproche *nm* reproach.

reproducir(se) *vt-vpr* to reproduce.

reptar *vi* to crawl.

reptil *nm* reptile.

república *nf* republic.

repuesto *nm* spare part.

repugnante *adj* repugnant.

reputación *nf* reputation.

requesón *nm* cottage cheese.

requisito *nm* requisite.

resaca *nf* hangover.

resbalar(se) *vi-vpr* 1 *(deslizarse)* to slide. 2 *(sin querer)* to slip.

resbalón *nm* slip.

rescatar *vt* 1 *(salvar)* to rescue. 2 *(recuperar)* to recover.

rescate *nm* 1 *(de persona)* rescue. 2 *(dinero)* ransom.

resentimiento *nm* resentment.

reserva *nf* 1 *(de plazas)* booking, reservation. 2 *(provisión)* reserve. 3 *(vino)* vintage. 4 *(de animales)* reserve. ► *nmf (deportista)* reserve, substitute. • **sin reservas** unreservedly, wholeheartedly.

reservar *vt (plazas)* to book, reserve. ► *vpr* **reservarse** *(conservarse)* to save oneself.

resfriado *nm (con congestión)* cold; *(poco importante)* chill.

resfriarse *vpr* to catch a cold.

resguardo *nm (recibo)* receipt.

residencia *nf* residence. ■ **residencia de ancianos** residential home; **residencia de estudiantes** GB hall of residence; US dormitory.

residir *vi* 1 *(habitar)* to reside, live. 2 *(radicar)* to lie: *es ahí donde reside el problema*, that's where the problem lies.

residuo *nm* residue. ■ **residuos radiactivos** radioactive waste.

resignarse *vpr* to resign oneself.

resina *nf* resin.

resistencia *nf* 1 *(de material)* resistance. 2 *(de persona)* endurance. 3 *(oposición)* reluctance, opposition.

resistente *adj* resistant.
resistir *vt* **1** *(no ceder, aguantar)* to withstand. **2** *(tolerar)* to stand, bear. ► *vpr* **resistirse 1** *(negarse)* to refuse. **2** *(forcejear)* to resist. **3** *(oponerse)* to offer resistance.
resolver *vt* *(problema)* to solve.
respaldo *nm* **1** *(de asiento)* back. **2** *(apoyo)* support, backing.
respectivo,-a *adj* respective.
respecto *nm*. • **al respecto** on the matter, about; **con respecto a** with regard to, regarding.
respetar *vt* to respect.
respeto *nm* respect.
respiración *nf* breathing. ▪ **respiración boca a boca** mouth-to-mouth resuscitation.
respirar *vi* to breathe.
responder *vt-vi* to answer, reply.
responsabilidad *nf* responsibility.
responsable *adj* responsible.
respuesta *nf* *(contestación)* answer, reply; *(reacción)* response.
resta *nf* substraction.
restablecerse *vpr* *(recuperarse)* to recover, get better.
restante *adj* remaining.
restar *vt* to subtract.
restauración *nf* **1** *(de muebles etc.)* restoration. **2** *(hostelería)* catering.

restaurante *nm* restaurant.
resto *nm* **1** *(lo que queda)* rest. **2** *(en matemáticas)* remainder. ► *nm pl* **restos** *(gen)* remains; *(de comida)* leftovers.
resultado *nm* result.
resultar *vi* **1** *(funcionar)* to work. **2** *(ocurrir, ser)* to turn out to be. **3** *(salir)* to come out: *resultar herido*, to be wounded. • **resulta que** it turns out that.
resumen *nm* summary. • **en resumen** in short.
resumir *vt* to summarize.
retablo *nm* altarpiece.
retina *nf* retina.
retirada *nf* **1** withdrawal. **2** MIL retreat.
retirar *vt* *(apartar)* to withdraw. ► *vpr* **retirarse 1** *(tropas)* to retreat. **2** *(apartarse)* to withdraw. **3** *(jubilarse)* to retire.
retiro *nm* **1** *(jubilación)* retirement. **2** *(pensión)* pension.
reto *nm* challenge.
retocar *vt* to touch up.
retorcer *vt* *(doblar)* to twist. ► *vpr* **retorcerse** *(de dolor)* to writhe; *(de risa)* to double up.
retorno *nm* return.
retransmisión *nf* broadcast.
retransmitir *vt* to broadcast.
retrasar *vt* **1** *(salida, proceso)* to delay, put off. **2** *(reloj)* to put back. ► *vi-vpr* **retrasar-(se)** **1** *(ir atrás)* to fall behind.

2 *(llegar tarde)* to be late. **3** *(reloj)* to be slow.

retraso *nm* **1** *(de tiempo)* delay. **2** *(subdesarrollo)* backwardness.

retrato *nm* **1** portrait. **2** *(foto)* photograph. ▪ **retrato robot** identikit picture.

retrete *nm* toilet, lavatory.

retroceder *vi* to go back.

retrovisor *nm* rear-view mirror.

reuma *nm* rheumatism.

reunión *nf* meeting.

reunir(se) *vt-vpr (personas)* to meet; *(cosas)* to get together.

revelado *nm* developing.

revelar *vt* **1** *(descubrir)* to reveal. **2** *(fotos)* to develop.

reventar(se) *vt-vpr (estallar)* to burst.

reventón *nm* **1** *(de tubería)* burst. **2** *(de neumático)* blowout.

reverencia *nf (inclinación)* bow; *(flexión de piernas)* curtsy.

revés *nm* **1** *(reverso)* back, reverse. **2** *(bofetada)* slap. **3** *(contrariedad)* misfortune. **4** *(en tenis etc.)* backhand. • **al revés** **1** *(todo lo contrario)* on the contrary. **2** *(en orden inverso)* the other way round. **3** *(lo de dentro fuera)* inside out. **4** *(lo delantero detrás)* back to front. **5** *(boca abajo)* upside down, the wrong way up.

revisar *vt (teoría, edición)* to revise; *(cuenta)* to check.

revisión *nf (de teoría, edición)* revision. ▪ **revisión médica** checkup.

revisor,-ra *nm,f* ticket inspector. ▪ **revisor ortográfico** spellchecker.

revista *nf* **1** *(publicación)* magazine, review. **2** *(espectáculo)* revue.

revolcarse *vpr* to roll about.

revolución *nf* revolution.

revólver *nm* revolver.

revolver *vt* **1** *(remover)* to stir; *(agitar)* to shake. **2** *(desordenar)* to mess up.

revuelta *nf (revolución)* revolt, riot.

revuelto *nm* scrambled eggs.

rey *nm* king. ▪ **los Reyes Magos** the Three Kings, the Three Wise Men.

rezagarse *vpr* to fall behind.

rezar *vi* to pray.

riachuelo *nm* stream.

riada *nf* flood.

ribera *nf* **1** *(de río)* bank. **2** *(de mar)* seashore.

rico,-a *adj* **1** *(gen)* rich. **2** *(sabroso)* tasty, delicious.

ridículo,-a *adj* ridiculous.

riego *nm* irrigation, watering. ▪ **riego sanguíneo** blood circulation.

riel *nm* rail.

rienda *nf (brida)* rein.

riesgo *nm* risk, danger.

rifar *vt* to raffle.
rifle *nm* rifle.
rígido,-a *adj* rigid.
rigor *nm* GB rigour, US rigor.
rima *nf* rhyme.
rímel *nm* mascara.
rincón *nm* corner.
rinoceronte *nm* rhinoceros.
riña *nf* 1 *(pelea)* fight. 2 *(discusión)* quarrel.
riñón *nm* kidney.
río *nm* river. • **río abajo** downstream; **río arriba** upstream.
risa *nf* laugh.
ritmo *nm* 1 *(compás)* rhythm. 2 *(velocidad)* pace, speed.
rito *nm* rite.
rival *nmf* rival.
rizado,-a *adj* curly.
rizo *nm* curl.
robar *vt* *(banco, persona)* to rob; *(objeto)* to steal; *(casa)* to burgle, break into.
roble *nm* oak tree.
robo *nm* *(a banco, persona)* robbery; *(de objeto)* theft; *(en casa)* burglary.
robot *nm* robot.
roca *nf* rock.
roce *nm* 1 *(señal - en superficie)* scuff mark; *(- en piel)* chafing mark. 2 *(contacto físico)* light touch.
rocío *nm* dew.
rodaja *nf* slice.
rodaje *nm* 1 *(de película)* filming, shooting. 2 *(de vehículo)* running-in.

rodar *vi* *(dar vueltas)* to roll, turn. ► *vt* 1 *(película)* to shoot. 2 *(coche)* to run in.
rodear *vt* 1 *(cercar)* to surround, encircle. 2 *(desviarse)* to make a detour.
rodeo *nm* 1 *(desvío)* detour. 2 *(elusión)* evasiveness.
rodilla *nf* knee.
roedor *nm* rodent.
rogar *vt* 1 *(suplicar)* to beg. 2 *(pedir)* to ask, request.
rojo,-a *adj* red. ► *nm* **rojo** red.
rollo *nm* 1 *(de tela, papel)* roll. 2 *fam* *(aburrimiento)* drag, bore, pain.
románico,-a *adj-mn* Romanesque.
romántico,-a *adj-nm,f* romantic.
rombo *nm* rhombus.
romero *nm* rosemary.
rompecabezas *nm* 1 *(juego)* puzzle. 2 *(problema)* riddle.
rompeolas *nm* breakwater.
romper(se) *vt-vpr* *(gen)* to break; *(papel, tela)* to tear; *(cristal)* to smash. ► *vt* *(relaciones)* to break off.
ron *nm* rum.
roncar *vi* to snore.
ronda *nf* 1 *(patrulla)* patrol. 2 *(de policía)* beat. 3 *(de bebidas, cartas)* round.
rondar *vt-vi* 1 *(vigilar)* to patrol. 2 *(merodear)* to prowl around. 3 *(cifra)* to be about.
ronquido *nm* snore.

ropa *nf* clothes. ▪ **ropa interior** underwear.

rosa *adj-nm (color)* pink. ▶ *nf (flor)* rose.

rosado *adj-nm (vino)* rosé.

rosal *nm* rosebush.

rosca *nf (de tuerca)* thread.

roscón *nm* ring-shaped roll or cake.

rosquilla *nf* doughnut.

rostro *nm fml* face.

roto,-a *adj* broken.

rotonda *nf* roundabout.

rótula *nf* knee-cap.

rotulador *nm* felt-tip pen.

rótulo *nm* 1 *(etiqueta)* label. 2 *(letrero)* sign. 3 *(anuncio)* poster, placard.

rotura *nf* 1 *(de objeto)* breakage. 2 *(de hueso)* fracture.

roulotte *nf* caravan.

rozadura *nf* scratch.

rozar *vt-vi (tocar ligeramente)* to touch, brush. ▶ *vt (raer)* to rub against: *el zapato me rozaba*, my shoe was rubbing.

rubéola *nf* German measles, rubella.

rubí *nm* ruby.

rubio,-a *adj (hombre)* blond; *(mujer)* blonde.

ruborizarse *vpr* to blush.

rúbrica *nf* 1 *(firma)* flourish. 2 *(título)* title.

rueda *nf (de vehículo)* wheel. ▪ **rueda de recambio** spare wheel.

ruedo *nm* bullring.

ruego *nm* request.

rugby *nm* rugby.

rugir *vi* to roar.

ruido *nm* noise.

ruina *nf* ruin: *al borde de la ruina*, on the brink of ruin; *el edificio amenazaba ruina*, the building was about to collapse. ▶ *nf pl* **ruinas** ruins. ▪ **en ruinas** in ruins.

ruiseñor *nm* nightingale.

rulo *nm (para pelo)* curler.

rumba *nf* rumba.

rumbo *nm* course, direction. ▪ **con rumbo a** bound for; **sin rumbo** aimlessly.

rumiante *adj-nm* ruminant.

rumor *nm* 1 *(noticia, voz)* GB rumour; US rumor. 2 *(murmullo)* murmur.

rumorearse *vi* GB to be rumoured; US to be rumored.

rupestre *adj (planta)* rock; *(pintura)* cave.

ruptura *nf* 1 *(de acuerdo)* breaking. 2 *(de relación)* breaking-off; *(de matrimonio)* break-up.

rural *adj* rural, country.

Rusia *nf* Russia.

ruso,-a *adj* Russian. ▶ *nm,f (persona)* Russian. ▶ *nm* **ruso** *(idioma)* Russian.

rústico,-a *adj* rustic.

ruta *nf* route.

rutina *nf* routine.

rutinario,-a *adj* monotonous.

S

sábado *nm* Saturday.
sabana *nf* savannah.
sábana *nf* sheet.
saber *nm* knowledge. ▸ *vt-vi* (*conocer*) to know. ▸ *vt* 1 (*poder*) can: *sabe tocar el piano*, she can play the piano. 2 (*tener noticias de*) to hear: *hace mucho que no sé nada de ellos*, I haven't heard anything from them for ages. 3 (*enterarse*) to find out: *cuando supe que era su cumpleaños...*, when I found out it was her birthday... ▸ *vi* (*tener sabor a*) to taste. ● **a saber** *fml* namely; **hacer saber** to inform; **saber mal a ALGN**: *le supo mal que se fueran sin ella*, she was upset that they went without her; **que yo sepa** as far as I know.
sabio,-a *adj* learned, wise.
sable *nm* sabre.
sabor *nm* 1 (*gusto*) taste. 2 (*gusto añadido*) GB flavour, US flavor. ● **tener sabor** to taste.
sabroso,-a *adj* tasty.
sacacorchos *nm* corkscrew.
sacapuntas *nm* pencil sharpener.
sacar *vt* 1 (*poner fuera*) to take out. 2 (*extraer*) to extract, pull out: *fui al dentista a sacarme una muela*, I went to the dentist to have a tooth out. 3 (*moda*) to introduce, bring out: *han sacado un nuevo disco*, they have brought out a new record. 4 (*entrada, pasaporte*) to get: *he sacado las entradas para el concierto*, I've bought the tickets for the concert. 5 (*tenis*) to serve; (*fútbol - al principio*) to kick off; (*durante el partido*) to take the kick. ● **sacar adelante** 1 (*proyecto*) to carry out. 2 (*hijos*) to bring up.
sacarina *nf* saccharine.
sacerdote *nm* priest.
saciar *vt* (*hambre*) to satiate; (*sed*) to quench.
saco *nm* 1 (*bolsa*) sack, bag. 2 (*contenido*) sackful, bagful. ■ **saco de dormir** sleeping bag.
sacramento *nm* sacrament.
sacrificarse *vpr* to make sacrifices.
sacrificio *nm* sacrifice.
sacudir *vt* (*agitar*) to shake.
safari *nm* safari.
sagrado,-a *adj* 1 (*religioso*) holy. 2 (*que merece respeto*) sacred.
sal *nf* 1 (*condimento*) salt. 2 (*gracia*) wit. ■ **sal de mesa** table salt; **sales de baño** bath salts.
sala *nf* 1 (*habitación*) room. 2 (*sala de estar*) living room. 3 (*de hospital*) ward. 4 (*de tribu-*

nal) courtroom. **5** *(cine)* cinema. ▪ **sala de espera** waiting room; **sala de estar** living room; **sala de fiestas** nightclub, discotheque.

salado,-a *adj* **1** *(con sal)* salted. **2** *(con demasiada sal)* salty. **3** *(no dulce)* GB savoury; US savory.

salamandra *nf* salamander.

salar *vt* to salt.

salario *nm* salary, wages.

salchicha *nf* sausage.

salchichón *nm* salami.

saldo *nm* **1** *(de una cuenta)* balance. **2** *(liquidación)* sale.

salero *nm (recipiente)* saltcellar.

salida *nf* **1** *(acto)* departure. **2** *(de personas)* exit, way out; *(de aire, gas)* vent; *(de agua)* outlet. **3** *(de autopista)* exit. **4** DEP start. **5** *(excursión)* trip, outing. ▪ **salida de emergencia** emergency exit; **salida del sol** sunrise; **salida nula** false start; **salidas internacionales** international departures; **salidas nacionales** domestic departures.

salir *vi* **1** *(ir de dentro para afuera)* to go out. **2** *(venir de dentro para fuera)* to come out. **3** *(partir)* to leave: *el autobús sale a las tres*, the bus leaves at three. **4** *(aparecer)* to appear: *salir en los periódicos*, to be in the newspapers. **5** *(resultar)* to turn out, to be: *la*

tarta te ha salido perfecta, the cake has turned out perfect. **6** *(del trabajo, colegio)* to leave, come out. **7** *(producto)* to come out, be released. **8** *(sol)* to rise. ► *vpr* **salirse 1** *(soltarse, desviarse)* to come off. **2** *(líquido)* to leak, leak out. • **salir a ALGN** to take after SB; **salir adelante** to be successful; **salir con ALGN** to go out with SB; **salir ganando con algo** to do well out of STH; **salir perdiendo** to lose out.

saliva *nf* saliva.

salmón *nm* salmon.

salmonete *nm* red mullet.

salón *nm* **1** *(en casa)* living room, lounge. **2** *(público)* hall. ▪ **salón de actos** assembly hall; **salón de belleza** beauty salon; **salón recreativo** amusement arcade.

salpicadero *nm* dashboard.

salpicar *vt* to splash.

salpicón *nm.* ▪ **salpicón de marisco** seafood salad.

salsa *nf* **1** sauce. **2** *(baile)* salsa.

salsera *nf* gravy boat.

saltamontes *nm* grasshopper.

saltar *vi* **1** *(botar)* to jump. **2** *(al agua)* to dive. **3** *(desprenderse)* to come off. ► *vt (valla etc.)* to jump (over). ► *vpr* **saltarse 1** *(ley etc)* to ignore. **2** *(omitir)* to skip, miss out.

salto *nm* 1 *(gen)* jump. 2 *(de trampolín)* dive. • **dar un salto** to jump. ■ **salto con pértiga** pole vault; **salto de agua** waterfall, falls *pl*; **salto de altura** high jump; **salto de cama** negligée; **salto de esquí** ski-jump; **salto de longitud** long jump; **salto mortal** somersault.

salud *nf* health. ► *interj* ¡**salud!** *(al brindar)* cheers!; *(al estornudar)* bless you!

saludar *vt-vi* to say hello to. • **le saluda atentamente** 1 *(si no conocemos el nombre)* yours faithfully. 2 *(si conocemos el nombre)* yours sincerely.

saludo *nm* 1 *(gen)* greeting. 2 *(entre militares)* salute. ► *nm pl* **saludos** best wishes.

salvación *nf* salvation.

salvaje *adj (gen)* wild; *(pueblo)* savage, uncivilized. ► *nmf* savage.

salvamanteles *nm* table mat.

salvamento *nm* rescue.

salvar *vt* to save, rescue. ► *vpr* **salvarse** *(sobrevivir)* to survive. • ¡**sálvese quien pueda!** every man for himself!

salvavidas *nm* life belt.

salvo *prep* except, except for. • **estar a salvo** to be safe and sound; **ponerse a salvo** to reach safety; **salvo que** unless.

san *adj* → santo,-a.

sanción *nf* 1 *(multa)* fine. 2 *(castigo)* sanction: *una sanción de cuatro partidos*, a four-game suspension.

sandalia *nf* sandal.

sandía *nf* watermelon.

sándwich *nm* sandwich.

sangrar *vt-vi* to bleed.

sangre *nf* blood. • **a sangre fría** in cool blood. ■ **sangre fría** sangfroid, calmness.

sangría *nf (bebida)* sangria.

sanidad *nf* public health.

sanitarios *nm pl* bathroom fittings.

sano,-a *adj* healthy. • **sano y salvo** safe and sound.

santo,-a *adj* 1 *(lugar, vida, misa)* holy. 2 *(con nombre)* Saint. 3 *(para enfatizar)* blessed: *todo el santo día*, the whole day long. ► *nm,f* saint.

sapo *nm* toad.

saque *nm* 1 *(tenis)* service. 2 *(fútbol)* kick-off. ■ **saque de banda** throw-in; **saque de esquina** corner.

sarampión *nm* measles.

sardina *nf* sardine.

sargento *nm* sergeant.

sarpullido *nm* rash.

sartén *nf* GB frying pan; US skillet.

sastre,-a *nm,f (hombre)* tailor; *(mujer)* dressmaker.

satélite *nm* satellite.

satén *nm* satin.

satisfacción *nf* satisfaction.

satisfacer *vt* to satisfy.

satisfecho,-a *adj* satisfied.

sauce *nm* willow. ■ **sauce llorón** weeping willow.

sauna *nf* sauna.

saxofón *nm* saxophone.

sazonar *vt* to season.

se[1] *pron* **1** *(reflexivo - a él mismo)* himself; *(- a ella misma)* herself; *(- a usted mismo)* yourself; *(- a ellos mismos)* themselves; *(- a ustedes mismos)* yourselves. **2** *(recíproco)* one another, each other. **3** *(en pasivas e impersonales)*: *se dice que...*, it is said that...; *se suspendió el partido*, the match was postponed; *se habla español*, Spanish spoken.

se[2] *pron (objeto indirecto - a él)* him; *(- a ella)* her; *(cosa)* it; *(- a usted/ustedes)* you; *(- a ellos/ellas)* them.

secador *nm* dryer. ■ **secador de pelo** hair-dryer.

secadora *nf* clothes-dryer, tumble-dryer.

secar *vt (pelo, ropa, piel)* to dry; *(lágrimas, vajilla)* to wipe.

sección *nf* **1** *(división)* section. **2** *(en tienda, oficina)* department.

seco,-a *adj* **1** *(no mojado)* dry. **2** *(frutos, flores)* dried. **3** *(golpe, ruido)* sharp. ● **a secas** simply, just; **en seco** sharply, suddenly.

secretaría *nf* secretary's office.

secretario,-a *nm,f* secretary: *secretario,-a de dirección*, executive secretary.

secreto,-a *adj* secret. ► *nm* **secreto** secret.

secta *nf* sect.

sector *nm* **1** *(zona)* area. **2** *(de la industria)* sector.

secuela *nf* consequence.

secuencia *nf* sequence.

secuestro *nm* **1** *(de persona)* kidnapping. **2** *(de avión)* highjacking.

secundario,-a *adj* secondary.

sed *nf* thirst. ● **tener sed** to be thirsty.

seda *nf* silk. ■ **seda dental** dental floss.

sedal *nm* fishing line.

sedante *adj-nm* sedative.

sede *nf* **1** *(de organización)* headquarters; *(de empresa)* head office. **2** *(del gobierno)* seat. **3** *(de acontecimiento)* venue.

seducir *vt* to seduce.

segar *vt* to reap.

segmento *nm* segment.

seguido,-a *adj* **1** *(acompañado)* followed. **2** *(consecutivo)* consecutive: *dos días seguidos*, two days running. ► *adv* straight on. ● **en seguida** at once, immediately.

seguidor,-ra *nm,f* follower.

seguir *vt* **1** *(gen)* to follow. **2** *(continuar)* to continue. ► *vi* **1** *(proseguir)* to go on: *siga to-*

do recto hasta la plaza, go straight on until you come to the square. **2** *(permanecer)* to remain: *siguió de pie*, he remained standing. **3** *(estar todavía)* to be still: *sigue enfermo*, he's still sick.

según *prep (de acuerdo con)* according to. ► *adv* **1** *(depende de)* depending on: *según lo que digan*, depending on what they say. **2** *(como)* just as: *todo quedó según estaba*, everything stayed just as it was. **3** *(a medida que)* as: *según iban entrando se les daba una copa*, as they came in they were given a drink.

segundero *nm* second hand.

segundo,-a *num* second. ► *nm* **segundo** second.

seguridad *nf* **1** *(contra accidentes)* safety. **2** *(contra robos, ataques)* security. **3** *(certeza)* certainty. **4** *(confianza)* confidence. ● **con toda seguridad** definitely. ■ **Seguridad Social** National Health Service.

seguro,-a *adj* **1** *(físicamente)* safe. **2** *(estable)* secure. **3** *(fiable)* reliable: *un método muy seguro*, a very reliable method. **4** *(cierto)* definite: *aún no es seguro que venga*, it's not definite that he's coming yet. **5** *(convencido)* confident, sure, certain: *estoy seguro de que no va a defraudarnos*, I'm

sure he won't let us down. ► *nm* **seguro 1** *(contrato, póliza)* insurance. **2** *(mecanismo)* safety catch, safety device. ► *adv (sin duda)* for sure, definitely: *lo sé seguro*, I know for sure. ● **seguro que...** I bet...

seis *num* six; *(en fechas)* sixth. ● **son las seis** it's six o'clock.

seiscientos,-as *num* six hundred.

seísmo *nm* earthquake.

selección *nf* selection. ■ **selección nacional** national team.

seleccionar *vt* to select.

selecto,-a *adj:* *un club selecto*, an exclusive club; *vinos selectos*, fine wines, choice wines; *ante un público selecto*, before a selected audience.

sellar *vt* to seal.

sello *nm* **1** *(de correos)* stamp. **2** *(de estampar, precinto)* seal. **3** *(distintivo)* hallmark. ■ **sello discográfico** record label.

selva *nf* jungle.

semáforo *nm* traffic lights.

semana *nf* week. ■ **Semana Santa** Easter.

semanal *adj* weekly.

semanario *nm* weekly magazine.

sembrar *vt (con semillas)* to sow; *(con plantas)* to plant.

semejante *adj (parecido)* similar. ► *nm* fellow being.

semen *nm* semen.

semestre *nm* six-month period; *(en educación)* semester.
semifinal *nf* semifinal.
semilla *nf* seed.
senado *nm* senate.
senador,-ra *nm,f* senator.
sencillo,-a *adj* 1 *(fácil)* simple. 2 *(persona)* natural, unaffected.
sendero *nm* path.
seno *nm* *(pecho)* breast.
sensación *nf* 1 *(percepción)* feeling. 2 *(efecto)* sensation.
sensacional *adj* sensational.
sensato,-a *adj* sensible.
sensibilidad *nf* sensitivity.
sensible *adj* sensitive.
sentar *vi* 1 *(comida)* to agree: *el chocolate no me sienta bien*, chocolate doesn't agree with me. 2 *(ropa)* to suit: *esa corbata te sienta bien*, that tie suits you. 3 *(hacer efecto)* to do: *un poco de aire fresco te sentará bien*, a bit of fresh air will do you good. ► *vpr* **sentarse** to sit down.
sentencia *nf* *(condena)* sentence. • **dictar sentencia** to pass sentence.
sentido *nm* 1 *(vista, oído, etc)* sense. 2 *(dirección)* direction: *una calle de sentido único*, a one-way street. 3 *(juicio)* consciousness. 4 *(significado)* meaning. • **perder el sentido** to faint; **recobrar el sentido** to regain consciousness;

tener sentido to make sense. ■ **sentido común** common sense; **sentido del humor** sense of humour (US humor).
sentimiento *nm* feeling.
sentir *vt* 1 *(lamentar)* to regret. 2 *(oír)* to hear. ► *vt-vpr* **sentir(se)** to feel. • **¡lo siento!** I'm sorry!; **sentirse mal** to feel ill.
seña *nf* sign. ► *nf pl* **señas** address. • **hacer señas** to signal, gesture.
señal *nf* 1 *(indicio)* sign. 2 *(marca)* mark. 3 *(signo)* signal. 4 *(por teléfono)* tone: *no había señal*, there was no dialling tone. ■ **señal de tráfico** road sign.
señalar *vt* 1 *(indicar)* to show. 2 *(marcar)* to mark: *señálalo en rojo*, mark it in red. 3 *(hacer notar)* to point to. 4 *(con el dedo)* to point at.
señor *nm* 1 *(hombre)* man; *(caballero)* gentleman. 2 *(en tratamientos)* sir; *(delante de apellido)* Mr: *el señor Pérez*, Mr Pérez.
señora *nf* 1 *(mujer)* woman; *(dama)* lady. 2 *(esposa)* wife. 4 *(en tratamientos)* madam; *(delante de apellido)* Mrs: *la señora Gómez*, Mrs Gómez; *señoras y señores*, ladies and gentlemen.
señorita *nf* 1 *(mujer joven)* young lady. 2 *(delante de ape-*

llido) Miss: **la señorita López**, Miss López. **3** *(profesora)* teacher.

separación *nf* **1** *(acción)* separation. **2** *(espacio)* gap.

separar *vt* to separate. ▶ *vpr* **separarse** *(de una persona)* to separate, split up.

sepia *nf* cuttlefish.

septiembre *nm* September.

séptimo,-a *num* seventh.

sepultar *vt* to bury.

sepultura *nf* grave.

sequía *nf* drought.

ser *vi* **1** *(gen)* to be. **2** *(pertenecer)* to belong: **el cuadro es de Picasso**, the painting is by Picasso. **3** *(material)* to be made of: **la mesa es de madera**, the table is made of wood. ▶ *aux* to be. • **a no ser que** unless; **a poder ser** if possible; **de no ser por...** had it not been for...; **érase una vez** once upon a time; **es más** furthermore; **sea como sea** in any case. ▪ **ser humano** human being; **ser vivo** living creature.

sereno,-a *adj* calm.

serial *nm* serial.

serie *nf* series.

serio,-a *adj* **1** *(persona, enfermedad)* serious. **2** *(formal)* reliable.

serpiente *nf* snake. ▪ **serpiente de cascabel** rattlesnake.

serrar *vt* to saw.

serrín *nm* sawdust.

servicio *nm* **1** *(atención)* service. **2** *(criados)* servants. **3** *(juego)* set. **4** *(tenis)* serve, service. **5** *(retrete)* toilet. ▪ **servicio a domicilio** home delivery service; **servicio militar** military service.

servidor *nm* INFORM server.

servilleta *nf* napkin, serviette.

servir *vt* **1** *(comida)* to serve: *¿ya le sirven?*, are you being served? **2** *(bebida)* to pour: *¿te sirvo yo?*, shall I pour? ▶ *vi* **1** *(ser útil)* to be useful. **2** *(trabajar)* to serve. ▶ *vpr* **servirse 1** *(comida)* to help oneself: **sírvase usted mismo**, help yourself. **2** *(utilizar)* to use. • **servir de** to be used as; **servir para** to be used for.

sesenta *num* sixty.

sesión *nf* **1** *(reunión)* session, meeting. **2** *(de película)* showing.

seso *nm* brain, brains.

seta *nf* mushroom; *(no comestible)* toadstool.

setecientos,-as *num* seven hundred.

setenta *num* seventy.

setiembre *nm* September.

seto *nm* hedge.

sexo *nm* sex.

sexto,-a *num* sixth.

short *nm* shorts.

si[1] *conj* if. • **si bien** although; **si no** otherwise.

si² *nm (nota musical)* ti, si, B.

sí¹ *pron (él)* himself; *(ella)* herself; *(cosa)* itself; *(uno mismo)* oneself; *(plural)* themselves.

sí² *adv* **1** *(en respuestas)* yes. **2** *(sustituye al verbo)*: **ella no irá, pero yo sí**, she won't go, but I will. ► *nm* yes

sida *nm* AIDS.

sidra *nf* cider.

siempre *adv* always. • **para siempre** forever; **siempre que** whenever; **siempre y cuando** provided, as long as.

sien *nf* temple.

sierra *nf* **1** *(herramienta)* saw. **2** *(cordillera)* mountain range.

siesta *nf* siesta, afternoon nap.

siete *num* seven; *(en fechas)* seventh. ► *nm (rasgón)* tear.

sifón *nm (bebida)* soda water.

sigla *nf* acronym.

siglo *nm* century.

significado *nm* meaning.

significar *vt* to mean.

signo *nm (señal)* sign.

siguiente *adj* following, next.

sílaba *nf* syllable.

silbar *vi* **1** *(con los labios, viento)* to whistle. **2** *(abuchear)* to hiss.

silbato *nm* whistle.

silbido *nm* whistle.

silencio *nm* silence. • **guardar silencio** to keep quiet.

silicona *nf* silicone.

silla *nf* chair. ▪ **silla de montar** saddle.

sillín *nm* saddle.

sillón *nm* armchair.

silueta *nf* **1** *(contorno)* silhouette. **2** *(figura)* figure: **te realza la silueta**, it shows off your figure.

silvestre *adj* wild.

símbolo *nm* symbol.

simétrico,-a *adj* symmetric.

similar *adj* similar.

simpático,-a *adj* nice.

simple *adj* **1** *(sencillo)* simple. **2** *(puro)* mere: **con una simple llamada**, with just a phone call.

simultáneo,-a *adj* simultaneous.

sin *prep* **1** *(gen)* without. **2** *(por hacer)*: **está sin planchar**, it has not been ironed. • **sin embargo** however.

sincero,-a *adj* sincere.

sindicato *nm* trade union.

sinfonía *nf* symphony.

singular *adj* **1** *(único)* singular, single. **2** *(excepcional)* extraordinary. **3** *(raro)* peculiar.

siniestro *nm (accidente)* accident. • **fue declarado siniestro total** it was declared a write-off.

sino *conj* but.

sinónimo *nm* synonym.

sintético,-a *adj* synthetic.

síntoma *nm* symptom.

sintonizar *vt* to tune in to.

sinvergüenza *nmf* cheeky devil.

siquiera *conj.* • **ni siquiera** not even.

sirena *nf* 1 *(alarma)* siren. 2 *(ninfa)* mermaid.

sirviente,-a *nm,f* servant.

sistema *nm* system.

sitio *nm* 1 *(lugar)* place. 2 *(espacio)* space, room.

situación *nf* situation.

situar *vt* to situate, locate.

sobaco *nm* armpit.

soborno *nm* 1 *(acción)* bribery. 2 *(regalo)* bribe.

sobra *nf* excess, surplus. ► *nf pl* **sobras** leftovers. • **de sobra** more than enough.

sobrar *vi* 1 *(quedar)* to be left over. 2 *(sin aprovechar)* to be more than enough. 3 *(estar de más)* to be superfluous.

sobre *prep* 1 *(encima)* on, upon: *el jarrón está sobre la mesa*, the vase is on the table. 2 *(por encima)* over, above: *el helicóptero volaba sobre la ciudad*, the helicopter flew over the city. 3 *(acerca de)* on, about: *hablar sobre algo*, to talk about STH. 4 *(alrededor de)* around, about: *llegaré sobre las once*, I'll get there at about eleven o'clock. ► *nm* 1 *(de carta)* envelope. 2 *(envoltorio)* packet: *sopa de sobre*, packet soup. 3 *(paquete pequeño)* sachet: *sobre de azúcar*, sachet of sugar. • **sobre todo** above all, especially.

sobremesa *nf* *(charla)* after-lunch chat; *(hora)* afternoon.

sobresaliente *nm* *(calificación)* A, first.

sobresalir *vi* 1 *(destacarse)* to stand out. 2 *(estar saliente)* to stick out. 3 *(abultar)* to protrude.

sobrevivir *vi* to survive.

sobrino,-a *nm,f* *(chico)* nephew; *(chica)* niece.

sobrio,-a *adj* sober, temperate.

social *adj* social.

sociedad *nf* society. ■ **sociedad anónima** GB limited company; US incorporated company; **sociedad limitada** private limited company.

socio,-a *nm,f* 1 *(de un grupo)* member. 2 *(de empresa)* partner.

sociología *nf* sociology.

socorrer *vt* to help, aid.

socorrista *nmf* *(en la playa)* lifeguard.

socorro *nm* help, aid, assistance. ► *interj* ¡socorro! help! • **pedir socorro** to ask for help.

soda *nf* soda water.

sofá *nm* sofa, settee.

software *nm* software.

soga *nf* rope.

soja *nf* soya bean.

sol[1] *nm* 1 *(astro)* sun. 2 *(luz)* sunlight, sunshine. • **tomar el sol** to sunbathe.

sol² *nm (nota)* sol, G.

solapa *nf* **1** *(de chaqueta)* lapel. **2** *(de sobre, libro)* flap.

solar¹ *adj* solar

solar² *nm (terreno)* plot.

soldado *nm* soldier.

soldar *vt (unir)* to weld; *(con estaño)* to solder.

soledad *nf* **1** *(estado)* solitude. **2** *(sentimiento)* loneliness.

solemne *adj* solemn.

soler *vi* **1** *(presente)* to be in the habit of doing: *soler hacer*, to usually do. **2** *(pasado)*: *solía ir a correr*, he used to go running.

solicitar *vt* **1** *(pedir)* to request. **2** *(trabajo)* to apply for.

solidaridad *nf* solidarity.

sólido,-a *adj* solid.

solitario,-a *adj* **1** *(sin compañía)* solitary. **2** *(sentimiento)* lonely. **3** *(lugar)* deserted. ► *nm* **solitario** solitaire.

sólo *adv* only.

solo,-a *adj* **1** *(sin compañía)* alone: *vive sola*, she lives alone. **2** *(solitario)* lonely: *se siente muy solo*, he feels very lonely. **3** *(único)* one, single: *una sola persona*, one single person. ► *nm* **solo** **1** *fam (café)* black coffee. **2** *(canción)* solo. ► *adv* **solo** only.

solomillo *nm* sirloin.

soltar *vt* **1** *(dejar suelto)* to let go of. **2** *(poner en libertad)* to set free, release. **3** *(desatar)* to undo, unfasten. ► *vpr* **soltarse** **1** *(desatarse)* to come undone. **2** *(desprenderse)* to come off.

soltero,-a *nm,f (hombre)* bachelor; *(mujer)* single woman.

solución *nf* solution.

solucionar *vt* to solve.

sombra *nf* **1** *(lugar sin sol)* shade. **2** *(silueta)* shadow. ■ **sombra de ojos** eye shadow.

sombrero *nm* hat.

sombrilla *nf (de mano)* parasol; *(de playa)* sunshade.

someter *vt* **1** *(subyugar)* to subdue. **2** *(exponer)* to subject: *someter algo a prueba*, to put STH to test. ► *vpr* **someterse** **1** *(rendirse)* to surrender: *el país tuvo que someterse al invasor*, the country had to surrender to the invader. **2** *(tratamiento etc.)* to undergo.

somier *nm* bed base.

somnífero *nm* sleeping pill.

sonajero *nm* rattle.

sonámbulo,-a *adj-nm,f* sleepwalker.

sonar *vi* **1** *(con timbrazos)* to ring; *(con campanadas)* to strike; *(con pitido)* to beep. **2** *(ponerse en marcha)* to go off. **3** *(conocer vagamente)* to sound familiar: *su cara me suena*, her face is familiar. ► *vpr* **sonarse** to blow one's nose.

sonda *nf* probe.

sondeo *nm* poll.

sonido *nm* sound.

sonreír *vi* to smile.

sonrisa *nf* smile.

soñar *vt-vi* to dream.

sopa *nf* soup.

sopera *nf* soup tureen.

soplar *vi* to blow.

soportar *vt* **1** *(sostener)* to support. **2** *(aguantar)* to put up with: *¿cómo lo soportas?*, how can you put up with him? **3** *(tolerar)* to stand: *no soporto a esta chica*, I can't stand this girl.

soprano *nmf* soprano.

sorbete *nm* sorbet.

sorbo *nm* sip.

sordo,-a *adj* **1** *(persona)* deaf. **2** *(sonido, dolor)* dull.

sordomudo,-a *adj* deaf and dumb. ▶ *nm,f* deaf mute.

sorprendente *adj* surprising.

sorprender *vt* to surprise.

sorpresa *nf* surprise.

sortear *vt* **1** *(echar a suertes)* to draw lots for; *(rifar)* to raffle. **2** *(obstáculos)* to get round.

sorteo *nm* *(de lotería)* draw; *(rifa)* raffle.

sortija *nf* ring.

soso,-a *adj* **1** *(sin sabor)* tasteless. **2** *(sin sal)*: *está soso*, it needs salt. **3** *(aburrido)* dull.

sospecha *nf* suspicion.

sospechar *vt* to suspect.

sospechoso,-a *nm,f* suspect.

sostén *nm* **1** *(apoyo)* support. **2** *(prenda)* bra, brassiere.

sostener *vt* **1** *(aguantar)* to support, hold up. **2** *(sujetar)* to hold. **3** *(conversación, reunión)* to have. **4** *(opinión)* to maintain, affirm.

sótano *nm* **1** *(usado como almacén)* cellar. **2** *(planta)* basement.

stop *nm* stop sign.

su *adj (de él)* his; *(de ella)* her; *(de usted/ustedes)* your; *(de ellos)* their; *(de animales, cosas)* its.

suave *adj* **1** *(piel, tela, color, voz)* soft. **2** *(superficie)* smooth. **3** *(brisa, persona)* gentle. **4** *(clima, sabor, detergente)* mild.

suavizante *nm* **1** *(para ropa)* fabric softener. **2** *(para pelo)* conditioner.

subasta *nf* auction.

subcampeón,-ona *nm,f* runner-up.

subida *nf* **1** *(ascenso)* ascent; *(a montaña)* climb. **2** *(pendiente)* slope. **3** *(aumento)* rise.

subir *vi* **1** *(a coche)* to get in; *(a tren, autobús, avión)* to get on. **2** *(aumentar)* to rise. ▶ *vt* **1** *(escalar)* to climb. **2** *(mover arriba)* to carry up, take up. **3** *(incrementar)* to put up. ▶ *vpr*

subirse 1 *(a coche)* to get in; *(a tren, autobús, avión)* to get on; *(a caballo)* to mount. **2**

(trepar) to climb. **3** *(elevar)* to pull up: **súbete los calcetines**, pull your socks up.

submarinismo *nm* scuba diving.

submarino *nm* submarine

subrayar *vt* **1** *(con una línea)* to underline. **2** *(recalcar)* to emphasize.

subsidio *nm* subsidy, aid. ■ **subsidio de desempleo** unemployment benefit.

subterráneo,-a *adj* subterranean, under-ground.

suburbano,-a *adj* suburban.

suburbio *nm* *(barrio pobre)* slum area; *(barrio de las afueras)* poor suburb.

subvención *nf* subsidy, grant.

suceder *vi* **1** *(acontecer)* to happen. **2** *(seguir)* to follow. ► *vt (sustituir)* to succeed.

sucesivo,-a *adj* consecutive, successive. • **en lo sucesivo** from now on.

suceso *nm* **1** *(hecho)* event, happening. **2** *(incidente)* incident.

sucesor,-ra *nm,f* **1** *(en un puesto)* successor. **2** *(heredero)* heir; *(heredera)* heiress.

suciedad *nf* dirt.

sucio,-a *adj* dirty.

sucursal *nf* branch office.

Sudamérica *nf* South America.

sudamericano,-a *adj* South American.

sudar *vi* to sweat.

sudor *nm* sweat.

sudoroso,-a *adj* sweaty.

suegro,-a *nm,f (hombre)* father-in-law; *(mujer)* mother-in-law.

suela *nf* sole.

sueldo *nm* salary, pay.

suelo *nm* **1** *(en la calle)* ground; *(de interior)* floor. **2** *(tierra)* soil.

suelto,-a *adj (no sujeto)* loose; *(desatado)* undone. ► *nm* **suelto** *(cambio)* small change.

sueño *nm* **1** *(ganas de dormir)* sleepiness: **tengo mucho sueño**, I'm very sleepy. **2** *(lo soñado)* dream.

suero *nm* **1** *(de la sangre)* serum. **2** *(solución salina)* saline solution.

suerte *nf* **1** *(fortuna)* luck. **2** *(azar)* chance: **fue la suerte la que me llevó hasta ti**, it was fate that led me to you. • **tener suerte** to be lucky; **tener mala suerte** to be unlucky.

suéter *nm* sweater.

suficiente *adj-pron* enough.

sufrir *vt* **1** *(padecer)* to suffer. **2** *(ser sujeto de)* to have; *(operación)* to undergo: **sufrir un accidente**, to have an accident.

sugerir *vt* to suggest.

suicidarse *vpr* to commit suicide.

suicidio *nm* suicide.

sujetador *nm* bra, brassiere.

sujetar *vt* **1** *(agarrar)* to hold. **2** *(fijar)* to fix, secure.

sujeto,-a *adj (fijo)* fastened. ▶ *nm* **sujeto 1** *(de verbo)* subject. **2** *(persona)* fellow.

suma *nf* sum, amount.

sumar *vt* to add up.

sumergir *vt (meter en líquido)* to submerge; *(con fuerza)* to plunge; *(rápidamente)* to dip. ▶ *vpr* **sumergirse** *(submarinista)* to go underwater, dive; *(submarino)* to dive.

suministrar *vt* to provide, supply.

suministro *nm* supply.

súper *nm* **1** *fam (supermercado)* supermarket. **2** *(gasolina)* GB four-star petrol; US regular.

superar *vt* **1** *(exceder)* to surpass, exceed. **2** *(obstáculo etc)* to overcome. **3** *(récord)* to break. **4** *(prueba)* to pass.

superficie *nf* surface.

superior *adj* **1** *(de arriba)* upper. **2** *(mayor)* greater. **3** *(mejor)* superior.

supermercado *nm* supermarket.

superviviente *nmf* survivor.

suplemento *nm* supplement.

suplente *adj-nmf* substitute.

suplicar *vt* to beg.

suponer *vt* **1** *(creer)* to suppose. **2** *(dar por sentado)* to assume. **3** *(acarrear)* to entail.

supositorio *nm* suppository.

suprimir *vt (noticia)* to suppress; *(ley, impuestos)* to abolish; *(palabras, texto)* to delete.

supuesto,-a *adj* **1** *(falso)* supposed, assumed. **2** *(presunto)* alleged. • **por supuesto** of course.

sur *adj-nm* south.

surgir *vi* to arise, appear.

surtido *nm* assortment.

surtidor *nm* **1** *(fuente)* fountain. **2** *(chorro)* jet, spout. ■ **surtidor de gasolina** GB petrol pump; US gas pump.

suscribir *vt* **1** *(contrato)* to sign. **2** *(opinión)* to subscribe. ▶ *vpr* **suscribirse** *(a una revista)* to subscribe to.

suscripción *nf* subscription.

suspender *vt* **1** *(aplazar)* to postpone. **2** *(examen)* to fail. **3** *(cancelar)* to suspend.

suspense *nm* suspense.

suspensión *nf* **1** *(de coche)* suspension. **2** *(cancelación)* suspension.

suspenso *nm* fail.

suspiro *nm* sigh.

sustancia *nf* substance.

sustantivo *nm* noun.

sustitución *nf* **1** *(transitoria)* substitution. **2** *(permanente)* replacement.

sustituir *vt* **1** *(transitoriamente)* to substitute. **2** *(permanentemente)* to replace.

susto *nm* fright, scare.

suyo,-a *adj (de él)* of his; *(de ella)* of hers; *(de usted/ustedes)* of yours; *(de ellos)* of theirs. ▶ *pron (de él)* his; *(de ella)* hers; *(de usted/ustedes)* yours; *(de ellos,-as)* theirs.

T

tabaco *nm* 1 *(planta, hoja)* tobacco. 2 *(cigarrillos)* cigarettes: *el tabaco es malo para la salud*, smoking damages your health. ▪ **tabaco negro** black tobacco; **tabaco rubio** Virginia tobacco.
tábano *nm* horsefly.
taberna *nf* pub, bar.
tabique *nm* partition wall. ▪ **tabique nasal** nasal bone.
tabla *nf* 1 *(de madera pulida)* board; *(de madera basta)* plank. 2 *(índice)* table. ▶ *nf pl* **tablas** *(ajedrez)* stalemate, draw. ▪ **tabla de planchar** ironing board; **tabla de surf** surfboard; **tabla de windsurf** sailboard.
tablero *nm* board. ▪ **tablero de ajedrez** chessboard.
tableta *nf* 1 *(de chocolate)* bar. 2 *(pastilla)* tablet.
tablón *nm* plank. ▪ **tablón de anuncios** notice board.
taburete *nm* stool.

tachar *vt* to cross out.
taco *nm* 1 *(para calzar)* wedge. 2 *(para tornillo)* Rawlplug®. 3 *(de entradas)* book; *(de billetes)* wad. 4 *(de billar)* cue. 5 *(de jamón, etc)* cube, piece. 6 *(en botas de fútbol)* stud. 7 *fam (palabrota)* swearword.
tacón *nm* heel.
táctica *nf* tactics.
tacto *nm* 1 *(sentido)* touch. 2 *(textura)* feel. 3 *(delicadeza)* tact.
tal *adj* such: *en tales condiciones*, in such conditions; *tal día*, such and such a day; *te llamó un tal García*, someone called García phoned you. ▶ *pron (cosa)* something; *(persona)* someone, somebody. • **con tal de que** so long as, provided; **¿qué tal?** how are things?; **tal como** just as; **tal cual** just as it is; **tal vez** perhaps, maybe.
taladro *nm (herramienta)* drill; *(barrena)* gimlet.
talar *vt* to fell, cut down.
talco *nm* talc.
talento *nm* talent.
talla *nf* 1 *(estatura)* height; *(altura moral etc)* stature. 2 *(de prenda)* size: *¿qué talla usas?*, what size are you? 3 *(escultura)* carving, sculpture. • **dar la talla** *(ser competente)* to measure up.
tallarines *nm pl* noodles.

taller *nm* 1 *(de artesano, profesional)* workshop. 2 *(de pintor)* studio. 3 *(industrial)* factory. ■ **taller de coches** garage.

tallo *nm* stem, stalk.

talón *nm* 1 *(de pie, calzado)* heel. 2 *(cheque)* GB cheque; US check.

tamaño *nm* size.

también *adv* also, too, as well.

tambor *nm* 1 *(instrumento)* drum. 2 *(de lavadora)* drum. 3 *(de detergente)* drum, giant size pack.

tampoco *adv* neither, nor, not... either.

tampón *nm* 1 *(de entintar)* inkpad. 2 *(absorbente)* tampon.

tan *adv* 1 so; *(después de sustantivo)* such: **no quiero una moto tan grande**, I don't want such a big motorbike; **¡son unos chicos tan malos!**, they are such naughty boys. 2 *(con adjetivos o adverbios)* so: **no comas tan deprisa**, don't eat so quickly. 3 *(comparativo)* as... as: **es tan alto como tú**, he's as tall as you are. 4 *(consecutivo)* so: **pasó tan deprisa que no lo vi**, he went by so fast that I didn't see him. ● **tan sólo** only.

tanda *nf* 1 *(conjunto)* batch, lot. 2 *(serie)* series, course. 3 *(turno)* shift.

tanque *nm* tank.

tanto,-a *adj* 1 *(con incontables)* so much; *(con contables)* so many. 2 *(en comparaciones - incontables)* as much; *(- contables)* as many. 3 *(en cantidades aproximadas)* odd: **tiene treinta y tantos años**, he's thirty something. ► *pron (incontables)* so much; *(contables)* so many. ► *adv* 1 *(cantidad)* so much. 2 *(tiempo)* so long. 3 *(frecuencia)* so often. ► *nm* 1 *(punto)* point. 2 *(cantidad imprecisa)* so much, a certain amount. ● **a las tantas** very late; **al tanto** informed, up to date; **no es para tanto** it's not that bad; **por lo tanto** therefore; **¡y tanto!** oh yes!, certainly! ■ **tanto por ciento** percentage.

tapa *nf* 1 *(cubierta - de caja, olla)* lid; *(-de tarro)* top. 2 *(de libro)* cover. 3 *(de comida)* appetizer.

tapar *vt* 1 *(cubrir)* to cover. 2 *(abrigar)* to wrap up. 3 *(cerrar - olla, tarro)* to put the lid on; *(- botella)* to put the top on. 4 *(ocultar)* to hide; *(vista)* to block. ► *vpr* **taparse** *(cubrirse)* to cover oneself up; *(abrigarse)* to wrap up.

tapete *nm* table runner.

tapia *nf* 1 *(cerca)* garden wall. 2 *(muro)* wall.

tapicería *nf* upholstery.

tapiz *nm* tapestry.

tapón *nm* **1** *(de goma, vidrio)* stopper; *(de botella)* cap, cork; *(de lavabo, bañera)* plug. **2** *(en baloncesto)* block.

taquilla *nf* **1** *(de tren, etc.)* ticket office, booking office; *(de teatro, cine)* box-office. **2** *(en vestuario, colegio)* locker.

tardar *vt (emplear tiempo)* to take: **tardé tres años**, it took me three years. ► *vi (demorar)* to take long: **se tarda más en tren**, it takes longer by train.

tarde *nf* **1** *(hasta las seis)* afternoon. **2** *(después de las seis)* evening. ► *adv* late. ● **llegar tarde** to be late; **más tarde** later; **¡buenas tardes!** **1** *(más temprano)* good afternoon. **2** *(hacia la noche)* good evening.

tarea *nf* task, job.

tarifa *nf* **1** *(precio)* tariff, rate; *(en transporte)* fare. **2** *(lista de precios)* price list

tarjeta *nf* card. ● **pagar con tarjeta** to pay by credit card. ▪ **tarjeta de embarque** boarding card; **tarjeta de visita 1** *(personal)* GB visiting card; US calling card. **2** *(profesional)* business card; **tarjeta telefónica** phone card; **tarjeta postal** postcard.

tarro *nm (recipiente)* jar, pot.

tarta *nf (pastel)* cake; *(de hojaldre)* tart, pie.

tartamudo,-a *nm,f* stutterer, stammerer.

tartera *nf* lunch box.

tasa *nf* **1** *(precio)* fee, charge. **2** *(impuesto)* tax. **4** *(índice)* rate.

tasca *nf* bar, pub.

tatuaje *nm* tattoo.

taxi *nm* taxi, cab.

taxímetro *nm* taximeter, clock.

taxista *nmf* taxi driver, cab driver.

taza *nf* **1** *(recipiente)* cup. **2** *(de retrete)* bowl.

tazón *nm* bowl.

te *pron* **1** *(complemento directo)* you; *(complemento indirecto)* you, for you. **2** *(reflexivo)* yourself.

té *nm* tea: **té con limón**, lemon tea.

teatro *nm* **1** *(sala)* GB theatre; US theater. **2** *(género)* drama. ● **hacer teatro** to play, act.

tebeo *nm* comic.

techo *nm* ceiling. ● **los sin techo** the homeless.

tecla *nf* key.

teclado *nm* keyboard.

técnica *nf* **1** *(tecnología)* technology. **2** *(habilidad)* technique, method.

técnico,-a *adj* technical. ► *nm,f* technician.

tecnología *nf* technology.

teja *nf (en tejado)* tile.

tejado *nm* roof.

tejanos *nm pl* jeans.

tejido *nm* **1** *(tela)* fabric, material. **2** *(en anatomía)* tissue.
tejón *nm* badger.
tela *nf* **1** *(tejido)* material, fabric, cloth; *(retal)* piece of material. **2** *(cuadro)* painting.
telaraña *nf* cobweb, spider's web.
tele *nf fam* telly, TV.
telecomunicaciones *nf pl* telecommunications.
telediario *nm* news.
teleférico *nm* cable car.
telefonista *nmf* telephone operator.
teléfono *nm* **1** *(aparato)* telephone, phone. **2** *(número)* phone number. • **contestar al teléfono** to answer the phone; **estar hablando por teléfono** to be on the phone; **llamar a ALGN por teléfono** to phone SB, ring SB. ■ **teléfono inalámbrico** cordless telephone; **teléfono móvil** mobile phone, US cellular phone; **teléfono público** public phone.
telegrama *nm* telegram, cable.
telenovela *nf* soap opera.
telesilla *nf* chair lift.
telespectador,-ra *nm,f* viewer.
telesquí *nm* ski lift.
teletexto *nm* Teletext®.
televisar *vt* to televise.
televisión *nf* **1** *(sistema)* television. **2** *fam (aparato)* television set. • **ver la televisión** to watch television.
televisor *nm* television set.
télex *nm* telex.
telón *nm* curtain.
tema *nm* **1** *(asunto)* subject. **2** *(canción)* song. ■ **temas de actualidad** current affairs.
temblar *vi* **1** *(de frío)* to shiver; *(de miedo)* to tremble. **2** *(voz)* to quiver.
temblor *nm* tremor, shudder. ■ **temblor de tierra** earthquake.
temer *vt* to fear, be afraid of.
temor *nm* fear.
temperamento *nm* temperament, nature.
temperatura *nf* temperature.
tempestad *nf* storm.
templado,-a *adj (agua, comida)* lukewarm; *(clima, temperatura)* mild, temperate.
templo *nm* temple.
temporada *nf* **1** *(en artes, deportes, moda)* season. **2** *(período)* period, time: *voy a pasar una temporada en casa de mis abuelos,* I'm going to live with my grandparents for a time. ■ **temporada alta** high season; **temporada baja** low season.
temporal *adj* temporary. ▶ *nm* storm.
temprano *adv* early.
tenazas *nf pl* pincers; *(para la comida)* tongs.

tendedero nm (cuerda) clothes-line; (lugar) drying place.

tendencia nf tendency, inclination.

tender vt 1 (puente) to build; (vía, cable) to lay. 2 (ropa, colada) to hang out. 3 (mano) to stretch out, hold out. 4 (emboscada, trampa) to lay. ► vi to tend. ► vpr **tenderse** (tumbarse) to lie down.

tendero,-a nm,f shopkeeper.

tendón nm tendon, sinew.

tenedor nm fork.

tener vt 1 (posesión) to have, have got. 2 (coger) to take: **ten esto**, take this. 3 (sensación, sentimiento) to be, feel: **tengo calor**, I'm hot; **tengo hambre**, I'm hungry; **tengo sed**, I'm thirsty. 4 (edad, tamaño) to be: **tiene diez años**, he's ten, he's ten years old. 5 (celebrar) to hold: **tener una reunión**, to hold a meeting. ► aux **tener que** 1 (obligación- a otra persona) to have to. 2 (- a uno mismo) must.

teniente nm lieutenant. ■ **teniente de alcalde** deputy mayor.

tenis nm tennis. ■ **tenis de mesa** table tennis.

tenista nmf tennis player.

tenor nm (cantante) tenor.

tensión nf 1 (gen) tension. 2 (sanguínea) pressure. ■ **tensión arterial** blood pressure.

tenso,-a adj 1 (cable, cuerda) taut. 2 (persona, músculo) tense. 3 (relaciones) strained.

tentación nf temptation.

tentáculo nm tentacle.

tentativa nf attempt.

teñir vt to dye.

teoría nf theory.

terapia nf therapy.

tercer num → tercero,-a.

tercero,-a num third. ■ **tercera edad** old age.

tercio nm third.

terciopelo nm velvet.

terco,-a adj obstinate, stubborn.

terminal adj terminal. ► nf 1 (gen) terminal. 2 (de autobuses) terminus.

terminar vt-vi (acabar) to finish. ► vi (ir a parar) to end up, end. ► vpr **terminarse** 1 (finalizar) to finish, be over. 2 (agotarse) to run out: **se nos ha terminado el papel**, we've run out of paper.

término nm 1 (final) end, finish. 2 (plazo, palabra) term. ● **en otros términos** in other words; **en primer término** in the foreground; **en términos generales** generally speaking; **poner término a algo** to put an end to STH; **por término medio** on average. ■ **término municipal** municipal area.

termita nf termite.

termo *nm* thermos (flask).

termómetro *nm* thermometer.

termostato *nm* thermostat.

ternera *nf* veal.

ternero,-a *nm,f* calf.

ternura *nf* tenderness.

terraplén *nm* embankment.

terraza *nf* **1** *(balcón)* terrace. **2** *(azotea)* roof terrace. **3** *(de un café)*: **en la terraza de un bar**, outside a bar.

terremoto *nm* earthquake.

terreno *nm* **1** *(tierra)* piece of land, ground; *(solar)* plot, site. **2** *(superficie)* terrain. **3** *(de cultivo)* soil; *(campo)* field. **4** *(ámbito)* field, sphere. ■ **terreno de juego** pitch.

terrestre *adj* **1** *(vida, transporte)* land, terrestrial. **2** *(animal, vegetación)* land.

terrible *adj* terrible, awful.

territorio *nm* territory.

terrón *nm* lump.

terror *nm* terror.

terrorismo *nm* terrorism.

tertulia *nf* gathering. ■ **tertulia televisiva** talk show.

tesis *nf* thesis.

tesoro *nm* **1** *(cosas de valor)* treasure. **2** *(del Estado)* treasury, exchequer.

test *nm* test. ■ **test de embarazo** pregnancy test.

testamento *nm* will, testament. • **hacer testamento** to make one's will.

testículo *nm* testicle.

testificar *vt-vi* to testify.

testigo *nmf* witness. ▶ *nm* DEP baton.

testimonio *nm* testimony. ■ **falso testimonio** perjury.

tetera *nf* teapot.

tetilla *nf (de biberón)* teat.

tetina *nf* teat.

tetrabrik® *nm* carton.

textil *adj* textile.

texto *nm* text.

ti *pron* you.

tía *nf (pariente)* aunt.

tibia *nf* tibia, shinbone.

tibio,-a *adj* tepid, lukewarm.

tiburón *nm* shark.

tic *nm* tic, twitch.

tiempo *nm* **1** *(período, momento)* time. **2** *(meteorológico)* weather. **3** *(parte de partido)* half. **4** *(gramatical)* tense. • **a tiempo** in time; **al mismo tiempo** at the same time; **del tiempo 1** *(fruta)* in season. **2** *(bebida)* at room temperature; **¿qué tiempo hace?** what's the weather like? ■ **tiempo libre** spare time; **tiempo muerto** time out.

tienda *nf* **1** GB shop; US store. **2** *(de campaña)* tent. ■ **tienda de comestibles** grocer's.

tierno,-a *adj* **1** *(blando)* tender, soft. **2** *(reciente)* fresh.

tierra *nf* **1** *(superficie sólida)* land. **2** *(terreno cultivado)* soil, land. **3** *(sustancia)* earth, soil. **4** *(zona de origen)*: **en mi tierra**, where I come from. **5** *(suelo)* ground. **6 la Tierra** *(planeta)* the Earth. • **tierra adentro** inland; **tomar tierra** to land. ▪ **tierra firme** terra firma.

tieso,-a *adj* **1** *(rígido)* stiff, rigid. **2** *(erguido)* upright, erect.

tiesto *nm* flowerpot.

tifón *nm* typhoon.

tigre *nm* tiger.

tijeras *nf pl* scissors.

tila *nf* lime-blossom tea.

timar *vt* to swindle.

timbre *nm* **1** *(de la puerta)* bell. **2** *(sello)* stamp. • **llamar al timbre** to ring the bell.

tímido,-a *adj* shy.

timo *nm* swindle, fiddle.

timón *nm* *(de barco)* rudder.

tímpano *nm* eardrum.

tinta *nf* ink.

tinte *nm* **1** *(colorante)* dye. **2** *(tintorería)* dry-cleaner's.

tinto,-a *adj* *(vino)* red. ▶ *nm* **tinto** red wine.

tintorería *nf* dry-cleaner's.

tío *nm* *(pariente)* uncle.

tiovivo *nm* merry-go-round, roundabout.

típico,-a *adj* typical.

tipo *nm* **1** *(clase)* sort, kind. **2** *(de interés, etc.)* rate. **3** *(de hombre)* build, physique; *(de mujer)* figure.

tira *nf* strip. • **la tira** *fam* a lot, loads.

tirada *nf* **1** *(impresión)* print run. **2** *(jugada)* throw. • **de una tirada** in one go.

tirado,-a *adj* **1** *fam (precio)* dirt cheap. **2** *fam (problema, examen)* dead easy. • **dejar tirado a ALGN** to leave SB in the lurch.

tirador *nm* *(de puerta)* knob; *(de cajón)* handle.

tirantes *nm pl* **1** *(de vestido)* straps. **2** *(de pantalón)* GB braces; US suspenders.

tirar *vt* **1** *(lanzar)* to throw; *(tiro)* to fire; *(bomba)* to drop. **2** *(dejar caer)* to drop. **3** *(desechar)* to throw away. **4** *(derribar)* to knock down; *(casa, árbol)* to pull down; *(vaso, botella)* to knock over. ▶ *vi* **1** *(cuerda, puerta)* to pull: **tira de la cadena**, pull the chain. **2** *(en juegos)*: **tira tú**, it's your turn, it's your go. **3** *fam (funcionar)* to work, run. **4** *(disparar)* to shoot. ▶ *vpr* **tirarse** *(lanzarse)* to throw oneself. ▪ **tira y afloja** give and take.

tirita® *nf* GB plaster; US Band-aid®.

tiritar *vi* to shiver, shake.

tiro *nm* **1** *(lanzamiento)* throw. **2** *(disparo, ruido)* shot. **3** *(herida)* bullet wound. **4** *(de caballos)* team. **5** *(de chimenea)* draught. • **a tiro 1** *(de arma)* within range. **2** *(a mano)* within reach; **sentar como**

un tiro a ALGN 1 *(comida)* not to agree with SB. 2 *(comentario)* to make SB really upset. ▪ **tiro al blanco** target shooting; **tiro con arco** archery.

tirón *nm* 1 *(acción)* tug: *sufrió un tirón en un músculo*, he pulled a muscle. 2 *(robo)* bag-snatching. • **de un tirón** *fam* in one go.

tiroteo *nm* shooting.

títere *nm* puppet, marionette.

titular *adj* appointed, official. ▶ *nmf* 1 *(en deporte)* first-team player. 2 *(de cuenta, pasaporte)* holder. ▶ *nm (de prensa)* headline. ▶ *vpr* **titularse** *(obra, película)* to be called.

título *nm* 1 *(gen)* title. 2 *(académico)* degree; *(diploma)* certificate, diploma. 4 *(acción)* bond, security.

tiza *nf* chalk.

toalla *nf* towel.

toallero *nm* towel rail.

tobillo *nm* ankle.

tobogán *nm* slide.

tocadiscos *nm* record player.

tocador *nm (mueble)* dressing table. ▪ **tocador de señoras** powder room.

tocar *vt* 1 *(gen)* to touch. 2 *(hacer sonar - instrumento, canción)* to play; *(- timbre)* to ring; *(- bocina)* to blow, honk; *(- campanas)* to ring. ▶ *vi* 1 *(corresponder)* to be one's turn: *¿a*

quién le toca ahora?, whose turn is it now? 2 *(caer en suerte)* to win.

tocino *nm* 1 *(grasa)* lard. 2 *(carne)* bacon.

todavía *adv* 1 *(tiempo -en frases afirmativas)* still; *(-en frases negativas)* yet. 2 *(para reforzar)* even: *esto todavía te gustará más*, you'll enjoy this even more.

todo,-a *adj* 1 *(gen)* all. 2 *(por completo)* whole: *participó toda la clase*, the whole class took part. 3 *(cada)* every: *todos los veranos*, every summer. 4 *(enfático)* quite. ▶ *pron* 1 **todo** *(sin exclusión)* all, everything. 2 **todos,-as** everybody, everyone. ▶ *adv* all. • **del todo** completely; **estar en todo** to be really with it; **todos nosotros/ vosotros/ ellos** all of us/you/ them.

todoterreno *nm* all-terrain vehicle.

toldo *nm* awning.

tolerancia *nf* tolerance.

tolerar *vt* to tolerate.

toma *nf* 1 *(acción)* taking. 2 *(dosis)* dose. 3 *(captura)* capture. 4 *(grabación)* recording. 5 *(de imágenes)* take. ▪ **toma de contacto** initial contact; **toma de corriente** power point; **toma de posesión** takeover; **toma de tierra** GB earth wire; US ground wire.

tomar vt 1 (gen) to take. 2 (comida, bebida, baño) to have: ¿quieres tomar algo?, would you like a drink? ► vpr **tomarse** (vacaciones, comentario) to take. • **tomarla con ALGN** to have it in for SB; **tomar por** to take for.

tomate nm tomato. • **ponerse como un tomate** to go as red as a beetroot.

tómbola nf tombola.

tomillo nm thyme.

tomo nm volume.

ton. • **sin ton ni son** without rhyme or reason.

tonel nm barrel, cask.

tonelada nf ton.

tónica nf 1 (bebida) tonic. 2 (tendencia) tendency, trend.

tónico nm tonic.

tono nm 1 (de sonido, voz) tone. 2 (de color) shades. • **a tono con** in tune with; **bajar el tono** to lower one's voice; **subir el tono** to speak louder.

tontería nf 1 (dicho, hecho) silly thing, stupid thing. 2 (insignificancia) little thing.

tonto,-a adj silly.

tope nm 1 (límite) limit, end. 2 (objeto) stop: **el tope de la puerta**, the doorstop. • **a tope** 1 fam (lleno) packed. 2 (al máximo) flat out.

tópico nm commonplace, cliché. • **de uso tópico** for external use.

topo nm mole.

toquilla nf shawl.

tórax nm thorax.

torbellino nm whirlwind.

torcedura nf sprain.

torcer vt 1 (cuerda, brazo) to twist. 2 (inclinar) to slant. ► vi (girar) to turn: **tuerce a la derecha**, turn right. ► vpr **torcerse** 1 to sprain: **se torció el tobillo**, she sprained her ankle. 2 (plan) to fall through.

tordo nm (pájaro) thrush.

torear vt-vi (toro) to fight.

torero,-a nm,f bullfighter.

tormenta nf storm.

tornado nm tornado.

torneo nm tournament.

tornillo nm screw.

torniquete nm tourniquet.

torno nm (de carpintero) lathe; (de alfarero) potter's wheel. • **en torno a** 1 (alrededor de) around. 2 (acerca de) about, concerning.

toro nm bull.

torpe adj (patoso) clumsy.

torre nf 1 (de edificio) tower. 2 (de ajedrez) rook, castle. ▪ **torre de control** control tower.

torrente nm torrent.

torrija nf French toast.

torta nf 1 (dulce) cake. 2 fam (bofetón) slap. • **ni torta** not a thing; **pegarse una torta** to give oneself a bump.

tortazo nm 1 (bofetón) slap. 2 (golpe) thump.

tortícolis *nf* stiff neck.

tortilla *nf* GB omelette; US omelet. ■ **tortilla de patatas** Spanish omelette; **tortilla francesa** plain omelette.

tórtola *nf* dove.

tortuga *nf* 1 *(de tierra)* GB tortoise; US turtle. 2 *(marina)* turtle.

tortura *nf* torture.

tos *nf* cough. ■ **tos ferina** whooping cough.

toser *vi* to cough.

tostada *nf* piece of toast.

tostadora *nf* toaster.

tostar *vt (pan)* to toast; *(café)* to roast.

total *adj-nm* total.

tóxico,-a *adj* toxic.

trabajador,-ra *adj* hardworking. ▶ *nm,f* worker.

trabajar *vi-vt* to work.

trabajo *nm* 1 *(gen)* work. 2 *(tarea)* task, job. 3 *(empleo)* job. 4 *(para clase)* essay, project. ■ **trabajos manuales** handicrafts.

tracción *nf* traction. ■ **tracción delantera/trasera** front/rear-wheel drive.

tractor *nm* tractor.

tradición *nf* tradition.

tradicional *adj* traditional.

traducción *nf* translation. ■ **traducción automática** machine translation; **traducción simultánea** simultaneous translation.

traducir *vt* to translate.

traductor,-ra *nm,f* translator.

traer(se) *vt-vpr* to bring. • **traerse algo entre manos** to be busy with STH; **me trae sin cuidado** I couldn't care less; **traérselas** *fam* to be really difficult.

traficante *nmf* dealer, trafficker.

tráfico *nm* traffic.

tragaperras *nf* slot machine.

tragar(se) *vt-vpr* 1 *(comida, medicina)* to swallow. 2 *(creer)* to fall for it.

tragedia *nf* tragedy.

trago *nm* 1 *(sorbo)* swig. 2 *(bebida)* drink. • **echar un trago** to have a drink; **pasar un mal trago** to have a bad time of it.

traicionar *vt* to betray.

traidor,-ra *nm,f* traitor.

tráiler *nm* 1 *(película)* trailer. 2 *(vehículo)* GB articulated lorry; US trailer truck.

traje *nm* 1 *(de hombre)* suit. 2 *(de mujer)* dress. ■ **traje de baño** bathing suit, bathing costume; **traje de etiqueta** evening dress; **traje de luces** bullfighter's costume; **traje espacial** spacesuit.

trama *nf (argumento)* plot.

tramar *vt (preparar)* to plot: *estarán tramando algo*, they must be up to something.

trámite *nm* **1** *(paso)* step. **2** *(negociación)* procedure. **3** *(formalismo)* formality: *es puro trámite*, it's purely a formality.

tramo *nm* **1** *(de carretera)* stretch, section. **2** *(de escalera)* flight.

trampa *nf* **1** *(para cazar)* trap. **2** *(engaño)* trap, trick. • **hacer trampas** to cheat.

trampolín *nm* **1** *(de piscina)* springboard, diving board. **2** *(de esquí)* ski jump.

tramposo,-a *nm,f* cheat.

tranquilidad *nf* **1** *(paz)* quiet, piece. **2** *(calma)* calm.

tranquilizante *nm* tranquillizer.

tranquilizar(se) *vt-vpr (alguien nervioso)* to calm down; *(alguien preocupado)* to set one's mind at rest.

tranquilo,-a *adj* **1** *(persona, voz, mar)* calm. **2** *(lugar, momento)* quiet, peaceful. • **dejar a ALGN tranquilo** to leave SB alone; **¡tranquilo!** **1** *(cálmate)* take it easy! **2** *(no te preocupes)* don't worry!

transatlántico,-a *adj* transatlantic. ▶ *nm* **transatlántico** liner.

transbordador *nm* ferry. ▪ **transbordador espacial** space shuttle.

transbordo *nm (de pasajeros)* change; *(de equipajes)* transfer. • **hacer transbordo** to change.

transcurrir *vi* to pass, elapse.

transeúnte *nmf* passer-by.

transferencia *nf* transfer.

transformador *nm* transformer.

transformar(se) *vt-vpr* to change.

transfusión *nf* transfusion.

transición *nf* transition.

transistor *nm* transistor.

transitivo,-a *adj* transitive.

tránsito *nm* **1** *(tráfico)* traffic. **2** *(acción)* passage, transit.

transmisión *nf* **1** *(gen)* transmission. **2** *(de radio etc)* broadcast.

transmisor,-ra *adj* transmitting. ▶ *nm,f* transmitter.

transmitir *vt* **1** *(gen)* to transmit. **2** *(por radio etc.)* to broadcast.

transparencia *nf* **1** *(gen)* transparency. **2** *(diapositiva)* slide.

transparentarse *vpr (blusa, vestido)* to be see-through.

transparente *adj* transparent.

transpirar *vi* to perspire.

transportar *vt (gen)* to transport; *(en barco)* to ship.

transporte *nm* transport.

transportista *nmf* haulier.

tranvía *nm* GB tram; US streetcar.

trapecio *nm (de circo, gimnasia)* trapeze.

trapecista *nmf* trapeze artist.

trapo *nm (paño)* cloth. ► *nm pl* **trapos** clothes. ■ **trapo de cocina** tea towel; **trapo del polvo** dust cloth.

tráquea *nf* trachea.

tras *prep* **1** *(después de)* after: **día tras día**, day after day. **2** *(detrás de)* behind: **se escondió tras la puerta**, she hid behind the door.

trasero,-a *adj* back, rear.

trasladar *vt* **1** *(desplazar)* to move. **2** *(de cargo etc.)* to transfer. ► *vpr* **trasladarse 1** *(persona)* to go. **2** *(mudarse)* to move.

traslado *nm* **1** *(mudanza)* move. **2** *(de cargo)* transfer.

trasnochar *vi* to stay up late.

traspasar *vt* **1** *(atravesar)* to go through, pierce. **2** *(negocio, jugador)* to transfer. ● **"Se traspasa"** "For sale".

traspaso *nm* **1** *(de negocio)* sale. **2** *(de jugador, competencias)* transfer. **3** *(precio)* takeover fee.

trasplante *nm* transplant.

trastero *nm* lumber room.

trasto *nm (cosa)* piece of junk. ► *nm pl* **trastos** *(utensilios)* tackle.

trastorno *nm* **1** disruption; *(molestia)* inconvenience. **2** *(enfermedad)* disorder.

tratado *nm* **1** *(pacto)* treaty. **2** *(estudio)* treatise.

tratamiento *nm* **1** *(gen)* treatment. **2** *(título)* title, form of address. ■ **tratamiento de textos** word processing.

tratar *vt* **1** *(gen)* to treat. **2** *(asunto, relación)* to deal with. ► *vi (relacionarse)* to be acquainted. ► *vpr* **tratarse 1** *(ser cuestión)* to be about: **tratándose de ti...**, seeing as it's you... **2** *(tener relación)* to be friendly with. ● **tratar de 1** *(intentar)* to try to. **2** *(dirigirse a)* to address as: **nos tratamos de usted**, we address each other as "usted". **3** *(versar)* to be about.

trato *nm* **1** *(de personas)* manner, treatment. **2** *(contacto)* contact. **3** *(acuerdo)* agreement. **4** *(comercial)* deal. ● **cerrar un trato** to close a deal; **¡trato hecho!** it's a deal! ■ **malos tratos** ill-treatment.

través *nm*. ● **a través de 1** *(mediante)* through. **2** *(de un lado a otro)* across.

travesía *nf* **1** *(viaje)* voyage, crossing. **2** *(calle)* street.

trayecto *nm* **1** *(distancia)* distance, way. **2** *(recorrido)* route: **el autobús cubría el trayecto Madrid-Burgos**, the bus was doing the Madrid-Burgos run. **3** *(viaje)* journey: **el trayecto entre Barcelona y Mallorca**, the journey between Barcelona and Majorca.

trayectoria *nf* 1 *(recorrido)* trajectory. 2 *(evolución)* line, course. ■ **trayectoria profesional** career.

trébol *nm* 1 *(hierba)* clover. 2 *(naipes)* club.

trece *num* thirteen; *(en fechas)* thirteenth.

tregua *nf* 1 MIL truce. 2 *(descanso)* respite, rest.

treinta *num* thirty; *(en fechas)* thirtieth.

tremendo,-a *adj* 1 *(terrible)* terrible, dreadful. 2 *(muy grande)* tremendous.

tren *nm* 1 *(ferrocarril)* train. 2 *(ritmo)* speed, pace: *a este tren no llegaremos*, we won't get there at this speed. ■ **tren de cercanías** suburban train; **tren de aterrizaje** undercarriage; **tren de lavado** car wash.

trenza *nf* GB plait; US braid.

trepar *vt-vi* to climb.

tres *num* three; *(en fechas)* third. ■ **tres en raya** GB noughts and crosses; US tic-tac-toe.

trescientos,-as *num* three hundred.

tresillo *nm* three-piece suite.

triángulo *nm* triangle.

tribu *nf* tribe.

tribuna *nf* 1 *(plataforma)* platform, rostrum. 2 stand.

tribunal *nm* 1 *(gen)* court. 2 *(de examen)* board of examiners.

triciclo *nm* tricycle.

trigo *nm* wheat.

trillizo,-a *nm,f* triplet.

trimestre *nm* 1 *(académico)* term. 2 *(tres meses)* quarter.

trinchar *vt* to carve.

trinchera *nf* trench.

trineo *nm* *(de perros)* sleigh; *(para jugar)* sledge.

trío *nm* trio.

tripa *nf* 1 *(estómago)* stomach. 2 *(panza)* belly.

triple *adj-nm* triple. ■ **triple salto** triple jump.

tripulación *nf* crew.

tripulante *nmf* crew member.

tripular *vt* to man.

triste *adj* sad.

tristeza *nf* sadness.

triturar *vt* *(ajo, minerales)* to crush; *(-papel)* to shred.

triunfar *vi* 1 *(tener éxito)* to succeed. 2 *(ganar)* to win.

triunfo *nm* 1 *(victoria)* triumph, victory; *(en deportes)* win. 2 *(éxito)* success. 3 *(naipes)* trump.

trocear *vt* to cut up.

trofeo *nm* trophy.

trombón *nm* trombone.

trompa *nf* 1 *(instrumento)* horn. 2 *(de elefante)* trunk.

trompeta *nf* trumpet.

tronco *nm* trunk.

trono *nm* throne.

tropa *nf* troops, soldiers.

tropezar(se) *vi-vpr* to trip.

tropical *adj* tropical.

trote *nm* *(de caballo)* trot.

trozo *nm* piece, chunk.

trucha *nf* trout.

truco *nm* trick. • **coger el truco** to get the knack.

trueno *nm* clap of thunder.

tu *adj* your.

tú *pron* you.

tuberculosis *nf* tuberculosis.

tubería *nf* (de agua) pipe; (de gas, petróleo) pipeline.

tubo *nm* tube. ▪ **tubo de ensayo** test tube; **tubo de escape** exhaust pipe; **tubo digestivo** alimentary canal.

tuerca *nf* nut.

tuerto,-a *adj* one-eyed.

tulipán *nm* tulip.

tumba *nf* 1 (mausoleo) tomb. 2 (fosa) grave.

tumbarse *vpr* to lie down.

tumbona *nf* (de playa) deckchair; (para tumbarse) lounger.

tumor *nm* GB tumour; US tumor.

túnel *nm* tunnel. ▪ **túnel de lavado** car wash.

túnica *nf* tunic.

tupé *nm* quiff.

turbina *nf* turbine.

turbio,-a *adj* cloudy.

turismo *nm* 1 (actividad) tourism. 2 (industria) tourist trade, tourist industry. 3 (coche) car.

turista *nmf* tourist.

turístico,-a *adj* tourist.

turnarse *vpr* to take turns.

turno *nm* 1 (en cola, lista) turn. 2 (de trabajo) shift.

turrón *nm* nougat.

tutor,-ra *nm,f* 1 JUR guardian. 2 (profesor) tutor.

tuyo,-a *adj* of yours. ▶ *pron* yours.

U

u *conj* or.

UCI *abr* (*Unidad de Cuidados Intensivos*) ICU, intensive care unit.

úlcera *nf* ulcer.

último,-a *adj* 1 (gen) last. 2 (más reciente) latest: *las últimas noticias*, the latest news. 3 (más alejado) furthest; (de más abajo) bottom, lowest; (de más arriba) top; (de más atrás) back: *vive en el último piso*, he lives on the top floor. 4 (definitivo) final: *mi última oferta*, my final offer. • **a la última** up to date; **estar en las últimas** 1 (moribundo) to be at death's door. 2 (arruinado) to be down and out; **por último** finally.

ultramarinos *nm pl* (tienda) grocer's; (comestibles) groceries.

umbral *nm* threshold.

un,-a *det* a, an. ▶ *adj* one.

unanimidad *nf* unanimity.
undécimo,-a *num* eleventh.
único,-a *adj* **1** *(solo)* only. **2** *(extraordinario)* unique.
unidad *nf* **1** unit. **2** *(cohesión)* unity.
uniforme *adj (velocidad, ritmo)* uniform; *(temperatura, superficie)* even. ▶ *nm* uniform.
unión *nf* union.
unir *vt* **1** *(juntar)* to join. **2** *(enlazar)* to link.
universal *adj* universal.
universidad *nf* university.
universitario,-a *adj* university. ▶ *nm,f (en curso)* university student; *(con título)* university graduate.
universo *nm* universe.
uno,-a *adj (número)* one. ▶ *pron* **1** one. **2** *(impersonal)* one, you: *en estos casos, uno no sabe qué hacer*, you don't know what to do in these situations. ▶ *nm (número)* one; *(en fechas)* first. ▶ *adj pl* **unos,-as 1** some. **2** *(aproximado)* about, around: *seremos unos veinte*, there will be around twenty of us. • **de uno en uno** one by one; **es la una** it's one o'clock.
untar *vt (crema, pomada)* to smear; *(mantequilla, queso)* to spread.
uña *nf* nail.
urbanización *nf* **1** *(proceso)* urbanization. **2** *(conjunto residencial)* housing development, housing estate.
urbano,-a *adj* urban.
urgencia *nf* **1** *(prisa)* urgency. **2** *(asunto)* emergency. ▶ *nf pl* **urgencias** casualty.
urgente *adj* **1** *(llamada, asunto)* urgent. **2** *(carta)* express.
urna *nf* **1** *(para votar)* ballot box. **2** *(para cenizas)* urn. **3** *(para objetos valiosos)* glass case.
urraca *nf* magpie.
urticaria *nf* rash.
usado,-a *adj* **1** *(gastado)* worn out, old. **2** *(de segunda mano)* secondhand, used.
usar *vt* **1** *(utilizar)* to use. **2** *(prenda)* to wear. • **de usar y tirar** disposable.
uso *nm* **1** *(utilización)* use. **2** *(de prenda)* wearing: *es obligatorio el uso del cinturón de seguridad*, seat belts must be worn.
usted *pron fml* you.
usual *adj* usual, customary.
usuario,-a *nm,f* user.
utensilio *nm* **1** *(de cocina)* utensil. **2** *(herramienta)* tool.
útero *nm* uterus.
útil *adj* useful.
utilización *nf* use.
utilizar *vt* to use, utilize.
uva *nf* grape.
UVI *abr (Unidad de Vigilancia Intensiva)* ICU, intensive care unit.

V

vaca *nf* **1** *(animal)* cow. **2** *(carne)* beef.

vacaciones *nf pl* holiday; GB holidays; US vacation. • **irse de vacaciones** to go on holiday (US vacation).

vacante *nf* vacancy.

vaciar *vt* **1** *(recipiente)* to empty. **2** *(contenido)* to pour away, pour out.

vacilar *vi* to hesitate.

vacío,-a *adj* **1** *(recipiente, lugar)* empty. **2** *(no ocupado)* unoccupied. ► *nm* **vacío 1** *(abismo)* void, emptiness. **2** *(en física)* vacuum. • **envasado al vacío** vacuum-packed.

vacuna *nf* vaccine.

vacunar *vt* to vaccinate.

vado *nm* **1** *(de río)* ford. **2** *(en calle)* garage entrance. ■ **"Vado permanente"** "Keep clear".

vagabundo,-a *nm,f* tramp.

vagina *nf* vagina.

vago,-a[1] *nm,f* idler, loafer.

vago,-a[2] *adj (impreciso)* vague.

vagón *nm* **1** *(para pasajeros)* GB carriage, coach; US car. **2** *(para mercancías)* GB wagon, goods van; US boxcar, freight car. ■ **vagón restaurante** restaurant car.

vaho *nm* steam; GB vapour; US vapor. ► *nm pl* **vahos** MED inhalation.

vaina *nf* **1** *(de espada)* sheath, scabbard. **2** *(de guisante, judía)* pod.

vainilla *nf* vanilla.

vaivén *nm* swaying, swinging.

vajilla *nf* **1** *(gen)* dishes, crockery. **2** *(juego completo)* dinner service.

vale *nm (de compra)* voucher. ► *interj* OK, all right.

valer *vi* **1** *(tener valor)* to be worth. **2** *(costar)* to cost: *¿cuánto vale?*, how much is it? **3** *(ser válido)* to be valid. **4** *(servir)* to be useful, be of use: *no vale para director*, he's no use as a manager. • **no vale** it's no good; **vale más…** it's better…: *más te vale no llegar tarde*, you'd better not arrive late.

válido,-a *adj* valid.

valiente *adj* brave.

valioso,-a *adj* valuable.

valla *nf* **1** *(cerca)* fence, barrier. **2** *(en atletismo)* hurdle. ■ **valla publicitaria** GB hoarding; US billboard.

valle *nm* valley.

valor *nm* **1** *(gen)* value. **2** *(precio)* price. **3** *(coraje)* courage; GB valour; US valor. ► *nm pl* **valores** *(financieros)* securities, bonds. • **¡qué valor!** what a nerve!; **sin ningún valor** worthless, worth nothing.

valorar *vt* to value.

válvula *nf* valve.

vender

vampiro *nm* vampire.

vanguardia *nf* **1** *(en arte etc.)* avant-garde. **2** MIL vanguard.

vano,-a *adj* **1** *(inútil)* vain, useless. **2** *(ilusorio)* illusory, futile. • **en vano** in vain.

vapor *nm* steam; GB vapour; US vapor. • **al vapor** steamed.

vaquero *nm* GB cowherd; US cowboy. ► *nm pl* **vaqueros** jeans.

variable *adj* variable.

variante *nf (carretera)* bypass.

variar *vt-vi* to vary, change. • **para variar** for a change.

varicela *nf* chickenpox.

variedad *nf* variety. ► *nf pl* **variedades** *(espectáculo)* variety show.

varilla *nf* **1** *(palito)* stick, rod. **2** *(de paraguas)* rib.

varios,-as *adj* some, several.

variz *nf* varicose vein.

varón *nm* male, man.

vasija *nf* vessel.

vaso *nm* **1** *(de cristal)* glass. **2** *(de papel, plástico)* cup. **3** *(sanguíneo)* vessel.

vasto,-a *adj* vast, immense.

vatio *nm* watt.

vaya *interj* **1** well! **2** *(con sustantivos)* what a...: **¡vaya casa!**, what a house!

vecino,-a *nm,f* **1** *(de edificio, calle)* GB neighbour; US neighbor. **2** *(habitante - de barrio)* resident; *(- de ciudad)* inhabitant.

veda *nf* close season.

vegetación *nf* vegetation.

vegetal *adj-nm* plant.

vegetariano,-a *adj-nm,f* vegetarian.

vehículo *nm* vehicle.

veinte *num* twenty; *(en fechas)* twentieth.

vejez *nf* old age.

vejiga *nf* bladder.

vela¹ *nf (de cera)* candle. • **pasar la noche en vela** to have a sleepless night.

vela² *nf (de barco)* sail.

velada *nf* evening.

velarse *vpr (foto)* to get fogged.

velatorio *nm* wake, vigil.

velero *nm* sailing boat.

veleta *nf* weathercock.

vello *nm* hair.

velo *nm* veil.

velocidad *nf* **1** *(rapidez)* speed, velocity. **2** *(marcha)* gear.

velódromo *nm* cycle track.

veloz *adj* fast, quick, swift.

vena *nf* vein.

vencedor,-ra *nm,f* winner.

vencer *vt* **1** *(derrotar)* to beat. **2** *(militarmente)* to defeat. ► *vi* **1** *(gen)* to win. **2** *(deuda)* to fall due.

venda *nf* bandage.

vendaje *nm* bandaging.

vendar *vt* to bandage.

vendedor,-ra *nm,f (hombre)* salesman; *(mujer)* saleswoman.

vender *vt* to sell. • **"Se vende"** "For sale".

vendimia *nf* grape harvest.
veneno *nm (químico, vegetal)* poison; *(de animal)* venom.
venenoso *adj* poisonous.
venganza *nf* revenge.
vengarse *vpr* to take revenge.
venir *vi* 1 *(gen)* to come. 2 *(estar)* to be: *mi teléfono viene en la guía*, my phone number is in the book. • **venir bien** to be suitable: *¿te viene bien esta tarde?*, does this afternoon suit you?; **venir mal** not to be convenient: *a esa hora me viene mal*, that time isn't convenient; **venirse abajo** 1 *(edificio)* to collapse, fall down. 2 *(persona)* to go to pieces; **¡venga!** come on!
venta *nf* 1 *(transacción)* sale, selling. 2 *(hostal)* roadside inn. • **"En venta"** "For sale".
ventaja *nf* advantage.
ventana *nf* window. • **doble ventana** double-glazed window.
ventanilla *nf* 1 *(de coche, sobre, en banco)* window. 2 *(de cine)* box office.
ventilador *nm* fan.
ventilar *vt (habitación, ropa)* to air.
ventisca *nf* snowstorm, blizzard.
ventosa *nf* sucker.
ver *vt* 1 *(percibir, mirar)* to see. 2 *(televisión)* to watch. ► *vpr* **verse** *(con ALGN)* to meet,

see each other: *nos vemos bastante a menudo*, we see each other quite often. • **a ver** let's see; **hacer ver algo** to pretend STH; **¡hay que ver!** would you believe it!; **no poder ver** not to be able to stand: *no puede ver a su primo*, she can't stand her cousin; **véase** see.
veraneante *nmf* summer resident.
veranear *vi* to spend the summer.
veraneo *nm* GB summer holiday; US summer vacation.
verano *nm* summer.
veras *adv.* • **de veras** really, truly.
verbena *nf (fiesta)* dance.
verbo *nm* verb.
verdad *nf* 1 truth. 2 *(confirmación)*: *es bonita, ¿verdad?*, she's pretty, isn't she? • **de verdad** 1 *(en serio)* really. 2 *(como debe ser)* real.
verdadero,-a *adj* true, real.
verde *adj* 1 *(color, tela, ojos)* green. 2 *(fruta)* unripe. 3 *fam (chiste)* blue, dirty. ► *nm (color)* green. • **poner verde a ALGN** *fam* to run SB down.
verdulería *nf* greengrocer's.
verdura *nf* vegetables *pl.*
veredicto *nm* verdict.
vergüenza *nf* 1 *(culpabilidad)* shame. 2 *(bochorno)* embarrassment.

verificar *vt* to verify.
verja *nf* railing.
vermut *nm* vermouth.
verruga *nf* wart.
versión *nf* version. • **en versión original** original language version.
verso *nm* verse.
vértebra *nf* vertebra.
vertebral *adj* vertebral.
vertedero *nm* dump, tip.
vertical *adj-nf* vertical.
vértice *nm* vertex.
vértigo *nm* vertigo.
vesícula *nf* vesicle.
vespa® *nf* scooter.
vestíbulo *nm* hall.
vestido *nm* dress. ■ **vestido de noche** evening dress; **vestido de novia** wedding dress.
vestimenta *nf* clothes.
vestir *vt* 1 *(llevar)* to wear. 2 *(a alguien)* to dress. ► *vpr* **vestirse** to get dressed.
vestuario *nm* 1 *(ropa)* wardrobe, clothes. 2 *(camerino)* dressing room; *(en gimnasio etc.)* GB changing room; US locker room.
veterano,-a *adj-nm,f* veteran.
veterinario,-a *nm,f* GB veterinary surgeon, vet; US veterinarian.
vez *nf* 1 *(ocasión)* time. 2 *(turno)* turn. • **a la vez** at the same time; **a veces** sometimes; **alguna vez** 1 *(en afirmación)* sometimes. 2 *(en pregunta)* ever; **de vez en cuando** from time to time; **dos veces** twice; **en vez de** instead of; **muchas veces** often; **otra vez** again; **rara vez** seldom, rarely; **tal vez** perhaps, maybe.
vía *nf* 1 *(camino)* road, way; *(calle)* street. 2 *(de tren - raíl)* track, line; *(- andén)* platform. • **por vía oral** to be taken orally. ■ **vía de acceso** slip road; **vía pública** thoroughfare; **vías respiratorias** respiratory tract.
viable *adj* viable.
viajante *nm* commercial traveller.
viajar *vi* to travel.
viaje *nm* journey, trip. • **¡buen viaje!** have a good journey!; **estar de viaje** to be away; **irse de viaje** to go on a journey, go on a trip. ■ **viaje de novios** honeymoon.
viajero,-a *(pasajero)* passenger, *(aventurero)* traveller.
víbora *nf* viper.
vibrar *vi* to vibrate.
viceversa *adv* viceversa.
vicio *nm* 1 *(corrupción)* vice, corruption. 2 *(mala costumbre)* bad habit.
víctima *nf* victim.
victoria *nf* 1 *(gen)* victory, triumph. 2 *(en partido)* win.
vid *nf* vine.

vida *nf* **1** *(de ser vivo)* life. **2** *(medios)* living: **se gana la vida como escritor**, he earns a living as a writer. • **en mi/ tu/su/la vida** never.

vídeo *nm* video. • **grabar algo en vídeo** to tape STH.

videocámara *nf* camcorder.

videocasete *nm* video cassette.

videoclip *nm* video.

videoclub *nm* video shop.

videojuego *nm* video game.

vidriera *nf* *(obra artística)* stained glass window.

vidrio *nm* glass.

viejo,-a *adj* *(persona)* old, aged; *(cosa)* old. ▶ *nm,f* *(hombre)* old man; *(mujer)* old woman. • **hacerse viejo** to get old.

viento *nm* wind

vientre *nm* belly, abdomen.

viernes *nm* Friday.

viga *nf* **1** *(de madera)* beam, rafter. **2** *(de acero)* girder.

vigente *adj* in use, in force.

vigilante *nmf* *(hombre)* watchman; *(mujer)* watchwoman.

vigilar *vt-vi* **1** *(ir con cuidado)* to watch. **2** *(con armas)* to guard.

vigor *nm* GB vigour; US vigor. • **en vigor** in force.

villa *nf* **1** *(casa)* villa. **2** *(pueblo)* small town.

villancico *nm* Christmas carol.

vinagre *nm* vinegar.

vinagreras *nf pl* cruet stand.

vinagreta *nf* vinaigrette.

vino *nm* wine. ▪ **vino blanco** white wine; **vino de Jerez** sherry; **vino rosado** rosé wine; **vino tinto** red wine.

viña *nf* vineyard.

viñedo *nm* vineyard.

viñeta *nf* **1** *(dibujo)* cartoon. **2** *(tira)* comic strip.

violar *vt* **1** *(acuerdo, derecho)* to violate. **2** *(persona)* to rape.

violencia *nf* violence.

violento,-a *adj* violent.

violeta *adj-nm* *(color)* violet. ▶ *nf* *(flor)* violet.

violín *nm* violin.

violinista *nmf* violinist.

violonchelo *nm* cello.

virgen *adj* **1** *(persona)* virgin. **2** *(cinta)* blank. **3** *(en estado natural)* unspoilt. ▶ *nf* virgin.

virtual *adj* virtual.

virtud *nf* virtue.

viruela *nf* smallpox.

virus *nm* virus.

visado *nm* visa.

vísceras *nf pl* viscera.

visera *nf* *(de gorra)* peak; *(de casco)* visor.

visible *adj* visible.

visión *nf* sight, vision. • **ver visiones** to dream, see things.

visita *nf* **1** *(acción)* visit. **2** *(visitante)* visitor, guest.

visitante *nmf* visitor.

visitar *vt* **1** *(ir a casa de)* to visit. **2** *(enfermo)* to see.

visón *nm* mink.

víspera *nf* **1** *(día anterior)* day before. **2** *(de fiesta)* eve.

vista *nf* **1** *(sentido)* sight, vision. **2** *(panorama)* view. • **con vistas a 1** *(jardín, calle)* overlooking. **2** *(beneficios, resultados)* with a view to; **conocer de vista** to know by sight; **estar a la vista** to be evident; **hasta la vista** good-bye, so long; **salta a la vista que...** it is obvious that...

visto,-a *adj* seen. • **por lo visto** as it seems; **ser lo nunca visto** to be unheard of. ■ **visto bueno** approval.

vitamina *nf* vitamin.

vitrina *nf* **1** *(en casa)* glass cabinet, display cabinet. **2** *(de exposición)* glass case, showcase. **3** *(escaparate)* shop window.

viudo,-a *nm,f (hombre)* widower; *(mujer)* widow.

viva *interj* hurrah!

víveres *nm pl* food, provisions.

vivero *nm* **1** *(de plantas)* nursery. **2** *(de peces)* fish farm.

vivienda *nf* **1** *(alojamiento)* housing, accommodation. **2** *(morada)* home; *(- casa)* house; *(- piso)* GB flat; US apartment.

viviente *adj* living, alive.

vivir *vi* to live. ► *vt (pasar)* to live through: *los que vivieron la guerra,* those who

lived through the war. • **vivir de** to live on: *vive de su pensión,* she lives on her pension.

vivo,-a *adj* **1** *(con vida)* alive, living. **2** *(color)* bright, vivid. **3** *(animado)* lively. • **en vivo** *(programa)* live.

vocabulario *nm* vocabulary.

vocación *nf* vocation.

vocal *adj* vocal. ► *nf (letra, sonido)* vowel. ► *nmf (de comité)* member.

vodka *nm* vodka.

volante *nm* **1** *(de vehículo)* steering wheel. **2** *(documento)* note: *pedí un volante para el especialista de la piel,* I asked to be referred to the skin specialist.

volar *vi* to fly. ► *vt (hacer explotar)* to blow up. • **volando** in a rush: *tuve que desayunar volando,* I had to eat my breakfast in a hurry.

volcán *nm* volcano.

volcar *vt* to knock over. ► *vi* to overturn. ► *vpr* **volcarse** *(entregarse)* to devote oneself.

voleibol *nm* volleyball.

voltereta *nf* somersault.

volumen *nm* volume. • **bajar/subir el volumen** to turn the volume down/up. ■ **volumen de negocios** turnover.

voluntad *nf* **1** *(de decidir)* will. **2** *(propósito)* intention, purpose. **3** *(deseo)* wish.

voluntario,-a *adj* voluntary.
▸ *nm,f* volunteer.
volver *vt* **1** *(dar vuelta a)* to
turn (over); *(hacia abajo)* to
turn upside down; *(de fuera a
dentro)* to turn inside out. **2**
(convertir) to turn, make: *me
vuelve loco*, he drives me
mad. ▸ *vi (regresar)* to come
back, go back. ▸ *vpr* **volverse 1** *(darse la vuelta)* to
turn (round): *se volvió hacia
mí*, he turned towards me. **2**
(convertirse) to turn, become:
se ha vuelto loco, he's gone
mad. • **volver en sí** to recover
consciousness, come round;
volverse atrás to back out.
vomitar *vi* to vomit, be sick.
vosotros,-as *pron* you. ▪
vosotros,-as mismos,-as
yourselves.
votación *nf* vote, voting.
votar *vi* to vote.
voto *nm* vote.
voz *nf* **1** *(gen)* voice. **2** *(grito)*
shout: *no me des esas voces*,
don't shout! • **a media voz**
in a whisper; **en voz alta**
aloud; **en voz baja** in a low
voice.
vuelo *nm* flight. ▪ **vuelo sin
motor** gliding.
vuelta *nf* **1** *(giro)* turn: *da
una vuelta a la llave*, give
the key one turn. **2** *(en un circuito)* lap. **3** *(paseo a pie)*
walk, stroll: *ir a dar una

vuelta*, to go for a walk. **4**
(paseo en coche) drive. **5** *(regreso)* return: *la vuelta la
haremos en tren*, we'll come
back by train. **6** *(dinero de
cambio)* change: *quédese con
la vuelta*, keep the change.
• **a la vuelta** on the way
back; **dar la vuelta 1** *(alrededor)* to go round. **2** *(girar)* to
turn round. **3** *(de arriba abajo)*
to turn upside down. **4** *(de
dentro a fuera)* to turn inside
out; **estar de vuelta** to be
back. ▪ **vuelta al mundo**
round-the-world trip; **vuelta ciclista** cycle race.
vuestro,-a *adj* your, of
yours. ▸ *pron* yours.
vulgar *adj* **1** *(grosero)* vulgar. **2**
(corriente) common, general.

W-X

Walkman® *nm* Walkman®.
wáter *nm fam* toilet.
waterpolo *nm* water polo.
W.C. *abr (retrete)* WC, toilet.
web *nf* **1** *(sitio)* website. **2**
(página) webpage.
whisky *nm* whisky; *(irlandés)*
whiskey.
windsurf *nm* windsurfing.
xenofobia *nf* xenophobia.
xilófono *nm* xylophone.

Y

y *conj* **1** *(gen)* and. **2** *(con hora)* past: *son las tres y cuarto*, it's a quarter past three. **3** *(con números)*: *cuarenta y cuatro*, forty-four.

ya *adv* **1** *(con pasado)* already: *ya lo sabía*, I already knew. **2** *(con presente)* now: *es preciso actuar ya*, it is vital that we act now. **3** *(ahora mismo)* immediately, at once. **4** *(luego)* later: *ya veremos*, we'll see. **5** *(uso enfático)*: *ya lo sé*, I know; *ya entiendo*, I see. • **ya no** not any more, no longer; **ya que** since.

yacimiento *nm* bed, deposit. ▪ **yacimiento arqueológico** archaeological site.

yate *nm* *(a motor)* pleasure cruiser; *(de vela)* yacht.

yegua *nf* mare.

yema *nf* **1** *(de huevo)* yolk. **2** *(del dedo)* fingertip.

yerno *nm* son-in-law.

yeso *nm* **1** *(mineral)* gypsum. **2** *(en construcción)* plaster.

yo *pron* **1** *(sujeto)* I. **2** *(objeto, con preposición)* me. • **yo mismo** myself.

yoga *nm* yoga.

yogur *nm* yoghurt.

yóquey *nm* jockey.

yugular *adj-nf* jugular.

yunque *nm* anvil.

Z

zafiro *nm* sapphire.

zamarra *nf* sheepskin jacket.

Zambia *nf* Zambia.

zambullirse *vpr* to dive.

zanahoria *nf* carrot.

zancada *nf* stride.

zancadilla *nf* *(para caer)* trip.

zanja *nf* ditch, trench.

zapatería *nf* GB shoe shop; US shoe store.

zapatilla *nf* slipper. ▪ **zapatillas de deporte** trainers.

zapato *nm* shoe. ▪ **zapatos de tacón** high-heeled shoes.

zar *nm* tsar, czar.

zarpa *nf* paw.

zarpar *vi* to set sail.

zarza *nf* bramble.

zarzamora *nf* *(planta)* blackberry bush; *(fruto)* blackberry.

zócalo *nm* skirting board.

zona *nf* area, zone. ▪ **zona azul** pay-and-display parking area; **zona verde** park.

zoo *nm* zoo.

zoología *nf* zoology.

zoológico *nm* zoo.

zorro,-a *nm,f* *(animal)* fox.

zueco *nm* clog.

zumbido *nm* **1** *(de insecto)* buzzing. **2** *(de motor)* humming.

zumo *nm* juice.

zurda *nf* *(mano)* left hand.

zurdo,-a *adj* left-handed.